Golf Digest's Best Places to Play

Fodor's Travel Publications, Inc.
New York • Toronto • London • Sydney • Auckland

Copyright © 1994 by GOLF DIGEST

All rights reserved under International and Pan-American Copyright conventions. Distributed by Random House, Inc., New York. No illustrations or other portions of this book may be reproduced in any form without written permission from the publishers.

Published by Fodor's Travel Publications, Inc.

Fodor's is a registered trademark of Fodor's Travel Publications, Inc.

ISBN 0-679-02862-5
First Edition

Special Sales
Fodor's Travel Publications are available at special discounts for bulk purchases for sales promotions or premiums. Special editions, including personalized covers, excerpts of existing guides, and corporate imprints, can be created in large quantities for special needs. For more information, contact your local bookseller or write to Special Markets, Fodor's Travel Publications, 201 East 50th Street, New York, N. Y. 10022.

MANUFACTURED IN THE UNITED STATES OF AMERICA
10 9 8 7 6 5 4 3 2 1

Cover photograph by Jim Moriarty,
taken at Jackson Hole (Wyo.) Golf and Tennis Club.

Welcome to Golf Digest's Best Places to Play

GOLF DIGEST has published an annual listing of Places to Play since 1963, but it's never been anything like this, and neither has anyone else's listing of courses in the United States, Canada and the Caribbean.

This survey is unique because it was done by 10,000 of the magazine's subscribers, who rated 1,700 courses—the first and biggest undertaking of its type in golf history. With no vested interests at stake, they offered candid appraisals and comments on courses ranging from posh resorts to local munys. The subscribers critiqued everything, from the playing conditions to the attitude of the shop staff to the food in the grill. They found the bargains and the rip-offs and everything in between.

The constant theme running through the reader comments was service, service and more service. What they expected for their green fees was courtesy from the staff, reliable tee times, a comfortable pace of play, acceptable playing conditions and reasonable refreshments at reasonable prices.

They not only rated the quality of a course, but also how it stacked up as a value relative to other courses in the area. Course quality is measured in stars. The 25 "Super Values"—our highest honor—and 100 "Great Values" are also marked with symbols. You won't want to miss any of them.

Beyond providing locations and phone numbers, this book includes the range of green fees, which credit cards are accepted, whether walking is allowed at any time and, if the facility has a practice range, whether it has grass or rubber-mat tees. There's information on yardage, par and USGA Slope ratings, as well as whether the course offers caddies and on-site housing. It also indicates which courses have appeared on any of GOLF DIGEST's widely respected and quoted course rankings and surveys.

In short, this book includes everything golfers need to know about a course before spending their hard-earned cash to play it. We think you'll find it indispensable.

—THE EDITORS

How to Use This Guide

★★★ **ANYWHERE GOLF COURSE**
Centerville—PU—408–000–3213 (25 mi. from Somewhere).
Season: Year-round. **High:** June–Oct. **Caddies:** Yes.
Green fee: $50–$99. **Credit cards:** V, AMEX, MC, DISC.
Lodging on site: Yes. **Reduced fees:** Weekdays, Low Season, Twilight
Play, Resort Guests.
Unrestricted walking: Yes. **Range:** Yes (mats).
Holes: 18. **Par:** 72. **Yards:** 6,116–5,576. **Slope:** 124–120.
Comments: "Good-time course . . . Spectacular first tee . . . No yardage
markers . . . Has all-day rates, a good value if you go around twice."

EXPLANATION:

★★★—A rating of the golf experience by GOLF DIGEST subscribers. See
  ratings chart below.
Centerville: Course location
PU: Public, semi-private, daily fee or municipal or R: Resort
(25 mi. from Somewhere): Distance from nearest major town.
Season: Months the facility is open for play.
High: The busy season, when prices are typically higher.
Caddies: Whether caddies are available.
Green fee: Fees during the season divided into four groups—Under $20; $20
  to $49; $50 to $99; and more than $100. Unless otherwise noted, fee
  includes cart rental.
Credit cards: V—Visa, M—MasterCard, AMEX—American Express,
  DISC—Discover, or "None" if credit cards are not accepted.
Lodging on site: If lodging is available on the property.
Reduced fees: Times or situations when discount fees are available; call
  ahead for details.
Unrestricted walking: If walking is allowed without restriction, at any
  time.
Range: If a practice range is available. Unless noted as "mat," the range has
  grass tees.
Holes: The number of holes available for play.
Yards: Yardage listed from the back and forward tees.
Slope: U.S. Golf Association Slope rating from both back and forward tees.
Comments: A representative sample of comments made by GOLF DIGEST
  subscribers.

Ratings chart

★ It's golf, but just barely.
★★ Good, not great, but not a rip-off, either.
★★★ Very good. Tell a friend it's worth getting off the interstate to play.
★★★★ Outstanding. Plan your next vacation around it.
★★★★★ Golf at its absolute best. Pay any price at least once in your life.
½ The equivalent of one-half star.

*—Course not yet rated by GOLF DIGEST subscribers.

The Five-star Courses

Blackwolf Run (River), Kohler, Wis.
Cog Hill Golf & Country Club (No. 4), Lemont, Ill.
Pebble Beach Golf Links, Pebble Beach, Calif.
Pinehurst (N.C.) Resort & Country Club (No. 2)
Spyglass Hill Golf Course, Pebble Beach, Calif.
Troon North Golf Club, Scottsdale, Ariz.

The Super Values

 Indicates one of just 25 courses whose combined "Golf Experience" and "Value" scores earned it our highest honor as a Super Value.

Bethpage State Park Golf Courses (Black), Farmingdale, N.Y.
Blackwolf Run (River), Kohler, Wis.
Cog Hill Golf & Country Club (No. 4), Lemont, Ill.
Desert Canyon Golf Resort, Orondo, Wash.
Farm Neck Golf Club, Oak Bluffs, Martha's Vineyard, Mass.
Gibson Bay Golf Course, Richmond, Ky.
The Homestead (Cascades), Hot Springs, Va.
Kananaskis Country Golf Course (Mt. Kidd), Alberta
Kananaskis Country Golf Course (Mt. Lorette), Alberta
Lakewood Shores Resort (Gailes), Oscoda, Mich.
Linville (N.C.) Golf Club
Montauk (N.Y.) Downs State Park Golf Course
Painted Dunes Desert Golf Course, El Paso
Pinehurst (N.C.) Resort & Country Club (No. 2)
Piñon Hills Golf Course, Farmington, N.M.
Princeville Resort (Prince), Princeville, Kauai, Hawaii
Reynolds Plantation Club (Great Waters), Greensboro, Ga.
Sandpines, Florence, Ore.
Sea Island Golf Club (Plantation/Seaside),
  St. Simons Island, Ga.
Sultan's Run Golf Course, Jasper, Ind.
Timberton Golf Club, Hattiesburg, Miss.
Tokatee Golf Club, Blue River, Ore.
Troon North Golf Club, Scottsdale, Ariz.
Valley View Golf Course, Layton, Utah
Wyncote Golf Club, Oxford, Pa.

The Great Values

 Indicates one of 100 courses whose combined "Golf Experience" and "Value" scores earned it an honor as a Great Value.

Annbriar Golf Course, Waterloo, Ill.
Arnold Palmer's Bay Hill Club & Lodge, Orlando, Fla.
Barton Creek Resort & Country Club (Fazio), Austin, Tex.

Blackwolf Run (Meadow Valleys), Kohler, Wis.
Breckenridge (Colo.) Golf Club
Brudenell River Provincial Golf Course,
 Montague, Prince Edward Island
Bryan Park and Golf Club (Champions), Brown Summit, N.C.
Bunker Hills Golf Course, Coon Rapids, Minn.
Carambola Golf Club, St. Croix, Virgin Islands
Casa de Campo (Teeth of the Dog),
 La Romana, Dominican Republic
Castlegar Golf Club, Castlegar, British Columbia
Cedar Creek Country Club, Onalaska, Wis.
Coeur d'Alene (Idaho) Resort Golf Course
Country Club at Woodloch Springs, Hawley, Pa.
Crumpin-Fox Club, Bernardston, Mass.
D'Arcy Ranch Golf Club, Alberta
Eagle's Landing Golf Course, Berlin, Md.
Eaglesticks Golf Club, Zanesville, Ohio
Edgewood Municipal Golf Course, Fargo, N.D.
Emerald Dunes Golf Club, West Palm Beach, Fla.
Fairfield Glade (Tenn.) Resort (Stonehenge)
Fairfield Glade (Tenn.) Resort (Heatherhurst)
Fields Ferry Golf Club, Calhoun, Ga.
Forest Ridge Golf Club, Broken Arrow, Okla.
Georgia Veterans State Park Golf Course, Cordele, Ga.
Golden Horseshoe Golf Club (Gold), Williamsburg, Va.
Golf Club of Jacksonville (Fla.)
The Golf Courses of Kenton County (Fox Run),
 Independence, Ky.
Grand National Golf Club (Lake), Opelika, Ala.
Grand National Golf Club (Links), Opelika, Ala.
The Greenbrier (Greenbrier), White Sulphur Springs, W. Va.
Heather Glen Golf Links, North Myrtle Beach, S.C.
Heritage Club, Pawleys Island, S.C.
Heritage Hills Golf Course, McCook, Neb.
Heron Lakes Golf Course (Great Blue), Portland, Ore.
**Horseshoe Bay (Tex.) Resort & Conference Center
 (Applerock)**
**Horseshoe Bay (Tex.) Resort & Conference Center (Ram
 Rock)**
Howell Park Golf Course, Farmingdale, N.J.
Indian Canyon Golf Course, Spokane, Wash.
Indigo Run Golf Club, Hilton Head, S.C.
Innisbrook Hilton Resort (Copperhead), Palm Harbor, Fla.
Innisbrook Hilton Resort (Island), Palm Harbor, Fla.
Jackson Hole (Wyo.) Golf & Tennis Club
Kapalua Golf Club (Plantation), Maui, Hawaii
Kayak Point Golf Course, Stanwood, Wash.
Kearney Hill Golf Links, Lexington, Ky.
Keith Hills Country Club, Buies Creek, N.C.
Lake Arrowhead Golf Course, Nekoosa, Wis.
Legacy Golf Links, Aberdeen, N.C.
Legends Club of Tennessee (North), Franklin, Tenn.
Legends Club of Tennessee (South), Franklin, Tenn.
Lick Creek Golf Course, Pekin, Ill.
The Links at Key Biscayne (Fla.)
The Links at Northfork, Ramsey, Minn.
Los Caballeros Golf Club, Wickenburg, Ariz.
Magnolia Grove Golf Club (Crossings), Semmes, Ala.
Magnolia Grove Golf Club (Falls), Semmes, Ala.
Marcus Pointe Golf Club, Pensacola, Fla.
Mariana Butte Golf Course, Loveland, Colo.

Marriott at Sawgrass Resort (Marsh Landing),
  Ponte Vedra Beach, Fla.
Mauna Kea Golf Course, Kohala Coast, Hawaii
McCormick Woods Golf Course, Port Orchard, Wash.
Meadowbrook Golf Course, Rapid City, S.D.
Minot (N.D.) Country Club
Olde Mill Golf Course, Laurel Fork, Va.
Osprey Cove Golf Club, St. Marys, Ga.
Palisades Country Club, Clermont, Fla.
Pasatiempo Golf Club, Santa Cruz, Calif.
Pelican's Nest Golf Club, Bonita Springs, Fla.
Pinehurst (N.C.) Resort & Country Club (No. 7)
The Pines at Grand View Lodge, Nisswa, Minn.
Poppy Hills Golf Course, Pebble Beach, Calif.
Princeville Resort (Makai), Princeville, Kauai, Hawaii
Pumpkin Ridge Golf Club (Ghost Creek), Cornelius, Ore.
Rams Hill Country Club, Borrego Springs, Calif.
Redhawk Golf Club, Temecula, Calif.
Riverdale Golf Courses (Dunes), Brighton, Colo.
San Ignacio Golf Club, Green Valley, Ariz.
Sea Trail Plantation (Rees Jones), Sunset Beach, N.C.
Sedona (Ariz.) Golf Resort
Seven Oaks Golf Club, Hamilton, N.Y.
The Sound Golf Links, Hertford, N.C.
Squaw Valley Golf Course, Glen Rose, Tex.
Sugarloaf Golf Club, Carrabassett Valley, Me.
Sunbrook Golf Club, St. George, Utah
Swan Point Yacht & Country Club, Issue, Md.
Tanglewood Park Golf Club (Championship),
  Clemmons, N.C.
Treetops Sylvan Resort (Fazio), Gaylord, Mich.
University of New Mexico Golf Course, Albuquerque
University Ridge Golf Course, Verona, Wis.
Waikapu Sandalwood Golf Course, Wailuku, Maui, Hawaii
Waikele Golf Club, Waipahu, Oahu, Hawaii
Wailua Golf Course, Lihue, Kauai, Hawaii
The Walt Disney World Resort (Osprey Ridge),
  Lake Buena Vista, Fla.
Waterville (Me.) Country Club
Westchase Golf Club, Tampa, Fla.
Wild Dunes Resort (Links), Isle of Palms, S.C.
Wild Wing Plantation (Wood Stork), Myrtle Beach, S.C.
Wild Wing Plantation (Hummingbird), Myrtle Beach, S.C.
Wintergreen Resort (Stoney Creek), Wintergreen, Va.

America's 100
Greatest Golf Courses
As ranked by GOLF DIGEST

FIRST 10

Pine Valley Golf Club, Pine Valley, N.J.
Pebble Beach Golf Links, Pebble Beach, Calif.
Augusta National Golf Club, Augusta, Ga.
Cypress Point Club, Pebble Beach, Calif.
Shinnecock Hills Golf Club, Southampton, N.Y.
Oakmont Country Club, Oakmont, Pa.

Winged Foot Golf Club (West), Mamaroneck, N.Y.
Shadow Creek Golf Club, North Las Vegas, Nev.
Muirfield Village Golf Club, Dublin, Ohio
Merion Golf Club (East), Ardmore, Pa.

SECOND 10

Pinehurst Country Club (No. 2), Pinehurst, N.C.
The Olympic Club (Lake), San Francisco
Medinah Country Club (No. 3), Medinah, Ill.
Crystal Downs Country Club, Frankfort, Mich.
Oak Hill Country Club (East), Rochester, N.Y.
Oakland Hills Country Club (South), Bloomfield Hills, Mich.
The Country Club (Open), Brookline, Mass.
Wade Hampton Golf Club, Cashiers, N.C.
Seminole Golf Club, North Palm Beach, Fla.
Baltusrol Golf Club (Lower), Springfield, N.J.

THIRD 10

Quaker Ridge Golf Club, Scarsdale, N.Y.
National Golf Links, Southampton, N.Y.
Southern Hills Country Club, Tulsa, Okla.
Winged Foot Golf Club (East), Mamaroneck, N.Y.
Prairie Dunes Country Club, Hutchinson, Kan.
Spyglass Hill Golf Club, Pebble Beach, Calif.
San Francisco Golf Club, San Francisco
Garden City Golf Club, Garden City, N.Y.
The Honors Course, Chattanooga
Peachtree Golf Club, Atlanta

FOURTH 10

Blackwolf Run Golf Club (River), Kohler, Wis.
Cherry Hills Country Club, Englewood, Colo.
Chicago Golf Club, Wheaton, Ill.
The Golf Club, New Albany, Ohio
Scioto Country Club, Columbus, Ohio
Valhalla Golf Club, Louisville, Ky.
Los Angeles Country Club (North), Los Angeles
Forest Highlands Golf Club, Flagstaff, Ariz.
Riviera Country Club, Pacific Palisades, Calif.
Sycamore Hills Golf Club, Fort Wayne, Ind.

FIFTH 10

Laurel Valley Golf Club, Ligonier, Pa.
Castel Pines Golf Club, Castle Rock, Colo.
The Prince Golf & Country Club, Princeville, Kauai, Hawaii
Long Cove Club, Hilton Head Island, S.C.
Butler National Golf Club, Oak Brook, Ill.
Maidstone Club, East Hampton, N.Y.
Colonial Country Club, Fort Worth
Inverness Club, Toledo, Ohio
Plainfield Country Club, Plainfield, N.J.
Shoal Creek, Shoal Creek, Ala.

SIXTH 10

Black Diamond (Quarry), Lecanto, Fla.
Oak Tree Golf Club, Edmond, Okla.
Desert Mountain (Renegade), Scottsdale, Ariz.
Wannamoisett Country Club, Rumford, R.I.
Troon Golf & Country Club, Scottsdale, Ariz.
Bellerive Country Club, St. Louis
Hazeltine National Golf Club, Chaska, Minn.
Haig Point Club (Calibogue), Daufuskie Island, S.C.
TPC at Sawgrass (Stadium), Ponte Vedra Beach, Fla.
Barton Creek Country Club (Fazio), Austin, Texas

SEVENTH 10

Point O'Woods Golf & Country Club, Benton Harbor, Mich.
Baltimore Country Club (East), Timonium, Md.
Salem Country Club, Peabody, Mass.
Somerset Hills Country Club, Bernardsville, N.J.
Troon North Golf Club, Scottsdale, Ariz.
Greenville Country Club (Chanticleer), Greenville, S.C.
Desert Highlands Golf Club, Scottsdale, Ariz.
Cog Hill Golf & Country Club (No. 4), Lemont, Ill.
Mauna Kea Golf CSE., Kohala Coast, Hawaii
Harbour Town Golf Links, Hilton Head Island, S.C.

EIGHTH 10

Camargo Club, Indian Hill, Ohio
Interlachen Country Club, Edina, Minn.
Congressional Country Club (Blue), Bethesda, Md.
Sahalee Country Club (South/North), Redmond, Wash.
Kittansett Club, Marion, Mass.
Crooked Stick Golf Club, Carmel, Ind.
Aronimink Golf Club, Newtown Square, Pa.
Old Marsh Golf Club, Palm Beach Gardens, Fla.
Sherwood Country Club, Thousand Oaks, Calif.
Bay Hill Club, Orlando, Fla.

NINTH 10

Milwaukee Country Club, Milwaukee
Eugene Country Club, Eugene, Ore.
Pasatiempo Golf Club, Santa Cruz, Calif.
Olympia Fields Country Club (North), Olympia Fields, Ill.
Wynstone Golf Club, North Barrington, Ill.
Stanwich Club, Greenwich, Conn.
Desert Mountain (Cochise), Scottsdale, Ariz.
Kauai Lagoons (Kiele), Lihue, Kauai, Hawaii
Canterbury Golf Club, Shaker Heights, Ohio
Saucon Valley Country Club (Grace), Bethlehem, Pa.

TENTH 10

NCR Country Club (South), Kettering, Ohio
Grandfather Golf & Country Club, Linville, N.C.
PGA West Golf Club (Stadium), La Quinta, Calif.

Desert Forest Golf Club, Carefree, Ariz.
Cascades Golf Club, Hot Springs, Va.
Jupiter Hills Club (Hills), Tequesta, Fla.
Skokie Country Club, Glencoe, Ill.
Country Club of North Carolina (Dogwood), Pinehurst
Ridgewood Country Club (East/West), Paramus, N.J.
Wild Dunes (Links), Isle of Palms, S.C.

America's 75 Best Resort Courses
As ranked by GOLF DIGEST

FIRST 25

Pebble Beach, Pebble Beach, Calif.
Pinehurst (No. 2), Pinehurst, N.C.
The Ocean Course, Kiawah Island, S.C.
Kapalua (Plantation), Kapalua, Maui, Hawaii
Prince Golf & Country Club, Princeville, Kauai, Hawaii
Spyglass Hill, Pebble Beach, Calif.
TPC at Sawgrass (Stadium), Ponte Vedra, Fla.
Mauna Kea, Kohala Coast, Hawaii
Harbour Town, Hilton Head Island, S.C.
Jackson Hole, Jackson Hole, Wyo.
Coeur d'Alene Resort, Coeur d'Alene, Idaho
The Homestead (Cascades), Hot Springs, Va.
Wild Dunes (Links), Isle of Palms, S.C.
Stonehenge, Fairfield Glade, Tenn.
Kauai Lagoons (Kiele), Lihue, Kauai, Hawaii
PGA West (Stadium), La Quinta, Calif.
Bay Hill (Challenger/Champion), Orlando, Fla.
Semiahmoo, Blaine, Wash.
Shanty Creek (Legend), Bellaire, Mich.
Sunriver (North), Sunriver, Ore.
Barton Creek (Fazio), Austin, Tex.
Innisbrook (Copperhead), Tarpon Springs, Fla.
Pinehurst (No. 7), Pinehurst, N.C.
Spanish Bay, Pebble Beach, Calif.
The Kings' Course, Waikoloa, Hawaii

SECOND 25

Samoset, Rockport, Me.
Treetops Sylvan (Jones), Gaylord, Mich.
Ventana Canyon (Mountain), Tucson
The Broadmoor (East), Colorado Springs, Colo.
Golden Horseshoe (Gold), Williamsburg, Va.
Kapalua (Village), Kapalua, Maui, Hawaii
Donald Ross Memorial, Harbor Springs, Mich.
The Greenbrier (Greenbrier), White Sulphur Springs, W. Va.
Stoney Creek, Wintergreen, Va.
PGA West (Nicklaus Resort), La Quinta, Calif.
Kapalua (Bay), Kapalua, Maui, Hawaii
Tamarron, Durango, Colo.
Eagle Ridge (South), Galena, Ill.
Eagle Ridge (North), Galena, Ill.

Horseshoe Bay (Ram Rock), Horseshoe Bay, Tex.
Keystone Ranch, Keystone, Colo.
Doral (Blue), Miami
Marriott's Bay Point (Lagoon Legend),
   Panama City Beach, Fla.
Turtle Point, Kiawah Island, S.C.
The Concord (Monster), Kiamesha Lake, N.Y.
Port Ludlow, Port Ludlow, Wash.
The New Course at Grand Cypress, Orlando, Fla.
Princeville Makai (Ocean/Lakes), Princeville, Kauai, Hawaii
Teton Pines, Jackson, Wyo.
Grand Traverse (Bear), Acme, Mich.

THIRD 25

Long Point, Amelia Island, Fla.
The Boulders (North), Carefree, Ariz.
Singletree, Edwards, Colo.
Osprey Point, Kiawah Island, S.C.
Grand Cypress (North/South), Orlando, Fla.
Callaway Gardens (Mountain View), Pine Mountain, Ga.
Palm Beach Polo (Dunes), West Palm Beach, Fla.
The Broadmoor (West), Colorado Springs, Colo.
La Paloma (Ridge/Canyon), Tucson
Sun Valley, Sun Valley, Idaho
Walt Disney World (Palm), Lake Buena Vista, Fla.
Sea Island (Plantation/Seaside), St. Simons Island, Ga.
Sugarloaf, Carrabassett Valley, Me.
Radisson Elkhorn Sun Valley, Sun Valley, Idaho
Desert Inn, Las Vegas
Wailea (Blue), Wailea, Maui, Hawaii
Ko Olina, Ewa Beach, Oahu, Hawaii
La Quinta Hotel (Citrus), La Quinta, Calif.
New Seabury (Blue), New Seabury, Mass.
Grenelefe (West), Haines City, Fla.
Innisbrook (Island), Tarpon Springs, Fla.
PGA National (Champion), Palm Beach Gardens, Fla.
Salishan, Gleneden Beach, Ore.
Boyne Highlands (Heather), Harbor Springs, Mich.
La Quinta Hotel (Dunes), La Quinta, Calif.

America's 75
Best Public Golf Courses
As ranked by GOLF DIGEST
Listed alphabetically

FIRST 25

Bull Creek (Wh./Bl.), Midland, Ga.
Cantigny (Premier), Wheaton, Ill.
The Captains, Brewster, Mass.
Cochiti Lake, Cochiti Lake, N.M.
Cog Hill (No. 4), Lemont, Ill.
Eastmoreland, Portland, Ore.
Edgewood Tahoe, Stateline, Nev.

Forest Preserve National, Oak Forest, Ill.
Hog Neck (Ch.), Easton, Md.
Hominy Hill, Colts Neck, N.J.
Hyland Hills (Gld.), Westminster, Colo.
Indian Canyon, Spokane, Wash.
Jackson Hole, Jackson Hole, Wyo.
Kemper Lakes, Hawthorn Woods, Ill.
Otter Creek, Columbus, Ind.
Pasatiempo, Santa Cruz, Calif.
Pine Meadow, Mundelein, Ill.
Richter Park, Danbury, Conn.
Riverdale (Dunes), Brighton, Colo.
Sandpiper, Goleta, Calif.
Sentryworld, Stevens Point, Wis.
Spook Rock, Ramapo, N.Y.
Tanglewood Park (Championship), Clemmons, N.C.
Tokatee, Blue River, Ore.
Wailua, Kauai, Hawaii

SECOND 25

Bear Creek (Masters), Houston, Tex.
Bethpage (Black), Farmingdale, N.Y.
Brown County, Oneida, Wis.
Colony West (Ch.), Tamarac, Fla.
Desert Dunes, Palm Springs, Calif.
Eagle Bend, Bigfork, Mont.
Eastwood, Fort Myers, Fla.
Edinburgh USA, Brooklyn Park, Minn.
Heather Glen (Nos. 1/2), Little River, S.C.
Heritage, Pawleys Island, S.C.
Howell Park, Farmingdale, N.J.
Hunter's Creek, Orlando, Fla.
Kayak Point, Stanwood, Wash.
Key Biscayne, Key Biscayne, Fla.
Lagoon Park, Montgomery, Ala.
Marsh Harbour, Calabash, N.C.
McCormick Woods, Port Orchard, Wash.
Meadowbrook, Rapid City, S.D.
Montauk Downs, Montauk, N.Y.
Oyster Bay, Sunset Beach, N.C.
Pecan Valley, San Antonio, Tex.
The Pit, Pinehurst, N.C.
Torrey Pines (So.), La Jolla, Calif.
TPC of Scottsdale (Stadium), Scottsdale, Ariz.
West Palm Beach, West Palm Beach, Fla.

THIRD 25

Alvamar, Lawrence, Kan.
Ancil Hoffman, Carmichael, Calif.
Arrowhead, Littleton, Colo.
Blue Ash, Blue Ash, Ohio
Eagle Creek (Ch.), Indianapolis
Fall Creek Falls, Pikeville, Tenn.
Golden Ocala, Ocala, Fla.
Grand Haven, Grand Haven, Mich.
Heron Lakes (White/Blue), Portland, Ore.
High Pointe, Williamsburg, Mich.

Hulman Links, Terre Haute, Ind.
Incline Village, Incline Village, Nev.
Golf Club of Indiana, Zionsville, Ind.
Jones Creek, Evans, Ga.
Lawsonia Links (West/East), Green Lake, Wis.
Lick Creek, Pekin, Ill.
Majestic Oaks, Ham Lake, Minn.
Moreno Valley Ranch (Mountain/Lake), Moreno Valley, Calif.
Oak Hollow, High Point, N.C.
Pole Creek, Winter Park, Colo.
Rattle Run, St. Clair, Mich.
Stone Mountain (Stonemont/Woodmont), Stone Mountain, Ga.
Timber Ridge, East Lansing, Mich.
Torrey Pines (No.), La Jolla, Calif.
University of New Mexico (South), Albuquerque, N.M.

★★★AUBURN LINKS
Auburn—PU—205-887-5151 (60 mi. from Montgomery).
Season: Year-round. **High:** March-Aug. **Caddies:** No.
Green fee: $20-$49. **Credit cards:** V, MC.
Lodging on site: No. **Reduced fees:** No.
Unrestricted walking: Yes. **Range:** Yes (grass).
Holes: 18. **Par:** 72. **Yards:** 7,145-5,320. **Slope:** 130.
Comments: "Narrow; play the white tees unless you're a long hitter . . .
Bent-grass greens . . . Great shape all year . . . Some tough tee shots . . .
Easy to lose balls in wooded areas . . . With front 9 revisions, will be
excellent . . . Excellent staff . . . Best for the money."

★★BAY OAKS GOLF CLUB
Bayou La Batre—PU—205-824-2429 (10 mi. from Mobile).
Season: Year-round. **High:** Nov.-March. **Caddies:** No.
Green fee: Under $20. **Credit cards:** V, MC.
Lodging on site: No. **Reduced fees:** Weekdays.
Unrestricted walking: Yes. **Range:** Yes (grass).
Holes: 18. **Par:** 72. **Yards:** 6,208-5,422. **Slope:** 124-122.

★★★½ BENT BROOK GOLF COURSE
Bessemer—PU—205-424-2368 (10 mi. from Birmingham).
Season: Year-round. **High:** May-Oct. **Caddies:** No.
Green fee: $20-$49. **Credit cards:** V, AMEX, DISC, MC.
Lodging on site: No. **Reduced fees:** No.
Unrestricted walking: No. **Range:** Yes (mats).
Holes: 27. **Par:** 35/36/35. **Yards:** 3,570/3,483/3,364.
Comments: "My idea of a first-class daily fee . . . Mixture of easy and
tough holes . . . Very good holes . . . Wide open hitting areas . . . Splendid
greens . . . Rough not too high . . . No carts in fairways, wears you out."

★★★½ COTTON CREEK CLUB
EAST/NORTH/WEST 9s
Gulf Shores—PU—205-968-7766 (40 mi. from Mobile).
Season: Year-round. **High:** March-Oct. **Caddies:** No.
Green fee: $20-$49. **Credit cards:** V, MC.
Lodging on site: No. **Reduced fees:** Weekdays, Low Season.
Unrestricted walking: No. **Range:** Yes (grass).
Holes: 27. **Par:** 36/36/36. **Yards:** 3,512/3,516/3,459.
Comments: "Well-balanced design . . . Challenging but not a killer . . .
Adaptable to all games . . . Best-kept course I've ever played . . . Staff
friendly . . . Good driving range . . . Costly."

★★★EAGLE POINT GOLF CLUB
Birmingham—PU—205-991-9070 (15 mi. from Birmingham).
Season: Year-round. **High:** Year-round. **Caddies:** No.
Green fee: $20-$49. **Credit cards:** V, AMEX, MC.
Lodging on site: No. **Reduced fees:** Weekdays.
Unrestricted walking: Yes. **Range:** Yes (mats).
Holes: 18. **Par:** 71. **Yards:** 6,470-4,691. **Slope:** 127-108.
Comments: "Holes too close together . . . Balls everywhere . . . Well
maintained . . . Difficult to walk . . . No pull carts."

★★½ GLENLAKES COUNTRY CLUB
Foley—PU—205-943-8000, 800-264-8333 (45 mi. from Mobile).
Season: Year-round. **High:** June-Aug. **Caddies:** Yes.
Green fee: $20-$49. **Credit cards:** V, MC.
Reduced fees: Weekdays, Low Season, Resort Guests, Twilight Play.
Unrestricted walking: No. **Range:** Yes (grass).
Holes: 18. **Par:** 71. **Yards:** 6,580-5,019. **Slope:** 130-120.
Comments: "Uneven . . . You get two courses in one . . . Back 9 much
better than front . . . Rinky dink . . . Don't like blind lay-up holes."

★★★½ GOOSE POND COLONY GOLF COURSE
Scottsboro—PU—205-574-5353 (40 mi. from Huntsville).
Season: Year-round. **High:** Spring/Aug.-Sept. **Caddies:** No.
Green fee: Under $20. **Credit cards:** V, DISC, MC.
Lodging on site: Yes. **Reduced fees:** Weekdays.
Unrestricted walking: Yes. **Range:** Yes (grass).
Holes: 18. **Par:** 72. **Yards:** 6,843-5,368. **Slope:** 119-115.
Comments: "Well-kept secret . . . Beautiful, along backwaters of Tennessee River; very playable . . . Woods, water, rolling terrain, spectacular par 3s . . . Good bent-grass greens . . . Excellent pro shop staff . . . Northern Alabama's finest golf value . . . You'll want to play it again."

GRAND NATIONAL GOLF CLUB
Opelika—PU—205-749-9042, 800-949-4444 (55 mi. from Montgomery).
Season: Year-round. **High:** March-Oct. **Caddies:** No.
Green fee: $20-$49. **Credit cards:** V, AMEX, DISC, MC.
Reduced fees: Weekdays, Low Season, Twilight Play.
Unrestricted walking: Yes. **Range:** Yes (grass).
★★★★ LAKE COURSE
Holes: 18. **Par:** 72. **Yards:** 7,089-4,910. **Slope:** 138-123.
Comments: "World class . . . Beautiful, great shape, great value . . . Superb . . . Water on nine holes . . . Needs more pit stops."
★★★★ LINKS COURSE
Holes: 18. **Par:** 72. **Yards:** 7,311-4,843. **Slope:** 141-125.
Selected as runner-up for Best New Public Course of 1993 by GOLF DIGEST.
Comments: "Tour quality . . . A 'must-see' . . . Water on 13 holes . . . Natural scenery . . . No two holes alike . . . Too much for the average player . . . Purple tees are for pros only."
SHORT COURSE*
Holes: 18. **Par:** 54. **Yards:** 3,328-1,863.
Green fee: Under $20.

★★½ GULF SHORES GOLF CLUB
Gulf Shores—PU—205-968-7366.
Season: Year-round. **High:** Jan.-Aug. **Caddies:** No.
Green fee: $20-$49. **Credit cards:** V, MC.
Lodging on site: No. **Reduced fees:** Weekdays.
Unrestricted walking: No. **Range:** Yes (grass).
Holes: 18. **Par:** 72. **Yards:** 6,570-5,522. **Slope:** 122-121.
Comments: "Nice older course . . . Old style . . . Needs upgrading . . . If greens were ever cut, it'd be great . . . Small clubhouse . . . Biggest fox squirrels in the world."

★★★½ GULF STATE PARK GOLF COURSE
Gulf Shores—R—205-948-4653 (50 mi. from Mobile).
Season: Year-round. **Caddies:** No.
Green fee: Under $20. **Credit cards:** V, AMEX, MC.
Lodging on site: Yes. **Reduced fees:** Resort Guests.
Unrestricted walking: Yes. **Range:** Yes (grass).
Holes: 18. **Par:** 72. **Yards:** 6,563-5,310. **Slope:** Unrated.
Comments: "Excellent maintenance for a state park . . . You'll need every club . . . Hidden jewel, friendly staff . . . Excellent for seniors . . . The best deal around."

HAMPTON COVE GOLF CLUB
Owens Cross Roads—PU—205-551-1818 (8 mi. from Huntsville).
Season: Year-round. **High:** April-Oct. **Caddies:** No.
Green fee: $20-$49. **Credit cards:** V, AMEX, DISC, MC.
Lodging on site: No. **Reduced fees:** Twilight Play.
Unrestricted walking: No. **Range:** Yes (grass).
★★★½ HIGHLANDS COURSE
Holes: 18. **Par:** 72. **Yards:** 7,262-4,773. **Slope:** 134-118.
Comments: "Great course, outstanding scenery . . . A jewel . . . Staff very

friendly . . . Too many lakes and bunkers . . . Penal. Demoralizes average golfers . . . No water to drink or wash balls out on course."

★★★RIVER COURSE
Holes: 18. **Par:** 72. **Yards:** 7,507-5,283. **Slope:** 135-118.
Comments: "Great fun . . . Large Bermuda greens . . . 16 water holes . . . Premium on iron play . . . Extremely nice."

SHORT COURSE*
Holes: 18. **Par:** 54. **Yards:** 3,635-1,861.
Green fee: Under $20.

★★HUNTSVILLE MUNICIPAL GOLF COURSE
Huntsville—PU—205-883-3647.
Season: Year-round. **High:** April-Oct. **Caddies:** No.
Green fee: Under $20. **Credit cards:** No.
Lodging on site: No. **Reduced fees:** No.
Unrestricted walking: Yes. **Range:** Yes (mats).
Holes: 18. **Par:** 72. **Yards:** 6,408-4,909. **Slope:** 122-109.
Comments: "A goat ranch . . . No challenge . . . The model airplanes are distracting."

★★★ISLE DAUPHINE GOLF CLUB
Dauphin Island—PU—205-861-2433 (30 mi. from Mobile).
Season: Year-round. **High:** Feb.-May. **Caddies:** No.
Green fee: Under $20. **Credit cards:** V, MC.
Lodging on site: No. **Reduced fees:** Weekdays.
Unrestricted walking: Yes. **Range:** No.
Holes: 18. **Par:** 72. **Yards:** 6,620-5,619. **Slope:** 123-122.
Comments: "A true American links . . . Right on the gulf . . . Windy . . . Challenging . . . Not in good shape . . . Lots of sand."

★★★½ LAGOON PARK GOLF COURSE
Montgomery—PU—205-271-7000.
Season: Year-round. **High:** April-Aug. **Caddies:** No.
Green fee: Under $20. **Credit cards:** V, DISC, MC.
Lodging on site: No. **Reduced fees:** Weekdays, Low Season.
Unrestricted walking: Yes. **Range:** Yes (grass).
Holes: 18. **Par:** 72. **Yards:** 6,673-5,342. **Slope:** 124-113.
Comments: "What a quality public course should be . . . Large greens, narrow fairways . . . Low cost . . . Tough . . . Challenging . . . Lots of traps . . . Overrated . . . Slowest play in town."

★★½ LAKEPOINT RESORT
Eufaula—R—205-687-6677 (50 mi. from Columbus, Ga.).
Season: Year-round. **High:** March-May. **Caddies:** No.
Green fee: $20-$49. **Credit cards:** V, AMEX, MC.
Lodging on site: Yes. **Reduced fees:** Resort Guests.
Unrestricted walking: Yes. **Range:** Yes (grass).
Holes: 18. **Par:** 72. **Yards:** 6,752-5,363. **Slope:** 123.
Comments: "Some nuts-and-bolts holes . . . Hospitality is A-plus."

★★THE LINKSMAN GOLF CLUB
Mobile—PU—205-661-0018.
Season: Year-round. **High:** March-June. **Caddies:** No.
Green fee: Under $20. **Credit cards:** V, AMEX, DISC, MC.
Reduced fees: Weekdays, Resort Guests, Twilight Play.
Unrestricted walking: Yes. **Range:** Yes (mats).
Holes: 18. **Par:** 72. **Yards:** 6,275-5,416. **Slope:** 123-121.
Comments: "Disappointing . . . Lacks imagination."

MAGNOLIA GROVE GOLF CLUB
Semmes—PU—205-645-0075 (2 mi. from Mobile).
Season: Year-round. **High:** April-Oct. **Caddies:** No.
Green fee: $20-$49. **Credit cards:** V, AMEX, DISC, MC.
Lodging on site: No. **Reduced fees:** Weekdays, Twilight Play.

Unrestricted walking: No. **Range:** Yes (grass).

★★★★CROSSINGS COURSE

Holes: 18. **Par:** 72. **Yards:** 7,150-5,184. **Slope:** Unrated.
Comments: "Great new course . . . Each hole isolated from the rest . . .
Difficult bunkers, elevated greens . . . Tough, tough, tough."

★★★★FALLS COURSE

Holes: 18. **Par:** 72. **Yards:** 7,240-5,253. **Slope:** Unrated.
Comments: "First-rate all around . . . Splendid, magnificent, beautiful . . .
Great course, great clubhouse, great people . . . What more could you want?
. . . Easier of the Magnolias."

SHORT COURSE*

Holes: 18. **Par:** 54. **Yards:** 3,140-1,829.
Green fee: Under $20.

MARRIOTT'S LAKEWOOD GOLF CLUB

Point Clear—R—205-990-6312 (40 mi. from Mobile).
Season: Year-round. **High:** Spring/Fall. **Caddies:** No.
Green fee: $50-$99. **Credit cards:** V, AMEX, DISC, MC.
Lodging on site: Yes. **Reduced fees:** Resort Guests.
Unrestricted walking: No. **Range:** Yes (mats).

★★★AZALEA COURSE

Holes: 18. **Par:** 72. **Yards:** 6,770-5,307. **Slope:** 128-118.
Comments: "Best in the area . . . Beautiful live oaks . . . Just an average
resort course . . . Extremely overpriced."

★★★DOGWOOD COURSE

Holes: 18. **Par:** 71. **Yards:** 6,676-5,532. **Slope:** 124-122.
Comments: "Some great holes, some bland ones . . . Pretty island green
. . . Staff very professional."

★½ McFARLAND PARK GOLF CLUB

Florence—PU—205-760-6428 (120 mi. from Birmingham).
Season: Year-round. **High:** May-Oct. **Caddies:** No.
Green fee: Under $20. **Credit cards:** V, MC.
Lodging on site: No. **Reduced fees:** Low Season.
Unrestricted walking: Yes. **Range:** Yes (mats).
Holes: 18. **Par:** 72. **Yards:** 6,660-5,741. **Slope:** Unrated.
Comments: "Limited facilities . . . Tends to flood . . . Elevated greens."

★½ OAK MOUNTAIN STATE PARK GOLF COURSE

Pelham—PU—205-663-6731 (15 mi. from Birmingham).
Season: Year-round. **High:** May-Sept. **Caddies:** No.
Green fee: Under $20. **Credit cards:** V, AMEX, MC.
Lodging on site: Yes. **Reduced fees:** No.
Unrestricted walking: Yes. **Range:** Yes (grass).
Holes: 18. **Par:** 72. **Yards:** 6,748-5,540. **Slope:** 127-124.
Comments: "Good course, not so good service . . . Typical public opera-
tion . . . Perfectly average course . . . Boring . . . Noisy road holes."

★★THE OAKS GOLF CLUB

Muscle Shoals—PU—205-381-1231 (45 mi. from Huntsville).
Season: Year-round. **High:** April-Sept. **Caddies:** No.
Green fee: $20-$49. **Credit cards:** V, MC.
Lodging on site: No. **Reduced fees:** Weekdays.
Unrestricted walking: No. **Range:** Yes (grass).
Holes: 18. **Par:** 70. **Yards:** 6,056-4,911. **Slope:** 117-107.
Comments: "New course, raw . . . Large greens . . . Lots of lakes . . .
Lacks character . . . 18 holes on 90 acres . . . Too short!"

★★½ OLYMPIA SPA & GOLF RESORT

Dothan—R—205-677-3326.
Season: Year-round. **High:** Spring. **Caddies:** No.
Green fee: $20-$49. **Credit cards:** V, AMEX, DISC, MC.
Lodging on site: Yes. **Reduced fees:** Weekdays, Resort Guests.
Unrestricted walking: No. **Range:** Yes (grass).

Holes: 18. **Par:** 72. **Yards:** 7,400-5,470. **Slope:** 123-113.
Comments: "Old but good . . . Probably too long . . . Excellent personnel . . . Accommodations poor."

OXMOOR VALLEY GOLF CLUB
Birmingham—PU—205-942-1177, 800-949-4444.
Season: Year-round. **High:** April-Oct. **Caddies:** No.
Green fee: $20-$49. **Credit cards:** All Major.
Lodging on site: No. **Reduced fees:** Twilight Play.
Unrestricted walking: No. **Range:** Yes (grass).
★★½ **RIDGE COURSE**
Holes: 18. **Par:** 72. **Yards:** 7,018-4,869. **Slope:** 140-130.
Comments: "Excellent target golf . . . Forced carries, divided fairways . . . Good variety . . . Tight, extra steep, blind shots . . . Big greens . . . A must play . . . First trip around is definitely not enjoyable . . . World class goat hill . . . Sadistic . . . Not suited for duffers . . . Good staff . . . Great views."
★★★ **VALLEY COURSE**
Holes: 18. **Par:** 72. **Yards:** 7,299-4,866. **Slope:** 135-118.
Comments: "Country club atmosphere . . . Walking for mountain goats only . . . Some blind tee shots . . . Too easy to lose balls . . . Severely tiered greens . . . Automatic three-putts . . . Plain vanilla."
SHORT COURSE*
Holes: 18. **Par:** 54. **Yards:** 3,154-1,990.
Green fee: Under $20.

★★½ **STILL WATERS RESORT**
Dadeville—R—205-825-7021, 800-633-4954 (58 mi. from Montgomery).
Season: Year-round. **High:** March-Oct. **Caddies:** No.
Green fee: $20-$49. **Credit cards:** V, AMEX, DISC, MC.
Lodging on site: Yes. **Reduced fees:** Weekdays, Low Season, Twilight.
Unrestricted walking: No. **Range:** Yes (grass).
Holes: 18. **Par:** 72. **Yards:** 6,407-5,287. **Slope:** 124-125.
Comments: "Great facilities, great people . . . Narrow but fun . . . Has been let go . . . Has lost character . . . Minimal attention."

★★½ **TERRAPIN HILLS GOLF ESTATES**
Ft. Payne—PU—205-845-4624 (45 mi. from Chattanooga, Tenn.).
Season: Year-round. **High:** April-May/Aug.-Oct. **Caddies:** No.
Green fee: Under $20. **Credit cards:** V, MC.
Lodging on site: No. **Reduced fees:** Weekdays.
Unrestricted walking: No. **Range:** Yes (grass).
Holes: 18. **Par:** 71. **Yards:** 6,696-5,278. **Slope:** 118.
Comments: "Short, fun . . . Excellent pro shop and personnel."

ALASKA

★½ ANCHORAGE GOLF COURSE
Anchorage—PU—907-522-3363.
Season: May-Oct. **High:** July-Aug. **Caddies:** No.
Green fee: $20-$49. **Credit cards:** MC, V.
Lodging on site: No. **Reduced fees:** No.
Unrestricted walking: No. **Range:** Yes (grass).
Holes: 18. **Par:** 72. **Yards:** 6,616-4,848. **Slope:** 130-119.
Ranked 2nd in Alaska by GOLF DIGEST.
Comments: "Narrow . . . Forest-lined fairways . . . Rocks for yardage markers . . . Higher green fees for nonresidents . . . Mandatory carts, but you can walk on Mondays and Tuesdays . . . Poor practice range."

★★★ EAGLEGLEN GOLF COURSE
Elmendorf AFB—PU—907-552-3821 (Anchorage).
Season: May-Oct. **High:** June-Aug. **Caddies:** No.
Green fee: $20-$49. **Credit cards:** V, MC.
Lodging on site: No. **Reduced fees:** Twilight Play.
Unrestricted walking: Yes. **Range:** Yes (grass).
Holes: 18. **Par:** 72. **Yards:** 6,689-5,457. **Slope:** 129-123.
Ranked 1st in Alaska by GOLF DIGEST.
Comments: "On grounds of Elmendorf Air Force Base . . . Excellent challenge . . . Water and rough . . . Fun to play . . . Military has priority . . . Worth a trip to Alaska . . . Watch for moose droppings."

★★ MOOSE RUN GOLF COURSE
Anchorage—PU—907-428-0056.
Season: May-Oct. **High:** No. **Caddies:** No.
Green fee: $20-$49. **Credit cards:** V, MC.
Lodging on site: No. **Reduced fees:** Twilight Play.
Unrestricted walking: Yes. **Range:** Yes (grass).
Holes: 18. **Par:** 72. **Yards:** 6,499-5,382. **Slope:** 119-120.
Ranked 3rd in Alaska by GOLF DIGEST.
Comments: "Greens are small . . . Military gets preferred tee times."

★★ PALMER GOLF COURSE
Anchorage—PU—907-745-4653 (42 mi. from Anchorage).
Season: May-Sept. **High:** May-Aug. **Caddies:** No.
Green fee: $20-$49. **Credit cards:** V, MC.
Lodging on site: No. **Reduced fees:** Weekday, Twilight Play.
Unrestricted walking: Yes. **Range:** Yes (grass).
Holes: 18. **Par:** 72. **Yards:** 7,125-5,895. **Slope:** 132.
Comments: "Glacial winds add challenge . . . It's windy most of the time."

ANTELOPE HILLS GOLF COURSES

Prescott—PU—602-776-7888, 800-972-6818.
Season: Year-round. **High:** April-Oct. **Caddies:** No.
Green fee: $20-$49. **Credit cards:** V, MC.
Reduced fees: Weekdays, Low Season, Resort Guests, Twilight Play.
Unrestricted walking: Yes. **Range:** Yes (grass).
★★★**NORTH COURSE**
Holes: 18. **Par:** 72. **Yards:** 6,778-6,087. **Slope:** 131-126.
Comments: "Traditional layout . . . Small greens . . . Fast, sloping greens
. . . Higher up, plays shorter than the card."
★★★**SOUTH COURSE**
Holes: 18. **Par:** 72. **Yards:** 7,014-5,560. **Slope:** 124-113.
Comments: "New . . . Is developing into a beautiful course."

★★★½ DESERT HILLS GOLF COURSE

Yuma—PU—602-344-4653 (160 mi. from San Diego).
Season: Year-round. **High:** Nov.-April. **Caddies:** No.
Green fee: Under $20. **Credit cards:** No.
Lodging on site: No. **Reduced fees:** Low Season.
Unrestricted walking: Yes. **Range:** Yes (grass).
Holes: 18. **Par:** 72. **Yards:** 6,853-5,726. **Slope:** 115-122.
Comments: "Arizona's best municipal . . . It's walkable."

LONDON BRIDGE GOLF CLUB

Lake Havasu—PU—602-855-2719 (150 mi. from Las Vegas).
Season: Year-round. **High:** Nov.-March. **Caddies:** No.
Green fee: $20-$49. **Credit cards:** V, MC.
Lodging on site: No. **Reduced fees:** No.
Unrestricted walking: No. **Range:** Yes (mats).
★★★**LONDON BRIDGE COURSE**
Holes: 18. **Par:** 71. **Yards:** 6,618-6,166. **Slope:** 122-114.
9-hole par-3 Queen's Bay Course also.
Comments: "Better maintenance could add a lot."
★★**STONEBRIDGE COURSE**
Holes: 18. **Par:** 71. **Yards:** 6,298-5,766. **Slope:** 114-109.
Comments: "Shorter than other London Bridge course . . . Helps the ego."

★★★★LOS CABALLEROS GOLF CLUB

Wickenburg—R—602-684-2704 (56 mi. from Phoenix).
Season: Year-round. **High:** Feb.-April. **Caddies:** No.
Green fee: $50-$99. **Credit cards:** No.
Lodging on site: Yes. **Reduced fees:** Low Season, Resort Guests.
Unrestricted walking: No. **Range:** Yes (grass).
Holes: 18. **Par:** 72. **Yards:** 6,962-5,690. **Slope:** 136-123.
Ranked 15th in Top 20 courses in Arizona by GOLF DIGEST.
Comments: "Superb . . . A well-kept secret . . . Great scenery . . . Chal-
lenging . . . Top quality . . . Fine course for small community . . . A 'must
play' . . . Perfect example of desert golf . . . Some funky holes . . . Fastest
greens in the West."

★★★★SEDONA GOLF RESORT

Sedona—R—602-284-9355 (90 mi. from Phoenix).
Season: Year-round. **High:** March-Nov. **Caddies:** No.
Green fee: $50-$99. **Credit cards:** V, MC.
Reduced fees: Weekdays, Low Season, Twilight Play.
Unrestricted walking: No. **Range:** Yes (grass).
Holes: 18. **Par:** 71. **Yards:** 6,642-5,030. **Slope:** 130-119.
Ranked 9th in Arizona by GOLF DIGEST.
Comments: "Scenery-scenery-scenery . . . Beautiful Red Rock Country
. . . Fantastic Red Rock vistas . . . Views and golf holes take your breath
away . . . Terrific sights, good golf challenge . . . Great test from back tees
. . . Fast greens . . . Good staff, amenities lacking . . . Checkerboard flags
hard to see."

PHOENIX/SCOTTSDALE AREA

★★AHWATUKEE COUNTRY CLUB

Phoenix—PU—602-893-1161.
Season: Year-round. **High:** Jan.-May **Caddies:** No.
Green fee: $50-$99. **Credit cards:** V, AMEX, MC.
Reduced fees: Weekdays, Low Season, Twilight Play.
Unrestricted walking: No. **Range:** Yes (grass).
Holes: 18. **Par:** 72. **Yards:** 6,713-5,506. **Slope:** 124-118.
Comments: "Still one of the best-kept secrets in Phoenix . . . Great summer rates . . . Don't bother."

ARIZONA BILTMORE COUNTRY CLUB

Phoenix—R—602-955-9655.
Season: Year-round. **High:** Jan.-May. **Caddies:** No.
Green fee: $50-$99. **Credit cards:** All Major.
Lodging on site: Yes. **Reduced fees:** Low Season.
Unrestricted walking: No. **Range:** Yes (grass).
★★½ ADOBE COURSE
Holes: 18. **Par:** 72. **Yards:** 6,767-6,101. **Slope:** 121-116.
Comments: "Too many trees."
★★★LINKS COURSE
Holes: 18. **Par:** 71. **Yards:** 6,300-4,747. **Slope:** 122-115.
Comments: "Perfect vacation course . . . Good test, nice environment . . . Fun course, all types of holes . . . Difficult to get tee times."

★★½ THE ARIZONA GOLF RESORT

Mesa—R—602-832-1661 (25 mi. from Phoenix).
Season: Year-round. **High:** Jan.-March. **Caddies:** No.
Green fee: $20-$49. **Credit cards:** All Major.
Lodging on site: Yes. **Reduced fees:** Weekdays, Low Season, Resort Guests, Twilight Play.
Unrestricted walking: No. **Range:** Yes (grass).
Holes: 18. **Par:** 71. **Yards:** 6,574-6,195. **Slope:** 123-117.
Comments: "Ordinary . . . Wide open, good course for average golfers . . . Stupid doglegs in and out of housing development . . . Well maintained . . . Needs to green up."

THE BOULDERS

Carefree—R—602-488-9028 (33 mi. from Phoenix).
Season: Year-round. **High:** Feb.-May. **Caddies:** No.
Green fee: $100 and up. **Credit cards:** All Major.
Lodging on site: Yes. **Reduced fees:** Low Season.
Unrestricted walking: No. **Range:** Yes (grass).
★★★★BOULDERS NORTH COURSE
Holes: 18. **Par:** 72. **Yards:** 6,731-4,893. **Slope:** 135-113.
Ranked 52nd in America's 75 Best Resort Courses by GOLF DIGEST.
Comments: "What a resort setting . . . Golf in the real desert . . . When they say boulders, they mean boulders! . . . Reasonable landing areas, plays fast . . . Better than the South, but no golfing value . . . Very expensive, yet difficult to get on . . . Overpriced getaway."
★★★★BOULDERS SOUTH COURSE
Holes: 18. **Par:** 71. **Yards:** 6,589-4,715. **Slope:** 137-107.
Ranked 12th in Arizona by GOLF DIGEST.
"Unbelievable . . . Simply the best . . . Best desert format in all of Arizona . . . All aspects first class . . . Outstanding . . . Good pro shop."

★★½ DOBSON RANCH GOLF CLUB

Mesa—PU—602-644-2291 (15 mi. from Phoenix).
Season: Year-round. **High:** Dec.-April. **Caddies:** No.
Green fee: Under $20. **Credit cards:** No.
Lodging on site: No. **Reduced fees:** Low Season, Twilight Play.
Unrestricted walking: Yes. **Range:** Yes (grass).

Holes: 18. **Par:** 72. **Yards:** 6,593-5,598. **Slope:** 117-116.
Comments: "Best shape for a public course . . . Beautiful greens . . . Cheap green fee . . . Difficult to get on . . . A guaranteed 6-hour round."

★½ ENCANTO GOLF COURSE
Phoenix—PU—602-253-3963.
Season: Year-round. **High:** Dec.-March. **Caddies:** No.
Green fee: $20-$49. **Credit cards:** No.
Lodging on site: No. **Reduced fees:** Low Season, Twilight Play.
Unrestricted walking: Yes. **Range:** Yes (grass).
Holes: 18. **Par:** 70. **Yards:** 6,500-6,324. **Slope:** 111-105.
Also 9-hole par-30 course on the property.

★★½ ESTRELLA GOLF COURSE
Goodyear—PU—602-932-3714 (15 mi. from Phoenix).
Season: Year-round. **High:** Jan.-April. **Caddies:** No.
Green fee: $20-$49. **Credit cards:** V, MC.
Reduced fees: Weekdays, Low Season, Twilight Play.
Unrestricted walking: Yes. **Range:** Yes (grass).
Holes: 18. **Par:** 71. **Yards:** 6,415-5,374. **Slope:** 118-112.
Comments: "Traditional design . . . Easy . . . Tough par 4s are a challenge."

★★ THE FOOTHILLS GOLF CLUB
Phoenix—PU—602-460-4653.
Season: Year-round. **High:** Jan.-April. **Caddies:** No.
Green fee: $50-$99. **Credit cards:** V, AMEX, DISC, MC.
Reduced fees: Weekdays, Low Season, Twilight Play.
Unrestricted walking: No. **Range:** Yes (grass).
Holes: 18. **Par:** 72. **Yards:** 6,967-5,213. **Slope:** 117-110.
Comments: "Very playable, good value . . . Not too bad . . . Always seems to be in process of improving . . . Hot, but enjoyable . . . Gee, could you put these houses a little closer to the fairways? I can't see what they're eating . . . Not worth the price."

★★½ FOUNTAIN HILLS GOLF CLUB
Fountain Hills—PU—602-837-1173 (12 mi. from Scottsdale).
Season: Year-round. **High:** Jan.-April 15th. **Caddies:** No.
Green fee: $50-$99. **Credit cards:** V, AMEX, MC.
Lodging on site: No. **Reduced fees:** Low Season, Twilight Play.
Unrestricted walking: No. **Range:** Yes (grass).
Holes: 18. **Par:** 71. **Yards:** 6,087-5,035. **Slope:** 119-112.
Comments: "Scenic . . . Lots of rolling hills . . . Elevated tees and greens."

★★★ GAINEY RANCH GOLF CLUB
DUNES/LAKES/ARROYO 9s
Scottsdale—R—602-951-0896.
Season: Year-round. **High:** Oct.-May. **Caddies:** No.
Green fee: $100 and up. **Credit cards:** All Major.
Lodging on site: Yes. **Reduced fees:** No.
Unrestricted walking: No. **Range:** Yes (grass).
Holes: 27. **Par:** 72. **Yards:** 6,800-6,252. **Slope:** 128-123.
Comments: "Short courses."

★★★ GOLD CANYON GOLF CLUB
Apache Junction—R—602-982-9449, 800-624-6445 (22 mi. from Phoenix).
Season: Year-round. **High:** Jan.-March. **Caddies:** No.
Green fee: $50-$99. **Credit cards:** All Major.
Lodging on site: Yes. **Reduced fees:** Low Season, Resort Guests, Twilight Play.
Unrestricted walking: No. **Range:** Yes (grass).
Holes: 18. **Par:** 71. **Yards:** 6,398-4,876. **Slope:** 135-112.
Comments: "Spectacular . . . A secret few people know about . . . Breath-taking   views of Superstition Mountains . . . A must play for all visitors . .

Most exciting and enjoyable . . . Great back 9 . . . Back a roller-coaster ride that makes drive from Phoenix worth it . . . Love that back 9 . . . An abomination . . . Overrated."

★★★½ HILLCREST GOLF CLUB
Sun City West—R—602-584-1500 (10 mi. from Phoenix).
Season: Year-round. **High:** Nov.-May. **Caddies:** No.
Green fee: $50-$99. **Credit cards:** V, AMEX, MC.
Lodging on site: Yes. **Reduced fees:** Weekdays, Low Season, Resort Guests, Twilight Play.
Unrestricted walking: No. **Range:** Yes (grass).
Holes: 18. **Par:** 72. **Yards:** 6,960-5,880. **Slope:** 127-119.
Comments: "Long and challenging . . . Staff is very good . . . Caters to Sun City retirees . . . Fun track at a fair price . . . Very good practice area."

★★★KARSTEN GOLF COURSE
Tempe—PU—602-921-8070 (5 mi. from Phoenix).
Season: Year-round. **High:** Jan.-May. **Caddies:** No.
Green fee: $50-$99. **Credit cards:** V, AMEX, DISC.
Lodging on site: No. **Reduced fees:** Weekdays, Low Season.
Unrestricted walking: No. **Range:** Yes (grass).
Holes: 18. **Par:** 72. **Yards:** 7,057-4,760. **Slope:** 128-106.
Course owned by Arizona State University. Ranked 19th in Arizona by GOLF DIGEST.
Comments: "Typical Dye design . . . Great test of skill . . . All golfers should play this once . . . Mounds instead of trees, on both sides of fairways—not fun . . . Arizona links . . . Very tight, almost cramped . . . Spotty maintenance . . . Best clubhouse staff ever encountered . . . Appreciates your business . . . Needs a restaurant . . . Horrible power-line skyline."

★★★THE LEGEND GOLF RESORT AT ARROWHEAD
Glendale—R—602-561-0953, 800-468-7918 (5 mi. from Phoenix).
Season: Year-round. **High:** Jan.-April. **Caddies:** No.
Green fee: $50-$99. **Credit cards:** V, AMEX, MC.
Reduced fees: Weekdays, Low Season, Twilight Play.
Unrestricted walking: No. **Range:** Yes (grass).
Holes: 18. **Par:** 72. **Yards:** 7,005-5,233. **Slope:** 129-119.
Comments: "A great Palmer course . . . Staffing is sparse at times."

MARRIOTT'S CAMELBACK GOLF CLUB
Scottsdale—R—602-948-6770, 800-242-2635.
Season: Year-round. **High:** Jan.-April. **Caddies:** No.
Green fee: $50-$99. **Credit cards:** All Major.
Lodging on site: Yes. **Reduced fees:** Weekdays, Low Season, Resort Guests, Twilight Play.
Unrestricted walking: No. **Range:** Yes (grass).
★★INDIAN BEND COURSE
Holes: 18. **Par:** 72. **Yards:** 7,014-5,917. **Slope:** 116-118.
Comments: "Excellent staff and pro shop . . . Conditions questionable . . . Boring . . . Precious little shade . . First 11 holes usually dead into the wind . . . Pricey . . . Food service sometimes lacking."
★★★PADRE COURSE
Holes: 18. **Par:** 71. **Yards:** 6,559-5,626. **Slope:** 117-117.
Comments: "Nice layout, good greens . . . Comfortable place to play . . . Old-style Arizona golf . . . They know how to treat guests."

★★MARYVALE MUNICIPAL GOLF COURSE
Phoenix—PU—602-846-4022.
Season: Year-round. **High:** Dec.-April. **Caddies:** No.
Green fee: $20-$49. **Credit cards:** V, AMEX, DISC, MC.
Reduced fees: Weekdays, Low Season, Twilight Play.
Unrestricted walking: Yes. **Range:** Yes (grass).
Holes: 18. **Par:** 72. **Yards:** 6,539-5,656. **Slope:** 116-111.
Comments: "Flat . . . Uninteresting . . . Cheap."

McCORMICK RANCH GOLF CLUB
Scottsdale—PU—602-948-0260.
Season: Year-round. **High:** Jan.-April. **Caddies:** No.
Green fee: $50-$99. **Credit cards:** V, MC.
Lodging on site: No. **Reduced fees:** Low Season, Twilight Play.
Unrestricted walking: No. **Range:** Yes (grass).
★★★**PALM COURSE**
Holes: 18. **Par:** 72. **Yards:** 7,032-5,210. **Slope:** 133-120.
Comments: "Good attention to details."
★★½ **PINE COURSE**
Holes: 18. **Par:** 72. **Yards:** 7,013-5,367. **Slope:** 133-120.
Comments: "Overpriced in season."

★★★★**OCOTILLO GOLF CLUB**
BLUE/WHITE/GOLD 9s
Chandler—R—602-275-4355 (30 mi. from Phoenix).
Season: Year-round. **High:** Jan.-April. **Caddies:** No.
Green fee: $50-$99. **Credit cards:** V, AMEX, MC.
Lodging on site: No. **Reduced fees:** Low Season, Twilight Play.
Unrestricted walking: No. **Range:** Yes (grass).
Holes: 27. **Par:** 36/35/36. **Yards:** 3,325/3,208/3,404.
Comments: "Magnificent . . . Brilliant layout . . . Memorable . . . Lush, watery . . . Best secret in Arizona . . . Lots of water . . . 14 miles of shoreline . . . Bring your ball retriever . . . Where did they get all that water in Arizona? . . . Good conditions . . . Outstanding value . . . Good summer specials . . . Patio amenities acceptable."

★★★**ORANGE TREE GOLF RESORT**
Scottsdale—R—602-948-3730, 800-228-0386.
Season: Year-round. **High:** Jan.-April. **Caddies:** No.
Green fee: $50-$99. **Credit cards:** V, AMEX, MC.
Lodging on site: Yes. **Reduced fees:** Weekdays, Low Season, Resort Guests, Twilight Play.
Unrestricted walking: No. **Range:** Yes (grass).
Holes: 18. **Par:** 72. **Yards:** 6,762-5,632. **Slope:** 122-116.
Comments: "Good resort layout . . . Best unknown course in Arizona . . . A true delight . . . Plush . . . Former country club . . . Disappointing . . . Overcrowded, pace of play a problem."

★★★½ **PAPAGO GOLF COURSE**
Phoenix—PU—602-275-8428.
Season: Year-round. **High:** Jan.-April. **Caddies:** No.
Green fee: $20-$49. **Credit cards:** No.
Lodging on site: No. **Reduced fees:** Low Season, Twilight Play.
Unrestricted walking: Yes. **Range:** Yes (grass).
Holes: 18. **Par:** 72. **Yards:** 7,068-5,781. **Slope:** 132-119.
Comments: "What a treat . . . Great muny . . . Best city course in Phoenix . . . The original desert design of Arizona . . . Superb staff . . . Crowded . . . Overplayed."

★★★**THE PHOENICIAN GOLF CLUB**
Scottsdale—R—602-423-2449.
Season: Year-round. **High:** Late Aug.-June. **Caddies:** No.
Green fee: $100 and up. **Credit cards:** All Major.
Lodging on site: Yes. **Reduced fees:** Low Season, Resort Guests.
Unrestricted walking: No. **Range:** Yes (grass).
Holes: 18. **Par:** 71. **Yards:** 6,487-6,033. **Slope:** 134-128.
Comments: "Fun resort course . . . Great resort . . . Good service . . . Staff was excellent, well trained! . . . Superb treatment . . . Spotty greens . . . Too short . . . Too easy for better players . . . Pricey."

★★★½ THE POINTE GOLF CLUB
AT LOOKOUT MOUNTAIN
Phoenix—R—602-866-6356.
Season: Year-round. **High:** Jan.-April. **Caddies:** No.
Green fee: $100 and up. **Credit cards:** All Major.
Lodging on site: Yes. **Reduced fees:** Low Season, Resort Guests, Twilight Play.
Unrestricted walking: No. **Range:** Yes (grass).
Holes: 18. **Par:** 72. **Yards:** 6,617-4,552. **Slope:** 131-113.
Comments: "Nicest course in Phoenix, well kept . . . Beautiful . . . Excellent, all-round facilities . . . Great total resort . . . Overpriced, underwatered . . . For price I paid, worst conditions."

★★ THE POINTE GOLF CLUB ON SOUTH MOUNTAIN
Phoenix—R—602-431-6480.
Season: Year-round. **High:** Feb.-April. **Caddies:** No.
Green fee: $50-$99. **Credit cards:** All Major.
Lodging on site: Yes. **Reduced fees:** Weekdays, Low Season, Twilight Play.
Unrestricted walking: No. **Range:** No.
Holes: 18. **Par:** 70. **Yards:** 6,003-4,550. **Slope:** 117-107.
Comments: "Weird layout . . . Must play target golf . . . Trick holes . . . Targets, targets, targets . . . 18th hole is a joke . . . Tough to gauge distances . . . Terribly high green fee."

★★★ RED MOUNTAIN RANCH COUNTRY CLUB
Mesa—PU—602-985-0285 (15 mi. from Phoenix).
Season: Year-round. **High:** Jan.-March. **Caddies:** No.
Green fee: $100 and up. **Credit cards:** V, AMEX, MC.
Lodging on site: No. **Reduced fees:** Low Season, Twilight Play.
Unrestricted walking: No. **Range:** Yes (grass).
Holes: 18. **Par:** 72. **Yards:** 6,797-5,603. **Slope:** 134-119.
Comments: "Typical Pete Dye target golf . . . Difficult Pete Dye . . . Great Pete Dye . . . Nice track . . . My favorite . . . Some impossible pins . . . Some impossible holes . . . Good value . . . Excellent staff . . . Major design flaws . . . Penal mounding . . . A piece of garbage . . . People who live nearby don't play here . . . Desert golf at its worst."

RIO VERDE COUNTRY CLUB
Rio Verde—PU—602-471-9420 (7 mi. from Scottsdale).
Season: Year-round. **High:** Dec.-April. **Caddies:** No.
Green fee: $50-$99. **Credit cards:** V, MC.
Lodging on site: Yes. **Reduced fees:** Low Season, Resort Guests.
Unrestricted walking: No. **Range:** Yes (mats).
★★★ QUAIL RUN COURSE
Holes: 18. **Par:** 72. **Yards:** 6,524-6,228. **Slope:** 116-113.
Comments: "Back tees make course much more interesting."
★★★ WHITE WING COURSE
Holes: 18. **Par:** 71. **Yards:** 6,456-6,053. **Slope:** 123-112.

★★★ SCOTTSDALE COUNTRY CLUB
NORTH/SOUTH/EAST 9s
Scottsdale—R—602-948-6911.
Season: Year-round. **High:** Feb.-April. **Caddies:** No.
Green fee: $50-$99. **Credit cards:** V, AMEX, MC.
Reduced fees: Weekdays, Low Season, Resort Guests, Twilight Play.
Unrestricted walking: No. **Range:** No.
Holes: 27. **Par:** 35/35/36. **Yards:** 3,021/3,064/3,271.
Comments: "Nice layout . . . Pleasant surprise . . . Doesn't have the reputation of other area biggies . . . Well maintained . . . North and South 9s great; East just so-so."

★★★ STONECREEK GOLF CLUB
Paradise Valley—R—602-953-9110.

ARIZONA

Season: Year-round. **High:** Jan.-May. **Caddies:** No.
Green fee: $50-$99. **Credit cards:** All Major.
Lodging on site: No. **Reduced fees:** Weekdays, Low Season.
Unrestricted walking: No. **Range:** Yes (grass).
Holes: 18. **Par:** 71. **Yards:** 6,839-5,098. **Slope:** 133-118.
Comments: "Fun, but tough . . . Small elevated greens . . . Stone creeks are severe penalties for off-line shots . . . Can't play the course without a yardage booklet . . . Best staff and pro shop in the valley, but they need to improve pace of play."

★★★½ SUPERSTITION SPRINGS GOLF CLUB
Mesa—PU—602-985-5622 (20 mi. from Phoenix).
Season: Year-round. **High:** Jan.-April. **Caddies:** No.
Green fee: $50-$99. **Credit cards:** V, AMEX, MC.
Reduced fees: Weekdays, Low Season, Twilight Play.
Unrestricted walking: No. **Range:** Yes (grass).
Holes: 18. **Par:** 72. **Yards:** 7,005-6,405. **Slope:** 135-132.
Comments: "Very modern design . . . Long . . . Challenging . . . Better than average . . . Expect some surprises . . . No. 9 is a super hole . . . The 18th is the best hole in the state . . . In poor condition."

★★½ TATUM RANCH GOLF CLUB
Cave Creek—R—602-585-2399 (10 mi. from Phoenix).
Season: Year-round. **High:** Jan.-April. **Caddies:** No.
Green fee: $50-$99. **Credit cards:** V, AMEX, MC.
Lodging on site: No. **Reduced fees:** Low Season, Twilight Play.
Unrestricted walking: No. **Range:** Yes (grass).
Holes: 18. **Par:** 72. **Yards:** 6,870-5,609. **Slope:** 128-116.
Comments: "Nice place to play . . . Lots of desert areas along the sides . . . Very playable . . . Fun for all levels . . . Extremely well groomed . . . Underappreciated . . . Average course . . . Featureless."

TOURNAMENT PLAYERS CLUB OF SCOTTSDALE
Scottsdale—R—602-585-3800.
Season: Year-round. **High:** Jan.-April. **Caddies:** No.
Green fee: Under $20. **Credit cards:** V, AMEX, MC.
Lodging on site: Yes. **Reduced fees:** Low Season, Twilight Play.
Unrestricted walking: Yes. **Range:** Yes (grass).
DESERT COURSE*
Holes: 18. **Par:** 71. **Yards:** 6,552-4,715. **Slope:** 112-109.
★★★½ STADIUM COURSE
Scottsdale—R—602-585-3600.
Green fee: $100 and up. **Unrestricted walking:** No.
Holes: 18. **Par:** 71. **Yards:** 6,992-5,567. **Slope:** 130-122.
Home of the PGA Tour's Phoenix Open. Ranked in Second 25 of America's 75 Best Public Courses by GOLF DIGEST.
Comments: "Super . . . Nice Morrish-Weiskopf layout . . . Something to be proud of . . . Different from normal Arizona courses . . . Demands shot placement . . . Slow greens . . . Cartpaths too far from fairways and greens; slows play . . . Conditioning is the only drawback . . . Cost a factor . . . You're paying for that TPC name . . . Don't play in summer months, even though it's cheaper . . . They try to rush you through . . . Try walking with an electric caddie."

★★★★★ TROON NORTH GOLF CLUB
Scottsdale—PU—602-585-5300.
Season: Year-round. **High:** Nov.-May. **Caddies:** No.
Green fee: $100 and up. **Credit cards:** V, AMEX, MC.
Lodging on site: No. **Reduced fees:** Low Season.
Unrestricted walking: No. **Range:** Yes (grass).
Holes: 18. **Par:** 72. **Yards:** 7,008-5,050. **Slope:** 146-116.
Ranked 65th in America's 100 Greatest Golf Courses by GOLF DIGEST.
Comments: "Superb . . . Classy . . . Exhilarating . . . Best public facility in America . . . It doesn't get any better . . . Weiskopf's best . . . Next to

ARIZONA

Desert Mountain, the finest ever in Arizona . . . It's the best . . . Second only to Pebble Beach . . . The epitome of a desert course . . . Very, very beautiful . . . Lots of desert areas . . . Little mercy on hooks or slices, yet very fair . . . Exceptional condition . . . Pure pleasure . . . Excellent reception by staff . . . They need a real clubhouse . . . Extremely expensive . . . No better way to spend your money."

WIGWAM RESORT
Litchfield Park—R—602-272-4653 (15 mi. from Phoenix).
Season: Year-round. **High:** March-May. **Caddies:** Yes.
Green fee: $50-$99. **Credit cards:** V, AMEX, DISC, MC.
Lodging on site: Yes. **Reduced fees:** Low Season.
Unrestricted walking: No. **Range:** Yes (grass).
★★BLUE COURSE
Holes: 18. **Par:** 70. **Yards:** 6,030-5,235. **Slope:** 118-118.
Comments: "Much gentler than Gold . . . Uninspiring . . . Esthetically dull . . . Could be better maintained . . . Always seems crowded."
★★★½ GOLD COURSE
Holes: 18. **Par:** 72. **Yards:** 7,021-5,673. **Slope:** 133-128.
Ranked 16th in Arizona by GOLF DIGEST.
Comments: "Super resort course . . . Great course . . . Top notch . . . Very long . . . Beautiful setting . . . Too penal . . . Rough gets so high it spoils the views . . . Lousy conditions . . . Hard traps."
★★★WEST COURSE
Holes: 18. **Par:** 72. **Yards:** 6,867-5,821. **Slope:** 119-117.
Comments: "OK, but it's not the Gold . . . Skip it. Play the Gold instead."

TUCSON AREA

★★ARTHUR PACK DESERT GOLF COURSE
Tucson—PU—602-744-3322.
Season: Year-round. **High:** Dec.-May. **Caddies:** No.
Green fee: Under $20. **Credit cards:** V, MC.
Lodging on site: No. **Reduced fees:** Low Season, Twilight Play.
Unrestricted walking: Yes. **Range:** Yes (grass).
Holes: 18. **Par:** 72. **Yards:** 6,900-6,500. **Slope:** 118-108.

★★★½ CANOA HILLS GOLF COURSE
Green Valley—PU—602-648-1880 (20 mi. from Tucson).
Season: Year-round. **High:** Jan.-April. **Caddies:** No.
Green fee: $20-$49. **Credit cards:** V, MC.
Lodging on site: No. **Reduced fees:** Low Season, Twilight Play.
Unrestricted walking: No. **Range:** Yes (grass).
Holes: 18. **Par:** 72. **Yards:** 6,599-5,158. **Slope:** 117-112.

EL CONQUISTADOR COUNTRY CLUB
Tucson—R—602-544-7800.
Season: Year-round. **High:** Feb.-April. **Caddies:** No.
Green fee: $100 and up. **Credit cards:** V, AMEX, DISC, MC.
Lodging on site: Yes. **Reduced fees:** No.
Unrestricted walking: No. **Range:** Yes (grass).
★★★½ SUNRISE COURSE
Holes: 18. **Par:** 72. **Yards:** 6,819-5,255. **Slope:** 123-116.
Comments: "Great resort . . . Fairly new . . . Still maturing."
★★★SUNSET COURSE
Holes: 18. **Par:** 72. **Yards:** 6,763-5,328. **Slope:** 123-114.

★★EL RIO GOLF COURSE
Tucson—PU—602-623-6783.
Season: Year-round. **High:** Nov.-April. **Caddies:** No.
Green fee: Under $20. **Credit cards:** No.
Lodging on site: No. **Reduced fees:** No.

Unrestricted walking: Yes. **Range:** Yes (grass).
Holes: 18. **Par:** 70. **Yards:** 6,418-6,113. **Slope:** 110-108.

RANDOLPH GOLF COURSE
Tucson—PU—602-325-2811.
Season: Year-round. **High:** Jan.-April. **Caddies:** No.
Green fee: Under $20. **Credit cards:** No.
Lodging on site: No. **Reduced fees:** Low Season, Twilight Play.
Unrestricted walking: Yes. **Range:** Yes (mats).
★★★NORTH COURSE
Holes: 18. **Par:** 72. **Yards:** 6,902-5,972. **Slope:** 128-124.
Host site of the LPGA's Ping/Welch's Championship.
Comments: "Excellent test from the back tees . . . Very good for the public golf crowd . . . Always busy."
★★½ SOUTH COURSE
Holes: 18. **Par:** 70. **Yards:** 6,229-5,568. **Slope:** 101-108.
Comments: "Bargain-basement Tucson golf."

★★★½ SAN IGNACIO GOLF CLUB
Green Valley—PU—602-648-3468 (25 mi. from Tucson).
Season: Year-round. **High:** Dec.-May. **Caddies:** No.
Green fee: $20-$49. **Credit cards:** No.
Lodging on site: No. **Reduced fees:** Low Season, Twilight Play.
Unrestricted walking: No. **Range:** Yes (mats).
Holes: 18. **Par:** 71. **Yards:** 6,704-5,200. **Slope:** 129-112.
Comments: "Stunning desert views . . . Fine design."

★★SILVERBELL GOLF COURSE
Tucson—PU—602-743-7284.
Season: Year-round. **High:** Oct.-April. **Caddies:** No.
Green fee: Under $20. **Credit cards:** V, MC.
Reduced fees: Weekdays, Low Season, Twilight Play.
Unrestricted walking: Yes. **Range:** Yes (grass).
Holes: 18. **Par:** 72. **Yards:** 6,900-6,400. **Slope:** 120-110.

★★★½ STARR PASS GOLF CLUB
Tucson—PU—602-622-6060.
Season: Year-round. **High:** Jan.-May. **Caddies:** No.
Green fee: $50-$99. **Credit cards:** V, AMEX, MC.
Lodging on site: Yes. **Reduced fees:** Low Season.
Unrestricted walking: No. **Range:** Yes (grass).
Holes: 18. **Par:** 72. **Yards:** 7,010-5,210. **Slope:** 139-121.
Formerly known as TPC at Starpass. Home of the PGA Tour's Northern Telecom Open. Ranked 17th in Arizona by Golf Digest.
Comments: "Nice desert layout . . . A good track in most spots . . . You'll need good shotmaking skills to score . . . Some blind shots . . . Nice off-season specials."

★★★½ SUN CITY VISTOSO GOLF CLUB
Tucson—PU—602-825-3110.
Season: Year-round. **High:** Nov.-April. **Caddies:** No.
Green fee: $50-$99. **Credit cards:** V, MC.
Lodging on site: No. **Reduced fees:** Low Season.
Unrestricted walking: No. **Range:** Yes (grass).
Holes: 18. **Par:** 72. **Yards:** 6,723-5,109. **Slope:** 137-110.

★★★½ TUCSON NATIONAL GOLF RESORT
ORANGE/GOLD/GREEN 9s
Tucson—R—602-297-2271, 800-528-4856.
Season: Year-round. **High:** Jan.-May. **Caddies:** No.
Green fee: $50-99. **Credit cards:** AMEX, DC, MC.
Lodging on site: Yes. **Reduced fees:** Weekdays, Low Season, Resort Guests.

Unrestricted walking: No. **Range:** Yes (grass).
Holes: 27. **Par:** 36/37/36. **Yards:** 3,470-3,638-3,222.
Ranked 20th in Arizona by GOLF DIGEST.

VENTANA CANYON GOLF & RACQUET CLUB

Tucson—R—602-577-2115, 800-828-5701.
Season: Year-round. **High:** Oct.-April. **Caddies:** No.
Green fee: $100 and up. **Credit cards:** All Major.
Lodging on site: Yes. **Reduced fees:** Low Season, Resort Guests.
Unrestricted walking: No. **Range:** Yes (grass).
★★★½ **CANYON COURSE**
Holes: 18. **Par:** 72. **Yards:** 6,969-4,919. **Slope:** 137-121.
Course used by Loews Ventana Canyon Resort.
Comments: "A genuine pleasure . . . Go in the off-season. It's still spectacular."
★★★½ **MOUNTAIN COURSE**
Holes: 18. **Par:** 72. **Yards:** 6,984-4,709. **Slope:** 149-117.
Ranked 28th in America's 75 Best Resort Courses by GOLF DIGEST.
Comments: "Target golf in the desert . . . Great views . . . Hard rounds . . . Best of the Arizona desert courses . . . Difficult for average players . . . Unbelievably long distances between holes . . . Very, very slow . . . Decent rates in the off-season."

★★★½ THE WESTIN LA PALOMA
RIDGE/CANYON/HILL 9s

Tucson—R—602-299-1500, 800-222-1249.
Season: Year-round. **High:** Jan.-May. **Caddies:** No.
Green fee: $50-$99. **Credit cards:** All Major.
Lodging on site: Yes. **Reduced fees:** Low Season.
Unrestricted walking: No. **Range:** Yes (grass).
Holes: 27. **Par:** 36/36/36. **Yards:** 3,554/3,434/3,463.
Ridge/Canyon Course ranked 59th in America's 75 Best Resort Courses by GOLF DIGEST.
Comments: "Three great 9s . . . Tough, but fun . . . Great finishing holes on Canyon over canyon . . . Wide variety of holes for different classes of golfers . . . Nicest course in Tucson . . . Nice, but a step below the best . . . Forecaddie program good idea . . . Too many forced carries."

★★½ BEN GEREN REGIONAL PARK GOLF COURSE
Fort Smith—PU—501-646-5301.
Season: Year-round. **High:** May-Aug. **Caddies:** No.
Green fee: Under $20. **Credit cards:** No.
Lodging on site: No. **Reduced fees:** Twilight Play.
Unrestricted walking: Yes. **Range:** Yes (mats).
Holes: 18. **Par:** 72. **Yards:** 6,782-5,023. **Slope:** 120-104.
Comments: "Nice . . . Good greens . . . Well maintained for a city-run outfit . . . Fairways need help . . . Very flat, bad for drainage."

★½ BURNS PARK GOLF COURSE
North Little Rock—PU—501-758-5800.
Season: Year-round. **High:** June-Aug. **Caddies:** No.
Green fee: Under $20. **Credit cards:** No.
Lodging on site: No. **Reduced fees:** Weekdays, Twilight Play.
Unrestricted walking: Yes. **Range:** Yes (grass).
Holes: 18. **Par:** 71. **Yards:** 6,350-5,830. **Slope:** 106-103.
Additional 9-hole course also on property.
Comments: "Forget it . . . Usually too crowded . . . Rock hard."

CHEROKEE VILLAGE GOLF CLUB
Cherokee Village—PU—501-257-2555 (135 mi. from Little Rock).
Season: Year-round. **High:** May-Sept. **Caddies:** No.
Green fee: Under $20. **Credit cards:** V, MC.
Lodging on site: Yes. **Reduced fees:** No.
Unrestricted walking: No. **Range:** Yes (grass).
★★★SOUTH COURSE
Holes: 18. **Par:** 70. **Yards:** 7,058-5,270. **Slope:** 128-116.
Club also has private North Course.
Comments: "Beautiful . . . Hilly . . . Challenging . . . Undergoing some reconstruction."

★★DAWN HILL GOLF AND RACQUET CLUB
Siloam Springs—R—501-524-4838, 800-423-3786 (30 mi. from Fayetteville). **Season:** Year-round. **High:** April-Oct. **Caddies:** No.
Green fee: Under $20. **Credit cards:** V, AMEX.
Lodging on site: Yes. **Reduced fees:** Weekdays, Resort Guests.
Unrestricted walking: No. **Range:** Yes (grass).
Holes: 18. **Par:** 72. **Yards:** 6,806-5,307. **Slope:** 114-110.
Comments: "Sloping greens make for difficult approach shots . . . Out of the way . . . Worth it if you're in the area, but play during the week."

★★½ DEGRAY LAKE RESORT STATE PARK GOLF COURSE
Bismarck—PU—501-865-2807 (18 mi. from Hot Springs).
Season: Year-round. **High:** April-Sept. **Caddies:** No.
Green fee: Under $20. **Credit cards:** V, AMEX, DISC, MC.
Lodging on site: Yes. **Reduced fees:** Weekdays.
Unrestricted walking: Yes. **Range:** Yes (grass).
Holes: 18. **Par:** 72. **Yards:** 6,975-5,731. **Slope:** 134-125.
Comments: "Very hilly . . . Lots of interesting terrain to negotiate . . . Holes 1 and 10 call for your best John Daly-type drives over valleys . . . Slow greens . . . Ragged but nice . . . Never crowded . . . Should be better . . . Bring your RV."

HOT SPRINGS GOLF & COUNTRY CLUB
Hot Springs—R—501-624-2661 (60 mi. from Little Rock).
Season: Year-round. **High:** April-Oct. **Caddies:** No.
Green fee: $20-$49. **Credit cards:** V, AMEX, MC.
Reduced fees: Weekdays, Low Season, Resort Guests, Twilight Play.
Unrestricted walking: Yes. **Range:** Yes (grass).
★★★ARLINGTON COURSE
Holes: 18. **Par:** 72. **Yards:** 6,646-6,206. **Slope:** 127-137.
Comments: "Fabulous . . . Requires both fades and draws . . . Uncrowded . . . A superior value . . . Depends on rough height for difficulty."

ARKANSAS

★★★ MAJESTIC COURSE
Holes: 18. **Par:** 72. **Yards:** 6,715-5,541. **Slope:** 131-121.
Comments: "Historic old course . . . Nice fairways . . . Not tight at all . . .
Great greens . . . Bring your hot putter . . . Very nice finishing hole . . .
Could use refurbishing."

★★★½ MOUNTAIN RANCH COUNTRY CLUB
Fairfield Bay—R—501-884-3400 (85 mi. from Little Rock).
Season: Year-round. **High:** May-Aug. **Caddies:** No.
Green fee: $20-$49. **Credit cards:** V, AMEX, DISC, MC.
Lodging on site: Yes. **Reduced fees:** Low Season, Resort Guests.
Unrestricted walking: No. **Range:** Yes (grass).
Holes: 18. **Par:** 72. **Yards:** 6,780-5,134. **Slope:** 129-121.
Comments: "Great test of shotmaking . . . Most beautiful in the state . . .
Difficult course . . . If it gets you down, it won't let you up."

★★★ PRAIRIE CREEK COUNTRY CLUB
Rogers—PU—501-925-2414.
Season: Year-round. **High:** April-Sept. **Caddies:** No.
Green fee: Under $20. **Credit cards:** No.
Lodging on site: No. **Reduced fees:** Weekdays, Twilight Play.
Unrestricted walking: Yes. **Range:** Yes (grass).
Holes: 18. **Par:** 72. **Yards:** 6,574-5,921. **Slope:** 129-118.
Comments: "Instead of front and back 9s, it has top and bottom 9s . . . First
along top of foothills . . . Hit it too far left or right, ball drops 40 feet below
. . . Watch out for snakes . . . Bottom 9 in valley with plenty of water
hazards . . . Could be truly outstanding with some hands-on maintenance."

★★½ RED APPLE INN AND COUNTRY CLUB
Heber Springs—R—501-362-3131, 800-255-8900 (65 mi. from Little Rock).
Season: Year-round. **High:** May-Oct. **Caddies:** No.
Green fee: $20-$49. **Credit cards:** V, AMEX, DISC, MC.
Lodging on site: Yes. **Reduced fees:** No.
Unrestricted walking: No. **Range:** Yes (grass).
Holes: 18. **Par:** 71. **Yards:** 6,450-5,137. **Slope:** 121-110.
Comments: "One of the better resort courses in the South . . . Some great
golf holes . . . Only game in town, nothing else in the area . . . Nice hotel
with excellent food . . . Mandatory cart is stupid . . . Can walk after 5 p.m.
. . . So spread out, you wouldn't want to walk it."

★½ FURNACE CREEK INN & RANCH RESORT

Death Valley—R—619-786-2301.
Season: Oct.-July. **High:** Jan.-April. **Caddies:** No.
Green fee: $20-$49. **Credit cards:** All Major.
Lodging on site: Yes. **Reduced fees:** Low Season, Resort Guests.
Unrestricted walking: Yes. **Range:** Yes (grass).
Holes: 18. **Par:** 70. **Yards:** 6,031-5,203. **Slope:** 103-111.
Lowest golf course in the world at 214 feet below sea level.

★★★ GRAEAGLE MEADOWS GOLF COURSE

Graeagle—R—916-836-2323 (60 mi. from Reno).
Season: April-Nov. **High:** July-Sept. **Caddies:** No.
Green fee: $20-$49. **Credit cards:** V, MC.
Lodging on site: Yes. **Reduced fees:** Twilight Play.
Unrestricted walking: Yes. **Range:** Yes (grass).
Holes: 18. **Par:** 72. **Yards:** 6,680-5,640. **Slope:** 118-118.
Comments: "Great secret . . . There's still undiscovered treasure in the Sierras . . . Beautiful setting . . . Great scenery, great area . . . Wide open, elevation 4,000 feet . . . Fire away."

★★★ HESPERIA GOLF & COUNTRY CLUB

Hesperia—PU—619-244-9301 (8 mi. from Victorville).
Season: Year-round. **High:** Year-round. **Caddies:** No.
Green fee: Under $20. **Credit cards:** V, MC.
Lodging on site: No. **Reduced fees:** No.
Unrestricted walking: Yes. **Range:** Yes (mats).
Holes: 18. **Par:** 72. **Yards:** 6,996-6,136. **Slope:** 133-124.

★★★ HORSE THIEF GOLF & COUNTRY CLUB

Tehachapi—R—805-822-5581, 800-244-0864 (60 mi. from Bakersfield).
Season: Year-round. **High:** Summer. **Caddies:** No.
Green fee: $20-$49. **Credit cards:** V, AMEX, DISC, MC.
Lodging on site: Yes. **Reduced fees:** Weekdays, Low Season, Resort Guests, Twilight Play.
Unrestricted walking: Yes. **Range:** Yes (mats).
Holes: 18. **Par:** 72. **Yards:** 6,678-5,677. **Slope:** 124-124.
Comments: "Unknown . . . Unique . . . Unusual scenery . . . Big rocks . . . Fun experience . . . Golf package an outstanding value."

★★★½ LA CONTENTA GOLF CLUB

Valley Springs—PU—209-772-1081 (30 mi. east of Stockton).
Season: Year-round. **High:** March-Nov. **Caddies:** No.
Green fee: $20-$49. **Credit cards:** V, MC.
Lodging on site: No. **Reduced fees:** Weekdays, Twilight Play.
Unrestricted walking: Yes. **Range:** No.
Holes: 18. **Par:** 72. **Yards:** 6,500-5,257. **Slope:** 127-120.
Comments: "Big-time fun . . . Hills everywhere . . . Some great par 3s . . . Resort amenities for reasonable cost . . . Helpful pro shop staff . . . Near a Federal park, too many tourists."

LAKE SHASTINA GOLF RESORT

Weed—R—916-938-3205, 800-358-4653 (60 mi. from Redding).
Season: Year-round. **High:** May-Sept. **Caddies:** No.
Green fee: $20-$49. **Credit cards:** V, AMEX, MC.
Lodging on site: Yes. **Reduced fees:** Low Season, Resort Guests, Twilight Play.
Unrestricted walking: Yes. **Range:** Yes (mats).

★★★ CHAMPIONSHIP COURSE

Holes: 18. **Par:** 72. **Yards:** 6,969-5,530. **Slope:** 126-117.
Resort has a shorter 9 holes called the Scottish Links Course.
Comments: "Super layout . . . Spectacular mountain views . . . Uncrowded . . . Excellent service from parking lot to 1st tee."

★★★LAKE TAHOE GOLF COURSE
South Lake Tahoe—R—916-577-0788 (70 mi. from Reno).
Season: May-Oct. **High:** Summer. **Caddies:** No.
Green fee: $20-$49. **Credit cards:** V, MC.
Lodging on site: No. **Reduced fees:** Twilight Play.
Unrestricted walking: No. **Range:** Yes (grass).
Holes: 18. **Par:** 71. **Yards:** 6,706-5,687. **Slope:** 120-115.
Comments: "Attractive mountain course . . . Good test . . . Eye-popping scenery . . . Great new clubhouse."

★★MODESTO CREEKSIDE GOLF CLUB
Modesto—PU—209-571-5123 (70 mi. from Sacramento).
Season: Year-round. **High:** May-Aug. **Caddies:** No.
Green fee: Under $20. **Credit cards:** No.
Lodging on site: No. **Reduced fees:** Weekdays.
Unrestricted walking: Yes. **Range:** Yes (grass).
Holes: 18. **Par:** 72. **Yards:** 6,610-5,496. **Slope:** 115-108.

★★½ MOUNTAIN SPRINGS GOLF CLUB
Sonora—PU—209-532-1000 (74 mi. from Stockton).
Season: Year-round. **High:** March-Oct. **Caddies:** No.
Green fee: $20-$49. **Credit cards:** V, MC.
Reduced fees: Weekdays, Low Season, Twilight Play.
Unrestricted walking: Yes. **Range:** Yes (grass).
Holes: 18. **Par:** 72. **Yards:** 6,783-5,195. **Slope:** 128-112.
Comments: "Very hilly . . . Need every club . . . Too many blind shots."

★★★½ NORTHSTAR-AT-TAHOE RESORT GOLF COURSE
Truckee—R—916-562-2490 (40 mi. from Reno).
Season: May-Oct. **High:** July-Aug. **Caddies:** No.
Green fee: $50-$99. **Credit cards:** V, AMEX, DISC, MC.
Lodging on site: Yes. **Reduced fees:** Low Season, Resort Guests, Twilight Play.
Unrestricted walking: No. **Range:** Yes (mats).
Holes: 18. **Par:** 72. **Yards:** 6,897-5,470. **Slope:** 135-134.
Comments: "Fantastic views . . . Exciting high altitude golf . . . Dr. Jekyll-Mr. Hyde course . . . Front and back 9s quite different . . . Front lulls you to sleep, then watch out! . . . Great place to play . . . Super staff."

★★★PLUMAS PINES COUNTRY CLUB
Blairsden—PU—916-836-1420 (63 mi. from Reno).
Season: April-Oct. **High:** Summer. **Caddies:** No.
Green fee: $50-$99. **Credit cards:** V, AMEX, MC.
Lodging on site: Yes. **Reduced fees:** Weekdays, Low Season, Twilight Play.
Unrestricted walking: No. **Range:** Yes (grass).
Holes: 18. **Par:** 72. **Yards:** 6,504-5,106. **Slope:** 127-122.

★★★½ SONOMA GOLF CLUB
Sonoma—PU—707-996-0300.
Season: Year-round. **High:** April-Oct. **Caddies:** Yes.
Green fee: $50-$99. **Credit cards:** V, MC, AMEX.
Reduced fees: Weekdays, Low Season, Twilight Play.
Unrestricted walking: Yes. **Range:** Yes (grass).
Holes: 18. **Par:** 72. **Yards:** 7,069-5,519. **Slope:** 135-128.
Comments: "Classic old course . . . Much improved with recent remodeling . . . Well maintained . . . Love it . . . Wish it was cheaper."

★★★TAHOE DONNER GOLF CLUB
Truckee—R—916-587-9440 (40 mi. from Reno).
Season: May-Oct. **High:** July-Aug. **Caddies:** No.
Green fee: $50-$99. **Credit cards:** V, MC.
Lodging on site: No. **Reduced fees:** Low Season, Twilight Play.

Unrestricted walking: Yes. **Range:** Yes (mats).
Holes: 18. **Par:** 72. **Yards:** 6,952-6,487. **Slope:** 130-127.

SACRAMENTO AREA

★★★ANCIL HOFFMAN GOLF COURSE
Carmichael—PU—916-482-5660.
Season: Year-round. **High:** Nov.-Feb. **Caddies:** No.
Green Fee: Under $20. **Credit cards:** No.
Lodging on site: No. **Reduced Fees:** Weekdays, Twilight Play.
Unrestricted Walking: Yes. **Range:** Yes (grass).
Holes: 18. **Par:** 72. **Yards:** 6,794-5,954. **Slope:** 123-123.
Ranked in Third 25 of America's 75 Best Public Courses by GOLF DIGEST.
Comments: "Tough course, nice people, good price . . . Good location, good design . . . Crowded."

★½ BING MALONEY GOLF COURSE
Sacramento—PU—916-428-9401.
Season: Year-round. **High:** May-Aug. **Caddies:** No.
Green Fee: Under $20. **Credit cards:** V, DISC, MC.
Lodging on site: No. **Reduced Fees:** Weekdays, Twilight Play.
Unrestricted Walking: Yes. **Range:** Yes (mats).
Holes: 18. **Par:** 72. **Yards:** 6,281-5,972. **Slope:** 106-121.

★★CHERRY ISLAND GOLF COURSE
Elverta—PU—916-991-0770.
Season: Year-round. **High:** July-Sept. **Caddies:** No.
Green Fee: Under $20. **Credit cards:** No.
Lodging on site: No. **Reduced Fees:** Weekdays, Twilight Play.
Unrestricted Walking: Yes. **Range:** Yes (mats).
Holes: 18. **Par:** 72. **Yards:** 6,562-5,163. **Slope:** 124-117.
Comments: "Once trees are fully grown, course will be too hard . . . Barely acceptable . . . Anticlimactic."

★★★DRY CREEK RANCH GOLF COURSE
Galt—PU—209-745-4653 (25 mi. from Sacramento).
Season: Year-round. **High:** April-Sept. **Caddies:** No.
Green Fee: $20-$49. **Credit cards:** V, MC.
Lodging on site: No. **Reduced Fees:** Weekdays, Twilight Play.
Unrestricted Walking: Yes. **Range:** Yes (grass).
Holes: 18. **Par:** 72. **Yards:** 6,773-5,952. **Slope:** 129-128.
Comments: "Good course for the price . . . Good winter course . . . All-around good course . . . Average appearance . . . Some testy holes . . . Challenging rough . . . 18th is a monster . . . Needs better maintenance."

HAGGIN OAKS GOLF COURSE
Sacramento—PU—916-481-4506.
Season: Year-round. **High:** April-Oct. **Caddies:** No.
Green Fee: Under $20. **Credit cards:** V, DISC, MC.
Lodging on site: No. **Reduced Fees:** Weekdays, Twilight Play.
Unrestricted Walking: Yes. **Range:** Yes (mats).
★★NORTH COURSE
Holes: 18. **Par:** 72. **Yards:** 6,860-5,853. **Slope:** 115-111.
Comments: "Nice people, good price . . . Par-5 18th offers lots of options . . . Poorly maintained."
★★SOUTH COURSE
916-481-4508.
Holes: 18. **Par:** 72. **Yards:** 6,600-5,732. **Slope:** 113-113.
Comments: "Classic 1930s style . . . For the amount of play, in good shape . . . 9th doesn't finish at the clubhouse . . . 13th hole no good."

RANCHO MURIETA COUNTRY CLUB
Rancho Murieta—R—916-354-3440 (25 mi. from Sacramento).

Season: Year-round. **High:** Summer. **Caddies:** No.
Green Fee: $50-$99. **Credit cards:** V, AMEX, MC.
Lodging on site: Yes. **Reduced Fees:** Resort Guests.
Unrestricted Walking: No. **Range:** Yes (mats).
Site of Senior PGA Tour tournament.

★★NORTH COURSE
Holes: 18. **Par:** 72. **Yards:** 6,839-5,608. **Slope:** 131-136.

★★SOUTH COURSE
Holes: 18. **Par:** 72. **Yards:** 6,886-5,527. **Slope:** 127-122.
Comments: "Superb setting, natural, challenging . . . Hard to get on anymore . . . Poor facilities . . . Very poor condition."

★★★RANCHO SOLANO GOLF COURSE
Fairfield—PU—707-429-4653 (40 mi. from Sacramento).
Season: Year-round. **High:** May-Sept. **Caddies:** No.
Green Fee: $20-$49. **Credit cards:** V, AMEX, DISC, MC.
Lodging on site: No. **Reduced Fees:** Weekdays, Twilight Play.
Unrestricted Walking: Yes. **Range:** Yes (mats).
Holes: 18. **Par:** 72. **Yards:** 6,705-5,206. **Slope:** 127-117.
Comments: "Big greens . . . Too large . . . Long . . . Good condition."

SAN FRANCISCO AREA

★★½ ADOBE CREEK GOLF CLUB
Petaluma—PU—707-765-3000 (30 mi. from San Francisco).
Season: Year-round. **High:** May-Oct. **Caddies:** No.
Green fee: $50-$99. **Credit cards:** V, MC.
Lodging on site: No. **Reduced fees:** Weekdays, Low Season.
Unrestricted walking: No. **Range:** Yes (grass).
Holes: 18. **Par:** 72. **Yards:** 6,963-5,027. **Slope:** 126-115.
Comments: "New, good greens, tough fairways . . . Windy, flat, lifeless . . . Precious few trees . . . Odd driving range hours."

★★½ BENNETT VALLEY GOLF CLUB
Santa Rosa—PU—707-528-3673.
Season: Year-round. **High:** April-Oct. **Caddies:** No.
Green fee: Under $20. **Credit cards:** V, MC.
Lodging on site: No. **Reduced fees:** Weekdays, Twilight Play.
Unrestricted walking: Yes. **Range:** Yes (mats).
Holes: 18. **Par:** 72. **Yards:** 6,538-5,958. **Slope:** 112-116.
Comments: "Well maintained, nice people, great price . . . Priced so anyone can play there . . . Best greens in the county."

★★★BODEGA HARBOUR GOLF LINKS
Bodega Bay—R—707-875-3538 (20 mi. from Santa Rosa).
Season: Year-round. **High:** July-Oct. **Caddies:** Yes.
Green fee: $50-$99. **Credit cards:** V, MC.
Lodging on site: Yes. **Reduced fees:** Weekdays, Low Season, Resort Guests, Twilight Play.
Unrestricted walking: Yes. **Range:** No.
Holes: 18. **Par:** 70. **Yards:** 6,220-4,749. **Slope:** 130-120.
Comments: "Nice views, tricky course, ugly price . . . A well-kept secret more should play . . . Average front 9, great back . . . Front side a waste . . . Great finishing holes . . . Real test on a windy day . . . Tough to walk."

CHARDONNAY CLUB
Napa—PU—707-257-8950, 800-788-0136 (35 mi. from San Francisco).
Season: Year-round. **High:** May-Oct. **Caddies:** No.
Green fee: $50-$99. **Credit cards:** V, AMEX, DISC, MC.
Reduced fees: Weekdays, Low Season, Twilight Play.
Unrestricted walking: No. **Range:** Yes (grass).

★★★THE VINEYARDS COURSE
Holes: 18. **Par:** 71. **Yards:** 6,811-5,200. **Slope:** 133-126.

Club also has another 18-hole course, Club Shakespeare Napa Valley, open only to members.
Comments: "Good course . . . Every shot in your repertoire is needed . . . Bad shots are penalized . . . Like any good Chardonnay, getting better with age . . . Too fancy . . . Fairly mundane . . . Advertises 'golf in the Scottish tradition,' but they won't let you walk . . . Greens too narrow, like putting on a bowling alley . . . 18th hole unfair . . . Waste of a round."

CHUCK CORICA GOLF COMPLEX
Alameda—PU—510-522-4321 (12 mi. from San Francisco).
Season: Year-round. **High:** May-Nov. **Caddies:** No.
Green fee: Under $20. **Credit cards:** No.
Lodging on site: No. **Reduced fees:** Weekdays, Twilight Play.
Unrestricted walking: Yes. **Range:** Yes (mats).
★★½ JACK CLARK COURSE
Holes: 18. **Par:** 71. **Yards:** 6,559-5,473 **Slope:** 119-110.
Comments: "Almost the equal of Earl Fry."
★★★EARL FRY COURSE
Holes: 18. **Par:** 71. **Yards:** 6,141-5,560. **Slope:** 119-114.
Additional 9-hole par-3 course available.
Comments: "Old style . . . Great muny."

★★★½ FOUNTAINGROVE RESORT & COUNTRY CLUB
Santa Rosa—R—707-579-4653 (55 mi. from San Francisco).
Season: Year-round. **High:** April-Oct. **Caddies:** No.
Green fee: $50-$99. **Credit cards:** V, AMEX, MC.
Lodging on site: No. **Reduced fees:** Weekdays.
Unrestricted walking: No. **Range:** Yes (grass).
Holes: 18. **Par:** 72. **Yards:** 6,797-5,644. **Slope:** 132-128.
Comments: "A real gem . . . Varied terrain . . . Excellent design, just needs maturation . . . Tough course in good condition . . . Best in Santa Rosa . . . Best in Sonoma County . . . Unique Oriental theme in clubhouse . . . Nice course, but far too expensive. . . Need 90-degree cart rule."

★★★½ HALF MOON BAY GOLF LINKS
Half Moon Bay—PU—415-726-4438 (30 mi. from San Francisco).
Season: Year-round. **High:** April-Oct. **Caddies:** No.
Green fee: $50-$99. **Credit cards:** V, MC.
Unrestricted walking: No. **Range:** No.
Holes: 18. **Par:** 72. **Yards:** 7,131-5,740. **Slope:** 136-124.
Comments: "The poor man's Pebble Beach . . . Remote seaside location . . . Pretty ocean views . . . Beautifully maintained . . . Nice greens . . . Nice finishing hole . . . Classical 18th . . . 18th is outstanding . . . Overall, front is better than back . . . Only one or two great holes . . . No driving range, poor restaurant . . . Too many condos."

★★½ HARDING PARK GOLF CLUB
San Francisco—PU—415-664-4690.
Season: Year-Round. **High:** May-Oct. **Caddies:** No.
Green fee: $20-$49. **Credit cards:** All Major.
Lodging on site: No. **Reduced fees:** Twilight Play.
Unrestricted walking: Yes. **Range:** Yes (mats).
Holes: 18. **Par:** 72. **Yards:** 6,743-6,187. **Slope:** 124-120.
Comments: "A once-great muny . . . Former Tour stop . . . 1930s-style architecture . . . Well laid out, great setting . . . Crummy maintenance . . . Mediocre greens . . . Lousy fairways . . . Too many people, very slow play."

★★★LAS POSITAS GOLF COURSE
Livermore—PU—510-443-3122.
Season: Year-round. **High:** March-Oct. **Caddies:** No.
Green fee: $20-$49. **Credit cards:** V, MC.

Lodging on site: No. **Reduced fees:** Twilight Play.
Unrestricted walking: Yes. **Range:** Yes (mats).
Holes: 18. **Par:** 72. **Yards:** 6,725-5,270. **Slope:** 126-120.
Also has 9-hole executive course.
Comments: "Fun course, well kept . . . Fast track, not too tough . . . Good operation . . . Needs permanent pro shop . . . New clubhouse will help."

★★★½ OAKHURST COUNTRY CLUB
Clayton—PU—510-672-9737 (3 mi. from Concord).
Season: Year-round. **High:** March-Nov. **Caddies:** No.
Green fee: $50-$99. **Credit cards:** V, DISC, MC.
Lodging on site: No. **Reduced fees:** Weekdays, Twilight Play.
Unrestricted walking: No. **Range:** Yes (grass).
Holes: 18. **Par:** 72. **Yards:** 6,739-5,285. **Slope:** 132-123.
Comments: "A genuine sleeper . . . Good design . . . Difficult, but fair . . . Needs maturation . . . Greens still so hard . . . Priced a little high."

OAKMONT GOLF CLUB
Santa Rosa—PU—707-539-0415.
Season: Year-round. **High:** March-Oct. **Caddies:** No.
Green fee: $20-$49. **Credit cards:** V, MC.
Reduced fees: Weekdays, Low Season, Resort Guests, Twilight Play.
Unrestricted walking: Yes. **Range:** Yes (grass).
★★★WEST COURSE
Holes: 18. **Par:** 72. **Yards:** 6,379-5,573. **Slope:** 120-128.
Club also has 18-hole executive-length East Course.

★½ PEACOCK GAP GOLF & COUNTRY CLUB
San Rafael—PU—415-453-4940 (12 mi. from San Francisco).
Season: Year-round. **High:** March-Oct. **Caddies:** No.
Green fee: $20-$49. **Credit cards:** V, MC.
Lodging on site: No. **Reduced fees:** Twilight Play.
Unrestricted walking: Yes. **Range:** Yes (mats).
Holes: 18. **Par:** 71. **Yards:** 6,354-5,629. **Slope:** 121-128.
Comments: "Flavorless . . . Too crowded."

★½ SHARP PARK GOLF COURSE
Pacifica—PU—415-359-3380 (5 mi. from San Francisco).
Season: Year-round. **High:** April-Nov. **Caddies:** No.
Green fee: $20-$49. **Credit cards:** No.
Lodging on site: No. **Reduced fees:** Weekdays, Twilight Play.
Unrestricted walking: Yes. **Range:** No.
Holes: 18. **Par:** 72. **Yards:** 6,273-6,095. **Slope:** 115-120.
Comments: "Cheap, poorly maintained . . . 'Poor man's Pebble Beach?'—No way!"

SILVERADO COUNTRY CLUB & RESORT
Napa—R—707-257-0200 (50 mi. from San Francisco).
Season: Year-round. **High:** Spring/Fall. **Caddies:** No.
Green fee: $50-$99. **Credit Cards:** All Major.
Lodging on site: Yes. **Reduced fees:** Low Season, Resort Guests, Twilight Play.
Unrestricted walking: No. **Range:** Yes (mats).
★★★NORTH COURSE
Holes: 18. **Par:** 72. **Yards:** 6,900-5,857 **Slope:** 131-128.
Comments: "What a weekend . . . Longer, but less difficult than South . . . Better than the South . . . Big name, poorly maintained . . . Disappointing conditions . . . Overrated because it hosts Senior Tour event."
★★★½ SOUTH COURSE
Holes: 18. **Par:** 72. **Yards:** 6,685-5,672. **Slope:** 129-123.
Comments: "Elegant setting . . . Shorter, more difficult . . . Fun to play . . . Wish it was cheaper . . . A little too snooty."

★★SUNNYVALE MUNICIPAL GOLF COURSE
Sunnyvale—PU—408-738-3666 (5 mi. from San Jose).
Season: Year-round. **High:** May-Aug. **Caddies:** No.
Green fee: $20-$49. **Credit cards:** No.
Lodging on site: No. **Reduced fees:** Weekdays, Twilight Play.
Unrestricted walking: Yes. **Range:** No.
Holes: 18. **Par:** 70. **Yards:** 6,249-5,305. **Slope:** 119-114.
Comments: "Decent muny . . . Busy . . . Not much of an experience . . . Great for local play."

★★★WINDSOR GOLF CLUB
Windsor—PU—707-838-7888 (50 mi. from San Francisco).
Season: Year-round. **High:** May-Oct. **Caddies:** No.
Green fee: $20-$49. **Credit cards:** V, MC.
Lodging on site: No. **Reduced fees:** Weekdays, Twilight Play.
Unrestricted walking: Yes. **Range:** Yes (grass).
Holes: 18. **Par:** 72. **Yards:** 6,650-5,116. **Slope:** 126-125.
Comments: "Nice area, nicer value . . . Short course . . . Well maintained . . . Great shot values . . . Greens are sparse . . . Needs work . . . Fairways and tees in good condition . . . Easy to walk."

MONTEREY AREA

★★★APTOS SEASCAPE GOLF COURSE
Aptos—PU—408-688-3213 (25 mi. from San Jose).
Season: Year-round. **High:** June-Oct. **Caddies:** No.
Green fee: $50-$99. **Credit cards:** V, AMEX, MC.
Reduced fees: Weekdays, Low Season, Twilight Play.
Unrestricted walking: Yes. **Range:** Yes (mats).
Holes: 18. **Par:** 72. **Yards:** 6,116-5,576. **Slope:** 124-120.
Comments: "Good-time course . . . No yardage markers . . . Has all-day rates, a good value if you go around twice . . . A sleeper."

FORT ORD GOLF COURSE
Fort Ord—PU—408-242-3268 (7 mi. from Monterey).
Season: Year-round. **High:** May-Sept. **Caddies:** No.
Green fee: $50-$99. **Credit cards:** V, MC.
Lodging on site: Yes. **Reduced fees:** Weekdays, Twilight Play.
Unrestricted walking: Yes. **Range:** Yes (mats).
★★★½ BAYONET COURSE
Holes: 18. **Par:** 72. **Yards:** 6,982-5,680. **Slope:** 132-134.
Comments: "Great undiscovered course . . . Tough course first time out . . . Incredibly challenging . . . No O.B. or water, few traps . . . Devilish monster . . . The one to play in Monterey . . . Needs to clean up a little . . . Desultory maintenance . . . Can't wait 'til the Army up and leaves."
BLACKHORSE COURSE*
Holes: 18. **Par:** 72. **Yards:** 6,396-5,613. **Slope:** 120-129.

★★½ LAGUNA SECA GOLF CLUB
Monterey—PU—408-373-3701.
Season: Year-round. **High:** April-Oct. **Caddies:** No.
Green fee: $50-$99. **Credit cards:** V, AMEX, MC.
Reduced fees: Weekdays, Low Season, Twilight Play.
Unrestricted walking: Yes. **Range:** No.
Holes: 18. **Par:** 72. **Yards:** 6,125-5,186. **Slope:** 123-119.
Comments: "Another secret, more should play . . . I'd play it again."

★★★★½ THE LINKS AT SPANISH BAY
Pebble Beach—R—408-647-7500.
Season: Year-round. **High:** April-Oct. **Caddies:** Yes.
Green fee: $100 and up. **Credit cards:** All Major.
Lodging on site: Yes. **Reduced fees:** Resort Guests, Twilight Play.
Unrestricted walking: No. **Range:** Yes (grass).

SANTA BARBARA AREA

★★★THE ALISAL RANCH GOLF COURSE
Solvang—R—805-688-4215 (40 mi. from Santa Barbara).
Season: Year-round. **High:** June-Aug. **Caddies:** No.
Green fee: $50-$99. **Credit cards:** V, AMEX, MC.
Lodging on site: Yes. **Reduced fees:** Resort Guests.
Unrestricted walking: Yes. **Range:** Yes (mats).
Holes: 18. **Par:** 72. **Yards:** 6,396-5,709. **Slope:** 121-127.
Comments: "Good course . . . Two different types of courses . . . Each 9 different . . . Greens don't hold well . . . Good staff."

★★★★LA PURISIMA GOLF COURSE
Lompoc—PU—805-735-8395 (52 mi. from Santa Barbara).
Season: Year-round. **High:** Jan.-March. **Caddies:** No.
Green fee: $50-$99. **Credit cards:** V, MC.
Lodging on site: No. **Reduced fees:** Weekdays, Twilight Play.
Unrestricted walking: Yes. **Range:** Yes (grass).
Holes: 18. **Par:** 72. **Yards:** 7,105-5,763. **Slope:** 142-131.
Comments: "Tough track . . . Long and difficult . . . Fun and challenging . . . One of Muir Graves' best . . . A total experience . . . Holes keep getting better as you play along . . . Stay straight . . . Play early in the morning or else . . . Windy every p.m. . . . Difficult to walk . . . Too tough for most amateurs . . . Enjoyable, though very humbling . . . Resort-type amenities at a super value . . . Courteous staff."

★★★MORRO BAY GOLF COURSE
Morro Bay—PU—805-772-4341 (15 mi. from San Luis Obispo).
Season: Year-round. **High:** May-Aug. **Caddies:** No.
Green fee: Under $20. **Credit cards:** V, MC.
Lodging on site: Yes. **Reduced fees:** Weekdays, Twilight Play.
Unrestricted walking: Yes. **Range:** Yes (mats).
Holes: 18. **Par:** 72. **Yards:** 6,113-5,671. **Slope:** 116-117.
Comments: "Busy, busy course but worth the effort to play."

★★★½ OJAI VALLEY INN & COUNTRY CLUB
Ojai—R—805-646-5511, 800-422-6524 (30 mi. from Santa Barbara).
Season: Year-round. **High:** Spring/Fall. **Caddies:** No.
Green fee: $50-$99. **Credit cards:** All Major.
Lodging on site: Yes. **Reduced fees:** Resort Guests, Twilight Play.
Unrestricted walking: Yes. **Range:** Yes (grass).
Holes: 18. **Par:** 70. **Yards:** 6,235-5,225. **Slope:** 123-123.
Home of Senior PGA Tour's GTE West Classic.
Comments: "What a golfing experience should be . . . Short, tight . . . Beautiful oaks . . . Much improved since refurbishing . . . Perfect course for seniors . . . The best course in southern California . . . Still a secret . . . Very nice, but very slow play . . . A great resort."

★★★RIVER COURSE AT THE ALISAL
Solvang—PU—805-688-6042 (35 mi. from Santa Barbara).
Season: Year-round. **High:** Spring/Fall. **Caddies:** No.
Green fee: $20-$49. **Credit cards:** V, AMEX, MC.
Lodging on site: No. **Reduced fees:** Weekdays.
Unrestricted walking: Yes. **Range:** Yes (mats).
Holes: 18. **Par:** 72. **Yards:** 6,830-5,815. **Slope:** 126-122.

★★★SAN LUIS BAY RESORT GOLF COURSE
Avila Beach—PU—805-595-2307 (10 mi. from San Luis Obispo).
Season: Year-round. **High:** June-Aug. **Caddies:** No.
Green fee: $20-$49. **Credit cards:** V, MC.
Lodging on site: No. **Reduced fees:** Weekdays, Twilight Play.
Unrestricted walking: Yes. **Range:** Yes (grass).

Holes: 18. **Par:** 71. **Yards:** 6,443-5,116. **Slope:** 122-121.
Comments: "Unusual seaside layout . . . One of best in area . . . Remember, this is seafood and wine country."

★★★★SANDPIPER GOLF COURSE
Goleta—PU—805-968-1541 (100 mi. from Los Angeles).
Season: Year-round. **High:** May-Oct. **Caddies:** No.
Green fee: $50-$99. **Credit cards:** V, MC.
Lodging on site: No. **Reduced fees:** Weekdays, Twilight Play.
Unrestricted walking: Yes. **Range:** Yes (grass).
Holes: 18. **Par:** 72. **Yards:** 7,067-5,723. **Slope:** 135-125.
Ranked in First 25 of America's 75 Best Public Courses by GOLF DIGEST.
Comments: "Beautiful, challenging course . . . Excellent links . . . Many gully carries . . . 13th hole toughest on earth . . . Course you want to play again and again . . . Best in the area . . . Second-best ocean course in California . . . The Pebble Beach of southern California . . . Pebble's baby brother . . . As good as Pebble . . . Ocean holes better than at Pebble . . . Ocean views I can afford . . . Outstanding course that let price get out of hand . . . Price has spiraled in recent years."

★★SANTA BARBARA GOLF CLUB
Santa Barbara—PU—805-687-7087.
Season: Year-round. **High:** May-Sept. **Caddies:** No.
Green fee: Under $20. **Credit cards:** V, MC.
Lodging on site: No. **Reduced fees:** Weekdays.
Unrestricted walking: Yes. **Range:** Yes (mats).
Holes: 18. **Par:** 70. **Yards:** 6,009-5,536. **Slope:** 103-99.

★★★SOULE PARK GOLF COURSE
Ojai—PU—805-646-5633 (16 mi. from Ventura).
Season: Year-round. **High:** June-Aug. **Caddies:** No.
Green fee: $20-$49. **Credit cards:** V, MC.
Lodging on site: Yes. **Reduced fees:** Weekdays.
Unrestricted walking: Yes. **Range:** Yes (grass).
Holes: 18. **Par:** 72. **Yards:** 6,398-5,894. **Slope:** 107-115.
Comments: "Resort level muny . . . An affordable publinx value . . . Surprisingly good food."

LOS ANGELES AREA

BROOKSIDE GOLF CLUB
Pasadena—PU—818-796-8151.
Season: Year-round. **High:** April-Oct. **Caddies:** No.
Green fee: $20-$49. **Credit cards:** V, MC.
Reduced fees: Weekdays, Low Season, Twilight Play.
Unrestricted walking: Yes. **Range:** Yes (mats).
★★★C.W. KOINER COURSE
Holes: 18. **Par:** 72. **Yards:** 6,888-6,124. **Slope:** 125-121.
★★E.O. NAY COURSE
Holes: 18. **Par:** 70. **Yards:** 6,060-5,389. **Slope:** 112-117.
Comments: "Golf in the shadow of the Rose Bowl . . . Great golf shop."

★½ CHESTER WASHINGTON GOLF COURSE
Los Angeles—PU—213-779-2803.
Season: Year-round. **High:** June-Aug. **Caddies:** No.
Green fee: Under $20. **Credit cards:** No.
Lodging on site: No. **Reduced fees:** Weekdays.
Unrestricted walking: Yes. **Range:** Yes (mats).
Holes: 18. **Par:** 70. **Yards:** 6,348-5,646. **Slope:** 107-115.
Formerly known as Western Avenue Golf Course.

COSTA MESA COUNTRY CLUB
Costa Mesa—PU—714-540-7500.
Season: Year-round. **High:** Year-round. **Caddies:** No.
Green fee: $20-$49. **Credit cards:** No.
Lodging on site: No. **Reduced fees:** Weekdays, Twilight Play.
Unrestricted walking: Yes. **Range:** Yes (mats).
★½ LOS LAGOS COURSE
Holes: 18. **Par:** 72. **Yards:** 6,542-5,925. **Slope:** 116-121.
★½ MESA LINDA COURSE
Holes: 18. **Par:** 70. **Yards:** 5,486-4,591. **Slope:** 104-115.

★★½ CYPRESS GOLF CLUB
Los Alamitos—PU—714-527-1800 (3 mi. from Long Beach).
Season: Year-round. **High:** Aug.-Oct. **Caddies:** No.
Green fee: $50-$99. **Credit cards:** All Major.
Lodging on site: No. **Reduced fees:** Weekdays, Twilight Play.
Unrestricted walking: No. **Range:** Yes (mats).
Holes: 18. **Par:** 71. **Yards:** 6,500-4,569. **Slope:** 140-117.
Comments: "Dye design . . . No scenic beauty . . . Fairways separated by
steep mounds that wear thin . . . Up and down, every shot . . . Water on 15
holes . . . Too many hazards on a very small plot . . . Expensive fees . . .
You drive through a horse barn to get to back 9 . . . Carts must stay on
concrete . . . Good dining."

EL PRADO GOLF COURSES
Chino—PU—909-597-1753 (10 mi. from Riverside).
Season: Year-round. **High:** Year-round. **Caddies:** No.
Green fee: $20-$49. **Credit cards:** No.
Lodging on site: No. **Reduced fees:** Weekdays, Twilight Play.
Unrestricted walking: Yes. **Range:** Yes (grass).
★★BUTTERFIELD STAGE COURSE
Holes: 18. **Par:** 72. **Yards:** 6,508-5,503. **Slope:** 108-118.
Comments: "Greens in great shape . . . Surroundings detract."
★★½ CHINO CREEK COURSE
Holes: 18. **Par:** 72. **Yards:** 6,671-5,596. **Slope:** 114-115.
Comments: "Good for a county course . . . Fairways unkept."

★★EL RANCHO VERDE COUNTRY CLUB
Rialto—PU—909-875-5346 (5 mi. from San Bernardino).
Season: Year-round. **High:** Year-round. **Caddies:** No.
Green fee: $20-$49. **Credit cards:** V, MC.
Reduced fees: Weekdays, Low Season, Twilight Play.
Unrestricted walking: Yes. **Range:** Yes (grass).
Holes: 18. **Par:** 72. **Yards:** 6,800-5,589. **Slope:** 124-118.
Comments: "Good operation . . . Poor facilities."

★★½ EL RIVINO COUNTRY CLUB
Riverside—PU—909-684-8905 (3 mi. from San Bernardino).
Season: Year-round. **High:** Year-round. **Caddies:** No.
Green fee: $20-$49. **Credit cards:** V, MC.
Lodging on site: No. **Reduced fees:** Weekdays, Twilight Play.
Unrestricted walking: No. **Range:** No.
Holes: 18. **Par:** 73. **Yards:** 6,466-5,863. **Slope:** 111-113.
Comments: "Not extremely difficult . . . Some water, not often seen . . .
First hole is a par 6 . . . Coffee shop has only vending machines."

★★★½ ELKINS RANCH GOLF CLUB
Fillmore—PU—805-524-1440 (30 mi. from Ventura).
Season: Year-round. **High:** April-Oct. **Caddies:** No.
Green fee: $20-$49. **Credit cards:** No.
Lodging on site: No. **Reduced fees:** Twilight Play.
Unrestricted walking: Yes. **Range:** Yes (mats).

Holes: 18. **Par:** 71. **Yards:** 6,302-5,650. **Slope:** 115-118.
Comments: "Classic layout . . . A gem hidden in the orange groves . . . Average front 9, fine back 9 . . . Best hamburger of any snack bar . . . OK for the average hacker . . . Didn't live up to advance billing."

GREEN RIVER GOLF CLUB
Corona—PU—714-970-8411 (20 mi. from Anaheim).
Season: Year-round. **High:** June-Aug. **Caddies:** No.
Green fee: $50-$99. **Credit Cards:** V, MC.
Lodging on Site: No. **Reduced fees:** Twilight Play.
Unrestricted walking: Yes. **Range:** Yes (mats).
★★½ **ORANGE COURSE**
Holes: 18. **Par:** 71. **Yards:** 6,416-5,744. **Slope:** 119-120.
★★½ **RIVERSIDE COURSE**
Holes: 18. **Par:** 71. **Yards:** 6,275-5,467. **Slope:** 117-115.
Comments: "Incredibly slow play . . . Could use much better marshaling."

GRIFFITH PARK
Los Angeles—PU—213-664-2255.
Season: Year-round. **High:** Year-round. **Caddies:** No.
Green fee: Under $20. **Credit cards:** V, AMEX, DISC, MC.
Lodging on site: No. **Reduced fees:** Twilight Play.
Unrestricted walking: Yes. **Range:** Yes (mats).
★★ **HARDING GOLF COURSE**
Holes: 18. **Par:** 72. **Yards:** 6,536-6,028. **Slope:** 112-118.
Comments: "Wonderful surroundings . . . For the amount of play, they're in considerably fine shape . . . Short, but well bunkered . . . Difficult at times . . . Hard to get on . . . Price increased recently."
★★½ **WILSON GOLF COURSE**
Holes: 18. **Par:** 72. **Yards:** 6,942-6,330. **Slope:** 115-119.
Comments: "Each hole a different challenge . . . Super price."

INDUSTRY HILLS SHERATON RESORT
City of Industry—R—818-810-4653 (20 mi. from Los Angeles).
Season: Year-round. **High:** Spring/Fall. **Caddies:** No.
Green fee: $50-$99. **Credit cards:** All Major.
Lodging on site: Yes. **Reduced fees:** Weekdays, Low Season, Resort Guests, Twilight Play.
Unrestricted walking: No. **Range:** Yes (mats).
★★★½ **DWIGHT D. EISENHOWER COURSE**
Holes: 18. **Par:** 72. **Yards:** 7,181-5,589. **Slope:** 149-126.
Comments: "Long, tough, interesting . . . Lots of long-iron greens . . . One of southern California's best . . . PGA Tour should take a look-see, or maybe it's too tough for them . . . Ridiculously hard. Not golf . . . Unfair fairways . . . Tight . . . Cartpath rule makes for a torturous round . . . A standard 6-hour round . . . Smoggy."
★★★ **BABE DIDRIKSON ZAHARIAS COURSE**
Holes: 18. **Par:** 71. **Yards:** 6,778-5,363. **Slope:** 144-123.
Comments: "Tough, fair, beautiful . . . A goodie . . . Narrow . . . If you're driving badly, forget it . . . Unfair rough. How can you play when you can't find your ball? . . . Bring lots of balls . . . A lot of play, but always in good shape . . . Once you tee off, it's 11 holes before the first rest room."

★★ **JURUPA HILLS COUNTRY CLUB**
Riverside—PU—909-685-7214.
Season: Year-round. **High:** June-Aug. **Caddies:** No.
Green fee: $20-$49. **Credit cards:** V, MC.
Lodging on site: No. **Reduced fees:** Weekdays.
Unrestricted walking: No. **Range:** Yes (grass).
Holes: 18. **Par:** 70. **Yards:** 6,022-5,773. **Slope:** 109-117.

★★½ **LOS ROBLES GOLF COURSE**
Thousand Oaks—PU—805-495-6421 (40 mi. from Los Angeles).
Season: Year-round. **High:** June-Aug. **Caddies:** No.

Green fee: $20-$49. **Credit cards:** No.
Lodging on site: No. **Reduced fees:** Weekdays, Twilight Play.
Unrestricted walking: Yes. **Range:** Yes (mats).
Holes: 18. **Par:** 70. **Yards:** 6,274-5,333. **Slope:** 118-117.
Comments: "Nice old-time layout . . . Best-priced public course in the area
. . . Too crowded, too slow . . . Beautiful oaks."

★★★½ MALIBU COUNTRY CLUB
Malibu—PU—818-889-6680.
Season: Year-round. **High:** June-Aug. **Caddies:** No.
Green fee: $50-$99. **Credit cards:** V, MC.
Lodging on site: No. **Reduced fees:** Weekdays.
Unrestricted walking: No. **Range:** No.
Holes: 18. **Par:** 72. **Yards:** 6,740-5,627. **Slope:** 130-120.
Comments: "Beautiful . . . Serene . . . Lot of character . . . A few tricky
holes . . . Lakes and canyons challenge accuracy . . . Local knowledge helps
. . . Short par 5s . . . Not overplayed."

★★★MONARCH BEACH GOLF LINKS
Dana Point—R—714-240-8247 (60 mi. from Los Angeles).
Season: Year-round. **High:** April-Oct. **Caddies:** No.
Green fee: $100 and up. **Credit cards:** V, AMEX, MC.
Lodging on site: No. **Reduced fees:** No.
Unrestricted walking: No. **Range:** Yes (mats).
Holes: 18. **Par:** 70. **Yards:** 6,224-4,984. **Slope:** 128-115.
Comments: "A delight for all . . . Right on the coast . . . Good links feel
. . . For these prices, don't bother . . . Like playing darts, too much sand . . .
No clubhouse . . . No practice range . . . In awful shape."

★★★½ MORENO VALLEY RANCH GOLF CLUB
MOUNTAIN/LAKE/VALLEY 9s
Moreno Valley—PU—909-924-4444 (10 mi. from Riverside).
Season: Year-round. **High:** Jan.-March. **Caddies:** No.
Green fee: $50-$99. **Credit cards:** V, AMEX, DISC, MC.
Reduced fees: Weekdays, Low Season, Twilight Play.
Unrestricted walking: No. **Range:** Yes (mats).
Holes: 27. **Par:** 36/36/36. **Yards:** 3,333/3,351/3,547.
Mountain/Lake 18 ranked in Third 25 of America's Best Public Courses by
GOLF DIGEST.
Comments: "Good test . . . Interesting, but in poor condition . . . Water
problems in winter . . . Mountain and Lake 9s a plus, Valley 9 a minus . . .
Many design faults . . . Too expensive."

★★★PALOS VERDES COUNTRY CLUB
Palos Verdes Estates—PU—310-375-2759.
Season: Year-round. **High:** June-Aug. **Caddies:** No.
Green fee: $50-$99. **Credit cards:** V, MC, AMEX.
Lodging on site: No. **Reduced fees:** No.
Unrestricted walking: No. **Range:** No.
Holes: 18. **Par:** 71. **Yards:** 6,116-5,506. **Slope:** 131-128.
Comments: "Sporty . . . Exposed to ocean winds . . . Layout changes by
the hour . . . Takes far too long to play, but worth it . . . Private on
weekends."

PELICAN HILL GOLF CLUB
Newport Coast—R—714-760-0707 (45 mi. from Los Angeles).
Season: Year-round. **High:** Year-round. **Caddies:** No.
Green fee: $100 and up. **Credit cards:** All Major.
Lodging on site: No. **Reduced fees:** Twilight Play.
Unrestricted walking: No. **Range:** Yes (grass).
★★★★THE OCEAN COURSE
Holes: 18. **Par:** 70. **Yards:** 6,634-5,240. **Slope:** 138-121.
Selected Best New Resort Course of 1992 by GOLF DIGEST.

Comments: "Gorgeous . . . On a heavenly site . . . Has Pebble's distracting views . . . An inland links . . . Lots of character . . . Great challenge . . . Fun . . . One of California's best . . . Kind of expensive, but you'll like it . . . Worth every dollar . . . Overrated for price . . . Great, but not worth $120 a round . . . Nice to play on an immaculately maintained empty golf course, empty because it's so overpriced."

THE LINKS COURSE*
Holes: 18. **Par:** 71. **Yards:** 6,856-4,950. **Slope:** 142-112.
New second 18 opened in late 1993.

★★★RANCHO PARK GOLF COURSE
Los Angeles—PU—310-839-4374.
Season: Year-round. **High:** April-Oct. **Caddies:** No.
Green fee: Under $20. **Credit cards:** No.
Lodging on site: No. **Reduced fees:** Weekdays, Twilight Play.
Unrestricted walking: Yes. **Range:** Yes (mats).
Holes: 18. **Par:** 71. **Yards:** 6,585-5,928. **Slope:** 124-122.
Also has a 9-hole par-3 course.
Comments: "The best golf value in America . . . No better course in Los Angeles for the money . . . Great layout, and cheap . . . But takes 6 hours . . . May handle more rounds each year than any other course . . . Has a tee-time priority scheme that is beyond awful . . . Cliques seem to have all the weekend tee times tied up."

SEPULVEDA GOLF COURSE
Encino—PU—818-986-4560 (20 mi. from Los Angeles).
Season: Year-round. **High:** April-Oct. **Caddies:** No.
Green fee: Under $20. **Credit cards:** No.
Lodging on site: No. **Reduced fees:** Weekdays, Twilight Play.
Unrestricted walking: Yes. **Range:** Yes (mats).
★½ BALBOA COURSE
Holes: 18. **Par:** 72. **Yards:** 6,328-5,890. **Slope:** 107-115.
★½ ENCINO COURSE
Holes: 18. **Par:** 72. **Yards:** 6,863-6,133. **Slope:** 112-119.

★★★½ TIJERAS CREEK GOLF CLUB
Rancho Santa Margarita—PU—714-589-9793 (45 mi. from Los Angeles).
Season: Year-round. **High:** Aug.-Sept. **Caddies:** No.
Green fee: $50-$99. **Credit cards:** V, MC.
Lodging on site: No. **Reduced fees:** Twilight Play.
Unrestricted walking: No. **Range:** Yes (grass).
Holes: 18. **Par:** 72. **Yards:** 6,601-5,130. **Slope:** 125-115.
Comments: "New and interesting . . . Lots of fun . . . Two personalities—fun front, dangerous back . . . Like night and day . . . Traditional front, target back . . . Back 9 is the best in Orange County . . . Makes you think before every swing . . . Very tough . . . Too many trick holes . . . Greens sometimes need work."

★★★TUSTIN RANCH GOLF CLUB
Tustin—PU—714-730-1611 (2 mi. from Irvine).
Season: Year-round. **High:** May-Oct. **Caddies:** No.
Green fee: $50-$99. **Credit cards:** V, AMEX, MC.
Lodging on site: No. **Reduced fees:** Twilight Play.
Unrestricted walking: No. **Range:** Yes (mats).
Holes: 18. **Par:** 72. **Yards:** 6,736-5,204. **Slope:** 129-101.
Comments: "Good layout . . . Nothing more . . . Multi-tiered greens require accurate approaches . . . OK for mid- to high-handicappers, boring for low handicappers . . . Will get better as trees grow . . . Fees are a little high . . . Waste of time, no fun."

PALM SPRINGS AREA

★★½ DESERT PRINCESS COUNTRY CLUB & RESORT
LA VISTA/EL CIELO/LOS LAGOS 9s
Cathedral City—R—619-322-2280 (5 mi. from Palm Springs).
Season: Year-round. **High:** Jan.-March. **Caddies:** No.
Green fee: $50-$99. **Credit cards:** All Major.
Lodging on site: Yes. **Reduced fees:** Weekdays, Low Season, Resort Guests.
Unrestricted walking: No. **Range:** Yes (grass).
Holes: 27. **Par:** 36/36/36. **Yards:** 3,422/3,342/3,245.
Comments: "Lush, but can be windy . . . Very windy . . . Too windy . . . No trees in the middle of the course . . . Newest 9 is a beautiful Princess."

★★★½ THE FIELD GOLF CLUB
Desert Hot Springs—PU—619-251-5366 (10 mi. from Palm Springs).
Season: Year-round. **High:** Jan.-Feb. **Caddies:** No.
Green fee: $50-$99. **Credit cards:** V, MC.
Reduced fees: Weekdays, Low Season, Resort Guests, Twilight Play.
Unrestricted walking: No. **Range:** Yes (grass).
Holes: 18. **Par:** 73. **Yards:** 7,004-5,359. **Slope:** 137-119.
Formerly known as Desert Dunes Golf Club. Ranked in Second 25 of America's 75 Best Public Courses by GOLF DIGEST.
Comments: "Sprawling . . . Unreal . . . Scottish style . . . Blind shots over desert washes . . . Takes remembering holes to do well . . . Very windy."

★½ INDIAN SPRINGS COUNTRY CLUB
La Quinta—PU—619-775-3360.
Season: Year-round. **High:** Jan.-April. **Caddies:** No.
Green fee: $20-$49. **Credit cards:** V, MC.
Lodging on site: No. **Reduced fees:** Weekdays, Low Season.
Unrestricted walking: Yes. **Range:** Yes (grass).
Holes: 18. **Par:** 71. **Yards:** 6,601-6,023. **Slope:** 105-113.
Comments: "Older desert course . . . Postage-stamp greens."

INDIAN WELLS GOLF RESORT
Indian Wells—R—619-346-4653 (19 mi. from Palm Springs).
Season: Year-round. **High:** Jan.-April. **Caddies:** No.
Green fee: $100 and up. **Credit Cards:** V, AMEX, MC.
Lodging on Site: Yes. **Reduced fees:** Weekdays, Low Season, Twilight Play.
Unrestricted walking: No. **Range:** Yes. (grass).
★★★EAST COURSE
Holes: 18. **Par:** 72. **Yards:** 6,665-5,521. **Slope:** 118-113.
★★★WEST COURSE
Holes: 18. **Par:** 72. **Yards:** 6,480-5,400. **Slope:** 116-111.
Site of Senior PGA Tour's Gulfstream Aerospace Invitational in 1993.
Comments: "For public courses, both are in good condition . . . Ludicrously expensive for public courses."

LA QUINTA HOTEL GOLF CLUB
La Quinta—PU—619-564-7620 (20 mi. from Palm Springs).
Season: Year-round. **High:** Oct.-May. **Caddies:** No.
Green fee: $100 and up. **Credit Cards:** V, AMEX, MC.
Lodging on Site: Yes. **Reduced fees:** Low Season, Resort Guests, Twilight Play.
Unrestricted walking: No. **Range:** Yes (grass).
Also has 18-hole Mountain Course, which may be restricted to members only.
★★★½ CITRUS COURSE
Holes: 18. **Par:** 72. **Yards:** 7,106-5,106. **Slope:** 135-112.
Ranked 68th in America's 75 Best Resort Courses by GOLF DIGEST.

Comments: "You can pick and eat grapefruit between holes."
★★★½ DUNES COURSE
La Quinta—R—619-564-7610.
High season: Oct.-May.
Holes: 18. **Par:** 72. **Yards:** 6,861-5,024. **Slope:** 139-107.
Ranked 75th in America's 75 Best Resort Courses by GOLF DIGEST.
Comments: "Challenging . . . Exceptional golf . . . Picture-perfect golf . . . Plenty of water and sand hazards . . . Take extra balls . . . Excellent service . . . Not as great as Mountain course, but very good."

★★½ LAWRENCE WELK'S DESERT OASIS COUNTRY CLUB
LAKE VIEW/MOUNTAIN VIEW/RESORT 9s
Cathedral City—PU—619-328-6571 (10 mi. from Palm Springs).
Season: Year-round. **High:** Jan.-April. **Caddies:** No.
Green fee: $50-$99. **Credit cards:** V, AMEX, DISC, MC.
Reduced fees: Weekdays, Low Season, Twilight Play.
Unrestricted walking: No. **Range:** Yes (grass).
Holes: 27. **Par:** 36/36/36. **Yards:** 3,197/3,308/3,169.
Comments: "Disappointing . . . Have let course get seedy."

MARRIOTT'S DESERT SPRINGS RESORT & SPA
Palm Desert—R—619-341-2211.
Season: Year-round. **High:** Oct.-April. **Caddies:** No.
Green fee: $100 and up. **Credit cards:** All Major.
Lodging on site: Yes. **Reduced fees:** Low Season, Resort Guests, Twilight Play.
Unrestricted walking: No. **Range:** Yes (grass).
★★★½ PALMS COURSE
Holes: 18. **Par:** 72. **Yards:** 6,761-5,492. **Slope:** 124-116.
Comments: "Ted Robinson's best . . . Better than PGA West . . . Play in the summer when heat is up, but crowds, prices are down."
★★★½ VALLEY COURSE
Holes: 18. **Par:** 72. **Yards:** 6,679-5,330. **Slope:** 124-110.
Comments: "On a par with the Palm . . . Excellent treatment."

★★★MARRIOTT'S RANCHO LAS PALMAS RESORT
NORTH/SOUTH/WEST 9s
Rancho Mirage—R—619-862-4551.
Season: Year-round. **High:** Jan.-April. **Caddies:** No.
Green fee: $50-$99. **Credit cards:** All Major.
Lodging on site: Yes. **Reduced fees:** Low Season.
Unrestricted walking: No. **Range:** Yes (grass).
Holes: 27. **Par:** 36/35/34. **Yards:** 3,004/3,015/2,554.
Comments: "Good resort course . . . Very tight, but elegant design . . . Back and forth across a wash."

★★½ MESQUITE GOLF & COUNTRY CLUB
Palm Springs—PU—619-323-1502.
Season: Year-round. **High:** Nov.-May. **Caddies:** No.
Green fee: $50-$99. **Credit cards:** V, AMEX, MC.
Reduced fees: Weekdays, Low Season, Twilight Play.
Unrestricted walking: No. **Range:** Yes (grass).
Holes: 18. **Par:** 72. **Yards:** 6,328-5,244. **Slope:** 117-118.
Comments: "Pleasant amenities . . . Lots of water . . . Made mainly for senior golfers . . . Seriously overpriced for what they have."

★★★½ MISSION HILLS NORTH GOLF COURSE
Rancho Mirage—R—619-770-9496, 800-358-2211.
Season: Year-round. **High:** Oct.-May. **Caddies:** No.
Green fee: $100 and up. **Credit cards:** V, AMEX, MC.
Lodging on site: Yes. **Reduced fees:** Weekdays, Low Season, Resort Guests, Twilight Play.
Unrestricted walking: No. **Range:** Yes (grass).
Holes: 18. **Par:** 72. **Yards:** 7,062-4,907. **Slope:** 134-118.

Comments: "Absolutely wonderful experience . . . A desert links . . . Scenic tee to green . . . Fair, playable . . . Fairways funnel to the center . . . Superb all the way around . . . Very expensive . . . How can it be so windy and so hot at the same time?"

★★★MISSION LAKES COUNTRY CLUB
Desert Hot Springs—PU—619-329-8061 (10 mi. from Palm Springs).
Season: Year-round. **High:** Dec.-April. **Caddies:** No.
Green fee: $50-$99. **Credit cards:** V, MC.
Lodging on site: Yes. **Reduced fees:** Weekdays, Low Season.
Unrestricted walking: No. **Range:** Yes (grass).
Holes: 18. **Par:** 71. **Yards:** 6,737-5,390. **Slope:** 131-122.
Comments: "Hard walking 11 through 13, but worth it for the view . . . 11th hole alone is worth the price of admission."

★★★½ OAK VALLEY GOLF CLUB
Beaumont—PU—909-769-7200 (20 mi. from Palm Springs).
Season: Year-round. **High:** Oct.-March. **Caddies:** No.
Green fee: $20-$49. **Credit cards:** V, AMEX, MC.
Lodging on site: No. **Reduced fees:** Weekdays, Twilight Play.
Unrestricted walking: No. **Range:** Yes (grass).
Holes: 18. **Par:** 72. **Yards:** 7,000-5,494. **Slope:** 136-122.
Comments: "Relatively new, potential to become a classic . . . Incredible track . . . Excellent elevation changes . . . No boring holes . . . Fantastic front, back not as good."

PGA WEST RESORT
La Quinta—R—619-564-7170 (25 mi. from Palm Springs).
Season: Year-round. **High:** Jan.-April. **Caddies:** No.
Green fee: $100 and up. **Credit cards:** All Major.
Reduced fees: Weekdays, Low Season, Resort Guests, Twilight Play.
Unrestricted walking: No. **Range:** Yes (grass).
★★★½ JACK NICKLAUS RESORT COURSE
Holes: 18. **Par:** 72. **Yards:** 7,126-5,043. **Slope:** 138-116.
Ranked 35th in America's 75 Best Resort Courses by GOLF DIGEST.
Comments: "Typical Nicklaus, for 4-handicappers and less only . . . Too tough for true 18-handicappers . . . Tough as the Stadium Course . . . A lot of water holes for a desert course . . . Well groomed . . . Excessively priced . . . Run professionally . . . Yardage sensors in the ground speed up play."
★★★★TPC STADIUM COURSE
Reduced fees: Low Season.
Holes: 18. **Par:** 72. **Yards:** 7,261-5,087. **Slope:** 151-124.
Ranked 93rd in America's 100 Greatest Golf Courses and 16th in America's 75 Best Resort Courses by GOLF DIGEST.
Comments: "So you say you want a challenge? . . . The Golf Course from Hell . . . Recommended for all golf enthusiasts . . . Not for weaklings . . . Great design . . . Another Pete Dye railroad-tie wonder . . . Incredible layout . . . Not just for good players . . . Average golfer can score from appropriate tees . . . Must think on every shot . . . Not as pretty or as enjoyable as the Nicklaus . . . Too pricey . . . No fun . . . Ridiculous costs."

★★½ PALM DESERT RESORT COUNTRY CLUB
Palm Desert—R—619-345-2791.
Season: Nov.-Sept. **High:** Nov.-March. **Caddies:** No.
Green fee: $50-$99. **Credit cards:** V, AMEX, MC.
Lodging on site: Yes. **Reduced fees:** Weekdays, Twilight Play.
Unrestricted walking: No. **Range:** Yes (grass).
Holes: 18. **Par:** 72. **Yards:** 6,571-5,670. **Slope:** 112-112.
Comments: "Nothing fancy . . . Monster greens."

★★½ PALM SPRINGS GOLF COURSE
Palm Springs—PU—619-328-1005.
Season: Year-round. **High:** Jan.-May. **Caddies:** No.
Green fee: $20-$49. **Credit cards:** V, MC.

Reduced fees: Weekdays, Low Season, Twilight Play.
Unrestricted walking: No. **Range:** Yes (grass).
Holes: 18. **Par:** 72. **Yards:** 6,460-6,044. **Slope:** 107-115.

★★★★REDHAWK GOLF CLUB

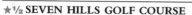

Temecula—PU—909-695-1424 (28 mi. from Riverside).
Season: Year-round. **High:** Oct.-May. **Caddies:** No.
Green fee: $50-$99. **Credit cards:** V, MC.
Lodging on site: No. **Reduced fees:** Twilight Play.
Unrestricted walking: No. **Range:** Yes (grass).
Holes: 18. **Par:** 72. **Yards:** 7,070-5,495. **Slope:** 142-135.
Comments: "A jewel . . . Beautiful . . . Immaculate . . . Outstanding . . . Best new course in southern California . . . Golf in Heaven should be so good . . . Great track, great shape, great price . . . Great variety . . . Great layout, best around . . . Tricky, tiered greens make this course . . . Very tough . . . Perfect lies . . . It's a long drive, but worth the time and money."

★½ SEVEN HILLS GOLF COURSE

Hemet—PU—909-925-4815.
Season: Year-round. **High:** Jan.-April. **Caddies:** No.
Green fee: $20-49. **Credit cards:** V, MC.
Lodging on site: No. **Reduced fees:** Weekdays, Twilight Play.
Unrestricted walking: Yes. **Range:** Yes (grass).
Holes: 18. **Par:** 72. **Yards:** 6,600-5,500. **Slope:** 118-115.

★★★SOBOBA SPRINGS COUNTRY CLUB

San Jacinto—PU—909-654-9354 (30 mi. from Palm Springs).
Season: Year-round. **High:** Oct.-May. **Caddies:** No.
Green fee: $20.-49. **Credit cards:** V, MC.
Lodging on site: No. **Reduced fees:** Weekdays, Twilight play.
Unrestricted walking: No. **Range:** Yes (grass).
Holes: 18. **Par:** 73. **Yards:** 6,826-5,829. **Slope:** 124-123.
Comments: "Desmond Muirhead's best . . . Interesting holes . . . Not too tough . . . You need all types of shots . . . More grass, please."

★★½ SUN CITY PALM SPRINGS GOLF CLUB

Bermuda Dunes—PU—619-772-2200 (10 mi. from Palm Springs).
Season: Year-round. **High:** Oct.-May. **Caddies:** No.
Green fee: $50-$99. **Credit cards:** V, MC.
Lodging on site: No. **Reduced fees:** Low Season, Twilight Play.
Unrestricted walking: No. **Range:** Yes (grass).
Holes: 18. **Par:** 72. **Yards:** 6,720-5,305. **Slope:** 131-118.

★★★SUN LAKES COUNTRY CLUB

Banning—PU—909-845-2135 (18 mi. from Palm Springs).
Season: Year-round. **High:** April-Oct. **Caddies:** No.
Green fee: $20-$49. **Credit cards:** V, MC.
Lodging on site: No. **Reduced fees:** Twilight Play.
Unrestricted walking: No. **Range:** Yes (grass).
Holes: 18. **Par:** 72. **Yards:** 7,017-5,497. **Slope:** 132-118.

★★★½ THE WESTIN MISSION HILLS RESORT GOLF COURSE

Rancho Mirage—R—619-328-3198, 800-358-2211.
Season: Year-round. **High:** Oct.-May. **Caddies:** No.
Green fee: $100 and up. **Credit cards:** V, AMEX, MC.
Lodging on site: Yes. **Reduced fees:** Weekdays, Low Season, Resort Guests, Twilight Play.
Unrestricted walking: No. **Range:** Yes (grass).
Holes: 18. **Par:** 70. **Yards:** 6,706-4,841. **Slope:** 137-107.
Comments: "Terrific Pete Dye course . . . Waterlogged."

CALIFORNIA

SAN DIEGO AREA

★★★½ **CARLTON OAKS COUNTRY CLUB**
Santee—R—619-448-8500, 800-831-6757 (18 mi. from San Diego).
Season: Year-round. **High:** Feb.-June. **Caddies:** No.
Green fee: $50-$99. **Credit cards:** V, AMEX, MC.
Lodging on site: Yes. **Reduced fees:** Resort Guests.
Unrestricted walking: No. **Range:** Yes (mats).
Holes: 18. **Par:** 72. **Yards:** 7,088-4,548. **Slope:** 144-114.
Comments: "Great renovation . . . Vastly improved . . . A great test . . .
Need all clubs . . . Nasty from the tips . . . Best fairways in San Diego
County . . . Carts must stay on paths—Bummer . . . Great inn."

★★½ **CARMEL HIGHLAND DOUBLETREE
GOLF & TENNIS RESORT**
San Diego—R—619-672-9100, 800-622-9223.
Season: Year-round **High:** Jan.-Aug. **Caddies:** No.
Green fee: $50-$99. **Credit cards:** All Major.
Lodging on site: Yes. **Reduced fees:** Weekdays, Low Season, Resort
Guests, Twilight Play.
Unrestricted walking: No. **Range:** Yes (mats).
Holes: 18. **Par:** 72. **Yards:** 6,418-5,429. **Slope:** 123-125.

★★½ **CARMEL MOUNTAIN RANCH COUNTRY CLUB**
San Diego—PU—619-487-9224.
Season: Year-round. **High:** Feb.-April. **Caddies:** No.
Green fee: $50-$99. **Credit cards:** V, AMEX, MC.
Lodging on site: No. **Reduced fees:** Weekdays, Twilight Play.
Unrestricted walking: No. **Range:** Yes (mats).
Holes: 18. **Par:** 72. **Yards:** 6,615-5,282. **Slope:** 136-118.
Comments: "Goofy golf . . . Fairways too narrow for housing develop-
ment . . . O.B. left and right on almost every hole . . . Rocks stick out of
traps . . . Some carries too long for short hitters . . . Too far between holes
. . . Improvements being made."

★★½ **CASTLE CREEK COUNTRY CLUB**
Escondido—PU—619-749-2422.
Season: Year-round. **High:** Jan.-May. **Caddies:** No.
Green fee: $20-$49. **Credit cards:** V, MC.
Lodging on site: No. **Reduced fees:** Weekdays, Twilight Play.
Unrestricted walking: Yes. **Range:** Yes (grass).
Holes: 18. **Par:** 72. **Yards:** 6,254-5,476. **Slope:** 124-125.

★★★ **CORONADO GOLF COURSE**
Coronado—PU—619-435-3121 (2 mi. from San Diego).
Season: Year-round. **High:** June-Aug./Nov.-Jan. **Caddies:** No.
Green fee: $20-$49. **Credit cards:** No.
Lodging on site: No. **Reduced fees:** Twilight Play.
Unrestricted walking: Yes. **Range:** Yes (mats).
Holes: 18. **Par:** 72. **Yards:** 6,700-5,784. **Slope:** 124-126.
Comments: "A walk in the park . . . Terrific public outing . . . Not hard
. . . Fun and cool . . . Magnificent weather . . . Ocean breezes . . . Great test
in the wind . . . In good shape for amount of play . . . No one can dislike this
course."

★★½ **EASTLAKE COUNTRY CLUB**
Chula Vista—PU—619-482-5757 (20 mi. from San Diego).
Season: Year-round. **High:** Feb.-July. **Caddies:** No.
Green fee: $20-$49. **Credit cards:** V, MC.
Lodging on site: No. **Reduced fees:** Twilight Play.
Unrestricted walking: Yes. **Range:** Yes (grass).
Holes: 18. **Par:** 72. **Yards:** 6,606-5,118. **Slope:** 116-114.

★★½ FALLBROOK GOLF CLUB

Fallbrook—PU—619-728-8334 (45 mi. from San Diego).
Season: Year-round. **High:** Nov.-March. **Caddies:** No.
Green fee: $20-$49. **Credit cards:** V, DISC, MC.
Lodging on site: No. **Reduced fees:** Weekdays, Twilight Play.
Unrestricted walking: Yes. **Range:** Yes (mats).
Holes: 18. **Par:** 72. **Yards:** 6,223-5,597. **Slope:** 117-119.
Comments: "Only a fair course . . . Back side is beautiful . . . Green fee too high for what they offer."

★★★★ FOUR SEASONS RESORT AVIARA

Carlsbad—R—619-929-0077 (25 mi. from San Diego).
Season: Year-round. **High:** April-Sept. **Caddies:** No.
Green fee: $50-$99. **Credit cards:** V, AMEX, MC.
Lodging on site: No. **Reduced fees:** Twilight Play.
Unrestricted walking: No. **Range:** Yes (grass).
Holes: 18. **Par:** 72. **Yards:** 7,007-5,007. **Slope:** 141-119.
Comments: "Lovely setting . . . Unbelievable beauty . . . 18 individually great holes . . . Best design I've played . . . Immaculate . . . Very mature for a new course . . . Excellent teaching school . . . Gorgeous clubhouse."

LA COSTA RESORT & SPA

Carlsbad—R—619-438-9111 (25 mi. from San Diego).
Season: Year-round. **High:** April-May. **Caddies:** Yes.
Green fee: $50-$99. **Credit Cards:** All Major.
Lodging on site: Yes. **Reduced fees:** Twilight Play.
Unrestricted walking: No. **Range:** Yes (grass).

★★★½ NORTH COURSE

Holes: 18. **Par:** 72. **Yards:** 6,987-5,939. **Slope:** 137-134.
Comments: "Tough courses . . . Very expensive . . . If you have to ask, you can't afford it.."

★★★½ SOUTH COURSE

Holes: 18. **Par:** 72. **Yards:** 6,894-5,612. **Slope:** 138-129.
Comments: "Wonderful shape . . . Good views . . . Excellent service . . . The spa is better than either of the courses . . . Too stuffy."

★★★½ MOUNT WOODSON COUNTRY CLUB

Ramona—PU—619-788-3555 (30 mi. from San Diego).
Season: Year-round. **High:** Year-round. **Caddies:** No.
Green fee: $50-$99. **Credit cards:** V, AMEX, MC.
Lodging on site: No. **Reduced fees:** Weekdays, Twilight Play.
Unrestricted walking: No. **Range:** No.
Holes: 18. **Par:** 70. **Yards:** 6,180-4,441. **Slope:** 130-108.
Comments: "Fascinating . . . One of the most beautiful, unique courses ever . . . Most novel course in California . . . Most challenging short course ever . . . Short iron game, nothing great, but fun . . . Spectacular, but gimmicky . . . Holes between boulders . . . Worth seeing."

★★ OCEANSIDE GOLF COURSE

Oceanside—PU—619-433-1360 (30 mi. from San Diego).
Season: Year-round. **High:** April-July. **Caddies:** No.
Green fee: $20-$49. **Credit cards:** V, MC.
Lodging on site: No. **Reduced fees:** Twilight Play.
Unrestricted walking: Yes. **Range:** Yes (grass).
Holes: 18. **Par:** 72. **Yards:** 6,450-5,398. **Slope:** 118-116.

★★★ PALA MESA RESORT

Fallbrook—R—619-728-5881, 800-722-4700 (60 mi. from San Diego).
Season: Year-round. **High:** May-Aug. **Caddies:** No.
Green fee: $50-$99. **Credit cards:** All Major.
Lodging on site: Yes. **Reduced fees:** Weekdays, Resort Guests, Twilight Play.

Unrestricted walking: No. **Range:** Yes (grass).
Holes: 18. **Par:** 72. **Yards:** 6,528-5,848. **Slope:** 131-133.
Comments: "A favorite . . . Super design and maintenance . . . 6-hour rounds on weekends . . . Fine amenities . . . Service very good . . . Above average costs . . . Great package deals . . . Has slipped recently, now heavy emphasis on group play."

★★★½ RAMS HILL COUNTRY CLUB

Borrego Springs—SP—619-767-5124 (70 mi. from San Diego).
Season: Nov.-Sept. **High:** Nov.-April. **Caddies:** No.
Green fee: $50-$99. **Credit cards:** V, AMEX, MC.
Lodging on site: Yes. **Reduced fees:** Low Season, Resort Guests, Twilight Play.
Unrestricted walking: No. **Range:** Yes (grass).
Holes: 18. **Par:** 72. **Yards:** 6,866-5,694. **Slope:** 133-119.
Comments: "Well designed, fun for all . . . Best maintained in southern California . . . Good attentive staff . . . Package plans great."

RANCHO BERNARDO INN AND COUNTRY CLUB

San Diego—R—619-487-0700, 800-662-6439 (20 mi. from San Diego).
Season: Year-round. **High:** Oct.-May. **Caddies:** No.
Green fee: $50-$99. **Credit cards:** V, AMEX, DISC, MC.
Lodging on site: Yes. **Reduced fees:** Weekdays, Low Season, Resort Guests, Twilight Play.
Unrestricted walking: No. **Range:** Yes (grass).
★★½ WEST COURSE
Holes: 18. **Par:** 72. **Yards:** 6,458-5,448. **Slope:** 122-119.
Club also has a 27-hole executive layout, the Oaks North Course.
Comments: "Nice resort course . . . Nice people . . . Best bet for snowbirds . . . A real sleeper . . . A real yawner until 18 . . . Shaggy greens . . . Great restaurant . . . Excellent food, outstanding facilities."

RANCHO SAN DIEGO GOLF CLUB

El Cajon—PU—619-442-9891 (20 Mi. From San Diego).
Season: Year-round. **High:** March-Oct. **Caddies:** No.
Green fee: $20-$49. **Credit cards:** V, MC.
Lodging on Site: No. **Reduced fees:** Weekdays, Twilight Play.
Unrestricted walking: Yes. **Range:** Yes (mats).
★★½ IVANHOE COURSE
Holes: 18. **Par:** 72. **Yards:** 7,011-5,624. **Slope:** 129-116.
Comments: "One of best public access values in San Diego area . . . Best greens in county . . . Shoddy . . . In poor shape."
★★ MONTE VISTA COURSE
Holes: 18. **Par:** 71. **Yards:** 6,110-5,407. **Slope:** 108-109.
Comments: "Golf carts barely work, cart bridges falling apart. But then, what do you expect for $25?"

★★★ SAN LUIS REY DOWNS GOLF RESORT

Bonsall—R—619-758-9699 (40 mi. from San Diego).
Season: Year-round. **High:** Year-round. **Caddies:** No.
Green fee: $20-$49. **Credit cards:** V, AMEX, MC.
Lodging on site: Yes. **Reduced fees:** Weekdays, Low Season, Resort Guests, Twilight play.
Unrestricted walking: No. **Range:** Yes (grass).
Holes: 18. **Par:** 72. **Yards:** 6,750-5,493. **Slope:** 128-124.

★★★ SAN VICENTE INN & GOLF CLUB

Ramona—R—619-789-3477 (40 mi. from San Diego).
Season: Year-round. **High:** March-May. **Caddies:** Yes.
Green fee: $20-$49. **Credit cards:** V, AMEX, MC.
Lodging on site: Yes. **Reduced fees:** Weekdays, Twilight Play.
Unrestricted walking: No. **Range:** Yes (mats).
Holes: 18. **Par:** 72. **Yards:** 6,610-5,543. **Slope:** 123-128.

Comments: "Great views, great rates, great value . . . Very relaxing . . . Much too overbooked."

SINGING HILLS COUNTRY CLUB
El Cajon—R—619-442-3425 (17 mi. from San Diego).
Season: Year-round. **High:** Jan.-June. **Caddies:** No.
Green fee: $20-$49. **Credit cards:** V, AMEX, DISC, MC.
Lodging on site: Yes. **Reduced fees:** Low Season, Resort Guests, Twilight Play.
Unrestricted walking: Yes. **Range:** Yes (mats).
★★★OAK GLEN COURSE
Holes: 18. **Par:** 71. **Yards:** 6,200-5,308. **Slope:** 112-112.
Comments: "Good experience . . . Nice resort course for any range handicap . . . Crowded . . . Green fee too high . . . Tank tops in style here."
★★★½ WILLOW GLEN COURSE
Club also has 18-hole, par-3 Pine Glen Course.
Holes: 18. **Par:** 72. **Yards:** 6,600-5,585. **Slope:** 124-122.
Comments: "Excellent golf factory in crowded metro area . . . Local favorite . . . Beautiful . . . Well kept . . . Nice experience . . . Staff does excellent job with crowded course . . . Slow, slow, slow."

★★★½ STEELE CANYON GOLF CLUB
CANYON/RANCH/MEADOW 9s
Jamul—PU—619-441-6900 (20 mi. from San Diego).
Season: Year-round. **High:** Jan.-April. **Caddies:** No.
Green fee: $20-$49. **Credit cards:** V, AMEX, MC.
Lodging on site: No. **Reduced fees:** Weekdays, Twilight Play.
Unrestricted walking: No. **Range:** Yes (grass).
Holes: 27. **Par:** 36/36/36. **Yards:** 3,206/3,535/3,466.
Comments: "Three striking 9s . . . Every hole an adventure . . . Must think your way around . . . Great design, much bump and run . . . Exciting . . . Fantastic layout . . . Will become great when it matures . . . Be ready to be humbled . . . Tough, bring lots of balls . . . Excellent shape . . . Fair price . . . Not too much fun . . . Unplayable the first time out."

TORREY PINES GOLF COURSE
La Jolla—PU—619-452-3226 (5 mi. from San Diego).
Season: Year-round. **High:** June-Sept. **Caddies:** No.
Green fee: $20-$49. **Credit cards:** V, MC.
Lodging on site: Yes. **Reduced fees:** Weekdays, Twilight Play.
Unrestricted walking: No. **Range:** Yes (grass).
★★★NORTH COURSE
Holes: 18. **Par:** 72. **Yards:** 6,647-6,118. **Slope:** 129-121.
Both courses host PGA Tour's Buick Invitational of California. Ranked in Third 25 of America's 75 Best Public Courses by GOLF DIGEST.
Comments: "Fine municipal . . . Traditional design . . . Easy to play . . . Easy to walk . . . Great coastline views . . . Sporadic maintenance . . . Always crowded . . . Very rough greens . . . Overrated."
★★★½ SOUTH COURSE
Holes: 18. **Par:** 72. **Yards:** 7,033-6,463. **Slope:** 136-128.
Ranked in Second 25 of America's 75 Best Public Courses by GOLF DIGEST.
Comments: "On the ocean . . . Has challenged the best . . . Tough course, poorly maintained in spots . . . Great views . . . San Diego's best scenery . . . Costs are up . . . Best value of any top-ranked course."

★½ WHISPERING PALMS LODGE & COUNTRY CLUB
EAST/SOUTH/NORTH 9s
Rancho Santa Fe—R—619-756-3255, 800-378-4653
(20 mi. from San Diego).
Season: Year-round. **High:** April-Oct. **Caddies:** No.
Green fee: $20-$49. **Credit cards:** All Major.
Lodging on site: Yes. **Reduced fees:** Resort Guests, Twilight Play.
Unrestricted walking: No. **Range:** No.
Holes: 27 **Par:** 36/36/35 **Yards:** 3,119/3,324/3,022.
Comments: "Not much . . . Too expensive for what you get."

★★★½ ARROWHEAD GOLF CLUB
Littleton—PU—303-973-9614 (30 mi. from Denver).
Season: March-Nov. **High:** May-Sept. **Caddies:** No.
Green fee: $50-$99. **Credit cards:** V, AMEX, MC.
Lodging on site: No. **Reduced fees:** Low Season, Twilight Play.
Unrestricted walking: No. **Range:** Yes (mats).
Holes: 18. **Par:** 70. **Yards:** 6,682-5,465. **Slope:** 134-123.
Ranked in Third 25 of America's 75 Best Public Courses by GOLF DIGEST.
Comments: "Spectacular setting . . . Holes among red rock towers . . .
Breathtaking . . . Unmatched location . . . Should be a national park . . .
Most scenic course in Colorado . . . One of the most beautiful anywhere . . .
Unbelievable wildlife . . . At almost $4 a hole, it'd better be outstanding . . .
Worth the money . . . Beautiful course in pathetic condition . . . Greens in
poor shape . . . Fairways below average . . . Second-rate facilities at these
prices? . . . Overpriced . . . Do once for sure."

★★ASPEN GOLF COURSE
Aspen—PU—303-925-2145.
Season: April-Oct. **High:** Summer. **Caddies:** No.
Green fee: $20-$49. **Credit cards:** V, DISC, MC.
Lodging on site: No. **Reduced fees:** Low Season.
Unrestricted walking: Yes. **Range:** Yes (grass).
Holes: 18. **Par:** 71. **Yards:** 7,165-6,469. **Slope:** 125-118.
Comments: "Beautiful views . . . Well run and maintained . . . Poor layout
. . . A disappointment . . . Flat . . . Rather boring, lots of similar holes."

★★★½ BATTLEMENT MESA GOLF CLUB
Battlement Mesa—R—303-285-7274 (35 mi. from Glenwood Springs).
Season: March-Nov. **High:** Summer. **Caddies:** No.
Green fee: $20-$49. **Credit cards:** V, AMEX, DISC, MC.
Lodging on site: Yes. **Reduced fees:** Weekdays, Low Season.
Unrestricted walking: No. **Range:** Yes (grass).
Holes: 18. **Par:** 72. **Yards:** 7,309-5,386. **Slope:** 132-112.
Comments: "Great course . . . Great views . . . Great staff . . . Long
course with large greens . . . Fair course for everyone . . . Only problem is
afternoon winds . . . Don't spread the word about this one."

★★★BEAVER CREEK GOLF CLUB
Beaver Creek—R—303-949-7123 (110 mi. from Denver).
Season: May-Oct. **High:** May-Sept. **Caddies:** No.
Green fee: $50-$99. **Credit cards:** All Major.
Lodging on site: Yes. **Reduced fees:** Low Season.
Unrestricted walking: No. **Range:** Yes (grass).
Holes: 18. **Par:** 70. **Yards:** 6,646-5,202. **Slope:** 133-121.
Comments: "Mountain golf at its best . . . An engineering *tour de force* . . .
So pretty . . . Short . . . No woods needed . . . 2nd and 3rd holes could be
improved . . . Last six holes excellent . . . Lots of through-the-housing
blahs, but some exceptional holes . . . Yardage marking not too good . . .
They should keep clubhouse open later."

★★★★BRECKENRIDGE GOLF CLUB
Breckenridge—PU—303-453-9104 (80 mi. from Denver).
Season: May-Oct. **High:** Summer. **Caddies:** No.
Green fee: $50-$99. **Credit cards:** V, AMEX, MC.
Lodging on site: No. **Reduced fees:** Twilight Play.
Unrestricted walking: No. **Range:** Yes (grass).
Holes: 18. **Par:** 72. **Yards:** 7,279-5,980. **Slope:** 146-128.
Comments: "Awesome . . . Incredible . . . A special experience . . . A real
winner . . . Long, beautiful mountain course . . . Great views . . . Not
normal Nicklaus . . . Jack's only municipal . . . Excellent test . . . Real
tough from the macho tees . . . Too demanding on the bogey golfer . . .
Greens not good, poorly designed for elevation factor . . . Afternoon weather can be a problem . . . Too popular . . . Crowded, short season."

THE BROADMOOR

Colorado Springs—R—719-577-5790, 800-634-7711.
Season: Year-round. **High:** Summer. **Caddies:** Yes.
Green fee: $50-$99. **Credit cards:** All Major.
Lodging on site: Yes. **Reduced fees:** No.
Unrestricted walking: No. **Range:** Yes (grass).

★★★★EAST COURSE

Holes: 18. **Par:** 72. **Yards:** 7,218-5,920. **Slope:** 128-126.
Ranked 29th in America's 75 Best Resort Courses by GOLF DIGEST. Site of the 1995 USGA Women's Open.
Comments: "Old standby . . . Good reputation . . . Finest around . . . Established, heavily treed . . . Best of the three . . . Tough greens to read . . . They break uphill, toward Cheyenne Mountain . . . Top-notch facilities . . . Great hotel, bad restaurants."

★★★SOUTH COURSE

Holes: 18. **Par:** 72. **Yards:** 6,781-4,834. **Slope:** 135-117.
Comments: "Wonderful . . . Interesting . . . Beautiful scenery . . . Plays short at mile-high altitude . . . Too expensive . . . Not very 'public,' must stay at the hotel."

★★★★WEST COURSE

Holes: 18. **Par:** 72. **Yards:** 6,937-5,505. **Slope:** 134-121.
Ranked 58th in America's 75 Best Resort Courses by GOLF DIGEST.
Comments: "Golf in Heaven . . . Fantastic . . . Hard to take in the scenery while playing . . . All three courses are significantly different in feel and architecture . . . Best-maintained courses in Colorado."

★★★★THE CLIFFS AT TAMARRON RESORT

Durango—R—303-259-2000.
Season: April-Nov. **High:** June-Oct. **Caddies:** No.
Green fee: $50-$99. **Credit cards:** All Major.
Lodging on site: Yes. **Reduced fees:** Low Season.
Unrestricted walking: No. **Range:** Yes (mats).
Holes: 18. **Par:** 72. **Yards:** 6,885-5,350. **Slope:** 144-127.
Ranked 37th in America's 75 Best Resort Courses by GOLF DIGEST.
Comments: "Most beautiful mountaintop golf in Colorado . . . Interesting holes, lovely views . . . Especially beautiful in fall . . . Outstanding accommodations . . . Best resort in Colorado for the value."

★★★COAL CREEK GOLF COURSE

Louisville—PU—303-666-7888 (4 mi. from Boulder).
Season: Year-round. **High:** April-Sept. **Caddies:** No.
Green fee: Under $20. **Credit cards:** V, MC.
Lodging on site: No. **Reduced fees:** Twilight Play.
Unrestricted walking: Yes. **Range:** Yes (grass).
Holes: 18. **Par:** 72. **Yards:** 6,957-6,009. **Slope:** 134-122.
Comments: "Outstanding muny . . . Tough test in wind . . . Great greens . . . Good from blues, too short from white tees . . . So much hidden water discourages aggressive play . . . Homes too close to fairways . . . Tough to get on."

★★½COPPER CREEK GOLF CLUB

Copper Mountain—R—303-968-2882 (80 mi. from Denver).
Season: June-Oct. **High:** Summer. **Caddies:** No.
Green fee: $50-$99. **Credit cards:** All Major.
Lodging on site: Yes. **Reduced fees:** Low Season, Resort Guests, Twilight Play.
Unrestricted walking: No. **Range:** Yes (grass).
Holes: 18. **Par:** 70. **Yards:** 6,094-5,159. **Slope:** 124-110.
Course is highest 18-hole course in N. America at an elevation of 9,700 feet.
Comments: "Worst course in Vail Summit area, but fun . . . Picturesque, can play tough . . . Must be accurate . . . Short with trick holes . . . Contrived . . . Blind, severe doglegs."

★★★EAGLE VAIL GOLF CLUB

Eagle Vail—PU—303-949-5267 (128 mi. from Denver).
Season: May-Oct. **High:** Summer. **Caddies:** No.
Green fee: $50-$99. **Credit cards:** V, AMEX, MC.
Lodging on site: No. **Reduced fees:** Low Season, Twilight Play.
Unrestricted walking: No. **Range:** Yes (grass).
Holes: 18. **Par:** 72. **Yards:** 6,819-4,856. **Slope:** 131-114.
Comments: "Fun course . . . A 'must play' . . . Spectacular holes . . . Big elevation changes . . . Love all the elevated tees . . . Enjoy! . . . Beautiful, but not a great course . . . Fair conditioning . . . Too many houses, not enough view . . . Too many trick-shot holes . . . Last four are gimmicky."

★★½ EAGLES NEST GOLF COURSE

Silverthorne—PU—303-468-0681 (67 mi. from Denver).
Season: May-Oct. **High:** Summer. **Caddies:** No.
Green fee: $50-$99. **Credit cards:** V, MC.
Reduced fees: Weekdays, Low Season, Resort Guests, Twilight Play.
Unrestricted walking: No. **Range:** Yes (grass).
Holes: 18. **Par:** 72. **Yards:** 7,024-5,556. **Slope:** 141-126.
Comments: "Best mountain views in the state . . . A fall spectacular . . . Most severe elevations in America . . . Mountain goats love it . . . Great course . . . Pretty, but unfair holes . . . Overly protected small greens, narrow fairways . . . Way too many blind shots . . . Two holes poorly designed . . . A couple of holes ruin the course . . . Waste of time . . . Don't even bother."

★★ESTES PARK GOLF COURSE

Estes Park—PU—303-586-8146 (60 mi. from Denver).
Season: April-Oct. **High:** Summer. **Caddies:** No.
Green fee: $20-$49. **Credit cards:** V, MC.
Lodging on site: No. **Reduced fees:** Low Season, Twilight Play.
Unrestricted walking: Yes. **Range:** Yes (grass).
Holes: 18. **Par:** 71. **Yards:** 6,326-5,869. **Slope:** 118-109.
Comments: "Easiest mountain course . . . Doesn't feel like a mountain course . . . Elk are interesting influence on play during spring."

★★★½ GRANDOTE GOLF & COUNTRY CLUB

La Veta—PU—719-742-3122, 800-762-9513 (45 mi. from Pueblo).
Season: April-Oct. **High:** Summer. **Caddies:** Yes.
Green fee: $20-$49. **Credit cards:** V, MC.
Lodging on site: No. **Reduced fees:** Weekdays.
Unrestricted walking: Yes. **Range:** Yes (grass).
Holes: 18. **Par:** 72. **Yards:** 7,085-5,608. **Slope:** 133-117.
Comments: "Fantastic for such a remote area . . . At foothills of Spanish Peaks, great beauty surrounds course . . . Dramatic, yet playable . . . Prettiest course in Colorado . . . Best-kept secret in Colorado . . . Wonderful greens . . . Narrow fairways . . . Almost unplayable rough."

★★GREAT SAND DUNES COUNTRY CLUB

Mosca—R—719-378-2357, 800-284-9213 (100 mi. from Pueblo).
Season: May-Oct. **High:** Summer. **Caddies:** No.
Green fee: $20-$49. **Credit cards:** V, AMEX, DISC, MC.
Lodging on site: Yes. **Reduced fees:** No.
Unrestricted walking: Yes. **Range:** Yes (grass).
Holes: 18. **Par:** 72. **Yards:** 6,816-5,840. **Slope:** 127-119.
Comments: "Not much character . . . Every hole's the same . . . Big mosquitos were a bother."

HYLAND HILLS GOLF COURSES

Westminster—PU—303-428-6526 (8 mi. from Denver).
Season: Year-round. **High:** May-Sept. **Caddies:** No.
Green fee: Under $20. **Credit cards:** V, AMEX, MC.
Lodging on site: No. **Reduced fees:** No.
Unrestricted walking: Yes. **Range:** Yes (grass).

COLORADO

★★★½ GOLD COURSE
Holes: 18. **Par:** 72. **Yards:** 7,101-5,737. **Slope:** 132-134.
Ranked in First 25 of America's 75 Best Public Courses by GOLF DIGEST.
Comments: "Colorado's finest municipal facility . . . Fun course to play
. . . Great since redesign . . . New 17th is a great hole . . . Smallish greens
. . . Nice practice area and driving range . . . Always working to improve
. . . Too many rounds . . . Hard to get a tee time."
BLUE COURSE*
Holes: 9. **Par:** 37. **Yards:** 3,498-3,097.
There are also two separate 9-hole, par-3 courses, the North and South.

★★★½ INVERNESS GOLF COURSE
Englewood—R—303-799-9660 (15 mi. from Denver).
Season: Year-round. **High:** Summer. **Caddies:** No.
Green fee: $50-$99. **Credit cards:** All Major.
Lodging on site: Yes. **Reduced fees:** Twilight Play.
Unrestricted walking: Yes. **Range:** Yes (grass).
Holes: 18. **Par:** 70. **Yards:** 6,948-6,407. **Slope:** 136-129.
Comments: "Fine course . . . Great facilities . . . Long par 4s . . . Perfect
greens . . . Fastest greens in Colorado."

★★★½ KEYSTONE RANCH GOLF COURSE
Keystone—R—303-468-4250, 800-451-5930 (70 mi. from Denver).
Season: June-Sept. **High:** July-Aug. **Caddies:** No.
Green fee: $50-$99. **Credit cards:** All Major.
Lodging on site: Yes. **Reduced fees:** Low Season, Resort Guests,
Twilight Play.
Unrestricted walking: No. **Range:** Yes (mats).
Holes: 18. **Par:** 72. **Yards:** 7,090-5,720. **Slope:** 136-119.
Ranked 41st in America's 75 Best Resort Courses by GOLF DIGEST.
Comments: "Gorgeous . . . Inspiring natural setting . . . Good mountain
test, some excellent holes . . . Outstanding in all ways . . . Needs a set of
senior tees . . . Play in the morning before the winds blow . . . Expensive
due to short season . . . Overrated."

★★½ LAKE VALLEY GOLF CLUB
Longmont—PU—303-444-2114 (2 mi. from Boulder).
Season: Year-round. **High:** March-Oct. **Caddies:** No.
Green fee: $20-$49. **Credit cards:** V, MC.
Reduced fees: Weekdays, Low Season, Twilight Play.
Unrestricted walking: Yes. **Range:** Yes (grass).
Holes: 18. **Par:** 70. **Yards:** 6,725-5,713. **Slope:** 121-119.
Comments: "Wide open but good . . . Great front 9 . . . Can be tough on
high handicappers . . . Easy to get on . . . Most year-round course in Colo-
rado . . . Friendly service."

★★★ MARIANA BUTTE GOLF COURSE
Loveland—PU—303-669-5800 (60 mi. from Denver).
Season: Year-round. **High:** Summer. **Caddies:** No.
Green fee: $20-$49. **Credit cards:** V, MC.
Lodging on site: No. **Reduced fees:** Weekdays, Twilight Play.
Unrestricted walking: Yes. **Range:** Yes (mats).
Holes: 18. **Par:** 72. **Yards:** 6,572-5,067. **Slope:** 130-117.
Comments: "Wonderful setting, sensitive design . . . Terrific . . . Uses
terrain beautifully . . . Stunning views from atop buttes . . . Equal to
Arrowhead . . . Every level can enjoy it . . . Second best public course in
Colorado . . . Will soon be the best . . . Fun, easy to walk, not too long . . .
Greens very true . . . Great value . . . Best bargain in Colorado."

GREAT VALUE

★★★ PINE CREEK GOLF CLUB
Colorado Springs—PU—719-594-9999.
Season: Year-round. **High:** May-Sept. **Caddies:** No.
Green fee: $20-$49. **Credit cards:** V, MC.
Lodging on site: No. **Reduced fees:** Weekdays.

Unrestricted walking: Yes. **Range:** Yes (grass).
Holes: 18. **Par:** 72. **Yards:** 7,194-6,040. **Slope:** 132-121.
Comments: "Delightful . . . A pleasure to play . . . Wonderfully creative . . . A challenge on every hole . . . No two holes alike . . . Native rough, tricky greens . . . Good condition . . . Needs clubhouse."

★★★PLUM CREEK GOLF & COUNTRY CLUB

Castle Rock—PU—303-688-2611, 800-488-2612 (12 mi. from Denver).
Season: March-Nov. **High:** May-Sept. **Caddies:** No.
Green fee: $50-$99. **Credit cards:** V, AMEX, MC.
Reduced fees: Weekdays, Low Season, Twilight Play.
Unrestricted walking: No. **Range:** Yes (grass).
Holes: 18. **Par:** 72. **Yards:** 6,633-4,881. **Slope:** 136-129.
Comments: "Good challenge . . . Some tough holes . . . Play smart, use every club . . . A fair test, only fair condition . . . Nestled along train tracks . . . Lots of railroad ties . . . Design sometimes unfair . . . Target golf . . . Gimmicks used too often . . . Pete Dye kicked my butt . . . Can't drive on grass, but must 'hurry, hurry' . . . Too much walking, even with a cart . . . Not very interesting."

★★★★POLE CREEK GOLF CLUB

Winter Park—PU—303-726-8847 (70 mi. from Denver).
Season: May-Oct. **High:** Summer. **Caddies:** No.
Green fee: $20-$49. **Credit cards:** V, MC.
Lodging on site: No. **Reduced fees:** Low Season, Twilight Play.
Unrestricted walking: Yes. **Range:** Yes (grass).
Holes: 18. **Par:** 72. **Yards:** 7,107-5,006. **Slope:** 135-129.
Selected Best New Public Course of 1984 and ranked in Third 25 of America's 75 Best Public Courses by GOLF DIGEST.
Comments: "Very tough cat out in thick woods . . . A natural . . . Magnificent views . . . Great layout always in top shape . . . A thinking player's course . . . Great diversity of holes from pines to prairie to mountain creeks . . . Best public course in the state, no contest . . . Hard to get to, hard to get on . . . Great food . . . Great trout fishing."

★★★½ PTARMIGAN GOLF CLUB

Ft. Collins—PU—303-226-6600 (50 mi. from Denver).
Season: Year-round. **High:** May-Aug. **Caddies:** No.
Green fee: $20-$49. **Credit cards:** V, MC.
Lodging on site: No. **Reduced fees:** No.
Unrestricted walking: Yes. **Range:** Yes (grass).
Holes: 18. **Par:** 72. **Yards:** 7,201-6,586. **Slope:** 135-128.
Comments: "A Nicklaus sleeper . . . A Nicklaus masterpiece . . . Fair, can use many different clubs . . . Long, sandy . . . Too many carries over sand . . . Bring your sand wedge . . . No trees . . . Lots of O.B.s . . . Don't hit the silo . . . Worth driving to . . . Nice but sparce . . . Dumb design, not everyone can hit it like Jack."

★★★RIFLE CREEK GOLF COURSE

Rifle—PU—303-625-1093 (60 mi. from Grand Junction).
Season: March-Dec. **High:** May-Sept. **Caddies:** No.
Green fee: $20-$49. **Credit cards:** V, MC.
Reduced fees: Weekdays, Low Season, Twilight Play.
Unrestricted walking: Yes. **Range:** Yes (grass).
Holes: 18. **Par:** 72. **Yards:** 6,250-5,150. **Slope:** 123-109.
Comments: "Two different 9s . . . Old flat, new rocky . . . New front 9—Wow! . . . Most unusual front 9 anywhere . . . Very challenging . . . Requires a lot of skill . . . Worth stopping by on way to Battlement Mesa."

RIVERDALE GOLF COURSES

Brighton—PU—303-659-6700 (10 mi. from Denver).
Season: Year-round. **High:** May-Aug. **Caddies:** No.
Green fee: $20-$49. **Credit cards:** V, MC.
Lodging on site: No. **Reduced fees:** No.
Unrestricted walking: Yes. **Range:** Yes (grass).

★★★★DUNES COURSE

Holes: 18. **Par:** 72. **Yards:** 7,100–4,902. **Slope:** 130–109.

Ranked in First 25 of America's 75 Best Public Courses and runner-up for Best New Public Course of 1986 by GOLF DIGEST. Site of 1993 USGA Public Links Championship.

Comments: "Excellent design . . . Scottish links in Colorado . . . Tight fairways, unforgiving rough . . . Rough seems two feet high . . . Grist for straight hitters . . . Easy if you stay off the golds . . . Always in good shape . . . Metro Denver's best public course . . . Best deal in Colorado . . . Great practice area . . . Not for everyone . . . Very ugly surroundings."

★★½ KNOLLS COURSE

Green fee: Under $20.

Holes: 18. **Par:** 71. **Yards:** 6,756–5,931. **Slope:** 118–117.

Comments: "Nothing special . . . Good original design, improvements backfired . . . Wide fairways . . . Canals not in view from tee boxes makes for a frustrating round."

★★★SHERATON STEAMBOAT RESORT

Steamboat Springs—R—303-879-2220.

Season: May-Oct. **High:** Summer. **Caddies:** No.

Green fee: $50-$99. **Credit card:** All Major.

Lodging on site: Yes. **Reduced fees:** Low Season, Resort Guests, Twilight Play.

Unrestricted walking: No. **Range:** Yes (grass).

Holes: 18. **Par:** 72. **Yards:** 6,906–5,647. **Slope:** 134–127.

Comments: "Just great . . . Great resort course . . . Great bargains . . . Great town . . . Prettiest setting in Colorado . . . Bring your camera."

★★★½ SINGLETREE GOLF CLUB

Edwards—R—303-926-3533 (120 mi. from Denver).

Season: April-Oct. **High:** Summer. **Caddies:** No.

Green fee: $50-$99. **Credit cards:** V, MC.

Reduced fees: Low Season, Resort Guests, Twilight Play.

Unrestricted walking: No. **Range:** Yes (grass).

Holes: 18. **Par:** 71. **Yards:** 7,059–5,293. **Slope:** 138–115.

Ranked 53rd in America's 75 Best Resort Courses by GOLF DIGEST.

Comments: "Truly great . . . A real treat . . . Worth a trip . . . Nice wide fairways . . . Best putting surfaces in the mountains . . . Watch out for sagebrush . . . Gets more expensive every year . . . Bring your gold card."

★★★SKYLAND COUNTRY CLUB

Crested Butte—PU—303-349-6131, 800-628-5496.

Season: May-Oct. **High:** Summer. **Caddies:** No.

Green fee: $50-$99. **Credit cards:** V, AMEX, MC.

Lodging on site: Yes. **Reduced fees:** Low Season, Resort Guests, Twilight Play.

Unrestricted walking: No. **Range:** Yes (grass).

Holes: 18. **Par:** 72. **Yards:** 7,208–5,747. **Slope:** 129–123.

Comments: "Beautiful experience . . . Awesome views . . . Long, well-trapped course . . . Scottish look on back 9 . . . 9,000-foot elevation makes you feel strong again . . . Too far, too little, too costly."

★★THE SNOWMASS CLUB GOLF COURSE

Snowmass Village—R—303-923-3148.

Season: April-Oct. **High:** Summer. **Caddies:** No.

Green fee: $50-$99. **Credit cards:** V, AMEX, DISC, MC.

Lodging on site: Yes. **Reduced fees:** Low Season, Resort Guests, Twilight Play.

Unrestricted walking: No. **Range:** Yes (grass).

Holes: 18. **Par:** 72. **Yards:** 6,894–5,008. **Slope:** 134–116.

Comments: "Expensive, poor layout, poor condition."

★★½ THORNCREEK GOLF CLUB

Thornton—PU—303-450-7055 (10 mi. from Denver).

Season: Year-round. **High:** May-Sept. **Caddies:** No.
Green fee: $20-$49. **Credit cards:** V, AMEX, MC.
Lodging on site: No. **Reduced fees:** Twilight Play.
Unrestricted walking: Yes. **Range:** Yes (mats).
Holes: 18. **Par:** 72. **Yards:** 7,268-5,547. **Slope:** 136-120.
Comments: "Tough course, no personality . . . Good course, bad management . . . Poor conditions for a 5-year-old . . . Some holes have no landing areas . . . Greens seem hard as a rock . . . Slow, slow, slow . . . Get rid of fivesomes."

★★★VAIL GOLF CLUB
Vail—PU—303-479-2260.
Season: May-Oct. **High:** July-Aug. **Caddies:** No.
Green fee: $50-$99. **Credit cards:** V, MC.
Lodging on site: No. **Reduced fees:** Low Season.
Unrestricted walking: No. **Range:** Yes (grass).
Holes: 18. **Par:** 71. **Yards:** 7,100-5,318. **Slope:** 121-114.
Comments: "Good valley course in high mountains . . . Great scenery . . . Hey, it's Vail . . . Best conditions of any summit course . . . Fun to play . . . Easy course, next to interstate . . . Highway noise is a downer . . . Busy in short season . . . Not worth the price."

★★★½ WALKING STICK GOLF COURSE
Pueblo—PU—719-584-3400.
Season: Year-round. **High:** May-Sept. **Caddies:** No.
Green fee: Under $20. **Credit cards:** V, MC.
Lodging on site: No. **Reduced fees:** Weekdays, Twilight Play.
Unrestricted walking: Yes. **Range:** Yes (grass).
Holes: 18. **Par:** 72. **Yards:** 7,147-5,181. **Slope:** 130-114.
Comments: "A great find . . . Terrific natural design . . . Prairie with ravines . . . A true test . . . Well-kept greens . . . As much fun as I've ever had on a golf course . . . May be the best public course ever . . . A tad dry, otherwise very good . . . Can carry, but ride . . . A significant hike if you walk . . . All-day green fee . . . Worth twice the price. . . . We need more Arthur Hills courses in Colorado."

★★WELLSHIRE MUNICIPAL GOLF COURSE
Denver—PU—303-757-1352.
Season: March-Nov. **High:** Summer. **Caddies:** No.
Green fee: Under $20. **Credit cards:** No.
Lodging on site: No. **Reduced fees:** No.
Unrestricted walking: Yes. **Range:** Yes (mats).
Holes: 18. **Par:** 72. **Yards:** 6,542-5,890. **Slope:** 121-116.
Comments: "Old private club went public generations ago . . . Let go . . . Unkempt bombing range . . . Always very crowded . . . Always plays slow . . . Some challenging holes, but poor greens . . . Replacing sprinkler system . . . Far too much ground under repair . . . Outsiders pay extra . . . A joke."

CONNECTICUT

★★½ BLACKLEDGE COUNTRY CLUB
Hebron—PU—203-228-0250 (10 mi. from Hartford).
Season: March-Dec. **High:** May-Sept. **Caddies:** No.
Green fee: $20-$49. **Credit cards:** No.
Lodging on site: No. **Reduced fees:** Weekdays, Twilight Play.
Unrestricted walking: Yes. **Range:** Yes (grass).
Holes: 18. **Par:** 72. **Yards:** 6,853-5,518. **Slope:** 123-116.
Comments: "Picturesque . . . Wide open . . . Fairly easy . . . Well trapped, good condition . . . Improving conditions every year . . . Much improved from 5 years ago . . . Good exercise, hard walking . . . Strange layout . . . No character . . . Not distinguished in any way."

★★½ H. SMITH RICHARDSON GOLF COURSE
Fairfield—PU—203-255-6094 (5 mi. from Bridgeport).
Season: April-Dec. **High:** Summer. **Caddies:** No.
Green fee: $20-$49. **Credit cards:** No.
Lodging on site: No. **Reduced fees:** Weekdays.
Unrestricted walking: Yes. **Range:** Yes (grass).
Holes: 18. **Par:** 72. **Yards:** 6,676-6,323. **Slope:** 127-124.
Comments: "Good muny . . . Only two or three weak holes . . . Beautifully maintenanced . . . Remarkably landscaped . . . Too long a wait to play . . . Archaic ball-rack system for tee times . . . Tough to get on."

★★½ LYMAN MEADOW GOLF CLUB
Middlefield—PU—203-349-8055 (20 mi. from Hartford).
Season: March-Nov. **High:** May-Sept. **Caddies:** No.
Green fee: $20-$49. **Credit cards:** V, MC.
Lodging on site: No. **Reduced fees:** No.
Unrestricted walking: Yes. **Range:** Yes (grass).
Holes: 18. **Par:** 72. **Yards:** 7,011-5,812. **Slope:** 129-122.
Comments: "Good layout . . . Not Robert Trent Jones at his best . . . Back is watery . . . Course condition erratic . . . In danger of going downhill . . . Tees very poor . . . Bad sand . . . Terrible greens . . . Often wet . . . They are improving . . . Now adding 18 more, designed by Gary Player . . . Easy walking . . . Good prices in pro shop."

★★½ NORWICH GOLF COURSE
Norwich—PU—203-889-6973 (40 mi. from Hartford).
Season: Year-round. **High:** May-Sept. **Caddies:** No.
Green fee: $20-$49. **Credit cards:** No.
Lodging on site: No. **Reduced fees:** Twilight Play.
Unrestricted walking: Yes. **Range:** Yes (mats).
Holes: 18. **Par:** 71. **Yards:** 6,133-5,848. **Slope:** 119-117.
Comments: "Quirky . . . Stretch of four dull holes doesn't fit rest of course . . . Two very nice holes, 16 and 17 . . . Much improved layout . . In outstanding condition . . . Terrific greens."

★★★ PORTLAND GOLF COURSE
Portland—PU—203-342-2833 (20 mi. from Hartford).
Season: March-Dec. **High:** April-Oct. **Caddies:** No.
Green fee: $20-$49. **Credit cards:** No.
Lodging on site: No. **Reduced fees:** Weekdays, Low Season.
Unrestricted walking: Yes. **Range:** Yes (grass).
Holes: 18. **Par:** 71. **Yards:** 6,213-5,802. **Slope:** 124-121.
Comments: "Short and hilly . . . Interesting . . . Must have good wedge game . . . Blind shots, different doglegs . . . Very pretty and semi-different . . . Excellent greens . . . Very consistent maintenance . . . Always in tip-top shape . . . Need yardage markers installed."

★★★★ RICHTER PARK GOLF COURSE
Danbury—PU—203-792-2552.
Season: April-Nov. **High:** Summer. **Caddies:** No.
Green fee: $20-$49. **Credit cards:** No.

practice area . . . Excellent service . . . Gives complete report before teeing off on what to look for . . . Slightly overrated . . . Water those fairways!"

★★★INDIAN BAYOU GOLF & COUNTRY CLUB
SEMINOLE/CHOCTAW/CREEK 9s
Destin—PU—904-837-6191 (30 mi. from Pensacola).
Season: Year-round. **High:** March-July. **Caddies:** No.
Green fee: $20-$49. **Credit cards:** V, AMEX, MC.
Lodging on site: No. **Reduced fees:** Low Season.
Unrestricted walking: No. **Range:** Yes (grass).
Holes: 27. **Par:** 36/36/36. **Yards:** 3,541/3,417/3,475.
Comments: "Excellent . . . Good fun . . . Good for juniors . . . Lots of sand, but fairly open for errant shots . . . Tough putting . . . Seminole 9 is demanding . . . New Creek 9 especially challenging . . . Not for duffers . . . Could use accessible refreshment stand at the turn."

★★★KILLEARN COUNTRY CLUB & INN
SOUTH/EAST/NORTH 9s
Tallahassee—R—904-893-2144, 800-476-4101.
Season: Year-round. **High:** Feb.-May. **Caddies:** No.
Green fee: $20-$49. **Credit cards:** All Major.
Lodging on site: Yes. **Reduced fees:** Low Season, Twilight Play.
Unrestricted walking: No. **Range:** Yes (grass).
Holes: 27. **Par:** 36/36/36. **Yards:** 3,532/3,493/3,367.

★★★★MARCUS POINTE GOLF CLUB
Pensacola—PU—904-484-9770.
Season: Year-round. **High:** Feb.-May. **Caddies:** No.
Green fee: $20-$49. **Credit cards:** V, MC.
Lodging on site: No. **Reduced fees:** No.
Unrestricted walking: No. **Range:** Yes (grass).
Holes: 18. **Par:** 72. **Yards:** 6,732-6,200. **Slope:** 129-125.
Comments: "Tremendous . . . Short, but very good . . . A real pleasure . . . Tough traps . . . Great greens . . . Good service from pro and staff . . . Nicest people in Florida."

MARRIOTT'S BAY POINT RESORT
Panama City Beach—R—904-234-3307 (100 mi. from Tallahassee).
Season: Year-round. **High:** March-June. **Caddies:** No.
Green fee: $50-$99. **Credit cards:** V, MC, AMEX.
Lodging on site: Yes. **Reduced fees:** Weekdays, Low Season, Resort Guests, Twilight Play.
Unrestricted walking: No. **Range:** Yes (grass).
★★★½ THE LAGOON LEGEND
Holes: 18. **Par:** 72. **Yards:** 6,885-4,942. **Slope:** 152-127
Ranked 43rd in America's 75 Best Resort Courses by GOLF DIGEST.
Comments: "Warning: Not for the faint-of-heart . . . Real challenge with long carries over marshes . . . All-out golf warfare. Loved it . . . Very demanding . . . May be too tough . . . The place to go next time you think you're really getting good . . . Lots of laughs . . . Not designed for amateurs . . . Difficult for no apparent reason . . . At least three island greens and innumerable carries over water to tiny targets . . . Bring a ball retriever . . . No. 18 is impossible . . . A little too tricked up . . . OK if you don't mind losing a dozen balls and shooting 10 strokes over your handicap."
★★★CLUB MEADOWS COURSE
Holes: 18. **Par:** 72. **Yards:** 6,913-4,999. **Slope:** 126-118.
Comments: "Country-club style golf . . . Almost too much grass . . . Good shape . . . Not what I expected . . . After Lagoon Legend, a cinch."

★★½ PERDIDO BAY GOLF COURSE
Pensacola—R—904-492-1223.
Season: Year-round. **High:** Feb.-April. **Caddies:** No.
Green fee: $20-$49. **Credit cards:** V, MC.
Lodging on site: Yes. **Reduced fees:** Weekdays, Low Season, Twilight Play.

Unrestricted walking: No. **Range:** Yes (grass).
Holes: 18. **Par:** 72. **Yards:** 7,154-5,476. **Slope:** 125-117.
Comments: "Average all the way . . . Alligators throughout . . . Bad greens, bad service . . . Too much play."

SANDESTIN RESORT
Destin—R—904-267-8155, 800-277-0800 (40 mi. from Pensacola).
Season: Year-round. **High:** March-Aug. **Caddies:** No.
Green fee: $20-$49. **Credit cards:** All Major.
Lodging on site: Yes. **Reduced fees:** Low Season, Resort Guests, Twilight Play.
Unrestricted walking: No. **Range:** Yes (grass).
★★★½ **BAYTOWNE GOLF CLUB**
TROON/DUNES/HARBOR 9s
Holes: 27. **Par:** 36/36/36. **Yards:** 3,593/3,603/3,368.
Comments: "Outstanding golf and resort . . . Very challenging . . . Wide variety of 9s for all levels . . . Tough, but fair . . . Good greens . . . Relaxing atmosphere . . . Has become expensive."
★★★½ **THE LINKS COURSE**
904-267-8144.
Holes: 18. **Par:** 72. **Yards:** 6,710-4,969. **Slope:** 124-115.
Comments: "An excellent adventure . . . Water makes it difficult . . . Difficult in wind . . . Narrow landing areas . . . Well maintained . . . Perfect fairways and greens . . . Better of the two courses."

★★½ **SANTA ROSA GOLF & BEACH CLUB**
Santa Rosa Beach—PU—904-267-2229.
Season: Year-round. **High:** April-Aug. **Caddies:** No.
Green fee: $20-$49. **Credit cards:** All Major.
Lodging on site: No. **Reduced fees:** Twilight Play.
Unrestricted walking: No. **Range:** Yes (grass).
Holes: 18. **Par:** 72. **Yards:** 6,608-4,920. **Slope:** 127-110.
Comments: "Hidden treasure on the Gulf Coast . . . Great dunes course . . . Fairways look like they've never been kept up . . . Lots of bad grass in fairways . . . Unforgiving off the fairways . . . Lots of construction, but never any progress."

★★★ **SHALIMAR POINTE GOLF & COUNTRY CLUB**
Shalimar—PU—904-651-1416, 800-964-2833 (45 mi. from Pensacola).
Season: Year-round. **High:** June-Aug./Jan.-March. **Caddies:** No.
Green fee: $20-$49. **Credit cards:** V, AMEX, MC.
Reduced fees: Weekdays, Low Season, Resort Guests, Twilight Play.
Unrestricted walking: No. **Range:** Yes (mats).
Holes: 18. **Par:** 72. **Yards:** 6,765-5,427. **Slope:** 125-115.
Comments: "Mature, tough, a great value . . . Much more difficult after redesign . . . Could use more esthetics . . . Only negative is that walking is not allowed . . . Maintained inconsistently . . . Contrived toughness . . . Too many bunkers . . . Too many waste areas . . . Residential growth is narrowing playing areas."

★★½ **SHOAL RIVER COUNTRY CLUB**
Crestview—PU—904-689-1111 (40 mi. from Pensacola).
Season: Year-round. **High:** Summer. **Caddies:** No.
Green fee: $20-$49. **Credit cards:** V, MC.
Lodging on site: No. **Reduced fees:** Low Season, Twilight Play.
Unrestricted walking: No. **Range:** Yes (grass).
Holes: 18. **Par:** 72. **Yards:** 6,782-5,183. **Slope:** 136-124.
Comments: "Excellent greens . . . Best, softest greens ever . . . Greens great, rest of course terrible . . . Marginal amenities."

TIGER POINT GOLF & COUNTRY CLUB
Gulf Breeze—PU—904-932-1333, 800-477-4833 (8 mi. from Pensacola).
Season: Year-round. **High:** Feb.-April. **Caddies:** No.

FLORIDA

Green fee: $20-$49. **Credit cards:** V, AMEX, MC.
Reduced fees: Weekdays, Low Season, Resort Guests, Twilight Play.
Unrestricted walking: No. **Range:** Yes (grass).
★★★½ **EAST COURSE**
Holes: 18. **Par:** 72. **Yards:** 7,033-5,209. **Slope:** 145-132.
Comments: "Good challenge from back tees . . . A good out-and-back layout . . . Very hard, but fair . . . Too long, too much water . . . Brings you back down to earth."
★★½ **WEST COURSE**
Holes: 18. **Par:** 71. **Yards:** 6,736-5,314. **Slope:** 118-117.
Comments: "Nothing compared to the East."

NORTHEAST REGION

AMELIA ISLAND PLANTATION
Amelia Island—R—904-277-5907, 800-874-6878 (30 mi. from Jacksonville).
Season: Year-round. **High:** Feb.-April. **Caddies:** No.
Green fee: $50-$99. **Credit cards:** All Major.
Lodging on site: Yes. **Reduced fees:** Low Season, Twilight Play.
Unrestricted walking: No. **Range:** Yes (grass).
★★★ **AMELIA LINKS**
OAKMARSH/OYSTERBAY/OCEANSIDE 9s
Holes: 27. **Par:** 36/36/35. **Yards:** 3,308/3,194/2,832.
Comments: "Short, tricked up . . . Forced carries over marsh are way too hard for average tourist . . . Too tight and quirky."
★★★½ **LONG POINT CLUB**
Holes: 18. **Par:** 72. **Yards:** 6,775-6,068. **Slope:** 127-121.
Ranked 51st in America's 75 Best Resort Courses by GOLF DIGEST.
Comments: "Great track . . . Excellent . . . Terrific . . . Challenging . . . Pretty . . . Immaculate . . . Playable . . . Expensive."

CIMARRONE GOLF & COUNTRY CLUB*
Jacksonville—PU—904-287-2000, 800-541-3473.
Season: Year-round. **High:** Spring/Fall. **Caddies:** No.
Green fee: $20-$49. **Credit cards:** V, AMEX, MC.
Lodging on site: No. **Reduced fees:** Weekdays, Twilight Play.
Unrestricted walking: No. **Range:** Yes (grass).
Holes: 18. **Par:** 72. **Yards:** 6,891-4,707. **Slope:** 128-119.

★★★ **CYPRESS KNOLL GOLF CLUB**
Palm Coast—PU—904-437-5807, 800-874-2101
(30 mi. from Daytona Beach).
Season: Year-round. **High:** Jan.-May. **Caddies:** No.
Green fee: $20-$49. **Credit cards:** V, MC.
Lodging on site: No. **Reduced fees:** Low Season, Resort Guests.
Unrestricted walking: No. **Range:** Yes (grass).
Holes: 18. **Par:** 72. **Yards:** 6,591-5,171. **Slope:** 130-117.
Comments: "Very hard target course . . . Too unforgiving . . . Prices too high . . . Don't get hungry or thirsty."

★★ **FERNANDINA BEACH MUNICIPAL GOLF COURSE**
WEST/SOUTH/NORTH 9s
Fernandina Beach—PU—904-277-7370 (50 mi. from Jacksonville).
Season: Year-round. **High:** Jan.-Sept. **Caddies:** No.
Green fee: $20-$49. **Credit cards:** No.
Lodging on site: No. **Reduced fees:** No.
Unrestricted walking: No. **Range:** Yes (grass).
Holes: 27. **Par:** 37/36/35. **Yards:** 3,709/3,318/3,094.

★★★½ **THE GOLF CLUB AT AMELIA ISLAND**
Amelia Island—R—904-277-8015, 800-245-4224 (30 mi. from Jacksonville).
Season: Year-round. **High:** March-Oct. **Caddies:** No.
Green fee: $50-$99. **Credit cards:** V, AMEX, MC.

Lodging on site: Yes. **Reduced fees:** Twilight Play.
Unrestricted walking: No. **Range:** Yes (grass).
Holes: 18. **Par:** 72. **Yards:** 6,681-5,039. **Slope:** 127-122.
Previously known as Summer Beach Golf Club.
Comments: "One of the best in Florida . . . Exquisitely maintained."

★★★½ THE GOLF CLUB AT CYPRESS HEAD
Port Orange—PU—904-756-5449 (3 mi. from Daytona Beach).
Season: Year-round. **High:** Dec.-April. **Caddies:** No.
Green fee: $20-$49. **Credit cards:** V, MC.
Reduced fees: Weekdays, Low Season, Twilight Play.
Unrestricted walking: No. **Range:** Yes (mats).
Holes: 18. **Par:** 72. **Yards:** 6,814-4,890. **Slope:** 133-110.
Comments: "Design allows for fair test for all levels . . . Long and strange carries."

★★★★ GOLF CLUB OF JACKSONVILLE
Jacksonville—PU—904-779-0800 (12 mi. from Jacksonville).
Season: Year-round. **High:** March-May. **Caddies:** No.
Green fee: $20-$49. **Credit cards:** V, AMEX, MC.
Lodging on site: No. **Reduced fees:** Weekdays, Twilight Play.
Unrestricted walking: No. **Range:** Yes (grass).
Holes: 18. **Par:** 71. **Yards:** 6,620-5,021. **Slope:** 120-112.
Comments: "Simply awesome . . . Jacksonville's great secret . . . Well designed . . . Strong test from tips . . . Great set of greens . . . Smooth and fast . . . Too short from white tees . . . Poor food."

★★★½ HALIFAX PLANTATION GOLF CLUB
Ormond Beach—PU—904-676-9600 (15 mi. from Daytona Beach).
Season: Year-round. **High:** Nov.-April. **Caddies:** No.
Green fee: $20-$49. **Credit cards:** V, AMEX, MC.
Lodging on site: No. **Reduced fees:** Low Season, Twilight Play.
Unrestricted walking: No. **Range:** Yes (grass).
Holes: 18. **Par:** 72. **Yards:** 7,128-4,971. **Slope:** 129-113.
Comments: "Nice track . . . Maintained like a private club . . . Best new course in 1993."

★½ JACKSONVILLE BEACH GOLF COURSE
Jacksonville—PU—904-249-8600 (10 mi. from Jacksonville).
Season: Year-round. **High:** Spring/Fall. **Caddies:** No.
Green fee: Under $20. **Credit cards:** V, MC.
Lodging on site: No. **Reduced fees:** Weekdays, Twilight Play.
Unrestricted walking: No. **Range:** Yes (grass).
Holes: 18. **Par:** 72. **Yards:** 6,510-5,245. **Slope:** 119-114.
Comments: "Open, easy course, some water . . . Deteriorating . . . No water on rough equals a sand pit off fairways . . . Gets too much play . . . Backs up too much."

MARRIOTT AT SAWGRASS RESORT
Ponte Vedra Beach—R—904-285-7777, 800-457-4653.
Season: Year-round. **High:** March-May. **Caddies:** No.
Green fee: $100 and up. **Credit cards:** All Major.
Lodging on site: Yes. **Reduced fees:** Low Season.
Unrestricted walking: No. **Range:** Yes (grass).
★★★½ MARSH LANDING COURSE
Holes: 18. **Par:** 72. **Yards:** 6,841-6,001. **Slope:** 131-120.
Comments: "First class . . . Lifestyles of the rich and famous . . . Beautiful, very expensive . . . Wish I lived there . . . Fantastic . . . Great example of working with the environment."
★★★ OAK BRIDGE COURSE
Holes: 18. **Par:** 70. **Yards:** 6,383-4,869. **Slope:** 126-116.
Comments: "Generic Florida golf . . . Shotmaker's special . . . Rough rough."

FLORIDA

★★★★**SAWGRASS COUNTRY CLUB**
EAST/WEST/SOUTH 9s
Holes: 27. **Par:** 36/36/36. **Yards:** 3,240/3,198/3,263.
Comments: "Fascinating . . . Very involving course . . . As nice as they come . . . World class all the way . . . A lagoon at every turn . . . What a treat . . . Difficult when windy, which is most of the time."

★★★★½ **TPC AT SAWGRASS STADIUM COURSE**
Holes: 18. **Par:** 72. **Yards:** 6,857-5,034. **Slope:** 135-123.
Ranked 59th in America's 100 Greatest Golf Courses and 7th in America's 75 Best Resort Courses by GOLF DIGEST.
Comments: "Once-in-a-lifetime thrill . . . You gotta play it . . . Incredible . . . Intimidating . . . Whew! Is this hard! . . . Too hard. Who cares? . . . What a kick . . . The best in target golf . . . Forget the score, just have fun . . . No. 17 will haunt me for the rest of my life . . . Overpriced and overrated . . . Only 17 and 18 are memorable . . . Just money hungry."

★★★½ **TPC AT SAWGRASS VALLEY COURSE**
Holes: 18. **Par:** 72. **Yards:** 6,864-5,126. **Slope:** 129-117.
Comments: "Tough if you're hooking it that day . . . More forgiving than Stadium . . . Better than its famous sister . . . Staff treats you great."

★★★**MATANZAS WOODS GOLF CLUB**
Palm Coast—R—904-446-6330, 800-874-2101
(30 mi. from Daytona Beach).
Season: Year-round. **High:** Jan.-May. **Caddies:** No.
Green fee: $20-$49. **Credit cards:** V, MC.
Lodging on site: No. **Reduced fees:** Low Season, Resort Guests.
Unrestricted walking: No. **Range:** Yes (grass).
Holes: 18. **Par:** 72. **Yards:** 6,985-5,407. **Slope:** 126-118.
Comments: "Quiet . . . Enjoyable . . . Challenging, lots of water . . . Solid design . . . Island 18th . . . Great hot dogs . . . Only problem: Out of my brand of beer . . . Sterile . . . Contrived . . . A bulldozer course . . . Looks like 900 other Florida courses . . . Snack bar opens too late, closes too early."

★★★**MILL COVE GOLF CLUB**
Jacksonville—PU—904-646-4653.
Season: Year-round. **High:** March-May. **Caddies:** No.
Green fee: $20-$49. **Credit cards:** V, AMEX, MC.
Reduced fees: Weekdays, Low Season, Twilight Play.
Unrestricted walking: No. **Range:** Yes (grass).
Holes: 18. **Par:** 71. **Yards:** 6,622-4,719. **Slope:** 124-112.
Comments: "Good public course in good shape . . . Interesting use of natural features . . . Run-of-the-mill . . . Not extremely long . . . Tight fairways . . . 18 holes on 14 holes worth of land . . . Routinely overbooked."

★★½ **PALM HARBOR GOLF CLUB**
Palm Coast—SP—904-445-0845, 800-874-2101
(30 mi. from Daytona Beach).
Season: Year-round. **High:** Jan.-May. **Caddies:** No.
Green fee: $20-$49. **Credit cards:** V, MC.
Lodging on site: No. **Reduced fees:** Low Season, Resort Guests.
Unrestricted walking: No. **Range:** Yes (grass).
Holes: 18. **Par:** 72. **Yards:** 6,572-5,346. **Slope:** 120-117.
Comments: "Pleasant . . . Comfortable . . . Crossover at 10 causes delays . . . No vending machines, out of luck if snack bar closed."

★★★**PINE LAKES COUNTRY CLUB**
Palm Coast—R—904-445-0852, 800-874-2101
(30 mi. from Daytona Beach).
Season: Year-round. **High:** Jan.-May. **Caddies:** No.
Green fee: $20-$49. **Credit cards:** V, MC.
Lodging on site: No. **Reduced fees:** Low Season, Resort Guests.
Unrestricted walking: No. **Range:** Yes (grass).
Holes: 18. **Par:** 72. **Yards:** 7,074-5,166. **Slope:** 126-124.

Comments: "Pleasant Palmer surprise . . . Truly fine design . . . Short, but not easy . . . Good shape . . . Just remodeled greens."

★★ PONCE DE LEON GOLF & CONFERENCE RESORT
St. Augustine—R—904-829-5314, 800-824-2821 (30 mi. from Jacksonville).
Season: Year-round. **High:** Feb.-May/Oct.-Nov. **Caddies:** No.
Green fee: $50-$99. **Credit cards:** V, AMEX, MC.
Lodging on site: Yes. **Reduced fees:** Low Season, Resort Guests, Twilight Play.
Unrestricted walking: No. **Range:** Yes (grass).
Holes: 18. **Par:** 72. **Yards:** 6,878-5,315. **Slope:** 131-125.
Comments: "Nostalgic . . . Modified Donald Ross . . . Front is woodsy, back is like a links . . . Back on Intracoastal Waterway . . . Just needs some grass in the fairways . . . Deathly slow . . . Heavy mosquito infestation . . . Once was enough."

PONTE VEDRA INN & CLUB
Ponte Vedra—R—904-285-2044 (20 mi. from Jacksonville).
Season: Year-round. **High:** Feb.-May/Oct.-Nov. **Caddies:** No.
Green fee: $50-$99. **Credit cards:** V, AMEX, MC.
Lodging on site: Yes. **Reduced fees:** Low Season.
Unrestricted walking: No. **Range:** Yes (grass).
★★½ LAGOON COURSE
Holes: 18. **Par:** 70. **Yards:** 5,239-4,571. **Slope:** 110-113.
★★★ OCEAN COURSE
Holes: 18. **Par:** 72. **Yards:** 6,573-5,237. **Slope:** 120-119.
Comments: "Great stuff . . . A fun afternoon . . . Above average . . . Very slooooow greens . . . Wonderful resort . . . Staff mediocre."

★★★½ RAVINES GOLF & COUNTRY CLUB
Middleburg—R—904-282-7888 (13 mi. from Orange Park).
Season: Year-round. **High:** Spring. **Caddies:** No.
Green fee: $20-$49. **Credit cards:** V, AMEX, MC.
Lodging on site: Yes. **Reduced fees:** Weekdays, Twilight Play.
Unrestricted walking: No. **Range:** Yes (grass).
Holes: 18. **Par:** 72. **Yards:** 6,733-4,817. **Slope:** 133-120.
Par-3 executive course available.
Comments: "Nothing like it in Florida . . . Florida's best . . . Great topography . . . A mountain course . . . Great change of pace . . . Lots o' fun . . . Latest remodeling is excellent . . . Reworked greens . . . Off the beaten path . . . Reputation scares average players away."

★★★½ ST. JOHNS COUNTY GOLF COURSE
Eckton—PU—904-825-4900 (8 mi. from St. Augustine).
Season: Year-round. **High:** Jan.-April. **Caddies:** No.
Green fee: Under $20. **Credit cards:** V, MC.
Lodging on site: No. **Reduced fees:** Twilight Play.
Unrestricted walking: No. **Range:** Yes (grass).
Holes: 18. **Par:** 72. **Yards:** 6,926-5,173. **Slope:** 130-117.
Comments: "Best public course in Florida . . . Great layout . . . Getting better all the time . . . Several great holes . . . Great scenery, great birds . . . Lots of water means challenging shots . . . Out of the way, worth the trip . . . Wide open, few trees, some boring holes."

★★½ SPRUCE CREEK COUNTRY CLUB
Daytona Beach—PU—904-756-6114.
Season: Year-round. **High:** Oct.-April. **Caddies:** No.
Green fee: $20-$49. **Credit cards:** V, MC.
Lodging on site: No. **Reduced fees:** Low Season.
Unrestricted walking: No. **Range:** Yes (grass).
Holes: 18. **Par:** 71. **Yards:** 6,637-5,157. **Slope:** 125-121.

★★★½ SUGAR MILL COUNTRY CLUB
RED/WHITE/BLUE 9s
New Smyrna Beach—PU—904-426-5210 (15 mi. from Daytona).
Season: Year-round. **High:** Jan-April. **Caddies:** No.
Green fee: $50-$99. **Credit cards:** V, MC.
Lodging on site: No. **Reduced fees:** Low Season.
Unrestricted walking: No. **Range:** Yes (grass).
Holes: 27. **Par:** 36/36/36 **Yards:** 3,356/3,410/3,339.
Comments: "Real fine Sugar . . . Beautiful . . . Long and narrow . . .
Greatly maintained . . . Keeps your interest."

★WEST MEADOWS GOLF CLUB
Jacksonville—PU—904-781-4834 (10 mi. from Jacksonville).
Season: Year-round. **High:** Spring/Fall. **Caddies:** No.
Green fee: Under $20. **Credit cards:** No.
Lodging on site: No. **Reduced fees:** Weekdays, Twilight Play.
Unrestricted walking: No. **Range:** Yes (grass).
Holes: 18. **Par:** 72. **Yards:** 6,197-5,6480. **Slope:** 110-115.

WILLOW LAKES GOLF CLUB
Jacksonville—PU—904-771-6656 (3 mi. from Jacksonville).
Season: Year-round. **High:** Feb.-June. **Caddies:** No.
Green fee: $20-$49. **Credit cards:** V, AMEX, MC.
Reduced fees: Weekdays, Low Season, Twilight Play.
Unrestricted walking: No. **Range:** Yes (grass).
★TROON COURSE
Holes: 18. **Par:** 72. **Yards:** 6,543-5,496. **Slope:** 123-114.
Comments: "Friendly . . . Economical . . . Poor conditioning."
LAKEWOOD COURSE*
Holes: 9. **Par:** 36. **Yards:** 2,880-2,525.

★★★½ WINDSOR PARKE GOLF CLUB
Jacksonville—PU—904-223-4653.
Season: Year-round. **High:** March-May. **Caddies:** No.
Green fee: $50-$99. **Credit cards:** V, AMEX, MC.
Lodging on site: No. **Reduced fees:** Weekdays, Twilight Play.
Unrestricted walking: No. **Range:** Yes (grass).
Holes: 18. **Par:** 72. **Yards:** 6,740-5,206. **Slope:** 133-123.
Comments: "Lush . . . Every hole is different . . . Undulating fairways and
greens . . . Smooth greens . . . Front tougher than back . . . Trouble lurks at
every turn . . . Bring extras . . . Nice practice area . . . Good course suffer-
ing from too much play . . . Staff very helpful, courteous . . . Didn't meet
my expectations."

CENTRAL REGION

★★★★½ ARNOLD PALMER'S BAY HILL CLUB & LODGE
CHALLENGER/CHAMPION/CHARGER 9s
Orlando—R—407-876-2429.
Season: Year-round. **High:** Nov.-April. **Caddies:** Yes.
Green fee: $100 and up. **Credit cards:** V, AMEX, MC.
Lodging on site: Yes. **Reduced fees:** No.
Unrestricted walking: No. **Range:** Yes (grass).
Holes: 27. **Par:** 36/36/36. **Yards:** 3,580/3,534/3,115.
Challenger/Champion ranked 80th in America's 100 Greatest Golf Courses
and 17th in America's 75 Best Resort Courses by GOLF DIGEST.
Comments: "Awesome . . . Premier golf property . . . Top quality . . .
Great surprise for Florida . . . Best in Florida . . . Long, tough, immaculate
. . . Cautious play is rewarded . . . Unlike so many Florida courses, it
actually has rough . . . Makes you feel like a pro . . . Watch Arnie practice
. . . Great hospitality, great food . . . Outstanding, but expensive."

★★BELLA VISTA GOLF & YACHT CLUB
Howey-in-the-Hills—PU—904-324-3233, 800-955-7001
(35 mi. from Orlando).
Season: Year-round. **High:** Jan.-April. **Caddies:** No.
Green fee: $20-$49. **Credit cards:** All Major.
Reduced fees: Weekdays, Low Season, Twilight Play.
Unrestricted walking: No. **Range:** Yes (grass).
Holes: 18. **Par:** 71. **Yards:** 6,400-5,386. **Slope:** 119-123.
Comments: "A little too cramped . . . Too short and jammed in . . . Wear a helmet."

★★★COUNTRY CLUB AT SILVER SPRINGS SHORES
Ocala—PU—904-687-2828 (50 mi. from Orlando).
Season: Year-round. **High:** Jan.-April. **Caddies:** No.
Green fee: $20-$49. **Credit cards:** V, AMEX, DISC, MC.
Reduced fees: Weekdays, Low Season, Twilight Play.
Unrestricted walking: No. **Range:** Yes (grass).
Holes: 18. **Par:** 72. **Yards:** 6,857-5,188. **Slope:** 131-120.
Comments: "Difficult, very fast greens . . . Great course, but three or four boring holes . . . In better shape than in years past."

DAYTONA BEACH GOLF COURSE
Daytona Beach—PU—904-258-3119 (60 mi. from Orlando).
Season: Year-round. **High:** Sept.-May. **Caddies:** No.
Green fee: Under $20. **Credit cards:** V.
Lodging on site: No. **Reduced fees:** Low Season, Twilight Play.
Unrestricted walking: Yes. **Range:** Yes (mats).
★½ NORTH COURSE
Holes: 18. **Par:** 72. **Yards:** 6,567-5,247. **Slope:** 111-122.
Comments: "Poor public facility . . . Fairways/greens often burned out."
★½ SOUTH COURSE
Holes: 18. **Par:** 71. **Yards:** 6,229-5,346. **Slope:** 106-118.
Comments: "Have had trouble with some greens recently."

★★★½ DELTONA HILLS GOLF & COUNTRY CLUB
Deltona—PU—904-789-4911 (30 mi. from Orlando).
Season: Year-round. **High:** Jan.-April. **Caddies:** No.
Green fee: $20-$49. **Credit cards:** All Major.
Reduced fees: Weekdays, Low Season, Twilight Play.
Unrestricted walking: No. **Range:** Yes (grass).
Holes: 18. **Par:** 72. **Yards:** 6,841-5,882. **Slope:** 125-132.
Comments: "Super . . . Rolling hills . . . Like the Carolinas . . . Lush fairways and greens . . . Best in central Florida . . . Water only on the 9th . . . Pleasant people . . . Busy, hard to get tee times."

★★DODGER PINES COUNTRY CLUB
Vero Beach—PU—407-569-4400 (90 mi. from Palm Beach).
Season: Year-round. **High:** Jan.-March. **Caddies:** No.
Green fee: $20-$49. **Credit cards:** V, AMEX, MC.
Lodging on site: Yes. **Reduced fees:** Low Season, Twilight Play.
Unrestricted walking: No. **Range:** Yes (grass).
Holes: 18. **Par:** 73. **Yards:** 6,692-5,776. **Slope:** 122-124.
Comments: "No variety . . . 3rd is 670-yard par 6 . . . What's the point of a par 6?"

★★★EKANA GOLF CLUB
Oviedo—PU—407-366-1211 (15 mi. from Orlando).
Season: Year-round. **High:** Dec.-April. **Caddies:** No.
Green fee: $20-$49. **Credit cards:** V, MC.
Reduced fees: Weekdays, Low Season, Twilight Play.
Unrestricted walking: No. **Range:** Yes (grass).
Holes: 18. **Par:** 72. **Yards:** 6,683-5,544. **Slope:** 130-128.
Comments: "Second best-kept secret in central Florida . . . Woodsy . . .

Great wildlife . . . Some target holes . . . Forced carries impossible for a high handicapper . . . Shots won't hold . . . Lacks full-size pro shop."

★★★½ FALCON'S FIRE GOLF CLUB
Kissimmee—PU—407-239-5445 (6 mi. from Orlando).
Season: Year-round. **High:** Jan.-April. **Caddies:** No.
Green fee: $50-$99. **Credit cards:** V, AMEX, MC.
Lodging on site: No. **Reduced fees:** Low Season, Twilight Play.
Unrestricted walking: No. **Range:** Yes (grass).
Holes: 18. **Par:** 72. **Yards:** 6,901-5,417. **Slope:** 125-118.
Comments: "Long, challenging, good condition . . . No bad lies . . . New course, weak greens . . . Tourist wear and tear already . . . Will get better with age . . . First-class operation . . . Carts have ball washers, all the amenities . . . Valet parking in the parking lot! . . . Valet parking? Bah!"

★★★½ GOLDEN OCALA GOLF COURSE
Ocala—PU—904-622-0100 (80 mi. from Orlando).
Season: Year-round. **High:** Dec.-April. **Caddies:** No.
Green fee: $20-$49. **Credit cards:** No.
Lodging on site: No. **Reduced fees:** Low Season, Twilight Play.
Unrestricted walking: No. **Range:** Yes (grass).
Holes: 18. **Par:** 72. **Yards:** 6,735-5,595. **Slope:** 132-124.
Has eight replica holes patterned after famous holes around the world. Ranked in Third 25 of America's 75 Best Public Courses by GOLF DIGEST.
Comments: "Fun to play famous holes . . . Such a worldly adventure . . . Most excellent . . . Funky . . . Underloved . . . A diverse test . . . Great memorable holes at reasonable price . . . Signature holes worth the trip . . . Great fun once a year . . . You'll never tire of it . . . Good course over all, not just the novelty of repro holes . . . Non-replica holes are the best . . . Using makeshift clubhouse."

GRAND CYPRESS RESORT
Orlando—R—407-239-3620.
Season: Year-round. **High:** Oct.-April. **Caddies:** Yes.
Green fee: $100 and up. **Credit cards:** All Major.
Lodging on site: Yes. **Reduced fees:** Low Season, Twilight Play.
Unrestricted walking: No. **Range:** Yes (grass).
★★★★NORTH/SOUTH/EAST 9s
Holes: 27. **Par:** 36/36/36. **Yards:** 3,521/3,472/3,434.
Caddies available with 48 hours' notice. North/South 18 Best New Resort Course of 1984 and ranked 55th in America's 75 Best Resort Courses by GOLF DIGEST.
Comments: "Moundular . . . Holes lined with hillocks . . . A moonscape . . . Perfect shape . . . Like hitting off a carpet . . . Everyone should experience it at least once . . . Best overall golfing experience in Florida . . . Jack made it too hard . . . Shallow greens make it tough . . . Great, but expensive . . . Can afford it once a year, maybe . . . Restaurant is overpriced . . . High-priced drinks . . . You need an expense account just for refreshments."
★★★★½ THE NEW COURSE AT GRAND CYPRESS
Unrestricted walking: Yes.
Holes: 18. **Par:** 72. **Yards:** 6,773-5,314. **Slope:** 126-117.
Caddies available with 48 hours' notice.
Ranked 47th in America's 75 Best Resort Courses by GOLF DIGEST.
Comments: "Terrific rendition of St. Andrews . . . The next best thing to it . . . Nicklaus gives great copy . . . Jack did himself proud here . . . Refreshingly different . . . Saves a trip to Scotland . . . Scotland at a fraction of the cost . . . Super course, not shy on fees."

GRENELEFE GOLF & TENNIS RESORT
Grenelefe—R—813-422-7511 (25 mi. from Disney World).
Season: Year-round. **High:** Jan.-April. **Caddies:** No.
Green fee: $50-$99. **Credit cards:** All Major.
Lodging on site: Yes. **Reduced fees:** Weekdays, Low Season, Twilight Play.

Unrestricted walking: No. **Range:** Yes (grass).

★★★½ EAST COURSE
Holes: 18. **Par:** 72. **Yards:** 6,802-5,094. **Slope:** 123-114.
Comments: "Three of the most beautiful courses ever . . . All pleasant and very challenging . . . Staff bent over backward to please . . . Great place to stay . . . Service and amenities is what Grenelefe is all about."

★★★½ SOUTH COURSE
Holes: 18. **Par:** 71. **Yards:** 6,869-5,174. **Slope:** 124-115.
Comments: "Many good holes . . . A few gimmicked up with sand and water . . . Great course, but not worth the premium."

★★★★WEST COURSE
Holes: 18. **Par:** 72. **Yards:** 7,325-5,398. **Slope:** 130-118.
Ranked 70th in America's 75 Best Resort Courses by GOLF DIGEST.
Comments: "Good tough golf course . . . Traditional layout . . . Could play a U.S. Open here . . . Better be long and straight . . . Bring your big lumber . . . Bunkers, bunkers and more bunkers . . . Challenging hills . . . 16 to 18 is a great finish . . . This one humbles."

★★★½ THE HABITAT GOLF COURSE
Valkaria—PU—407-952-6312 (12 mi. from Melbourne).
Season: Year-round. **High:** Nov.-April. **Caddies:** No.
Green fee: $20-$49. **Credit cards:** V, MC.
Lodging on site: No. **Reduced fees:** Low Season.
Unrestricted walking: Yes. **Range:** Yes (grass).
Holes: 18. **Par:** 72. **Yards:** 6,836-4,969. **Slope:** 129-115.
Comments: "Golf on a nature walk . . . Fine course . . . Developing into a great one . . . A great public value."

★★★★HUNTER'S CREEK GOLF COURSE
Orlando—PU—407-240-4653.
Season: Year-round. **High:** Jan.-March. **Caddies:** No.
Green fee: $50-$99. **Credit cards:** V, MC.
Lodging on site: No. **Reduced fees:** Low Season, Twilight Play.
Unrestricted walking: No. **Range:** Yes (grass).
Holes: 18. **Par:** 72. **Yards:** 7,432-5,755. **Slope:** 127-120.
Ranked in Second 25 of America's 75 Best Public Courses by GOLF DIGEST.
Comments: "Great, great test . . . Long target golf, go figure . . . All you want from the back . . . A ton of water . . . Bring extra clubs . . . Hard first time around . . . Need local knowledge of correct landing areas . . . Tough on short hitters . . . Clubhouse is too small."

HUNTINGTON HILLS GOLF & COUNTRY CLUB*
Lakeland—PU—813-859-3689 (75 mi. from Orlando).
Season: Year-round. **High:** Jan.-March. **Caddies:** No.
Green fee: $20-$49. **Credit cards:** V, AMEX, DISC, MC.
Lodging on site: No. **Reduced fees:** Twilight Play.
Unrestricted walking: No. **Range:** Yes (grass).
Holes: 18. **Par:** 72. **Yards:** 6,679-5,129. **Slope:** 122-115.

★★★½ INDIGO LAKES GOLF & TENNIS CLUB
Daytona Beach—R—904-254-3607, 800-223-4161 (50 mi. from Orlando).
Season: Year-round. **High:** Jan.-April. **Caddies:** No.
Green fee: $20-$49. **Credit cards:** All Major.
Lodging on site: Yes. **Reduced fees:** Low Season, Resort Guests, Twilight Play.
Unrestricted walking: No. **Range:** Yes (grass).
Holes: 18. **Par:** 72. **Yards:** 7,168-5,159. **Slope:** 128-123.
Comments: "Big greens, super course . . . Impeccable . . . One of Florida's best resort courses . . . Surprisingly nice . . . Much better since rework two years ago . . . Solid, relaxing . . . A lot of sand, a lot of grief . . . Nice, but noisy during Daytona 500 week."

★★INTERNATIONAL GOLF CLUB
Orlando—R—407-239-6909.
Season: Year-round. **High:** Nov.-April. **Caddies:** No.
Green fee: $50-$99. **Credit cards:** V, MC.
Lodging on site: No. **Reduced fees:** Resort Guests, Twilight Play.
Unrestricted walking: No. **Range:** Yes (mats).
Holes: 18. **Par:** 72. **Yards:** 6,776-5,077. **Slope:** 117-107.
Comments: "Nothing spectacular, just average holes . . . Lots of sand . . .
Not very exciting . . . Deep woods border narrow fairways . . . Short, way
overpriced . . . Highway robbery on cart prices."

★★½ KISSIMMEE BAY COUNTRY CLUB
Kissimmee—PU—407-348-3614 (10 mi. from Orlando).
Season: Year-round. **High:** Jan.-April. **Caddies:** No.
Green fee: $50-$99. **Credit cards:** V, DISC, MC.
Reduced fees: Weekdays, Low Season, Twilight Play.
Unrestricted walking: No. **Range:** Yes (grass).
Holes: 18. **Par:** 71. **Yards:** 6,846-5,171. **Slope:** 125-122.
Comments: "Nicest new course in central Florida . . . Something for everyone . . . Short, reachable par 5s . . . Yardages on scorecard a joke . . .
Watch out for low-flying airplanes . . . Poor, very poor."

★★★THE LINKS OF LAKE BERNADETTE
Zephyrhills—PU—813-788-4653 (25 mi. from Tampa).
Season: Year-round. **High:** Nov.-April. **Caddies:** No.
Green fee: $20-$49. **Credit cards:** V, MC.
Lodging on site: No. **Reduced fees:** Weekdays, Low Season.
Unrestricted walking: No. **Range:** No.
Holes: 18. **Par:** 71. **Yards:** 6,392-5,031. **Slope:** 117-118.
Comments: "Short, very tricky . . . Very fast greens . . . Greens too
difficult for most . . . Very playable . . . Pleasant staff."

★★★MARRIOTT'S ORLANDO WORLD CENTER
Orlando—R—407-238-8661 (10 mi. from Orlando).
Season: Year-round. **High:** Oct.-April. **Caddies:** No.
Green fee: $50-$99. **Credit cards:** V, AMEX, DISC, MC.
Lodging on site: Yes. **Reduced fees:** Low Season, Twilight Play.
Unrestricted walking: No. **Range:** Yes (grass).
Holes: 18. **Par:** 71. **Yards:** 6,307-5,048. **Slope:** 121-115.
Comments: "Good Joe Lee layout . . . Well conditioned . . . Tight, lots of
water . . . Playable the first time . . . Service with a smile . . . But they let
too many play, so expect long delays."

★½ MAYFAIR COUNTRY CLUB
Sanford—PU—407-322-2531 (15 mi. from Orlando).
Season: Year-round. **High:** Dec.-April. **Caddies:** No.
Green fee: $20-$49. **Credit cards:** V, DISC, MC.
Lodging on site: No. **Reduced fees:** Weekdays, Low Season.
Unrestricted walking: No. **Range:** Yes (grass).
Holes: 18. **Par:** 72. **Yards:** 6,375-5,223. **Slope:** 119-115.
Comments: "Beginner's course . . . Isn't taken care of . . . Poor shape,
slow greens . . . I always go somewhere else."

★★★½ METROWEST COUNTRY CLUB
Orlando—PU—407-299-1099.
Season: Year-round. **High:** Jan.-April. **Caddies:** No.
Green fee: $50-$99. **Credit cards:** V, AMEX, MC.
Lodging on site: No. **Reduced fees:** Low Season, Twilight Play.
Unrestricted walking: No. **Range:** Yes (grass).
Holes: 18. **Par:** 72. **Yards:** 7,051-5,323. **Slope:** 126-117.
Comments: "Mid-handicapper's paradise . . . Minimum of water for Florida . . . Best fairways in Orlando . . . Best greens in the state . . . Wide open,
no rough . . . High level of maintenance . . . Very plush . . . Nice people
. . . Worth playing . . . The extras make this one a must."

MISSION INN RESORT
Howey-in-the-Hills—R—904-324-3101, 800-874-9053
(30 mi. from Orlando).
Season: Year-round. **High:** Winter/Spring. **Caddies:** No.
Green fee: $50-$99. **Credit cards:** All Major.
Lodging on site: Yes. **Reduced fees:** Low Season, Resort Guests.
Unrestricted walking: No. **Range:** Yes (grass).
★★★½ EL CAMPEON COURSE
Holes: 18. **Par:** 72. **Yards:** 6,842-5,038. **Slope:** 134-122.
Comments: "Tops! . . . Wow, what a dream . . . Actual hills . . . Amazing hills . . . An island green . . . The thinking golfer's challenge . . . A true test for the average golfer . . . The better of the 2 at Mission Inn . . . Worth the trip to the middle of nowhere . . . Well maintained but overpriced."
★★★ LAS COLINAS COURSE
Holes: 18. **Par:** 72. **Yards:** 6,867-4,500. **Slope:** 128-109.
Comments: "Fun open course . . . Interesting . . . Give it five years and a good mowing . . . Very buggy . . . Great place to stay . . . Fine resort, fine dining."

★★★★ PALISADES COUNTRY CLUB
Clermont—PU—904-394-0085 (30 mi. from Orlando).
Season: Year-round. **High:** Jan.-April. **Caddies:** No.
Green fee: $20-$49. **Credit cards:** V, MC.
Reduced fees: Weekdays, Low Season, Twilight Play.
Unrestricted walking: No. **Range:** Yes (grass).
Holes: 18. **Par:** 72. **Yards:** 7,002-5,537. **Slope:** 127-122.
Comments: "Best-kept secret in central Florida . . . Best for your money . . . Very creative design . . . Good-sized hills . . . Like playing in some other state . . . Difficult greens . . . Everything you'd want . . . Break out your long irons . . . Remote but worth it."

(GREAT VALUE)

PELICAN BAY COUNTRY CLUB
Daytona Beach—PU—904-788-6496 (40 mi. from Orlando).
Season: Year-round. **High:** Dec.-April. **Caddies:** No.
Green fee: $20-$49. **Credit cards:** V, MC.
Reduced fees: Weekdays, Low Season, Twilight Play.
Unrestricted walking: No. **Range:** No.
★★★ SOUTH COURSE
Holes: 18. **Par:** 72. **Yards:** 6,630-5,278. **Slope:** 123-126.
Club also has 18-hole North Course for members only.
Comments: "Fun to play . . . Somewhat interesting . . . Nothing but narrow fairways . . . Excellent and inexpensive."

PLANTATION INN & GOLF RESORT
Crystal River—R—904-795-7211 (40 mi. from Gainesville).
Season: Year-round. **High:** Feb.-April. **Caddies:** No.
Green fee: $20-$49. **Credit cards:** All Major.
Lodging on site: Yes. **Reduced fees:** Low Season, Resort Guests, Twilight Play.
Unrestricted walking: No. **Range:** Yes (grass).
★★ CHAMPIONSHIP COURSE
Holes: 18. **Par:** 72. **Yards:** 6,502-5,395. **Slope:** 126-122.
Resort also has 9-hole par-34 Lagoons Course.
Comments: "Not much to brag about as a resort course . . . Fairly short, plenty of water . . . In poor shape recently."

★★½ POINCIANA GOLF & RACQUET RESORT
Kissimmee—R—407-933-5300, 800-331-7743 (30 mi. from Orlando).
Season: Year-round. **High:** Jan.-March. **Caddies:** No.
Green fee: $20-$49. **Credit cards:** V, AMEX, MC.
Lodging on site: Yes. **Reduced fees:** Low Season, Resort Guests, Twilight Play.

Unrestricted walking: No. **Range:** Yes (grass).
Holes: 18. **Par:** 72. **Yards:** 6,700-4,988. **Slope:** 125-118.
Comments: "Interesting holes . . . Many trees, much water . . . Low fees . . . Very accommodating pro staff."

★★★RIVER BEND GOLF CLUB
Ormond Beach—PU—904-673-6000 (3 mi. from Daytona Beach).
Season: Year-round. **High:** Jan.-April. **Caddies:** No.
Green fee: $20-$49. **Credit cards:** V, MC.
Lodging on site: No. **Reduced fees:** Low Season, Twilight Play.
Unrestricted walking: No. **Range:** Yes (grass).
Holes: 18. **Par:** 72. **Yards:** 6,821-5,112. **Slope:** 126-120.
Comments: "Pretty course . . . Fun for medium handicappers . . . Everyone likes it . . . Beautiful fairways . . . Heavy woods off fairways . . . Very nice, but holds rain too much."

★RIVIERA COUNTRY CLUB
Ormond Beach—PU—904-677-2464 (2 mi. from Daytona).
Season: Year-round. **High:** Jan.-April. **Caddies:** No.
Green fee: $20-$49. **Credit cards:** V, MC.
Lodging on site: No. **Reduced fees:** Low Season.
Unrestricted walking: No. **Range:** Yes (grass).
Holes: 18. **Par:** 71. **Yards:** 6,302-5,207. **Slope:** 113-122.
Comments: "Hardly The Riviera Country Club . . . A cow pasture . . . Fairly easy, but great people."

★★★ROYAL OAK GOLF CLUB
Titusville—PU—407-268-1550 (40 mi. from Orlando).
Season: Year-round. **High:** Jan.-March. **Caddies:** No.
Green fee: $20-$49. **Credit cards:** All Major.
Reduced fees: Weekdays, Low Season, Twilight Play.
Unrestricted walking: No. **Range:** Yes (grass).
Holes: 18. **Par:** 71. **Yards:** 6,709-5,471. **Slope:** 126-120.

SANDRIDGE GOLF CLUB
Vero Beach—PU—407-770-5000 (70 mi. from West Palm Beach).
Season: Year-round. **High:** Jan.-April. **Caddies:** No.
Green fee: $20-$49. **Credit cards:** No.
Reduced fees: Weekdays, Low Season, Twilight Play.
Unrestricted walking: No. **Range:** Yes (grass).
★★DUNES COURSE
Holes: 18. **Par:** 72. **Yards:** 6,817-4,944. **Slope:** 123-109.
Comments: "Good, not great . . . Nice rolling fairways . . . Was nice at one time, but is getting dog-eared."
★★★LAKES COURSE
Holes: 18. **Par:** 72. **Yards:** 6,138-4,625. **Slope:** 120-109.
Comments: "Good course in good shape . . . Lots of water."

★★★½ SEVEN HILLS GOLFERS CLUB
Spring Hill—PU—904-688-8888 (55 mi. from Tampa).
Season: Year-round. **High:** Jan.-April. **Caddies:** No.
Green fee: $20-$49. **Credit cards:** No.
Lodging on site: No. **Reduced fees:** Low Season, Twilight Play.
Unrestricted walking: No. **Range:** Yes (grass).
Holes: 18. **Par:** 72. **Yards:** 6,715-4,902. **Slope:** 126-109.
Comments: "Nice gem close to Tampa . . . Worth the drive up U.S. 19 . . . Superb terrain . . . Beautiful rolls . . . Looks like North Carolina . . . Solid fun . . . Nice quick greens . . . Less than a 4-hour round."

★★½ SHERMAN HILLS GOLF CLUB
Brooksville—PU—904-544-0990 (35 mi. from Tampa).
Season: Year-round. **High:** Winter/Spring. **Caddies:** No.
Green fee: $20-$49. **Credit cards:** No.
Reduced fees: Weekdays, Low Season, Twilight Play.

Unrestricted walking: No. **Range:** Yes (grass).
Holes: 18. **Par:** 72. **Yards:** 6,778-4,959. **Slope:** 118-110.
Comments: "Beautiful new course . . . Great condition . . . Back 9 has no trees, great for big wild-hitters . . . Not yet well known, will be difficult to keep it that way."

SPRING LAKE GOLF & TENNIS RESORT*
OSPREY/HAWK/EAGLE 9s
Sebring—R—813-655-0101, 800-635-7277 (70 mi. from Orlando).
Season: Year-round. **High:** Jan.-March. **Caddies:** No.
Green fee: $20-$49. **Credit cards:** V, AMEX, DISC, MC.
Lodging on site: Yes. **Reduced fees:** Low Season, Resort Guests, Twilight Play.
Unrestricted walking: No. **Range:** Yes (mats).
Holes: 27. **Par:** 35/36/36. **Yards:** 3,128/3,400/3,270.
Club claims to have the world's largest green on Osprey.

THE WALT DISNEY WORLD RESORT
Lake Buena Vista—R—407-824-2270 (15 mi. from Orlando).
Season: Year-round. **High:** Jan.-April. **Caddies:** No.
Green fee: $50-$99. **Credit cards:** V, AMEX, MC.
Lodging on site: Yes. **Reduced fees:** Twilight Play.
Unrestricted walking: No. **Range:** Yes (grass).
★★★½ EAGLE PINES COURSE
Holes: 18. **Par:** 72. **Yards:** 6,722-4,838. **Slope:** 131-116.
Comments: "Not as severe as most Pete Dye courses . . . Fun Pete Dye . . . Several challenging water holes . . . Greens a bit much . . . Meticulously groomed . . . Just what a course should be . . . Has a Carolinas' flavor."
★★★ LAKE BUENA VISTA COURSE
Holes: 18. **Par:** 72. **Yards:** 6,829-5,176. **Slope:** 128-120.
Comments: "Most fun of the Disney family . . . Best over all . . . Condos have detracted from its golfing pleasure."
★★★½ MAGNOLIA COURSE
Holes: 18. **Par:** 72. **Yards:** 7,190-5,414. **Slope:** 133-123.
Site of final round of PGA Tour's Walt Disney World/Oldsmobile Golf Classic. Previous rounds rotated among three courses.
Comments: "Great course . . . Beautiful shape and beautiful scenery . . .What more could you ask for? . . . Most overrated of the Disneys . . . Overplayed, needs a rest . . . Tourist trap . . . Too crowded and expensive."
★★★★ OSPREY RIDGE COURSE
Holes: 18. **Par:** 72. **Yards:** 7,101-5,402. **Slope:** 135-124.
Comments: "Best of the new breed . . . Good addition to the Disney fold . . . It's Fazio. 'Nuff said . . . Just what you'd expect from Tom Fazio . . . Just beautiful . . . Wonderful . . . Lots of manufactured roll to the land . . . Owns the toughest par 3 in the Magic Kingdom . . . Good carry required on most holes . . . Hard for seniors, but interesting and well kept . . . Very slow . . . 6-hour rounds . . . Worth the ticket."
OAK TRAIL COURSE*
Holes: 9. **Par:** 36. **Yards:** 2,913-2,532.
Only course at Walt Disney World that allows walking.

GREAT VALUE

★★★★ PALM COURSE
Holes: 18. **Par:** 72. **Yards:** 6,957-5,398. **Slope:** 133-124.
Ranked 61st in America's 75 Best Resort Courses by GOLF DIGEST.
Comments: "Very serene . . . Lots of wildlife . . . Not Mickey Mouse . . . Best of the original three . . . For long hitters . . . Lots of water . . . Fun decisions . . . Break out the scuba gear . . . Front 9 OK, back 9 outstanding . . . High priced and worth it . . . Too many cartpaths."

WORLD WOODS GOLF CLUB
Brooksville—PU—904-796-5500 (65 mi. from Tampa).
Season: Year-round. **High:** Jan.-May. **Caddies:** No.
Green fee: $100 and up. **Credit cards:** V, MC.
Lodging on site: No. **Reduced fees:** No.
Unrestricted walking: No. **Range:** Yes (grass).

PINE BARRENS COURSE*
Holes: 18. **Par:** 71. **Yards:** 6,905-5,300. **Slope:** 134-132.
ROLLING OAKS COURSE*
Holes: 18. **Par:** 72. **Yards:** 6,985-5,245. **Slope:** 131-128.
Club also has a 9-hole short course, a 3-hole practice course plus 2 complete practice ranges.

TAMPA/ST. PETERSBURG

★★½ BARDMOOR NORTH GOLF CLUB
Largo—PU—813-397-0483 (5 mi. from St. Petersburg).
Season: Year-round. **High:** Jan.-April. **Caddies:** Yes.
Green fee: $50-$99. **Credit cards:** V, AMEX, MC.
Reduced fees: Weekdays, Low Season, Twilight Play.
Unrestricted walking: No. **Range:** Yes (grass).
Holes: 18. **Par:** 72. **Yards:** 6,960-5,569. **Slope:** 126-118.
Comments: "Has gone downhill since JCPenney tournament left . . . Bare tees, old carts . . . Beat-up greens . . . Design deserves better conditioning."

★★½ BELLEVIEW MIDO COUNTRY CLUB
Belleair—R—813-581-5498 (25 mi. from Tampa).
Season: Year-round. **High:** Feb.-April. **Caddies:** No.
Green fee: $50-$99. **Credit cards:** All Major.
Lodging on site: Yes. **Reduced fees:** Low Season, Resort Guests.
Unrestricted walking: No. **Range:** Yes (grass).
Holes: 18. **Par:** 72. **Yards:** 6,550-5,601. **Slope:** 118-119.
Comments: "Ross course . . . Not really very interesting . . . Lose the carts. Let us walk this dead-flat Florida course."

★★★★ BLOOMINGDALE GOLFERS CLUB
Valrico—PU—813-685-4105 (15 mi. from Tampa).
Season: Year-round. **High:** Dec.-April. **Caddies:** No.
Green fee: $50-$99. **Credit cards:** V, AMEX, MC.
Reduced fees: Weekdays, Low Season, Twilight Play.
Unrestricted walking: No. **Range:** Yes (mats).
Holes: 18. **Par:** 72. **Yards:** 7,165-5,506. **Slope:** 137-129.
Comments: "Excellent greens . . . Best greens in Florida . . . No gimmes . . . Probably the best group of par 5s around . . . Very good course . . . Overpriced."

CITRUS HILLS GOLF AND COUNTRY CLUB
Hernando—PU—904-746-4425 (90 mi. from Tampa).
Season: Year-round. **High:** Dec.-April. **Caddies:** No.
Green fee: $20-$49. **Credit cards:** V, MC.
Lodging on site: Yes. **Reduced fees:** Low Season, Twilight Play.
Unrestricted walking: No. **Range:** Yes (grass).
★★ MEADOWS COURSE
Holes: 18. **Par:** 70. **Yards:** 5,885-4,585. **Slope:** 115-112.
★★½ OAKS COURSE
Holes: 18. **Par:** 70. **Yards:** 6,323-4,647. **Slope:** 120-114.
Comments: "Good unknown . . . Built through large oaks . . . Very hilly for Florida . . . Pretty . . . Long and narrow . . . In decent shape."

★★½ DUNEDIN COUNTRY CLUB
Dunedin—PU—813-733-7836 (20 mi. from Tampa).
Season: Year-round. **High:** Dec.-April. **Caddies:** No.
Green fee: $20-$49. **Credit cards:** No.
Lodging on site: No. **Reduced fees:** Twilight Play.
Unrestricted walking: No. **Range:** Yes (grass).
Holes: 18. **Par:** 72. **Yards:** 6,565-5,726. **Slope:** 125-124.
Comments: "Old Scottish design . . . Itty-bitty greens . . . Very difficult rough."

★★★THE EAGLES COUNTRY CLUB
FOREST/OAKS/LAKE 9s
Odessa—PU—813-920-6681 (15 mi. from Tampa).
Season: Year-round. **High:** Jan.-April. **Caddies:** No.
Green fee: $20-$49. **Credit cards:** V, MC.
Lodging on site: No. **Reduced fees:** No.
Unrestricted walking: No. **Range:** Yes (grass).
Holes: 27. **Par:** 36/36/36. **Yards:** 3,504/3,564/3,630.
Comments: "Very enjoyable . . . Three 9s set in large, cypress forest . . .
Shot placement important . . . Forest and Lake are best."

THE GOLF CLUB AT CYPRESS CREEK
Ruskin—R—813-634-8888 (15 mi. from Tampa).
Season: Year-round. **High:** Jan.-March. **Caddies:** No.
Green fee: $20-$49. **Credit cards:** V, MC.
Lodging on site: Yes. **Reduced fees:** Low Season, Resort Guests,
Twilight Play.
Unrestricted walking: No. **Range:** Yes (grass).
★★★CYPRESS CREEK COURSE
Holes: 18. **Par:** 72. **Yards:** 6,839-4,640. **Slope:** 133-114.
Comments: "Pleasant natural environment . . . Hit it straight . . . Pot
bunkers . . . Fun starts at the greens . . . Super people."
UPPER CREEK COURSE*
Holes: 18. **Par:** 63. **Yards:** 3,505-2,022.

★★★IMPERIAL LAKES GOLF CLUB
Palmetto—PU—813-747-4653 (20 mi. from Tampa).
Season: Year-round. **High:** Nov.-April. **Caddies:** No.
Green fee: $20-$49. **Credit cards:** V, MC.
Lodging on site: No. **Reduced fees:** Low Season, Twilight Play.
Unrestricted walking: No. **Range:** Yes (grass).
Holes: 18. **Par:** 72. **Yards:** 7,008-5,270. **Slope:** Unrated-117.
Comments: "Good design . . . Just average conditioning . . . Monstrous
9th is a 550-yarder around a lake."

INNISBROOK HILTON RESORT
Palm Harbor—R—813-942-2000 (20 mi. from Tampa).
Season: Year-round. **High:** Nov.-April. **Caddies:** No.
Green fee: $100 and up. **Credit cards:** All Major.
Lodging on site: Yes. **Reduced fees:** Low Season, Resort Guests.
Unrestricted walking: No. **Range:** Yes (grass).

GREAT VALUE

★★★★COPPERHEAD COURSE
Holes: 18. **Par:** 71. **Yards:** 7,087-5,506. **Slope:** 140-128.
Ranked 22nd in America's 75 Best Resort Courses by GOLF DIGEST.
Comments: "Not your typical Florida flats . . . Something you'll never
forget . . . As good as you'll find in Florida . . . Several outstanding holes
. . . Has all the shots . . . If you can play well here, you can play anywhere
. . . Exceptional beauty . . . Super service."

GREAT VALUE

★★★★ISLAND COURSE
Holes: 18. **Par:** 72. **Yards:** 6,999-5,860. **Slope:** 133-130.
Ranked 71st in America's 75 Best Resort Courses by GOLF DIGEST.
Comments: "The poor man's Augusta National . . . Hills, pines and water
. . . Each 9 is different, has great character . . . Slippery greens . . . Not as
strong as Copperhead, but more playable for most of us."
★★★SANDPIPER COURSE
FIRST/SECOND/THIRD 9s
Holes: 27. **Par:** 35/35/35. **Yards:** 3,002/2,967/3,243.
Comments: "Short course with long par 3s . . . Toughest 'easy course' in
the world . . . Best-run resort in the U.S. . . . Nice ambiance . . . The whole
experience was a delight, if expensive."

★★½ LANSBROOK GOLF CLUB
Palm Harbor—PU—813-784-7333 (20 mi. from Tampa).
Season: Year-round. **High:** Jan.-April. **Caddies:** No.

Green fee: $20-$49. **Credit cards:** V, MC.
Lodging on site: No. **Reduced fees:** Low Season, Twilight Play.
Unrestricted walking: No. **Range:** Yes (grass).
Holes: 18. **Par:** 72. **Yards:** 6,630-5,180. **Slope:** 126-119.
Comments: "Not long, somewhat open . . . Just enough water to keep it interesting . . . Many greens redone in past two years . . . Always improving . . . Room for errors . . . Just OK . . . Monotonous, only one dogleg . . . Food service poor."

★★★MANGROVE BAY GOLF CLUB
St. Petersburg—PU—813-893-7800.
Season: Year-round. **High:** Jan.-April. **Caddies:** No.
Green fee: $20-$49. **Credit cards:** V, DISC, MC.
Lodging on site: No. **Reduced fees:** Low Season, Twilight Play.
Unrestricted walking: Yes. **Range:** Yes (grass).
Holes: 18. **Par:** 72. **Yards:** 6,779-5,172. **Slope:** 120-112.
Comments: "Terrific muny . . . Top notch . . . Affordable surprise . . . Nice shape, but uninteresting . . . Overplayed, overpriced."

★½ ROCKY POINT GOLF COURSE
Tampa—PU—813-884-5141.
Season: Year-round. **High:** Dec.-April. **Caddies:** No.
Green fee: $20-$49. **Credit cards:** V, MC.
Lodging on site: No. **Reduced fees:** Low Season, Twilight Play.
Unrestricted walking: Yes. **Range:** No.
Holes: 18. **Par:** 71. **Yards:** 6,489-4,910. **Slope:** 122-111.
Comments: "Too pinched. Gave up too much land when reconstructing . . . Mixture of very easy and very hard holes . . . Has two rinky-dink par 3s . . . Condition of greens is a crapshoot."

SADDLEBROOK RESORT
Wesley Chapel—R—813-973-1111, 800-729-8383 (20 mi. from Tampa).
Season: Year-round. **High:** Dec.-April. **Caddies:** No.
Green fee: $100 and up. **Credit cards:** All Major.
Lodging on site: Yes. **Reduced fees:** Low Season, Resort Guests.
Unrestricted walking: No. **Range:** Yes (grass).
★★★PALMER COURSE
Holes: 18. **Par:** 71. **Yards:** 6,469-5,212. **Slope:** 126-121.
Comments: "Great variety in terrain . . . Rolling mounds, uneven lies in fairways . . . Too many hills in fairways . . . Great getaway spot."
★★★SADDLEBROOK COURSE
Holes: 18. **Par:** 70. **Yards:** 6,603-5,183. **Slope:** 124-124.
Comments: "Better than Palmer . . . More playable . . . Dull layout, poor condition for the price."

SEVEN SPRINGS GOLF & COUNTRY CLUB
New Port Richey—PU—813-376-0035 (12 mi. from Tampa).
Season: Year-round. **High:** Jan.-April. **Caddies:** No.
Green fee: $20-$49. **Credit cards:** V, MC.
Lodging on site: No. **Reduced fees:** Low Season, Twilight Play.
Unrestricted walking: No. **Range:** Yes (grass).
★★½ CHAMPIONSHIP COURSE
Holes: 18. **Par:** 72. **Yards:** 6,566-5,250. **Slope:** 123-112.
Comments: "Extremely narrow . . . Greens 10 on the Stimpmeter . . . Very good in off-season."
EXECUTIVE COURSE*
Holes: 18. **Par:** 64. **Yards:** 4,310-4,030. **Slope:** 112-113.

★★★½ SEVILLE GOLF & COUNTRY CLUB
Brooksville—PU—904-596-7888 (65 mi. from Tampa).
Season: Year-round. **High:** Jan.-April. **Caddies:** No.
Green fee: $20-$49. **Credit cards:** V, MC.
Lodging on site: No. **Reduced fees:** Low Season, Twilight Play.

Unrestricted walking: No. **Range:** Yes (grass).
Holes: 18. **Par:** 72. **Yards:** 7,140-5,236. **Slope:** 138-126.
Comments: "Unique golfing experience . . . A pleasant and unexpected surprise . . . One of the most interesting ever . . . Cut from sandhills . . . Deep sand traps . . . Natural sand traps . . . The Pine Valley of Florida . . . Requires a variety of accurate, thoughtful shots . . . Best value in the area . . . Maintenance needs attention . . . Great course in very poor shape . . . Greens are rough . . . Good people, no food service."

★½ SPRING HILL GOLF CLUB
Spring Hill—PU—904-683-2261 (55 mi. from Tampa).
Season: Year-round. **High:** Jan.-April. **Caddies:** No.
Green fee: $20-$49. **Credit cards:** No.
Lodging on site: No. **Reduced fees:** Low Season, Twilight Play.
Unrestricted walking: No. **Range:** Yes (grass).
Holes: 18. **Par:** 72. **Yards:** 6,917-5,588. **Slope:** 133-127.
Comments: "Design is terrific, but course always in terrible condition . . . Must have zero maintenance budget."

STOUFFER VINOY GOLF CLUB*
St. Petersburg—R—813-896-8000.
Season: Year-round. **High:** Oct.-May. **Caddies:** No.
Green fee: $50-$99. **Credit cards:** All Major.
Lodging on site: Yes. **Reduced fees:** Twilight Play.
Unrestricted walking: No. **Range:** Yes (grass).
Holes: 18. **Par:** 70. **Yards:** 6,267-4,818. **Slope:** 118-111.

★★½ SUMMERFIELD GOLF CLUB
Riverview—PU—813-671-3311 (22 mi. from Tampa).
Season: Year-round. **High:** Nov.-May. **Caddies:** No.
Green fee: $20-$49. **Credit cards:** V, MC.
Lodging on site: No. **Reduced fees:** Low Season.
Unrestricted walking: No. **Range:** Yes (grass).
Holes: 18. **Par:** 71. **Yards:** 6,883-5,139. **Slope:** 125-114.
Comments: "Novel design . . . Like two separate courses . . . Many surprise hazards . . . Used to be better. Has gone downhill condition-wise."

★TARPON SPRINGS GOLF CLUB
Tarpon Springs—PU—813-937-6906.
Season: Year-round. **High:** Jan.-April. **Caddies:** No.
Green fee: $20-$49. **Credit cards:** No.
Lodging on site: No. **Reduced fees:** Low Season, Twilight Play.
Unrestricted walking: No. **Range:** Yes (grass).
Holes: 18. **Par:** 72. **Yards:** 6,099-5,338. **Slope:** 112-110.
Comments: "The worst . . . The pits . . . Don't bother."

★★UNIVERSITY OF SOUTH FLORIDA GOLF COURSE
Tampa—PU—813-974-2071.
Season: Year-round. **High:** Oct.-March. **Caddies:** No.
Green fee: $20-$49. **Credit cards:** V, MC.
Lodging on site: No. **Reduced fees:** Weekdays, Low Season.
Unrestricted walking: Yes. **Range:** No.
Holes: 18. **Par:** 72. **Yards:** 6,962-5,349. **Slope:** 131-115.
Comments: "Tight, small greens . . . In better shape than in the past."

★★★½ WESTCHASE GOLF CLUB
Tampa—PU—813-854-2331.
Season: Year-round. **High:** Dec.-April. **Caddies:** No.
Green fee: $20-$49. **Credit cards:** V, AMEX, DISC, MC.
Lodging on site: No. **Reduced fees:** Weekdays.
Unrestricted walking: No. **Range:** Yes (grass).
Holes: 18. **Par:** 72. **Yards:** 6,710-5,205. **Slope:** 130-121.
Comments: "Nice new course . . . Demands all the shots . . . Always in superb condition . . . Best new course in Florida."

★**WHISPERING OAKS COUNTRY CLUB**
Ridge Manor—PU—904-583-4233, 800-453-4799 (40 mi. from Tampa).
Season: Year-round. **High:** Nov.-April. **Caddies:** No.
Green fee: $20-$49. **Credit cards:** V, MC.
Lodging on site: No. **Reduced fees:** Low Season, Twilight Play.
Unrestricted walking: No. **Range:** Yes (grass).
Holes: 18. **Par:** 72. **Yards:** 6,313-6,055. **Slope:** 123-118.
Comments: "Weedy fairways, bare areas on tees and greens."

SARASOTA, BRADENTON, VENICE

BOBBY JONES GOLF COMPLEX
Sarasota—PU—813-955-8097.
Season: Year-round. **High:** Dec.-April. **Caddies:** No.
Green fee: Under $20. **Credit cards:** V, MC.
Lodging on site: No. **Reduced fees:** Low Season, Twilight Play.
Unrestricted walking: No. **Range:** Yes (mats).
★½ **AMERICAN COURSE**
Holes: 18. **Par:** 71. **Yards:** 6,009-4,453. **Slope:** 117-107.
Comments: "Terrible shape . . . If Bobby Jones were alive, he'd want his
name removed."
★½ **BRITISH COURSE**
Holes: 18. **Par:** 72. **Yards:** 6,468-5,695. **Slope:** 111-115.
Complex includes 9-hole par-30 Gillespie Course.
Comments: "Flat, uninteresting, poor shape . . . Has lost its British flavor
. . . Poorly managed, but inexpensive."

★★★**CALUSA LAKES GOLF COURSE**
Nokomis—PU—813-484-8995 (5 mi. from Sarasota).
Season: Year-round. **High:** Jan.-April. **Caddies:** No.
Green fee: $20-$49. **Credit cards:** V, MC.
Lodging on site: No. **Reduced fees:** Low Season, Twilight Play.
Unrestricted walking: No. **Range:** Yes (grass).
Holes: 18. **Par:** 72. **Yards:** 6,760-5,197. **Slope:** 124-118.
Comments: "Cut through forest . . . Feels like North Carolina . . . A
pretty course in need of water."

★½ **CAPRI ISLES GOLF CLUB**
Venice—PU—813-485-3371 (15 mi. from Sarasota).
Season: Year-round. **High:** Nov.-May. **Caddies:** No.
Green fee: $20-$49. **Credit cards:** V, MC.
Lodging on site: No. **Reduced fees:** Low Season, Twilight Play.
Unrestricted walking: No. **Range:** Yes (grass).
Holes: 18. **Par:** 72. **Yards:** 6,472-5,894. **Slope:** 123-122.
Comments: "Grand old dame of west Florida has seen better days."

★★★½ **THE CLUB AT OAK FORD**
MYRTLE/PALMS/LIVE OAK 9s
Sarasota—PU—813-371-3680 (60 mi. from Tampa).
Season: Year-round. **High:** Jan.-April. **Caddies:** No.
Green fee: $20-$49. **Credit cards:** V, MC.
Lodging on site: No. **Reduced fees:** Low Season.
Unrestricted walking: No. **Range:** Yes (grass).
Holes: 27. **Par:** 36/36/36. **Yards:** 3,404/3,349/3,330
Comments: "Second best in the area . . . Good relatively new test . . . two
holes among the best anywhere . . . Palms great until the last three . . . Too
many carries over jungle. Not good . . . Out in the woods."

★★**FOXFIRE GOLF CLUB**
PINE/PALM/OAK 9s
Sarasota—PU—813-921-7757 (60 mi. from Tampa).
Season: Year-round. **High:** Nov.-April. **Caddies:** No.
Green fee: $20-$49. **Credit cards:** V, MC.

Lodging on site: No. **Reduced fees:** Low Season.
Unrestricted walking: Yes. **Range:** Yes (grass).
Holes: 27. **Par:** 36/36/36. **Yards:** 3,017/3,196/3,084.
Comments: "All three 9s extremely fair . . . Not too long . . . Not well maintained . . . Bakes out like a rock . . . No smoking rule on the course. Gimme a break."

LONGBOAT KEY CLUB
Longboat Key—R—813-383-9571 (3 mi. from Sarasota).
Season: Year-round. **High:** Dec.-May. **Caddies:** No.
Green fee: $50-$99. **Credit cards:** V, AMEX, MC.
Lodging on site: Yes. **Reduced fees:** Low Season.
Unrestricted walking: No. **Range:** Yes (grass).
★★★½ **HARBOURSIDE COURSE**
RED/WHITE/BLUE 9s
Holes: 27. **Par:** 36/36/36. **Yards:** 3,323/3,426/3,386.
Comments: "Your standard variety resort course . . . Lots of water hazards and sand traps."
★★★½ **ISLANDSIDE COURSE**
Holes: 18. **Par:** 72. **Yards:** 6,792-5,198. **Slope:** 138-121.
Comments: "Pristine . . . Everything very good . . . Better than Harbourside."

★★★½ **THE RIVER CLUB**
Bradenton—PU—813-751-4211 (45 mi. south of Tampa).
Season: Year-round. **High:** Jan.-April. **Caddies:** No.
Green fee: $20-$49. **Credit cards:** V, MC.
Lodging on site: No. **Reduced fees:** Low Season, Twilight Play.
Unrestricted walking: No. **Range:** Yes (grass).
Holes: 18. **Par:** 72. **Yards:** 7,004-5,252. **Slope:** 133-122.
Comments: "Fine layout . . . A sparkler . . . Rustic . . . Lots of mounds . . . Nos. 10 and 18 are unfair, require long carries over wastelands."

★★★½ **ROSEDALE GOLF & COUNTRY CLUB**
Bradenton—PU—813-756-0004 (30 mi. from Tampa).
Season: Year-round. **High:** Jan.-April. **Caddies:** No.
Green fee: $20-$49. **Credit cards:** V, MC.
Lodging on site: No. **Reduced fees:** Low Season.
Unrestricted walking: No. **Range:** Yes (grass).
Holes: 18. **Par:** 72. **Yards:** 6,779-5,169. **Slope:** 130-120.
Comments: "Great new tight layout . . . Extremely narrow fairways . . . Still unfinished. Will be very good when done."

★★½ **SARASOTA GOLF CLUB**
Sarasota—PU—813-371-2431.
Season: Year-round. **High:** Nov.-April. **Caddies:** No.
Green fee: $20-$49. **Credit cards:** V, MC.
Lodging on site: No. **Reduced fees:** Low Season, Twilight Play.
Unrestricted walking: No. **Range:** Yes (grass).
Holes: 18. **Par:** 72. **Yards:** 7,112-5,592. **Slope:** 117-116.
Comments: "Great for duffers . . . Lots of improvements made in 1993 . . . The pride of Sarasota."

★★★ **TATUM RIDGE GOLF LINKS**
Sarasota—PU—813-378-4211.
Season: Year-round. **High:** Jan.-Easter. **Caddies:** No.
Green fee: $20-$49. **Credit cards:** V, MC.
Lodging on site: No. **Reduced fees:** Low Season, Twilight Play.
Unrestricted walking: No. **Range:** Yes (grass).
Holes: 18. **Par:** 72. **Yards:** 6,757-5,149. **Slope:** 124-114.
Comments: "Very intriguing . . . Links style . . . All that's missing are some bagpipes . . . Short enough to score on, long enough to test any golfer . . . Not for everyone . . . Par-5 13th, one of the best."

FLORIDA

★★★WATERFORD GOLF CLUB
Venice—PU—813-484-6621 (15 mi. from Sarasota).
Season: Year-round. **High:** Jan.-April. **Caddies:** No.
Green fee: $20-$49. **Credit cards:** V, MC.
Lodging on site: No. **Reduced fees:** Low Season.
Unrestricted walking: No. **Range:** Yes (grass).
Holes: 18. **Par:** 72. **Yards:** 6,601-5,242. **Slope:** 124-116.
Comments: "Playable . . . Fair to everyone . . . Plays very slow."

SOUTHWEST REGION

ADMIRAL LEHIGH GOLF & RESORT
Lehigh—R—813-369-2121 (17 mi. from Fort Myers).
Season: Year-round. **High:** Jan.-April. **Caddies:** No.
Green fee: $20-$49. **Credit cards:** V, AMEX, DISC, MC.
Lodging on site: Yes. **Reduced fees:** Low Season, Twilight Play.
Unrestricted walking: No. **Range:** Yes (mats).
★NORTH COURSE
Holes: 18. **Par:** 71. **Yards:** 6,303-5,353. **Slope:** 119-121.
Comments: "Hard to say whether resort or course needs more work . . . Lots of bare spots . . . Weeds in the greens."
SOUTH COURSE AT MIRROR LAKES*
813-369-1322.
Lodging on site: No. **Range:** Yes (grass).
Holes: 18. **Par:** 72. **Yards:** 6,941-5,677. **Slope:** 123-125.

★★½ CAPE CORAL GOLF & TENNIS RESORT
Cape Coral—R—813-542-7879, 800-648-1475 (110 mi. from Tampa).
Season: Year-round. **High:** Oct.-May. **Caddies:** No.
Green fee: $50-$99. **Credit cards:** V, AMEX, DISC, MC.
Lodging on site: Yes. **Reduced fees:** Low Season, Resort Guests, Twilight Play.
Unrestricted walking: No. **Range:** Yes (grass).
Holes: 18. **Par:** 72. **Yards:** 6,649-5,464. **Slope:** 112-119.
Comments: "Beauty and the beast . . . Has seen better days . . . Fairways really need work . . . Generally plays slow . . . Courteous crew."

★★½ CORAL OAKS GOLF COURSE
Cape Coral—PU—813-283-4100 (15 mi. from Fort Myers).
Season: Year-round. **High:** Dec.-April. **Caddies:** No.
Green fee: $20-$49. **Credit cards:** V, DISC, MC.
Lodging on site: No. **Reduced fees:** Low Season, Twilight Play.
Unrestricted walking: No. **Range:** Yes (grass).
Holes: 18. **Par:** 72. **Yards:** 6,623-4,803. **Slope:** 123-117.
Comments: "Excellent layout, but grazing cows could maintain it better . . . Great for all skill levels . . . Poor design . . . Too many golfers."

★★★½ EASTWOOD GOLF COURSE
Fort Myers—PU—813-275-4848.
Season: Year-round. **High:** Dec.-April. **Caddies:** No.
Green fee: $20-$49. **Credit cards:** No.
Lodging on site: No. **Reduced fees:** Low Season, Twilight Play.
Unrestricted walking: No. **Range:** Yes (grass).
Holes: 18. **Par:** 72. **Yards:** 6,772-5,116. **Slope:** 130-116.
Ranked in Second 25 of America's 75 Best Public Courses by GOLF DIGEST.
Comments: "Excellent muny . . . The best in southwest Florida . . . Best public course in the state . . . Best city course in America . . . Attractive and well kept . . . Makes my day."

★★½ FORT MYERS COUNTRY CLUB
Fort Myers—PU—813-936-2457.
Season: Year-round. **High:** Dec.-April. **Caddies:** No.
Green fee: $20-$49. **Credit cards:** No.

Reduced fees: Weekdays, Low Season, Twilight Play.
Unrestricted walking: Yes. **Range:** Yes (grass).
Holes: 18. **Par:** 71. **Yards:** 6,414-5,135. **Slope:** 118-117.
Comments: "Donald Ross course . . . Nice track . . . Greens make it challenging . . . Beautifully maintained . . . Newly renovated . . . Walking anytime . . . Fun even when play is slow . . . Reasonably priced, if you can get a tee time."

★★★½ GATEWAY GOLF CLUB
Fort Myers—PU—813-561-1010.
Season: Year-round. **High:** Feb.-April. **Caddies:** No.
Green fee: $50-$99. **Credit cards:** V, AMEX, MC.
Reduced fees: Low Season, Resort Guests, Twilight Play.
Unrestricted walking: No. **Range:** Yes (grass).
Holes: 18. **Par:** 72. **Yards:** 6,974-5,323. **Slope:** 130-120.
Comments: "Fun course, keeps your interest . . . Beautiful, challenging . . . Immaculate . . . Country club conditions, country club prices."

GOLDEN GATE COUNTRY CLUB*
Naples—R—813-455-1010, 800-277-0017.
Season: Year-round. **High:** Nov.-April. **Caddies:** No.
Green fee: $20-$49. **Credit cards:** V, AMEX, DISC, MC.
Lodging on site: Yes. **Reduced fees:** Low Season, Resort Guests, Twilight Play.
Unrestricted walking: No. **Range:** Yes (grass).
Holes: 18. **Par:** 72. **Yards:** 6,570-5,374. **Slope:** 124-125.

★★★½ THE GOLF CLUB AT MARCO
Marco Island—R—813-793-6060 (100 mi. from Miami).
Season: Year-round. **High:** Jan.-April. **Caddies:** No.
Green fee: $50-$99. **Credit cards:** All Major.
Lodging on site: Yes. **Reduced fees:** Low Season.
Unrestricted walking: No. **Range:** Yes (grass).
Holes: 18. **Par:** 72. **Yards:** 6,898-5,416. **Slope:** 137-122.
Comments: "Cut from the Everglades . . . Very playable . . . Biggest mosquitos in the world."

★★★★LELY FLAMINGO ISLAND CLUB
Naples—R—813-793-2223 (40 mi. from Fort Myers).
Season: Year-round. **High:** Nov.-April. **Caddies:** No.
Green fee: $50-$99. **Credit cards:** All Major.
Lodging on site: No. **Reduced fees:** Low Season, Twilight Play.
Unrestricted walking: No. **Range:** Yes (grass).
Holes: 18. **Par:** 72. **Yards:** 7,171-5,377. **Slope:** 135-126.
Comments: "Wonderful . . . The pick of the litter . . . One of the tops . . . One of the three best in southwest Florida . . . Extremely picturesque . . . Bring your camera . . . For the price, can't beat it . . . Too expensive for a public course . . . Isn't worth the green fee."

★★½ LOCHMOOR COUNTRY CLUB
North Fort Myers—PU—813-995-0501 (5 mi. from Fort Myers).
Season: Year-round. **High:** Jan.-April. **Caddies:** No.
Green fee: $20-$49. **Credit cards:** V, MC.
Reduced fees: Low Season, Resort Guests, Twilight Play.
Unrestricted walking: No. **Range:** Yes (grass).
Holes: 18. **Par:** 72. **Yards:** 6,908-5,152. **Slope:** 128-116.

MARCO SHORES COUNTRY CLUB*
Marco Island—PU—813-394-2581 (5 mi. from Naples).
Season: Year-round. **High:** Jan.-April. **Caddies:** No.
Green fee: $50-$99. **Credit cards:** V, MC.
Reduced fees: Low Season, Resort Guests, Twilight Play.
Unrestricted walking: No. **Range:** Yes (grass).
Holes: 18. **Par:** 72. **Yards:** 6,879-5,634. **Slope:** 125-121.

★★★NAPLES BEACH HOTEL & GOLF CLUB
Naples—R—813-261-2222, 800-237-7600 (40 mi. from Fort Myers).
Season: Year-round. **High:** Jan.-April. **Caddies:** No.
Green fee: $50-$99. **Credit cards:** All Major.
Lodging on site: Yes. **Reduced fees:** Low Season, Resort Guests.
Unrestricted walking: No. **Range:** Yes (grass).
Holes: 18. **Par:** 72. **Yards:** 6,462-5,267. **Slope:** 122-115.
Comments: "Lovely old setting right on the gulf . . . Pleasant . . . Sweet
. . . Conditions vary . . . Course gets heavy play . . . Fairways and greens
best shape ever . . . Was better before Hurricane Andrew stopped by . . .
Staff is very helpful."

★½ PALM RIVER COUNTRY CLUB
Naples—PU—813-597-6082.
Season: Year-round. **High:** Jan.-March. **Caddies:** No.
Green fee: $20-$49. **Credit cards:** V, MC.
Lodging on site: No. **Reduced fees:** Low Season, Twilight Play.
Unrestricted walking: No. **Range:** No.
Holes: 18. **Par:** 72. **Yards:** 6,718-5,830. **Slope:** 120-121.
Comments: "Needs much better grooming . . . Always a snail's pace of
play . . . OK if there's nowhere else to play."

★★★★PELICAN'S NEST GOLF CLUB
HURRICANE/GATOR/SEMINOLE 9s
Bonita Springs—PU—813-947-4600, 800-952-6378
(15 mi. from Fort Myers).
Season: Year-round. **High:** Jan.-March. **Caddies:** Yes.
Green fee: $50-$99. **Credit cards:** V, AMEX, MC.
Lodging on site: No. **Reduced fees:** Low Season, Twilight Play.
Unrestricted walking: No. **Range:** Yes (grass).
Holes: 27. **Par:** 36/36/36. **Yards:** 3,459/3,491/3,478.
Fourth 9 holes scheduled to open in early 1994.
Comments: "South Florida's best . . . Likable courses . . . Quite difficult
yet fun . . . Beautiful and fair . . . More water than grass . . . Bring extra
sleeves . . . Good conditioning in an expensive setting . . . Worth every
penny . . . Best-managed public club ever seen . . . Happy staff."

GREAT VALUE

★★★½ VINES GOLF & COUNTRY CLUB
Fort Myers—PU—813-267-7003.
Season: Year-round. **High:** Nov.-April. **Caddies:** No.
Green fee: $50-$99 **Credit cards:** V, AMEX, MC.
Lodging on site: No. **Reduced fees:** Low Season.
Unrestricted walking: No. **Range:** Yes (grass).
Holes: 18. **Par:** 72. **Yards:** 7,029-5,254. **Slope:** 135-119.
Comments: "Friendly . . . Difficult for the average guy."

SOUTHEAST REGION

★★★ATLANTIS COUNTRY CLUB
Atlantis—R—407-968-1300 (5 mi. from West Palm Beach).
Season: Year-round. **High:** Jan.-March. **Caddies:** No.
Green fee: $50-$99. **Credit cards:** V, MC.
Lodging on site: Yes. **Reduced fees:** Low Season, Resort Guests.
Unrestricted walking: No. **Range:** Yes (grass).
Holes: 18. **Par:** 72. **Yards:** 6,477-5,258. **Slope:** 125-123.
Comments: "Tight, tree lined, old style . . . Carolina style . . . Much
harder than appears from scorecard . . . Always in tip-top shape . . . Very
friendly staff . . . Poor practice facilities."

★★BAYSHORE GOLF COURSE
Miami—PU—305-532-3350.
Season: Year-round. **High:** Dec.-March. **Caddies:** No.
Green fee: $20-$49. **Credit cards:** V, MC.

Reduced fees: Weekdays, Low Season, Twilight Play.
Unrestricted walking: No. **Range:** Yes (mats).
Holes: 18. **Par:** 72. **Yards:** 6,903-5,538. **Slope:** 127-120.
Additional 9-hole par-3 course.
Comments: "Older golfers' favorite . . . Better shape than it used to be, but still boring."

★★½ BILTMORE GOLF COURSE
Coral Gables—PU—305-460-5364 (3 mi. from Miami).
Season: Year-round. **High:** Nov.-April. **Caddies:** No.
Green fee: $20-$49. **Credit cards:** V, AMEX, MC.
Lodging on site: Yes. **Reduced fees:** Low Season, Twilight Play.
Unrestricted walking: No. **Range:** Yes (grass).
Holes: 18. **Par:** 71. **Yards:** 6,642-5,820. **Slope:** 119-122.
Comments: "Still spotty conditions . . . Bad design . . . 6-hour round . . . New 18th totally out of character."

BOCA RATON RESORT & CLUB
Boca Raton—R—407-395-3000, 800-327-0101, (22 mi. from Palm Beach).
Season: Year-round. **High:** Oct.-May. **Caddies:** No.
Green fee: $50-$99. **Credit cards:** All Major.
Lodging on site: Yes. **Reduced fees:** Low Season, Twilight Play.
Unrestricted walking: No. **Range:** Yes (grass).
COUNTRY CLUB COURSE*
Holes: 18. **Par:** 72. **Yards:** 6,564-5,565. **Slope:** 126-124.
★★½ RESORT COURSE
Holes: 18. **Par:** 71. **Yards:** 6,682-5,518. **Slope:** 122-124.
Comments: "A classic . . . Lots of history . . . Beautiful . . . Old-fashioned temptations . . . A nice experience . . . Excellent service . . . Short . . . Nothing special . . . Not too interesting."

★★BOYNTON BEACH MUNICIPAL GOLF COURSE
RED/WHITE/BLUE 9s
Boynton Beach—PU—407-969-2201 (10 mi. from West Palm Beach).
Season: Year-round. **High:** Nov.-April. **Caddies:** No.
Green fee: $20-$49. **Credit cards:** No.
Lodging on site: No. **Reduced fees:** Low Season.
Unrestricted walking: No. **Range:** Yes (grass).
Holes: 27. **Par:** 35/36/30. **Yards:** 3,070/3,261/2,018.
Comments: "Short, but watch out . . . Typical crowded muny . . . Nil practice area."

★½ THE BREAKERS GOLF CLUB
Palm Beach—R—407-659-8407.
Season: Year-round. **High:** Nov.-May. **Caddies:** Yes.
Green fee: $50-$99. **Credit cards:** All Major.
Lodging on site: Yes. **Reduced fees:** No.
Unrestricted walking: No. **Range:** Yes (grass).
Holes: 18. **Par:** 70. **Yards:** 6,017-5,582. **Slope:** 119-122.
Comments: "Old traditional layout . . . Just fun . . . Good for resort play . . . Run down . . . Charges are high."

★★★BREAKERS WEST GOLF CLUB
West Palm Beach—R—407-790-7020.
Season: Year-round. **High:** Dec.-April. **Caddies:** No.
Green fee: $50-$99. **Credit cards:** V, AMEX, MC.
Lodging on site: No. **Reduced fees:** Low Season.
Unrestricted walking: No. **Range:** Yes (grass).
Holes: 18. **Par:** 71. **Yards:** 7,017-5,536. **Slope:** 133-114.

COLONY WEST COUNTRY CLUB
Tamarac—PU—305-726-8430 (5 mi. from Fort Lauderdale).
Season: Year-round. **High:** Nov.-April. **Caddies:** No.
Green fee: $50-$99. **Credit cards:** V, AMEX, MC.

Reduced fees: Weekdays, Low Season, Twilight Play.
Unrestricted walking: No. **Range:** No.
★★★½ **CHAMPIONSHIP COURSE**
Holes: 18. **Par:** 71. **Yards:** 7,271-4,810. **Slope:** 138-127.
Ranked in Second 25 of America's 75 Best Public Courses by GOLF DIGEST.
Comments: "Total pleasure . . . Toughest in south Florida . . . Demands both length and accuracy . . . Great, but condos make it ugly . . . Pretty well maintained . . . Has gone down past few years . . . Evidently maintenance budget was 1st victim of the recession . . . Chewed up tees and greens, poor fairways . . . Nice, but no memorable holes . . . Very, very overrated."
GLADES COURSE*
Unrestricted walking: Yes.
Holes: 18. **Par:** 65. **Yards:** 4,207-3,855.
Comments: "Short, walking course with small, fast greens."

CRYSTAL LAKE COUNTRY CLUB
Pompano Beach—PU—305-943-2902 (10 mi. from Fort Lauderdale).
Season: Year-round. **High:** Nov.-May. **Caddies:** No.
Green fee: $20-$49. **Credit cards:** V, MC, AMEX.
Lodging on site: No. **Reduced fees:** Twilight Play, Low Season.
Unrestricted walking: No. **Range:** Yes (mats).
★★**SOUTH COURSE**
Holes: 18. **Par:** 72. **Yards:** 6,610-5,458 **Slope:** 120-121.
TAM O'SHANTER NORTH COURSE*
Holes: 18. **Par:** 70. **Yards:** 6,360-5,205. **Slope:** 119-118.

★★½ **CYPRESS CREEK COUNTRY CLUB**
Boynton Beach—PU—407-737-6880 (10 mi. from West Palm Beach).
Season: Year-round. **High:** Jan.-April. **Caddies:** No.
Green fee: $20-$49. **Credit cards:** V, MC.
Lodging on site: No. **Reduced fees:** Weekdays, Low Season.
Unrestricted walking: No. **Range:** Yes (grass).
Holes: 18. **Par:** 72. **Yards:** 6,808-5,530. **Slope:** 113-109.
Comments: "Very good layout . . . Used to be best public course in area, now too expensive . . . Top practice area, clubhouse and help . . . Needs a greenkeeper."

DEER CREEK GOLF CLUB*
Deerfield Beach—PU—305-421-5550 (10 mi. from Fort Lauderdale).
Season: Year-round. **High:** Dec.-April. **Caddies:** Yes.
Green fee: $50-$99. **Credit cards:** V, AMEX, MC.
Reduced fees: Weekdays, Low Season, Resort Guests, Twilight Play.
Unrestricted walking: No. **Range:** Yes (grass).
Holes: 18. **Par:** 72. **Yards:** 7,058-5,331. **Slope:** 134-122.
Comments: "Undergoing complete renovation . . . Hilly fairways, unusual for Florida . . . Excellent pro shop and restaurant."

★★½ **DELRAY BEACH GOLF CLUB**
Delray Beach—PU—407-243-7380 (20 mi. from West Palm Beach).
Season: Year-round. **High:** Nov.-April. **Caddies:** No.
Green fee: $20-$49. **Credit cards:** V, MC.
Lodging on site: No. **Reduced fees:** Low Season.
Unrestricted walking: No. **Range:** Yes (mats).
Holes: 18. **Par:** 72. **Yards:** 6,907-5,189. **Slope:** 126-117.
Comments: "Old Donald Ross could stand some changes . . . Would be nicer looking if better maintained."

DIPLOMAT RESORT COUNTRY CLUB*
Hallendale—PU—305-457-2082 (5 mi. from Fort Lauderdale).
Season: Year-round. **High:** Dec.-April. **Caddies:** No.
Green fee: $20-$49. **Credit cards:** V, MC.
Lodging on site: No. **Reduced fees:** Low Season.
Unrestricted walking: No. **Range:** Yes.
Holes: 18. **Par:** 72. **Yards:** 6,624-5,404. **Slope:** 115-110.

★★½ DON SHULA'S HOTEL AND GOLF CLUB
Miami Lakes—PU—305-821-1151.
Season: Year-round. **High:** Dec.-April. **Caddies:** No.
Green fee: $20-$49. **Credit cards:** All Major.
Lodging on site: Yes. **Reduced fees:** No.
Unrestricted walking: Yes. **Range:** Yes (grass).
Holes: 18. **Par:** 72. **Yards:** 7,022-5,639. **Slope:** 124-120.
Comments: "Good course . . . Requires golfer to think . . . Good shape sometimes, other times it's rough . . . Trees need trimming . . . Staff not very helpful . . . Stick to football."

DORAL RESORT & COUNTRY CLUB
Miami—R—305-592-2000.
Season: Year-round. **High:** Jan.-April/Oct.-Dec. **Caddies:** Yes.
Green fee: $50-$99, except Blue. **Credit cards:** All Major.
Lodging on site: Yes. **Reduced fees:** Low Season, Resort Guests.
Unrestricted walking: No. **Range:** Yes (mats).
★★★★BLUE COURSE
Green fee: $100 and up.
Holes: 18. **Par:** 72. **Yards:** 6,939-5,786. **Slope:** 127-124.
Site of the PGA Tour's Doral-Ryder Open. Ranked 42nd in America's 75 Best Resort Courses by GOLF DIGEST.
Comments: "Still the Blue Monster . . . The hometown champ . . . Best ever . . . No. 1 in south Florida . . . Pure class . . . You need a complete game to enjoy it . . . Value for your money can't be beat . . . Best Bermuda greens anywhere . . . Memorable for many reasons . . . 18th is a legend . . . Highly overrated . . . Has deteriorated . . . Great hype, poor greenkeeping . . . Lousy conditions for the price . . . Green fee outrageous."
★★★½ GOLD COURSE
Holes: 18. **Par:** 70. **Yards:** 6,361-5,422. **Slope:** 127-122.
Comments: "Impressive . . . Very good since the redesign . . . Extremely long and hard . . . Great shot variety . . . Overlooked . . . As good as the Blue . . . Better than the Blue . . . Tougher than the Blue . . . Has tarnished in recent years."
★★★RED COURSE
Holes: 18. **Par:** 71. **Yards:** 6,210-5,254. **Slope:** 118-118.
Comments: "More playable for short hitters than the others . . . Development has chopped this one up . . . Overplayed . . . Poor maintenance."
★★WHITE COURSE
Holes: 18. **Par:** 72. **Yards:** 6,208-5,286. **Slope:** 117-116.
Club also has 9-hole par-3 Green Course.
Comments: "Ugh! What a golf factory."

★★DOUG FORD'S LACUNA GOLF CLUB
Lake Worth—PU—407-433-3006 (5 mi. from West Palm Beach).
Season: Year-round. **High:** Nov.-May. **Caddies:** No.
Green fee: $20-$49. **Credit cards:** V, MC.
Lodging on site: No. **Reduced fees:** Low Season.
Unrestricted walking: No. **Range:** Yes (grass).
Holes: 18. **Par:** 71. **Yards:** 6,700-5,119. **Slope:** 121-111.
Comments: "Decent design, poorly managed . . . Not well maintained."

★★★★½ EMERALD DUNES GOLF CLUB
West Palm Beach—R—407-684-4653.
Season: Year-round. **High:** Dec.-April. **Caddies:** No.
Green fee: $100 and up. **Credit cards:** V, AMEX, MC.
Lodging on site: No. **Reduced fees:** Weekdays, Low Season.
Unrestricted walking: No. **Range:** Yes (grass).
Holes: 18. **Par:** 72. **Yards:** 7,006-4,676. **Slope:** 129-126.
Comments: "Super . . . Terrific . . . Excellent . . . The perfect place . . . Best in south Florida . . . Best public experience east of the Mississippi . . . Makes you think . . . No homes . . . Pro-style greens . . . Interesting, but much too expensive . . . Another great, overpriced Fazio layout . . . Prices have spiraled in its first four years."

FONTAINEBLEAU GOLF COURSE
Miami—PU—305-221-5181.
Season: Year-round. **High:** Nov.-March. **Caddies:** No.
Green fee: $20-$49. **Credit cards:** V, MC.
Reduced fees: Weekdays, Low Season, Twilight Play.
Unrestricted walking: No. **Range:** Yes (mats).
★½ **EAST COURSE**
Holes: 18. **Par:** 72. **Yards:** 7,035-5,586. **Slope:** 122-119.
Comments: "A true blue-collar operation . . . Fairways and greens in bad shape."
★½ **WEST COURSE**
Holes: 18. **Par:** 72. **Yards:** 6,944-5,565. **Slope:** 120-118.
Comments: "Poor management of large crowds."

GOLF CLUB OF MIAMI
Miami—PU—305-829-8456.
Season: Year-round. **High:** Dec.-March. **Caddies:** No.
Green fee: $20-$49. **Credit cards:** V, AMEX.
Reduced fees: Weekdays, Low Season, Resort Guests, Twilight Play.
Unrestricted walking: No. **Range:** Yes. (grass).
★★★½ **EAST COURSE**
Holes: 18. **Par:** 70. **Yards:** 6,353-5,025. **Slope:** 124-117.
Comments: "Best public facility for the price in all of Florida . . . Very narrow, nicely maintained."
SOUTH COURSE*
Holes: 18. **Par:** 62. **Yards:** 5,200-4,900. **Slope:** Unrated.
Comments: "Best executive course ever."
★★★½ **WEST COURSE**
Holes: 18. **Par:** 72. **Yards:** 7,017-5,298. **Slope:** 130-123.
Comments: "Best in the area, second only to Doral . . . Toughest around . . . Great par 3s, all over water . . . Great practice range."

★★½ GRAND PALMS GOLF & COUNTRY CLUB
GRAND/ROYAL/SABAL 9s
Pembrooke Pines—R—305-437-3334 (5 mi. from Fort Lauderdale).
Season: Year-round. **High:** Nov.-April. **Caddies:** No.
Green fee: $20-$49. **Credit cards:** All Major.
Lodging on site: Yes. **Reduced fees:** Weekday, Low Season, Resort Guests, Twilight Play.
Unrestricted walking: No. **Range:** Yes (grass).
Holes: 27. **Par:** 36/36/36. **Yards:** 3,337/3,420/3,306.
Comments: "Lousy, several terrible holes . . . Bad design on some holes . . . Too much water, too little landing area . . . Fairways hard as concrete . . . Still planting trees . . . Needs to age."

JACARANDA GOLF CLUB
Plantation—PU—305-472-5836 (12 mi. from Fort Lauderdale).
Season: Year-round. **High:** Nov.-May. **Caddies:** No.
Green fee: $50-$99. **Credit cards:** V, AMEX, MC.
Reduced fees: Weekdays, Low Season, Twilight Play.
Unrestricted walking: No. **Range:** Yes (grass).
★★½ **EAST COURSE**
Holes: 18. **Par:** 72. **Yards:** 7,170-5,668. **Slope:** 130-121.
Comments: "Nice staff . . . Total pleasure . . . Every hole feels like a 625-yard par 5."
★★½ **WEST COURSE**
Holes: 18. **Par:** 72. **Yards:** 6,729-5,314. **Slope:** 135-129.
Comments: "Greens hold, putt true . . . Lots of traps, too hard for the novice . . . Only things missing from both are 40 acres and some cows."

KEY WEST RESORT GOLF COURSE*
Key West—PU—305-294-5232 (140 mi. from Miami).
Season: Year-round. **High:** Dec.-April. **Caddies:** No.

Green fee: $20-$49. **Credit cards:** MC, V, AMEX.
Lodging on site: No. **Reduced fees:** Low Season, Twilight Play.
Unrestricted walking: No. **Range:** Yes (grass).
Holes: 18. **Par:** 70. **Yards:** 6,526-5,183. **Slope:** 122-118.
Comments: "Next nearest course is 100 miles away."

★½ LAKE WORTH GOLF CLUB
Lake Worth—PU—407-582-9713 (7 mi. from West Palm Beach).
Season: Year-round. **High:** Jan.-March. **Caddies:** No.
Green fee: $20-$49. **Credit cards:** No.
Reduced fees: Weekdays, Low Season, Twilight Play.
Unrestricted walking: Yes. **Range:** No.
Holes: 18. **Par:** 70. **Yards:** 6,113-5,423. **Slope:** 116-113.
Comments: "A real scarcity—a course that allows walking."

★★★★½ THE LINKS AT KEY BISCAYNE
Key Biscayne—PU—305-361-9129 (1 mi. from Miami).
Season: Year-round. **High:** Nov.-March. **Caddies:** No.
Green fee: $50-$99. **Credit cards:** V, AMEX, MC.
Lodging on site: No. **Reduced fees:** Low Season, Twilight Play.
Unrestricted walking: No. **Range:** Yes (grass).
Holes: 18. **Par:** 72. **Yards:** 7,070-5,690. **Slope:** 138-129.
Ranked in Second 25 of America's 75 Best Public Courses by GOLF DIGEST.
Comments: "Terrific visual course . . . Always a great time . . . Coming back after the hurricane . . . Better after the hurricane . . . Best muny in south Florida . . . Best when the wind blows . . . Difficult in three-club winds . . . Cured me of my hydrophobia! . . . Good, but doesn't compare to Eastwood . . . Hot and buggy . . . Poorly operated . . . Complicated starting-time system . . . Stuffy attitude."

PGA NATIONAL GOLF CLUB
Palm Beach Gardens—R—407-627-1800 (15 mi. from West Palm Beach).
Season: Year-round. **High:** Jan.-April. **Caddies:** No.
Green fee: $50-$99. **Credit cards:** V, AMEX, MC.
Lodging on site: Yes. **Reduced fees:** Low Season.
Unrestricted walking: No. **Range:** Yes (grass).
★★★½ CHAMPION COURSE
Green fee: $100 and up.
Holes: 18. **Par:** 72. **Yards:** 7,022-5,377. **Slope:** 142-121.
Ranked 72nd in America's 75 Best Resort Courses by GOLF DIGEST.
Comments: "A true champion . . . Great challenge . . . A must . . . Super hard . . . Nicklaus should have left Fazio alone . . . 15 and 17 too much alike . . . Too expensive for us locals . . . Don't miss the downstairs coffee shop."
★★★ESTATE COURSE
Lake Park—R—407-627-1614.
Lodging on site: No.
Holes: 18. **Par:** 72. **Yards:** 6,784-4,955. **Slope:** 131-118.
Previously known as Stonewal Golf Club.
Comments: "A hidden jewel . . . Well maintained . . . Great greens . . . Best Bermuda greens in Florida . . . Dinkiest 19th hole in America."
★★★GENERAL COURSE
Holes: 18. **Par:** 72. **Yards:** 6,768-5,324. **Slope:** 134-122.
Comments: "Tough, good for long hitters . . . Several forced carries from the fairways."
★★★½ HAIG COURSE
Holes: 18. **Par:** 72. **Yards:** 6,806-5,645. **Slope:** 132-121.
Comments: "Best of the lot . . . Better than the Champion for the money . . . Less expensive . . . Not Fazio's best work . . . Greens being reworked."
★★★SQUIRE COURSE
Holes: 18. **Par:** 72. **Yards:** 6,478-5,114. **Slope:** 130-119.
Comments: "Tight, short, water-laden . . . Overpriced."

PALM AIRE SPA RESORT*
Pompano Beach—R—305-968-2775.
Season: Year-round. **High:** Nov.-April. **Caddies:** No.
Green fee: $20-$49. **Credit cards:** V, MC.
Lodging on site: Yes. **Reduced fees:** No.
Unrestricted walking: No. **Range:** Yes (grass).
THE PALMS COURSE
Holes: 18. **Par:** 72. **Yards:** 6,932-5,432. **Slope:** 128-120.
THE PINES COURSE
Holes: 18. **Par:** 72. **Yards:** 6,610-5,232. **Slope:** 122-115.
THE SABALS COURSE
Holes: 18. **Par:** 60. **Yards:** 3,401-3,069. **Slope:** Unrated.

★★½ PALM BEACH GARDENS MUNICIPAL GOLF COURSE
Palm Beach Gardens—PU—407-775-2556 (8 mi. from West Palm Beach).
Season: Year-round. **High:** Dec.-April. **Caddies:** No.
Green fee: $20-$49. **Credit cards:** No.
Lodging on site: No. **Reduced fees:** No.
Unrestricted walking: No. **Range:** Yes (grass).
Holes: 18. **Par:** 72. **Yards:** 6,375-4,663. **Slope:** 125-110.
Comments: "Affordable golf in a high-priced area . . . Good test of skills . . . Unusual layout . . . Tight, difficult . . . Designed, I think, by Daniel Boone . . . You'll need a guide the first time out . . . Very penal."

PALM BEACH POLO & COUNTRY CLUB
West Palm Beach—R—407-798-7401.
Season: Year-round. **High:** Dec.-April. **Caddies:** No.
Green fee: $50-$99. **Credit cards:** All Major.
Lodging on site: Yes. **Reduced fees:** Low Season.
Unrestricted walking: No. **Range:** Yes (grass).
★★★½ CYPRESS COURSE
Holes: 18. **Par:** 72. **Yards:** 7,116-5,172. **Slope:** 138-121.
Comments: "Tough course, lots of possibilities . . . Tournament character . . . Great greens . . . Rambo golf at its worst."
★★★½ DUNES COURSE
Holes: 18. **Par:** 72. **Yards:** 7,050-5,516. **Slope:** 132-122.
Ranked 57th in America's 75 Best Resort Courses by GOLF DIGEST.
Comments: "Even better set of greens."
OLDE COURSE*
Holes: 9. **Par:** 36. **Yards:** 3,461.

POMPANO BEACH GOLF COURSE
Pompano Beach—PU—305-781-0426 (8 mi. from Fort Lauderdale).
Season: Year-round. **High:** Dec.-April. **Caddies:** No.
Green fee: $20-$49. **Credit cards:** No.
Lodging on site: No. **Reduced fees:** Low Season, Twilight Play.
Unrestricted walking: Yes. **Range:** Yes (grass).
★★PINES COURSE
Holes: 18. **Par:** 72. **Yards:** 6,886-5,980. **Slope:** 117-117.
Comments: "For city course kept up very well . . . New clubhouse and restaurant very nice."
★★PALMS COURSE
Holes: 18. **Par:** 71. **Yards:** 6,356-5,523. **Slope:** 106-108.

★★½ RAINTREE GOLF RESORT
Pembroke Pines—R—305-432-4400, 800-346-5332 (8 mi. from Fort Lauderdale).
Season: Year-round. **High:** Nov.-April. **Caddies:** No.
Green fee: $20-$49. **Credit cards:** MC, V, AMEX, DISC.
Lodging on site: Yes. **Reduced fees:** Weekdays, Low Season, Resort Guest, Twilight Play.
Unrestricted walking: No. **Range:** Yes (grass).
Holes: 18. **Par:** 72. **Yards:** 6,661-5,382. **Slope:** 126-122.

Comments: "A '6-6-6' layout, six of each kind of par . . . Too many similar holes . . . Hard greens, won't hold."

★★ROLLING HILLS HOTEL & GOLF RESORT
Fort Lauderdale—R—305-475-0400, 800-327-7735.
Season: Year-round. **High:** Jan.-April. **Caddies:** No.
Green fee: $20-$49. **Credit cards:** V, AMEX, MC.
Lodging on site: Yes. **Reduced fees:** Weekdays, Low Season, Resort Guests, Twilight Play.
Unrestricted walking: No. **Range:** Yes (mats).
Holes: 18. **Par:** 72. **Yards:** 6,905-5,630. **Slope:** 124-121.
Comments: "Old course sitting on its laurels . . . Nice movie set . . . Was once great, now run-down . . . Nice rolling fairways . . . Only course in south Florida with elevated tees/greens . . . It's been all downhill since its "Caddyshack" heyday . . . Four types of grass on each green . . . Could be more fun with Bill Murray around . . . Didn't see any gophers."

TURNBERRY ISLE RESORT & CLUB
Aventura-North Miami Beach—R—305-932-6200, 800-327-7028.
Season: Year-round. **High:** Nov.-May. **Caddies:** No.
Green fee: $50-$99. **Credit cards:** All Major.
Lodging on site: Yes. **Reduced fees:** Low Season.
Unrestricted walking: No. **Range:** Yes (grass).
★★NORTH COURSE
Holes: 18. **Par:** 70. **Yards:** 6,323-4,991. **Slope:** 127-112.
Comments: "Good, but too expensive for what is offered."
★★★SOUTH COURSE
Holes: 18. **Par:** 72. **Yards:** 7,003-5,581. **Slope:** 140-121.
Comments: "Worth a night's stay to play . . . Not much except for the finishing holes . . . Awfully busy in winter."

★★★½ WEST PALM BEACH COUNTRY CLUB
West Palm Beach—PU—407-582-2019.
Season: Year-round. **High:** Dec.-April. **Caddies:** No.
Green fee: $20-$49. **Credit cards:** No.
Lodging on site: No. **Reduced fees:** Twilight Play.
Unrestricted walking: No. **Range:** Yes (mats).
Holes: 18. **Par:** 72. **Yards:** 6,800-5,884. **Slope:** 124-121.
Ranked in Second 25 of America's 75 Best Public Courses by GOLF DIGEST.
Comments: "Great Dick Wilson muny . . . Best pure public course in America . . . Good layout, extra good value, wait wait wait . . . Could have more challenge . . . No water hazards . . . Greens not consistent . . . Hard to get tee times . . . New restricted walking policy unfortunate."

★★★WESTCHESTER GOLF AND COUNTRY CLUB
Boynton Beach—PU—407-734-6300 (10 mi. from West Palm Beach).
Season: Year-round. **High:** Nov.-May. **Caddies:** No.
Green fee: $20-$49. **Credit cards:** V, DISC, MC.
Lodging on site: No. **Reduced fees:** Weekdays, Low Season.
Unrestricted walking: No. **Range:** Yes (grass).
Holes: 18. **Par:** 72. **Yards:** 6,760-4,886. **Slope:** 128-111.
Comments: "Good layout, good greens . . . Water everywhere . . . Good value in summer, expensive in winter."

★★★WINSTON TRAILS GOLF CLUB
Lake Worth—PU—407-439-3700 (15 mi. from West Palm Beach).
Season: Year-round. **High:** Nov.-April. **Caddies:** No.
Green fee: $50-$99. **Credit cards:** V, AMEX, MC.
Reduced fees: Weekdays, Low Season, Twilight Play.
Unrestricted walking: No. **Range:** Yes (grass).
Holes: 18. **Par:** 72. **Yards:** 6,820-5,378. **Slope:** 123-117.
Comments: "Fine Joe Lee layout at reasonable cost . . . Check it out . . . Best of the new ones . . . Shows promise . . . Oversized greens . . . Hole designs all very similar . . . Polite staff."

BACON PARK GOLF COURSE*
LIVE OAK/MAGNOLIA/CYPRESS 9s
Savannah—PU—912-354-2625.
Season: Year-round. **High:** April-Aug. **Caddies:** No.
Green fee: Under $20. **Credit cards:** V, MC.
Lodging on site: No. **Reduced fees:** Weekdays, Twilight Play.
Unrestricted walking: No. **Range:** Yes (grass).
Holes: 27. **Par:** 36/36/36. **Yards:** 3,423/3,317/3,256.

★★★½ BARRINGTON HALL GOLF CLUB
Macon—PU—912-757-8358.
Season: Year-round. **High:** March-Nov. **Caddies:** No.
Green fee: $20-$49. **Credit cards:** V, MC.
Lodging on site: No. **Reduced fees:** Weekdays.
Unrestricted walking: Yes. **Range:** Yes (grass).
Holes: 18. **Par:** 72. **Yards:** 7,062-5,012. **Slope:** 131-118.
Comments: "One of the prettiest ever . . . Very narrow . . . Thick trees and underbrush . . . Premium on shot placement . . . Rolling hills."

BULL CREEK GOLF COURSE
Columbus—PU—706-561-1614.
Season: Year-round. **High:** Spring/Summer. **Caddies:** No.
Green fee: Under $20. **Credit cards:** V, MC.
Lodging on site: No. **Reduced fees:** Weekdays.
Unrestricted walking: Yes. **Range:** Yes (grass).
★★★ EAST COURSE
Holes: 18. **Par:** 72. **Yards:** 6,705-5,430. **Slope:** 127-118.
Comments: "Best value in Georgia . . . Prefer the old 9 to the new one."
★★★½ WEST COURSE
Holes: 18. **Par:** 72. **Yards:** 6,921-5,385. **Slope:** 130-117.
Ranked in First 25 of America's 75 Best Public Courses by GOLF DIGEST.
Comments: "A challenge from any tee box . . . Inexpensive."

CALLAWAY GARDENS RESORT
Pine Mountain—R—404-663-2281 (70 mi. from Atlanta).
Season: Year-round. **High:** Spring/Fall. **Caddies:** No.
Green fee: $50-$99. **Credit cards:** V, AMEX, MC.
Lodging on site: Yes. **Reduced fees:** Low Season, Twilight Play.
Unrestricted walking: No. **Range:** Yes (grass).
★★½ GARDENS VIEW COURSE
Holes: 18. **Par:** 72. **Yards:** 6,392-5,848. **Slope:** 121-123.
Comments: "Mainly for short hitters . . . Excellent accommodations."
★★★½ LAKE VIEW COURSE
Holes: 18. **Par:** 70. **Yards:** 6,006-5,452. **Slope:** 115-122.
Comments: "Medium difficulty . . . Very challenging . . . Good fun . . . Best greens of year . . . Play is too slow."
★★★½ MOUNTAIN VIEW COURSE
Holes: 18. **Par:** 72. **Yards:** 7,057-5,848. **Slope:** 138-122.
Home of the PGA Tour's Buick Southern Open. Ranked 56th in America's 75 Best Resort Courses by GOLF DIGEST.
Comments: "Long, tough course . . . Beautiful . . . Top drawer . . . Simply excellent . . . Georgia is always on my mind because of Callaway . . . Don't play in summer, the crowned greens become impossible to hold."

★★½ CENTENNIAL GOLF CLUB
Acworth—PU—404-975-1000 (30 mi. from Atlanta).
Season: Year-round. **High:** May-Sept. **Caddies:** No.
Green fee: $20-$49. **Credit cards:** V, AMEX, DISC, MC.
Lodging on site: No. **Reduced fees:** Weekdays, Twilight Play.
Unrestricted walking: No. **Range:** Yes (grass).
Holes: 18. **Par:** 72. **Yards:** 6,900-5,095. **Slope:** 134-122.
Comments: "Nice variety . . . Shotmaker's course . . . May have the best greens in the state . . . Great finishing hole . . . First few holes rather dull, gets interesting from No. 5 on . . . Boring . . . Tricked up . . . Designed like

there was not a lot of land, holes bunched together . . . Parallel holes . . . 5-hour rounds the norm . . . Would rather be deer hunting on it."

★★½ THE CHAMPIONS CLUB OF ATLANTA
Alpharetta—PU—404-343-9700 (20 mi. from Atlanta).
Season: Year-round. **High:** April-Oct. **Caddies:** No.
Green fee: $50-$99. **Credit cards:** V, MC.
Lodging on site: No. **Reduced fees:** Twilight Play.
Unrestricted walking: No. **Range:** Yes (grass).
Holes: 18. **Par:** 72. **Yards:** 6,725-4,470. **Slope:** 130-111.
Comments: "A true experience . . . Very good . . . Short . . . A little on the easy side . . . Needs better conditioning . . . Nice facilities."

★★★½ CHATEAU ELAN GOLF CLUB
Braselton—R—404-339-9838, 800-233-9463 (30 mi. from Atlanta).
Season: Year-round. **High:** Spring/Fall. **Caddies:** No.
Green fee: $20-$49. **Credit cards:** V, AMEX, MC.
Lodging on site: Yes. **Reduced fees:** Weekdays, Low Season, Resort Guests.
Unrestricted walking: No. **Range:** Yes (grass).
Holes: 18. **Par:** 71. **Yards:** 7,030-5,092. **Slope:** 136-124.
Comments: "A gorgeous sleeper . . . One of Atlanta area's best . . . Outstanding design and condition . . . Good as any private club . . . One of the best conditioned ever . . . No matter what time of year . . . The poor man's Augusta National . . . Need to stay on the short stuff . . . Rough impossibly high . . . First-class treatment . . . Great service, but somewhat pricey."

★★★CHICOPEE WOODS GOLF COURSE
Gainesville—PU—404-534-7322.
Season: Year-round. **High:** April-Aug. **Caddies:** No.
Green fee: $20-$49. **Credit cards:** V, AMEX, MC.
Reduced fees: Weekdays, Low Season, Twilight Play.
Unrestricted walking: Yes. **Range:** Yes (grass).
Holes: 18. **Par:** 72. **Yards:** 7,040-5,001. **Slope:** 135-117.
Comments: "Super layout . . . Great greens . . . Very hilly . . . Long carries . . . One of best values in Atlanta . . . Higher fees for non-county residents."

★★★½ EAGLE WATCH GOLF CLUB
Woodstock—PU—404-591-1000 (35 mi. from Atlanta).
Season: Year-round. **High:** March-Oct. **Caddies:** No.
Green fee: $50-$99. **Credit cards:** V, AMEX, MC.
Reduced fees: Weekdays, Low Season, Twilight Play.
Unrestricted walking: No. **Range:** Yes (grass).
Holes: 18. **Par:** 72. **Yards:** 6,896-6,044. **Slope:** 136-133.
Comments: "Exciting routing of holes . . . Neat par 5s . . . Very few flat lies . . . Outstanding service . . . Well kept but costly . . . Due to its 'value' I go less often."

★★★½ FIELDS FERRY GOLF CLUB
Calhoun—PU—706-625-5666 (50 mi. from Atlanta).
Season: Year-round. **High:** April-Sept. **Caddies:** No.
Green fee: $20-$49. **Credit cards:** V, MC.
Lodging on site: No. **Reduced fees:** Weekdays.
Unrestricted walking: Yes. **Range:** Yes (grass).
Holes: 18. **Par:** 72. **Yards:** 6,750-5,355. **Slope:** 125-120.

Comments: "Strategically-placed bunkers . . . Great par 3s . . . Open . . . Very little rough . . . Few shade trees . . . Tough to lose balls . . . Easy walk . . . Worth the drive."

★★★GEORGIA VETERANS STATE PARK GOLF COURSE
Cordele—PU—912-276-2377 (45 mi. from Macon).
Season: Year-round. **High:** April-Oct. **Caddies:** No.

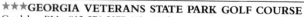

Green fee: $20-$49. **Credit cards:** V, MC.
Lodging on site: Yes. **Reduced fees:** Weekdays.
Unrestricted walking: Yes. **Range:** Yes (grass).
Holes: 18. **Par:** 72. **Yards:** 7,088-5,180. **Slope:** 130-124.
Comments: "Great new state course . . . Very pleasant . . . Very friendly staff . . . Still young, promises to be one of the best."

★★★THE HAMPTON CLUB

St. Simons Island—PU—912-634-0255 (70 mi. from Jacksonville, Fla.).
Season: Year-round. **High:** Sept.-March. **Caddies:** No.
Green fee: $50-$99. **Credit cards:** V, AMEX, MC.
Reduced fees: Low Season, Resort Guests, Twilight Play.
Unrestricted walking: No. **Range:** Yes (grass).
Holes: 18. **Par:** 72. **Yards:** 6,465-5,233. **Slope:** 130-120.
Comments: "Picturesque . . . Beautiful layout with marsh and island views . . . Great marsh holes . . . Island holes are super . . . Outstanding greens . . . Overhyped . . . Some poor holes cramped into small area."

★★★HARD LABOR CREEK STATE PARK GOLF COURSE

Rutledge—PU—706-557-3006 (55 mi. from Atlanta).
Season: Year-round. **High:** April-June. **Caddies:** No.
Green fee: $20-$49. **Credit cards:** V, MC.
Lodging on site: Yes. **Reduced fees:** Twilight Play.
Unrestricted walking: Yes. **Range:** Yes (grass).
Holes: 18. **Par:** 72. **Yards:** 6,437-6,043. **Slope:** 125-119.
Comments: "Lovely, challenging, cheap . . . Probably the best value for the money in Georgia . . . Much improved . . . Can golf and camp."

★★INNSBRUCK GOLF CLUB OF HELEN

Helen—R—404-878-2100, 800-642-2709 (90 mi. from Atlanta).
Season: Year-round. **High:** April-Oct. **Caddies:** No.
Green fee: $20-$49. **Credit cards:** V, AMEX, MC.
Lodging on site: Yes. **Reduced fees:** Low Season, Resort Guests, Twilight Play.
Unrestricted walking: No. **Range:** Yes (grass).
Holes: 18. **Par:** 72. **Yards:** 6,798-5,174. **Slope:** 130-129.
Comments: "Alpine golf at its best . . . Memorable holes . . . Love it in the fall . . . Watch out for deer . . . Terrible course . . . One to avoid."

JEKYLL ISLAND GOLF CLUB

Jekyll Island—PU—912-635-2368 (65 mi. from Jacksonville, Fla.).
Season: Year-round. **High:** Feb.-April. **Caddies:** No.
Green fee: $20-$49. **Credit cards:** V, DISC, MC.
Lodging on site: No. **Reduced fees:** Low Season.
Unrestricted walking: Yes. **Range:** Yes (grass).
★★★INDIAN MOUND COURSE
Holes: 18. **Par:** 72. **Yards:** 6,596-5,345. **Slope:** 127-122.
Comments: "Great . . . Best public course in Georgia . . . All three Jekylls are fun . . . Well maintained . . . Have great packages . . . Very good values . . . Have lots of bugs."
★★★OLEANDER COURSE
Holes: 18. **Par:** 72. **Yards:** 6,679-5,654. **Slope:** 128-124.
Comments: "Championship quality course . . . The best of both links and inland . . . Good bunkering . . . Lots of trees . . . Best of the three Jekylls . . . Only Augusta is better in Georgia . . . Watch for gators."
★★½ PINE LAKES COURSE
Holes: 18. **Par:** 72. **Yards:** 6,802-5,742. **Slope:** 130-124.
Has 9-hole Oceanside Course.
Comments: "Simple but loads of fun . . . Flat . . . Unoriginal . . . Traps need work."

★★★★JONES CREEK GOLF CLUB

Evans—PU—706-860-4228 (2 mi. from Augusta).

Season: Year-round. **High:** Spring/Fall. **Caddies:** No.
Green fee: $20-$49. **Credit cards:** V, AMEX, MC.
Lodging on site: No. **Reduced fees:** Weekdays, Twilight Play.
Unrestricted walking: No. **Range:** Yes (grass).
Holes: 18. **Par:** 72. **Yards:** 7,008-5,430. **Slope:** 137-130.
Ranked in Third 25 of America's 75 Best Public Courses by GOLF DIGEST.
Comments: "Fantastic . . . Delightful . . . Every hole is great . . . Second only to Augusta . . . Augusta National Junior . . . Best public course in the state . . . Challenging bent-grass greens . . . Superb greens . . . Some difficult hilly holes . . . Better be accurate . . . Always tip-top shape . . . Great shape in spring, poor shape by fall."

★★LAKE ARROWHEAD RESORT & COUNTRY CLUB
Waleska—R—404-479-5505 (55 mi. from Atlanta).
Season: Year-round. **High:** April-Oct. **Caddies:** No.
Green fee: $20-$49. **Credit cards:** V, AMEX, MC.
Lodging on site: Yes. **Reduced fees:** Weekdays, Resort Guests.
Unrestricted walking: No. **Range:** Yes (grass).
Holes: 18. **Par:** 72. **Yards:** 6,400-4,468. **Slope:** 135-117.
Comments: "Views spectacular . . . Short par 4s . . . Needs maintenance badly . . . Not much."

★★★½ LAKE LANIER HILTON RESORT
Lake Lanier—R—404-945-8787 (35 mi. from Atlanta).
Season: Year-round. **High:** March-Oct. **Caddies:** No.
Green Fee: $20-$49. **Credit cards:** All Major.
Lodging on site: Yes. **Reduced Fees:** Low Season.
Unrestricted Walking: No. **Range:** Yes (grass).
Holes: 18. **Par:** 72. **Yards:** 6,341-4,935. **Slope:** 124-117.
Comments: "Great esthetics . . . Extraordinarily beautiful . . . Great views of Lake Lanier . . . The Pebble Beach of the southeast . . . Cheaper and more fun than PineIsle . . . More challenging than most resort courses . . . Designer must like water . . . 13 water holes . . . One giant water hazard . . . Too many forced carries . . . Terrifying water carries . . . Too little acreage . . . Several strange shots . . . Tough for short hitters."

★★★LANE CREEK GOLF CLUB
Bishop—PU—706-769-6699 (45 mi. from Atlanta).
Season: Year-round. **High:** April-June. **Caddies:** No.
Green fee: $20-$49. **Credit cards:** V, MC.
Lodging on site: No. **Reduced fees:** Weekdays, Twilight Play.
Unrestricted walking: Yes. **Range:** Yes (grass).
Holes: 18. **Par:** 72. **Yards:** 6,725-5,195. **Slope:** 125-119.

★★★★OSPREY COVE GOLF CLUB
St. Marys—PU—912-882-5575, 800-352-5575 (35 mi. from Jacksonville, Fla.). **Season:** Year-round. **High:** Jan.-July. **Caddies:** No.
Green fee: $20-$49. **Credit cards:** V, AMEX, MC.
Lodging on site: No. **Reduced fees:** Weekdays, Twilight Play.
Unrestricted walking: No. **Range:** Yes (grass).
Holes: 18. **Par:** 72. **Yards:** 6,791-5,263. **Slope:** 130-120.
Comments: "Stunning . . . Great vistas, great price . . . Great design . . . McCumber at his best . . . Marsh everywhere . . . A must . . . Golf and service both first class . . . No competition comes close."

REYNOLDS PLANTATION CLUB
Greensboro—R—706-467-3159 (78 mi. from Atlanta).
Season: Year-round. **High:** April-Oct. **Caddies:** No.
Green fee: $50-$99. **Credit cards:** V, AMEX, MC, DIS.
Lodging on site: Yes. **Reduced fees:** No.
Unrestricted walking: No. **Range:** Yes (grass).

★★★½ PLANTATION COURSE
Holes: 18. **Par:** 72. **Yards:** 6,656-5,162. **Slope:** 125-117.
Ranked 14th in Georgia by GOLF DIGEST.

Comments: "Tight . . . Very scenic . . . Some breathtaking holes . . . Tough but fair . . . Great from the blues . . . Excellent back 9 . . . Excellent shape . . . Warm clubhouse and staff."

★★★½ GREAT WATERS COURSE

706-485-0235.

Holes: 18. **Par:** 72. **Yards:** 7,048-5,057. **Slope:** 140-118.

Selected as runner-up for Best New Resort Course of 1993 by GOLF DIGEST.

Comments: "Excellent Nicklaus design . . . One of Jack's best . . . Outstanding in every facet . . . Terrific views of Lake Oconee . . . Good test of all levels . . . As fine as you'll ever play . . . What a challenge . . . Everyone should play this course . . . The Pebble Beach of Georgia."

★★★RIVERPINES GOLF CLUB

Alpharetta—PU—404-442-5960 (25 mi. from Atlanta).

Season: Year-round. **High:** June-Aug. **Caddies:** No.

Green fee: $20-$49. **Credit cards:** V, AMEX, MC.

Lodging on site: No. **Reduced fees:** No.

Unrestricted walking: No. **Range:** Yes (mats).

Holes: 18. **Par:** 70. **Yards:** 6,511-4,279. **Slope:** 126-114.

Comments: "Short but excellent for its 1st year . . . Strictly golf . . . Treats golf as a business, not as a pastime . . . Cold atmosphere."

★★★ST. SIMONS ISLAND CLUB

St. Simons Island—PU—912-638-5130 (70 mi. from Jacksonville, Fla.).

Season: Year-round. **High:** March-May. **Caddies:** Yes.

Green fee: $20-$49. **Credit cards:** V, MC.

Lodging on site: No. **Reduced fees:** Low Season.

Unrestricted walking: No. **Range:** Yes (grass).

Holes: 18. **Par:** 72. **Yards:** 6,490-5,361. **Slope:** 133-124.

Comments: "Traditional design . . . Very narrow . . . Lots of water hazards . . . Beautiful woods . . . Length not a great factor, premium on accuracy . . . Don't skip this if at The Cloister."

★★★SCONTI GOLF CLUB
CHOCTAW/CHEROKEE/CREEK 9s

Big Canoe—R—706-268-5103 (50 mi. from Atlanta).

Season: Year-round. **High:** April-Oct. **Caddies:** No.

Green fee: $20-$49. **Credit cards:** V, AMEX, DISC, MC.

Lodging on site: Yes. **Reduced fees:** Weekdays.

Unrestricted walking: No. **Range:** Yes (grass).

Holes: 27. **Par:** 36/36/36. **Yards:** 3,200/3,171/3,076.

SEA ISLAND GOLF CLUB

St. Simons Island—R—912-638-5118 (75 mi. from Savannah).

Season: Year-round. **High:** March/April/Oct. **Caddies:** Yes.

Green fee: $50-$99. **Credit cards:** V, MC.

Lodging on site: Yes. **Reduced fees:** Resort Guests.

Unrestricted walking: No. **Range:** Yes (grass).

★★★½ MARSHSIDE 9/RETREAT 9

Holes: 18. **Par:** 72. **Yards:** 6,518-5,056. **Slope:** 130-111.

Comments: "A good test . . . Variety of interesting holes . . . Overshadowed by the other 18, but just as fun."

★★★★PLANTATION 9/SEASIDE 9

Holes: 18. **Par:** 72. **Yards:** 6,710-5,200. **Slope:** 133-110.

Ranked 62nd in America's 75 Best Resort Courses by GOLF DIGEST.

Comments: "Tradition reigns . . . The resort alone is worth the experience . . . Seaside is a unique 9 . . . Excellent condition . . . Good management of pace of play . . . Lacks character on some holes . . . Poor value."

★★½ SEA PALMS GOLF & TENNIS RESORT
TALL PINES/GREAT OAKS/SEA PALMS WEST 9s

St. Simons Island—R—912-638-9041 (68 mi. from Jacksonville, Fla.).

Season: Year-round. **High:** March-Oct. **Caddies:** No.

Green fee: $50-$99. **Credit cards:** V, AMEX, MC.

Lodging on site: Yes. **Reduced fees:** Low Season, Resort Guests, Twilight Play
Unrestricted walking: No. **Range:** Yes (grass).
Holes: 27. **Par:** 36/36/37. **Yards:** 3,253/3,405/2,945.
Comments: "OK, not what you expect for a resort . . . Run-down in places, needs attention to greens . . . Lacks character on some holes."

★★½ SKY VALLEY GOLF CLUB
Sky Valley—R—706-746-5303, 800-437-2416 (120 mi. from Atlanta).
Season: Year-round. **High:** May-Oct. **Caddies:** No.
Green fee: $20-$49. **Credit cards:** All Major.
Lodging on site: Yes. **Reduced fees:** Low Season, Twilight Play.
Unrestricted walking: No. **Range:** Yes (grass).
Holes: 18. **Par:** 72. **Yards:** 6,388-5,066. **Slope:** 136-127.
Comments: "Terrific mountain course . . . Beautiful surroundings . . . Too short . . . Needs some TLC."

★★★½ SOUTHBRIDGE GOLF CLUB
Savannah—PU—912-651-5455.
Season: Year-round. **High:** March-Oct. **Caddies:** No.
Green fee: $20-$49. **Credit cards:** V, MC, AMEX, DISC.
Lodging on site: No. **Reduced fees:** Weekdays, Low Season.
Unrestricted walking: No. **Range:** Yes (grass).
Holes: 18. **Par:** 72. **Yards:** 6,990-5,181. **Slope:** 136-118.
Comments: "Fair course . . . Always tremendous shape . . . Tough par 3s, can take risks or play safe . . . A true test of putting skills . . . Can't wait to play again . . . Too much mounding."

★★★SOUTHERNESS GOLF CLUB
Stockbridge—PU—404-808-6000 (20 mi. from Atlanta).
Season: Year-round. **High:** May-Oct. **Caddies:** No.
Green Fee: $20-$49. **Credit cards:** V, AMEX, MC.
Lodging on site: No. **Reduced Fees:** Weekdays, Twilight Play.
Unrestricted Walking: No. **Range:** Yes (grass).
Holes: 18. **Par:** 72. **Yards:** 6,766-4,956. **Slope:** 127-119.
Comments: "Another jewel . . . Best public facility in Atlanta . . . Don't miss it when in town . . . Great variety of holes . . . Terrific test . . . Three white-knuckle finishing holes over water . . . Service even better than the course . . . Very nice but remote, and too pricey . . . Bad shape . . . Clover in rough . . . Lost balls just inches off fairway."

STONE MOUNTAIN PARK GOLF COURSE
Stone Mountain—R—404-498-5715 (12 mi. from Atlanta).
Season: Year-round. **High:** April-Oct. **Caddies:** No.
Green fee: $20-$49. **Credit cards:** All Major.
Lodging on site: Yes. **Reduced fees:** No.
Unrestricted walking: No. **Range:** Yes (grass).
★★★LAKEMONT/WOODMONT COURSE
Holes: 18. **Par:** 72. **Yards:** 6,595-5,231. **Slope:** 131-120.
Comments: "Gorgeous . . . Shotmaker's course . . . Scenic but too short . . . Two or three holes just plain goofy . . . Expect 5½-hour rounds . . . Didn't like paying to get into park just to get to the course."
★★★STONEMONT COURSE
Holes: 18. **Par:** 72. **Yards:** 6,683-5,020. **Slope:** 133-121.
Ranked in Third 25 of America's 75 Best Public Courses by GOLF DIGEST.
Comments: "Everything you look for in a course . . . Interesting turns and hills . . . Good greens . . . Good shape . . . Good value . . . Poor management, weekend rounds take almost 6 hours . . . Course is packed."

★★★½ STOUFFER PINEISLE RESORT
Lake Lanier Islands—R—404-945-8922 (40 mi. from Atlanta).
Season: Year-round. **High:** April-Oct. **Caddies:** No.
Green fee: $50-$99. **Credit cards:** All Major.

Lodging on site: Yes. **Reduced fees:** No.
Unrestricted walking: No. **Range:** Yes (grass).
Holes: 18. **Par:** 72. **Yards:** 6,527-5,297. **Slope:** 122-116.
Comments: "Great family resort . . . Big time enjoyment . . . Terrific combo of lakes and hills . . . Extremely hilly . . . Hard greens . . . Very contrived . . . Costly . . . Slow play . . . Watch out for goose droppings . . . What's all the fuss about?"

★½ SUGAR HILL GOLF CLUB

Sugar Hill—PU—404-271-0519 (36 mi. from Atlanta).
Season: Year-round. **High:** May-July. **Caddies:** No.
Green fee: $20-$49. **Credit cards:** V, MC.
Lodging on site: No. **Reduced fees:** Weekdays, Twilight Play.
Unrestricted walking: No. **Range:** Yes (mats).
Holes: 18. **Par:** 72. **Yards:** 6,423-4,207. **Slope:** 129-112.

WINDSTONE GOLF CLUB*

Ringgold—PU—615-894-1231 (10 mi. from Chattanooga).
Season: Year-round. **High:** April-Oct. **Caddies:** No.
Green fee: $20-$49. **Credit cards:** V, AMEX, DISC, MC.
Lodging on site: No. **Reduced fees:** Weekdays, Low Season.
Unrestricted walking: Yes. **Range:** Yes (grass).
Holes: 18. **Par:** 72. **Yards:** 6,626-4,669. **Slope:** 119-108.

BIG ISLAND

★★★½ BEACH GOLF CLUB
Waikoloa—R—808-885-6060 (25 mi. from Kailua-Kona).
Season: Year-round. **High:** Dec.-May. **Caddies:** No.
Green fee: $50-$99. **Credit cards:** All Major.
Lodging on site: Yes. **Reduced fees:** Resort Guests.
Unrestricted walking: No. **Range:** Yes (grass).
Holes: 18. **Par:** 70. **Yards:** 6,566-5,958. **Slope:** 133-126.
Comments: "Shortest and resortiest at Waikoloa . . . Lots of lava fun . . . Service now minimal, but easily forgiven because of the great golf."

★★★ HAPUNA GOLF COURSE
Kohala Coast—R—808-882-1035 (36 mi. from Kailua-Kona).
Season: Year-round. **High:** Dec.-Feb. **Caddies:** No.
Green fee: $50-$99. **Credit cards:** All Major.
Lodging on site: Yes. **Reduced fees:** Resort Guests.
Unrestricted walking: No. **Range:** Yes (grass).
Holes: 18. **Par:** 72. **Yards:** 6,875-5,067. **Slope:** 134-117.
Comments: "Good layout but long distance treks between greens and tees . . . 75 percent harder when wind is up . . . Expect 40 m.p.h. winds."

★★★ THE KINGS' GOLF CLUB
Waikoloa—R—808-885-4647 (25 mi. from Kailua-Kona).
Season: Year-round. **High:** Dec.-May. **Caddies:** No.
Green fee: $50-$99. **Credit cards:** All Major.
Lodging on site: Yes. **Reduced fees:** Resort Guests.
Unrestricted walking: No. **Range:** Yes (grass).
Holes: 18. **Par:** 72. **Yards:** 7,074-5,459. **Slope:** 133-119.
Ranked 25th in America's 75 Best Resort Courses and selected as runner-up for Best New Resort Course of 1990 by GOLF DIGEST.
Comments: "The best in Hawaii . . . Use of lava rock as rough creates a spectacular contrast . . . Green against black. What a sight . . . Tradewinds and 95 bunkers add interesting element, make it a bear . . . Difficult greens . . . Compared to other island green fees, this is a pretty good deal."

★★★ KONA COUNTRY CLUB
Kailua—R—808-322-2595.
Season: Year-round. **High:** Jan.-April. **Caddies:** No.
Green fee: $50-$99. **Credit cards:** All Major.
Reduced fees: Low Season, Resort Guests, Twilight Play.
Unrestricted walking: No. **Range:** Yes (mats).
Holes: 18. **Par:** 72. **Yards:** 6,579-5,499. **Slope:** 129-117.
Comments: "Windblown . . . Many awkward lies . . . Used to be a great deal. No longer."

★★★½ MAKALEI HAWAII COUNTRY CLUB
Kailua—PU—808-325-6625.
Season: Year-round. **High:** Nov.-April. **Caddies:** No.
Green fee: $100 and up. **Credit cards:** All Major.
Lodging on site: No. **Reduced fees:** Twilight Play.
Unrestricted walking: No. **Range:** Yes (grass).
Holes: 18. **Par:** 72. **Yards:** 7,061-5,242. **Slope:** 143-125.

★★★★½ MAUNA KEA GOLF COURSE
Kohala Coast—R—808-882-5888 (32 mi. from Kailua-Kona).
Season: Year-round. **High:** Jan.-April. **Caddies:** No.
Green fee: $100 and up. **Credit cards:** V, AMEX, MC.
Lodging on site: Yes. **Reduced fees:** Resort Guests.
Unrestricted walking: No. **Range:** Yes (grass).
Holes: 18. **Par:** 72. **Yards:** 7,114-5,277. **Slope:** 143-121.
Ranked 69th in America's 100 Greatest Golf Courses and 8th in America's 75 Best Resort Courses by GOLF DIGEST.

Comments: "Unbelievable . . . Outstanding . . . Still a classic . . . Best views on the Big Island . . . Best course on the Big Island . . . Is there any better? . . . Challenging terrain . . . Some holes canyon-like . . . Four toughest par 3s anywhere . . . Over-the-ocean hole incredible . . . Condition is exemplary . . . I could play here twice a day, forever . . . If you've got the bucks, it's heaven."

MAUNA LANI RESORT
Kohala Coast—R—808-885-6655 (35 mi. from Kailua-Kona).
Season: Year-round. **High:** Dec.-March. **Caddies:** No.
Green fee: $100 and up. **Credit cards:** All Major.
Lodging on site: Yes. **Reduced fees:** No.
Unrestricted walking: No. **Range:** Yes (grass).
★★★★NORTH COURSE
Holes: 18. **Par:** 72. **Yards:** 6,993-5,474. **Slope:** 136-124.
Comments: "Great course . . . A beauty . . . A real joy . . . A piece of art . . . Love that lava . . . Excellent for resort golfers . . . Preferred original 18 . . . Much better before . . . Not up to expectations."
★★★★SOUTH COURSE
Holes: 18. **Par:** 72. **Yards:** 7,029-5,331. **Slope:** 133-122.
Home of the Senior PGA Tour's Senior Skins game. Ranked 10th in Hawaii by GOLF DIGEST.
Comments: "Stunning . . . Memorable . . . A favorite, scenic-wise . . . Relaxed golf in a classy setting . . . Fair test . . . A little tame . . . A real Frankenstein, pieces shoved together . . . Very, very expensive . . . Thank goodness for Kamaaina (local resident) rates!"

★½ SEAMOUNTAIN GOLF COURSE
Pahala—R—808-928-6222 (58 mi. from Hilo).
Season: Year-round. **High:** Jan.-March. **Caddies:** No.
Green fee: $20-$49. **Credit cards:** V, AMEX, MC.
Lodging on site: Yes. **Reduced fees:** Low Season, Resort Guests.
Unrestricted walking: No. **Range:** Yes (grass).
Holes: 18. **Par:** 72. **Yards:** 6,500-5,663. **Slope:** 136-116.
Comments: "Sleepy location . . . Nice people . . . Poor service . . . Hours from any population center."

★★VOLCANO GOLF & COUNTRY CLUB
Volcano National Park—PU—808-967-7331 (32 mi. from Hilo).
Season: Year-round. **High:** July-Sept. **Caddies:** No.
Green fee: $50-$99. **Credit cards:** All Major.
Lodging on site: No. **Reduced fees:** No.
Unrestricted walking: No. **Range:** Yes (grass).
Holes: 18. **Par:** 72. **Yards:** 6,250-5,449. **Slope:** 128-117.
Located in Hawaii Volcano National Park.
Comments: "Unique . . . When was the last time you played along side a volcano? . . . Not well kept . . . Kind of ragged . . . Not so good."

★★½ WAIKOLOA VILLAGE GOLF CLUB
Waikoloa—R—808-883-9621 (26 mi. from Kona).
Season: Year-round. **High:** Nov.-March. **Caddies:** No.
Green fee: $50-$99. **Credit cards:** All Major.
Lodging on site: Yes. **Reduced fees:** Resort Guests, Twilight Play.
Unrestricted walking: No. **Range:** Yes (grass).
Holes: 18. **Par:** 72. **Yards:** 6,687-5,558. **Slope:** 129-120.
Comments: "Top drawer . . . Enjoyable . . . Only decent place on the big island that people of modest means can afford . . . Wind controls the score . . . Terrible bunkers."

OAHU

★½ ALA WAI GOLF COURSE
Honolulu—PU—808-734-3656.

Season: Year-round. **High:** June-Aug. **Caddies:** No.
Green fee: $20-$49. **Credit cards:** No.
Lodging on site: No. **Reduced fees:** Twilight Play.
Unrestricted walking: Yes. **Range:** Yes (mats).
Holes: 18. **Par:** 70. **Yards:** 6,020-5,011. **Slope:** 115-119.

★★HAWAII KAI GOLF COURSE
Honolulu—PU—808-395-2358.
Season: Year-round. **High:** Year-round. **Caddies:** No.
Green fee: $50-$99. **Credit cards:** All Major.
Lodging on site: No. **Reduced fees:** Twilight Play.
Unrestricted walking: No. **Range:** Yes (mats).
Holes: 18. **Par:** 72. **Yards:** 6,686-5,719. **Slope:** 126-121.
Comments: "Average course . . . Play too heavy . . . 6-hour rounds."

★★HAWAII PRINCE GOLF CLUB
A/B/C 9s
Ewa Beach—R—808-944-4567 (20 mi. from Honolulu).
Season: Year-round. **High:** Dec.-March. **Caddies:** No.
Green fee: $100 and up. **Credit cards:** All Major.
Reduced fees: Weekdays, Low Season, Resort Guests, Twilight Play.
Unrestricted walking: No. **Range:** Yes (grass).
Holes: 27. **Par:** 36/36/36. **Yards:** 3,518/3,620/3,604.
Comments: "Good layouts . . . Well conditioned . . . Easy courses . . .
Too boring."

★★★½ KO OLINA GOLF CLUB
Kapolei—R—808-676-5300 (20 mi. from Honolulu).
Season: Year-round. **High:** Year-round. **Caddies:** No.
Green fee: $100 and up. **Credit cards:** All Major.
Lodging on site: Yes. **Reduced fees:** Resort Guests, Twilight Play.
Unrestricted walking: No. **Range:** Yes (grass).
Holes: 18. **Par:** 72. **Yards:** 6,867-5,358. **Slope:** 135-122.
Ranked 67th in America's 75 Best Resort Courses by GOLF DIGEST. Site of
LPGA Hawaiian Ladies Open.
Comments: "Most fun ever . . . Fun without too much frustration . . .
Worth playing once . . . Good shotmaking . . . Some beautiful holes, espe-
cially No. 18 . . . Too many blind landing areas from back tees . . . Very
expensive, even for residents."

★★★½ THE LINKS AT KUILIMA
Kahuku—R—808-293-8574 (45 mi. from Honolulu).
Season: Year-round. **High:** Jan.-March. **Caddies:** No.
Green fee: $100 and up. **Credit cards:** All Major.
Lodging on site: Yes. **Reduced fees:** Resort Guests.
Unrestricted walking: No. **Range:** Yes (grass).
Holes: 18. **Par:** 72. **Yards:** 7,199-4,851. **Slope:** 141-120.
Comments: "Excellent . . . Great location . . . Quiet, peaceful, rarely
crowded . . . When God created wind, he put it here . . . Tough wind . . .
With maturity, greens will be as good as any . . . Local residents get a break
on green fees."

★★★MAKAHA VALLEY COUNTRY CLUB
Waianae—PU—808-695-9578 (55 mi. from Honolulu).
Season: Jan.-Dec. **High:** Dec.-March. **Caddies:** No.
Green fee: $50-$99. **Credit cards:** All Major.
Lodging on site: No. **Reduced fees:** Low Season.
Unrestricted walking: No. **Range:** Yes (grass).
Holes: 18. **Par:** 71. **Yards:** 6,369-5,720. **Slope:** 133-120.

★★MILILANI GOLF CLUB
Mililani—PU—808-623-2222 (25 mi. from Honolulu).
Season: Year-round. **High:** Jan./Feb./June. **Caddies:** No.
Green fee: $50-$99. **Credit cards:** All Major.

Lodging on site: No. **Reduced fees:** Weekdays, Twilight Play.
Unrestricted walking: No. **Range:** Yes (mats).
Holes: 18. **Par:** 72. **Yards:** 6,455-5,985. **Slope:** 121.
Comments: "Great escape . . . Not busy, good value . . . Layout challenging . . . Greens always bumpy . . . Tee boxes were terrible . . . Slow play."

★★½ OLOMANA GOLF LINKS
Waimanalo—PU—808-259-7926.
Season: Year-round. **High:** Jan.-Aug. **Caddies:** No.
Green fee: $50-$99. **Credit cards:** V, AMEX, MC.
Lodging on site: No. **Reduced fees:** No.
Unrestricted walking: No. **Range:** Yes (mats).
Holes: 18. **Par:** 72. **Yards:** 6,326-5,465. **Slope:** 129-131.
Comments: "Wet and wild with a view . . . Short but enjoyable . . . Lots of sneaky water on the back 9 . . . Excellent greens . . . Good pace of play."

★★★½ PALI MUNICIPAL GOLF COURSE
Kaneohe—PU—808-261-9784 (9 mi. from Honolulu).
Season: Year-round. **High:** May-Oct. **Caddies:** No.
Green fee: $20-$49. **Credit cards:** No.
Lodging on site: No. **Reduced fees:** Twilight Play.
Unrestricted walking: Yes. **Range:** Yes (grass).
Holes: 18. **Par:** 72. **Yards:** 6,494-6,080. **Slope:** 127-133.
Comments: "Great layout . . . Unsung beauty . . . Nice muny . . . Needs better upkeep . . . Walk or ride, the best bargain in town . . . Mostly locals play here . . . Long waits, too crowded . . . Bring your umbrella."

★★½ PEARL COUNTRY CLUB
Aiea—PU—808-487-3802 (6 mi. from Honolulu).
Season: Year-round. **High:** Year-round. **Caddies:** No.
Green fee: $50-$99. **Credit cards:** V, AMEX, MC.
Lodging on site: No. **Reduced fees:** Twilight Play.
Unrestricted walking: No. **Range:** Yes (mats).
Holes: 18. **Par:** 72. **Yards:** 6,750-5,489. **Slope:** 128-118.
Comments: "Challenging layout . . . Nice, hilly . . . Greens average to good . . . Allow too many nonplayer tourists to play."

★★★½ SHERATON MAKAHA RESORT & COUNTRY CLUB
Waianae—R—808-695-9544.
Season: Year-round. **High:** Jan.-March. **Caddies:** No.
Green fee: $100 and up. **Credit cards:** All Major.
Lodging on site: Yes. **Reduced fees:** Weekdays, Low Season, Resort Guests, Twilight Play.
Unrestricted walking: No. **Range:** Yes (mats).
Holes: 18. **Par:** 72. **Yards:** 7,091-5,880. **Slope:** 139-129.
Comments: "The best on Oahu . . . A must when on Oahu . . . Beautiful canyons . . . Great golf, great food . . . Starting tee-offs from both 9s makes for 6-hour rounds . . . Overpriced . . . Slow play."

★★★½ WAIKELE GOLF CLUB
Waipahu—PU—808-676-9000 (15 mi. from Honolulu).
Season: Year-round. **High:** Jan.-Feb. **Caddies:** No.
Green fee: $50-$99. **Credit cards:** V.
Lodging on site: No. **Reduced fees:** Twilight Play.
Unrestricted walking: No. **Range:** Yes (grass).
Holes: 18. **Par:** 72. **Yards:** 6,663-5,226. **Slope:** 126-113.
Comments: "Just opened . . . Friendly staff . . . Great facilities . . . They raided the white stake warehouse for this course."

GREAT VALUE

MOLOKAI

★★★½ KALUAKOI GOLF COURSE
Maunaloa—R—808-552-2739.

Season: Year-round. **High:** Dec.-March. **Caddies:** No.
Green fee: $50-$99. **Credit cards:** All Major.
Lodging on site: Yes. **Reduced fees:** Resort Guests.
Unrestricted walking: No. **Range:** Yes (grass).
Holes: 18. **Par:** 72. **Yards:** 6,600-5,461. **Slope:** 129-119.
Comments: "If you want beauty and solitude . . . The best getaway . . .
No waiting . . . Talk about lonely! . . . Six holes on the ocean . . . No two
holes alike . . . Better learn to play in the wind . . . Of all the courses in
Hawaii, this is the one we talk about the most."

KAUAI

KAUAI LAGOONS RESORT
Lihu—R—808-241-6000, 800-634-6400.
Season: Year-round. **High:** Jan.-March. **Caddies:** No.
Green fee: $100 and up. **Credit cards:** All Major.
Lodging on site: Yes. **Reduced fees:** Resort Guests.
Unrestricted walking: No. **Range:** Yes (grass).
★★★★KIELE COURSE
Holes: 18. **Par:** 72. **Yards:** 7,070-5,417. **Slope:** 137-123.
Ranked 88th in America's 100 Greatest Golf Courses, selected Best New
Resort Course of 1989 and ranked 15th in America's 75 Best Resort Courses
by GOLF DIGEST.
Comments: "Unique . . . Super views . . . The best ever, anywhere . . .
Ultimate scenery and service in golf . . . Extremely interesting . . . Scenic
Nicklaus . . . Very solid . . . Lots of sand . . . Pinpoint drives . . . Not fun
for high handicappers . . . Too pricey to ever play twice."
★★★LAGOONS COURSE
Lihue—R—808-241-6000, 800-634-6400.
Season: Year-round. **High:** Jan.-March. **Caddies:** No.
Green fee: $100 and up. **Credit cards:** All Major.
Lodging on site: Yes. **Reduced fees:** Resort Guests.
Unrestricted walking: No. **Range:** Yes (grass).
Holes: 18. **Par:** 72. **Yards:** 6,942-5,607. **Slope:** 135-116.
Comments: "Nice . . . Playable . . . Too open . . . Lacking services expected at such a price."

★★★KIAHUNA GOLF CLUB
Poipu—R—808-742-9595 (14 mi. from Lihue).
Season: Year-round. **High:** Jan.-Feb. **Caddies:** No.
Green fee: $20-$49. **Credit cards:** V, AMEX, MC.
Lodging on site: No. **Reduced fees:** No.
Unrestricted walking: No. **Range:** Yes (grass).
Holes: 18. **Par:** 70. **Yards:** 6,353-4,871. **Slope:** 128-111.
Comments: "Recovered from Iniki . . . White tees too easy, play from the
blues . . . Big disappointment . . . Very bland . . . Easy to forget."

★★★POIPU BAY RESORT GOLF COURSE
Koloa—R—808-742-9489 (16 mi. from Lihue).
Season: Year-round. **High:** Jan.-May. **Caddies:** No.
Green fee: $100 and up. **Credit cards:** All Major.
Lodging on site: Yes. **Reduced fees:** Resort Guests, Twilight Play.
Unrestricted walking: No. **Range:** Yes (grass).
Holes: 18. **Par:** 72. **Yards:** 6,959-5,241. **Slope:** 132-121.
Ranked 6th in Top 10 in Hawaii by GOLF DIGEST.
Comments: "Scenic seaside links . . . Typical resort course . . . Open, few
trees, big greens . . . Wind and elevation changes play mental games . . .
Bring wind clubs . . . 2nd round was half price!"

PRINCEVILLE RESORT
Princeville—R—808-826-3580 (36 mi. from Lihue).
Season: Year-round. **High:** Year-round. **Caddies:** No.
Green fee: $50-$99. **Credit cards:** V, AMEX, MC.

Lodging on site: Yes. **Reduced fees:** Resort Guests, Twilight Play.
Unrestricted walking: No. **Range:** Yes (grass).

★★½ THE MAKAI COURSE
OCEAN/LAKES/WOODS 9s
Holes: 27. **Par:** 36/36/36. **Yards:** 3,467/3,433/3,445.
Ranked 48th in America's 75 Best Resort Courses by GOLF DIGEST.
Comments: "Not bad . . . Not quite the Prince but good . . . Scenic . . .
Playable . . . Three beautiful 9s . . . Good variety of holes . . . No crowds
. . . Different after Iniki, still nice."

★★★★½ THE PRINCE COURSE
808-826-5000.
Holes: 18. **Par:** 72. **Yards:** 7,309-5,338. **Slope:** 145-127.
Ranked 43rd in America's 100 Greatest Golf Courses, selected Best New
Resort Course of 1990 and ranked 5th in America's 75 Best Resort Courses
by GOLF DIGEST.
Comments: "Paradise! . . . Spectacular scenery . . . Spectacular course . . .
Magnificent . . . The complete course. Diverse, fair, scenic, hard . . . The
best in Hawaii . . . Regardless of cost . . . Most beautiful in the world . . .
The most challenging . . . Super, super, super . . . Yes! Yes! Yes! . . . Jungle
holes . . . Hard, hard, hard . . . Only for single digits . . . Extremely difficult, steep and narrow . . . Would love to see PGA Tour event there . . . Let
me at it. I'll get even . . . Everything absolutely excellent . . . They treat you
like a king . . . Really like this one . . . Too bad I can't afford it more than
once a year."

★★★½ WAILUA GOLF COURSE
Lihue—PU—808-241-6666.
Season: Year-round. **High:** Jan.-April. **Caddies:** No.
Green fee: Under $20. **Credit cards:** No.
Lodging on site: No. **Reduced fees:** Weekdays, Twilight Play.
Unrestricted walking: Yes. **Range:** Yes (mats).
Holes: 18. **Par:** 72. **Yards:** 6,981-5,974. **Slope:** 136-122.
Site of U.S. Public Links Championship in 1996 and ranked in First 25 of
America's Best Public Courses by GOLF DIGEST.
Comments: "Best muny in Hawaii . . . Best test for the price . . . Best golf
value in the islands . . . Best bargain in America . . . Unlike Princeville, not
tricked up . . . Pretty basic services . . . A little frayed . . . Must have
heaviest play in the islands . . . Would love to get on it someday."

MAUI

KAANAPALI GOLF COURSES
Lahaina—R—808-661-3691 (30 mi. from Kahului).
Season: Year-round. **High:** Dec.-April. **Caddies:** No.
Green fee: $100 and up. **Credit cards:** All Major.
Lodging on site: Yes. **Reduced fees:** Low Season, Resort Guests, Twi-
light Play.
Unrestricted walking: No. **Range:** Yes (grass).

★★★½ NORTH COURSE
Holes: 18. **Par:** 71. **Yards:** 6,994-5,417. **Slope:** 134-123.
Comments: "Excellent . . . Very scenic and well kept . . . Great location
. . . A bear . . . Exceptional staff . . . Spotty condition . . . Thin lies . . . Not
impressive . . . Tourist oriented . . . Worth about one-third what they
charge . . . Costs way too much . . . But you're on vacation."

★★★SOUTH COURSE
Holes: 18. **Par:** 71. **Yards:** 6,555-5,485. **Slope:** 127-120.

KAPALUA GOLF CLUB
Lahaina—R—808-669-8044.
Season: Year-round. **High:** Year-round. **Caddies:** Yes.
Green fee: $50-$99. **Credit cards:** V, AMEX, DISC, MC.
Lodging on site: Yes. **Reduced fees:** Resort Guests, Twilight Play.
Unrestricted walking: No. **Range:** Yes (grass).

Site of Kapalua International on PGA schedule.

★★★½ THE BAY COURSE
Holes: 18. **Par:** 72. **Yards:** 6,600-5,124. **Slope:** 140-115.
Ranked 36th in America's 75 Best Resort Courses by GOLF DIGEST.
Comments: "Gorgeous . . . Great location . . . Windblown . . . Scenic . . .
Well planned . . . Pleasant golfing . . . Expensive views . . . Too expensive
for non-hotel players . . . Wish it was cheaper . . . Overrated tourist trap."

★★★★½ THE PLANTATION COURSE
Holes: 18. **Par:** 73. **Yards:** 7,263-5,627. **Slope:** 135-127.
Ranked 4th in America's 75 Best Resort Courses and selected as runner-up
for Best New Resort Course of 1991 by GOLF DIGEST.
Comments: "Wow . . . What a layout . . . Fantastic . . . Tremendous . . .
Best of the Kapaluas . . . The Augusta National of the Pacific . . . A true
golfing experience . . . All the shots . . . Nothing like it . . . Very windy and
rainy . . . Difficult greens . . . Fabulous caddies . . . Breathtaking views . . .
Ocean view from every hole . . . Watch whales jumping in winter . . . Best
clubhouse on the island, by far . . . Worth every penny . . . What a joke. Ball
rolls forever. You can putt from 30 yards off a green . . . A monument to
contrivance—blind shots and gullies . . . Tough for short hitters . . . Too
much for tourist play . . . Better for a camera than a club."

★★★½ THE VILLAGE COURSE
Holes: 18. **Par:** 71. **Yards:** 6,632-6,001. **Slope:** 135-132.
Ranked 31st in America's 75 Best Resort Courses by GOLF DIGEST.
Comments: "Scenic . . . Windy . . . Most beautiful ever . . . Definitely
worth playing . . . Need all your shots . . . Great shape . . . Weakest of the
three at Kapalua."

MAKENA RESORT GOLF COURSE
Makena—R—808-879-3344.
Season: Year-round. **High:** Nov.-June. **Caddies:** No.
Green fee: $100 and up. **Credit cards:** All Major.
Lodging on site: Yes. **Reduced fees:** Resort Guests, Twilight Play.
Unrestricted walking: No. **Range:** Yes (grass).

NORTH COURSE*
Holes: 18. **Par:** 72. **Yards:** 6,914-5,303. **Slope:** 139-128.

SOUTH COURSE*
Holes: 18. **Par:** 72. **Yards:** 6,986-5,503. **Slope:** 138-130.

★★½ PUKALANI COUNTRY CLUB
Pukalani—PU—808-572-1314 (16 mi. from Kahului).
Season: Year-round. **High:** Nov.-April. **Caddies:** No.
Green fee: $50-$99. **Credit cards:** V, MC.
Lodging on site: No. **Reduced fees:** Low Season.
Unrestricted walking: No. **Range:** Yes (grass).
Holes: 18. **Par:** 72. **Yards:** 6,494-5,574. **Slope:** 121-118.
Comments: "An absolute diamond-in-the-rough . . . Beautiful views . . .
Best for the money in Maui . . . 40 m.p.h. winds."

★★★ SILVERSWORD GOLF CLUB
Kihei—PU—808-874-0777 (10 mi. from Kahului).
Season: Year-round. **High:** Dec.-March. **Caddies:** No.
Green fee: $50-$99. **Credit cards:** V, MC.
Lodging on site: No. **Reduced fees:** Low Season, Twilight Play.
Unrestricted walking: No. **Range:** Yes (grass).
Holes: 18. **Par:** 71. **Yards:** 6,801-5,265. **Slope:** 124-118.
Comments: "Great course . . . Very affordable for Maui . . . Good for the
money . . . Fine alternative to those pricey resorts . . . Very mature greens
for a new course . . . Get out early; tradewinds tough . . . Needs trees for
balance . . . Dull . . . Limited . . . Greens not consistent."

★★ WAIEHU MUNICIPAL GOLF COURSE
Wailuku—PU—808-244-5934.
Season: Year-round. **High:** Nov.-March. **Caddies:** No.

Green fee: $20-$49. **Credit cards:** V, MC.
Lodging on site: No. **Reduced fees:** No.
Unrestricted walking: Yes. **Range:** Yes (mats).
Holes: 18. **Par:** 72. **Yards:** 6,330-5,511. **Slope:** 111-115.
Comments: "County course . . . $7 green fees for community residents. . .
Allows sixsomes . . . Lots of strong winds . . . Poor shape."

★★★½ WAIKAPU SANDALWOOD GOLF COURSE

Wailuku—PU—808-242-4653 (9 mi. from Kahului).
Season: Year-round. **High:** Nov.-May. **Caddies:** No.
Green fee: $50-$99. **Credit cards:** V, AMEX, MC.
Lodging on site: No. **Reduced fees:** No.
Unrestricted walking: No. **Range:** Yes (grass).
Holes: 18. **Par:** 72. **Yards:** 6,469-5,162. **Slope:** 129-118.
Comments: "Outstanding public course . . . Best run on Maui . . . Second-best value on Maui . . . Doesn't charge you the value of your house just to play . . . Ball and club cleaner on carts, also iced water and soft drinks . . . Didn't enjoy having to play behind sixsomes."

WAILEA GOLF CLUB

Kihei—R—808-879-2966 (17 mi. from Kahului).
Season: Year-round. **High:** Dec.-April. **Caddies:** No.
Green fee: $100 and up. **Credit cards:** All Major.
Lodging on site: Yes. **Reduced fees:** Resort Guests.
Unrestricted walking: No. **Range:** Yes (grass).
★★★½ BLUE COURSE
Holes: 18. **Par:** 72. **Yards:** 6,943-5,291. **Slope:** 129-117.
Ranked 66th in America's 75 Best Resort Courses by GOLF DIGEST.
Comments: "Interesting challenge . . . Wide and beautiful . . . Great oceanside course . . . Maui no ka hoi—Priced too high . . . Too snooty for me . . . Course workers don't bother to stop mowing while you hit."
GOLD COURSE*
Holes: 18. **Par:** 72. **Yards:** 6,810-5,644. **Slope:** 138-120.
ORANGE COURSE*
Holes: 18. **Par:** 72. **Yards:** 6,915-5,315. **Slope:** Unrated.

LANAI

★★★THE EXPERIENCE AT KOELE

Lanai—R—808-565-4653.
Season: Year-round. **High:** Dec.-May. **Caddies:** No.
Green fee: $50-$99. **Credit cards:** All Major.
Lodging on site: Yes. **Reduced fees:** Twilight Play.
Unrestricted walking: No. **Range:** Yes (grass).
Holes: 18. **Par:** 72. **Yards:** 7,017-5,425. **Slope:** 141-123.
Selected as runner-up for Best New Resort Course of 1992 and ranked 5th in Hawaii by GOLF DIGEST.
Comments: "May be the ultimate golf experience . . . Most beautiful I've ever seen . . . A scenic delight . . . Fun but difficult . . . Beautiful front 9 . . . Many excellent holes, some a bit gimmicky . . . Winds make it play more difficult than it looks . . . Excellent vacation . . . Needs a clubhouse."

★★½ AVONDALE GOLF CLUB
Hayden Lake—PU—208-772-2437 (40 mi. from Spokane, Wash.).
Season: March-Oct. **High:** June-Aug. **Caddies:** No.
Green fee: Under $20. **Credit cards:** V, MC.
Reduced fees: Weekdays, Low Season, Twilight Play.
Unrestricted walking: Yes. **Range:** Yes (mats).
Holes: 18. **Par:** 72. **Yards:** 6,525-5,719. **Slope:** 118-121.

★★★★½ COEUR D'ALENE RESORT GOLF COURSE
Coeur d'Alene—R—208-667-4653 (40 mi. from Spokane, Wash.).
Season: April-Nov. **High:** June-Sept. **Caddies:** Yes.
Green fee: $100 and up. **Credit cards:** All Major.
Lodging on site: Yes. **Reduced fees:** Low Season, Resort Guests.
Unrestricted walking: Yes. **Range:** Yes (grass).
Holes: 18. **Par:** 71. **Yards:** 6,309-4,446. **Slope:** 121-105.
Ranked 11th among America's 75 Best Resort Courses by GOLF DIGEST.
Comments: "Best place I've ever played . . . Right behind Pine Valley as the top golf destination in America . . . A wonderful experience . . . Maintained like a fine garden . . . Meticulous . . . Not a blade of grass out of shape . . . Like playing on one big golf green . . . Floating island green is a 'must see' . . . You'll be treated like royalty . . . Leisurely three-hour rounds . . . Carts and forecaddies . . . Incredibly expensive, but worth it once."

(GREAT VALUE)

★★★½ ELKHORN GOLF RESORT
Sun Valley—R—208-622-3309 (150 mi. from Boise).
Season: May-Oct. **High:** June-Sept. **Caddies:** No.
Green fee: $50-$99. **Credit cards:** All Major.
Lodging on site: Yes. **Reduced fees:** Low Season, Resort Guests, Twilight Play.
Unrestricted walking: No. **Range:** Yes (grass).
Holes: 18. **Par:** 72. **Yards:** 7,101-6,524. **Slope:** 133-128.
Ranked 64th among America's 75 Best Resort Courses by GOLF DIGEST.
Comments: "Exciting, scenic resort course . . . Two different 9s . . . Lots of sand . . . Some long carries from the back tees, but remember, the ball goes farther up here . . . Excellent pro shop staff . . . When I die, can I go here? . . . Not particularly interesting . . . Greens in bad shape."

★★★ PINECREST MUNICIPAL GOLF COURSE
Idaho Falls—PU—208-529-1485 (220 mi. from Salt Lake City).
Season: March-Nov. **High:** June-Aug. **Caddies:** No.
Green fee: Under $20. **Credit cards:** V, MC.
Lodging on site: No. **Reduced fees:** Weekdays.
Unrestricted walking: Yes. **Range:** No.
Holes: 18. **Par:** 70. **Yards:** 6,394-6,123. **Slope:** 116-125.
Comments: "Short but fine public layout . . . Old, narrow, interesting . . . Some of the ugliest sand on this side of the planet."

★★★ PURPLE SAGE GOLF COURSE
Caldwell—PU—208-459-2223 (25 mi. from Boise).
Season: March-Nov. **High:** March-Sept. **Caddies:** No.
Green fee: Under $20. **Credit cards:** No.
Lodging on site: No. **Reduced fees:** Weekdays.
Unrestricted walking: Yes. **Range:** Yes (grass).
Holes: 18. **Par:** 71. **Yards:** 6,747-5,343. **Slope:** 117-111.
Comments: "Nice course for out in the middle of nowhere . . . Good flat greens . . . Subtle greens . . . Always in fine shape."

★★★ QUAIL HOLLOW GOLF CLUB
Boise—PU—208-344-7807.
Season: Year-round. **High:** March-Sept. **Caddies:** No.
Green fee: Under $20. **Credit cards:** V, MC.
Lodging on site: No. **Reduced fees:** No.
Unrestricted walking: Yes. **Range:** Yes (grass).

Holes: 18. **Par:** 70. **Yards:** 6,600–4,530. **Slope:** 129-129.
Ranked 5th in Idaho by GOLF DIGEST.
Comments: "Odd layout—up, down, left, right . . . Blind shots . . . Very difficult . . . Don't walk it . . . Superb conditioning."

★★★½ SUN VALLEY RESORT GOLF COURSE

Sun Valley—R—208-622-2251.
Season: April-Oct. **High:** June-Oct. **Caddies:** No.
Green fee: $50-$99. **Credit cards:** All Major.
Lodging on site: Yes. **Reduced fees:** Low Season.
Unrestricted walking: No. **Range:** Yes (grass).
Holes: 18. **Par:** 72. **Yards:** 6,635-6,057. **Slope:** 128-122.
Ranked 60th in America's 75 Best Resort Courses by GOLF DIGEST.
Comments: "Tremendous . . . Great experience . . . Simply beautiful . . . Challenging . . . A great remodel . . . Better than Elkhorn . . . Birch trees and mountain streams . . . Bring your fishing pole."

★½ WARM SPRINGS GOLF COURSE

Boise—PU—208-343-5661.
Season: Year-round. **High:** May-Sept. **Caddies:** No.
Green fee: Under $20. **Credit cards:** V, AMEX, DISC, MC.
Lodging on site: No. **Reduced fees:** Weekdays, Twilight Play.
Unrestricted walking: Yes. **Range:** Yes (mats).
Holes: 18. **Par:** 72. **Yards:** 6,719-5,660. **Slope:** 113-113.
Comments: "Routine . . . Flat . . . Boring . . . Crowded . . . Slow."

★★★★ANNBRIAR GOLF COURSE
Waterloo—PU—618-939-4653 (18 mi. from St. Louis).
Season: Year-round. **High:** April-Oct. **Caddies:** No.
Green fee: $20-$49. **Credit cards:** V, MC.
Lodging on site: No. **Reduced fees:** Low Season.
Unrestricted walking: No. **Range:** Yes (grass).
Holes: 18. **Par:** 72. **Yards:** 6,841-4,792. **Slope:** 141-Unrated.
Comments: "Beautiful new course . . . Already excellent . . . Has it all . . . Offers a Pete Dye approach on front and an Augusta National look on the back . . . Will soon be the best public in southern Illinois."

ARBORETUM GOLF COURSE*
Buffalo Grove—PU—708-913-1112 (45 mi. from Chicago).
Season: March-Nov. **High:** May-Sept. **Caddies:** No.
Green fee: $20-$49. **Credit cards:** V, DISC, MC.
Lodging on site: No. **Reduced fees:** Weekdays, Low Season, Twilight Play.
Unrestricted walking: No. **Range:** No.
Holes: 18. **Par:** 72. **Yards:** 6,477-5,039. **Slope:** 132-118.

BALMORAL WOODS COUNTRY CLUB*
Crete—PU—708-672-7448 (40 mi. from Chicago).
Season: March-Nov. **High:** May-Sept. **Caddies:** No.
Green fee: $20-$49. **Credit cards:** V, AMEX, MC.
Lodging on site: No. **Reduced fees:** Weekdays.
Unrestricted walking: Yes. **Range:** Yes (grass).
Holes: 18. **Par:** 72. **Yards:** 6,683-5,282. **Slope:** 131-128.

★★★BIG RUN GOLF CLUB
Lockport—PU—815-838-1057 (35 mi. from Chicago).
Season: March-Nov. **High:** June-Aug. **Caddies:** No.
Green fee: $20-$49. **Credit cards:** V, MC.
Lodging on site: No. **Reduced fees:** Twilight Play.
Unrestricted walking: No. **Range:** No.
Holes: 18. **Par:** 72. **Yards:** 6,865-6,585. **Slope:** 129-126.
Comments: "Classic Midwest golf at a price . . . Very tough, long par 5s . . . Small mushroom-shaped greens . . . I hope there's one like this in heaven . . . Extremely hilly, tough to walk . . . Won't let you walk in summer . . . 9 and 18 are not good holes . . . Very unfair for short hitters . . . So much potential, so little care."

★★★★CANTIGNY GOLF AND TENNIS CLUB
WOODSIDE/LAKESIDE/HILLSIDE 9s
Wheaton—PU—708-668-3323 (30 mi. from Chicago).
Season: April-Oct. **High:** June-Aug. **Caddies:** No.
Green fee: $50-$99. **Credit cards:** V, AMEX, MC.
Lodging on site: No. **Reduced fees:** No.
Unrestricted walking: Yes. **Range:** Yes (grass).
Holes: 27. **Par:** 36/36/36. **Yards:** 3,422/3,287/3,338.
Woodside and Lakeside 9s named Best New Public Course of 1989 and ranked in First 25 of America's 75 Best Public Courses by GOLF DIGEST.
Comments: "Three neat nines . . . Beautiful setting . . . Most scenic course in Chicago area . . . Good facilities and good staff make for a pleasant day . . . Just plain fun . . . Not tremendously difficult but very good . . . Good tee time spacing . . . Hard to get a tee time . . . Need to control slow play . . . So-so condition . . . Polite people . . . Treat people like country club members . . . I saw 'Dick Tracy' on No. 18."

COG HILL GOLF & COUNTRY CLUB
Lemont—PU—708-257-5872 (30 mi. from Chicago).
Season: Year-round. **High:** May-Sept. **Caddies:** Yes.
Green fee: $20-$49. **Credit cards:** V, DISC, MC.

ILLINOIS

Reduced fees: Weekdays, Low Season, Twilight Play.
Unrestricted walking: Yes. **Range:** Yes (mats).
★★½ COURSE NO. 1
Holes: 18. **Par:** 71. **Yards:** 6,324–5,614. **Slope:** 117–114.
Comments: "A special place . . . Fun to play but very Plain Jane facilities
. . . Expect 5-hour rounds . . . Excellent condition . . . Greatest milk shakes
on the planet Earth."
★★★COURSE NO. 2
Holes: 18. **Par:** 72. **Yards:** 6,268–5,564. **Slope:** 120–118.
Comments: "Awesome Midwest beauty . . . Very playable . . . Challeng-
ing, OK price . . . Impossible to get on . . . Good walking course . . .
Walking allowed on weekends, not normal for around here . . . Used too
much . . . Good, not great . . . As good as No. 4."
★★½ COURSE NO. 3
Holes: 18. **Par:** 72. **Yards:** 6,437–5,321. **Slope:** 117–114.
Comments: "Excellent condition for a plain course . . . Very professional,
courteous starters."
★★★★★COURSE NO. 4
Season: April–Oct. **Green fee:** $50–$99. **Reduced fees:** No.
Holes: 18. **Par:** 72. **Yards:** 6,997–5,874. **Slope:** 142–134.
Home of PGA Tour's Western Open. Ranked 68th in America's 100 Great-
est and in First 25 of America's 75 Best Public Courses by GOLF DIGEST.
Comments: "The ultimate test . . . Beautiful, traditional . . . Incredible
golfing experience . . . A good lesson in humility . . . Dick Wilson's best
work . . . Worth the admission . . . Worth every penny . . . Worth going
out of your way to play . . . Deserves a U.S. Open . . . Bunkersville . . .
Like the Sahara Desert . . . Bunkers much better since sand was replaced for
Western . . . Pace of play is relatively fast . . . Probably the best value in
Illinois . . . Tops in every way . . . Excellent condition . . . They make you
feel very welcome . . . Joe Jemsek, don't change a thing."

★★½ EAGLE CREEK RESORT GOLF COURSE
Findlay—R—217-756-3456, 800-876-3245 (40 mi. from Decatur).
Season: Year-round. **High:** April–Oct. **Caddies:** No.
Green fee: $20–$49. **Credit cards:** All Major.
Lodging on site: Yes. **Reduced fees:** Weekdays, Low Season, Resort
Guests, Twilight Play.
Unrestricted walking: No. **Range:** Yes (grass).
Holes: 18. **Par:** 72. **Yards:** 6,908–5,901. **Slope:** 132–121.
Comments: "Nice resort course . . . Very young, but extremely challeng-
ing . . . Lots of rough edges . . . Still needs work . . . Time and money . . .
Take the family, even if they don't play golf."

EAGLE RIDGE INN & RESORT
Galena—R—815-777-5200 (210 mi. from Chicago).
Season: April–Oct. **High:** June–Sept. **Caddies:** No.
Green fee: $50–$99. **Credit cards:** All Major.
Lodging on site: Yes. **Reduced fees:** Resort Guests, Twilight Play.
Unrestricted walking: No. **Range:** Yes (grass).
Club also has new 9-hole East Course.
★★★½ NORTH COURSE
Holes: 18. **Par:** 72. **Yards:** 6,836–5,578. **Slope:** 134–127.
Ranked 39th in America's 75 Best Resort Courses by GOLF DIGEST.
Comments: "Fantastic . . . Beautiful . . . Routing is such that you feel like
you're the only one there . . . Elevation changes unique in Illinois . . . View
from seventh tee takes your breath away . . . Spectacular fall colors . . . No.
10 is tough, 18 is a good closer . . . Third green breaks uphill . . . Staff really
on the ball . . . Treat golfers great . . . Excellent getaway . . . Very scenic,
but not very challenging . . . Too much money to play."
★★★★SOUTH COURSE
Holes: 18. **Par:** 72. **Yards:** 6,762–5,609. **Slope:** 133–128.
Co-selection as Best New Resort Course of 1984 and ranked 38th in America's 75 Best Resort Courses by GOLF DIGEST.

Comments: "Not tremendously difficult, but scenic and fun . . . Worth driving from Chicago . . . Staff is invariably courteous, informed . . . Great food . . . Rent a cottage in the deep woods section . . . Rangers nonexistent."

★★★FOX CREEK GOLF CLUB
Edwardsville—PU—618-692-9400.
Season: Year-round. **High:** April-Oct. **Caddies:** No.
Green fee: $20-$49. **Credit cards:** V, MC.
Lodging on site: No. **Reduced fees:** Weekdays.
Unrestricted walking: No. **Range:** Yes (grass).
Holes: 18. **Par:** 72. **Yards:** 6,970-5,204. **Slope:** Unrated.
Comments: "Possibly the most challenging public course in the area . . . A lot of character. . . Best first-year course ever played . . . New, conditions still weak . . . A couple of holes squeezed in."

★★★GEORGE W. DUNNE NATIONAL GOLF COURSE
Oak Forest—PU—708-535-3377 (5 mi. from Chicago).
Season: April-Dec. **High:** May-Sept. **Caddies:** No.
Green fee: $20-$49. **Credit cards:** V, MC.
Lodging on site: No. **Reduced fees:** Weekdays, Twilight Play.
Unrestricted walking: Yes. **Range:** Yes (mats).
Holes: 18. **Par:** 72. **Yards:** 7,170-5,535. **Slope:** 134-121.
Formerly known as Forest Preserve National Golf Course. Ranked in First 25 of America's 75 Best Public Courses by GOLF DIGEST.
Comments: "Great layout, needs better conditioning . . . When maintained, tough as any . . . Overplayed and beat up . . . A lot like Doral's Blue Monster . . . The poor man's Kemper Lakes . . . Difficult for weekenders . . . Upkeep is poor . . . Shag carpet greens . . . Bad sand . . .Hard packed . . .No effort to improve . . . Players need to take better care of it . . . Green fee has tripled in four years . . . Almost no clubhouse."

★★GLENDALE LAKES GOLF COURSE
Glendale Heights—PU—708-260-0018 (25 mi. from Chicago).
Season: April-Dec. **High:** May-Sept. **Caddies:** No.
Green fee: $20-$49. **Credit cards:** V, AMEX, DISC, MC.
Lodging on site: No. **Reduced fees:** Weekdays, Twilight Play.
Unrestricted walking: No. **Range:** No.
Holes: 18. **Par:** 71. **Yards:** 6,150-5,390. **Slope:** 121-117.
Comments: "Average . . . Flat . . . Very tight, lots of water . . . Trick shot course . . .Always seems worn out . . . Hardpan lined with condos."

GLENWOODIE COUNTRY CLUB*
Glenwoodie—PU—708-758-1212 (25 mi. from Chicago).
Season: Year-round. **High:** April-Oct. **Caddies:** No.
Green fee: $20-$49. **Credit cards:** V, DISC, MC.
Reduced fees: Weekdays, Low Season, Twilight Play.
Unrestricted walking: Yes. **Range:** Yes (grass).
Holes: 18. **Par:** 72. **Yards:** 6,670-5,505. **Slope:** 120-118.

★★★GOLF CLUB OF ILLINOIS
Algonquin—PU—708-658-4400 (35 mi. from Chicago).
Season: April-Nov. **High:** June-Sept. **Caddies:** No.
Green fee: $50-$99. **Credit cards:** V, AMEX, MC.
Lodging on site: No. **Reduced fees:** Weekdays, Twilight Play.
Unrestricted walking: No. **Range:** Yes (grass).
Holes: 18. **Par:** 71. **Yards:** 7,011-4,896. **Slope:** 133-115.
Comments: "Unique . . . Not quite a true links . . . Not for below average golfers . . . Needs a lot of TLC . . . Pro shop always wants you back . . . A failed attempt at a links . . . Unusual but boring . . . All I remember is a long par 5 against the wind . . . Who needs a 680-yard hole?. . . All the construction around it hurts the experience."

ILLINOIS

★★HIGHLAND PARK GOLF COURSE
Bloomington—PU—309-823-4200.
Season: Year-round. **High:** Summer. **Caddies:** No.
Green fee: Under $20. **Credit cards:** V.
Lodging on site: No. **Reduced fees:** Twilight Play.
Unrestricted walking: Yes. **Range:** No.
Holes: 18. **Par:** 70. **Yards:** 5,725-5,530. **Slope:** 115-111.
Comments: "Eye-appealing course, but plays at a snail's pace . . . 5-hour rounds not uncommon . . . Extremely heavy play . . . Series of drivable par 4s on back 9 . . . Lots of good buys in the pro shop."

★★½ ILLINOIS STATE UNIVERSITY GOLF COURSE
Normal—PU—309-438-8065.
Season: March-Dec. **High:** June-Aug. **Caddies:** No.
Green fee: Under $20. **Credit cards:** V, MC.
Lodging on site: No. **Reduced fees:** Twilight Play.
Unrestricted walking: Yes. **Range:** Yes (mats).
Holes: 18. **Par:** 71. **Yards:** 6,326-5,781. **Slope:** 120-119.
Comments: "Fine university course . . . Awesome value at $10 . . . Good walking course, always in shape . . . Lots of sand traps . . . Big sand traps . . . Clubhouse only fair . . . Modest services."

INDIAN LAKES RESORT*
Bloomingdale—R—708-529-0200 (30 mi. from Chicago).
Season: April-Nov. **High:** June-Sept. **Caddies:** No.
Green fee: $20-$49. **Credit cards:** All Major.
Lodging on site: Yes. **Reduced fees:** Weekdays, Low Season, Twilight Play.
Unrestricted walking: No. **Range:** No.
IROQUOIS COURSE
Holes: 18. **Par:** 72. **Yards:** 6,580-6,239. **Slope:** 117.
SIOUX COURSE
Holes: 18. **Par:** 72. **Yards:** 6,564-6,225. **Slope:** 121.

★★★★KEMPER LAKES GOLF CLUB
Long Grove—PU—708-540-3450 (35 mi. from Chicago).
Season: April-Nov. **High:** June-Aug. **Caddies:** No.
Green fee: $50-$99. **Credit cards:** V, MC.
Lodging on site: No. **Reduced fees:** No.
Unrestricted walking: No. **Range:** Yes (grass).
Holes: 18. **Par:** 72. **Yards:** 7,217-5,634. **Slope:** 140-131.
Ranked in First 25 of America's 75 Best Public Courses by GOLF DIGEST.
Comments: "Great course, great facility, nice staff, but price is stiff for our area . . . Far too expensive . . . Priced because pro tournaments were held there . . . As good as it gets . . . You'd better be long off tee . . . Always a treat . . . 10-minute starting intervals add to enjoyment . . . No hackers, please . . . I love it (except for 18) . . . Cut those greens, put sand in the bunkers and course would be great . . . Hard to get tee times . . . Takes too long to play. . . Slow play ruins the experience . . . For a name course, nothing is memorable . . . Didn't like the course, but was treated well . . . Why all the fuss?"

★★★½ LICK CREEK GOLF COURSE
Pekin—PU—309-346-0077 (20 mi. from Peoria).
Season: April-Oct. **High:** Summer. **Caddies:** No.
Green fee: Under $20. **Credit cards:** V, MC.
Lodging on site: No. **Reduced fees:** Twilight Play.
Unrestricted walking: Yes. **Range:** Yes (grass).
Holes: 18. **Par:** 72. **Yards:** 6,909-5,729. **Slope:** 128-113.

Ranked in Third 25 of America's 75 Best Public Courses by GOLF DIGEST.
Comments: "Tough but fun . . . Lots of water . . . Great greens . . . You'd better know how to putt . . . Terrific course, terrific value . . . Fantastic shape for a public course . . . Too many forced carries."

MARENGO RIDGE COUNTRY CLUB*
Marengo—PU—815-923-2332 (35 mi. from Chicago).
Season: March-Dec. **High:** May-Sept. **Caddies:** No.
Green fee: $20-$49. **Credit cards:** V, MC.
Reduced fees: Weekdays, Low Season, Resort Guests, Twilight Play.
Unrestricted walking: Yes. **Range:** Yes (grass).
Holes: 18. **Par:** 72. **Yards:** 6,985-5,795. **Slope:** 125-105.

★★ MARRIOTT'S LINCOLNSHIRE RESORT
Lincolnshire—R—708-634-5935 (30 mi. from Chicago).
Season: April-Oct. **High:** June-Aug. **Caddies:** No.
Green fee: $20-$49. **Credit cards:** All Major.
Lodging on site: Yes. **Reduced fees:** Weekdays, Low Season, Twilight Play.
Unrestricted walking: No. **Range:** No.
Holes: 18. **Par:** 70. **Yards:** 6,313-4,892. **Slope:** 129-117.
Courses: "Short . . . Nothing exceptional . . . Two very different 9s . . . Weak front, good back . . . Front is too cramped, several tee areas in the path of errant balls . . . Back 9 gets tough quickly . . . Rock-hard greens . . . A few short holes but challenging . . . Nice atmosphere . . . Resort that doesn't get a lot of play . . . Secluded even though near the city."

NAPERBROOK GOLF COURSE*
Plainfield—PU—708-378-4215 (25 mi. from Chicago).
Season: March-Dec. **High:** June-Aug. **Caddies:** No.
Green fee: $20-$49. **Credit cards:** V, MC.
Lodging on site: No. **Reduced fees:** Weekdays.
Unrestricted walking: Yes. **Range:** Yes (grass).
Holes: 18. **Par:** 72. **Yards:** 6,755-6,089. **Slope:** 120-113.

★★½ NEWMAN GOLF COURSE
Peoria—PU—309-674-1663 (250 mi. from Chicago).
Season: March-Dec. **High:** June-Aug. **Caddies:** No.
Green fee: Under $20. **Credit cards:** V, MC.
Lodging on site: No. **Reduced fees:** Weekdays, Twilight Play.
Unrestricted walking: Yes. **Range:** No.
Holes: 18. **Par:** 71. **Yards:** 6,838-5,933. **Slope:** 119-114.
Comments: "Best challenge in Peoria . . . Think your way around this one . . . Recently added watering system, best shape it's ever been in . . . It plays in Peoria."

★½ NORDIC HILLS RESORT
Itasca—R—708-773-3510 (20 mi. from Chicago).
Season: April-Nov. **High:** June-Aug. **Caddies:** No.
Green fee: $20-$49. **Credit cards:** All Major.
Lodging on site: Yes. **Reduced fees:** Weekdays, Low Season, Twilight Play.
Unrestricted walking: No. **Range:** No.
Holes: 18. **Par:** 71. **Yards:** 5,910-5,331. **Slope:** 105-113.
Comments: "Short, undemanding . . . Nothing memorable . . . Two drivable par 4s plus a 90-yard par 3 . . . Too slow, too many outings . . . Dangerous course due to placement of tee boxes by greens . . . Gravel pits for sand traps . . . Shorter than card states . . . Good conference center . . . Typical impersonal resort atmosphere. Very expensive for what's offered."

★★★½ NORRIS A. ALDEEN GOLF CLUB
Rockford—PU—815-282-8728 (80 mi. from Chicago).
Season: April-Oct. **High:** June-Aug. **Caddies:** No.
Green fee: $20-$49. **Credit cards:** V, DISC, MC.
Lodging on site: No. **Reduced fees:** Twilight Play.
Unrestricted walking: Yes. **Range:** Yes (mats).
Holes: 18. **Par:** 72. **Yards:** 7,058-5,038. **Slope:** 122-113.

Comments: "Everything you'd want in a course, plus service . . . New, it is going to be great . . . Superb, reasonably priced."

OAK BROOK HILLS HOTEL & RESORT*
Oak Brook—R—708-850-5530 (25 mi. from Chicago).
Season: April-Dec. **High:** June-Sept. **Caddies:** No.
Green fee: $50-$99. **Credit cards:** All Major.
Lodging on site: Yes. **Reduced fees:** Weekdays, Low Season, Twilight Play.
Unrestricted walking: No. **Range:** No.
Holes: 18. **Par:** 70. **Yards:** 6,409-5,339. **Slope:** 121-114.

★★½ ODYSSEY GOLF COURSE
Tinley Park—PU—708-429-7400 (23 mi. from Chicago).
Season: April-Nov. **High:** June-Oct. **Caddies:** No.
Green fee: $50-$99. **Credit cards:** V, MC.
Reduced fees: Weekdays, Low Season, Twilight Play.
Unrestricted walking: No. **Range:** Yes (grass).
Holes: 18. **Par:** 72. **Yards:** 7,095-5,554. **Slope:** 128-112.
Comments: "Interesting, clubhouse under construction . . . Maintained well . . . Needs to mature, needs trees . . . Slicer's layout . . . Too far between holes."

★½ PHEASANT RUN RESORT GOLF COURSE
St. Charles—R—708-584-4914 (40 mi. from Chicago).
Season: Year-round. **High:** May-Oct. **Caddies:** No.
Green fee: $20-$49. **Credit cards:** All Major.
Lodging on site: Yes. **Reduced fees:** Weekdays, Low Season, Twilight Play.
Unrestricted walking: Yes. **Range:** Yes (grass).
Holes: 18. **Par:** 71. **Yards:** 6,315-5,452. **Slope:** 124-121.
Comments: "Very open, good for duffers . . . Short and uneventful . . . Flat, elevated greens . . . Front 9 is like a par-3 course . . . Yardage markers way off. . . Holes lack character . . . Gets ratty by September . . . This place used to be a cornfield . . . Course needs a lot of work."

★★★★ PINE MEADOW GOLF CLUB
Mundelein—PU—708-566-4653 (35 mi. from Chicago).
Season: Year-round. **High:** May-Aug. **Caddies:** Yes.
Green fee: $20-$49. **Credit cards:** V, DISC, MC.
Lodging on site: No. **Reduced fees:** Twilight Play.
Unrestricted walking: Yes. **Range:** Yes (mats).
Holes: 18. **Par:** 72. **Yards:** 7,141-5,335. **Slope:** 131-120.
Selected Best New Public Course of 1986 and ranked in First 25 of America's 75 Best Public Courses by GOLF DIGEST.
Comments: "Tee to green, one of the most beautiful, challenging courses around . . . In excellent shape . . . Neat, classy . . . Set on 200 acres . . . Killer rough, fast greens . . . Possibly better than Cog Hill No. 4 . . . Top notch . . . A better value than Kemper Lakes . . . Run like a smooth ship . . . Great practice area . . . Good course for all levels . . . Great despite extremely heavy play . . .Run-of-the-mill clubhouse . . . Forced fast pace of play . . . A hassle to get on."

★★★½ PRAIRIE VISTA GOLF COURSE
Bloomington—PU—309-823-4217.
Season: March-Nov. **High:** Summer. **Caddies:** Yes.
Green fee: Under $20. **Credit cards:** V
Lodging on site: No. **Reduced fees:** No.
Unrestricted walking: Yes. **Range:** Yes (mats).
Holes: 18. **Par:** 72. **Yards:** 6,745-5,224. **Slope:** 128-114.
Comments: "Incredible . . . Great design, great shape . . . Great for just 3 years old . . .Immature trees but great course . . . Style, quality and conditioning normally found at country clubs . . . No problem for walkers . . . You want to tell your friends about this place, but you don't want too many to find out about it."

119

★★★THE RAIL GOLF COURSE
Springfield—PU—217-525-0365 (100 mi. from St. Louis).
Season: March-Dec. **High:** June-Sept. **Caddies:** No.
Green fee: $20-$49. **Credit cards:** V, AMEX, MC.
Lodging on site: No. **Reduced fees:** No.
Unrestricted walking: Yes. **Range:** Yes (grass).
Holes: 18. **Par:** 72. **Yards:** 6,583-5,406. **Slope:** 120-116.
Site of LPGA State Farm Rail Classic.
Comments: "Nice layout, great value . . . Spacious . . . Generous fairways facilitate fast play . . . Good practice facility . . . Lots of bunkers . . . Steadily improving . . . Very polite staff . . . Worth a Saturday trip for 36 holes."

RUFFLED FEATHERS GOLF CLUB*
Lemont—PU—708-257-1000 (30 mi. from Chicago).
Season: March-Dec. **High:** May-Sept. **Caddies:** No.
Green fee: $50-$99. **Credit cards:** V, MC.
Lodging on site: No. **Reduced fees:** Twilight Play.
Unrestricted walking: No. **Range:** Yes (grass).
Holes: 18. **Par:** 72. **Yards:** 6,878-4,455. **Slope:** 134-105.

ST. ANDREWS GOLF & COUNTRY CLUB*
West Chicago—PU—708-231-3100 (30 mi. from Chicago).
Season: Year-round. **High:** April-Sept. **Caddies:** No.
Green fee: $20-$49. **Credit cards:** V, DISC, MC.
Reduced fees: Weekdays, Low Season, Twilight Play.
Unrestricted walking: Yes. **Range:** Yes (mats).
LAKEWOOD COURSE
Holes: 18. **Par:** 72. **Yards:** 6,666-5,353. **Slope:** 121-109.
ST. ANDREWS COURSE
Holes: 18. **Par:** 71. **Yards:** 6,759-5,138. **Slope:** 118-103.

SANDY HOLLOW GOLF COURSE*
Rockford—PU—815-987-8836 (90 mi. from Chicago).
Season: April-Oct. **High:** June-Aug. **Caddies:** No.
Green fee: $20-$49. **Credit cards:** No.
Lodging on site: No. **Reduced fees:** Weekdays, Twilight Play.
Unrestricted walking: Yes. **Range:** No.
Holes: 18. **Par:** 71. **Yards:** 6,228-5,882. **Slope:** 113-113.

★★★SEVEN BRIDGES GOLF CLUB
Woodridge—PU—708-964-7777 (20 mi. from Chicago).
Season: March-Nov. **High:** May-Oct. **Caddies:** No.
Green fee: $50-$99. **Credit cards:** V, AMEX, MC.
Lodging on site: No. **Reduced fees:** Twilight Play.
Unrestricted walking: No. **Range:** Yes (mats).
Holes: 18. **Par:** 72. **Yards:** 7,100-5,200. **Slope:** 132-113.
Comments: "Front 9 very good, back 9 very poor . . . These two 9s don't belong together . . . Dr. Jekyll/Mr. Hyde course . . . Too much water on back, unnecessarily penal . . . Holes 11, 12, 14 have no bailout . . . Very well managed . . . Service comparable to a country club . . . They treat you like a king . . . Pamper you to death . . . Still easy to get on . . . Pin placement chart on carts is great idea."

SILVER LAKE COUNTRY CLUB*
Orland Park—PU—708-349-6940 (25 mi. from Chicago).
Season: Year-round. **High:** April-Sept. **Caddies:** No.
Green fee: $20-$49. **Credit cards:** V, DISC, MC.
Lodging on site: No. **Reduced fees:** Twilight Play.
Unrestricted walking: Yes. **Range:** No.
NORTH COURSE
Holes: 18. **Par:** 72. **Yards:** 6,826-5,719. **Slope:** 116-116.

SOUTH COURSE
Holes: 18. **Par:** 70. **Yards:** 5,948-5,138. **Slope:** 108-109.
Also has a nine-hole executive course called Rolling Hills.

★★★½ SPENCER T. OLIN COMMUNITY GOLF COURSE
Alton—PU—618-465-3111 (22 mi. from St. Louis).
Season: Year-round. **High:** May-Sept. **Caddies:** No.
Green fee: $20-$49. **Credit cards:** V, AMEX, MC.
Lodging on site: Yes. **Reduced fees:** Weekdays, Low Season,
Twilight Play.
Unrestricted walking: No. **Range:** Yes (grass).
Holes: 18. **Par:** 72. **Yards:** 6,941-5,049. **Slope:** 132-117.
Course will host the 1996 U.S. Women's National Public Links.
Comments: "Best in area. Outstanding quality . . . Very fun and fair . . .
Excellent course conditions . . . Fits a variety of skill levels . . . Lots of
doglegs, very picturesque . . . A class operation . . . A pleasure to play . . .
Mandatory carts, ugh! . . . Marshals overdo rapid play."

SPRINGBROOK GOLF COURSE*
Naperville—PU—708-420-4215 (28 mi. from Chicago).
Season: March-Dec. **High:** June-Aug. **Caddies:** No.
Green fee: $20-$49. **Credit cards:** V, MC.
Lodging on site: No. **Reduced fees:** Weekdays.
Unrestricted walking: Yes. **Range:** Yes (grass).
Holes: 18. **Par:** 72. **Yards:** 6,896-6,459. **Slope:** 124-121.

STEEPLE CHASE GOLF CLUB*
Mundelein—PU—708-949-8900 (30 mi. from Chicago).
Season: April-Nov. **High:** May-Sept. **Caddies:** No.
Green fee: $20-$49. **Credit cards:** V, AMEX, DISC, MC.
Lodging on site: No. **Reduced fees:** Weekdays, Twilight Play.
Unrestricted walking: Yes. **Range:** No.
Holes: 18. **Par:** 72. **Yards:** 6,818-4,831. **Slope:** 129-113.

★★½ TAMARACK GOLF CLUB
Naperville—PU—708-904-4004 (35 mi. from Chicago).
Season: April-Dec. **High:** Summer. **Caddies:** No.
Green fee: $20-$49. **Credit cards:** V, AMEX, MC.
Lodging on site: No. **Reduced fees:** Weekdays, Twilight Play.
Unrestricted walking: No. **Range:** Yes (grass).
Holes: 18. **Par:** 70. **Yards:** 6,955-5,100. **Slope:** 131-114.
Comments: "Lot of water right, OB left. No thanks . . . Cartpaths only.
No thanks."

VILLAGE GREENS OF WOODBRIDGE*
Woodbridge—PU—708-985-3610 (20 mi. from Chicago).
Season: March-Nov. **High:** June-Aug. **Caddies:** No.
Green fee: $20-$49. **Credit cards:** V, MC.
Lodging on site: No. **Reduced fees:** Weekdays, Twilight Play.
Unrestricted walking: Yes. **Range:** Yes (grass).
Holes: 18. **Par:** 72. **Yards:** 6,650-5,847. **Slope:** 121-119.

WESTGATE VALLEY COUNTRY CLUB*
Palos Heights—PU—708-385-1810 (22 mi. from Chicago).
Season: Year-round. **High:** April-Oct. **Caddies:** No.
Green fee: $20-$49. **Credit cards:** No.
Reduced fees: Weekdays, Low Season, Twilight Play.
Unrestricted walking: Yes. **Range:** No.
EAST COURSE
Holes: 18. **Par:** 67. **Yards:** 5,336-5,150. **Slope:** 95-95.
WEST COURSE
Holes: 18. **Par:** 71. **Yards:** 6,399-6,300. **Slope:** 105-105.

★★½ CHRISTMAS LAKE GOLF CLUB
Santa Claus—PU—812-544-2271, 800-927-2571 (45 mi. from Evansville).
Season: Feb.-Dec. **High:** May-Sept. **Caddies:** No.
Green fee: $20-$49. **Credit cards:** V, MC.
Reduced fees: Weekdays, Low Season, Twilight Play.
Unrestricted walking: No. **Range:** Yes (grass).
Holes: 18. **Par:** 72. **Yards:** 7,191-6,660. **Slope:** 135-127.
Comments: "Long . . . Poorly maintained . . . Greens too slow."

★★EAGLE CREEK GOLF CLUB
Indianapolis—PU—317-297-3366.
Season: Year-round. **High:** May-Aug. **Caddies:** No.
Green fee: Under $20. **Credit cards:** V, MC.
Lodging on site: No. **Reduced fees:** Weekdays, Twilight Play.
Unrestricted walking: No. **Range:** Yes (grass).
Holes: 18. **Par:** 72. **Yards:** 7,159-5,800. **Slope:** 126-113.
Site of 1982 USGA Public Links Championship. Ranked in Third 25 of
America's 75 Best Public Courses by GOLF DIGEST. Club has additional 9-
hole, 2,980-yard course.
Comments: "Beautiful setting . . . Great layout but poorly kept. A real
shame . . . Many well-designed holes, conditions erratic . . . City has let this
place go . . . So much ground under repair, it's almost unplayable."

FRENCH LICK SPRINGS COUNTRY CLUB
French Lick—R—812-936-9300 (50 mi. from Louisville, Ky.).
Season: April-Oct. **High:** April-Oct. **Caddies:** No.
Green fee: $20-$49. **Credit cards:** All Major.
Lodging on site: Yes. **Reduced fees:** No.
Unrestricted walking: No. **Range:** No.
★★★COUNTRY CLUB COURSE
Holes: 18. **Par:** 70. **Yards:** 6,625-5,781. **Slope:** 119-121.
Comments: "Big greens . . . Great greens . . . Greens are wild . . . Tough-
est undulations I've ever played . . . Greens more severe than Augusta."
★½ VALLEY COURSE
Holes: 18. **Par:** 70. **Yards:** 6,056-5,687. **Slope:** 110-108.
Comments: "Flat, wide open, small greens . . . In absolutely terrible shape
. . . Not much of a golf course."

★★★GOLF CLUB OF INDIANA
Zionsville—PU—317-769-6388 (10 mi. from Indianapolis).
Season: Year-round. **High:** June-Aug. **Caddies:** No.
Green fee: $20-$49. **Credit cards:** No.
Lodging on site: No. **Reduced fees:** Low Season, Twilight Play.
Unrestricted walking: Yes. **Range:** Yes (grass).
Holes: 18. **Par:** 72. **Yards:** 7,084-5,498. **Slope:** 140-122.
Ranked in Third 25 of America's 75 Best Public Courses by GOLF DIGEST.
Comments: "Has everything except hills . . . Bunkers, water create diffi-
culty . . . Punitive but enjoyable . . . Best public course in Indy area . . .
Great shape all the time . . . Can easily walk and carry . . . Often crowded,
slow play . . . Limited pro shop."

★★★½ GRAND OAK GOLF CLUB
West Harrison—PU—812-637-3943 (30 mi. from Cincinnati).
Season: Feb.-Dec. **High:** April-Oct. **Caddies:** No.
Green fee: $20-$49. **Credit cards:** V, MC.
Lodging on site: No. **Reduced fees:** Weekdays.
Unrestricted walking: Yes. **Range:** Yes (grass).
Holes: 18. **Par:** 71. **Yards:** 6,440-4,842. **Slope:** 125-121.
Comments: "Neat layout . . . Beautiful holes, target golf . . . Walking
allowed, but not recommended unless you're in good shape."

★★★½ HULMAN LINKS GOLF COURSE
Terre Haute—PU—812-877-2096.
Season: March-Dec. **High:** April-Sept. **Caddies:** No.
Green fee: $20-$49. **Credit cards:** V, MC.
Lodging on site: No. **Reduced fees:** Low Season.
Unrestricted walking: Yes. **Range:** Yes (grass).
Holes: 18. **Par:** 72. **Yards:** 7,225-5,775. **Slope:** 144-134.
Ranked in Third 25 of America's 75 Best Public Courses by GOLF DIGEST.
Comments: "Great challenge . . . Good test . . . Demanding tee shots . . .
Difficult for all . . . Well conditioned . . . Best 17 holes for the price . . .
Only one bad hole . . . 11th hole is unfair . . . Never been there when they
didn't have part of it torn up."

LAKE HILLS GOLF CLUB*
FRONT/MIDDLE/BACK 9s
Lake Hills—PU—219-365-8601 (20 mi. from Chicago).
Season: March-Dec. **High:** March-Sept. **Caddies:** No.
Green fee: $20-$49. **Credit cards:** All Major.
Reduced fees: Weekdays, Low Season, Twilight Play.
Unrestricted walking: Yes. **Range:** Yes (mats).
Holes: 27. **Par:** 35/37/35. **Yards:** 3,083/2,805/3,088.

★★★½ THE LEGENDS OF INDIANA GOLF COURSE
Franklin—PU—317-736-8186 (10 mi. from Indianapolis).
Season: March-Nov. **High:** June-Sept. **Caddies:** No.
Green fee: $20-$49. **Credit cards:** V, MC.
Lodging on site: No. **Reduced fees:** Twilight Play.
Unrestricted walking: No. **Range:** Yes (grass).
Holes: 18. **Par:** 72. **Yards:** 7,044-5,420. **Slope:** 132-123.
Comments: "Young course, flat farmland, no trees . . . With seasoning,
could be great . . . Good course that pretends to be great . . . They needed
more room. Holes too close together."

★★★★½ OTTER CREEK GOLF COURSE
Columbus—PU—812-579-5227 (45 mi. from Indianapolis).
Season: March-Nov. **High:** April-Oct. **Caddies:** Yes.
Green fee: $50-$99. **Credit cards:** All Major.
Lodging on site: No. **Reduced fees:** Weekdays, Low Season.
Unrestricted walking: Yes. **Range:** Yes (grass).
Holes: 18. **Par:** 72. **Yards:** 7,258-5,690. **Slope:** 137-116.
Site of 1991 U.S. Public Links Championship. Ranked in First 25 of Ameri-
ca's 75 Best Public Courses by GOLF DIGEST.
Comments: "Magnificent . . . A premier course . . . A joy . . . Wonderful-
ly playable by all . . . Challenging and fair . . . The best publinks in Indiana
. . . A favorite in Hoosierland . . . Could host a U.S. Open . . . Golf at its
best. No tricks, no gimmicks . . . Each hole has a different character . . .
Staff is excellent . . . Excellent clubhouse fits surroundings . . . Very expensive for the area . . . All-day fee on Monday and Tuesday are great."

PEBBLE BROOK GOLF & COUNTRY CLUB
Noblesville—PU—317-896-5596 (25 mi. from Indianapolis).
Season: March-Nov. **High:** May-Sept. **Caddies:** No.
Green fee: $20-$49. **Credit cards:** V, MC.
Lodging on site: No. **Reduced fees:** Weekdays.
Unrestricted walking: No. **Range:** Yes (grass).
★★½ NORTH COURSE
Holes: 18. **Par:** 70. **Yards:** 6,492-5,806. **Slope:** 118-114.
Comments: "Longer, more mounding than South . . . No trees . . . A
study in how to trick-up a course . . . Out of the way, worth the trip."
★★½ SOUTH COURSE
Holes: 18. **Par:** 72. **Yards:** 6,557-5,261. **Slope:** 111-108.
Comments: "Short but well kept . . . Nothing special . . . Not enough
definition or character . . . Dull and uninteresting course."

★★★SALT CREEK GOLF CLUB
Nashville—PU—812-988-7888 (45 mi. from Indianapolis).
Season: March-Nov. **High:** May-Oct. **Caddies:** No.
Green fee: $20-$49. **Credit cards:** V, MC.
Lodging on site: No. **Reduced fees:** No.
Unrestricted walking: No. **Range:** Yes (grass).
Holes: 18. **Par:** 72. **Yards:** 6,407-5,001. **Slope:** 132-122.
Comments: "Brand new, but plays mature . . . Fine course, treelined . . .
Much variety . . . Interesting, playable for shorter hitters . . . Maintained
beautifully . . . Picturesque, set in famed Brown County . . . Beautiful in fall
. . . Staff is attentive and helpful . . . Back 9 short, 14 holes are repetitive . . .
Scenic, but not well designed. First 9 confusing."

★★★★SULTAN'S RUN GOLF COURSE
Jasper—PU—812-482-1009.
Season: Year-round. **High:** April-Oct. **Caddies:** No.
Green fee: $20-$49. **Credit cards:** V, MC.
Reduced fees: Weekdays, Low Season, Twilight Play.
Unrestricted walking: No. **Range:** Yes (grass).
Holes: 18. **Par:** 72. **Yards:** 7,000-5,400. **Slope:** 132-120.
Comments: "An absolutely beautiful course . . . Wonderful, exciting . . .
Unique . . . Excellent layout . . . In a few years will be best in area . . .
Greens a little too sloped . . . Hard to walk . . . Friendliest staff in years . . .
Happy to see you play."

SUPER VALUE

★★★WABASH VALLEY GOLF CLUB
Geneva—PU—219-368-7388 (45 mi. from Fort Wayne).
Season: March-Nov. **High:** June-Aug. **Caddies:** No.
Green fee: Under $20. **Credit cards:** V, MC.
Lodging on site: No. **Reduced fees:** Weekdays.
Unrestricted walking: Yes. **Range:** Yes (grass).
Holes: 18. **Par:** 71. **Yards:** 6,375-5,018. **Slope:** 117-106.
Comments: "Best public in northern Indiana . . . A great value."

★★★½ AMANA COLONIES GOLF COURSE
Amana—R—319-622-6222, 800-383-3636 (20 mi. from Cedar Rapids).
Season: Year-round. **High:** June-Aug. **Caddies:** No.
Green fee: $20-$49. **Credit cards:** V, AMEX, MC.
Lodging on site: Yes. **Reduced fees:** Weekdays, Low Season,
Twilight Play.
Unrestricted walking: No. **Range:** Yes (grass).
Holes: 18. **Par:** 72. **Yards:** 6,824-5,228. **Slope:** 136-115.
Comments: "A great resort course in Iowa? Believe it . . . Beautiful, hilly,
few flat lies . . . Esthetically spectacular . . . First class . . . Very tight, lots of
trees . . . Bring your straight stick . . . Excellent service, very nice . . . Great
experience . . . Maintained very well . . . A killer, too difficult . . . Hard
work . . . A real disappointment . . . You play the same hole over and over
. . . Heavy insect problem . . . Carts on paths a bummer . . . Makes play
slow and tedious . . . Just too much money to play it frequently."

GLYNNS CREEK GOLF COURSE*
Long Grove—PU—319-285-6444 (8 mi. from Davenport).
Season: April-Nov. **High:** June-Aug. **Caddies:** No.
Green fee: $20-$49. **Credit cards:** V, MC.
Lodging on site: No. **Reduced fees:** Weekdays, Twilight Play.
Unrestricted walking: No. **Range:** Yes (grass).
Holes: 18. **Par:** 72. **Yards:** 7,036-5,435. **Slope:** 131-Unrated.

JESTER PARK GOLF COURSE*
Granger—PU—515-999-2903 (10 mi. from Des Moines).
Season: March-Oct. **High:** May-Sept. **Caddies:** No.
Green fee: Under $20. **Credit cards:** V, MC.
Reduced fees: Weekdays, Low Season, Twilight Play.
Unrestricted walking: Yes. **Range:** Yes (grass).
Holes: 18. **Par:** 72. **Yards:** 6,801-6,062. **Slope:** 125.
9-hole par-3 course also.

★★★½ LAKE PANORAMA NATIONAL GOLF COURSE
Panora—R—515-755-2024, 800-766-7013 (45 mi. from Des Moines).
Season: April-Nov. **High:** May-Sept. **Caddies:** No.
Green fee: $20-$49. **Credit cards:** V, AMEX, MC.
Lodging on site: Yes. **Reduced fees:** No.
Unrestricted walking: No. **Range:** Yes (grass).
Holes: 18. **Par:** 72. **Yards:** 7,015-6,517. **Slope:** 131-126.
Comments: "One of Iowa's best . . . Fair test of golf . . . Nice, tough in the
wind . . . Long, has variety . . . Demanding second and third shots . . . A
pleasure to play . . . Quality personnel and service . . . Needs better
maintenance."

★★½ OKOBOJI VU GOLF COURSE
Spirit Lake—PU—712-337-3372.
Season: April-Oct. **High:** June-Sept. **Caddies:** No.
Green fee: $20-$49. **Credit cards:** No.
Reduced fees: Weekdays, Low Season, Twilight Play.
Unrestricted walking: Yes. **Range:** Yes (grass).
Holes: 18. **Par:** 70. **Yards:** 6,550-6,051. **Slope:** 113-113.
Course has a real 19th hole, a par 3 used for playoffs.
Comments: "Good vacation golf with the kids . . . Good value, not much
on amenities . . . Nice since they started watering fairways . . . Just average
. . . Poorly managed tee times."

★★½ PHEASANT RIDGE MUNICIPAL GOLF COURSE
Cedar Falls—PU—319-273-8647 (5 mi. from Waterloo).
Season: April-Oct. **High:** May-Sept. **Caddies:** No.
Green fee: Under $20. **Credit cards:** No.
Lodging on site: No. **Reduced fees:** Low Season, Twilight Play.
Unrestricted walking: Yes. **Range:** Yes (grass).

Holes: 18. **Par:** 72. **Yards:** 6,730-5,179. **Slope:** 122.
Comments: "Excellent public value . . . Nicely groomed, well-placed sand traps, otherwise wide open . . . Well conditioned but monotonous . . . No tree or rough trouble, not much water . . . No clubhouse."

SHORELINE GOLF COURSE*

Carter Lake—PU—712-347-5173 (2 mi. from Omaha).
Season: March-Nov. **High:** June-Aug. **Caddies:** No.
Green fee: Under $20. **Credit cards:** V, MC.
Lodging on site: No. **Reduced fees:** Weekdays, Low Season.
Unrestricted walking: Yes. **Range:** Yes (grass).
Holes: 18. **Par:** 72. **Yards:** 6,669-5,439. **Slope:** 124-107.
Comments: "Young course, maturing quickly . . . Each hole is different."

★★SQUAW CREEK GOLF COURSE

Marion—PU—319-398-5182, 800-373-8433 (2 mi. from Cedar Rapids).
Season: April-Nov. **High:** June-Sept. **Caddies:** No.
Green fee: Under $20. **Credit cards:** V, MC.
Lodging on site: No. **Reduced fees:** No.
Unrestricted walking: Yes. **Range:** Yes (grass).
Holes: 18. **Par:** 72. **Yards:** 6,629-5,574. **Slope:** 111-109.
Comments: "Good walking course . . . Easy but fun . . . Good for all types, has room for errors . . . Coming back after drought."

★★★VEENKER MEMORIAL GOLF COURSE

Ames—PU—515-294-6727 (35 mi. from Des Moines).
Season: March-Nov. **High:** June-Aug. **Caddies:** No.
Green fee: Under $20. **Credit cards:** All Major.
Lodging on site: No. **Reduced fees:** No.
Unrestricted walking: Yes. **Range:** Yes (grass).
Holes: 18. **Par:** 72. **Yards:** 6,543-6,086. **Slope:** 124-120.
Course owned by Iowa State University.
Comments: "Good old college course . . . One of the finest anywhere . . . Some outstanding holes . . . Very hilly . . . You'd never know you're in Iowa . . . Leave fairway, lose ball . . . Solid long irons a must . . . Every green is different . . . Takes a lot of local knowledge to score well."

★★★½ WAVELAND GOLF COURSE

Des Moines—PU—515-242-2911.
Season: March-Nov. **High:** May-Aug. **Caddies:** No.
Green fee: Under $20. **Credit cards:** No.
Lodging on site: No. **Reduced fees:** Twilight Play.
Unrestricted walking: Yes. **Range:** No.
Holes: 18. **Par:** 72. **Yards:** 6,648-6,419. **Slope:** 126-121.
Comments: "Classic old course being wasted by poor conditioning . . . Several excellent holes . . . Steep hills abound . . . Hundreds of mature ˙s . . . 'Timber' is often heard instead of 'Fore' . . . Could be outstanding with commitment from city . . . They're working hard to get it back on top . . . Finally, watered fairways! . . . Memorable holes, improving conditions."

★★½ WILLOW CREEK GOLF COURSE

Des Moines—PU—515-285-4558.
Season: Year-round. **High:** Summer. **Caddies:** No.
Green fee: Under $20. **Credit cards:** V, DISC, MC.
Lodging on site: Yes. **Reduced fees:** Weekdays.
Unrestricted walking: Yes. **Range:** Yes (grass).
Holes: 18. **Par:** 71. **Yards:** 6,465-6,146. **Slope:** 116-110.
Comments: "Complete complex, full 18, extra 9, executive 9 . . . Not too difficult . . . Nice driving range . . . Friendly staff . . . Customer oriented. Owners are always putting money back into the courses . . . You feel you are welcome . . . Mix of old holes with new ones doesn't blend . . . Too many back and forth holes . . . Hard greens, get too much use . . . Very hard to get tee times . . . Too many golfers at once. Ever heard of a ranger?"

★★★½ ALVAMAR GOLF COURSE
Lawrence—PU—913-842-1907 (20 mi. from Topeka).
Season: Year-round. **High:** May-Sept. **Caddies:** No.
Green fee: $20-$49. **Credit cards:** V, DISC, MC.
Reduced fees: Weekdays, Low Season, Twilight Play.
Unrestricted walking: Yes. **Range:** Yes.
Holes: 18. **Par:** 72. **Yards:** 7,096-5,489. **Slope:** 135-133.
Ranked in Third 25 of America's 75 Best Public Course by GOLF DIGEST.
Comments: "Superb course, superb value . . . Zoysia fairways, no bad lies
. . . Easy to walk, 4½-hour rounds maximum, good range and putting
green, friendly employees . . . Conditions always good, the best greens
anywhere . . . Nice, a challenge to score . . . When the wind blows, a real
test . . . Almost as good as private course next door . . . For the money, best
in the Midwest . . . They treat you right."

★★★½ DEER CREEK GOLF CLUB
Overland Park—PU—913-681-3100.
Season: Year-round. **High:** March-Nov. **Caddies:** No.
Green fee: $20-$49. **Credit cards:** V, DISC, MC.
Reduced fees: Weekdays, Low Season, Twilight Play.
Unrestricted walking: Yes. **Range:** No.
Holes: 18. **Par:** 72. **Yards:** 6,890-5,120. **Slope:** 137-113.
Comments: "Tremendous layout, cut through trees . . . Trent Jones Jr. did
OK here . . . Tight fairways, large greens . . . Good target golf . . . Tests all
the game. . . Creek comes into play a lot . . . Good restaurant."

★★★HERITAGE PARK GOLF COURSE
Olathe—PU—913-829-4653 (20 mi. from Kansas City).
Season: Year-round. **High:** April-Sept. **Caddies:** No.
Green fee: Under $20. **Credit cards:** V, MC.
Lodging on site: No. **Reduced fees:** Twilight Play.
Unrestricted walking: Yes. **Range:** Yes (grass).
Holes: 18. **Par:** 71. **Yards:** 6,876-5,181. **Slope:** 131-107.
Comments: "Long, hard, poorly maintained . . . Need to be accurate off
the tee; fairways too hard . . . No medium-length holes . . . Tough walking
course from greens to tees . . . Not designed for walking . . . They must
own stock in golf carts . . . Some greens poorly designed, slope away."

★½ HIDDEN LAKES GOLF COURSE
Derby—PU—316-788-2855 (4 mi. from Wichita).
Season: Year-round. **High:** April-Oct. **Caddies:** No.
Green fee: Under $20. **Credit cards:** V, AMEX, DISC, MC.
Lodging on site: No. **Reduced fees:** Weekdays, Twilight Play.
Unrestricted walking: Yes. **Range:** Yes (grass).
Holes: 18. **Par:** 72. **Yards:** 6,484-6,269. **Slope:** 122-120.
Comments: "Comes by its name well. Two over-water par 5s are good
challenges . . . Poorly maintained, poor service, poor amenities . . . Poor
greens, no fairways, a poor value at any price . . . Upkeep goes up and down
. . . Holds lots of outings . . . Practice of holding customer's drivers license
for cart rental is insulting."

★★PAWNEE PRAIRIE GOLF COURSE
Wichita—PU—316-722-6310.
Season: Year-round. **High:** May-Oct. **Caddies:** No.
Green fee: Under $20. **Credit cards:** No.
Lodging on site: No. **Reduced fees:** No.
Unrestricted walking: Yes. **Range:** Yes (grass).
Holes: 18. **Par:** 72. **Yards:** 7,363-5,928. **Slope:** 123-117.
Comments: "Playable course . . . Nice, good value . . . Long, can be
difficult for short hitters . . . Needs more trees . . . Fairways never have
come around . . . Will definitely improve with new irrigation."

KANSAS

★★★½ QUAIL RIDGE GOLF COURSE
Winfield—PU—316-221-5645 (35 mi. from Wichita).
Season: Year-round. **High:** March-Oct. **Caddies:** No.
Green fee: Under $20. **Credit cards:** V, MC.
Lodging on site: Yes. **Reduced fees:** Resort Guests.
Unrestricted walking: Yes. **Range:** Yes (grass).
Holes: 18. **Par:** 72. **Yards:** 6,850-5,350. **Slope:** 130-119.
Comments: "New course, great shape . . . Not a weed in sight."

★★★½ ROLLING MEADOWS GOLF COURSE
Junction City—PU—913-238-4303 (60 mi. from Topeka).
Season: Year-round. **High:** May-Aug. **Caddies:** No.
Green fee: Under $20. **Credit cards:** V, MC.
Lodging on site: No. **Reduced fees:** Weekdays, Twilight Play.
Unrestricted walking: Yes. **Range:** Yes (grass).
Holes: 18. **Par:** 72. **Yards:** 6,900-5,515. **Slope:** 120-116.
Comments: "Superb! . . . Seldom crowded, beautifully maintained . . .
Surprising . . . A hidden jewel . . . A great buy . . . Beautiful beech trees
. . . Just a fun course. . . Friendly staff . . . Beautiful in the fall."

SIM PARK GOLF COURSE*
Wichita—PU—316-267-5383.
Season: Year-round. **High:** March-Oct. **Caddies:** No.
Green fee: Under $20. **Credit cards:** V.
Lodging on site: No. **Reduced fees:** Twilight Play.
Unrestricted walking: Yes. **Range:** No.
Holes: 18. **Par:** 71. **Yards:** 6,330-5,867. **Slope:** 119-114.

SUNFLOWER HILLS GOLF COURSE*
Bonner Springs—PU—913-721-2727 (20 mi. from Kansas City).
Season: Year-round. **High:** May-Aug. **Caddies:** No.
Green fee: Under $20. **Credit cards:** V, MC.
Lodging on site: No. **Reduced fees:** Weekdays, Twilight Play.
Unrestricted walking: Yes. **Range:** No.
Holes: 18. **Par:** 72. **Yards:** 7,001-5,849. **Slope:** 124-118.

★★★½ TERRADYNE RESORT HOTEL
AND COUNTRY CLUB
Andover—R—316-733-5851 (5 mi. from Wichita).
Season: Year-round. **High:** May-Sept. **Caddies:** Yes.
Green fee: $20-$49. **Credit cards:** V, AMEX, MC.
Lodging on site: Yes. **Reduced fees:** Resort Guests.
Unrestricted walking: Yes. **Range:** Yes (grass).
Holes: 18. **Par:** 71. **Yards:** 6,800-6,136. **Slope:** 138-132.
Ranked 5th in Kansas by GOLF DIGEST.
Comments: "Links-type course, tough . . . Scottish style with long prairie
grass roughs . . . Like Prairie Dunes . . . You must keep it in the fairway . . .
Kansas version of target golf . . . Thick rough right off the fairway. Far too
difficult for average golfer . . . Great clubhouse . . . Friendly staff . . . Excel-
lent shape . . . Tremendous . . . Great fun."

★★WICHITA STATE UNIVERSITY GOLF COURSE
Wichita—PU—316-685-6601.
Season: Year-round. **High:** March-Oct. **Caddies:** No.
Green fee: Under $20. **Credit cards:** No.
Lodging on site: No. **Reduced fees:** Weekdays, Twilight Play.
Unrestricted walking: Yes. **Range:** Yes (grass).
Holes: 18. **Par:** 70. **Yards:** 6,407-5,475. **Slope:** 129-118.
Comments: "Formerly country club . . . Pasture pool . . . Weeds and dead
grass . . . Needs work on fairways and greens."

BARREN RIVER STATE PARK GOLF COURSE*
Lucas—R—502-646-4653 (30 mi. from Bowling Green).
Season: Year-round. **High:** April-Sept. **Caddies:** No.
Green fee: Under $20. **Credit cards:** All Major.
Lodging on site: Yes. **Reduced fees:** Weekdays.
Unrestricted walking: Yes. **Range:** Yes (grass).
Holes: 18. **Par:** 72. **Yards:** 6,440-4,919. **Slope:** 125-114.

★★½ BOOTS RANDOLPH GOLF COURSE
Cadiz—R—502-924-9076 (40 mi. from Paducah).
Season: Year-round. **High:** April-Oct. **Caddies:** No.
Green fee: Under $20. **Credit cards:** All Major.
Lodging on site: Yes. **Reduced fees:** Low Season, Twilight Play.
Unrestricted walking: Yes. **Range:** Yes (grass).
Holes: 18. **Par:** 72. **Yards:** 6,771-5,191. **Slope:** 131-121.
Located in Lake Barkley State Park.
Comments: "A little something for everyone . . . Not as good a shape as past . . . Mower must be broken . . . Needs some TLC . . . Don't like their new multi-tiered greens . . . Priced right."

CROOKED CREEK GOLF CLUB*
London—PU—606-877-4653 (75 mi. from Lexington).
Season: Year-round. **High:** April-Sept. **Caddies:** No.
Green fee: $20-$49. **Credit cards:** V, MC.
Lodging on site: No. **Reduced fees:** Weekdays, Low Season.
Unrestricted walking: Yes. **Range:** Yes (grass).
Holes: 18. **Par:** 72. **Yards:** 7,007-5,700. **Slope:** 134-122.

★★ GENERAL BURNSIDE STATE PARK GOLF COURSE
Burnside—PU—606-561-4104 (8 mi. from Somerset).
Season: Year-round. **High:** May-Sept. **Caddies:** No.
Green fee: Under $20. **Credit cards:** V, MC.
Lodging on site: No. **Reduced fees:** Low Season, Twilight Play.
Unrestricted walking: Yes. **Range:** No.
Holes: 18. **Par:** 71/75. **Yards:** 5,905. **Slope:** Unrated.

★★★½ GIBSON BAY GOLF COURSE
Richmond—PU—606-623-0225 (30 mi. from Lexington).

Season: Year-round. **High:** April-Sept. **Caddies:** No.
Green fee: Under $20. **Credit cards:** V, MC.
Reduced fees: Weekdays, Low Season, Twilight Play.
Unrestricted walking: Yes. **Range:** No.
Holes: 18. **Par:** 72. **Yards:** 7,113-4,869. **Slope:** 128-115.
Comments: "New . . . Testing but fair . . . Excellent condition . . . Inexpensive . . . Four or five tee boxes on every hole . . . Too hilly."

THE GOLF COURSES AT KENTON COUNTY
Independence—PU—606-371-3200 (10 mi. from Cincinnati).
Season: April-Oct. **High:** May-Sept. **Caddies:** No.
Green fee: $20-$49. **Credit cards:** V, MC.
Lodging on site: No. **Reduced fees:** No.
Unrestricted walking: No. **Range:** Yes (grass).
★★★½ FOX RUN COURSE
Holes: 18. **Par:** 72. **Yards:** 7,055-4,707. **Slope:** 143-122.
Comments: "Super course . . . Interesting holes, fairly difficult, fun . . . Best new course in years."
THE PIONEER COURSE*
Season: Year-round. **Green fee:** Under $20.
Reduced fees: Weekdays. **Unrestricted walking:** Yes.
Holes: 18. **Par:** 70. **Yards:** 6,059-5,336. **Slope:** 114-108.
THE WILLOWS COURSE*
Season: March-Nov. **Green fee:** Under $20.

Reduced fees: Weekdays. **Unrestricted walking:** Yes.
Holes: 18. **Par:** 72. **Yards:** 6,791-5,669. **Slope:** 130-123.

★★JUNIPER HILLS GOLF COURSE
Frankfort—PU—502-875-8559.
Season: Year-round. **High:** March-Oct. **Caddies:** No.
Green fee: Under $20. **Credit cards:** V, MC.
Lodging on site: No. **Reduced fees:** No.
Unrestricted walking: Yes. **Range:** No.
Holes: 18. **Par:** 70. **Yards:** 6,147-5,904. **Slope:** 104-106.
Comments: "OK course . . . Tough to walk."

★★★½ KEARNEY HILL GOLF LINKS
Lexington—PU—606-253-1981.
Season: Year-round. **High:** May-Oct. **Caddies:** No.
Green fee: $20-$49. **Credit cards:** V, MC.
Lodging on site: No. **Reduced fees:** Twilight Play.
Unrestricted walking: Yes. **Range:** No.
Holes: 18. **Par:** 72. **Yards:** 6,984-5,341. **Slope:** 128-118.
Ranked 5th in Kentucky by GOLF DIGEST.
Comments: "Great challenge for public course . . . Tough greens . . . A real test . . . Bravo! . . . Best public course in Kentucky . . . Close in quality to Indiana's Otter Creek . . . Different links for Senior Tour stop . . . Very hospitable golf shop staff . . . Uneven greens."

★★½ KENTUCKY DAM VILLAGE
STATE RESORT GOLF COURSE
Gilbertsville—R—502-362-8658 (25 mi. from Paducah).
Season: Year-round. **High:** June-Aug. **Caddies:** No.
Green fee: Under $20. **Credit cards:** No.
Lodging on site: Yes. **Reduced fees:** Twilight Play.
Unrestricted walking: Yes. **Range:** No.
Holes: 18. **Par:** 72. **Yards:** 6,704-5,094. **Slope:** 135-124.
Comments: "Not bad for a state park . . . Too much play."

★★½ LINCOLN HOMESTEAD STATE PARK GOLF COURSE
Springfield—PU—606-336-7461 (50 mi. from Louisville).
Season: Year-round. **High:** April-Sept. **Caddies:** No.
Green fee: $20-$49. **Credit cards:** V, MC.
Lodging on site: No. **Reduced fees:** Weekdays.
Unrestricted walking: Yes. **Range:** No.
Holes: 18. **Par:** 71. **Yards:** 6,400-5,472. **Slope:** 119-118.
Comments: "Too short . . . Bring in the cows."

★★½ MARRIOTT'S GRIFFIN GATE RESORT GOLF CLUB
Lexington—R—606-254-4101.
Season: Year-round. **High:** April-Oct. **Caddies:** No.
Green fee: $20-$49. **Credit cards:** All Major.
Lodging on site: Yes. **Reduced fees:** Weekdays, Low Season, Twilight Play.
Unrestricted walking: No. **Range:** Yes (mats).
Holes: 18. **Par:** 72. **Yards:** 6,801-4,979. **Slope:** 132-119.
Comments: "Short, good greens . . . Many great water shots . . . Fancy, but something lacking . . . Too pricey for 18 postage stamp greens . . . Some holes are forced . . . Cramped . . . Plenty of sand . . . More clover than an Irish Pub . . . Management could be more congenial."

MY OLD KENTUCKY HOME STATE PARK GOLF COURSE*
Bardstown—PU—502-349-6542 (41 mi. from Louisville).
Season: Year-round. **High:** June-Sept. **Caddies:** No.
Green fee: Under $20. **Credit cards:** V, DISC, MC.
Lodging on site: No. **Reduced fees:** Twilight Play.
Unrestricted walking: Yes. **Range:** Yes (grass).
Holes: 18. **Par:** 70. **Yards:** 6,065-5,239. **Slope:** 119-118.

★★½ NEVEL MEADE GOLF COURSE
Prospect—PU—502-228-9522 (15 mi. from Louisville).
Season: Year-round. **High:** May-Sept. **Caddies:** No.
Green fee: Under $20. **Credit cards:** V, MC.
Lodging on site: No. **Reduced fees:** Weekdays.
Unrestricted walking: Yes. **Range:** Yes (grass).
Holes: 18. **Par:** 72. **Yards:** 6,903-5,500. **Slope:** 119-114.
Comments: "Scottish links . . . Still growing in . . . Great walking . . . Yardages poorly marked . . . Hard to judge distances . . . Ho-hum course."

★★★★QUAIL CHASE GOLF CLUB
SOUTH/WEST/EAST 9s
Louisville—PU—502-239-2110.
Season: Year-round. **High:** April-Sept. **Caddies:** No.
Green fee: Under $20. **Credit cards:** V, MC.
Lodging on site: No. **Reduced fees:** Weekdays, Twilight Play.
Unrestricted walking: Yes. **Range:** Yes (grass).
Holes: 27. **Par:** 36/36/36. **Yards:** 3,274/3,241/3,512.
Comments: "Twenty-seven holes of great value . . . Quality layouts . . . Best value in Louisville . . . Beautiful . . . First hole on East is one of the prettiest in Louisville . . . Fair, extremely well maintained . . . Rugged, use a cart . . . Several blind shots, but well marked . . . True public course. Unlike others in area, they're not trying to go private . . . They cram in too many rounds . . . 5-hour rounds common."

★★TATES CREEK GOLF COURSE
Lexington—PU—606-272-3428.
Season: Year-round. **High:** March-Sept. **Caddies:** No.
Green fee: Under $20. **Credit cards:** No.
Lodging on site: No. **Reduced fees:** Twilight Play.
Unrestricted walking: Yes. **Range:** No.
Holes: 18. **Par:** 72. **Yards:** 6,240-5,260. **Slope:** 120-117.
Comments: "Typical public course . . . Cheapest golf in the U.S."

BAYOU OAKS GOLF COURSES
New Orleans—PU—504-483-9396.
Season: Year-round. **High:** April-June. **Caddies:** No.
Green fee: Under $20. **Credit cards:** No.
Lodging on site: No. **Reduced fees:** Twilight Play.
Unrestricted walking: Yes. **Range:** No.
Four-course complex was previously known as City Park Golf Club.
★★★½ CHAMPIONSHIP COURSE
Holes: 18. **Par:** 72. **Yards:** 7,061-6,013. **Slope:** 116-118.
Comments: "Old-style design, being refurbished . . . Makes you play all the shots . . . Had been in poor shape, lots of money spent on improving it . . . Vast improvements . . . New irrigation is a big plus . . . Now well maintained . . . Enjoyable . . . Gets too crowded."
★½ LAKESIDE COURSE
Holes: 18. **Par:** 70. **Yards:** 6,054-5,872. **Slope:** 110-113.
Comments: "Not very exciting . . . Short and flat . . . Good beginner's course."
★ LITTLE COURSE
Holes: 18. **Par:** 68. **Yards:** 4,921. **Slope:** 106-112.
★★½ WISNER COURSE
Holes: 18. **Par:** 72. **Yards:** 6,465-5,707. **Slope:** 111-116.
Comments: "Most scenic of the four . . . Big oaks and cypress . . . Tight front 9 . . . Has hardest opening hole at City Park . . . Do your scoring on the back side . . . City Park bunkers in bad shape . . . Gets too much play."

★½ CHENNAULT PARK GOLF COURSE
Monroe—PU—318-329-2454 (100 mi. from Shreveport).
Season: Year-round. **High:** May-Sept. **Caddies:** No.
Green fee: Under $20. **Credit cards:** No.
Lodging on site: No. **Reduced fees:**
Unrestricted walking: Yes. **Range:** Yes (grass).
Holes: 18. **Par:** 72. **Yards:** 7,044-5,783. **Slope:** 118-109.
Comments: "Set in Louisiana's 'hardwood bottomland' . . . Water on eight holes . . . Usually soggy . . . Very big greens . . . Needs sand traps . . . Needs some fairway grass . . . Jets nearby disturb concentration."

★★ HUNTINGTON PARK GOLF COURSE
Shreveport—PU—318-673-7765.
Season: Year-round. **High:** April-Sept. **Caddies:** No.
Green fee: Under $20. **Credit cards:** V, MC.
Lodging on site: No. **Reduced fees:** Twilight Play.
Unrestricted walking: Yes. **Range:** Yes (grass).
Holes: 18. **Par:** 72. **Yards:** 7,294-6,171. **Slope:** Unrated.
Comments: "Good layout . . . Big putting greens . . . No. 10 is one of the hardest in the state . . . A shame it's a muny . . . City hasn't maintained in accordance with fees collected . . . Course needs work . . . Pro shop has nothing to sell."

★★★ MALLARD COVE GOLF COURSE
Lake Charles—PU—318-491-1204 (135 mi. from Baton Rouge).
Season: Year-round. **High:** March-Sept. **Caddies:** No.
Green fee: Under $20. **Credit cards:** No.
Lodging on site: No. **Reduced fees:** Twilight Play.
Unrestricted walking: Yes. **Range:** Yes (grass).
Holes: 18. **Par:** 72. **Yards:** 6,803-5,294. **Slope:** 125-117.
Comments: "New grass on fairways . . . Wide open for wild drivers . . . Much water in play . . . Tough greens . . . Have to have a short game . . . Good facility . . . Good pro shop . . . Extremely heavy play."

★★★½ OAK HARBOR GOLF CLUB
Slidell—PU—504-646-0110 (28 mi. from New Orleans).
Season: Year-round. **High:** May-Sept. **Caddies:** No.
Green fee: $20-$49. **Credit cards:** AMEX.

Lodging on site: No. **Reduced fees:** Weekdays, Twilight Play.
Unrestricted walking: No. **Range:** Yes (grass).
Holes: 18. **Par:** 72. **Yards:** 6,896–5,305. **Slope:** 132–Unrated.
Comments: "Tough links-style . . . Mounds, water, sand . . . Wind makes it long . . . On Lake Pontchartrain, always windy . . . Great weekday rates . . . Tuesday twofers . . . Too many pointless O.B. stakes . . . Pros are excellent, need a full-time clubhouse . . . Maybe money problems hold it back."

★★★★SANTA MARIA GOLF COURSE
Baton Rouge—PU—504-792-9667.
Season: Year-round. **High:** April–Oct. **Caddies:** No.
Green fee: $20–$49. **Credit cards:** V, MC.
Lodging on site: No. **Reduced fees:** Twilight Play.
Unrestricted walking: Yes. **Range:** Yes (grass).
Holes: 18. **Par:** 72. **Yards:** 7,051–5,758. **Slope:** 134–128.
Comments: "Great architecture . . . Classic design, rolling hills . . . Challenging holes . . . Hands down, the parish's best . . . Quality, inexpensive golf . . . Used to be private . . . Needs work on fairways and tees . . . Getting better with age . . . Condition of greens varies from good to fair . . . Greens too hard . . . Used to be very picturesque but now developing surrounding land. Not as good as two years ago. "

★★½ TORO HILLS LODGE GOLF COURSE
Florien—R—318-586-4661, 800-533-5031 (20 mi. from Leesville).
Season: Year-round. **High:** April–Sept. **Caddies:** No.
Green fee: $20–$49. **Credit cards:** V, AMEX, DISC, MC.
Lodging on site: Yes. **Reduced fees:** Weekdays.
Unrestricted walking: No. **Range:** Yes (grass).
Holes: 18. **Par:** 72. **Yards:** 6,550–6,300. **Slope:** 120–118.
Comments: "Tiny and very tight with small greens . . . Made for the short hitter . . . Course management, not length, is the order of the day . . . Leave the driver home . . . Very hilly . . . Lots of tree trouble . . . Several blind shots to greens . . . Extremely relaxing . . . Watch for gnats . . . Isolated location."

★★★AROOSTOCK VALLEY COUNTRY CLUB
Fort Fairfield—PU—207-476-8083.
Season: May-Oct. **High:** July-Aug. **Caddies:** No.
Green fee: $20-$49. **Credit cards:** No.
Reduced fees: Low Season, Resort Guests, Twilight Play.
Unrestricted walking: Yes. **Range:** Yes (grass).
Holes: 18. **Par:** 72. **Yards:** 6,304-5,977. **Slope:** 118-115.
Comments: "Tough, hilly . . . Unique, parts of course are in Canada . . .
Well maintained . . . Can't recommend it."

★★½ BANGOR MUNICIPAL GOLF COURSE
Bangor—PU—207-941-0232.
Season: April-Nov. **High:** June-Aug. **Caddies:** No.
Green fee: Under $20. **Credit cards:** No.
Lodging on site: No. **Reduced fees:** Weekdays.
Unrestricted walking: Yes. **Range:** Yes (grass).
Holes: 27. **Par:** 35/36/36. **Yards:** 3,171/3,174/3,215.
Comments: "Good solid municipal . . . 3 super 9s . . . Fun to play . . .
Usually in good shape . . . Easy walking . . . Wide open . . . Not very
difficult . . . Fairways, greens sometimes ragged."

★★BETHEL INN & COUNTRY CLUB
Bethel—R—207-824-6276, 800-654-0125 (70 mi. from Portland).
Season: May-Oct. **High:** June-Aug. **Caddies:** No.
Green fee: $20-$49. **Credit cards:** V, AMEX, DISC, MC.
Lodging on site: Yes. **Reduced fees:** Low Season, Twilight Play.
Unrestricted walking: Yes. **Range:** No.
Holes: 18. **Par:** 72. **Yards:** 6,663-5,280. **Slope:** 131-111.
Comments: "A blend of old and new . . . Ego-boosting course . . . Very
dry, lots of roll in midsummer . . . Fun place . . . New 9 in poor condition
. . . Good change of pace . . . Much improved . . . Can't beat price or the
food . . . Inn accommodations top shelf."

★★★KEBO VALLEY GOLF COURSE
Bar Harbor—PU—207-288-3000 (45 mi. from Bangor).
Season: April-Oct. **High:** July-Sept. **Caddies:** No.
Green fee: $20-$49. **Credit cards:** V, MC.
Lodging on site: No. **Reduced fees:** Low Season.
Unrestricted walking: Yes. **Range:** No.
Holes: 18. **Par:** 70. **Yards:** 6,112-5,440. **Slope:** 130-121.
Oldest course in Maine.
Comments: "Grand old course, many interesting holes . . . Quaint historic
ambiance . . . A classic . . . Maine-type links, in forest of pines . . . More
demanding than it appears . . . Beware the black flies of May."

MINGO SPRINGS GOLF COURSE*
Rangeley—PU—207-864-5021 (125 mi. from Portland).
Season: May-Nov. **High:** July-Sept. **Caddies:** No.
Green fee: $20-$49. **Credit cards:** No.
Lodging on site: No. **Reduced fees:** Low Season.
Unrestricted walking: Yes. **Range:** Yes (grass).
Holes: 18. **Par:** 70. **Yards:** 5,923-5,334. **Slope:** 109.

★★★PENOBSCOT VALLEY COUNTRY CLUB
Orono—PU—207-866-2423 (2 mi. from Bangor).
Season: April-Oct. **High:** June-Aug. **Caddies:** No.
Green fee: $20-$49. **Credit cards:** V, MC.
Lodging on site: No. **Reduced fees:** No.
Unrestricted walking: Yes. **Range:** Yes (grass).
Holes: 18. **Par:** 72. **Yards:** 6,445-5,856. **Slope:** 123-126.
Comments: "Very good Donald Ross course . . . Straightforward . . .
Tricky greens . . . Always in good shape."

MAINE

★★½ POLAND SPRING COUNTRY CLUB
Poland Spring—R—207-998-6002 (20 mi. from Portland).
Season: May-Nov. **High:** June-Aug. **Caddies:** No.
Green fee: Under $20. **Credit cards:** V, DISC, MC.
Lodging on site: Yes. **Reduced fees:** Resort Guests.
Unrestricted walking: Yes. **Range:** No.
Holes: 18. **Par:** 71. **Yards:** 6,196-5,854. **Slope:** 119-117.
Oldest 18-hole resort course in U.S.
Comments: "Neat old course . . . Not today's type . . . Tiny greens, no
trickery, wonderful views . . . Forecaddies . . . Good change of pace . . .
Maintenance problems . . . Needs modernization . . . Very good resort."

★★RIVERSIDE MUNICIPAL GOLF COURSE
Portland—PU—207-797-3524.
Season: April-Nov. **High:** July-Aug. **Caddies:** No.
Green fee: Under $20. **Credit cards:** No.
Lodging on site: No. **Reduced fees:** Weekdays.
Unrestricted walking: Yes. **Range:** No.
Holes: 18. **Par:** 72. **Yards:** 6,370-6,052. **Slope:** 115-112.
Additional 9 holes available.
Comments: "Wide open and short but fun to play . . . Comfortable . . .
Too busy . . . Poorly maintained . . . Floods . . . City needs to put some
income back into it."

★★★SABLE OAKS GOLF CLUB
South Portland—R—207-775-6257.
Season: April-Nov. **High:** July-Sept. **Caddies:** No.
Green fee: $20-$49. **Credit cards:** V, MC.
Lodging on site: Yes. **Reduced fees:** Weekdays, Low Season,
Twilight Play.
Unrestricted walking: Yes. **Range:** No.
Holes: 18. **Par:** 70. **Yards:** 6,359-4,786. **Slope:** 134-118.
Ranked 5th in Maine by GOLF DIGEST.
Comments: "Up-and-comer . . . Good test of your game . . . Very nar-
row, demands target golf . . . Many blind shots, extreme slopes on greens,
difficult for area players . . . Several holes ridiculous . . . Par 5s are poor . . .
Forced carries make it unplayable for short hitters . . . Too much distance
from greens to next tee . . . Played it once, never again."

★★★½ SAMOSET RESORT GOLF CLUB
Rockport—R—207-594-1431 (42 mi. from Augusta).
Season: April-Nov. **High:** June-Aug. **Caddies:** No.
Green fee: $20-$49. **Credit cards:** V, AMEX, DISC, MC.
Lodging on site: Yes. **Reduced fees:** Low Season, Resort Guests.
Unrestricted walking: No. **Range:** No.
Holes: 18. **Par:** 70. **Yards:** 6,417-5,360. **Slope:** 125-117.
Ranked 26th in America's 75 Best Resort Courses by GOLF DIGEST.
Comments: "Outstanding New England ocean course . . . The Pebble
Beach of Maine . . . Great layout, great resort . . . Scenery is terrific . . .
Extraordinarily distracting views . . . Expensive but beautiful . . . A close
second to Sugarloaf for Best in State . . . Water not much of a factor . . .
Top resort and personnel . . . Some disappointing holes."

★★★★SUGARLOAF GOLF CLUB
Carrabassett Valley—R—207-237-2000 (100 mi. from Portland).
Season: May-Oct. **High:** July-Sept. **Caddies:** Yes.
Green fee: $20-$49. **Credit cards:** V, AMEX, MC.
Lodging on site: Yes. **Reduced fees:** Weekdays, Low Season, Resort
Guests, Twilight Play.
Unrestricted walking: Yes. **Range:** Yes (grass).
Holes: 18. **Par:** 72. **Yards:** 7,000-6,200. **Slope:** 137-136.
Ranked 63rd in America's 75 Best Resort Courses and ranked 1st in Maine
by GOLF DIGEST.

GREAT VALUE

Comments: "Tremendous course with dramatic shots . . . A mountain masterpiece . . . Must be straight and long . . . Excellent views . . . Outstanding scenery . . . Best in Maine . . . Best in New England . . . Unparalleled beauty . . . Downhill holes excellent . . . 10 and 11 are truly magnificent in autumn . . . Very impressive . . . Very hard for beginners . . . Bring extra balls, fairways steal 'em . . . Must take carts and keep them on path . . . Need cart just to get to next tee . . . I saw a bear on No. 2 tee last year . . . Moose and deer wander through . . . Too far away."

VA JO WAH GOLF COURSE*

Island Falls—R—207-463-2128 (85 mi. from Bangor).
Season: May-Oct. **High:** July-Sept. **Caddies:** No.
Green fee: Under $20. **Credit cards:** V, DISC, MC.
Lodging on site: Yes. **Reduced fees:** Low Season, Resort Guests, Twilight Play.
Unrestricted walking: Yes. **Range:** Yes (grass).
Holes: 18. **Par:** 72. **Yards:** 6,303-5,065. **Slope:** 121-117.

★★½ VAL HALLA GOLF COURSE

Cumberland—PU—207-829-2225 (12 mi. from Portland).
Season: April-Oct. **High:** July-Aug. **Caddies:** No.
Green fee: $20-$49. **Credit cards:** V, MC.
Lodging on site: No. **Reduced fees:** Weekdays.
Unrestricted walking: Yes. **Range:** Yes (mats).
Holes: 18. **Par:** 72. **Yards:** 6,569-5,554. **Slope:** 126-114.
Comments: "Not bad . . . Par 4s very similar . . . Staff tries hard . . . Bring your bug spray."

★★★★WATERVILLE COUNTRY CLUB

Waterville—PU—207-465-9861.
Season: April-Nov. **High:** June-Aug. **Caddies:** No.
Green fee: $20-$49. **Credit cards:** No.
Lodging on site: No. **Reduced fees:** No.

Unrestricted walking: Yes. **Range:** Yes (grass).
Holes: 18. **Par:** 70. **Yards:** 6,412-5,781. **Slope:** 124-125.
Comments: "Outstanding . . . Nice older course, well kept . . . Accuracy needed. Bring all your skills . . . Tough, fun to play . . . Excellent clubhouse amenities."

★★½ THE BAY CLUB

Berlin—PU—410-641-4081, 800-229-2582 (7 mi. from Ocean City).
Season: Year-round. **High:** May-Sept. **Caddies:** No.
Green fee: $20-$49. **Credit cards:** V, MC.
Reduced fees: Weekdays, Low Season, Twilight Play.
Unrestricted walking: No. **Range:** Yes (grass).
Holes: 18. **Par:** 72. **Yards:** 6,956-5,609. **Slope:** 126-118.
Comments: "Truly uninspiring round of golf . . . Fairways hard, greens not consistent . . . Too much water . . . Too expensive."

★★½ CLUSTERED SPIRES GOLF COURSE

Frederick—PU—301-694-6249 (40 mi. from Baltimore).
Season: Year-round. **High:** March-Oct. **Caddies:** No.
Green fee: $20-$49. **Credit cards:** V, MC.
Lodging on site: No. **Reduced fees:** Weekdays, Twilight Play.
Unrestricted walking: Yes. **Range:** Yes (grass).
Holes: 18. **Par:** 72. **Yards:** 6,769-5,230. **Slope:** 115-124.
Comments: "Good muny . . . Fair layout . . . Good walk, quick rounds."

★★★★ EAGLE'S LANDING GOLF COURSE

Berlin—PU—410-213-7277, 800-283-3846 (120 mi. from Baltimore).
Season: Year-round. **High:** April-Oct. **Caddies:** No.
Green fee: $20-$49. **Credit cards:** V, AMEX, MC.
Lodging on site: No. **Reduced fees:** Low Season, Twilight Play.
Unrestricted walking: Yes. **Range:** No.
Holes: 18. **Par:** 72. **Yards:** 7,003-4,896. **Slope:** 126-115.
Ranked 4th in Maryland by GOLF DIGEST.
Comments: "Fine new course . . . Terrific . . . Interesting . . . Great experience . . . Some outstanding holes . . . Tough shots through marshes . . . Requires care, thought . . . Wildlife in every direction."

★★★ THE GOLF CLUB AT WISP

McHenry—R—301-387-4911 (40 mi. from Cumberland).
Season: April-Nov. **High:** June-Sept. **Caddies:** No.
Green fee: $20-$49. **Credit cards:** V, DISC, MC.
Lodging on site: Yes. **Reduced fees:** Low Season, Resort Guests, Twilight Play.
Unrestricted walking: No. **Range:** Yes (mats).
Holes: 18. **Par:** 72. **Yards:** 7,122-5,666. **Slope:** 137-128.
Comments: "Long and demanding . . . Adequate test for any player."

★★½ HARBOURTOWNE GOLF RESORT

St. Michaels—R—410-745-5183, 800-446-9066 (40 mi. from Annapolis).
Season: Year-round. **High:** March-Nov. **Caddies:** No.
Green fee: $20-$49. **Credit cards:** No.
Lodging on site: Yes. **Reduced fees:** Weekdays, Low Season, Resort Guests.
Unrestricted walking: No. **Range:** Yes (grass).
Holes: 18. **Par:** 70. **Yards:** 6,271-5,036. **Slope:** 120-113.
Comments: "Nine links holes, nine woods holes . . . Architecturally poor design . . . Only a few holes are good . . . Bland until last four."

★★★★ HOG NECK GOLF COURSE

Easton—PU—410-822-6079 (60 mi. from Baltimore).
Season: Feb.-Dec. **High:** April-Sept. **Caddies:** No.
Green fee: $20-$49. **Credit cards:** No.
Lodging on site: No. **Reduced fees:** Twilight Play.
Unrestricted walking: Yes. **Range:** Yes (mats).
Holes: 18. **Par:** 72. **Yards:** 7,090-5,464. **Slope:** 125-118.
Also has 9-hole executive course. Ranked in First 25 of America's 75 Best Public Courses by GOLF DIGEST.

Comments: "Outstanding challenge, lots of variety . . . Excellent for all skill levels . . . From back tees a real monster . . . Pack some extra sleeves . . . Can't find a much better course . . . Front 9 open, back 9 tight . . . Great back 9 . . . First class all the way . . . Well groomed all the time . . . Well marshaled . . . Friendly staff . . . Course is nice, price is right . . . Watch out for horseflies at dusk."

★★★½ MOUNT PLEASANT GOLF CLUB
Baltimore—PU—410-254-5100.
Season: Year-round. **High:** May-Sept. **Caddies:** No.
Green fee: Under $20. **Credit cards:** V, MC
Lodging on site: No. **Reduced fees:** Weekdays, Twilight Play.
Unrestricted walking: Yes. **Range:** No.
Holes: 18. **Par:** 71. **Yards:** 6,757-5,489. **Slope:** 121-120.
Comments: "Well-kept secret . . . Old PGA Tour course . . . Tall trees, rolling hills on edge of city . . . Not bad for a city-run course . . . No pullcarts on weekends, but can carry . . . Best $12 I ever spent."

★★½ NASSAWANGO COUNTRY CLUB
Snow Hill—PU—410-632-3144 (18 mi. from Salisbury).
Season: Year-round. **High:** May-Aug. **Caddies:** No.
Green fee: Under $20. **Credit cards:** No.
Lodging on site: No. **Reduced fees:** No.
Unrestricted walking: No. **Range:** No.
Holes: 18. **Par:** 72. **Yards:** 6,643-5,760. **Slope:** 125-121.
Comments: "Affordable . . . Pleasant to play . . . No pushover."

★★NEEDWOOD GOLF COURSE
Derwood—PU—301-948-1075 (20 mi. from Washington D.C.).
Season: Year-round. **High:** April-Sept. **Caddies:** No.
Green fee: Under $20. **Credit cards:** V, MC.
Lodging on site: No. **Reduced fees:** Weekdays, Low Season.
Unrestricted walking: Yes. **Range:** Yes (mats).
Holes: 18. **Par:** 70. **Yards:** 6,254-5,112. **Slope:** 113-105.
Also a 9-hole executive course.
Comments: "Too short. Unlike its name, you don't 'need a wood' . . . Pro staff are excellent instructors."

★★½ NORTHWEST PARK GOLF COURSE
Wheaton—PU—301-598-6100 (10 mi. from Washington D.C.).
Season: Year-round. **High:** March-Oct. **Caddies:** No.
Green fee: Under $20. **Credit cards:** V, MC.
Lodging on site: No. **Reduced fees:** Weekdays, Low Season.
Unrestricted walking: Yes. **Range:** Yes (mats).
Holes: 18. **Par:** 72. **Yards:** 7,185-6,325. **Slope:** 122-126.
Also has par-34 'Inside 9'.
Comments: "Long but forgiving . . . If private, would be a Top 100 course. . . . No. 2 is a 481-yard par 4! . . . Terrible conditioning lately."

OCEAN CITY GOLF & YACHT CLUB
Berlin—PU—410-641-1779, 800-442-3570 (120 mi. from Baltimore).
Season: Year-round. **High:** April-Sept. **Caddies:** No.
Green fee: $20-$49. **Credit cards:** V, MC.
Reduced fees: Weekdays, Low Season, Resort Guests, Twilight Play.
Unrestricted walking: No. **Range:** Yes (grass).
★★½ BAYSIDE COURSE
Holes: 18. **Par:** 72. **Yards:** 6,526-5,396. **Slope:** 121-119.
Comments: "Scenic, but some bad holes . . . Poor maintenance, even for public course . . . Slow play not regulated."
★★½ SEASIDE COURSE
Holes: 18. **Par:** 73. **Yards:** 6,520-5,848. **Slope:** 115-119.
Comments: "Well-developed, good course . . . Greens, rough too high."

★★★PINE RIDGE GOLF COURSE
Lutherville—PU—410-252-1408 (10 mi. from Baltimore).
Season: Year-round. **High:** April-Oct. **Caddies:** No.
Green fee: Under $20. **Credit cards:** No.
Lodging on site: No. **Reduced fees:** Weekdays, Twilight Play.
Unrestricted walking: Yes. **Range:** Yes (mats).
Holes: 18. **Par:** 72. **Yards:** 6,820-5,732. **Slope:** 122-120.
Comments: "Built around a large reservoir . . . Beautiful scenery . . . Deer and ducks . . . Excellent course on edge of watershed . . . Tall trees, well manicured . . . Cheap . . . A model for all public courses . . . Went downhill after LPGA left . . . Inconsistent greens . . . Plan on 6 hours."

QUEENSTOWN HARBOR GOLF LINKS
Queenstown—PU—410-827-6611, 800-827-5257 (45 mi. from Baltimore).
Season: Year-round. **High:** April-Oct. **Caddies:** No.
Green fee: $20-$49. **Credit cards:** V, MC.
Lodging on site: No. **Reduced fees:** Weekdays, Twilight Play.
Unrestricted walking: Yes. **Range:** Yes (mats).
★★★★RIVER COURSE
Holes: 18. **Par:** 72. **Yards:** 7,110-5,026. **Slope:** 138-123.
Ranked 6th in Maryland by GOLF DIGEST.
Comments: "Outstanding new course . . . Beautiful . . . Well laid out . . . . . . Wetlands make it difficult . . . Good shape . . . Friendly . . . Fine facility . . . Too hard for average golfers . . . Need to speed up play . . . Make you keep carts on paths . . . Avoid snack bar prices . . . Nice course if you're rich."
LAKES COURSE*
Holes: 18. **Par:** 72. **Yards:** 6,600-4,800. **Slope:** NA.
New 9 to complete full second 18; to open mid-1994.

★★★RIVER RUN GOLF CLUB
Berlin—R—410-641-7200, 800-733-7786 (30 mi. from Salisbury).
Season: Year-round. **High:** May-Sept. **Caddies:** Yes.
Green fee: $20-$49. **Credit cards:** V, AMEX, MC.
Lodging on site: Yes. **Reduced fees:** Weekdays, Low Season, Twilight Play.
Unrestricted walking: No. **Range:** Yes (grass).
Holes: 18. **Par:** 71. **Yards:** 6,705-5,002. **Slope:** 128-117.
Comments: "Young course, will be very good . . . Beautiful, each hole different . . . A few tight driving holes . . . Great switch in design from front to back . . . Best layout near Ocean City . . . Excellent conditioning . . . Good to look at, fun to play, but not for short hitters . . . Yardage seems overstated."

★★★★SWAN POINT YACHT & COUNTRY CLUB

Issue—PU—301-259-0047 (50 mi. from Washington D.C.).
Season: Year-round. **High:** May-Sept. **Caddies:** No.
Green fee: $20-$49. **Credit cards:** No.
Lodging on site: No. **Reduced fees:** No.
Unrestricted walking: No. **Range:** Yes (grass).
Holes: 18. **Par:** 72. **Yards:** 6,761-5,009. **Slope:** 126-116.
Comments: "First-class layout . . . Outstanding in every way . . . Very difficult from back tees . . . Very attractive . . . Like being in South Carolina . . . Could be used for PGA Tour event . . . No waiting! . . . New clubhouse is beautiful . . . No opportunity to stop at clubhouse at crossover."

TURF VALLEY HOTEL & COUNTRY CLUB*
Ellicott City—R—410-465-1504 (10 mi. from Baltimore).
Season: Year-round. **High:** April-Nov. **Caddies:** No.
Green fee: $50-$99. **Credit cards:** All Major.
Lodging on site: Yes. **Reduced fees:** Weekdays, Low Season, Resort Guests, Twilight Play.
Unrestricted walking: No. **Range:** No.

MARYLAND

EAST COURSE
Holes: 18. **Par:** 71. **Yards:** 6,592-5,564. **Slope:** 128-131.
Comments: "Club has something for everybody . . . Variety with 45 holes . . . Great greens."
SOUTH COURSE
Holes: 18. **Par:** 70. **Yards:** 6,323-5,572. **Slope:** 113-126.
NORTH COURSE
Holes: 9. **Par:** 35. **Yards:** 3,434/3,111.
Second 9 holes under construction; scheduled to open late summer '94.

BALLYMEADE COUNTRY CLUB*
N. Falmouth—PU—508-540-4005 (60 mi. from Boston).
Season: Year-round. **High:** May-Sept. **Caddies:** No.
Green fee: $50-$99. **Credit cards:** V, AMEX, MC.
Reduced fees: Weekdays, Low Season, Twilight Play.
Unrestricted walking: No. **Range:** Yes (grass).
Holes: 18. **Par:** 72. **Yards:** 6,928-4,722. **Slope:** 137-112.

★★½ BASS RIVER GOLF COURSE
South Yarmouth—PU—508-398-9079 (75 mi. from Boston).
Season: Year-round. **High:** May-Sept. **Caddies:** No.
Green fee: $20-$49. **Credit cards:** V, MC.
Reduced fees: Weekdays, Low Season, Twilight Play.
Unrestricted walking: Yes. **Range:** No.
Holes: 18. **Par:** 72. **Yards:** 6,129-5,343. **Slope:** 124-111.
Comments: "Pretty old course . . . Good basic public course . . . Very tough in wind, good all-around test . . . Best kept on the Cape . . . Best greens on the Cape . . . Playable . . . Nothing noteworthy except perhaps as Jim Hallet's baptismal course . . . Especially good for beginners . . . Front 9 par 34, back 9 par 38 . . . Many blind shots."

★★★ BAYBERRY HILLS GOLF COURSE
West Yarmouth—PU—508-394-5597 (75 mi. from Boston).
Season: March-Dec. **High:** May-Sept. **Caddies:** No.
Green fee: $20-$49. **Credit cards:** V, MC.
Reduced fees: Weekdays, Low Season, Twilight Play.
Unrestricted walking: Yes. **Range:** Yes (grass).
Holes: 18. **Par:** 72. **Yards:** 7,172-5,275. **Slope:** 132-111.
Comments: "Nice little-known layout . . . Interesting . . . Exciting golf . . . Excellent condition . . . Outstanding with best practice area on Cape Cod . . . Nice and reasonable . . . Long walk, but well worth it . . . Very courteous staff . . . Excellent pro shop . . . Restaurant below par . . . Every hole plays the same, slow."

★★½ BRADFORD COUNTRY CLUB
Bradford—PU—508-372-8587 (25 mi. from Boston).
Season: March-Dec. **High:** May-Sept. **Caddies:** No.
Green fee: $20-$49. **Credit cards:** V, AMEX, MC.
Lodging on site: No. **Reduced fees:** Weekdays, Low Season.
Unrestricted walking: Yes. **Range:** No.
Holes: 18. **Par:** 70. **Yards:** 6,511-4,939. **Slope:** 141-129.
Comments: "Difficult course, fine conditioning . . . Good, but not great . . . Many forced carries, several awkward holes . . . Very difficult 12th hole . . . Par-5 12th is great . . . Disjointed layout . . . Front 9 Dr. Jekyll, Back 9 Mr. Hyde . . . Front is strange . . . Back is tighter and tougher . . . Almost impossible to walk."

★★½ CAPE COD COUNTRY CLUB
Hatchville—PU—508-563-9842 (60 mi. from Boston).
Season: Year-round. **High:** June-Sept. **Caddies:** No.
Green fee: $20-$49. **Credit cards:** V, MC.
Lodging on site: No. **Reduced fees:** Weekdays, Twilight Play.
Unrestricted walking: Yes. **Range:** No.
Holes: 18. **Par:** 71. **Yards:** 6,404-5,423. **Slope:** 122-119.
Comments: "Old-fashioned delight . . . Nice course with average facilities . . . Charming, small greens . . . Hills, hills, hills . . . Enjoyable, several elevated greens . . . Fun place, but on a hot day, ride . . . Front 9 is interesting . . . Back 9 short . . . Boring . . . Course needs maintenance."

★★★½ CAPTAINS GOLF COURSE
Brewster—PU—508-896-5100 (80 mi. from Boston).
Season: April-Dec. **High:** May-Oct. **Caddies:** No.
Green fee: $20-$49. **Credit cards:** No.

Reduced fees: Weekdays, Low Season, Twilight Play.
Unrestricted walking: Yes. **Range:** Yes (grass).
Holes: 18. **Par:** 72. **Yards:** 6,794-5,388. **Slope:** 130-117.
Selected Best New Public Course of 1985 and ranked in First 25 of America's 75 Best Public Courses by GOLF DIGEST.
Comments: "Fabulous . . . Great holes, great layout . . . Fair for all . . . Great course to walk for all ages . . . Good combination of design and conditioning . . . Holes set up well visually . . . Superbly conditioned . . . Greatest in the fall . . . Tough to get tee time . . . Weird call-in rules . . . Price is rising as fast as its fame . . . Rude marshals . . . Too busy . . . Five-hour rounds hurt . . . Clearly a public course, wide fairways, big greens."

COLONIAL GOLF CLUB*
Wakefield—R—617-245-9300 (10 mi. from Boston).
Season: March-Dec. **High:** May-Oct. **Caddies:** No.
Green fee: $20-$49. **Credit cards:** All Major.
Lodging on site: Yes. **Reduced fees:** Weekdays, Low Season, Twilight Play.
Unrestricted walking: No. **Range:** Yes (mats).
Holes: 18. **Par:** 70. **Yards:** 6,565-5,280. **Slope:** 130-109.

★★★½ CRANBERRY VALLEY GOLF COURSE
Harwich—PU—508-430-7560 (90 mi. from Boston).
Season: March-Dec. **High:** June-Oct. **Caddies:** No.
Green fee: $20-$49. **Credit cards:** No.
Lodging on site: No. **Reduced fees:** No.
Unrestricted walking: Yes. **Range:** Yes (grass).
Holes: 18. **Par:** 72. **Yards:** 6,745-5,518. **Slope:** 129-115.
Comments: "The Cape's outstanding public course . . . Excellent variety . . . Short but tight . . . A modern pleasure . . . Through woods . . . Well run, well maintained . . . Always in super state . . . Large greens, wide fairways, friendly atmosphere . . . Greens are tricky . . . Excellent all around . . . Fun to play . . . Great price . . . Should be the part of any Cape vacation . . . Lobster at the 19th hole!"

★★★★ CRUMPIN-FOX CLUB
Bernardston—PU—413-648-9101 (35 mi. from Springfield).
Season: April-Nov. **High:** June-Sept. **Caddies:** Yes.
Green fee: $20-$49. **Credit cards:** V, AMEX, DISC, MC.
Lodging on site: No. **Reduced fees:** Dinner Guests.
Unrestricted walking: Yes. **Range:** Yes (grass).
Holes: 18. **Par:** 72. **Yards:** 7,007-5,432. **Slope:** 141-131.
Ranked 6th in Massachusetts by GOLF DIGEST.
Comments: "First class all the way . . . Played as a 9-holer for years . . . New 9 equally tough . . . Very, very nice . . . Presents all the challenges . . . Layout is fantastic, needs conditioning . . . Compares to most Carolina resort courses . . . Not too long but difficult . . . Second shots are key . . . As good as it gets . . . Hard to find . . . Best course in the boonies . . . May be the best course in Massachusetts . . . The best pro shop in New England . . . Get the golf and dinner package . . . Value package with dinner is great . . . Great atmosphere . . . Expensive, but good . . . Overpriced and they really don't care . . . Long drive to hotels."

★★½ DENNIS HIGHLANDS GOLF COURSE
S. Dennis—PU—508-385-8347 (75 mi. from Boston).
Season: March-Nov. **High:** July-Sept. **Caddies:** No.
Green fee: $20-$49. **Credit cards:** V, MC.
Lodging on site: No. **Reduced fees:** Low Season, Twilight Play.
Unrestricted walking: Yes. **Range:** Yes (grass).
Holes: 18. **Par:** 71. **Yards:** 6,464-4,927. **Slope:** 118-112.
Comments: "Enjoyable New England course . . . Imaginative . . . Open fairways, tough greens . . . Bring your accurate tee ball . . . Playable . . . Great design, greens need work . . . Long par 3s . . . Nice course, nice

people, busy . . . Good layout, some tight holes . . . Front 9 tough to walk
. . . Very hilly . . . For my way of thinking, no character."

★★★DENNIS PINES GOLF COURSE
S. Dennis—PU—508-385-8347 (75 mi. from Boston).
Season: Year-round. **High:** July-Sept. **Caddies:** No.
Green fee: $20-$49. **Credit cards:** V, MC.
Lodging on site: No. **Reduced fees:** Low Season, Twilight Play.
Unrestricted walking: Yes. **Range:** Yes (mats).
Holes: 18. **Par:** 72. **Yards:** 7,029-5,798. **Slope:** 127-128.
Comments: "A modern pleasure . . . Surprisingly sporty . . . Good test
. . . Tight, requires more thinking . . . Sidehill lies . . . Best course in town
. . . Starters and food service staff excellent . . . Well run, good value . . .
Out of modern time's step . . . Many monotonous, dull holes . . . Could
have better maintenance . . . Better than Dennis Highlands but still ho-hum
. . . Cape Cod has better courses."

★★★★FARM NECK GOLF CLUB
Oak Bluffs—PU—508-693-3057 (80 mi. from Boston).
Season: April-Nov. **High:** June-Sept. **Caddies:** No.
Green fee: $50-$99. **Credit cards:** No.
Lodging on site: No. **Reduced fees:** Low Season.
Unrestricted walking: Yes. **Range:** Yes (grass).
Holes: 18. **Par:** 72. **Yards:** 6,709-6,094. **Slope:** 130-126.
Course located on Martha's Vineyard.
Comments: "Fabulous island course . . . Magnificent . . . One gorgeous
layout . . . On the water . . . Prettiest course in New England . . . Velvet
fairways . . Wonderfully challenging . . . Views of ocean, saltwater ponds,
marshes and birds . . . Like golfing in a wildlife sanctuary . . . Treatment
outstanding . . . Tranquil, unhurried feeling . . . Drinking water on every
other hole . . . Great off-season values."

GEORGE WRIGHT GOLF COURSE*
Hyde Park—PU—617-361-8313 (6 mi. from Boston).
Season: Year-round. **High:** April-Oct. **Caddies:** No.
Green fee: $20-$49. **Credit cards:** V, MC.
Lodging on site: No. **Reduced fees:** Weekdays.
Unrestricted walking: Yes. **Range:** No.
Holes: 18. **Par:** 70. **Yards:** 6,400-5,039. **Slope:** 126-115.

★★½ HYANNIS GOLF CLUB AT IYANOUGH HILLS
Hyannis—PU—508-362-2606 (60 mi. from Boston).
Season: Year-round. **High:** May-Oct. **Caddies:** No.
Green fee: $20-$49. **Credit cards:** All Major.
Reduced fees: Weekdays, Low Season, Resort Guests, Twilight Play.
Unrestricted walking: Yes. **Range:** Yes (mats).
Holes: 18. **Par:** 71. **Yards:** 6,514-5,149. **Slope:** 121-Unrated.
Comments: "Great views . . . Great greens . . . Not one flat lie . . . Some
strange kicks . . . Busy course, good for functions."

★★★MAPLEGATE COUNTRY CLUB
Bellingham—PU—508-528-6000 (30 mi. from Boston).
Season: April-Dec. **High:** May-Sept. **Caddies:** No.
Green fee: $20-$49. **Credit cards:** V, MC.
Lodging on site: No. **Reduced fees:** Twilight Play.
Unrestricted walking: No. **Range:** Yes (grass).
Holes: 18. **Par:** 72. **Yards:** 6,815-4,852. **Slope:** 133-124.
Comments: "Excellent course in second year of play . . . Great new layout
. . . An up-and-comer . . . Long walking course . . . Very tight, difficult
from back tees . . . Greens have a lot of contour . . . Varied terrain . . . Due
to recent opening, course not yet marked well."

★★★NEW ENGLAND COUNTRY CLUB
Bellingham—PU—508-883-2300 (20 mi. from Boston).

Season: April-Dec. **High:** Summer. **Caddies:** No.
Green fee: $20-$49. **Credit cards:** V, MC.
Lodging on site: No. **Reduced fees:** Twilight Play.
Unrestricted walking: No. **Range:** Yes (grass).
Holes: 18. **Par:** 71. **Yards:** 6,378-5,648. **Slope:** 129-125.
Comments: "Sweet course . . . Great secret, very accessible . . . Very demanding . . . Narrow and tough . . . Must be straight hitter . . . Positioning shots is a must . . . Some tough carries over swamps . . . Blue tees for scratch players only . . . No amenities . . . Mandatory carts . . . Paths only . . . Overpriced . . . Way too penal."

NEW SEABURY RESORT & CONFERENCE CENTER
New Seabury—R—508-477-9110 (78 mi. from Boston).
Season: Year-round. **High:** June-Aug. **Caddies:** No.
Green fee: $50-$99. **Credit cards:** V, AMEX, MC.
Lodging on site: Yes. **Reduced fees:** Low Season, Twilight Play.
Unrestricted walking: No. **Range:** Yes (grass).
★★★★BLUE COURSE
Holes: 18. **Par:** 72. **Yards:** 6,909-5,105. **Slope:** 130-106.
Ranked 69th in America's 75 Best Resort Courses by GOLF DIGEST.
Comments: "Still the best on Cape Cod . . . Fantastic . . . Delightful . . . A good challenge . . . Like two different courses . . . Each 9 has different character . . . Great front 9 . . . Windswept, seaside . . . Gorgeous . . . Windward holes very difficult . . . Relentless winds . . . Back side in thick trees . . . Bring your 1-iron . . . Easier par 3s would make it better . . . Hassle to get on . . . Unfair to average golfers."
★★★GREEN COURSE
Holes: 18. **Par:** 70. **Yards:** 5,930-5,105. **Slope:** 110-106.
Comments: "Good short layout . . . Easy, fun . . . Superb walking course . . . Better than just a 'second course' . . . Not good drainage."

★★★OCEAN EDGE GOLF CLUB
Brewster—R—508-896-5911 (90 mi. from Boston).
Season: Year-round. **High:** Summer. **Caddies:** No.
Green fee: $50-$99. **Credit cards:** V, AMEX, MC.
Lodging on site: Yes. **Reduced fees:** Weekdays, Low season.
Unrestricted walking: No. **Range:** Yes (grass).
Holes: 18. **Par:** 72. **Yards:** 6,665-5,098. **Slope:** 129-129.
Comments: "Nice course . . . Best test for your game on Cape Cod . . . Short but challenging . . . Position is everything . . . Water everywhere . . . You'll know if you can play after you play this course . . . Uniquely interesting . . . Easy availability, nice people . . . Great service . . . Great place to stay . . . Course with a lot of class . . . Needs upgrading . . . Won't let you walk . . . Overpriced condo-golf . . . Overbooked, several curious and difficult holes . . . Expensive . . . Slow play a problem . . . Tricked up . . . Poor condition . . . Cross-country hikes between holes."

★★★OLDE BARNSTABLE FAIRGROUNDS GOLF COURSE
Marston Mills—PU—508-420-1141 (5 mi. from Hyannis).
Season: Year-round. **High:** May-Oct. **Caddies:** No.
Green fee: $20-$49. **Credit cards:** No.
Lodging on site: No. **Reduced fees:** Weekdays.
Unrestricted walking: Yes. **Range:** Yes (mats).
Holes: 18. **Par:** 71. **Yards:** 6,503-5,162. **Slope:** 123-118.
Comments: "Very enjoyable, becoming popular . . . Good facilities, pro shop and range . . . Needs to grow in."

★★½ QUASHNET VALLEY COUNTRY CLUB
Mashpee—PU—508-477-4412 (55 mi. from Boston).
Season: Year-round. **High:** May-Oct. **Caddies:** No.
Green fee: $20-$49. **Credit cards:** V, MC.
Reduced fees: Weekdays, Low Season, Twilight Play.
Unrestricted walking: No. **Range:** Yes (mats).
Holes: 18. **Par:** 72. **Yards:** 6,602-5,108. **Slope:** 132-119.

Comments: "Fun place . . . Every hole different . . . Around cranberry bogs . . . Accuracy very important . . . On the tough side . . . Back 9 easier . . . Not a friendly place . . . Some holes lack personality . . . A dog patch."

★★ROUND HILL COUNTRY CLUB
East Sandwich—PU—508-888-3384 (60 mi. from Boston).
Season: Year-round. **High:** June-Sept. **Caddies:** No.
Green fee: $20-$49. **Credit cards:** V, MC.
Reduced fees: Weekdays, Low Season, Twilight Play.
Unrestricted walking: No. **Range:** Yes (grass).
Holes: 18. **Par:** 71. **Yards:** 6,157-4,842. **Slope:** 124-115.
Comments: "Nice facility . . . Was mountain goat course, new hole designs will help in future . . . Tough, swirling winds . . . All the shots . . . Front 9 OK, back 9 an endurance test . . . Designer should have stuck to road construction."

★★★½ SHAKER HILLS GOLF CLUB
Harvard—PU—508-772-2227 (35 mi. from Boston).
Season: April-Nov. **High:** June-Aug. **Caddies:** No.
Green fee: $20-$49. **Credit cards:** V, MC.
Lodging on site: No. **Reduced fees:** Weekdays, Twilight Play.
Unrestricted walking: No. **Range:** Yes (grass).
Holes: 18. **Par:** 71. **Yards:** 6,850-5,001. **Slope:** 135-116.
Ranked 4th in Massachusetts by GOLF DIGEST.
Comments: "Wonderful track . . . Challenging . . . Outstanding layout . . . Tall pines . . . Solid course, difficult par 5s . . . Very good public facility . . . Best in Boston area . . . A public country club . . . Best value in the area . . . Nicest staff . . . Rough conditions . . . Had problems with greens . . . Green fee a bit expensive . . . Play is too slow, active rangers needed."

★★★SHERATON TARA HOTEL & RESORT
TARA FERNCROFT COUNTRY CLUB
Danvers—R—508-777-5614 (20 mi. from Boston).
Season: April-Dec. **High:** Summer. **Caddies:** No.
Green fee: $50-$99. **Credit cards:** V, MC, AMEX, DISC.
Lodging on site: Yes. **Reduced fees:** No.
Unrestricted walking: No. **Range:** Yes (grass).
Holes: 18. **Par:** 72. **Yards:** 6,536-5,488. **Slope:** 133-118.
Has additional 9-hole par-3 course.
Comments: "Beautiful layout, plenty of sand and water . . . Front 9 flat, watery. Back 9 wooded, hilly . . . Underrated . . . Price very high, but enjoyable round can be found . . . Always an outing . . . Open to members and hotel guests only . . . Too many hidden water hazards."

STERLING COUNTRY CLUB*
Sterling—PU—508-422-3335 (12 mi. from Worcester).
Season: April-Nov. **High:** May-Sept. **Caddies:** No.
Green fee: $20-$49. **Credit cards:** V, AMEX, MC.
Reduced fees: Weekdays, Low Season, Twilight Play.
Unrestricted walking: No. **Range:** Yes (grass).
Holes: 18. **Par:** 71. **Yards:** 6,640-4,768. **Slope:** 136-115.

STOW ACRES COUNTRY CLUB
Stow—PU—508-568-8690 (25 mi. from Boston).
Season: March-Dec. **High:** April-Nov. **Caddies:** No.
Green fee: $20-$49. **Credit cards:** No.
Lodging on site: No. **Reduced fees:** Weekdays, Twilight Play.
Unrestricted walking: Yes. **Range:** Yes (mats).
★★★NORTH COURSE
Holes: 18. **Par:** 72. **Yards:** 6,909-6,011. **Slope:** 130-120.
Site of 1995 USGA Public Links Championship.
Comments: "Excellent competitive course . . . Long, 18 solid holes . . . Strategically it is tops . . . Each hole different, all clubs needed . . . Large greens . . . No gimmes here . . . Beautiful course to walk . . . Nice day in

the country . . . 9th hole is challenging . . . Holes tend to resemble each other . . . Should enforce dress code . . . Too many high handicappers playing a difficult course."

★★½ SOUTH COURSE

Holes: 18. **Par:** 72. **Yards:** 6,520-5,642. **Slope:** 120-116.

Comments: "Not quite as good as North . . . Easier than North . . . Prettier of the two . . . Generic front, back has plenty of character . . . A lot of different types of holes . . . Very enjoyable for mid-to-high handicaps . . . Slow players are given their money back, asked to leave . . . Neither course deserves previous high ranking . . . Poor condition because of overplay . . . Mountain goat back 9."

★★★ TACONIC GOLF CLUB

Williamstown—PU—413-458-3997 (35 mi. from Albany, N.Y.).
Season: April-Oct. **High:** April-Oct. **Caddies:** Yes.
Green fee: $50-$99. **Credit cards:** V, MC.
Lodging on site: No. **Reduced fees:** No.
Unrestricted walking: Yes. **Range:** Yes (grass).
Holes: 18. **Par:** 71. **Yards:** 6,614-5,202. **Slope:** 128-111.
Located on Williams College campus. Site of 1996 U.S. Senior Amateur.
Comments: "Classic New England mountain golf . . . As testing as it is beautiful."

★★★ TRULL BROOK GOLF COURSE

N. Tewksbury—PU—508-851-6731 (25 mi. from Boston).
Season: March-Nov. **High:** May-Sept. **Caddies:** No.
Green fee: $20-$49. **Credit cards:** V, MC.
Lodging on site: No. **Reduced fees:** Weekdays, Twilight Play.
Unrestricted walking: Yes. **Range:** No.
Holes: 18. **Par:** 72. **Yards:** 6,330-5,682. **Slope:** 115-118.
Comments: "Pretty, well kept, fun . . . Short, hilly, tough to walk . . . Typical New England . . . Well run and picturesque . . . Always in super state . . . Gets better with age . . . Very tough front 9 . . . Hard to get weekend tee times . . . Extremely heavy play, but stands up well."

★★½ A-GA-MING GOLF CLUB
Kewadin—R—616-264-5081, 800-678-0122 (22 mi. from Traverse City).
Season: April-Oct. **High:** July-Aug. **Caddies:** No.
Green fee: $20-$49. **Credit cards:** V, AMEX, DISC, MC.
Lodging on site: Yes. **Reduced fees:** Low Season, Twilight Play.
Unrestricted walking: No. **Range:** Yes (grass).
Holes: 18. **Par:** 72. **Yards:** 6,663-5,125. **Slope:** 129-118.
Comments: "Picturesque, fair course . . . Very scenic, very hilly . . .
Breathtaking vistas, breakneck speed putts . . . A relief from pricey resort
courses . . . Quirky, 10th hole absurd . . . No. 16 is a poor golf hole . . .
Too many blind shots . . . Should turn it back into a cherry orchard."

★★★ ANTRIM DELLS GOLF CLUB
Ellsworth—PU—616-599-2679, 800-872-8561 (40 mi. from Traverse City).
Season: April-Oct. **High:** July-Aug. **Caddies:** No.
Green fee: $20-$49. **Credit cards:** V, MC.
Lodging on site: No. **Reduced fees:** Low Season, Twilight Play.
Unrestricted walking: No. **Range:** Yes (grass).
Holes: 18. **Par:** 72. **Yards:** 6,606-5,493. **Slope:** 125-121.
Comments: "Nine wooded, 9 open . . . Ordinary, unexciting . . . Must be
straight hitter, unescapable woods . . . Reasonably priced, good value."

★★½ BAY VALLEY GOLF CLUB
Bay City—R—517-686-5400, 800-292-5028 (100 mi. from Detroit).
Season: April-Oct. **High:** July-Sept. **Caddies:** No.
Green fee: $20-$49. **Credit cards:** V, AMEX, DISC, MC.
Lodging on site: Yes. **Reduced fees:** Weekdays, Low Season,
Resort Guests.
Unrestricted walking: No. **Range:** Yes (grass).
Holes: 18. **Par:** 71. **Yards:** 6,610-5,151. **Slope:** 125-114.
Comments: "Good layout not taken care of . . . Take lots of balls, 13 water
holes . . . Back 9 has challenging stretch of 11th to 15th."

BOYNE HIGHLANDS RESORT
Harbor Springs—R—616-526-2171, 800-462-6963 (8 mi. from Petoskey).
Season: April-Nov. **High:** June-Aug. **Caddies:** No.
Green fee: $50-$99. **Credit cards:** All Major.
Lodging on site: Yes. **Reduced fees:** Weekdays, Low Season, Resort
Guests, Twilight Play.
Unrestricted walking: No. **Range:** Yes (grass).

★★★½ DONALD ROSS MEMORIAL COURSE
Holes: 18. **Par:** 72. **Yards:** 6,840-4,977. **Slope:** 131-117.
Course consists of reproductions, 17 Donald Ross-designed holes, plus one
from Scotland's Royal Dornoch, birthplace of Ross. Ranked 32nd in America's 75 Best Resort Courses by GOLF DIGEST.
Comments: "Clever idea, interesting if you've played Ross courses . . .
Great to play holes Ross had designed . . . Fantastic, every hole is famous
. . . Not to be missed . . . Like playing a museum . . . Matured into an
outstanding course . . . Very good test . . . Nice course, too expensive . . .
This may be sacrilegious, but I found it boring and below average."

★★★★ HEATHER COURSE
Holes: 18. **Par:** 72. **Yards:** 7,210-5,263. **Slope:** 131-111.
Ranked 74th in America's 75 Best Resort Courses by GOLF DIGEST.
Comments: "A classic . . . Great Trent Jones layout . . . Hard par, easy
bogey . . . Great stuff! A true pleasure . . . For the golf purist . . . Traps add
beauty . . . No gimmes . . . Good course but pricey . . . Nice atmosphere
. . . Still the best at Boyne."

★★★ MOOR COURSE
Holes: 18. **Par:** 72. **Yards:** 7,179-5,459. **Slope:** 131-118.
Comments: "Short, interesting test . . . Good shotmaking a must . . . No
variety on back 9, five par 4s of the same length."

BOYNE MOUNTAIN RESORT

Boyne Falls—R—616-549-2441, 800-462-6963 (18 mi. from Petoskey).
Season: April-Nov. **High:** June-Aug. **Caddies:** No.
Green fee: $50-$99. **Credit cards:** All Major.
Lodging on site: Yes. **Reduced fees:** Weekdays, Low Season, Resort Guests, Twilight Play.
Unrestricted walking: No. **Range:** Yes (grass).

★★★½ ALPINE COURSE

Holes: 18. **Par:** 72. **Yards:** 7,017-4,986. **Slope:** 129-114.
First tee is over a mile cart ride from clubhouse, atop Boyne Mountain. Course plays down the mountain from there.
Comments: "Beautiful . . . Spectacular scenery . . . Panoramic, enjoyable . . . Picturesque . . . Nice condition . . . Most fun course I have played . . . Fun playing down a mountain . . . As much fun as the Donald Ross Course, underrated . . . Boyne's owner Everett Kircher never did a second-rate thing in his life."

★★★ MONUMENT COURSE

Holes: 18. **Par:** 72. **Yards:** 7,086-4,904. **Slope:** 139-122.
Routed down a mountain, in a fashion similar to Alpine Course.
Comments: "Impressive . . . Scenic, challenging . . . Flashy . . . Toughest 1st hole in golf . . . Best 1st hole in the state . . . Almost too tough . . . A few mundane holes . . . Disappointing . . . Living off its ski resort reputation."

★★ CATTAILS GOLF CLUB

South Lyon—PU—313-486-8777 (25 mi. from Detroit).
Season: March-Nov. **High:** May-Sept. **Caddies:** No.
Green fee: $20-$49. **Credit cards:** V, MC.
Reduced fees: Weekdays, Low Season, Twilight Play.
Unrestricted walking: No. **Range:** Yes (grass).
Holes: 18. **Par:** 72. **Yards:** 6,418-4,987. **Slope:** 132-117.
Comments: "Requires too many placement shots . . . Brings long and short hitters together . . . Hard layout to manage game . . . Too difficult for average golfers . . . 10th is silliest hole in Michigan . . . No. 10 is a great hole . . . Ground doesn't drain . . . No locker facilities."

★★½ CRYSTAL MOUNTAIN RESORT
MOUNTAIN MEADOWS/MOUNTAIN RIDGE/
MOUNTAIN CREEK 9s

Thompsonville—R—616-378-2000 (30 mi. from Traverse City).
Season: April-Oct. **High:** June-Sept. **Caddies:** No.
Green fee: $20-$49. **Credit cards:** V, AMEX, DISC, MC.
Lodging on site: Yes. **Reduced fees:** Low Season, Resort Guests, Twilight Play.
Unrestricted walking: Yes. **Range:** Yes (grass).
Holes: 27. **Par:** 36/36/35. **Yards:** 3,301/3,451/3,019.
Comments: "Tight, small greens, blind tee shots, too tough for amateurs . . . Not crowded . . . Only blue tees challenging . . . Design didn't work."

★★★½ ELK RIDGE GOLF COURSE

Atlanta—PU—517-785-2275, 800-626-4355 (35 mi. from Gaylord).
Season: May-Oct. **High:** June-Aug. **Caddies:** No.
Green fee: $50-$99. **Credit cards:** V, DISC, MC.
Reduced fees: Weekdays, Low Season, Twilight Play.
Unrestricted walking: No. **Range:** Yes (grass).
Holes: 18. **Par:** 72. **Yards:** 7,058-5,261. **Slope:** 144-135.
Selected runner-up for Best New Public Course of 1991 and ranked 15th in Michigan by GOLF DIGEST.
Comments: "Got to play it to believe it . . . Fair course at fair price . . . Fabulous, breathtaking surroundings . . . Worth the money for the views . . . Wonderful course but no accommodations nearby . . . Great property but too many double doglegs . . . A better player's course . . . Target golf . . . Some holes impossible to reach . . . Many forced carries, hard for short

hitters . . . Carts must stay on paths . . . Elk and other wildlife everywhere
. . . A pig bunker on No. 10."

★★★THE FORTRESS
Frankenmuth—R—517-652-9229 (12 mi. from Saginaw).
Season: April-Nov. **High:** June-Sept. **Caddies:** No.
Green fee: $50-$99. **Credit cards:** All Major.
Reduced fees: Weekdays, Low Season, Resort Guests, Twilight Play.
Unrestricted walking: No. **Range:** Yes (grass).
Holes: 18. **Par:** 72. **Yards:** 6,813-4,837. **Slope:** 132-121.
Comments: "Great rework into 18 holes . . . Hard to believe it's only one
year old . . . Too squeezed in . . . Holes too close together . . . Some cart
paths handle two-way traffic . . . Rough too difficult . . . Run very well, but
not worth what they charge . . . Most helpful and courteous staff."

FOX HILLS COUNTRY CLUB
Plymouth—PU—313-453-7272.
Season: April-Oct. **High:** May-Sept. **Caddies:** No.
Green fee: $20-$49. **Credit cards:** All Major.
Reduced fees: Weekdays, Low Season, Twilight Play.
Unrestricted walking: Yes. **Range:** Yes (grass).
THE HILLS/THE WOODLANDS/THE LAKES 9s*
Holes: 27. **Par:** 35/35/36. **Yards:** 3,334/3,064/3,450.
★★½THE GOLDEN FOX COURSE
Unrestricted walking: No.
Holes: 18. **Par:** 72. **Yards:** 6,783-5,040. **Slope:** 136-122.
Comments: "Aptly named . . . Challenging yet playable . . . All day rates
make for a good value . . . Difficult to hold greens . . . Some little landing
areas."

★★★FOX RUN COUNTRY CLUB
Grayling—PU—517-384-4343 (3 mi. from Grayling).
Season: April-Oct. **High:** June-Aug. **Caddies:** No.
Green fee: $20-$49. **Credit cards:** V, MC.
Lodging on site: No. **Reduced fees:** Twilight Play.
Unrestricted walking: No. **Range:** Yes (grass).
Holes: 18. **Par:** 72. **Yards:** 6,207-4,809. **Slope:** 126-117.
Comments: "Lush, wooded, reasonable . . . Best conditioned public course
I've seen . . . Well designed, not overpriced . . . Friendly staff . . . Rock hard
greens, crowded, impossible to play . . . Close to boring."

GARLAND GOLF RESORT
Lewiston—R—517-786-2211, 800-968-0042 (30 mi. from Gaylord).
Season: April-Oct. **High:** June-Aug. **Caddies:** No.
Green fee: $50-$99. **Credit cards:** V, AMEX, DISC, MC.
Lodging on site: Yes. **Reduced fees:** Weekdays, Low Season, Resort
Guests, Twilight Play.
Unrestricted walking: No. **Range:** Yes (grass).
★★★½ MONARCH COURSE
Holes: 18. **Par:** 72. **Yards:** 7,145-4,860. **Slope:** 140-123.
Comments: "Beautifully done . . . Well-groomed fairways . . . Rewards
good shotmaking . . . Nice people . . . Pricey, no rainchecks . . . Spectacu-
lar clubhouse disguises vastly overrated tracks."
★★★½ REFLECTIONS COURSE
Holes: 18. **Par:** 72. **Yards:** 6,434-4,778. **Slope:** 120-110.
Comments: "Excellent mix of golf and scenery . . . Narrow fairways . . .
Interesting water holes . . . Six par 5s, six par 4s, six par 3s . . . Like a
wildlife sanctuary. A deer ran by the 18th, an eagle watched us putt on 11
. . . Trick course design, they think having trees blocking greens is cute and
challenging . . . Garland's a nice complex with nice courses. They just pack
too many in at one time. Frustrating."
★★★½ SWAMPFIRE COURSE
Holes: 18. **Par:** 72. **Yards:** 6,854-4,791. **Slope:** 138-121.

Comments: "Flat, wet, tough, beautiful . . . All I remember is water! . . . Too many water hazards . . . Course has little contour . . . Too many blind shots and gimmicky holes . . . Water in play on the first 10 holes . . . Toughest of the three . . . Too ordinary for this price . . . How many more can they build?"

★★★GRAND HAVEN GOLF CLUB
Grand Haven—PU—616-842-4040.
Season: April-Oct. **High:** June-Aug. **Caddies:** No.
Green fee: $20-$49. **Credit cards:** V, MC.
Lodging on site: No. **Reduced fees:** Low Season, Twilight Play.
Unrestricted walking: Yes. **Range:** Yes (grass).
Holes: 18. **Par:** 72. **Yards:** 6,789-5,536. **Slope:** 124-119.
Ranked in Third 25 of America's 75 Best Public Courses by GOLF DIGEST.
Comments: "Scenic. Price is right . . . Short but requires precision . . . Nice surprise, similar to North Carolina . . . One tight hole after another . . . You need tunnel vision to play this course . . . Always a joy to play, even from the trees. . . Scenic dunes. Balls findable."

GRAND TRAVERSE RESORT
Grand Traverse Village—R—616-938-1620, 800-748-0303
(5 mi. from Traverse City).
Season: April-Oct. **High:** June-Aug. **Caddies:** No.
Green fee: $50-$99. **Credit cards:** All Major.
Lodging on site: Yes. **Reduced fees:** Weekdays, Low Season, Resort Guests, Twilight Play.
Unrestricted walking: No. **Range:** Yes (grass).
★★★½ THE BEAR COURSE
Holes: 18. **Par:** 72. **Yards:** 7,065-5,281. **Slope:** 149-138.
Ranked 50th in America's 75 Best Resort Courses by GOLF DIGEST.
Comments: "Very difficult Nicklaus links . . . A monster, not a bear! . . . Too tough for average golfer . . . Toughest in the midwest . . . Beautifully maintained . . . Too hard, not fun . . . Unreasonable shots required . . . All hype . . . Root canals are more fun . . . Even Senior Tour played the whites . . . From the correct tees, not as tough as people say . . . Deserves all the accolades, but not the price . . . Not real pretty, a real lot of money . . . Extremely overpriced for any area. Lots of better choices nearby."
★★★SPRUCE RUN COURSE
Holes: 18. **Par:** 72. **Yards:** 6,741-5,139. **Slope:** 125-116.
Comments: "Accommodates most skill levels . . . Plush, too easy . . . Very fair, narrow only at greens or driving area, but not both . . . Better value than The Bear for mid-handicappers . . . Well maintained, more enjoyable than The Bear . . . A first class resort."

★★★½ GREYSTONE GOLF CLUB
Romeo—PU—313-752-7030 (30 mi. from Detroit).
Season: April-Nov. **High:** May-Oct. **Caddies:** No.
Green fee: $20-$49. **Credit cards:** V, AMEX, DISC, MC.
Reduced fees: Weekdays, Low Season, Twilight Play.
Unrestricted walking: No. **Range:** Yes (mats).
Holes: 18. **Par:** 72. **Yards:** 6,860-4,816. **Slope:** 131-120.
Second hole based on design of Joseph Kropinecki, winner of GOLF DIGEST's 1991 Armchair Architect par-3 competition.
Comments: "Excellent course, well maintained . . . Final three holes make this course a 'must play' . . . Fantastic finish . . . Maturity will increase rating . . . A few unfair landing areas . . . Staff has a great attitude."

★★½ HIDDEN VALLEY RESORT & CLUB
Gaylord—R—517-732-4653, 800-752-5510 (60 mi. from Traverse City).
Season: April-Oct. **High:** June-Aug. **Caddies:** No.
Green fee: $20-$49. **Credit cards:** V, AMEX, DISC, MC.
Lodging on site: Yes. **Reduced fees:** Weekdays, Low Season, Resort Guests, Twilight Play.
Unrestricted walking: No. **Range:** Yes (grass).

Holes: 18. **Par:** 71. **Yards:** 6,305-5,591. **Slope:** 121-113.
Comments: "Hilly, old style . . . Nice, scenic, not impossible to play . . .
Dull, boring holes . . . Not the resort quality of most courses in the same
price range . . .Poor cousin to great local courses."

★★★HIGH POINTE GOLF CLUB
Williamsburg—PU—616-267-9900, 800-753-7888
(5 mi. from Traverse City).
Season: May-Oct. **High:** July-Aug. **Caddies:** No.
Green fee: $20-$49. **Credit cards:** All Major.
Reduced fees: Weekdays, Low Season, Twilight Play.
Unrestricted walking: Yes. **Range:** Yes (grass).
Holes: 18. **Par:** 71. **Yards:** 6,849-5,258. **Slope:** 128-121.
Ranked in Third 25 of America's 75 Best Public Courses by GOLF DIGEST.
Comments: "An excellent course right under The Bear's nose, across the
highway . . . Nothing exceptional, very enjoyable . . . Too much contrast
between 9s . . . From flat to hilly . . . Back 9 much better . . . Front is
getting shabby . . . Fescue greens allowed for more undulations, took getting used to . . . Fescue greens putted terribly . . . Doak's joke . . . New
grass on the greens should help."

★★★½ HURON BREEZE GOLF & COUNTRY CLUB
Au Gres—PU—517-876-6868.
Season: April-Oct. **High:** June-Sept. **Caddies:** No.
Green fee: $20-$49. **Credit cards:** V, MC.
Lodging on site: No. **Reduced fees:** Weekdays.
Unrestricted walking: No. **Range:** Yes (grass).
Holes: 18. **Par:** 72. **Yards:** 6,806-5,075. **Slope:** 128-120.
Comments: "Very playable, inexpensive . . . Pleasant round of golf, no
surprises . . . Nice track . . . In beautiful setting and beautiful condition . . .
One block from Lake Huron . . . Golf shop staff very attentive."

★★★HURON GOLF CLUB
Ypsilanti—R—313-487-2441 (35 mi. from Detroit).
Season: March-Nov. **High:** June-Aug. **Caddies:** No.
Green fee: $20-$49. **Credit cards:** V, AMEX, MC.
Lodging on site: Yes. **Reduced fees:** Weekdays, Low Season,
Twilight Play.
Unrestricted walking: No. **Range:** Yes (grass).
Holes: 18. **Par:** 72. **Yards:** 6,755-5,185. **Slope:** 138-124.
Course owned by Eastern Michigan University.
Comments: "Thinker's course . . . Compares to best courses in Northern
Michigan . . . Short but not easy, lots of water holes . . . Tough from back
tees, greens roll nice, great price . . . Poor service from staff."

LAKEVIEW HILLS COUNTRY CLUB AND RESORT
Lexington—R—313-359-8901 (20 mi. from Port Huron).
Season: Year-round. **High:** May-Sept. **Caddies:** No.
Green fee: $20-$49. **Credit cards:** V, AMEX, MC.
Lodging on site: Yes. **Reduced fees:** Weekdays, Low Season.
Unrestricted walking: No. **Range:** Yes (grass).
★★★NORTH COURSE
Holes: 18. **Par:** 72. **Yards:** 6,852-4,995. **Slope:** 132-122.
★★½ SOUTH COURSE
Green fee: Under $20. **Reduced fees:** Weekdays, Low Season, Twilight
Play. **Unrestricted walking:** Yes.
Holes: 18. **Par:** 72. **Yards:** 6,290-4,707. **Slope:** 119-116.

LAKEWOOD SHORES RESORT
Oscoda—R—517-739-2075, 800-882-2493 (90 mi. from Saginaw).
Season: April-Nov. **High:** June-Sept. **Caddies:** No.
Green fee: $20-$49. **Credit cards:** V, MC.
Lodging on site: Yes. **Reduced fees:** Weekdays, Low Season, Resort
Guests, Twilight Play.

SUPER VALUE

Unrestricted walking: Yes. **Range:** Yes (grass).

★★★★½ THE GAILES COURSE

Holes: 18. **Par:** 72. **Yards:** 6,954-5,246. **Slope:** 137-132.

Selected America's Best New Resort Course of 1993 by GOLF DIGEST.

Comments: "True Scottish links . . . Enjoyable . . . Plucked from Scotland . . . Brand new, but plays like it's 10 years old . . . Best 'heathers course' in the state . . . Best value in north Michigan."

★★★THE RESORT COURSE

Holes: 18. **Par:** 72. **Yards:** 6,806-5,295. **Slope:** 120-115.

Comments: "Great traditional design . . . . . . Good staff . . . OK conditions . . . Nothing memorable, poor sister to The Gailes."

★★½ THE LINKS OF NOVI
EAST/SOUTH/WEST 9s

Novi—PU—313-380-9595 (20 mi. from Detroit).

Season: April-Nov. **High:** May-Sept. **Caddies:** No.

Green fee: $20-$49. **Credit cards:** V, MC.

Lodging on site: No. **Reduced fees:** Weekdays, Twilight Play.

Unrestricted walking: No. **Range:** Yes (mats).

Holes: 27. **Par:** 35/34/36. **Yards:** 3,209/2,805/3,288.

Comments: "Long and plain . . . Northern Michigan terrain on three holes . . . Nothing outstanding . . . Clubhouse and amenities nice, course has bad greens . . . Underbrush not cleaned out . . . Can you say 'Mosquito'? . . . Should work on customer service . . . Has nice course outings."

★★★★LITTLE TRAVERSE BAY GOLF CLUB

Harbor Springs—PU—616-526-6200.

Season: May-Oct. **High:** June-Sept. **Caddies:** No.

Green fee: $50-$99. **Credit cards:** V, MC.

Lodging on site: No. **Reduced fees:** Weekdays, Low Season.

Unrestricted walking: No. **Range:** Yes (grass).

Holes: 18. **Par:** 72. **Yards:** 6,865-6,191. **Slope:** 131-125.

Comments: "Beautiful scenery, spectacular views . . . Great views . . . Prettiest 18 in the state . . . Probably not a more beautiful course on earth . . . Back side is the best . . . Excellent condition for a new course . . . Greens too severe."

★★★MARSH RIDGE GOLF AND NORDIC SKI RESORT

Gaylord—R—517-732-6794, 800-968-2633.

Season: Year-round. **High:** May-Sept. **Caddies:** No.

Green fee: $20-$49. **Credit cards:** V, AMEX, MC.

Lodging on site: Yes. **Reduced fees:** Low Season, Resort Guests, Twilight Play.

Unrestricted walking: No. **Range:** Yes (grass).

Holes: 18. **Par:** 71. **Yards:** 6,062-4,324. **Slope:** 126-115.

Comments: "Excellent new course . . . Requires accuracy. "

★★★MATHESON GREENS GOLF COURSE

Northport—PU—616-386-5171 (25 mi. from Traverse City).

Season: May-Oct. **High:** July-Aug. **Caddies:** No.

Green fee: $20-$49. **Credit cards:** V, DISC, MC.

Lodging on site: No. **Reduced fees:** Low Season, Twilight Play.

Unrestricted walking: No. **Range:** Yes (mats).

Holes: 18. **Par:** 72. **Yards:** 6,609-4,716. **Slope:** 132-116.

Comments: "Interesting new course . . . Good short course . . . Nice views . . . Play blue tees for fair test."

MICHAYWE HILLS GOLF CLUB
★★★½ LAKE COURSE

Gaylord—R—517-939-8911, 800-322-6636 (45 mi. from Traverse City).

Season: April-Oct. **High:** June-Aug. **Caddies:** No.

Green fee: $50-$99. **Credit cards:** V, MC.

Lodging on site: Yes. **Reduced fees:** Weekdays, Low Season, Resort Guests, Twilight Play.

Unrestricted walking: No. **Range:** Yes (grass).
Holes: 18. **Par:** 72. **Yards:** 6,508-5,000. **Slope:** 141-130.
Comments: "Very interesting, lots of variety . . . A sleeper, wonderful . . . Wet and tough . . . Very difficult greens . . . Toughest course I ever played . . . Every hole is a challenge . . . Too tough, not fun . . . Unforgiving . . . Slim landing areas, bring your 3-wood . . . Too strict a dress code."

★★★PINES COURSE
Holes: 18. **Par:** 72. **Yards:** 6,835-5,901. **Slope:** 129-126.
Comments: "Nice course . . . Lush, short . . . Good test in fine shape . . . Speed governors on buggies means snail's pace."

★★★THE NATURAL
Gaylord—R—517-732-1785 (50 mi. from Traverse City).
Season: April-Oct. **High:** June-Aug. **Caddies:** No.
Green fee: $20-$49. **Credit cards:** V, MC.
Lodging on site: Yes. **Reduced fees:** Low Season, Resort Guests, Twilight Play.
Unrestricted walking: No. **Range:** Yes (grass).
Holes: 18. **Par:** 71. **Yards:** 6,300-4,830. **Slope:** Unrated.
Comments: "Nice but overplayed . . . Playable, enjoyable . . . Great shape . . . Tightly packed . . . Requires accuracy . . . Difficult to walk, but is permitted . . . Challenging carries over marsh . . . Too many marsh areas . . . Needs to fill in."

★★★PINE TRACE GOLF CLUB
Rochester Hills—PU—313-852-7100.
Season: April-Nov. **High:** May-Oct. **Caddies:** No.
Green fee: $20-$49. **Credit cards:** V, MC.
Lodging on site: No. **Reduced fees:** No.
Unrestricted walking: No. **Range:** Yes (mats).
Holes: 18. **Par:** 72. **Yards:** 6,610-4,974. **Slope:** 134-125.
Comments: "Best public in southeast Michigan . . . Best maintained course in area . . . Great course with some outstanding holes . . . Lots of forced carries, have to be strong off the tee . . . I love their Pace of Play policy . . . All groups timed, slow groups asked to leave . . . Great course ruined by surly, belligerent staff who assume you're going to play slowly . . . Carts-only-on-paths rule slows down play . . . Rangers have overbearing preoccupation with pace of play . . . Gestapo rangers . . . Feel pushed by time policy . . . Too concerned about slow play . . . Fast play enforcement is great . . . They keep play moving."

★★★½ POHLCAT GOLF COURSE
Mount Pleasant—R—517-773-4221 (65 mi. from Lansing).
Season: April-Nov. **High:** July-Sept. **Caddies:** No.
Green fee: $50-$99. **Credit cards:** V, MC.
Lodging on site: Yes. **Reduced fees:** Weekdays, Low Season, Resort Guests, Twilight Play.
Unrestricted walking: No. **Range:** Yes (grass).
Holes: 18. **Par:** 72. **Yards:** 6,810-5,140. **Slope:** 139-124.
Comments: "Nice new layout . . . Great holes, great fun, stalk 'The Cat' . . . Carry plenty of golf balls because of water risks . . . Few memorable holes, overpriced . . . No frills . . . Needs time to mature."

★★★RATTLE RUN GOLF COURSE
East China—PU—313-329-2070 (50 mi. from Detroit).
Season: April-Oct. **High:** May-Sept. **Caddies:** No.
Green fee: $20-$49. **Credit cards:** V, MC.
Lodging on site: No. **Reduced fees:** Weekdays, Low Season.
Unrestricted walking: No. **Range:** Yes (grass).
Holes: 18. **Par:** 72. **Yards:** 6,891-5,946. **Slope:** 139-134.
Ranked in Third 25 of America's 75 Best Public Courses by GOLF DIGEST.
Comments: "A neglected old maid . . . A sleeper in the boondocks . . . Maintenance has declined last two years . . . Questionable greens . . . Too soggy . . . Terrible clubhouse . . . With more upkeep, course could be world famous."

153

THE ROCK AT WOODMOOR*
Drummond Island—R—906-493-1006, 800-999-6343
(55 mi. from Sault Ste. Marie).
Season: May-Oct. **High:** June-Aug. **Caddies:** No.
Green fee: $50-$99. **Credit cards:** V, AMEX, DISC, MC.
Lodging on site: Yes. **Reduced fees:** Weekdays, Low Season, Resort
Guests, Twilight Play.
Unrestricted walking: No. **Range:** Yes (grass).
Holes: 18. **Par:** 71. **Yards:** 6,830-4,992. **Slope:** 140-126.
Comments: "Beautiful, secluded, magical . . . Remote location. First-class
golf destination resort."

★★½ SALEM HILLS GOLF CLUB
Northville—PU—313-437-2152 (12 mi. from Ann Arbor).
Season: April-Nov. **High:** May-Oct. **Caddies:** No.
Green fee: Under $20. **Credit cards:** No.
Reduced fees: Weekdays, Low Season, Twilight Play.
Unrestricted walking: No. **Range:** Yes (grass).
Holes: 18. **Par:** 72. **Yards:** 6,966-5,874. **Slope:** 121-116.
Comments: "Open but enjoyable . . . Excellent greens with subtle con-
touring . . . Long par 3s . . . Par-4 11th is outstanding . . . Bring an old pair
of shoes. Drains slowly."

★★★½ SCHUSS MOUNTAIN GOLF COURSE
Mancelona—R—616-587-9232 (25 mi. from Traverse City).
Season: April-Oct. **High:** June-Aug. **Caddies:** No.
Green fee: $50-$99. **Credit cards:** All Major.
Lodging on site: Yes. **Reduced fees:** Low Season, Resort Guests,
Twilight Play.
Unrestricted walking: No. **Range:** Yes (grass).
Holes: 18. **Par:** 72. **Yards:** 6,922-5,383. **Slope:** 124-119.
Comments: "Scenic, beautiful . . . First-class resort . . . Always in good
shape . . . Keeps your attention . . . Typical resort course from whites, no
bunkers in play, good conditions . . . Large level greens . . . Not quite
Legendary, but better value . . . Shop needs work."

SHANTY CREEK RESORT
Bellaire—R—616-533-8621, 800-678-4111 (35 mi. from Traverse City).
Season: April-Oct. **High:** June-Aug. **Caddies:** No.
Green fee: $50-$99. **Credit cards:** All Major.
Lodging on site: Yes. **Reduced fees:** Low Season, Resort Guests,
Twilight Play.
Unrestricted walking: No. **Range:** Yes (grass).
★½ SHANTY CREEK COURSE
Holes: 18. **Par:** 71. **Yards:** 6,276-4,545. **Slope:** 120-116.
Comments: "Open, little penalty for errant shots . . . Definitely The Leg-
end's ugly sister. . . Too many blind shots . . . Not worth the money . . .
Play The Legend again instead . . . Would be OK if the price was 20 bucks."
★★★★½ THE LEGEND COURSE
Holes: 18. **Par:** 72. **Yards:** 6,764-4,953. **Slope:** 135-119.
Ranked 19th in America's 75 Best Resort Courses by GOLF DIGEST.
Comments: "Best course in the state. Best value among pricey resorts . . .
Gorgeous . . . Most beautiful course ever . . . Wonderful . . . Exceptional
. . . Challenging, not impossible . . . Won't disappoint . . . Hills, trees,
babbling brooks . . . Bring a panoramic camera . . . Next hole is better than
the last . . . Where golfers would like to go when they die . . . Always in
good shape . . . It's perfect . . . Bring $$$ . . . Scenery makes the price
worth it . . . First-class resort . . . If only it wasn't so expensive."

★★★½ STONEBRIDGE GOLF CLUB
Ann Arbor—PU—313-429-8383 (30 mi. from Detroit).
Season: March-Dec. **High:** June-Sept. **Caddies:** No.
Green fee: $20-$49. **Credit cards:** V, MC.
Lodging on site: No. **Reduced fees:** Weekdays, Twilight Play.

Unrestricted walking: No. **Range:** Yes (grass).
Holes: 18. **Par:** 72. **Yards:** 6,932-5,075. **Slope:** 139-128.
Comments: "Great layout, needs to mature . . . Too new to tell . . . 16 holes have water . . . Great shots into greens. Sand and grass bunkers frame targets beautifully . . . No depth to greens, they don't hold."

★★★½ STONEHEDGE GOLF COURSE
Augusta—PU—616-731-2300 (120 mi. from Detroit).
Season: April-Oct. **High:** May-Sept. **Caddies:** No.
Green fee: $20-$49. **Credit cards:** V, MC.
Lodging on site: No. **Reduced fees:** Resort Guests.
Unrestricted walking: No. **Range:** Yes (grass).
Holes: 18. **Par:** 72. **Yards:** 6,650-5,191. **Slope:** 134-120.
Comments: "Jewel that not a lot of folks know about . . . Exciting but not severe . . . Scenic, can play different each time . . . Large greens . . . Not long, but tight . . . Unique stone fences . . . Can a roller coaster be a bore? This one can . . .Slowest putting greens in creation . . . They've gone corporate and lost their personal touch. Too bad."

★★ SYCAMORE HILLS GOLF CLUB
NORTH/SOUTH/WEST 9s
Macomb—PU—313-598-9500 (20 mi. from Detroit).
Season: April-Oct. **High:** May-Sept. **Caddies:** No.
Green fee: $20-$49. **Credit cards:** V, MC.
Reduced fees: Weekdays, Low Season, Twilight Play.
Unrestricted walking: No. **Range:** Yes (mats).
Holes: 27. **Par:** 36/36/36. **Yards:** 3,150/3,155/3,085.
Comments: "Too short, even from back tees . . . Nothing special . . . 27 holes on an 18-hole tract of land . . . Poorly managed, bad condition . . . Upscale pricing for poor layout . . . Course passable, pro shop zero."

★★ TAYLOR MEADOWS GOLF CLUB
Taylor—PU—313-295-0506 (12 mi. from Detroit).
Season: March-Dec. **High:** May-Sept. **Caddies:** No.
Green fee: $20-$49. **Credit cards:** V, MC.
Reduced fees: Weekdays, Low Season, Twilight Play.
Unrestricted walking: Yes. **Range:** No.
Holes: 18. **Par:** 71. **Yards:** 6,057-5,118. **Slope:** 114-110.
Comments: "Short, easy . . . Too tight, a shooting gallery . . . Greens are brick-like . . . Always busy, tough to get tee times."

★★★½ TIMBER RIDGE GOLF COURSE
East Lansing—PU—517-339-8000, 800-233-6669 (4 mi. from Lansing).
Season: March-Nov. **High:** May-Sept. **Caddies:** No.
Green fee: $50-$99. **Credit cards:** V, MC.
Reduced fees: Weekdays, Low Season, Twilight Play.
Unrestricted walking: No. **Range:** No.
Holes: 18. **Par:** 72. **Yards:** 6,497-5,048. **Slope:** 137-129.
Ranked in Third 25 of America's 75 Best Public Courses by GOLF DIGEST.
Comments: "Hills like up north . . . Great course design, same course up North would cost $20 more . . . Love it. Very scenic. Difficult but fair if you play smart . . . Small landing areas. Accuracy a must . . . Not crowded, not walkable . . . Tops in beauty, design and amenities . . . Last three holes are outstanding, other 15 are not remarkable . . . Lost-ball-jungles off fairways . . . Some great holes, some forced ones . . . Not kept up, run down . . . Excellent clubhouse."

TREETOPS SYLVAN RESORT
Gaylord—R—517-732-6711, 800-444-6711.
Season: May-Oct. **High:** Summer. **Caddies:** No.
Green fee: $50-$99. **Credit cards:** All Major.
Lodging on site: Yes. **Reduced fees:** Low Season, Resort Guests, Twilight Play.
Unrestricted walking: No. **Range:** Yes (grass).

Also has 9-hole par-3 course called Threetops.

★★★★FAZIO COURSE
Holes: 18. **Par:** 72. **Yards:** 6,832-5,039. **Slope:** 135-123.
Comments: "Very new, a little more open than Jones 18. Excellent condition . . . Terrific views, demanding layout . . . Great view, feel like you're on top of the world . . . Great place to take pictures, tough place to play golf . . . Holes start wide and funnel down . . . Fair . . . Playable, no tricks . . . Fits the land . . . Also great teaching staff."

★★★½ JONES COURSE
Holes: 18. **Par:** 71. **Yards:** 7,060-4,972. **Slope:** 146-124.
Ranked 27th in America's 75 Best Resort Courses by GOLF DIGEST.
Comments: "Scenic, difficult but not unreasonable . . . Great course to play, visually great . . . Excellent condition . . . Several holes not fair . . . Extremely difficult for average golfers . . . Long, tough, mean . . . Torture . . . Too many long carries . . . Punishing . . . A monster, almost unplayable . . . Open four years, greens are still too thin . . . Take aspirin before and after . . . Not a fun course to play . . . New greenkeeper has made a difference . . . 6th is prettiest hole anywhere . . . Takes your 'A' game, gives you back a 'C' game . . . Skip it and play their Fazio Course instead."

SMITH COURSE*
Holes: 18. **Par:** 70. **Yards:** 6,653-4,604. **Slope:** 137-118.

WILDERNESS VALLEY GOLF CLUB
Gaylord—R—616-585-7090
Season: April-Oct. **High:** July-Aug. **Caddies:** No.
Green fee: $20-$49. **Credit cards:** All Major.
Lodging on site: Yes. **Reduced fees:** Low Season, Twilight Play.
Unrestricted walking: No. **Range:** Yes (grass).

★★★½ BLACK FOREST COURSE
Holes: 18. **Par:** 73. **Yards:** 7,044-5,282. **Slope:** 140-127.
Ranked 7th in Michigan by GOLF DIGEST.
Comments: "An unknown gem . . . Great course, scenic, tough, huge bunkers . . . Bring sand wedge . . . Tom Doak's masterpiece, beautiful and fair . . . It was always there, Doak just found it . . . Layout and bunkers well done, but tiny greens may be too penal . . . Too tricked-up, must play numerous times to learn the course . . . Not player friendly, lost many balls . . . Bump-and-run not an option on several holes."

★★½ VALLEY COURSE
Unrestricted walking: Yes.
Holes: 18. **Par:** 71. **Yards:** 6,519-4,889. **Slope:** 126-115.
Comments: "Easy course, great for short hitters . . . Personable people . . . Doesn't compare to Black Forest."

★★½ BAKER NATIONAL GOLF COURSE
Medina—PU—612-473-0800 (18 mi. from Minneapolis).
Season: April-Oct. **High:** June-Aug. **Caddies:** Yes.
Green fee: $20-$49. **Credit cards:** V.
Lodging on site: No. **Reduced fees:** Weekdays.
Unrestricted walking: Yes. **Range:** Yes (grass).
Holes: 18. **Par:** 72. **Yards:** 6,752-5,395. **Slope:** 132-125.
Also has 9-hole executive course.
Comments: "Nice new back 9 . . . Wilderness setting . . . Good variety, good exercise for walkers . . . Excellent challenge . . . Very diversified . . . Difficult, too many uneven lies . . . Polite service, fun course . . . A good value . . . Very crowded, a few holes slow play considerably."

★★★½ BEMIDJI TOWN & COUNTRY CLUB
Bemidji—PU—218-751-9215 (150 mi. from Duluth).
Season: April-Oct. **High:** July-Aug. **Caddies:** No.
Green fee: $20-$49. **Credit cards:** V, MC.
Lodging on site: No. **Reduced fees:** Low Season, Resort Guests.
Unrestricted walking: Yes. **Range:** Yes (grass).
Holes: 18. **Par:** 72. **Yards:** 6,535-5,058. **Slope:** 127-120.
Comments: "Fun course . . . Has been redesigned . . . New update eliminated weak holes . . . Large red pines . . . Clover needs to go."

★★★ BRAEMAR GOLF COURSE
Edina—PU—612-941-2072 (12 mi. from Minneapolis).
Season: April-Nov. **High:** June-Aug. **Caddies:** No.
Green fee: Under $20. **Credit cards:** No.
Lodging on site: No. **Reduced fees:** No.
Unrestricted walking: Yes. **Range:** Yes (grass).
Holes: 18. **Par:** 71. **Yards:** 6,695-5,832. **Slope:** 124-129.
Also has 9-hole executive. Additional regulation 9 holes will open in 1994.
Comments: "Solid, well-manicured course . . . Long on distance, not much trouble . . . Long par 4s on front . . . Great teaching facility . . . South Minneapolis area's best, and getting better . . . City is constructing 9 additional holes, overlap some parts of existing course . . . Tee boxes are rough, uneven . . . Too much play, greens get spiked to death . . . Always crowded . . . Tough to get on unless you're an Edina resident."

BREEZY POINT RESORT
Breezy Point—R—218-562-7177, 800-950-4960 (140 mi. from Minneapolis). **Season:** April-Oct. **High:** June-Sept. **Caddies:** No.
Green fee: $20-$49. **Credit cards:** All Major.
Lodging on site: Yes. **Reduced fees:** Weekdays, Twilight Play.
Unrestricted walking: Yes. **Range:** Yes (grass).
★★CHAMPIONSHIP COURSE
Holes: 18. **Par:** 72. **Yards:** 6,600-5,718. **Slope:** 124-128.
Comments: "Excellent accommodations . . . Short, not very interesting . . . Front 9 dull . . . Back 9 some challenge . . . Too many tilted greens . . . Rather open except for last few holes . . . Not well kept."
TRADITIONAL COURSE*
Holes: 18. **Par:** 68. **Yards:** 5,200-5,127. **Slope:** 114-111.

★★★★BUNKER HILLS GOLF COURSE
NORTH/EAST/WEST 9s
Coon Rapids—PU—612-755-4141 (10 mi. from Minneapolis).
Season: April-Oct. **High:** June-Aug. **Caddies:** No.
Green fee: $20-$49. **Credit cards:** No.
Lodging on site: No. **Reduced fees:** Weekdays.
Unrestricted walking: Yes. **Range:** Yes (grass).
Holes: 27. **Par:** 36/36/36. **Yards:** 3,418/3,381/3,520.
Also has 9-hole executive course.
Comments: "Outstanding . . . Great challenge . . . Excellent . . . Flat, well bunkered . . . Nothing fancy, just good solid golf . . . Original course has

(GREAT VALUE)

MINNESOTA

quality holes . . . New 9 reminds me of Pinehurst . . . Not a Senior PGA Tour venue for nuttin' . . . Very cooperative staff, great with juniors . . . Long walks between holes . . . 'No thrills' golf . . . A little pricey."

★★½ CUYUNA COUNTRY CLUB
Deerwood—PU—218-534-3489 (15 mi. from Brainerd).
Season: April-Nov. **High:** June-Aug. **Caddies:** Yes.
Green fee: $20-$49. **Credit cards:** V, MC.
Lodging on site: No. **Reduced fees:** Weekdays, Twilight Play.
Unrestricted walking: Yes. **Range:** No.
Holes: 18. **Par:** 71. **Yards:** 6,273-5,627. **Slope:** 124-123.
Comments: "Old 9 from the 1920s, with new 9, which is too tight . . . Tough, fair, very scenic . . . Rough on the edges . . . Location is beautiful . . . Friendly staff."

★★★★EDINBURGH U.S.A.
Brooklyn Park—PU—612-424-7060 (15 mi. from Minneapolis).
Season: April-Oct. **High:** June-Aug. **Caddies:** No.
Green fee: $20-$49. **Credit cards:** V, AMEX, MC.
Lodging on site: No. **Reduced fees:** Twilight Play.
Unrestricted walking: Yes. **Range:** Yes (mats).
Holes: 18. **Par:** 72. **Yards:** 6,701-5,255. **Slope:** 132-124.
Ranked in Second 25 of America's 75 Best Public Courses by GOLF DIGEST.
Comments: "A jewel . . . Great test, lots of trouble . . . Bent-grass fairways, a lot of sand . . . Truest greens in Minnesota . . . Different personalities between 9s . . . The more it's played the more its design is appreciated . . . Fabulous for all but the men pros . . . Hard to get tee times, always busy . . . 5 hours of championship golf . . . Dot-to-dot golf . . . Too difficult for most hackers . . . No carts on grass."

★★½ ENGER PARK GOLF COURSE
FRONT/MIDDLE/BACK 9s
Duluth—PU—218-723-3452.
Season: May-Oct. **High:** June-Aug. **Caddies:** No.
Green fee: Under $20. **Credit cards:** No.
Lodging on site: No. **Reduced fees:** Low Season, Twilight Play.
Unrestricted walking: Yes. **Range:** Yes (grass).
Holes: 27. **Par:** 36/36/36. **Yards:** 3,304/3,130/3,195.
Comments: "Lots of character but only fair condition . . . New and reconstructed holes have no topsoil, just gravel and rocks on the surface . . . Nice layout poorly kept . . . Everything breaks toward Lake Superior."

FOX HOLLOW GOLF CLUB*
Rogers—PU—612-428-4468 (30 mi. from Minneapolis).
Season: April-Nov. **High:** July-Sept. **Caddies:** Yes.
Green fee: $20-$49. **Credit cards:** V, MC.
Lodging on site: No. **Reduced fees:** Weekdays.
Unrestricted walking: Yes. **Range:** Yes (grass).
Holes: 18. **Par:** 72. **Yards:** 6,701-5,161. **Slope:** 129-117.

★★½ FRANCIS A. GROSS GOLF COURSE
Minneapolis—PU—612-789-2542.
Season: April-Nov. **High:** June-Aug. **Caddies:** No.
Green fee: Under $20. **Credit cards:** No.
Lodging on site: No. **Reduced fees:** Twilight Play.
Unrestricted walking: Yes. **Range:** Yes (grass).
Holes: 18. **Par:** 71. **Yards:** 6,575-5,824. **Slope:** 120-121.
Comments: "Fine old respected course . . . Small greens . . . Lots of trees . . . Course in bad shape last year due to record rainfalls . . . City employees do a poor job of greenkeeping . . . Nothing fancy . . . Mature but bland."

★★½ INVER WOOD GOLF COURSE
Inver Grove Heights—PU—612-457-3667 (5 mi. from St. Paul).
Season: April-Oct. **High:** June-Aug. **Caddies:** No.

Green fee: $20-$49. **Credit cards:** V, MC.
Lodging on site: No. **Reduced fees:** No.
Unrestricted walking: Yes. **Range:** Yes (mats).
Holes: 18. **Par:** 72. **Yards:** 6,724-5,175. **Slope:** 135-130.
Also has 9-hole executive course.
Comments: "New course, needs a few years . . . Balls easily lost . . . Hilly, treelined . . . Rent a cart . . . Wants to be a championship course, but won't spend money on maintenance . . . Some long par 4s are trapped in front, some greens slope front to back."

★★IZATY'S GOLF & YACHT CLUB
Onamia—R—612-532-4575, 800-533-1728 (90 mi. from Minneapolis).
Season: April-Oct. **High:** June-Sept. **Caddies:** No.
Green fee: $20-$49. **Credit cards:** V, AMEX, MC, DISC.
Lodging on site: Yes. **Reduced fees:** Weekdays, Resort Guests, Twilight Play.
Unrestricted walking: Yes. **Range:** Yes (mats).
Holes: 18. **Par:** 72. **Yards:** 6,481-4,939. **Slope:** 132-127.
Comments: "Extremely difficult resort course . . . Tough, many water hazards . . . Too many acute doglegs . . . A Dye disaster, no bailouts any-where . . . Contrived . . . Overpriced lodge and green fee for a Dye redesign."

★★½ KELLER GOLF COURSE
St. Paul—PU—612-484-3011.
Season: April-Nov. **High:** May-Sept. **Caddies:** No.
Green fee: Under $20. **Credit cards:** No.
Lodging on site: No. **Reduced fees:** Weekdays, Twilight Play.
Unrestricted walking: Yes. **Range:** Yes (grass).
Holes: 18. **Par:** 72. **Yards:** 6,542-5,597. **Slope:** 127-123.
Comments: "Classic course, but always has trouble with maintenance of greens . . . Fun old course. Pros used to play there . . . Strictly blue collar. Poorly maintained greens, lacks definition between fairways and rough . . . Should be better for its age . . . Looking tired these days."

★★½ THE LAKES COURSE AT
RUTTGER'S BAY LAKE LODGE
Deerwood—R—218-678-2885 (100 mi. from Minneapolis).
Season: April-Oct. **High:** June-Aug. **Caddies:** Yes.
Green fee: $20-$49. **Credit cards:** V, DISC, MC.
Lodging on site: Yes. **Reduced fees:** Low Season, Resort Guests.
Unrestricted walking: Yes. **Range:** Yes (grass).
Holes: 18. **Par:** 72. **Yards:** 6,485-5,052. **Slope:** 124-122.
Comments: "Has possibilities, but layout of matching two different 9s doesn't work real well . . . The old 9 is better . . . Too many blind shots . . . Needs more seasoning . . . Needs better ranger control."

★★★½ THE LINKS AT NORTHFORK
Ramsey—PU—612-241-0506 (25 mi. from Minneapolis).
Season: April-Oct. **High:** June-Sept. **Caddies:** Yes.
Green fee: $20-$49. **Credit cards:** V, MC.
Lodging on site: No. **Reduced fees:** Weekdays, Twilight Play.
Unrestricted walking: Yes. **Range:** Yes (grass).
Holes: 18. **Par:** 72. **Yards:** 6,988-5,241. **Slope:** 122-114.
Has additional 3-hole practice loop.
Comments: "Super new course . . . Links style . . . Welcome break from trees and water . . . Different kind of course . . . When the wind is up, you're a goner . . . Rough too high . . . Excellent front 9, a couple of gimmick holes on the back."

MADDEN'S ON GULL LAKE
Brainerd—R—218-829-2811 (135 mi. from Minneapolis).
Season: April-Oct. **High:** July-Aug. **Caddies:** No.
Green fee: $20-$49. **Credit cards:** V, MC.

Lodging on site: Yes. **Reduced fees:** Weekdays, Resort Guests, Twilight Play.
Unrestricted walking: Yes. **Range:** Yes (grass).
Also has a 9-hole par-28 'Social 9.'
★★★PINE BEACH EAST COURSE
Holes: 18. **Par:** 72. **Yards:** 5,932-5,362. **Slope:** 111-116.
Comments: "Nice old resort course, open and easy . . . Very flat and crowded . . . Fun place for average golfers . . . Finest accommodations and amenities of any Minnesota course . . . A golf resort that puts the customer first . . . Great atmosphere . . . Mosquitos bad in early evening."
★★PINE BEACH WEST COURSE
Holes: 18. **Par:** 67. **Yards:** 5,070-4,585. **Slope:** 103-107.
Comments: "Good beginner's course . . . Easy, could be in better shape . . . Bad starting hole, a par 3."

MAJESTIC OAKS GOLF CLUB
Ham Lake—PU—612-755-2142 (20 mi. from Minneapolis).
Season: April-Oct. **High:** June-Aug. **Caddies:** No.
Green fee: Under $20. **Credit cards:** V, AMEX, MC.
Reduced fees: Weekdays, Low Season, Twilight Play.
Unrestricted walking: Yes. **Range:** Yes (grass).
Also 9-hole executive course.
★★GOLD COURSE
Holes: 18. **Par:** 72. **Yards:** 6,396-4,848. **Slope:** 122-118.
Comments: "New, needs time . . . Corporate outing course, opened too soon, no grass . . . Seems like this course is always ground under repair."
★★★½ PLATINUM COURSE
Green fee: $20-$49.
Holes: 18. **Par:** 72. **Yards:** 7,013-5,268. **Slope:** 132-124.
Ranked in Third 25 of America's 75 Best Public Courses by Golf Digest.
Comments: "Some of the tallest trees, some of the deepest bunkers . . . Needs more distinct fairways . . . Greens in poor shape . . . Run-down, no longer majestic . . . Management more interested in homesite development than the course."

★★MEADOWBROOK GOLF COURSE
Hopkins—PU—612-929-2077 (1 mi. from Minneapolis).
Season: April-Nov. **High:** May-Sept. **Caddies:** No.
Green fee: Under $20. **Credit cards:** No.
Lodging on site: No. **Reduced fees:** Low Season, Twilight Play.
Unrestricted walking: Yes. **Range:** Yes (grass).
Holes: 18. **Par:** 72. **Yards:** 6,593-5,610. **Slope:** 113-122.
Comments: "Older course, trees, small greens . . . Bumpy greens . . . Short, a lot of uphill and downhill shots . . . Lacks traps and big tee boxes . . . Not overly challenging, too wide open . . . Too many blind shots, slows play . . . Beat up, even for a public course."

MISSISSIPPI NATIONAL GOLF LINKS*
LOWLANDS/MIDLANDS/HIGHLANDS 9s
Red Wing—PU—612-388-1874 (55 mi. from Minneapolis).
Season: April-Oct. **High:** July-Aug. **Caddies:** No.
Green fee: $20-$49. **Credit cards:** V, MC.
Lodging on site: No. **Reduced fees:** No.
Unrestricted walking: Yes. **Range:** Yes (grass).
Holes: 27. **Par:** 35/36/35. **Yards:** 3,139/3,334/2,881.

★★★★½ THE PINES AT GRAND VIEW LODGE
Nisswa—R—218-963-3146, 800-432-3788 (140 mi. from Minneapolis).
Season: May-Sept. **High:** June-Aug. **Caddies:** No.
Green fee: $20-$49. **Credit cards:** V, AMEX, MC.
Lodging on site: Yes. **Reduced fees:** Weekdays, Low Season, Resort Guests, Twilight Play.

GREAT VALUE

Unrestricted walking: Yes. **Range:** Yes (grass).
Holes: 18. **Par:** 72. **Yards:** 6,832-5,132. **Slope:** 135-122.
9-hole par-35 Lodge Course nearby.
Comments: "A great, great course at a top resort . . . Absolutely flawless . . . A woodland beauty . . . Beautiful and challenging . . . Enthralling . . . Top 10 material . . . Some par 4s similar to Augusta National . . . Best designed course in Minnesota . . . If you like trees, you'll love The Pines . . . Great accommodations . . . Well worth the trip. Expensive but very scenic, very good . . . A true gem."

★SUNDANCE GOLF CLUB
Maple Grove—PU—612-420-4700 (15 mi. from Minneapolis).
Season: April-Nov. **High:** May-July **Caddies:** No.
Green fee: Under $20. **Credit cards:** V, AMEX, MC.
Lodging on site: No. **Reduced fees:** Weekdays.
Unrestricted walking: Yes. **Range:** Yes (grass).
Holes: 18. **Par:** 72. **Yards:** 6,446-5,548. **Slope:** 129-129.
Comments: "Overhyped cow pasture . . . Boring old cornfield . . . Not much to say except it opens early in the season . . . Peat bog. Not fun when wet . . . Selling full coolers of beer to take out on the course ruins the game."

★★★½ WEDGEWOOD GOLF CLUB
Woodbury—PU—612-731-4779 (10 mi. from St. Paul).
Season: April-Nov. **High:** June-Aug. **Caddies:** No.
Green fee: $20-$49. **Credit cards:** V, MC.
Lodging on site: No. **Reduced fees:** Weekdays.
Unrestricted walking: Yes. **Range:** Yes (mats).
Holes: 18. **Par:** 72. **Yards:** 6,735-5,150. **Slope:** 120-121.
Comments: "Ideal new course for all types of players . . . Always windy . . . Fast hard greens, a real challenge . . . Thinking golfer's design, mostly elevated tees add confidence . . . Excellent finishing holes . . . Interesting challenge, plays fast . . . Pleasant round . . . What every course should be . . . Improves every year . . . Mix of creative and dull holes . . . Housing first, golf second . . . Starting to get taken over by houses."

★★★½ WILLINGER'S GOLF CLUB
Northfield—PU—612-652-2500 (35 mi. from Minneapolis).
Season: April-Nov. **High:** June-Aug. **Caddies:** No.
Green fee: $20-$49. **Credit cards:** V, MC.
Lodging on site: No. **Reduced fees:** Weekdays, Twilight Play.
Unrestricted walking: Yes. **Range:** Yes (grass).
Holes: 18. **Par:** 72. **Yards:** 6,711-5,174. **Slope:** 131-126.
Comments: "Great new course . . . Great future . . . Best new course in years . . . Beautiful natural setting . . . Well maintained . . . Fast hard greens . . . A surprise in farm country . . . Superior layout. When mature, top 50 . . . Pro shop staff very helpful . . . A class act . . . Target course, can't be played the first time without a yardage book, which they don't have . . . Too many blind shots . . . Tough to walk, greens to tees."

THE BROADWATER BEACH GOLF CLUB
Gulfport—R—601-896-4482, 800-647-3964.
Season: Year-round. **High:** Jan.-April. **Caddies:** No.
Green fee: $20-$49. **Credit cards:** V, MC.
Lodging on site: No. **Reduced fees:** Twilight Play.
Unrestricted walking: No. **Range:** No.
★★SEA COURSE
Holes: 18. **Par:** 71. **Yards:** 6,001-5,403. **Slope:** 118-119.
Comments: "Needs sprucing up . . . Overgrown . . . Is this a course or a pasture?"
★★SUN COURSE
601-388-3672
Holes: 18. **Par:** 72. **Yards:** 7,190-5,485. **Slope:** Unrated.
Comments: "Not what it once was . . . Quality has really declined . . . Long, open, hardpan fairways . . . Good place for Army manuevers."

DIAMONDHEAD COUNTRY CLUB
Diamondhead—R—601-255-3910, 800-346-8741 (15 mi. from Gulfport).
Season: Year-round. **High:** Feb.-May **Caddies:** No.
Green fee: $20-$49. **Credit cards:** All Major.
Lodging on site: Yes. **Reduced fees:** Low Season, Resort Guests.
Unrestricted walking: No. **Range:** Yes (grass).
★★★CARDINAL COURSE
Holes: 18. **Par:** 72. **Yards:** 6,831-5,065. **Slope:** 132-117.
Comments: "A beauty . . . Great par 5, must carry water twice to reach it . . . Well kept . . . Greens need a little work."
★★½ PINE COURSE
Holes: 18. **Par:** 72. **Yards:** 6,860-5,359. **Slope:** 132-118.
Comments: "Big hitters' course . . . Long and narrow . . . Rolling terrain . . . Excellent fairways . . . Watch out for that fox who'll steal your ball."

★★★HICKORY HILL COUNTRY CLUB
Gautier—R—601-497-2372, 800-477-4044 (15 mi. from Biloxi).
Season: Year-round. **High:** Feb.-April. **Caddies:** No.
Green fee: $20-$49. **Credit cards:** V, AMEX, DISC, MC.
Lodging on site: Yes. **Reduced fees:** Weekdays, Low Season, Resort Guests, Twilight Play.
Unrestricted walking: No. **Range:** Yes (mats).
Holes: 18. **Par:** 72. **Yards:** 7,004-5,229. **Slope:** 128-113.
Comments: "The class of the Mississippi gulf coast, despite an inadequate practice area . . . A meal ticket is included in the green fee . . . Short, heavily wooded . . . Could stand to be modernized . . . Needs more bunkers."

★★★MISSISSIPPI STATE UNIVERSITY GOLF COURSE
Mississippi State—PU—601-325-3028 (67 mi. from Tupelo).
Season: Year-round. **High:** April-Sept. **Caddies:** No.
Green fee: Under $20. **Credit cards:** V, MC.
Lodging on site: No. **Reduced fees:** No.
Unrestricted walking: Yes. **Range:** Yes (grass).
Holes: 18. **Par:** 72. **Yards:** 6,926-5,443. **Slope:** 130-121.
Comments: "Wonderful . . . Best for the money anywhere . . . New course, needs to mature . . . Exceptional maintenance . . . Cheap fees . . . Firm Bermuda greens . . . Are always inconsistent."

★★OLE MISS GOLF CLUB
Oxford—PU—601-234-4816 (50 mi. from Tupelo).
Season: Year-round. **High:** March-Sept. **Caddies:** No.
Green fee: Under $20. **Credit cards:** V, MC.
Lodging on site: No. **Reduced fees:** Weekdays, Low Season.
Unrestricted walking: Yes. **Range:** Yes (grass).
Holes: 18. **Par:** 72. **Yards:** 6,682-5,276. **Slope:** 129-120.
Course owned by the University of Mississippi.
Comments: "Great old college layout . . . Needs a little polish."

MISSISSIPPI

★★½ PASS CHRISTIAN ISLES GOLF CLUB
Pass Christian—PU—601-452-3830 (10 mi. from Gulfport).
Season: Year-round. **High:** Year-round. **Caddies:** No.
Green fee: $20-$49. **Credit cards:** All Major.
Lodging on site: No. **Reduced fees:** No.
Unrestricted walking: No. **Range:** No.
Holes: 18. **Par:** 72. **Yards:** 6,480-5,428. **Slope:** 124-120.
Comments: "Nice little course . . . Small greens . . . Fairways need improvement . . . Making progress."

★½ PINE ISLAND COUNTRY CLUB
Ocean Springs—PU—601-875-1674 (45 mi. from Mobile, Ala.).
Season: Year-round. **High:** Feb.-April. **Caddies:** No.
Green fee: $20-$49. **Credit cards:** V, MC.
Lodging on site: No. **Reduced fees:** Low Season.
Unrestricted walking: No. **Range:** Yes (grass).
Holes: 18. **Par:** 71. **Yards:** 6,322-4,915. **Slope:** 129-109.
Comments: "Short, lots of water, marsh . . . Must choose shots carefully . . . Not much to say, but run-down."

★★SUNKIST COUNTRY CLUB
Biloxi—PU—601-388-3961.
Season: Year-round. **High:** Feb.-May. **Caddies:** No.
Green fee: $20-$49. **Credit cards:** V, DISC, MC.
Lodging on site: No. **Reduced fees:** Twilight Play.
Unrestricted walking: No. **Range:** Yes (grass).
Holes: 18. **Par:** 72. **Yards:** 6,276-5,457. **Slope:** 121-120.
Comments: "Small town course . . . Only a handful of interesting holes . . . Not much of a pro shop."

★★★★TIMBERTON GOLF CLUB
Hattiesburg—PU—601-584-4653 (80 mi. from New Orleans).
Season: Year-round. **High:** Feb.-Aug. **Caddies:** No.
Green fee: $20-$49. **Credit cards:** V, MC.
Lodging on site: No. **Reduced fees:** Weekdays.
Unrestricted walking: No. **Range:** Yes (grass).
Holes: 18. **Par:** 72. **Yards:** 7,003-5,439. **Slope:** 131-128.
Ranked 3rd in Mississippi by GOLF DIGEST.
Comments: "Great track . . . A beauty . . . Stadium-type . . . Extremely playable . . . Plays longer than the card . . . Keep it a secret . . . Will soon rank as No. 1 in Mississippi . . . Future Top 100 . . . U.S. Open potential . . . Super friendly staff—they like golfers . . . Par 3s are too similar."

★★½ TRAMARK GOLF COURSE
Gulfport—PU—601-863-7808.
Season: Year-round. **High:** Feb.-April. **Caddies:** No.
Green fee: Under $20. **Credit cards:** V, MC.
Lodging on site: No. **Reduced fees:** No.
Unrestricted walking: Yes. **Range:** Yes (grass).
Holes: 18. **Par:** 72. **Yards:** 6,350-5,256. **Slope:** 116-109.
Comments: "Cheap . . . Easy to walk . . . Not very interesting . . . Won't go back."

★★★½ WINDANCE COUNTRY CLUB
Gulfport—PU—601-832-4871 (60 mi. from New Orleans).
Season: Year-round. **High:** Feb.-May. **Caddies:** No.
Green fee: $50-$99. **Credit cards:** V, AMEX, MC.
Lodging on site: No. **Reduced fees:** No.
Unrestricted walking: No. **Range:** Yes (grass).
Holes: 18. **Par:** 72. **Yards:** 6,705-5,530. **Slope:** 128-114.
Comments: "Very good layout . . . Great greens . . . Plenty of water . . . Long journey to some tees."

★★★½ BENT CREEK GOLF COURSE
Jackson—PU—314-243-6060 (100 mi. from St. Louis).
Season: Year-round. **High:** April-Oct. **Caddies:** No.
Green fee: $20-$49. **Credit cards:** V, MC.
Reduced fees: Weekdays, Low Season, Resort Guests, Twilight Play.
Unrestricted walking: Yes. **Range:** Yes (mats).
Holes: 18. **Par:** 72. **Yards:** 7,000-5,038. **Slope:** 136-112.
Comments: "Best public course in Missouri . . . Unfortunately in the middle of nowhere . . . Target areas not well defined . . . Rough is unmanageable . . . Never crowded . . . The back 9 is a hill climb, very trying."

★★★CRYSTAL HIGHLANDS GOLF CLUB
Crystal City—PU—314-933-3880 (30 mi. from St. Louis).
Season: Year-round. **High:** April-Oct. **Caddies:** No.
Green fee: $20-$49. **Credit cards:** V, MC.
Reduced fees: Weekdays, Low Season, Twilight Play.
Unrestricted Walking: No. **Range:** Yes (grass).
Holes: 18. **Par:** 72. **Yards:** 6,542-4,953. **Slope:** 135-109.
Comments: "Excellent layout, conditioning a problem . . . Best for the money in St. Louis area . . . When rough matures, will be outstanding . . . Quality layout, but greens almost unfair . . . Small, fast . . . Gimmicky . . . Erratic fairways . . . Not great, but decent . . . Nothing spectacular, but a good challenge . . . Hard to get to . . . Too crowded."

★½ EAGLE SPRINGS GOLF COURSE
St. Louis—PU—314-355-7277.
Season: Year-round. **High:** May-Sept. **Caddies:** No.
Green fee: $20-$49. **Credit cards:** V, MC.
Reduced fees: Weekdays, Low Season, Twilight Play.
Unrestricted walking: Yes. **Range:** Yes (mats).
Holes: 18. **Par:** 72. **Yards:** 6,454-5,453. **Slope:** 113-112.
Also 9-hole par-3 course.
Comments: "OK, but some weak holes . . . Plagued by erosion . . . Conditioning needs improvement . . . Large greens, poor fairways . . . Very disappointing, not challenging at all . . . Course opened too early . . . Getting better, fairways not as rutted, greens better."

★★½ LAKE VALLEY GOLF & COUNTRY CLUB
Camdenton—PU—314-346-7218 (60 mi. from Jefferson City).
Season: Year-round. **High:** April-Oct. **Caddies:** No.
Green fee: $20-$49. **Credit cards:** V, MC.
Lodging on site: No. **Reduced fees:** Low Season.
Unrestricted walking: No. **Range:** Yes (grass).
Holes: 18. **Par:** 72. **Yards:** 6,405-6,103. **Slope:** 121-118.
Comments: "Short, but good for the money . . . Friendly . . . Fun course . . . Six par 3s, six par 4s, six par 5s . . . Not crowded, excellent greens."

THE LODGE OF FOUR SEASONS
Lake Ozark—R—314-365-8532, 800-843-5253.
Season: March-Nov. **High:** May-Sept. **Caddies:** No.
Green fee: $50-$99. **Credit cards:** V, AMEX, DISC, MC.
Lodging on site: Yes. **Reduced fees:** Weekdays, Low Season, Twilight Play.
Unrestricted walking: No. **Range:** Yes (grass).
★★★½ ROBERT TRENT JONES COURSE
Holes: 18. **Par:** 71. **Yards:** 6,406-5,289. **Slope:** 133-120.
Comments: "Good resort . . . Good course . . . Always a pleasure . . . Nos. 10 and 11 are unforgettable . . . Undulating greens . . . Plays well year-round. . . . Too expensive . . . Long distances between holes, lots of O.B. . . . Needs work, living on its reputation . . . Not worth the cost."
★★★½ SEASONS RIDGE COURSE
314-365-8544.

Holes: 18. **Par:** 72. **Yards:** 6,416-4,657. **Slope:** 130-118.
Comments: "Scenery is outstanding . . . Short, but hilly, tight and fun . . . Best in the Ozarks . . . Too young to really tell . . . Gets better every year . . . In two years will be hard to beat . . . Great, but too expensive for average player."

MARRIOTT'S TAN-TAR-A RESORT & GOLF CLUB
Osage Beach—R—314-348-8521, 800-826-8272 (80 mi. from Springfield).
Season: Year-round. **High:** April-Oct. **Caddies:** No.
Green fee: $50-$99. **Credit cards:** All Major.
Lodging on site: Yes. **Reduced fees:** Weekdays, Low Season, Resort Guests, Twilight Play.
Unrestricted walking: No. **Range:** Yes (grass).
★★½ **THE OAKS COURSE**
Holes: 18. **Par:** 71. **Yards:** 6,442-3,943. **Slope:** 143-103.
"Tough and scenic . . . Good job with questionable land . . . Gorgeous views, not challenging . . . More blind shots than I like in a resort course . . . All four par 3s are alike . . . Crabgrass growing on greens. You have to hunt for grass on tee boxes. All this and less for about $60 . . . Quality personnel and service . . . Takes too long to play . . . Too expensive . . . Beware the summer heat and humidity."
HIDDEN LAKES COURSE*
Holes: 9. **Par:** 35. **Yards:** 3,015-2,232.

★★½ NORTH PORT NATIONAL GOLF CLUB
Lake Ozark—R—314-365-1100 (45 mi. from Jefferson City).
Season: Year-round. **High:** April-Oct. **Caddies:** No.
Green fee: $50-$99. **Credit cards:** V, AMEX, MC.
Lodging on site: Yes. **Reduced fees:** Twilight Play.
Unrestricted walking: No. **Range:** Yes (grass).
Holes: 18. **Par:** 72. **Yards:** 7,150-5,252. **Slope:** 145-122.
Comments: "Not so great . . . Two different 9s, conditioning questionable, high cost . . . Hard to believe Arnold Palmer manages course . . . Opened too early, needs to grow in . . . Still young, will get better . . . Two years away from being in decent shape . . . Where's Arnie?"

PARADISE VALLEY GOLF & COUNTRY CLUB*
Valley Park—PU—314-225-5157 (20 mi. from St. Louis).
Season: Year-round. **High:** April-Sept. **Caddies:** No.
Green fee: Under $20. **Credit cards:** V, AMEX, MC.
Lodging on site: No. **Reduced fees:** Weekdays.
Unrestricted walking: No. **Range:** Yes (mats).
Holes: 18. **Par:** 70. **Yards:** 6,185-5,102. **Slope:** 112-108.

★★★QUAIL CREEK GOLF CLUB
St Louis—PU—314-487-1988.
Season: Year-round. **High:** April-Oct. **Caddies:** No.
Green fee: $20-$49. **Credit cards:** V, AMEX, MC.
Reduced fees: Weekdays, Low Season, Twilight Play.
Unrestricted walking: No. **Range:** Yes (mats).
Holes: 18. **Par:** 72. **Yards:** 6,984-5,244. **Slope:** 141-109.
Comments: "One of Hale Irwin's best designs . . . Easy layout, but some trick holes . . . Back 9 much more difficult . . . No. 15 is one of the best holes in the city . . . Very busy . . . Gets a bit brown due to St. Louis summers and fact course is in wetlands area . . . Cartpath rule necessitates long walks with two or three clubs . . . Too much money."

SOUTHVIEW GOLF CLUB*
Belton—PU—816-331-4042 (15 mi. from Kansas City).
Season: Year-round. **High:** April-Sept. **Caddies:** No.
Green fee: Under $20. **Credit cards:** No.
Lodging on site: No. **Reduced fees:** Weekdays.
Unrestricted walking: Yes. **Range:** Yes (mats).
Holes: 18. **Par:** 72. **Yards:** 6,594-5,805. **Slope:** 115-113.

★★SWOPE MEMORIAL GOLF COURSE

Kansas City—PU—816-523-9081.
Season: Year-round. **High:** April-Oct. **Caddies:** No.
Green fee: Under $20. **Credit cards:** V.
Lodging on site: No. **Reduced fees:** Weekdays, Twilight Play.
Unrestricted walking: Yes. **Range:** No.
Holes: 18. **Par:** 72. **Yards:** 6,274-4,517. **Slope:** 128-117.

WHITMOOR COUNTRY CLUB

St. Charles—PU—314-926-9622 (20 mi. from St. Louis).
Season: Year-round. **High:** April-Sept. **Caddies:** No.
Green fee: $20-$49. **Credit cards:** V, AMEX, DISC, MC.
Lodging on site: No. **Reduced fees:** Low Season, Twilight Play.
Unrestricted walking: No. **Range:** Yes (grass).
★★EAST COURSE
Holes: 18. **Par:** 71. **Yards:** 6,646-4,658. **Slope:** 132-110.
Club also has 18-hole West Course open only to members.
Comments: "Poor architecture, most drives and second shots leave sidehill lies . . . Not much character . . . Many greens ridiculously terraced . . . Too high a cost, too slow of play . . . Weekdays good, weekends expensive . . . Gets excessive play . . . Worn out, poor care . . . Turf quality lacking . . . Overbooked, slow."

BIG SKY GOLF CLUB*

Big Sky—R—406-995-4706 (38 mi. from Bozeman).
Season: May-Oct. **High:** July-Sept. **Caddies:** No.
Green fee: $20-$49. **Credit cards:** V, AMEX, DISC, MC.
Lodging on site: No. **Reduced fees:** No.
Unrestricted walking: Yes. **Range:** Yes (grass).
Holes: 18. **Par:** 72. **Yards:** 6,748-5,374. **Slope:** 111-104.

BUFFALO HILL GOLF CLUB

Kalispell—PU—406-756-4545.
Season: March-Nov. **High:** May-Sept. **Caddies:** No.
Green fee: $20-$49. **Credit cards:** V, MC.
Lodging on site: No. **Reduced fees:** No.
Unrestricted walking: Yes. **Range:** Yes (mats).
★★★½ **CHAMPIONSHIP COURSE**
Holes: 18. **Par:** 72. **Yards:** 6,525-5,258. **Slope:** 131-125.
Comments: "Great city course . . . Good spot to pop in unannounced."
CAMERON COURSE*
Holes: 9. **Par:** 35. **Yards:** 3,001-2,950.

★★★½ EAGLE BEND GOLF CLUB

Bigfork—PU—406-837-7302, 800-255-5641.
Season: April-Nov. **High:** June-Aug. **Caddies:** No.
Green fee: $20-$49. **Credit cards:** V, AMEX, DISC, MC.
Lodging on site: Yes. **Reduced fees:** Low Season, Twilight Play.
Unrestricted walking: Yes. **Range:** Yes (grass).
Holes: 18. **Par:** 72. **Yards:** 6,742-5,398. **Slope:** 124-122.
Ranked in Second 25 of America's 75 Best Public Courses and selected as
runner-up for Best New Public Course of 1989 by GOLF DIGEST.
Comments: "Gorgeous setting . . . Beautiful and tough . . . When in Montana, don't you dare miss this one."

LARCHMONT GOLF COURSE*

Missoula—PU—406-721-4416.
Season: March-Oct. **High:** March-Oct. **Caddies:** No.
Green fee: Under $20. **Credit cards:** V, MC.
Lodging on site: No. **Reduced fees:** Weekdays.
Unrestricted walking: Yes. **Range:** Yes (grass).
Holes: 18. **Par:** 72. **Yards:** 7,114-5,936. **Slope:** 116-118.

★★½ MEADOW LAKE GOLF RESORT

Columbia Falls—R—406-892-2111, 800-321-4653 (10 mi. from Kalispell).
Season: April-Oct. **High:** July-Sept. **Caddies:** No.
Green fee: $20-$49. **Credit cards:** V, AMEX, MC.
Lodging on site: Yes. **Reduced fees:** Resort Guests, Twilight Play.
Unrestricted walking: Yes. **Range:** Yes (grass).
Holes: 18. **Par:** 72. **Yards:** 6,701-5,488. **Slope:** 128-122.
Comments: "A little too built up with houses . . . A course being used to
sell time-shares."

★★½ POLSON COUNTRY CLUB

Polson—PU—406-883-2440.
Season: March-Nov. **High:** June-Sept. **Caddies:** No.
Green fee: $20-$49. **Credit cards:** V, MC.
Lodging on site: No. **Reduced fees:** No.
Unrestricted walking: Yes. **Range:** Yes (grass).
Holes: 18. **Par:** 72. **Yards:** 6,756-5,215. **Slope:** 119-114.
Comments: "Beautiful backdrops of Flathead Lake and the Montana sky
. . . Inexpensive and uncrowded, even in peak season."

MONTANA

RED LODGE GOLF COURSE*
Red Lodge—PU—406-446-3344 (60 mi. from Billings).
Season: May-Sept. **High:** June-Aug. **Caddies:** No.
Green fee: Under $20. **Credit cards:** V, MC.
Lodging on site: No. **Reduced fees:** No.
Unrestricted walking: Yes. **Range:** Yes (grass).
Holes: 18. **Par:** 72. **Yards:** 6,779-6,445. **Slope:** 115-115.

★★★WHITEFISH LAKE GOLF CLUB
MOUNTAIN/WOODS/LAKE 9s
Whitefish—PU—406-862-5960.
Season: April-Oct. **High:** June-Sept. **Caddies:** No.
Green fee: $20-$49. **Credit cards:** V, MC.
Lodging on site: Yes. **Reduced fees:** No.
Unrestricted walking: Yes. **Range:** Yes (mats).
Holes: 27. **Par:** 36/36/36. **Yards:** 3,110/2,847/3,090.
Fourth 9 scheduled to open in spring of 1994. Woods/Lake 18 ranked 4th in Montana by GOLF DIGEST.

★★½ APPLEWOOD GOLF COURSE
Omaha—PU—402-444-4656.
Season: Jan.-Dec. **High:** May-Aug. **Caddies:** No.
Green fee: Under $20. **Credit cards:** No.
Lodging on site: No. **Reduced fees:** No.
Unrestricted walking: Yes. **Range:** Yes (grass).
Holes: 18. **Par:** 72. **Yards:** 6,916-6,014. **Slope:** 117-126.
Comments: "Lots of play . . . Greens rough . . . A good muny in bad shape."

★★½ BENSON PARK GOLF COURSE
Omaha—PU—402-444-4626.
Season: Year-round. **High:** Summer. **Caddies:** No.
Green fee: Under $20. **Credit cards:** No.
Lodging on site: No. **Reduced fees:** Weekdays.
Unrestricted walking: Yes. **Range:** No.
Holes: 18. **Par:** 72. **Yards:** 6,814-6,085. **Slope:** 120-121.

★★½ GRAND ISLAND MUNICIPAL GOLF COURSE
Grand Island—PU—308-381-5340 (90 mi. from Lincoln).
Season: Year-round. **High:** Summer. **Caddies:** No.
Green fee: Under $20. **Credit cards:** No.
Lodging on site: No. **Reduced fees:** No.
Unrestricted walking: Yes. **Range:** Yes (grass).
Holes: 18. **Par:** 72. **Yards:** 6,752-5,484. **Slope:** 115-112.

★★★½ HERITAGE HILLS GOLF COURSE
McCook—PU—308-345-5032.
Season: Year-round. **High:** Summer. **Caddies:** No.
Green fee: Under $20. **Credit cards:** All Major.
Lodging on site: No. **Reduced fees:** No.
Unrestricted walking: Yes. **Range:** Yes (grass).
Holes: 18. **Par:** 72. **Yards:** 6,715-5,475. **Slope:** 133-120.
Comments: "Top quality . . . Sandhills scenic . . . The best public course in Nebraska."

GREAT VALUE

★★½ HOLMES PARK GOLF COURSE
Lincoln—PU—402-441-8960.
Season: March-Nov. **High:** May-Sept. **Caddies:** No.
Green fee: Under $20. **Credit cards:** V, MC.
Lodging on site: No. **Reduced fees:** Weekdays.
Unrestricted walking: Yes. **Range:** Yes (grass).
Holes: 18. **Par:** 72. **Yards:** 6,805-6,054. **Slope:** 126-131.

★★★½ INDIAN CREEK GOLF COURSE
Elkhorn—PU—402-289-0900 (5 mi. from Omaha).
Season: March-Dec. **High:** May-Aug. **Caddies:** No.
Green fee: $20-$49. **Credit cards:** V, MC.
Lodging on site: No. **Reduced fees:** Weekdays.
Unrestricted walking: Yes. **Range:** Yes (grass).
Holes: 18. **Par:** 72. **Yards:** 7,236-5,149. **Slope:** 127-114.
Comments: "Very long from back . . . Relatively new, still growing in."

★★ MAHONEY GOLF COURSE
Lincoln—PU—402-441-8969 (50 mi. from Omaha).
Season: April-Nov. **High:** May-Aug. **Caddies:** No.
Green fee: Under $20. **Credit cards:** All Major.
Lodging on site: No. **Reduced fees:** Weekdays.
Unrestricted walking: Yes. **Range:** Yes (grass).
Holes: 18. **Par:** 70. **Yards:** 6,459-5,585. **Slope:** 103-115.
Comments: "Very good shape, not expensive."

MIRACLE HILL GOLF AND TENNIS CENTER*
Omaha—PU—402-498-0220.
Season: Year-round. **High:** May-Aug. **Caddies:** No.
Green fee: Under $20. **Credit cards:** No.
Lodging on site: No. **Reduced fees:** Weekdays.
Unrestricted walking: Yes. **Range:** Yes (mats).
Holes: 18. **Par:** 70. **Yards:** 6,412-5,069. **Slope:** 129-117.

★★★THE PINES COUNTRY CLUB
Valley—PU—402-359-4311 (25 mi. from Omaha).
Season: March-Nov. **High:** May-Aug. **Caddies:** No.
Green fee: $20-$49. **Credit cards:** V, MC.
Lodging on site: No. **Reduced fees:** Weekdays.
Unrestricted walking: Yes. **Range:** Yes (grass).
Holes: 18. **Par:** 72. **Yards:** 6,650-5,370. **Slope:** 118-129.
Comments: "Excellent shape . . . A good test."

★★★PIONEERS GOLF COURSE
Lincoln—PU—402-441-8966.
Season: Year-round. **High:** May-Sept. **Caddies:** No.
Green fee: Under $20. **Credit cards:** V, MC.
Lodging on site: No. **Reduced fees:** Weekdays.
Unrestricted walking: Yes. **Range:** Yes (grass).
Holes: 18. **Par:** 71. **Yards:** 6,478-5,778. **Slope:** 112-110.
Comments: "Best muny in Lincoln."

★★★QUAIL RUN GOLF COURSE
Columbus—PU—402-564-1313 (80 mi. from Omaha).
Season: April-Oct. **High:** Summer. **Caddies:** No.
Green fee: Under $20. **Credit cards:** V, AMEX, DISC, MC.
Lodging on site: No. **Reduced fees:** No.
Unrestricted walking: Yes. **Range:** Yes (grass).
Holes: 18. **Par:** 72. **Yards:** 7,024-5,147. **Slope:** 140-125.

TIBURON GOLF CLUB*
Omaha—PU—402-895-2688.
Season: March-Oct. **High:** May-Aug. **Caddies:** No.
Green fee: $20-$49. **Credit cards:** V, AMEX, MC.
Lodging on site: No. **Reduced fees:** No.
Unrestricted walking: No. **Range:** Yes (grass).
Holes: 18. **Par:** 72. **Yards:** 7,005-5,435. **Slope:** 137-127.

★★★½ WOODLAND HILLS GOLF COURSE
Eagle—PU—402-475-4653 (15 mi. from Lincoln).
Season: Year-round. **High:** March-Oct. **Caddies:** No.
Green fee: Under $20. **Credit cards:** V, MC.
Lodging on site: No. **Reduced fees:** Weekdays, Twilight Play.
Unrestricted walking: No. **Range:** Yes (grass).
Holes: 18. **Par:** 71. **Yards:** 6,592-5,886. **Slope:** 125-118.
Ranked 3rd in Nebraska by GOLF DIGEST.
Comments: "A good layout, still filling in . . . Nice and easy tee times . . . Will be great in time."

ANGEL PARK GOLF CLUB

Las Vegas—PU—702-254-4653.

Season: Year-round. **High:** March-May/Oct. **Caddies:** No.

Green fee: $50-$99. **Credit cards:** V, AMEX, MC.

Lodging on site: No. **Reduced fees:** Low Season, Twilight Play.

Unrestricted walking: No. **Range:** Yes (mats).

Club also has "Cloud Nine" course, a unique 12-hole layout that imitates famous par 3s.

★★★MOUNTAIN COURSE

Holes: 18. **Par:** 71. **Yards:** 6,722-5,164. **Slope:** 128-119.

Comments: "Nice new course . . . Excellent condition year round . . . Super, but expensive . . . Nearly impossible carries when wind blows. And it's always blowing . . . Excellent staff, have never been treated better."

★★★PALM COURSE

Holes: 18. **Par:** 70. **Yards:** 6,530-4,570. **Slope:** 130-110.

Comments: "Par 70, but challenging . . . Was awful, but recent remodel job improved it immeasurably . . . Wonderful vistas . . . Great shot values."

★½ BLACK MOUNTAIN GOLF & COUNTRY CLUB

Henderson—PU—702-565-7933 (15 mi. from Las Vegas).

Season: Year-round. **High:** Jan.-May. **Caddies:** No.

Green fee: $20-$49. **Credit cards:** V, MC.

Lodging on site: No. **Reduced fees:** Low Season.

Unrestricted walking: No. **Range:** Yes (grass).

Holes: 18. **Par:** 72. **Yards:** 6,541-5,478. **Slope:** 123-125.

Comments: "Not one bit impressive."

★★CRAIG RANCH GOLF COURSE

North Las Vegas—PU—702-642-9700.

Season: Year-round. **High:** Feb.-June/Sept.-Nov. **Caddies:** No.

Green fee: Under $20. **Credit cards:** No.

Lodging on site: No. **Reduced fees:** No.

Unrestricted walking: Yes. **Range:** Yes (grass).

Holes: 18. **Par:** 70. **Yards:** 6,001-5,522. **Slope:** 105-101.

Comments: "Price is right, but course needs work . . . A zillion trees . . . Won't be back."

★★★½ DESERT INN HOTEL & COUNTRY CLUB

Las Vegas—R—702-733-4290, 800-634-6909.

Season: Year-round. **High:** Feb.-June. **Caddies:** No.

Green fee: $100 and up. **Credit cards:** All Major.

Lodging on site: Yes. **Reduced fees:** Weekdays, Resort Guests.

Unrestricted walking: No. **Range:** Yes (grass).

Holes: 18. **Par:** 72. **Yards:** 7,074-5,809. **Slope:** 134-115.

Ranked 65th in America's 75 Best Resort Courses by GOLF DIGEST.

Comments: "Expensive, but beautiful . . . Simple layout, astronomical prices . . . Architecture is dated . . . It's crazy what they charge here."

★½ DESERT ROSE GOLF COURSE

Las Vegas—PU—702-431-4653.

Season: Year-round. **High:** Spring/Fall. **Caddies:** No.

Green fee: $20-$49. **Credit cards:** V, MC.

Reduced fees: Weekdays, Low Season, Twilight Play.

Unrestricted walking: Yes. **Range:** Yes (mats).

Holes: 18. **Par:** 71. **Yards:** 6,511-5,458. **Slope:** 112-107.

Comments: "Deadly dull . . . For the money, one of the worst I've played . . . So many things need attention."

★★★★EDGEWOOD TAHOE GOLF COURSE

Stateline—PU—702-588-3566 (55 mi. from Reno).

Season: May-Oct. **High:** Summer. **Caddies:** No.

Green fee: $100 and up. **Credit cards:** V, AMEX, MC.

Lodging on site: No. **Reduced fees:** No.
Unrestricted walking: No. **Range:** Yes (grass).
Holes: 18. **Par:** 72. **Yards:** 7,491-5,749. **Slope:** 139-140.
Ranked in First 25 of America's 75 Best Public Courses by GOLF DIGEST.
Comments: "An absolute must play . . . Nevada's best . . . Second only to
Pebble Beach for beauty . . . Bring your Instamatic . . . Too popular . . .
Can be hard to get good tee times . . . Outstanding staff and facility . . . Too
many forced carries . . . Costs way too much."

★★EMERALD RIVER GOLF COURSE
Laughlin—PU—702-298-0061 (89 mi. from Las Vegas).
Season: Year-round. **High:** Feb.-Nov. **Caddies:** No.
Green fee: $50-$99. **Credit cards:** V, MC.
Lodging on site: No. **Reduced fees:** Weekdays, Low Season.
Unrestricted walking: No. **Range:** Yes (grass).
Holes: 18. **Par:** 72. **Yards:** 6,809-5,205. **Slope:** 144-129.
Comments: "Target golf of the worst kind . . . 8-irons off the tees . . .
Rock hard . . . Always hot, even in the morning . . . Bring your canteen."

HIGHLAND FALLS GOLF CLUB*
Las Vegas—PU—702-254-7010.
Season: Year-round. **High:** Oct.-May. **Caddies:** No.
Green fee: $50-$99. **Credit cards:** V, AMEX, MC.
Lodging on site: No. **Reduced fees:** Low Season, Twilight Play.
Unrestricted walking: No. **Range:** Yes (grass).
Holes: 18. **Par:** 72. **Yards:** 6,512-5,019. **Slope:** 126-112.

INCLINE VILLAGE GOLF RESORT
Incline Village—PU—702-832-1144 (30 mi. from Reno).
Season: May-Oct. **High:** July-Sept. **Caddies:** No.
Green fee: $50-$99. **Credit cards:** V, MC.
Lodging on site: No. **Reduced fees:** Twilight Play.
Unrestricted walking: No. **Range:** Yes (mats).
★★★½ CHAMPIONSHIP COURSE
Holes: 18. **Par:** 72. **Yards:** 6,915-5,350. **Slope:** 129-126.
Ranked in Third 25 of America's 75 Best Public Courses by GOLF DIGEST.
Comments: "Invigorating . . . Breathtaking . . . A great value for home-
owners, not for the rest of us . . . Hard to get to, you pay for the trouble
once you're there . . . Outstanding staff."
EXECUTIVE COURSE*
702-832-1150
Holes: 18. **Par:** 58. **Yards:** 3,513-3,002. **Slope:** 94-85.

★★LAKERIDGE GOLF COURSE
Reno—PU—702-825-2200.
Season: March-Dec. **High:** April-Oct. **Caddies:** No.
Green fee: $50-$99. **Credit cards:** V, MC.
Lodging on site: No. **Reduced fees:** Low Season, Twilight Play.
Unrestricted walking: No. **Range:** Yes (mats).
Holes: 18. **Par:** 71. **Yards:** 6,703-5,159. **Slope:** 127-119.
Comments: "Tops . . . Best place to play in Reno . . . Great signature hole
. . . Dramatic par-3 15th with island green and skyline views . . . A bit
pricey . . . Needs better maintenance."

★★LAS VEGAS GOLF CLUB
Las Vegas—PU—702-646-3003.
Season: Year-round. **High:** Oct.-Dec./March-May. **Caddies:** No.
Green fee: $20-$49. **Credit cards:** No.
Lodging on site: No. **Reduced fees:** Low Season, Twilight Play.
Unrestricted walking: Yes. **Range:** Yes (mats).
Holes: 18. **Par:** 72. **Yards:** 6,631-5,715. **Slope:** 114-113.
Comments: "Good public course for the money . . . Considering all the
play, is in very good shape."

★★★½ THE LEGACY GOLF CLUB
Henderson—R—702-897-2187 (5 mi. from Las Vegas).
Season: Year-round. **High:** Feb.-May/Sept.-Nov. **Caddies:** No.
Green fee: $50-$99. **Credit cards:** No.
Lodging on site: No. **Reduced fees:** Low Season, Twilight Play.
Unrestricted walking: No. **Range:** Yes (grass).
Holes: 18. **Par:** 72. **Yards:** 7,233-5,340. **Slope:** 136-120.
Comments: "A must when in Vegas . . . Excellent design . . . Some moonscape holes . . . Getting too developed . . . Only in Vegas: a 'deck of cards' set of tee boxes."

★★ THE MIRAGE GOLF CLUB
Las Vegas—R—702-369-7111.
Season: Year-round. **High:** Sept.-May. **Caddies:** No.
Green fee: $100 and up. **Credit cards:** V, AMEX, DISC, MC.
Reduced fees: Low Season, Resort Guests, Twilight Play.
Unrestricted walking: No. **Range:** Yes (mats).
Holes: 18. **Par:** 72. **Yards:** 7,078-6,163. **Slope:** 132-119.
Previously known as The Dunes Country Club.

★★★ PAINTED DESERT GOLF CLUB
Las Vegas—PU—702-645-2568.
Season: Year-round. **High:** Sept.-June. **Caddies:** No.
Green fee: $50-$99. **Credit cards:** V, MC.
Lodging on site: No. **Reduced fees:** Twilight Play.
Unrestricted walking: No. **Range:** Yes (mats).
Holes: 18. **Par:** 72. **Yards:** 6,840-5,711. **Slope:** 136-120.
Comments: "Nifty . . . Good, tough desert course . . . Best bet in Vegas . . . Too tight, no mercy . . . Slow greens . . . Constant home construction noise a problem . . . A little too far off the strip for tourists."

★★★½ PEPPERMILL PALMS GOLF COURSE
Mesquite—R—800-621-0187 (80 mi. from Las Vegas).
Season: Year-round. **High:** Jan.-May. **Caddies:** No.
Green fee: $50-$99. **Credit cards:** V, AMEX, DISC, MC.
Lodging on site: Yes. **Reduced fees:** Resort Guests.
Unrestricted walking: No. **Range:** Yes (grass).
Holes: 18. **Par:** 72. **Yards:** 7,022-5,162. **Slope:** 137-120.
Comments: "Beautiful oasis in the desert . . . Too good to be true . . . Very plush . . . Well groomed, but very long . . . Tough rough . . . Two totally different 9s . . . Front 9 so-so . . . Seemed forced and contrived . . . Flat . . . The 'water 9' . . . Back 9 fun . . . Hilly, interesting . . . Elevated tees and greens . . . Variation is fun . . . Very fine facility and staff."

★★½ ROSEWOOD LAKES MUNICIPAL GOLF COURSE
Reno—PU—702-857-2892.
Season: Year-round. **High:** April-Nov. **Caddies:** No.
Green fee: $20-$49. **Credit cards:** V, MC.
Lodging on site: No. **Reduced fees:** Low Season, Twilight Play.
Unrestricted walking: Yes. **Range:** Yes (grass).
Holes: 18. **Par:** 72. **Yards:** 6,693-5,082. **Slope:** 127-115.
Comments: "Narrow, surrounded by protected wetlands."

★★½ ROYAL KENFIELD COUNTRY CLUB
Henderson—PU—702-434-9009 (8 mi. from Las Vegas).
Season: Year-round. **High:** Oct.-May. **Caddies:** No.
Green fee: $50-$99. **Credit cards:** V, MC.
Reduced fees: Weekdays, Low Season, Twilight Play.
Unrestricted walking: No. **Range:** Yes (grass).
Holes: 18. **Par:** 72. **Yards:** 7,053-5,372. **Slope:** 135-125.
On its fourth name. Formerly called Paradise Valley Country Club, then Showboat Country Club and most recently Indian Wells Country Club.
Comments: "Former country club gone public . . . Tricked up a mature course."

★★★SAHARA COUNTRY CLUB
Las Vegas—PU—702-796-0013, 800-468-7918.
Season: Year-round. **High:** Nov.-May. **Caddies:** No.
Green fee: $50-$99. **Credit cards:** V, AMEX, MC.
Reduced fees: Weekdays, Low Season, Twilight Play.
Unrestricted walking: No. **Range:** Yes (mats).
Holes: 18. **Par:** 71. **Yards:** 6,815-5,741. **Slope:** 123-114.
Comments: "Fine older course . . . The poor man's Desert Inn . . . Good bargain over all."

★½ SIERRA SAGE GOLF COURSE
Reno—PU—702-972-1564.
Season: Year-round. **High:** May-Oct. **Caddies:** No.
Green fee: $20-$49. **Credit cards:** No.
Lodging on site: No. **Reduced fees:** Weekdays, Low Season.
Unrestricted walking: Yes. **Range:** Yes (mats).
Holes: 18. **Par:** 71. **Yards:** 6,650-5,573. **Slope:** 120-113.

SPRING CREEK GOLF COURSE*
Elko—PU—702-753-6331.
Season: March-Nov. **High:** Summer. **Caddies:** No.
Green fee: Under $20. **Credit cards:** V, MC.
Lodging on site: No. **Reduced fees:** No.
Unrestricted walking: Yes. **Range:** Yes (grass).
Holes: 18. **Par:** 71. **Yards:** 6,258-5,658. **Slope:** 125-119.

★★WASHOE COUNTY GOLF COURSE
Reno—PU—702-785-4286.
Season: Year-round. **High:** March-Oct. **Caddies:** No.
Green fee: Under $20. **Credit cards:** No.
Reduced fees: Weekdays, Low Season, Twilight Play.
Unrestricted walking: Yes. **Range:** Yes (mats).
Holes: 18. **Par:** 72. **Yards:** 6,695-5,973. **Slope:** 119-120.

★½ WILDCREEK GOLF COURSE
Sparks—PU—702-673-3100 (1 mi. from Reno).
Season: Feb.-Dec. **High:** May-Oct. **Caddies:** No.
Green fee: $20-$49. **Credit cards:** V, MC.
Lodging on site: No. **Reduced fees:** Low Season, Twilight Play.
Unrestricted walking: No. **Range:** Yes (grass).
Holes: 18. **Par:** 72. **Yards:** 6,932-5,472. **Slope:** 132-120.
Has 9-hole par-3 course on property.
Comments: "Good course before the drought. Play only if it's been re-grassed . . . Terrible fairway lies . . . Not rewarded for good shots . . . Need a guide to find your way around."

BETHLEHEM COUNTRY CLUB*
Bethlehem—PU—603-869-5745 (150 mi. from Boston).
Season: May-Oct. **High:** Summer. **Caddies:** No.
Green fee: Under $20. **Credit cards:** V, MC.
Lodging on site: No. **Reduced fees:** Twilight Play.
Unrestricted walking: Yes. **Range:** No.
Holes: 18. **Par:** 70. **Yards:** 5,746-5,616. **Slope:** 113-121.

★★★½ BRETWOOD GOLF COURSE
Keene—PU—603-352-7626 (55 mi. from Manchester).
Season: April-Nov. **High:** Summer. **Caddies:** No.
Green fee: $20-$49. **Credit Cards:** No.
Lodging on Site: No. **Reduced fees:** Weekdays.
Unrestricted walking: Yes. **Range:** Yes (Grass).
Holes: 18. **Par:** 72. **Yards:** 6,974-5,140. **Slope:** 134-120.
Ranked 5th in New Hampshire by GOLF DIGEST. Also has 9-hole par-36
South Course.
Comments: "A nice, fun course . . . Good condition, walkable, fast greens
. . . No regard for slow play, clubhouse facilities are poor."

★★★COUNTRY CLUB OF NEW HAMPSHIRE
North Sutton—PU—603-927-4246 (30 mi. from Concord).
Season: April-Nov. **High:** Summer. **Caddies:** No.
Green fee: $20-$49. **Credit cards:** V, MC.
Lodging on site: Yes. **Reduced fees:** Twilight Play.
Unrestricted walking: Yes. **Range:** Yes (grass).
Holes: 18. **Par:** 72. **Yards:** 6,900-6,300. **Slope:** 125-122.
Comments: "Classic layout . . . Picturesque mountain layout . . . A think-
ing person's golf course . . . Rolling hills and woods everywhere . . . Vary-
ing holes . . . Very plush for a public course . . . The state's best-kept secret
. . . A hidden gem . . . Good range, nice greens . . . Never crowded . . .
Punch card saves 20 percent . . . Coming up under new management . . .
9th hole doesn't bring you to the clubhouse."

★★★EASTMAN GOLF LINKS
Grantham—PU—603-863-4500 (42 mi. from Concord).
Season: May-Nov. **High:** Summer. **Caddies:** No.
Green fee: $20-$49. **Credit cards:** V, MC.
Lodging on site: Yes. **Reduced fees:** No.
Unrestricted walking: No. **Range:** Yes (mats).
Holes: 18. **Par:** 71. **Yards:** 6,731-5,369. **Slope:** 137-128.
Comments: "The best of New Hampshire . . . Great course, tight, in the
mountains . . . Spectacular views . . . Best in autumn . . . Almost too hard."

★★½ JACK O'LANTERN RESORT
Woodstock—R—603-745-3636 (60 mi. from Manchester).
Season: May-Oct. **High:** Aug.-Oct. **Caddies:** No.
Green fee: $20-$49. **Credit cards:** V, AMEX, DISC, MC.
Lodging on site: Yes. **Reduced fees:** Weekdays, Resort Guests, Twilight
Play.
Unrestricted walking: No. **Range:** Yes (mats).
Holes: 18. **Par:** 70. **Yards:** 5,990-4,830. **Slope:** 113-110.
Comments: "A favorite . . . Good resort, well managed, good price . . .
On the short side, many doglegs . . . Railroad goes right down the middle of
the course."

★MAPLEWOOD CASINO AND COUNTRY CLUB
Bethlehem—PU—603-869-3335 (6 mi. from Littleton).
Season: May-Oct. **High:** Aug.-Sept. **Caddies:** No.
Green fee: $20-$49. **Credit cards:** V, MC.
Lodging on site: No. **Reduced fees:** Weekdays, Twilight Play.
Unrestricted walking: Yes. **Range:** Yes (grass).
Holes: 18. **Par:** 72. **Yards:** 6,243-6,001. **Slope:** 119-113.

Comments: "You can walk! . . . Lack of tee times is a problem . . . Could be better conditioned . . . Nice, plus low rates . . . Has a par 6!"

★★MOUNT WASHINGTON GOLF CLUB

Bretton Woods—R—603-278-1000 (40 mi. from North Conway).
Season: May-Oct. **High:** July-Sept. **Caddies:** No.
Green fee: $20-$49. **Credit cards:** All Major.
Lodging on site: Yes. **Reduced fees:** Resort Guests.
Unrestricted walking: Yes. **Range:** No.
Holes: 18. **Par:** 71. **Yards:** 6,623-5,356. **Slope:** 123-119.
Has 9-hole par-35 Mount Pleasant course.
Comments: "Easy layout . . . Great prices . . . Great views from anywhere on the course . . . Poorly maintained, poorly marked . . . Not very good."

★★★½ THE PANORAMA GOLF COURSE

Dixville Notch—R—603-255-4961.
Season: May-Oct. **High:** July-Sept. **Caddies:** No.
Green fee: $20-$49. **Credit cards:** V, AMEX, DISC, MC.
Lodging on site: Yes. **Reduced fees:** Resort Guests.
Unrestricted walking: Yes. **Range:** No.
Holes: 18. **Par:** 72. **Yards:** 6,804-5,069. **Slope:** 136-124.
On the grounds of The Balsams Grand Resort Hotel. Has 9-hole par-32 Coashaukee Course.
Comments: "Awesome . . . Great setting . . . Mountain top . . . Terrific . . . Immaculate Donald Ross design . . . Great variety of holes . . . Most enjoyable from blue tees . . . Scenic wonderland . . . Outstanding views . . . A must . . . No fee to hotel guests . . . Hotel a bit expensive even after tourist season . . . Great getaway, relaxing . . . Great service . . . Conditioning can be bad early in season . . . Lots of insects in spring time."

★★½ PASSACONAWAY COUNTRY CLUB

Litchfield—PU—603-424-4653 (1 mi. from Manchester).
Season: April-Dec. **High:** May-Sept. **Caddies:** Yes.
Green fee: $20-$49. **Credit cards:** V, MC.
Lodging on site: No. **Reduced fees:** Weekdays.
Unrestricted walking: Yes. **Range:** Yes (mats).
Holes: 18. **Par:** 71. **Yards:** 6,855-5,364. **Slope:** 126-118.
Comments: "Front 9 very long, back 9 short . . . Front is back-and-forth . . . Back side is best . . . Deceptive . . . Good conditioning . . . Beautiful links style, not too difficult . . . Serious need of trees to divide fairways . . . Danger of being hit by balls, many holes too close together . . . Hard to get weekend tee times . . . Staff very accommodating . . . No chipping to practice green, how foolish!"

★★★½ PORTSMOUTH COUNTRY CLUB

Greenland—PU—603-436-9719 (45 mi. from Manchester).
Season: April-Nov. **High:** Summer. **Caddies:** No.
Green fee: $20-$49. **Credit cards:** V, MC.
Lodging on site: No. **Reduced fees:** Twilight Play.
Unrestricted walking: Yes. **Range:** Yes (grass).
Holes: 18. **Par:** 72. **Yards:** 7,050-6,202. **Slope:** 127-135.
Ranked 4th in New Hampshire by GOLF DIGEST.
Comments: "Beautiful oceanside course . . . Windy, long and tough . . . Great variety . . . The Pebble Beach of the Atlantic . . . The best in New Hampshire . . . Some very challenging holes . . . Beautifully kept, but over-priced . . . Easy to walk . . . Hard for nonmembers to get tee times . . . Pro shop has drive-through-window attitude."

★★★½ THE SHATTUCK GOLF COURSE

Jaffrey—PU—603-532-4300 (74 mi. from Boston).
Season: April-Nov. **High:** Summer. **Caddies:** No.
Green fee: $20-$49. **Credit cards:** V, MC.
Lodging on site: No. **Reduced fees:** Twilight Play.
Unrestricted walking: Yes. **Range:** Yes (grass).

Holes: 18. **Par:** 71. **Yards:** 6,701-4,632. **Slope:** 148-139.

Ranked 1st in New Hampshire by GOLF DIGEST.

Comments: "Target golf at its finest . . . Just great . . . Best in New England . . . Like Pine Valley, every golfer should play this one at least once . . . Excellent . . . Beautiful mountain layout, many carries over water . . . Good challenging course for low handicappers . . . Toughest in the area . . . Wild layout, but too penal for most . . . Impossible to play for average player . . . Almost unplayable . . . Ruined a good nature walk . . . Bring at least a dozen balls . . . Unfair to average golfer . . . Makes you swing defensively."

★★★½ SKY MEADOW COUNTRY CLUB

Nashua—PU—603-888-9000 (35 mi. from Boston).

Season: April-Nov. **High:** Summer. **Caddies:** No.

Green fee: $50-$99. **Credit cards:** V, AMEX, MC.

Lodging on site: No. **Reduced fees:** Weekdays.

Unrestricted walking: No. **Range:** Yes (grass).

Holes: 18. **Par:** 72. **Yards:** 6,590-5,127. **Slope:** 133-131.

Ranked 3rd in New Hampshire by GOLF DIGEST.

Comments: "Fine championship course . . . Thinking man's golf . . . Best in this area . . . Picturesque . . . Good condition, too . . . Good layout, some long carries, some room for error . . . Lots of places to lose balls . . . Many placement shots . . . No. 2 is best par 3 in New England . . . Not a walking course . . . Expensive, but beautiful . . . High price, but best in New England . . . Expensive 5-hour round . . . Clubhouse was well stocked . . . Play it soon, someday it will be private."

★★ WAUKEWAN GOLF CLUB

Meredith—PU—603-279-6661 (12 mi. from Laconia).

Season: May-Oct. **High:** Summer. **Caddies:** No.

Green fee: $20-$49. **Credit cards:** V, MC.

Lodging on site: No. **Reduced fees:** No.

Unrestricted walking: Yes. **Range:** Yes (grass).

Holes: 18. **Par:** 71. **Yards:** 5,753-5,010. **Slope:** 120-112.

Comments: "Interesting . . . Fair up-country track . . . Fun, especially for women . . . No tee times needed . . . Pleasant, but not well groomed."

★½ WAUMBEK GOLF CLUB

Jefferson—PU—603-586-7777.

Season: April-Nov. **High:** Summer. **Caddies:** No.

Green fee: Under $20. **Credit cards:** No.

Lodging on site: No. **Reduced fees:** Low Season, Twilight Play.

Unrestricted walking: Yes. **Range:** No.

Holes: 18. **Par:** 71. **Yards:** 5,874-4,772. **Slope:** 107-107.

Comments: "Rustic . . . A jewel in the rough . . . Very rough."

★★★ WENTWORTH BY THE SEA GOLF CLUB

Portsmouth—R—603-433-5010 (46 mi. from Boston).

Season: April-Nov. **High:** Summer. **Caddies:** Yes.

Green fee: $50-$99. **Credit cards:** V, AMEX, MC.

Lodging on site: No. **Reduced fees:** Weekdays, Low Season.

Unrestricted walking: Yes. **Range:** No.

Holes: 18. **Par:** 70. **Yards:** 6,162-5,145. **Slope:** 123-119.

Comments: "Grand old course . . . Great old scenery . . . Gorgeous ocean bay setting . . . Prettiest course in the Northeast . . . The Pebble Beach of New Hampshire . . . Fun course . . . Wind makes all the difference . . . Some very challenging holes . . . Requires strict control . . . Well worth a return trip . . . Beautifully maintained . . . Layout stinks . . . Too punitive . . . Awful greens . . . Trees in front of greens! . . . Lots of bugs."

177

★ ½ AVALON GOLF COURSE
Swanton—PU—609-465-4389, 800-643-4766 (25 mi. from Atlantic City).
Season: Year-round. **High:** May-Oct. **Caddies:** No.
Green fee: $50-$99. **Credit cards:** V, AMEX, MC.
Lodging on site: No. **Reduced fees:** Weekdays, Low Season.
Unrestricted walking: No. **Range:** Yes (mats).
Holes: 18. **Par:** 72. **Yards:** 6,325-5,896. **Slope:** 122-117.

★★★½ BLUE HERON PINES GOLF CLUB
Galloway—PU—609-965-4653 (18 mi. from Atlantic City).
Season: Year-round. **High:** May-Oct. **Caddies:** No.
Green fee: $50-$99. **Credit cards:** V, AMEX, DISC, MC.
Lodging on site: No. **Reduced fees:** Low Season.
Unrestricted walking: No. **Range:** Yes (grass).
Holes: 18. **Par:** 72. **Yards:** 6,777-5,053. **Slope:** 136-116.
Comments: "New . . . Great golf experience . . . No. 14 is the only bad hole, a poor attempt to put a 'Pine Valley' look in the track . . . Over-hyped."

BOWLING GREEN GOLF CLUB*
Milton—PU—201-697-8688 (50 mi. from New York City).
Season: March-Dec. **High:** Summer. **Caddies:** No.
Green fee: $20-$49. **Credit cards:** V, AMEX, MC.
Lodging on site: No. **Reduced fees:** Twilight Play.
Unrestricted walking: Yes. **Range:** Yes (mats).
Holes: 18. **Par:** 72. **Yards:** 6,689-4,966. **Slope:** 131-117.

★ ½ BRIGANTINE GOLF LINKS
Brigantine—PU—609-266-1388 (2 mi. from Atlantic City).
Season: Year-round. **High:** May-Sept. **Caddies:** Yes.
Green fee: $20-$49. **Credit cards:** V, MC.
Lodging on site: No. **Reduced fees:** Low Season, Twilight Play.
Unrestricted walking: No. **Range:** No.
Holes: 18. **Par:** 72. **Yards:** 6,520-6,233. **Slope:** 123-120.
Comments: "Too wide open with little penalty for errant shots . . . Winds through houses . . . Needs work . . . Lawn conditions . . . Overpriced . . . Not a great value when it's no fun."

★★★ CAPE MAY NATIONAL GOLF CLUB
Cape May—PU—609-884-1563 (40 mi. from Atlantic City).
Season: Year-round. **High:** May-Oct. **Caddies:** No.
Green fee: $50-$99. **Credit cards:** V, MC.
Lodging on site: No. **Reduced fees:** Low Season, Twilight Play.
Unrestricted walking: No. **Range:** Yes (mats).
Holes: 18. **Par:** 71. **Yards:** 6,807-6,083. **Slope:** 136-123.
Comments: "Neat links-type layout . . . Great variety of holes . . . Good course for all playing levels . . . Plenty of wind . . . Lots of water . . . Excellent par 3 over nature preserve . . . Still immature, but great potential . . . Superior staff."

★★★ CRYSTAL SPRINGS GOLF CLUB
Hamburg—PU—201-827-1444 (50 mi. from New York City).
Season: April- Dec. **High:** May-Oct. **Caddies:** No.
Green fee: $50-$99. **Credit cards:** V, AMEX, MC.
Lodging on site: No. **Reduced fees:** Weekdays, Twilight Play.
Unrestricted walking: No. **Range:** Yes (grass).
Holes: 18. **Par:** 72. **Yards:** 6,887-5,201. **Slope:** 132-123.
Comments: "Stunning, challenging . . . Hilly, tight . . . Beautiful and difficult . . . Unforgettable . . . Can't see another golfer when playing any hole . . . Excellent design . . . A 'must play,' but bring lots of balls . . . Par-3 10th one of the best . . . In an old quarry . . . Worth price just to see the quarry holes . . . Excellent professional staff . . . Very good practice area . . . Mounds everywhere . . . Extreme mounding is contrived . . . Like playing a

NEW JERSEY

moonscape . . . Rough too deep . . . Large penalties for small errors . . . Many forced carries . . . Strange greens . . . Difficult to walk, even with a pull cart . . . Overpriced for its location."

FLANDERS VALLEY GOLF CLUB
Flanders—PU—201-584-5382 (18 mi. from Morristown).
Season: April-Dec. **High:** Summer. **Caddies:** No.
Green fee: $50-$99. **Credit cards:** No.
Lodging on site: No. **Reduced fees:** Twilight Play.
Unrestricted walking: Yes. **Range:** No.
★★★½ RED/GOLD COURSE
Holes: 18. **Par:** 72. **Yards:** 6,770-5,540. **Slope:** 124-121.
Comments: "One of the best . . . Truest greens I've played on . . . Large greens make club selection a key . . . A long, uphill walk on the back . . . Too hilly for seniors . . . Being improved each year . . . Exceptional value for Morris County residents."
★★★½ WHITE/BLUE COURSE
Holes: 18. **Par:** 72. **Yards:** 6,765-5,534. **Slope:** 124-122.
Comments: "Great public course . . . Meticulously maintained, require length and creativity . . . Better than many private clubs . . . Heavily treed on both sides of fairways . . . Starters are annoying."

★★★½ GREAT GORGE COUNTRY CLUB
QUARRY/RAIL/LAKE 9s
McAfee—PU—201-827-5757 (50 mi. from New York City).
Season: March-Nov. **High:** May-Oct. **Caddies:** No.
Green fee: $50-$99. **Credit cards:** All Major.
Lodging on site: Yes. **Reduced fees:** Weekdays, Low Season, Resort Guests, Twilight
Unrestricted walking: No. **Range:** Yes (grass).
Holes: 27. **Par:** 35/36/36. **Yards:** 3,362/3,457/3,457.
Comments: "Pretty 27 . . . Very pleasurable . . . Interesting layouts . . . Lake and Quarry 9s are the best . . . Quarry especially good . . . Some terrific views and holes . . . Views on Quarry are great . . . Always well maintained, pretty in fall . . . Poor design, not worth the money . . . Slow greens, impersonal pro shop . . . Very congested."

★★ GREATE BAY RESORT AND COUNTRY CLUB
Somers Point—R—609-927-0066 (8 mi. from Atlantic City).
Season: Year-round. **High:** May-Sept. **Caddies:** No.
Green fee: $50-$99. **Credit cards:** V, AMEX, MC.
Lodging on site: Yes. **Reduced fees:** Low Season, Resort Guests, Twilight Play.
Unrestricted walking: No. **Range:** Yes (grass).
Holes: 18. **Par:** 71. **Yards:** 6,750-5,495. **Slope:** 130-126.
Comments: "Not worth the price . . . Overrated because LPGA plays there . . . Green speed seems like 1.5 on the Stimpmeter."

★ HILLSBOROUGH GOLF AND COUNTRY CLUB
Flemington—PU—908-369-3322 (12 mi. from Somerville).
Season: Year-round. **High:** April-Oct. **Caddies:** No.
Green fee: $20-$49. **Credit cards:** No.
Reduced fees: Weekdays, Low Season, Twilight Play.
Unrestricted walking: No. **Range:** Yes (grass).
Holes: 18. **Par:** 70. **Yards:** 5,860-5,445. **Slope:** 114-119.
Comments: "Poor excuse for a golf course . . . On a mountainside . . . Like playing on an inclined plane . . . Greens too fast . . . Overall poorly maintained . . . Not well managed."

★★★★ HOMINY HILL GOLF CLUB
Colts Neck—PU—908-462-9222 (50 mi. from Philadelphia).
Season: March-Dec. **High:** May-Oct. **Caddies:** No.
Green fee: $20-$49. **Credit cards:** No.

Lodging on site: No. **Reduced fees:** Weekdays, Twilight Play.
Unrestricted walking: Yes. **Range:** Yes (grass).
Holes: 18. **Par:** 72. **Yards:** 7,059-5,794. **Slope:** 132-128.
Ranked in First 25 of America's 75 Best Public Courses by GOLF DIGEST.
Comments: "Good Trent Jones layout in Horse Country . . . Strategic . . .
As good as any public course in America . . . Better than most resort courses
. . . One of the best in the state . . . Playable 5 minutes after a 30-minute
downpour . . . Long and tough . . . Difficult rough, makes for an interesting
game . . . For amount of traffic, outstanding."

★★★★HOWELL PARK GOLF COURSE
Farmingdale—PU—908-938-4771 (50 mi. from Newark).
Season: March-Dec. **High:** April-Oct. **Caddies:** No.
Green fee: $20-$49. **Credit cards:** No.
Lodging on site: No. **Reduced fees:** Weekdays, Twilight Play.
Unrestricted walking: Yes. **Range:** No.
Holes: 18. **Par:** 72. **Yards:** 6,885-5,693. **Slope:** 128-125.
Ranked in Second 25 of America's 75 Best Public Courses by GOLF DIGEST.
Comments: "A Jersey gem . . . Super layout . . . More fun than Hominy
Hill . . . One of best in the state . . . Challenge at every turn . . . Consistent
green speeds . . . Well cared for . . . Very, very good conditions . . . Coun-
try club-like fairways and greens . . . Good value for county residents . . .
Too crowded on weekends, but good during week."

MARRIOTT'S SEAVIEW RESORT
Absecon—R—609-748-7680 (8 mi. from Atlantic City).
Season: Year-round. **High:** April-Nov. **Caddies:** No.
Green fee: $50-$99. **Credit cards:** All Major.
Lodging on site: Yes. **Reduced fees:** Low Season.
Unrestricted walking: No. **Range:** Yes (grass).
★★½ BAY COURSE
Holes: 18. **Par:** 71. **Yards:** 6,263-5,586. **Slope:** 113-115.
Comments: "Beautiful and challenging unknown . . . Wide open, wind
becomes prominent factor . . . Fun, but no bargain . . . Not worth $75 . . .
Very uneventful . . . Bunkers not strategically placed . . . If it wasn't a
resort, they wouldn't get $10 for green fees . . . A letdown after the Pines
. . . Bay? What Bay? You mean that swamp? . . . Bring bug spray."
★★★½ PINES COURSE
Holes: 18. **Par:** 71. **Yards:** 6,885-5,837. **Slope:** 132-128.
Comments: "Beautiful . . . Well designed . . . Great scenery . . . Expensive . . . It's OK after gambling . . . Must be straight off the tee . . . Better of
the two at Seaview . . . Needs better conditioning . . . Good pro shop."

★★OCEAN COUNTY GOLF COURSE AT ATLANTIS
Tuckerton—PU—609-296-2444 (25 mi. from Atlantic City).
Season: Year-round. **High:** May-Sept. **Caddies:** No.
Green fee: $20-$49. **Credit cards:** No.
Lodging on site: No. **Reduced fees:** Weekdays, Twilight Play.
Unrestricted walking: No. **Range:** Yes (mats).
Holes: 18. **Par:** 72. **Yards:** 6,848-5,579. **Slope:** 134-124.
Comments: "So-so layout . . . Course improving steadily since county
takeover . . . An early season course . . . Play it in March . . . Too many
mosquitos . . . Insects will eat you alive."

RAMBLEWOOD COUNTRY CLUB*
RED/WHITE/BLUE 9s
Mt. Laurel—PU—609-235-2119 (5 mi. from Philadelphia).
Season: Year-round. **High:** May-Sept. **Caddies:** No.
Green fee: $20-$49. **Credit cards:** V, MC.
Reduced fees: Weekdays, Low Season, Twilight Play.
Unrestricted walking: No. **Range:** No.
Holes: 27. **Par:** 36/36/36. **Yards:** 3,491/3,392/3,232.

★★½ ANGEL FIRE COUNTRY CLUB
Angel Fire—R—505-377-3055 (150 mi. from Albuquerque).
Season: May-Oct. **High:** Summer. **Caddies:** No.
Green fee: $20-$49. **Credit cards:** V, AMEX, DISC, MC.
Lodging on site: Yes. **Reduced fees:** Low Season, Resort Guests.
Unrestricted walking: Yes. **Range:** Yes (mats).
Holes: 18. **Par:** 72. **Yards:** 6,624-5,328. **Slope:** 128-118.
Comments: "Beautiful . . . Unique experience at 8,400 feet."

★★½ ARROYO DEL OSO GOLF COURSE
Albuquerque—PU—505-884-7505.
Season: Year-round. **High:** May-Nov. **Caddies:** No.
Green fee: Under $20. **Credit cards:** All Major.
Lodging on site: No. **Reduced fees:** Twilight Play.
Unrestricted walking: Yes. **Range:** Yes (grass).
Holes: 18. **Par:** 72. **Yards:** 6,900-5,998. **Slope:** 121-129.
Also has additional "Dam 9" around flood control basin.
Comments: "Good muny operation . . . Nicely managed . . . Unimagina-
tive . . . Inconsistent . . . Bad sand traps . . . Too long for short hitters . . .
Too much traffic."

★★★★ COCHITI LAKE GOLF COURSE
Cochiti Lake—PU—505-465-2239 (50 mi. from Albuquerque).
Season: Year-round. **High:** March-Oct. **Caddies:** No.
Green fee: Under $20. **Credit cards:** V, DISC, MC.
Lodging on site: No. **Reduced fees:** Weekdays.
Unrestricted walking: Yes. **Range:** Yes (grass).
Holes: 18. **Par:** 72. **Yards:** 6,413-5,183. **Slope:** 131-117.
Ranked in First 25 of America's 75 Best Public Courses by GOLF DIGEST.
Comments: "Super . . . Great, high desert design . . . Superb setting . . .
Terrific vistas . . . Hilly . . . Very interesting, need cart . . . Cut from cedars
and piñons . . . As good as mountain golf gets . . . Fastest, toughest, nicest
greens around . . . Different and difficult . . . Delivers a beating."

★★★★ INN OF THE MOUNTAIN GODS GOLF COURSE
Mescalero—R—505-257-5141, 800-446-2963 (123 mi. from El Paso).
Season: March-Dec. **High:** May-Sept. **Caddies:** No.
Green fee: $50-$99. **Credit cards:** V, AMEX, DISC, MC.
Lodging on site: Yes. **Reduced fees:** Low Season.
Unrestricted walking: No. **Range:** Yes (grass).
Holes: 18. **Par:** 72. **Yards:** 6,834-5,478. **Slope:** 132-114.
Ranked 5th in New Mexico by GOLF DIGEST.
Comments: "Beautiful setting . . . Located on Indian land in a national
forest . . . Breathtaking experience . . . Fun course . . . Pretty hilly . . .
Some great water holes . . . An island fairway! . . . Greens always 11 to 12
on the Stimpmeter . . . Finishes with a terrific par 3."

★★½ LADERA GOLF COURSE
Albuquerque—PU—505-836-4449.
Season: Year-round. **High:** April-Sept. **Caddies:** No.
Green fee: Under $20. **Credit cards:** V, AMEX, MC.
Lodging on site: No. **Reduced fees:** Twilight Play.
Unrestricted walking: Yes. **Range:** Yes (grass).
Holes: 18. **Par:** 72. **Yards:** 7,060-5,966. **Slope:** 115-113.
Has 9-hole par-31 course.
Comments: "Very busy city-owned course . . . Interesting play . . . Good
for your confidence . . . Poorly run."

★★★½ THE LINKS AT SIERRA BLANCA
Ruidoso—PU—505-258-5330, 800-854-6571 (150 mi. from El Paso).
Season: Year-round. **High:** Summer. **Caddies:** No.
Green fee: $20-$49. **Credit cards:** V, AMEX, MC.
Reduced fees: Weekdays, Low Season, Twilight Play.

Unrestricted walking: No. **Range:** Yes (grass).
Holes: 18. **Par:** 72. **Yards:** 7,003-6,505. **Slope:** 136-131.
Comments: "Links in the mountains . . . Painted Dunes in the pines . . . Some Scottish holes, some invade forest . . . Very good practice facility . . . Good play for women."

★★LOS ALTOS GOLF COURSE
Albuquerque—PU—505-298-1897.
Season: Jan.-Dec. **High:** May-Aug. **Caddies:** No.
Green fee: Under $20. **Credit cards:** V, MC.
Lodging on site: No. **Reduced fees:** Weekdays.
Unrestricted walking: Yes. **Range:** Yes (grass).
Holes: 18. **Par:** 71. **Yards:** 6,460-6,180. **Slope:** 110-108.
Comments: "Short, mature, big trees . . . Easiest course in city . . . Good for high handicappers . . . Can get easily backed up."

★★★NEW MEXICO STATE UNIVERSITY GOLF COURSE
Las Cruces—PU—505-646-3219 (45 mi. from El Paso).
Season: Year-round. **High:** Spring/Fall. **Caddies:** No.
Green fee: Under $20. **Credit cards:** V, MC.
Lodging on site: No. **Reduced fees:** Twilight Play.
Unrestricted walking: Yes. **Range:** Yes (grass).
Holes: 18. **Par:** 72. **Yards:** 7,040-6,084. **Slope:** 133-121.
Comments: "Good, but hard ground . . . Nice layout."

★★★PARADISE HILLS GOLF CLUB
Albuquerque—PU—505-898-7001.
Season: Year-round. **High:** May-Oct. **Caddies:** No.
Green fee: $20-$49. **Credit cards:** V, MC.
Lodging on site: Yes. **Reduced fees:** Weekdays, Low Season, Twilight Play.
Unrestricted walking: Yes. **Range:** Yes (grass).
Holes: 18. **Par:** 72. **Yards:** 6,895-6,629. **Slope:** 118-116.
Comments: "Used to be a country club . . . Went through a $1 million renovation . . . Improvements extensive . . . Now best public course in Albuquerque . . . Mature and well manicured."

★★★★½ PIÑON HILLS GOLF COURSE
Farmington—PU—505-326-6066 (180 mi. from Albuquerque).
Season: Feb.-Dec. **High:** March-Oct. **Caddies:** No.
Green fee: Under $20. **Credit cards:** V, MC.
Lodging on site: No. **Reduced fees:** No.
Unrestricted walking: Yes. **Range:** Yes (grass).
Holes: 18. **Par:** 72. **Yards:** 7,249-6,239. **Slope:** 130-121.
Ranked 1st in New Mexico by GOLF DIGEST.
Comments: "One of the best, interesting and most challenging golf courses around . . . Fascinating . . . Well thought out . . . A shotmaker's course . . . Weaves through white cliffs . . . Last three holes on each 9 are extremely long and testing . . . Just great, worth taking a day off for . . . Head to the Four Corners and play it."

★★★★UNIVERSITY OF NEW MEXICO GOLF COURSE
Albuquerque—PU—505-277-4546.
Season: Year-round. **High:** April-Oct. **Caddies:** No.
Green fee: $20-$49. **Credit cards:** V, MC.
Lodging on site: No. **Reduced fees:** Weekdays, Twilight Play.
Unrestricted walking: Yes. **Range:** Yes (grass).
Holes: 18. **Par:** 72. **Yards:** 7,248-6,031. **Slope:** 138-120.
University also has 9-hole North Course adjacent to campus. Ranked in Third 25 of America's 75 Best Public Courses by GOLF DIGEST.
Comments: "Outstanding traditional course . . . An honest challenge . . . Championship caliber . . . Long, long, long . . . Lush, very little roll . . . Very thick rough . . . Rolling fairways with difficult greens."

★★★VALLE GRANDE GOLF COURSE
TAMARA/RIO GRANDE/CORONADO 9s

Bernalillo—PU—505-867-9464 (15 mi. from Albuquerque).
Season: Year-round. **High:** March-Oct. **Caddies:** No.
Green fee: $20-$49. **Credit cards:** All Major.
Reduced fees: Weekdays, Low Season, Twilight Play.
Unrestricted walking: Yes. **Range:** Yes (grass).
Holes: 27. **Par:** 36/35/36. **Yards:** 3,534/3,548/3,543.
Comments: "New . . . Wonderful . . . Coming along nicely . . . Awesome panoramas . . . Links-type . . . All natural—no trees . . . Tough greens . . . Hard fun . . . If you don't hit it straight, it'll be a long day."

★★½ ADIRONDACK GOLF & COUNTRY CLUB
Peru—PU—518-643-8403, 800-346-1761 (70 mi. from Montreal).
Season: March-Nov. **High:** Summer. **Caddies:** No.
Green fee: $20-$49. **Credit cards:** V, DISC, MC.
Reduced fees: Weekdays, Low Season, Resort Guests, Twilight Play.
Unrestricted walking: Yes. **Range:** Yes (grass).
Holes: 18. **Par:** 72. **Yards:** 6,851-5,069. **Slope:** 123-116.
Comments: "Young, great potential . . . Gorgeous location . . . Nice people . . . Facilities still not completed."

BETHPAGE STATE PARK GOLF COURSES
Farmingdale—PU—516-293-8899 (40 mi. from New York City).
Season: Year-round. **High:** May-Sept. **Caddies:** No.
Green fee: Under $20. **Credit cards:** V, MC, AMEX.
Lodging on site: No. **Reduced fees:** Twilight Play.
Unrestricted walking: Yes. **Range:** Yes (mats).

SUPER VALUE

★★★★½ BLACK COURSE
Holes: 18. **Par:** 71. **Yards:** 7,065-6,556. **Slope:** 144-146.
Ranked in Second 25 of America's 75 Best Public Courses by GOLF DIGEST.
Comments: "A legendary gem . . . The supreme test of golf . . . The Best! . . . Rivals Plainfield and Baltusrol . . . Has stood the test of time and remains a benchmark . . . Use every shot in the bag . . . Outstanding layout, needs more money to be perfect . . . Most difficult course in tri-state area. Only experienced players should play . . . Requires carries of 200 yards to reach some fairways . . . Brutal rough . . . Good condition for public course . . . No carts, no caddies . . . Very physically demanding . . . For $18, more golf than you can bear . . . A steal . . . Poor reservation system . . . Unless you arrive pre-dawn on weekends, expect 4- to 6-hour waits . . . And a 5½-hour round . . . A long day—bring lunch! . . . Worth the wait . . . I challenge anyone to find a tougher, truer test of golf . . . They should play a U.S. Open here . . . Needs rangers . . . If I had to choose only one course to play forever, this would be a very close second."

★★★BLUE COURSE
Holes: 18. **Par:** 72. **Yards:** 6,684-6,513. **Slope:** 126-124.
Comments: "Good front 9, fair back 9 . . . Long, but a step easier than the Black . . . Front 9 as tough as Black . . . Small greens, many trees . . . Just redone . . . Nice, but not overly inspiring . . . Need a cart . . . Surprisingly good condition . . . Battered tee boxes . . . Bethpage tee-off wait is the problem . . . Some areas not maintained well . . . Cheap, but slow . . . 6-hour waits, 6-hour rounds. Not worth it even if it was free."

★★★GREEN COURSE
Holes: 18. **Par:** 71. **Yards:** 6,267. **Slope:** 121.
Comments: "Short . . . Well laid out . . . Small greens . . . Sloping greens . . . Some pin placements are ridiculous . . . Tee areas like a rock . . . Like Black, does not allow electric carts or caddies and is physically demanding . . . Great value, but too long a wait . . . The car line starts early."

★★★½ RED COURSE
Holes: 18. **Par:** 70. **Yards:** 6,756-6,537. **Slope:** 127-125.
Comments: "Prettiest at Bethpage . . . As good as the Black, with carts . . . Good challenge . . . First hole is too tough . . . Wait on second tee is aggravating . . . Several long holes, especially 1, 9 and 15, but allows a good short game to shine . . . Very good shape . . . Best golf for the money . . . Nice, but can't compare to the Black . . . Disastrous tee-time system."

★★½ YELLOW COURSE
Holes: 18. **Par:** 71. **Yards:** 6,316-6,171. **Slope:** 121-120.
Comments: "Easiest of the five at Bethpage, very good shape . . . Little rough . . . Sporty . . . A senior's delight! . . . Basic and tedious . . . Unlike Black and Red, too open. Like Black and Red, overplayed . . . Extremely overworked . . . Except for the crowds, a nice place."

★★★BRISTOL HARBOUR GOLF CLUB
Canandaigua—R—716-396-2460 (40 mi. from Rochester).

Season: April-Nov. **High:** May-Sept. **Caddies:** No.
Green fee: $20-$49. **Credit cards:** V, MC.
Lodging on site: Yes. **Reduced fees:** Weekdays, Low Season, Resort Guests, Twilight Play.
Unrestricted walking: No. **Range:** Yes (grass).
Holes: 18. **Par:** 72. **Yards:** 6,692-6,095. **Slope:** 126-121.
Comments: "Best in the Finger Lakes . . . A scenic wonder . . . Distinctively different 9s . . . Open front, tight back . . . Front links, back forest . . . Back nicer than front . . . More challenging and scenic . . . Most scenic 9 anywhere . . . Great value . . . Friendly staff will bring you back . . . If only the greens would roll better . . . Needs cartpath paving . . . Needs more sand in traps."

CONCORD RESORT HOTEL

Kiamesha Lake—R—914-794-4000 (90 mi. from New York City).
Season: April-Nov. **High:** May-Sept. **Caddies:** No.
Green fee: $50-$99. **Credit cards:** All Major.
Lodging on site: Yes. **Reduced fees:** Resort Guests, Twilight Play.
Unrestricted walking: No. **Range:** Yes (grass).
Hotel also has 9-hole par-31 "Challenger Course."

★★★★ CHAMPIONSHIP COURSE

Holes: 18. **Par:** 72. **Yards:** 7,966-6,548. **Slope:** 142-129.
Ranked 45th in America's 75 Best Resort Courses by GOLF DIGEST.
Comments: "A wonderful experience . . . Humbling is the word . . . Nicknamed 'The Monster' . . . Monster is an understatement . . . The Monster was a treat to play . . . Definitely in the Monster Top 10 . . . Need big drives to score well . . . Difficult and immaculate . . . Bring comfortable shoes . . . Play the Red tees . . . Next to The Ocean Course at Kiawah, the hardest course ever played . . . Would be awesome if 500 yards shorter, and cheaper . . . Expensive, but worth the trip . . . Prices getting out of hand . . . Too expensive, but I enjoyed it . . . I hate to carry five clubs every time I get out of a cart . . . Slow play due to golfers in over their heads."

★★½ INTERNATIONAL COURSE

Holes: 18. **Par:** 71. **Yards:** 6,619-5,554. **Slope:** 127-125.
Comments: "Fun course . . . Not The Monster, but OK . . . Playable for middle handicappers . . . Greens poor . . . Cartpaths poor . . . 9-hole course here is an excellent beginner's course."

★½ DYKER BEACH GOLF COURSE

Brooklyn—PU—718-836-9722.
Season: Year-round. **High:** April-Nov. **Caddies:** No.
Green fee: Under $20. **Credit cards:** V, MC.
Lodging on site: No. **Reduced fees:** Weekdays, Twilight Play.
Unrestricted walking: Yes. **Range:** No.
Holes: 18. **Par:** 71. **Yards:** 6,548-5,696. **Slope:** 115-Unrated.
Comments: "Golf in Brooklyn? Yes, and thank goodness it's still there after all these years . . . Was birdies and burning autos . . . Since private takeover, much better . . . Vastly improved in three years . . . Still King of the 6-Hour Road . . . 'Dem Bums didn't go to L.A. but to Dyker . . . Not enough water to drink, lacks rangers . . . Good layout spoiled by slow play . . . Not bad for all the rounds played on it."

★★★ EN-JOIE GOLF CLUB

Endicott—PU—607-785-1661 (12 mi. from Binghamton).
Season: April-Dec. **High:** Summer. **Caddies:** No
Green fee: Under $20. **Credit cards:** V, MC.
Lodging on site: No. **Reduced fees:** Low Season.
Unrestricted walking: No. **Range:** Yes (mats).
Holes: 18. **Par:** 72. **Yards:** 7,016-5,205. **Slope:** 123-118.
Home of PGA Tour's B.C. Open.
Comments: "Exceptional play at reasonable prices . . . Tight, lots of water holes . . . A 'have-to-play-it-at-least-once' type . . . Well maintained, fun to

play . . . Not that tough for the pros . . . All-day green fee . . . Lacks character."

★★★GLEN OAK GOLF COURSE
East Amherst—PU—716-688-5454.
Season: April-Nov. **High:** Summer. **Caddies:** No.
Green fee: $20-$49. **Credit cards:** V, MC.
Lodging on site: No. **Reduced fees:** Weekdays, Low Season.
Unrestricted walking: No. **Range:** Yes (grass).
Holes: 18. **Par:** 72. **Yards:** 6,730-5,561. **Slope:** 129-118.
Comments: "Great course when it's maintained . . . Many changes in owners, some scrimped, some splurged . . . Great shape . . . Felt like I was playing on the tour . . . Very interesting for all levels . . . Many water hazards . . . Water could come into play more . . . Poor sand traps . . . For the price, you can't beat it."

★★★★GROSSINGER RESORT & COUNTRY CLUB
LAKE/VALLEY/VISTA 9s
Liberty—R—914-292-9000 (98 mi. from New York City).
Season: April-Oct. **High:** Summer. **Caddies:** No.
Green fee: $50-$99. **Credit cards:** V, AMEX, DISC, MC.
Lodging on site: Yes. **Reduced fees:** Weekdays, Resort Guests, Twilight Play.
Unrestricted walking: No. **Range:** Yes (mats).
Holes: 27. **Par:** 36/35/36. **Yards:** 3,357/3,401/3,288.
Comments: "Terrific mountain course . . . One of the most picturesque in the East . . . One of the best anywhere . . . Underrated . . . Overlooked . . . Solid, fair track . . . Everything you could want . . . Long and hard, even from the whites . . . Will wear you out . . . Interesting holes . . . No such thing as a level lie . . . Lightning greens . . . Lake is best of the three 9s . . . Well kept . . . Tough for newer players . . . New management . . . Prices shot up . . . Poor clubhouse."

★★★HILAND GOLF CLUB
Queensbury—PU—518-761-4653 (45 mi. from Albany).
Season: Year-round. **High:** April-Oct. **Caddies:** No.
Green fee: $20-$49. **Credit cards:** All Major.
Reduced fees: Weekdays, Low Season, Twilight Play.
Unrestricted walking: No. **Range:** Yes (mats).
Holes: 18. **Par:** 72. **Yards:** 6,843-5,677. **Slope:** 135-123.
Comments: "Young, beautiful . . . Great potential . . . Rarely crowded . . . Easy to fit in 36 holes a day . . . Great value after 2 p.m. . . . Well maintained . . . Greens spike-mark easily . . . Beautiful dining room and clubhouse . . . Manufactured course, too expensive . . . Not enough trees . . . Should reverse 9s."

★★½ KUTSHER'S COUNTRY CLUB
Monticello—R—914-794-6000.
Season: Year-round. **High:** May-Oct. **Caddies:** No.
Green fee: $20-$49. **Credit cards:** V, MC.
Lodging on site: Yes. **Reduced fees:** Resort Guests.
Unrestricted walking: No. **Range:** Yes (mats).
Holes: 18. **Par:** 72. **Yards:** 7,001-6,510. **Slope:** 123-118.
Comments: "Moderately challenging . . . Nice front, poor back . . . Great greens, terrible fairways . . . Poor condition . . . Good course, poor management . . . Could be sensational with some work . . . Poor customer relations . . . Need courteous help . . . Everybody has their hand out."

★★★½ LEATHERSTOCKING GOLF COURSE
Cooperstown—R—607-547-5275 (25 mi. from Utica).
Season: May-Oct. **High:** Summer. **Caddies:** No.
Green fee: $20-$49. **Credit cards:** V, AMEX, MC.
Lodging on site: Yes. **Reduced fees:** Resort Guests.

Unrestricted walking: No. **Range:** No.
Holes: 18. **Par:** 72. **Yards:** 6,388-5,175. **Slope:** 124.
Comments: "Good old-style design . . . Short, but tough . . . Front side is pretty . . . Hill holes are great . . . Nos. 17 and 18 are excellent closing holes . . . Memorable holes . . . Worth playing for the 18th hole alone . . . 18 is prettiest finishing hole in New York State."

★★★★MONTAUK DOWNS STATE PARK GOLF COURSE
Montauk—PU—516-668-1100 (125 mi. from New York City).
Season: April-Dec. **High:** Summer. **Caddies:** No.
Green fee: Under $20. **Credit cards:** V, AMEX, MC.
Lodging on site: No. **Reduced fees:** Twilight Play.
Unrestricted walking: Yes. **Range:** Yes (mats).
Holes: 18. **Par:** 72. **Yards:** 6,762-5,797. **Slope:** 133-135.
Ranked in Second 25 of America's 75 Best Public Courses by GOLF DIGEST.
Comments: "Great layout . . . Beautiful views . . . Prettiest on Long Island . . . A smaller Shinnecock Hills . . . Almost as good as Bethpage Black, without the long waits . . . Best value in New York . . . Difficulty depends on wind . . . Lots of wind and hills make it hard . . . Big greens . . . Very good conditions . . . Biggest problem is getting to the course . . . Long ride, but worth it . . . Class employees . . . Proves New York State can do some things right . . . Reservation roulette . . . Bring more balls . . . Nasty winds, blind second shots . . . Very slow play in July and August . . . Mow it shorter, will ya?"

SUPER VALUE

★★★NEVELE COUNTRY CLUB
Ellenville—R—914-647-7315, 800-647-6000 (90 mi. from New York City).
Season: April-Nov. **High:** Summer. **Caddies:** No.
Green fee: $20-$49. **Credit cards:** V, AMEX, MC.
Lodging on site: Yes. **Reduced fees:** Weekdays, Resort Guests.
Unrestricted walking: Yes. **Range:** Yes (grass).
Holes: 18. **Par:** 70. **Yards:** 6,532-4,570. **Slope:** 128-126.
Comments: "Sporty vacation course . . . Short, but enjoyable . . . Confusing, but fun . . . Nice, well run . . . But not equal to 9-hole Fallsview course next door . . . An average course at best . . . Too many lay-up tee shots . . . Poor drainage after rain . . . Terrible lockers and eating facilities."

★★★OYSTER BAY TOWN GOLF COURSE
Woodbury—PU—516-364-3977 (65 mi. from New York City).
Season: Year-round. **High:** March-Nov. **Caddies:** No.
Green fee: $20-$49. **Credit cards:** V, AMEX, MC.
Lodging on site: No. **Reduced fees:** Weekdays, Low Season.
Unrestricted walking: Yes. **Range:** Yes (mats).
Holes: 18. **Par:** 70. **Yards:** 6,351-5,109. **Slope:** 131-122.
Comments: "Short, narrow, hilly . . . Very tight, very tough . . . Incredibly challenging even though not long . . . Last three holes are awesome . . . Shoehorned in . . . A bad Fazio design . . . No excuse for greens this bad . . . Crowded . . . A green fee rip-off for nonresidents."

★★PEEK'N PEAK RECREATION CLUB
Clymer—R—716-355-4141 (20 mi. from Erie, Pa.).
Season: April-Nov. **High:** Summer. **Caddies:** No.
Green fee: $20-$49. **Credit cards:** All Major.
Lodging on site: Yes. **Reduced fees:** Weekdays.
Unrestricted walking: Yes. **Range:** Yes (grass).
Holes: 18. **Par:** 72. **Yards:** 6,260-5,328. **Slope:** Unrated.

★★RIVER OAKS GOLF CLUB
Grand Island—R—716-773-3336 (10 mi. from Niagara Falls).
Season: April-Nov. **High:** Summer. **Caddies:** No.
Green fee: $20-$49. **Credit cards:** V, AMEX, MC.
Lodging on site: Yes. **Reduced fees:** Weekdays.
Unrestricted walking: No. **Range:** Yes (grass).

Holes: 18. **Par:** 72. **Yards:** 7,389-5,747. **Slope:** 129-118.
Comments: "Built to host an LPGA event . . . Rolling fairways . . . Very long and demanding . . . Numerous improvements last two years."

★★★½ THE SAGAMORE RESORT & GOLF COURSE
Bolton Landing—R—518-644-9400 (65 mi. from Albany).
Season: April-Oct. **High:** Summer. **Caddies:** No.
Green fee: $50-$99. **Credit cards:** All Major.
Lodging on site: Yes. **Reduced fees:** No.
Unrestricted walking: No. **Range:** Yes (grass).
Holes: 18. **Par:** 70. **Yards:** 6,890-5,261. **Slope:** 130-122.
Comments: "A Donald Ross challenge . . . Great mountain setting . . . Very beautiful . . . Very difficult . . . Excellent use of natural terrain . . . Some real interesting golf . . . Each hole unto itself, a nice touch by Ross . . . Memorable 13th. Don't be left . . . Superbly maintained . . . Personnel outstanding . . . Great routing, but dress codes and mandatory carts absurd . . . Fees, especially for hotel rooms, are a bit steep."

★★★ SARATOGA SPA GOLF COURSE
Saratoga Springs—PU—518-584-2006 (20 mi. from Albany).
Season: April-Nov. **High:** Summer. **Caddies:** No.
Green fee: Under $20. **Credit cards:** V, MC.
Lodging on site: No. **Reduced fees:** Weekdays, Twilight Play.
Unrestricted walking: Yes. **Range:** Yes (grass).
Holes: 18. **Par:** 72. **Yards:** 7,025-5,663. **Slope:** 121.
Comments: "Best-kept secret among public courses . . . Great state-run course . . . A best buy . . . Pleasant . . . Very flat . . . Tight back 9 . . . Not many water hazards . . . Slow play due to large grounds . . . Always crowded . . . Packed! . . . Don't play in August, a mob scene . . . During Saratoga Thoroughbred season."

★★★ SEGALLA COUNTRY CLUB
Amenia—PU—914-373-9200 (25 mi. from Poughkeepsie).
Season: April-Nov. **High:** May-Sept. **Caddies:** No.
Green fee: $20-$49. **Credit cards:** V, MC.
Lodging on site: No. **Reduced fees:** Twilight Play.
Unrestricted walking: No. **Range:** Yes (mats).
Holes: 18. **Par:** 72. **Yards:** 6,617-5,601. **Slope:** 133-129.
Comments: "New and promising . . . Forgiving course. Not much water . . . Tough greens and rough . . . Very scenic . . . Needs only to mature . . . Slow greens, carts required."

★★★½ SEVEN OAKS GOLF CLUB
Hamilton—PU—315-824-1432 (41 mi. from Syracuse).
Season: April-Oct. **High:** Summer. **Caddies:** Yes.
Green fee: $20-$49. **Credit cards:** V, MC.
Lodging on site: No. **Reduced fees:** Resort Guests.
Unrestricted walking: Yes. **Range:** Yes (grass).
Holes: 18. **Par:** 72. **Yards:** 6,915-5,849. **Slope:** 128-125.
Course owned by Colgate University.

Comments: "Beautiful . . . Challenging . . . Good playing time . . . Nice course with little traffic . . . Need better yardage marking . . . Staff tends to make this layout unfairly difficult at times with U.S. Open rough, fast greens, etc. . . . Pro shop and food service both excellent."

★★★½ SPOOK ROCK GOLF COURSE
Suffern—PU—914-357-6466 (35 mi. from New York City).
Season: April-Nov. **High:** Summer. **Caddies:** No.
Green fee: $20-$49. **Credit cards:** No.
Lodging on site: No. **Reduced fees:** Twilight Play.
Unrestricted walking: Yes. **Range:** Yes (mats).
Holes: 18. **Par:** 72. **Yards:** 6,894-4,853. **Slope:** Unrated.
Ranked in First 25 of America's 75 Best Public Courses by GOLF DIGEST.

Comments: "*Creme de la creme* . . . Like a private club . . . Nice design . . . Major improvements over last year . . . Very tough opening par 4 . . . Good shape . . . Entertaining course, but needs marshals, takes too long to play . . . Favors those who fade . . . Highly overrated."

★★★SPRING LAKE GOLF CLUB
THUNDERBIRD FRONT and BACK/SANDPIPER 9s
Middle Island—PU—516-924-5115 (50 mi. from New York City).
Season: Year-round. **High:** Summer. **Caddies:** No.
Green fee: $20-$49. **Credit cards:** No.
Lodging on site: No. **Reduced fees:** Weekdays.
Unrestricted walking: No. **Range:** Yes (mats).
Holes: 27. **Par:** 36/36/36. **Yards:** 3,583/3,465/3,250.
Comments: "Good moderately priced round . . . Testy . . . Lots of water . . . Huge greens . . . Always in great shape . . . Must get up early for tee time, but worth it . . . 5-hour rounds . . . Rangers don't speed up play . . . Yardage markers are terrible."

★★½ SWAN LAKE GOLF CLUB
Manorville—PU—516-369-1818.
Season: Year-round. **High:** May-Oct. **Caddies:** No.
Green fee: $20-$49. **Credit cards:** No.
Lodging on site: No. **Reduced fees:** Twilight Play.
Unrestricted walking: No. **Range:** No.
Holes: 18. **Par:** 72. **Yards:** 7,011-5,245. **Slope:** 126-119.
Comments: "Easy to play . . . Always in great shape . . . Very, very large greens . . . Fairways forgiving . . . No rough . . . Lends itself to an enjoyable round . . . Employees very helpful."

★★★TARRY BRAE GOLF CLUB
South Fallsburg—PU—914-434-2620 (90 mi. from New York City).
Season: April-Oct. **High:** Summer. **Caddies:** No.
Green fee: $20-$49. **Credit cards:** No.
Lodging on site: No. **Reduced fees:** Weekdays, Resort Guests, Twilight Play.
Unrestricted walking: No. **Range:** Yes (grass).
Holes: 18. **Par:** 72. **Yards:** 6,888-6,270. **Slope:** 128-122.
Comments: "Very good mountain course . . . One of the Catskills' best . . . Great lake vistas . . . Woods left intact . . . Greens hold well . . . Reasonably priced . . . The best greater N.Y. City public course . . . Best value of any course . . . Good course if you have six hours to spare . . . Clubhouse needs modernization."

★★½ TENNANAH LAKE GOLF & TENNIS CLUB
Roscoe—PU—607-498-5502 (117 mi. from New York City).
Season: May-Oct. **High:** Summer. **Caddies:** No.
Green fee: $20-$49. **Credit cards:** V, AMEX, MC.
Lodging on site: Yes. **Reduced fees:** Weekdays, Resort Guests, Twilight Play.
Unrestricted walking: Yes. **Range:** No.
Holes: 18. **Par:** 72. **Yards:** 6,737-5,822. **Slope:** 121-115.
Comments: "Nice country course . . . Very scenic . . . Great views . . . Easiest course to get on, never a wait . . . Still developing amenities."

★★THOUSAND ISLANDS GOLF CLUB
Wellesley Island—R—315-482-9454 (100 mi. from Syracuse).
Season: April-Nov. **High:** May-Sept. **Caddies:** No.
Green fee: $20-$49. **Credit cards:** V, AMEX, MC.
Lodging on site: Yes. **Reduced fees:** Resort Guests.
Unrestricted walking: No. **Range:** Yes (grass).
Holes: 18. **Par:** 72. **Yards:** 6,250-6,050. **Slope:** 118-116.
Comments: "Interesting, but easy . . . Condition not always great."

★★½ TOWN OF WALLKILL GOLF CLUB
Middletown—PU—914-361-1022 (55 mi. from New York City).
Season: April-Dec. **High:** Summer. **Caddies:** No.
Green fee: $20-$49. **Credit cards:** No.
Lodging on site: No. **Reduced fees:** Weekdays, Twilight Play.
Unrestricted walking: Yes. **Range:** Yes (mats).
Holes: 18. **Par:** 72. **Yards:** 6,437-5,171. **Slope:** 128-122.
Comments: "Fun course . . . Abundance of different holes, doglegs abound
. . . Still a young course . . . Hasn't come into its own yet . . . Poor
sodding, rocks in fairways . . . Many blind shots, could be dangerous."

★½ VAN CORTLANDT GOLF COURSE
Bronx—PU—718-543-4595.
Season: Year-round. **High:** Summer. **Caddies:** No.
Green fee: Under $20. **Credit cards:** V, MC.
Lodging on site: No. **Reduced fees:** Weekdays, Twilight Play.
Unrestricted walking: Yes. **Range:** No.
Holes: 18. **Par:** 70. **Yards:** 6,122-5,421. **Slope:** 110-120.
Oldest public golf course in America.
Comments: "Most holes just long and straight, no interest . . . Two 600-
yard holes! . . . Too much walking between holes . . . An absolute zoo since
it was taken from city by a private company. Has become too expensive, too
time consuming . . . Has improved condition . . . Accurate distance markers
needed . . . Avoid weekends."

★★★ VILLA ROMA COUNTRY CLUB
Callicoon—R—914-887-5097 (80 mi. from Binghamton).
Season: April-Nov. **High:** May-Sept. **Caddies:** No.
Green fee: $20-$49. **Credit cards:** V, AMEX, DISC, MC.
Lodging on site: Yes. **Reduced fees:** Weekdays, Resort Guests,
Twilight Play.
Unrestricted walking: No. **Range:** Yes (grass).
Holes: 18. **Par:** 71. **Yards:** 6,231-4,797. **Slope:** 125-117.
Comments: "A little slice of Heaven . . . Short, but testing due to frequent
sidehill lies . . . Very scenic . . . Good condition, but short . . . Demanding
greens . . . All putts break toward the valley."

★★½ WHITEFACE INN RESORT GOLF COURSE
Lake Placid—R—518-523-2551, 800-422-6757.
Season: May-Oct. **High:** Summer. **Caddies:** No.
Green fee: $20-$49. **Credit cards:** V, AMEX, DISC, MC.
Lodging on site: Yes. **Reduced fees:** Resort Guests, Twilight Play.
Unrestricted walking: Yes. **Range:** Yes (grass).
Holes: 18. **Par:** 72. **Yards:** 6,490-5,635. **Slope:** 123.
Comments: "Traditional old course . . . Fun to play . . . Great mountain
air . . . Great views . . . Accommodations were mediocre."

★★½ WIND WATCH GOLF CLUB
Hauppauge—R—516-232-9850 (42 mi. from New York City).
Season: Year-round. **High:** May-Oct. **Caddies:** No.
Green fee: $50-$99. **Credit cards:** V, AMEX, DISC, MC.
Lodging on site: Yes. **Reduced fees:** Weekdays, Low Season, Resort
Guests, Twilight Play.
Unrestricted walking: No. **Range:** Yes (grass).
Holes: 18. **Par:** 71. **Yards:** 6,425-5,135. **Slope:** 133-118.
Comments: "Short, cute . . . One of the best on Long Island . . . Fair to all
men and women . . . Staff provides royal treatment . . . Spotty condition
. . . Overplayed . . . Long playing time . . . Greens not correct for ap-
proaches . . . Could be much better with proper care . . . Priced like a
resort, but not one."

★★★★BALD HEAD ISLAND CLUB
Bald Head Island—R—919-457-7310, 800-234-1666
(25 mi. from Wilmington).
Season: Year-round. **High:** May-Sept. **Caddies:** No.
Green fee: $50-$99. **Credit cards:** V, AMEX, MC.
Lodging on site: Yes. **Reduced fees:** Low Season, Resort Guests.
Unrestricted walking: No. **Range:** Yes (grass).
Holes: 18. **Par:** 72. **Yards:** 6,800-6,200. **Slope:** 143-136.
Comments: "Stunning . . . Tropical forest mixed with marsh . . . Great course, uncrowded . . . Lots of wildlife . . . If there's no wind, then it's a pussycat . . . Watch out for gators . . . Hard to get to, a pleasure to play . . . Great staff, never too busy . . . Don't tell too many people about it."

★★★BEACON RIDGE GOLF & COUNTRY CLUB
West End—PU—919-673-2950 (10 mi. from Pinehurst).
Season: Year-round. **High:** Spring/Fall. **Caddies:** No.
Green fee: $50-$99. **Credit cards:** V, MC.
Lodging on site: Yes. **Reduced fees:** Low Season, Resort Guests, Twilight Play.
Unrestricted walking: No. **Range:** Yes (grass).
Holes: 18. **Par:** 72. **Yards:** 6,600-4,800. **Slope:** 125-115.
Comments: "Short, demanding . . . Gene Hamm gem . . . No crowds, even on weekends!"

★★½ BEAU RIVAGE PLANTATION GOLF CLUB
Wilmington—R—919-392-9022, 800-628-7080.
Season: Year-round. **High:** April-May. **Caddies:** No.
Green fee: $20-$49. **Credit cards:** V, AMEX, DISC, MC.
Lodging on site: Yes. **Reduced fees:** Resort Guests, Twilight Play.
Unrestricted walking: No. **Range:** Yes (grass).
Holes: 18. **Par:** 72. **Yards:** 6,790-4,612. **Slope:** 136-114.
Comments: "Good test . . . Linkish . . . Natural setting . . . Fun if you know the course . . . Some ill-designed holes."

★½ BLACK MOUNTAIN GOLF COURSE
Black Mountain—PU—704-669-2710 (15 mi. from Asheville).
Season: Year-round. **High:** May-Oct. **Caddies:** No.
Green fee: Under $20. **Credit cards:** V, MC.
Lodging on site: No. **Reduced fees:** No.
Unrestricted walking: Yes. **Range:** No.
Holes: 18. **Par:** 71. **Yards:** 6,181-5,780. **Slope:** 116-Unrated.
No. 17 is world's longest par 6 at 747 yards.

★★★BOONE GOLF CLUB
Boone—PU—704-264-8760.
Season: April-Nov. **High:** June-Sept. **Caddies:** No.
Green fee: $20-$49. **Credit cards:** No.
Lodging on site: No. **Reduced fees:** No.
Unrestricted walking: No. **Range:** No.
Holes: 18. **Par:** 71. **Yards:** 6,401-5,172. **Slope:** 120-113.
Comments: "In the mountains, but not a mountain course . . . Surprisingly flat . . . Good course for the whole family."

★★BRICK LANDING PLANTATION
Ocean Isle Beach—R—919-754-5545, 800-438-3006
(20 mi. from N. Myrtle Beach).
Season: Year-round. **High:** Spring/Fall. **Caddies:** No.
Green fee: $20-$49. **Credit cards:** V, MC.
Lodging on site: Yes. **Reduced fees:** Low Season, Resort Guests, Twilight Play.
Unrestricted walking: No. **Range:** Yes (grass).
Holes: 18. **Par:** 72. **Yards:** 6,473-4,363. **Slope:** 141-116.
Comments: "Beautiful setting, water on 17 holes, ocean, waterway and

191

marsh . . . Somewhat short . . . Unfair to the average golfer . . . Too many lay-up shots . . . Dinky . . . Has a par 3 under 100 yards from the championship tee . . . Water, water, water . . . Poor design, tried too hard to make it tough . . . Six water hazards on one hole is ridiculous."

★★BRIERWOOD GOLF CLUB
Shallotte—PU—919-754-4660 (30 mi. from Wilmington).
Season: Year-round. **High:** Spring/Fall. **Caddies:** No.
Green fee: $20-$49. **Credit cards:** V, MC.
Lodging on site: Yes. **Reduced fees:** Low Season, Twilight Play.
Unrestricted walking: No. **Range:** No.
Holes: 18. **Par:** 72. **Yards:** 6,709-6,218. **Slope:** 121-114.

★★★½ BRUNSWICK PLANTATION GOLF LINKS
Calabash—R—919-287-7888, 800-848-0290 (25 mi. from Myrtle Beach).
Season: Year-round. **High:** March-Oct. **Caddies:** No.
Green fee: $20-$49. **Credit cards:** V, MC.
Lodging on site: No. **Reduced fees:** Low Season.
Unrestricted walking: No. **Range:** Yes (grass).
Holes: 18. **Par:** 72. **Yards:** 6,779-5,210. **Slope:** 131-115.

BRYAN PARK AND GOLF CLUB
Brown Summit—PU—919-375-2200 (10 mi. from Greensboro).
Season: Year-round. **High:** May-Oct. **Caddies:** No.
Green fee: $20-$49. **Credit cards:** V, MC.
Lodging on site: No. **Reduced fees:** Weekdays, Twilight Play.
Unrestricted walking: Yes. **Range:** Yes (mats).

GREAT VALUE

★★★★CHAMPIONS COURSE
Holes: 18. **Par:** 72. **Yards:** 7,135-5,395. **Slope:** 130-118.
Selected as runner-up for Best New Public Course of 1990 by GOLF DIGEST.
Comments: "A real treat . . . Super layout . . . Plays along a lake, winds definitely a factor . . . Use one extra club . . . Not unfair unless you constantly hit it crooked . . . Great course for a great price . . . Most for your money anywhere . . . The Greater Greensboro Open ought to go here."

★★½ PLAYERS COURSE
Holes: 18. **Par:** 72. **Yards:** 7,076-5,260. **Slope:** 128-115.
Comments: "Great track, poor conditioning."

★★½ THE CAPE GOLF & RACQUET CLUB
Wilmington—R—919-799-3110.
Season: Year-round. **High:** March/April/July/Oct. **Caddies:** No.
Green fee: $20-$49. **Credit cards:** V, MC.
Lodging on site: Yes. **Reduced fees:** Weekdays, Low Season, Resort Guests, Twilight Play.
Unrestricted walking: No. **Range:** Yes (grass).
Holes: 18. **Par:** 72. **Yards:** 6,790-5,108. **Slope:** 135-121.

★★½ CAROLINA LAKES GOLF COURSE
Sanford—PU—919-499-5421, 800-942-8633 (10 mi. from Fayetteville).
Season: Year-round. **High:** Spring/Fall. **Caddies:** No.
Green fee: Under $20. **Credit cards:** V, MC.
Lodging on site: No. **Reduced fees:** Weekdays, Low Season.
Unrestricted walking: Yes. **Range:** Yes (grass).
Holes: 18. **Par:** 70. **Yards:** 6,300-5,010. **Slope:** 117-110.
Comments: "Fun for short hitters . . . Good course for the average golfer."

★½ CAROLINA PINES GOLF & COUNTRY CLUB
New Bern—PU—919-444-1000.
Season: Year-round. **High:** April-Oct. **Caddies:** No.
Green fee: $20-$49. **Credit cards:** V, AMEX, MC.
Lodging on site: No. **Reduced fees:** Weekdays.
Unrestricted walking: Yes. **Range:** Yes (grass).
Holes: 18. **Par:** 72. **Yards:** 6,250-5,900. **Slope:** 115-111.
Comments: "Needs a lot of work."

★★★CAROLINA SHORES GOLF & COUNTRY CLUB
Calabash—PU—919-579-2181, 800-762-8813 (7 mi. from Myrtle Beach).
Season: Year-round. **High:** Spring/Fall. **Caddies:** No.
Green fee: $50-$99. **Credit cards:** V, MC.
Lodging on site: No. **Reduced fees:** Twilight Play.
Unrestricted walking: No. **Range:** Yes (grass).
Holes: 18. **Par:** 72. **Yards:** 6,783-6,231. **Slope:** 128-122.
Comments: "Holy sand trap! . . . Very unfair sand traps . . . There should be a law against so much sand."

★★★CLEGHORN PLANTATION GOLF
AND COUNTRY CLUB
Rutherfordton—PU—704-286-9117 (60 mi. from Charlotte).
Season: Year-round. **High:** April-May. **Caddies:** No.
Green fee: $20-$49. **Credit cards:** V, MC.
Lodging on site: Yes. **Reduced fees:** Weekdays.
Unrestricted walking: No. **Range:** Yes (grass).
Holes: 18. **Par:** 72. **Yards:** 6,903-4,751. **Slope:** 134-111.
Comments: "Always good golf . . . Different from other Carolina courses . . . Very tough test . . . Must stay in fairway . . . Great people."

★★★THE CLUB AT LONGLEAF
Southern Pines—PU—919-692-6100 (70 mi. from Raleigh).
Season: Year-round. **High:** March-May. **Caddies:** No.
Green fee: $50-$99. **Credit cards:** V, MC.
Lodging on site: Yes. **Reduced fees:** Low Season, Twilight Play.
Unrestricted walking: No. **Range:** Yes (grass).
Holes: 18. **Par:** 71. **Yards:** 6,600-4,719. **Slope:** 117-108.
Built on a former horse ranch. Much of front 9 plays among posts, rails and turns of old racetrack.
Comments: "Unique . . . Two 9s entirely different . . . Charming, short, very soft, very green . . . Fun course for average golfer . . . Pretty, but not much character . . . Shop/restaurant very good."

COLONY LAKE LURE GOLF RESORT
Lake Lure—R—704-625-2888 (5 mi. from Asheville).
Season: Year-round. **High:** April-Oct. **Caddies:** No.
Green fee: $20-$49. **Credit cards:** All Major.
Lodging on site: Yes. **Reduced fees:** Low Season, Resort Guests.
Unrestricted walking: No. **Range:** No.
★★★½ APPLE VALLEY COURSE
Holes: 18. **Par:** 72. **Yards:** 6,726-4,661. **Slope:** 138-114.
Comments: "One of the most beautiful mountain courses around."
★★★BALD MOUNTAIN COURSE
704-625-2626
Holes: 18. **Par:** 72. **Yards:** 6,575-4,808. **Slope:** 125-112.
Comments: "Scenery breathtaking . . . Beautifully maintained."

COUNTRY CLUB OF WHISPERING PINES
Whispering Pines—PU—919-949-2311 (60 mi. from Raleigh).
Season: Year-round. **High:** Spring/Fall. **Caddies:** No.
Green fee: $50-$99. **Credit cards:** V, AMEX, MC.
Lodging on site: Yes. **Reduced fees:** Low Season, Resort Guests.
Unrestricted walking: No. **Range:** Yes (grass).
★★★½ EAST COURSE
Holes: 18. **Par:** 72. **Yards:** 7,138-5,542. **Slope:** 130-119.
Comments: "Better than the West . . . Good clubhouse."
★★★WEST COURSE
Holes: 18. **Par:** 71. **Yards:** 6,363-5,135. **Slope:** 126-111.
Comments: "Not an early-season course."

★★★CYPRESS LAKES GOLF COURSE
Hope Mills—PU—919-483-0359 (8 mi. from Fayetteville).
Season: Year-round. **High:** Spring/Fall. **Caddies:** No.

Green fee: $20-$49. **Credit cards:** V, MC.
Lodging on site: No. **Reduced fees:** No.
Unrestricted walking: Yes. **Range:** Yes (grass).
Holes: 18. **Par:** 72. **Yards:** 7,240-6,615. **Slope:** 126-118.

★★★DEERCROFT GOLF & COUNTRY CLUB
Wagram—PU—919-369-3107 (12 mi. from Pinehurst).
Season: Year-round. **High:** Spring/Fall. **Caddies:** No.
Green fee: $20-$49. **Credit cards:** V, MC.
Lodging on site: No. **Reduced fees:** No.
Unrestricted walking: No. **Range:** Yes (grass).
Holes: 18. **Par:** 72. **Yards:** 6,745-5,443. **Slope:** 125-120.
Comments: "Delightful . . . Very fair layout . . . Always in good shape
. . . Best-kept secret in the Sandhills . . . Rough comes to fringe, forces you
to carry onto greens."

★★★★DEVILS RIDGE GOLF CLUB
Hilly Springs—PU—919-557-6100 (15 mi. from Raleigh).
Season: Year-round. **High:** June-Aug. **Caddies:** No.
Green fee: $20-$49. **Credit cards:** V, MC.
Lodging on site: No. **Reduced fees:** Twilight Play.
Unrestricted walking: No. **Range:** Yes (grass).
Holes: 18. **Par:** 72. **Yards:** 7,002-5,244. **Slope:** 138-121.
Comments: "Challenging . . . Most fun . . . Young, a comer . . . John
LaFoy's best . . . Unlimited potential . . . Large rolling greens make for a
different course each time out . . . No. 17 is a real killer."

★★½ ECHO FARMS GOLF & COUNTRY CLUB
Wilmington—PU—919-791-9318 (120 mi. from Raleigh).
Season: Year-round. **High:** Spring/Fall. **Caddies:** No.
Green fee: $20-$49. **Credit cards:** V, AMEX, MC.
Reduced fees: Weekdays, Low Season, Twilight Play.
Unrestricted walking: No. **Range:** Yes (grass).
Holes: 18. **Par:** 72. **Yards:** 7,014-5,142. **Slope:** 131-121.
Comments: "Long course, excellent fairways . . . Good greens, good staff
. . . Terrific front 9 . . . Great shape . . . Too tough for short hitters."

★★★½ THE EMERALD GOLF CLUB
New Bern—PU—919-633-4440, 800-424-4407 (115 mi. from Raleigh).
Season: Year-round. **High:** May-Sept. **Caddies:** No.
Green fee: $20-$49. **Credit cards:** V, MC.
Lodging on site: No. **Reduced fees:** Weekdays.
Unrestricted walking: No. **Range:** Yes (grass).
Holes: 18. **Par:** 72. **Yards:** 6,924-5,287. **Slope:** 125-119.
Comments: "A true surprise . . . Fine layout . . . Staff friendly . . . Ameni-
ties fair . . . Carts not allowed off paths . . . Burn those golf carts!"

★★★★ETOWAH VALLEY COUNTRY CLUB
SOUTH/WEST/NORTH 9s
Etowah—R—704-891-7141, 800-451-8174 (20 mi. from Asheville).
Season: Year-round. **High:** April-Oct. **Caddies:** No.
Green fee: $20-$49. **Credit cards:** V, MC.
Lodging on site: Yes. **Reduced fees:** Low Season.
Unrestricted walking: No. **Range:** Yes (grass).
Holes: 27. **Par:** 36/36/37. **Yards:** 3,507/3,601/3,404.
Comments: "Three great 9s . . . Extremely different 9s . . . Newest may
be a bit too easy . . . Tourist oriented . . . Staff aims to please . . . Excellent
accommodations . . . Package deals are too good to believe."

★½ FOX SQUIRREL COUNTRY CLUB
Southport—PU—919-845-2625 (23 mi. from Wilmington).
Season: Year-round. **High:** Feb.-July. **Caddies:** No.
Green fee: $20-$49. **Credit cards:** V, MC.
Lodging on site: No. **Reduced fees:** Low Season, Twilight Play.

Unrestricted walking: Yes. **Range:** No.
Holes: 18. **Par:** 72. **Yards:** 6,762-5,349. **Slope:** 125-110.
Comments: "Nice setting . . . Needs attention . . . Narrow . . . No fun . . . No practice facility."

FOXFIRE RESORT & COUNTRY CLUB
Jackson Springs—R—919-295-5555, 800-736-9347 (70 mi. from Raleigh).
Season: Year-round. **High:** March-May. **Caddies:** No.
Green fee: $20-$49. **Credit cards:** V, AMEX, MC.
Lodging on site: Yes. **Reduced fees:** Low Season, Twilight Play.
Unrestricted walking: No. **Range:** Yes (grass).
★★★**EAST COURSE**
Holes: 18. **Par:** 72. **Yards:** 6,780-6,377. **Slope:** 132-129.
Comments: "Good, lots of challenges . . . Harder than West Course . . . Big improvements in last five years."
★★½ **WEST COURSE**
Holes: 18. **Par:** 72. **Yards:** 6,742-6,321. **Slope:** 129-123.
Comments: "Rocky bunkers the only negative."

★★★**THE GAUNTLET AT ST. JAMES PLANTATION**
Southport—PU—910-253-3008, 800-247-4806 (25 mi. from Wilmington).
Season: Year-round. **High:** Nov.-April. **Caddies:** Yes.
Green fee: $20-$49. **Credit cards:** All Major.
Lodging on site: No. **Reduced fees:** Low Season, Twilight Play.
Unrestricted walking: No. **Range:** Yes (grass).
Holes: 18. **Par:** 72. **Yards:** 7,022-5,048. **Slope:** 142-119.
Comments: "Very difficult hidden gem . . . Very unusual . . . Typical Dye bunkers . . . Very friendly, hospitable staff . . . Swamp thing."

★½ **GREAT SMOKIES HILTON GOLF RESORT**
Asheville—R—704-253-5874.
Season: Year-round. **High:** April-Oct. **Caddies:** No.
Green fee: $20-$49. **Credit cards:** All Major.
Lodging on site: Yes. **Reduced fees:** Low Season, Resort Guests, Twilight Play.
Unrestricted walking: No. **Range:** No.
Holes: 18. **Par:** 70. **Yards:** 5,600-5,400. **Slope:** 116-111.
Comments: "Poorly designed . . . Too many acute doglegs . . . Too many lay ups . . . Too short . . . Tries to be too big for itself."

★★½ **GROVE PARK INN RESORT**
Asheville—R—704-252-2711, 800-438-5800.
Season: Year-round. **High:** April-Nov. **Caddies:** No.
Green fee: $20-$49. **Credit cards:** All Major.
Lodging on site: Yes. **Reduced fees:** No.
Unrestricted walking: No. **Range:** No.
Holes: 18. **Par:** 71. **Yards:** 6,550-5,000. **Slope:** 125-111.
Comments: "Neat course, but not long enough . . . Lots of fun . . . One bad hole, no range. Otherwise, beautiful . . . Fantastic resort . . . A favorite 'business overnight' spot . . . Accommodations great."

HAWKSNEST GOLF & SKI RESORT*
Seven Devils—PU—704-963-6561, 800-822-4295
(70 mi. from Winston-Salem).
Season: Year-round. **High:** July-Aug. **Caddies:** No.
Green fee: $20-$49. **Credit cards:** V, DISC, MC.
Reduced fees: Weekdays, Low Season, Twilight Play.
Unrestricted walking: No. **Range:** No.
Holes: 18. **Par:** 72. **Yards:** 6,244-4,799. **Slope:** 113-110.

★★½ **HIGH HAMPTON INN & COUNTRY CLUB**
Cashiers—R—704-743-2450 (65 mi. from Asheville).
Season: April-Nov. **High:** July-Oct. **Caddies:** No.

Green fee: $20-$49. **Credit cards:** V, AMEX, MC.
Lodging on site: Yes. **Reduced fees:** Resort Guests, Twilight Play.
Unrestricted walking: Yes. **Range:** Yes (mats).
Holes: 18. **Par:** 71. **Yards:** 6,012. **Slope:** Unrated.
Comments: "Picturesque . . . OK if you like old and rustic . . . Water and woods, no sand . . . Thatchy greens . . . Good course but dry county . . . Not well kept up . . . High Hampton prices . . . Food and rooms poor."

★★★½ HIGHLAND CREEK GOLF CLUB
Charlotte—PU—704-875-9000.
Season: Year-round. **High:** May-Nov. **Caddies:** No.
Green fee: $20-$49. **Credit cards:** V, AMEX, MC.
Lodging on site: No. **Reduced fees:** Weekdays, Twilight Play.
Unrestricted walking: No. **Range:** Yes (grass).
Holes: 18. **Par:** 72. **Yards:** 7,008-5,080. **Slope:** 133-122.
Comments: "A joy . . . Best public course in Charlotte . . . Fair test for any golfer . . . Should someday be in Top 20 in the nation."

★★★ HOLLY FOREST COUNTRY CLUB
Sapphire—R—704-743-1174 (60 mi. from Asheville).
Season: Year-round. **High:** May-Sept. **Caddies:** No.
Green fee: $20-$49. **Credit cards:** V, MC.
Lodging on site: Yes. **Reduced fees:** Low Season.
Unrestricted walking: No. **Range:** Yes (grass).
Holes: 18. **Par:** 70. **Yards:** 6,147-5,690. **Slope:** 119-118.
Comments: "Fun course . . . Beautiful . . . Play it for the scenery and the island par 3 . . . Several wonderful holes . . . Great shape . . . Nothing special . . . Six miles of cartpaths."

★★★½ HOUND EARS CLUB
Blowing Rock—R—704-963-4321 (90 mi. from Charlotte).
Season: April-Nov. **High:** June-Sept. **Caddies:** No.
Green fee: $20-$49. **Credit cards:** All Major.
Lodging on site: Yes. **Reduced fees:** None.
Unrestricted walking: No. **Range:** Yes (grass).
Holes: 18. **Par:** 72. **Yards:** 6,165-4,959. **Slope:** 113-108.
Comments: "Great place . . . Several good holes, superb food and service . . . Great views . . . Outstanding staff . . . Expensive, but worth it."

★★½ HYLAND HILLS RESORT
Southern Pines—R—919-692-3752.
Season: Year-round. **High:** Spring/Fall. **Caddies:** No.
Green fee: $20-$49. **Credit cards:** V, MC.
Lodging on site: Yes. **Reduced fees:** Twilight Play.
Unrestricted walking: No. **Range:** Yes (grass).
Holes: 18. **Par:** 72. **Yards:** 6,750-4,677. **Slope:** 120-109.
Comments: "Not of the same caliber as other Pinehurst courses . . . Always dry in wet weather . . . Biggest villain is slow play . . . Staff makes you feel important."

★★★ JEFFERSON LANDING
Jefferson—R—919-246-5555 (80 mi. from Winston-Salem).
Season: March-Nov. **High:** June-Sept. **Caddies:** No.
Green fee: $20-$49. **Credit cards:** All Major.
Lodging on site: Yes. **Reduced fees:** Weekdays, Low Season, Resort Guests, Twilight Play.
Unrestricted walking: No. **Range:** Yes (grass).
Holes: 18. **Par:** 72. **Yards:** 7,111-4,960. **Slope:** 121-103.
Comments: "A genuine find . . . A flat course in the mountains . . . New . . . Keep it a secret . . . Nice, but too expensive."

★★★½ KEITH HILLS COUNTRY CLUB
Buies Creek—PU—919-893-5051 (30 mi. from Raleigh).
Season: Year-round. **High:** Spring/Fall. **Caddies:** No.
Green fee: $20-$49. **Credit cards:** V, MC.

Lodging on site: No. **Reduced fees:** Weekdays.
Unrestricted walking: Yes. **Range:** Yes (grass).
Holes: 18. **Par:** 72. **Yards:** 6,660-5,225. **Slope:** 129-120.
Comments: "Great course . . . Beautifully landscaped . . . The way a course ought to look and play . . . Favors left-to-right play . . . A sleeper for I-95 travelers . . . A hidden gold mine . . . Always in super shape . . . Best-kept secret in North Carolina . . . Too many college kids on it."

★★★★LEGACY GOLF LINKS

Aberdeen—PU—919-944-8825, 800-344-8825 (70 mi. from Raleigh).
Season: Year-round. **High:** March-May. **Caddies:** No.
Green fee: $50-$99. **Credit cards:** V, AMEX, MC.
Lodging on site: No. **Reduced fees:** Low Season, Twilight Play.
Unrestricted walking: No. **Range:** Yes (grass).
Holes: 18. **Par:** 72. **Yards:** 6,989-4,948. **Slope:** 132-116.
First American design by Jack Nicklaus Jr.
Comments: "Wonderful . . . Great new design . . . Memorable . . . Understated . . . Super enjoyable . . . Good use of water hazards . . . Excellent range of holes . . . Wide variety without being tricked up . . . Now we know which Nicklaus can design."

★★★★½ LINVILLE GOLF CLUB

Linville—R—704-733-4363 (17 mi. from Boone).
Season: May-Oct. **High:** July-Aug. **Caddies:** No.
Green fee: $20-$49. **Credit cards:** V, MC.
Lodging on site: Yes. **Reduced fees:** No.
Unrestricted walking: No. **Range:** Yes (grass).
Holes: 18. **Par:** 72. **Yards:** 6,780-5,086. **Slope:** 135-117.
Comments: "A Donald Ross classic . . . Ross at his best . . . Many great holes . . . True test of placement and accuracy . . . Poa-annua greens maintained to perfection . . . Gorgeous scenery . . . Excellent course in a quaint little village . . . The granddaddy of Grandfather Mountain."

★★★½ LION'S PAW GOLF LINKS

Ocean Isle Beach—PU—919-287-1703, 800-233-1801
(50 mi. from Wilmington).
Season: Year-round. **High:** Spring/Fall. **Caddies:** No.
Green fee: $50-$99. **Credit cards:** V, MC.
Lodging on site: No. **Reduced fees:** Resort Guests, Twilight Play.
Unrestricted walking: No. **Range:** Yes (grass).
Holes: 18. **Par:** 72. **Yards:** 7,003-5,363. **Slope:** 138-118.
Comments: "Marvelous design . . . Two distinct courses in one—one tight, other linksy . . . Great condition, beautiful greens . . . Tough par 3s . . . Best in Myrtle Beach area . . . Staff extremely friendly."

★★★LOCKWOOD FOLLY GOLF LINKS

Holden Beach—R—919-842-5666, 800-443-7891
(26 mi. from Myrtle Beach).
Season: Year-round. **High:** April/July/Oct. **Caddies:** No.
Green fee: $50-$99. **Credit cards:** V, MC.
Lodging on site: Yes. **Reduced fees:** Low Season, Resort Guests.
Unrestricted walking: No. **Range:** Yes (grass).
Holes: 18. **Par:** 72. **Yards:** 6,835-6,149. **Slope:** 135-129.
Comments: "Really enjoyable . . . Lots of water . . . Interesting second hole . . . Doesn't get attention it should . . . Seldom crowded . . . Too many bunkers in fairways . . . Not in great shape."

★★★★MARSH HARBOUR GOLF LINKS

Calabash—PU—803-249-3449, 800-552-2660 (25 mi. from Myrtle Beach).
Season: Year-round. **High:** March-May. **Caddies:** No.
Green fee: $50-$99. **Credit cards:** V, AMEX, MC.
Lodging on site: No. **Reduced fees:** No.
Unrestricted walking: No. **Range:** Yes (grass).
Holes: 18. **Par:** 71. **Yards:** 6,690-4,795. **Slope:** 134-121.

Ranked in Second 25 of America's 75 Best Public Courses by GOLF DIGEST.
Comments: "Great layout . . . Always a treat . . . Every hole different . . .
Beautiful scenery . . . Outstanding test . . . What a homestretch! . . . Memorable holes . . . Famous 17th along marsh is magnificent . . . Best par 5
ever . . . No. 18 is one of the great underrated short par 4s in golf . . . Bring
your camera. If you can't shoot a good score, at least shoot some great
pictures . . . Great course, but getting pricey."

★★★½ MID PINES RESORT

Southern Pines—R—919-692-2114, 800-323-2114 (60 mi. from Raleigh).
Season: Year-round. **High:** Spring/Fall. **Caddies:** No.
Green fee: $50-$99. **Credit cards:** All Major.
Lodging on site: Yes. **Reduced fees:** Low Season, Resort Guests,
Twilight Play.
Unrestricted walking: No. **Range:** Yes (grass).
Holes: 18. **Par:** 72. **Yards:** 6,515-5,592. **Slope:** 127-128.
Comments: "Interesting, but neglected Donald Ross course . . . Like playing the past . . . Quiet getaway . . . Best resort course for the money in
Pinehurst . . . Great golf packages . . . Nice people run the pro shop . . .
Attention to customers is excellent."

★★★½ MOUNT MITCHELL GOLF CLUB

Burnsville—PU—704-675-5454 (55 mi. from Asheville).
Season: April-Nov. **High:** July-Aug. **Caddies:** No.
Green fee: $20-$49. **Credit cards:** V, MC.
Lodging on site: Yes. **Reduced fees:** Resort Guests.
Unrestricted walking: No. **Range:** No.
Holes: 18. **Par:** 72. **Yards:** 6,475-5,455. **Slope:** 121-116.
Comments: "Super little mountain course . . . Simply magnificent . . .
One of the best unknowns . . . Very scenic . . . Great condition."

★★★½ NAGS HEAD GOLF LINKS

Nags Head—R—919-441-8074, 800-851-9404
(80 mi. from Chesapeake, Va).
Season: Year-round. **High:** May-Oct. **Caddies:** No.
Green fee: $50-$99. **Credit cards:** V, MC.
Lodging on site: Yes. **Reduced fees:** Low Season, Resort Guests.
Unrestricted walking: No. **Range:** Yes (grass).
Holes: 18. **Par:** 71. **Yards:** 6,126-5,354. **Slope:** 130-123.
Comments: "Links at its best . . . Very Scottish . . . Ocean views, target
golf . . . Watch out for the winds . . . Ferocious . . . Tee off at dawn, hit the
beach by 11 o'clock . . . Too narrow, not enough land."

★★★½ NORTH SHORE COUNTRY CLUB

Sneads Ferry—R—919-327-2410, 800-828-5035 (30 mi. from Wilmington).
Season: Year-round. **High:** April-Oct. **Caddies:** No.
Green fee: $20-$49. **Credit cards:** V, MC.
Lodging on site: Yes. **Reduced fees:** Weekdays, Low Season,
Twilight Play.
Unrestricted walking: No. **Range:** Yes (grass).
Holes: 18. **Par:** 72. **Yards:** 6,866-5,039. **Slope:** 137-115.
Comments: "Always special . . . Fun to play . . . Lots of trees and water
. . . Requires long, straight carries . . . Reasonable rates . . . Friendly staff."

★★★½ OAK HOLLOW GOLF COURSE

High Point—PU—919-883-3260 (8 mi. from Greensboro).
Season: Year-round. **High:** April-Sept. **Caddies:** No.
Green fee: Under $20. **Credit cards:** V, MC.
Lodging on site: No. **Reduced fees:** Weekdays.
Unrestricted walking: Yes. **Range:** Yes (mats).
Holes: 18. **Par:** 72. **Yards:** 6,529-4,796. **Slope:** 121-119.
Ranked in Third 25 of America's 75 Best Public Courses by GOLF DIGEST.
Comments: "Affordable Pete Dye . . . Sort of tight, sort of hilly . . . Very

walkable . . . Challenging doglegs with water in play."

★★½ OAK ISLAND GOLF & COUNTRY CLUB
Caswell Beach—PU—919-278-5275 (23 mi. from Wilmington).
Season: Year-round. **High:** June-Oct. **Caddies:** No.
Green fee: $20-$49. **Credit cards:** V, MC.
Lodging on site: No. **Reduced fees:** Weekdays, Low Season.
Unrestricted walking: No. **Range:** Yes (grass).
Holes: 18. **Par:** 72. **Yards:** 6,608-5,437. **Slope:** 128-121.

★½ OAKWOOD HILLS GOLF CLUB
Pinebluff—R—919-281-3169 (80 mi. from Raleigh).
Season: Year-round. **High:** Spring/Fall. **Caddies:** No.
Green fee: Under $20. **Credit cards:** V, AMEX, MC.
Lodging on site: Yes. **Reduced fees:** Low Season, Resort Guests,
Twilight Play.
Unrestricted walking: Yes. **Range:** Yes (grass).
Holes: 18. **Par:** 72. **Yards:** 6,670-5,017. **Slope:** 127-103.

★★½ OCEAN ISLE BEACH GOLF COURSE
Ocean Isle Beach—PU—919-579-2610 (30 mi. from Myrtle Beach).
Season: Year-round. **High:** Spring/Fall. **Caddies:** No.
Green fee: $20-$49. **Credit cards:** V, MC.
Lodging on site: No. **Reduced fees:** Twilight Play.
Unrestricted walking: No. **Range:** Yes (grass).
Holes: 18. **Par:** 72. **Yards:** 6,626-5,075. **Slope:** 126-116.
Comments: "Fun little beach course . . . Staff good, helps singles get on
. . . Cheapest in Myrtle Beach area . . . Poorly maintained."

★★½ OLDE POINT COUNTRY CLUB
Hampstead—PU—919-270-2403 (18 mi. from Wilmington).
Season: Year-round. **High:** Spring/Fall. **Caddies:** No.
Green fee: $20-$49. **Credit cards:** V, AMEX, MC.
Lodging on site: Yes. **Reduced fees:** Weekdays, Low Season.
Unrestricted walking: No. **Range:** Yes (grass).
Holes: 18. **Par:** 72. **Yards:** 6,913-5,133. **Slope:** 136-115.
Comments: "Pretty . . . Pretty easy . . . Makes you feel like a pro . . . Well
maintained . . . Great par-5 11th . . . Watch for water hazards."

★★★★ OYSTER BAY GOLF LINKS
Sunset Beach—PU—919-579-3528, 800-552-2660
(25 mi. from Myrtle Beach).
Season: Year-round. **High:** Spring/Fall. **Caddies:** No.
Green fee: $50-$99. **Credit cards:** V, AMEX, MC.
Lodging on site: Yes. **Reduced fees:** No.
Unrestricted walking: No. **Range:** Yes (grass).
Holes: 18. **Par:** 71. **Yards:** 6,785-4,825. **Slope:** 137-117.
Selected as Best New Resort Course of 1983 and ranked in Second 25 of
America's 75 Best Public Courses by GOLF DIGEST.
Comments: "What a course! . . . One of the seaside elite . . . Fair, tough,
well laid out . . . A delightful challenge . . . Good combination of easy and
challenging holes . . . Best layout in North Carolina . . . Unbeaten vistas on
every hole . . . Guaranteed you'll see a gator . . . Sand and more sand . . .
Oyster-shell hazards . . . Expensive, but beautiful . . . Overplayed."

★★★½ PINE NEEDLES RESORT
Southern Pines—R—919-692-7111 (70 mi. from Raleigh).
Season: Year-round. **High:** Spring/Fall. **Caddies:** No.
Green fee: $50-$99. **Credit cards:** V, AMEX, MC.
Lodging on site: Yes. **Reduced fees:** Low Season, Resort Guests.
Unrestricted walking: No. **Range:** Yes (grass).
Holes: 18. **Par:** 71. **Yards:** 6,708-5,039. **Slope:** 131-118.
Site of 1996 U.S. Women's Open.
Comments: "Donald Ross at a reasonable rate . . . Fine layout . . . Very

fair, not too long . . . Forward markers give a big advantage . . . Wonderful atmosphere . . . The Bell family makes this a real pleasure . . . Excellent learning facility . . . Great food."

PINEHURST RESORT & COUNTRY CLUB

Pinehurst—R—919-295-8141 (70 mi. from Raleigh).
Season: Year-round. **High:** Spring/Fall. **Caddies:** Yes.
Green fee: $50-$99. **Credit cards:** All Major.
Lodging On site: Yes. **Reduced fees:** Low Season, Twilight Play.
Unrestricted walking: Yes. **Range:** Yes (grass).

★★★½ **NO. 1 COURSE**
Holes: 18. **Par:** 70. **Yards:** 5,780-5,329. **Slope:** 114-117.
Comments: "Short, full of Donald Ross tests . . . Not pretty enough for its high rates."

★★★★★ **NO. 2 COURSE**
Green fee: $100 and up.
Holes: 18. **Par:** 72. **Yards:** 7,020-5,966. **Slope:** 131-127.
Ranked 11th in America's 100 Greatest Golf Courses and 2nd in America's 75 Best Resort Courses by GOLF DIGEST.
Comments: "A national treasure . . . The Ultimate . . . The epitome of golf . . . Reeks of tradition . . . A classic . . . A monument to design ingenuity . . . Pure history . . . A real golf memory . . . The greatest ever . . . No. 2 is No. 1 in the Carolinas, maybe the U.S. . . . Heaven, with caddies . . . Holes have had only subtle changes. . . . Great place to stay and play . . . Very fair . . . Very expensive . . . At those prices, not very 'public' . . . You're paying for image . . . Sorry, I'm not into nostalgia."

★★★ **NO. 3 COURSE**
Holes: 18. **Par:** 70. **Yards:** 5,593-5,198. **Slope:** 112-114.
Comments: "Tiny greens . . . Overcrowded . . . Disinterested caddies."

★★★½ **NO. 4 COURSE**
Holes: 18. **Par:** 72. **Yards:** 6,919-5,696. **Slope:** 126-119.
Comments: "Wonderful old course . . . Back is best 9 at Pinehurst . . . Could play it every day . . . Underrated . . . $50 less than No. 2."

★★★ **NO. 5 COURSE**
Holes: 18. **Par:** 72. **Yards:** 6,827-5,658. **Slope:** 130-131.
Comments: "Could play this one every day."

★★★½ **NO. 6 COURSE**
Unrestricted walking: No.
Holes: 18. **Par:** 72. **Yards:** 7,157-5,430. **Slope:** 139-125.
Comments: "Pretty and playable . . . Very difficult from back tees . . . Toughest behind No. 2 . . . Wonderful recent improvements."

★★★★ **NO. 7.**
Green fee: $100 and up. **Unrestricted walking:** No.
Holes: 18. **Par:** 72. **Yards:** 7,114-4,924. **Slope:** 145-124.
Ranked 23rd in America's 75 Best Resort Courses by GOLF DIGEST.
Comments: "Another gem in the Pinehurst crown . . . Fun round of golf . . . A combination of Pine Valley and Edgewood Tahoe . . . 2nd best at Pinehurst . . . Better than No. 2 . . . Outstanding employee treatment . . . Fantastic, but too expensive . . . Not fun to play . . . Too damned hard."

★★★½ **THE PIT GOLF LINKS**
Pinehurst—PU—919-944-1600 (70 mi. from Raleigh).
Season: Year-round. **High:** March-May/Oct. **Caddies:** No.
Green fee: $50-$99. **Credit cards:** No.
Lodging on site: No. **Reduced fees:** Low Season, Twilight Play.
Unrestricted walking: No. **Range:** Yes (grass).
Holes: 18. **Par:** 72. **Yards:** 6,600-4,759. **Slope:** 139-120.
Ranked in Second 25 of America's 75 Best Public Courses by GOLF DIGEST.
Comments: "Truly different . . . The Pine Valley of the South . . . Unusual layout, must play more than once . . . Complete test of position play . . . Good gut check . . . Fun, must-be-seen course . . . Enjoyable, but short . . . Second-best course in Pinehurst . . . The ultimate tricked up course . . . 'La-la' golf . . . Goofy golf . . . Grand putt-putt . . . 6-hour rounds."

★★★½ REEMS CREEK GOLF CLUB
Weaverville—PU—704-645-4393 (12 mi. from Asheville).
Season: Year-round. **High:** March-Nov. **Caddies:** No.
Green fee: $20-$49. **Credit cards:** V, MC.
Lodging on site: No. **Reduced fees:** Weekdays, Low Season.
Unrestricted walking: No. **Range:** Yes (grass).
Holes: 18. **Par:** 72. **Yards:** 6,464-4,605. **Slope:** 133-114.
Comments: "Perfect mountain golf . . . Some blind shots . . . Scenic . . . 'Carts on path only' policy inconvenient."

★★½ RIVER BEND GOLF CLUB
Shelby—PU—704-482-4286 (40 mi. from Charlotte).
Season: Year-round. **High:** April-Oct. **Caddies:** No.
Green fee: $20-$49. **Credit cards:** V, MC.
Lodging on site: No. **Reduced fees:** Weekdays.
Unrestricted walking: No. **Range:** Yes (grass).
Holes: 18. **Par:** 72. **Yards:** 6,800-5,900. **Slope:** 130-117.

★★★½ SANDPIPER BAY GOLF & COUNTRY CLUB
Sunset Beach—R—919-579-9120, 800-356-5827
(15 mi. from Myrtle Beach).
Season: Year-round. **High:** Spring/Fall. **Caddies:** No.
Green fee: $20-$49. **Credit cards:** V, DISC, MC.
Reduced fees: Low Season, Resort Guests, Twilight Play.
Unrestricted walking: No. **Range:** Yes (grass).
Holes: 18. **Par:** 71. **Yards:** 6,503-4,869. **Slope:** 119-116.
Comments: "Good course lost in the glitz of Myrtle Beach . . . Very forgiving, easy to score on . . . Greens roll true . . . Fairways very nice . . . Good design . . . Five par 3s, five par 5s—fun . . . Great condition."

★★★ SEA SCAPE GOLF COURSE
Kitty Hawk—PU—919-261-2158 (75 mi. from Norfolk, Va.).
Season: Year-round. **High:** July-Aug. **Caddies:** No.
Green fee: $20-$49. **Credit cards:** V, MC.
Lodging on site: No. **Reduced fees:** Low Season.
Unrestricted walking: No. **Range:** Yes (grass).
Holes: 18. **Par:** 72. **Yards:** 6,483-5,536. **Slope:** 127-114.
Comments: "Golf in the sand dunes . . . Authentic links . . . A lot of sand . . . Very unique beach course, especially with northeast wind."

SEA TRAIL PLANTATION
Sunset Beach—R—919-579-4350, 800-624-6601.
Season: Year-round. **High:** Spring/Fall. **Caddies:** No.
Green fee: $50-$99. **Credit cards:** All Major.
Lodging on site: Yes. **Reduced fees:** Low Season, Resort Guests, Twilight Play.
Unrestricted walking: No. **Range:** Yes (grass).

(GREAT VALUE)

★★★½ DAN MAPLES COURSE
Holes: 18. **Par:** 72. **Yards:** 6,751-5,090. **Slope:** 121-108.
Comments: "Super layout . . . One of the best on the Grand Strand . . . Must play while in Myrtle . . . Nice, interesting . . . Well maintained . . . Good facilities."
★★★½ REES JONES COURSE
Holes: 18. **Par:** 72. **Yards:** 6,761-4,912. **Slope:** 132-115.
Comments: "Best of the three . . . Fun . . . Contoured fairways help . . . In great shape . . . Treated with respect . . . Mucho rough."
★★★½ WILLARD BYRD COURSE
Holes: 18. **Par:** 72. **Yards:** 6,750-4,717. **Slope:** 128-121.
Comments: "Good course . . . Beautifully manicured . . . Fun to play . . . Customer satisfaction high . . . Three great courses in one complex."

★★½ SILVER CREEK GOLF CLUB
Swansboro—PU—919-393-8058 (18 mi. from Morehead City).
Season: Year-round. **High:** May-Sept. **Caddies:** No.

Green fee: $20-$49. **Credit cards:** V, MC.
Lodging on site: No. **Reduced fees:** Low Season, Twilight Play.
Unrestricted walking: No. **Range:** Yes (grass).
Holes: 18. **Par:** 72. **Yards:** 6,526-4,962. **Slope:** 117-110.
Comments: "Too many forced carries for high handicappers to enjoy, but still the best track in this area . . . Easy to get tee times."

★★★½ THE SOUND GOLF LINKS

Hertford—PU—919-426-5555, 800-535-0704.
Season: Year-round. **High:** June-Aug. **Caddies:** No.
Green fee: $20-$49. **Credit cards:** V, MC.
Lodging on site: No. **Reduced fees:** None.
Unrestricted walking: No. **Range:** Yes (grass).
Holes: 18. **Par:** 72. **Yards:** 6,500-5,900. **Slope:** 124-119.

★★SPRINGDALE COUNTRY CLUB

Canton—R—704-235-8451, 800-553-3027 (11 mi. from Waynesville).
Season: Year-round. **High:** April-May. **Caddies:** No.
Green fee: $20-$49. **Credit cards:** V, MC.
Lodging on site: Yes. **Reduced fees:** Twilight Play.
Unrestricted walking: No. **Range:** No.
Holes: 18. **Par:** 72. **Yards:** 6,812-5,421. **Slope:** 126-113.
Comments: "Poor design, too many blind shots . . . Maintenance marginal . . . Green fee too high for these course conditions."

★★STAR HILL GOLF & COUNTRY CLUB
FIRST/SECOND/THIRD 9s

Swansboro—PU—919-393-8111 (25 mi. from Jacksonville, N.C.).
Season: Year-round. **High:** June-Sept. **Caddies:** No.
Green fee: $20-$49. **Credit cards:** All Major.
Lodging on site: No. **Reduced fees:** Low Season.
Unrestricted walking: No. **Range:** Yes (grass).
Holes: 27. **Par:** 36/36/35. **Yards:** 3,107/3,194/3,254.

★★★STONEY CREEK GOLF CLUB

Sedalia—PU—919-449-5688 (11 mi. from Greensboro).
Season: Year-round. **High:** Spring/Fall. **Caddies:** No.
Green fee: $20-$49. **Credit cards:** V, MC.
Lodging on site: No. **Reduced fees:** Weekdays.
Unrestricted walking: No. **Range:** Yes (grass).
Holes: 18. **Par:** 72. **Yards:** 7,016-5,190. **Slope:** 144-109.
Comments: "Routing just OK . . . Greens hard and convex."

★★★★TALAMORE AT PINEHURST

Southern Pines—PU—919-692-5884 (1 mi. from Pinehurst).
Season: Year-round. **High:** March-May. **Caddies:** No.
Green fee: $50-$99. **Credit cards:** V, MC.
Lodging on site: No. **Reduced fees:** Low Season.
Unrestricted walking: No. **Range:** Yes (grass).
Holes: 18. **Par:** 71. **Yards:** 6,802-4,903. **Slope:** 142-125.
Ranked 14th in North Carolina by GOLF DIGEST.
Comments: "Fabulous, fabulous . . . Primo course . . . Pleasing to play . . . I'd play it every day . . . Very challenging . . . May become a classic soon . . . Very difficult for average golfer . . . Didn't try the llama caddies."

TANGLEWOOD PARK GOLF CLUB

Clemmons—PU—919-766-5082 (5 mi. from Winston-Salem).
Season: Year-round. **High:** Spring/Fall. **Caddies:** No.
Green fee: $50-$99. **Credit cards:** None.
Lodging on site: Yes. **Reduced fees:** Resort Guests, Twilight Play.
Unrestricted walking: No. **Range:** Yes (mats).

★★★★½ CHAMPIONSHIP COURSE

Holes: 18. **Par:** 72. **Yards:** 7,022-5,119. **Slope:** 140-130.
Site of the 1974 PGA. Home of senior tour's Vantage Championship.

Ranked in First 25 of America's 75 Best Public Courses by GOLF DIGEST.
Comments: "Fantastic . . . Immaculate . . . A great experience . . . A solid test . . . Heavily bunkered . . . Too much sand . . . Few 'run-in' greens . . . Back more challenging than front . . . Best finishing holes anywhere."

★★★REYNOLDS COURSE
Green fee: $20-$49. **Unrestricted walking:** Yes.
Holes: 18. **Par:** 72. **Yards:** 6,469-5,203. **Slope:** 125-120.
Also an 18-hole par-3 course on the property.
Comments: "Tough to choose between these two . . . Do you want long or tight? . . . Reynolds much fairer than Championship."

★TOPSAIL GREENS COUNTRY CLUB
Hampstead—PU—919-270-2883 (15 mi. from Wilmington).
Season: Year-round. **High:** March-July/Sept.-Dec. **Caddies:** No.
Green fee: $20-$49. **Credit cards:** V, AMEX, MC.
Lodging on site: No. **Reduced fees:** Low Season, Twilight Play.
Unrestricted walking: No. **Range:** Yes (grass).
Holes: 18. **Par:** 71. **Yards:** 6,324-5,033. **Slope:** 121-113.
Comments: "Plain . . . Mediocre conditions . . . Staff is cordial, but the course is a goat track."

★★★WAYNESVILLE COUNTRY CLUB INN
Waynesville—R—704-452-4617 (25 mi. from Asheville).
Season: Year-round. **High:** April-Oct. **Caddies:** No.
Green fee: $20-$49. **Credit cards:** V, MC.
Lodging on site: Yes. **Reduced fees:** Low Season, Resort Guests, Twilight Play.
Unrestricted walking: No. **Range:** No.
Holes: 27. **Par:** 35/35/35. **Yards:** 2,969/2,829/2,974.
Comments: "The gem of the Smoky Mountains . . . Beautiful scenery . . . Three 9s of varying difficulty . . . Short, demands accuracy."

★★½ WHISPERING WOODS GOLF CLUB
Whispering Pines—PU—919-949-4653 (60 mi. from Raleigh).
Season: Year-round. **High:** Spring/Fall. **Caddies:** No.
Green fee: $20-$49. **Credit cards:** All Major.
Lodging on site: Yes. **Reduced fees:** Weekdays, Low Season.
Unrestricted walking: No. **Range:** No.
Holes: 18. **Par:** 70. **Yards:** 6,450-6,144. **Slope:** 115-110.
Comments: "Good, fun test of golf . . . Course is OK, resort isn't much."

★★★WOODBRIDGE GOLF LINKS
Kings Mountain—PU—704-482-0353 (30 mi. from Charlotte).
Season: Year-round. **High:** April-Oct. **Caddies:** No.
Green fee: $20-$49. **Credit cards:** V, MC.
Lodging on site: No. **Reduced fees:** No.
Unrestricted walking: No. **Range:** Yes (grass).
Holes: 18. **Par:** 72. **Yards:** 6,743-5,151. **Slope:** 131-116.
Comments: "Tough with wind . . . Covered cart bridges a nice touch."

★★★½ WOODLAKE COUNTRY CLUB
FIRST/SECOND/THIRD 9s
Vass—R—919-245-4686 (12 mi. from Fayetteville).
Season: Year-round. **High:** March-May. **Caddies:** No.
Green fee: $20-$49. **Credit cards:** V, MC.
Lodging on site: Yes. **Reduced fees:** Low Season, Resort Guests, Twilight Play.
Unrestricted walking: No. **Range:** Yes (mats).
Holes: 27. **Par:** 36/36/36. **Yards:** 3,389/3,623/3,422.
Third 9 actually has 10 holes, including an unusual "warm-up" hole.
Comments: "Scenic lakefront setting . . . Unusual holes . . . Lots of water, lots of sand, a true test . . . Great fun, great service."

★★★BOIS DE SIOUX GOLF COURSE
Wahpeton—PU—701-647-3526 (190 mi. from Minneapolis).
Season: April-Oct. **High:** June-Aug. **Caddies:** Yes.
Green fee: Under $20. **Credit cards:** No.
Lodging on site: No. **Reduced fees:** Weekdays.
Unrestricted walking: Yes. **Range:** Yes (grass).
Holes: 18. **Par:** 72. **Yards:** 6,670-6,489. **Slope:** 115-115.
Comments: "Nice greens . . . Front is too wide open . . . Nine holes in North Dakota, nine in Minnesota."

★★★½ EDGEWOOD MUNICIPAL GOLF COURSE

Fargo—PU—701-232-2824.
Season: April-Nov. **High:** June-Aug. **Caddies:** No.
Green fee: Under $20. **Credit cards:** No.
Lodging on site: No. **Reduced fees:** Weekdays, Twilight Play.
Unrestricted walking: Yes. **Range:** Yes (mats).
Holes: 18. **Par:** 71. **Yards:** 6,400-5,200. **Slope:** 122-115.
Ranked 3rd in North Dakota by GOLF DIGEST.
Comments: "Old course, great shape . . . Good looker . . . Busy, can't get on . . . Best value in North Dakota . . . A true gem for the money . . . Back side tends to flood in spring . . . Hit the ball straight. Most of the trees in North Dakota are on this course . . . Nicest, toughest muny for 100 miles in any direction . . . Worth the trip to Fargo . . . Comfy pro shop."

★★★½ MINOT COUNTRY CLUB
Minot—PU—701-839-6169.
Season: April-Nov. **High:** June-Aug. **Caddies:** No.
Green fee: $20-$49. **Credit cards:** V, MC.
Lodging on site: No. **Reduced fees:** Weekdays.
Unrestricted walking: Yes. **Range:** Yes (grass).
Holes: 18. **Par:** 72. **Yards:** 6,667-6,217. **Slope:** 124-121.
Ranked 5th in North Dakota by GOLF DIGEST.
Comments: "Well kept, a little too easy . . . Good walking course . . . Immaculate . . . Par 5s need work."

★★ATWOOD RESORT GOLF COURSE
Dellroy—R—216-735-2630 (25 mi. from Canton).
Season: Year-round. **High:** Summer. **Caddies:** No.
Green fee: Under $20. **Credit cards:** V, AMEX, MC.
Lodging on site: Yes. **Reduced fees:** No.
Unrestricted walking: Yes. **Range:** Yes (mats).
Holes: 18. **Par:** 70. **Yards:** 6,152-4,188. **Slope:** 102-91.
Comments: "Lots of hills . . . Excellent lodge . . . Staff is tops."

★★★½ AVALON LAKES GOLF COURSE
Warren—PU—216-856-8898 (50 mi. from Cleveland).
Season: April-Nov. **High:** Summer. **Caddies:** No.
Green fee: $20-$49. **Credit cards:** V, AMEX, MC.
Lodging on site: Yes. **Reduced fees:** No.
Unrestricted walking: No. **Range:** No.
Holes: 18. **Par:** 71. **Yards:** 6,868-5,324. **Slope:** 128-116.
LPGA Tour tournament site.
Comments: "Nice flat challenging course . . . Outstanding in every aspect
. . . Excellent, makes you use every club . . . Immaculate. . . Definitely
worth a second visit . . . Totally flat, water has nowhere to go. . . Fairways
like sponges after a rain. . . Too crowded. . . A shooting gallery."

★★★BENT TREE GOLF CLUB
Sunbury—PU—614-965-5140 (10 mi. from Columbus).
Season: Year-round. **High:** Summer. **Caddies:** No.
Green fee: $20-$49. **Credit cards:** V, MC.
Lodging on site: No. **Reduced fees:** Low Season, Twilight Play.
Unrestricted walking: No. **Range:** Yes (grass).
Holes: 18. **Par:** 72. **Yards:** 6,850-5,280. **Slope:** 119-113.
Comments: "Nice facility . . . Nice course. . . Numerous strategically
placed sand traps . . . Overpriced . . . An expensive day of golf . . . Too
wide open . . . Not real tough . . . Staff sets up holes too short to speed play
. . . Lousy traps. . . Lets back-9 tee-offs have priority. . . Too expensive".

★★★½ BLUE ASH GOLF COURSE
Cincinnati—PU—513-745-8577.
Season: Year-round. **High:** May-Sept. **Caddies:** No.
Green fee: Under $20. **Credit cards:** No.
Lodging on site: No. **Reduced fees:** Low Season.
Unrestricted walking: Yes. **Range:** No.
Holes: 18. **Par:** 72. **Yards:** 6,643-5,125. **Slope:** 127-124.
Ranked in Third 25 of America's 75 Best Public Courses by GOLF DIGEST.
Comments: "Long, hilly, tight . . . Good test of golf. . . Well taken care of
. . . One of the finest public courses . . . Bent-grass fairways kept in excel-
lent condition . . . Toughest four starting holes in the area . . . Bargain green
fee . . . Not much of a pro shop . . . Not enough land for layout."

★★½ DARBY CREEK GOLF COURSE
Marysville—PU—513-349-7491, 800-343-2729.
Season: Year-round. **High:** April-Sept. **Caddies:** No.
Green fee: $20-$49. **Credit cards:** No.
Reduced fees: Weekdays, Low Season, Twilight Play.
Unrestricted walking: No. **Range:** Yes (grass).
Holes: 18. **Par:** 72. **Yards:** 7,054-5,245. **Slope:** 119-109.
Comments: "Great course. . . Great price . . . Front 9 OK, back 9 tremen-
dous . . . Needs a few years."

★★★★EAGLESTICKS GOLF CLUB
Zanesville—PU—614-454-4900, 800-782-4493 (55 mi. from Columbus).
Season: April-Dec. **High:** May-Sept. **Caddies:** No.
Green fee: $20-$49. **Credit cards:** V, AMEX, MC.
Lodging on site: No. **Reduced fees:** Weekdays, Twilight Play.
Unrestricted walking: No. **Range:** Yes (grass).

GREAT VALUE

Holes: 18. **Par:** 70. **Yards:** 6,412-4,137. **Slope:** 120-99.
Ranked 14th in Ohio by GOLF DIGEST.
Comments: "Elegant . . . A pleasure. . . One of the best. . . Short but challenging . . . Unique accuracy course . . . Hilly, with beautiful holes everyone can play. . . Very playable. . . Not a backbreaker. . . Excellent greens . . . Well-groomed bent fairways . . . More than 100 bunkers . . . Outstanding personal attention . . . People are very friendly . . . Only drawback is it's too short . . . Too many short par 4s . . . Hard to find."

★★½ GLENVIEW GOLF COURSE
Cincinnati—PU—513-771-1747.
Season: Year-round. **High:** May-Aug. **Caddies:** No.
Green fee: Under $20. **Credit cards:** No.
Lodging on site: No. **Reduced fees:** Low Season.
Unrestricted walking: Yes. **Range:** Yes (mats).
Holes: 18. **Par:** 72. **Yards:** 6,859-5,196. **Slope:** 119-105.
Comments: "Pretty decent for a public course . . . Ordinary yet challenging. . . Plain front . . . So-so . . . Not well designed . . . Newer back 9 much better . . . Great 9 . . . Typical conditioning woes of a municipal, some good days, some bad. . . Good for a 5½-hour round."

★★★½ GRANVILLE GOLF COURSE
Granville—PU—614-587-4653 (35 mi. from Columbus).
Season: Year-round. **High:** April-Nov. **Caddies:** No.
Green fee: $20-$49. **Credit cards:** V, MC.
Lodging on site: No. **Reduced fees:** Weekdays, Low Season.
Unrestricted walking: No. **Range:** Yes (mats).
Holes: 18. **Par:** 71. **Yards:** 6,612-5,413. **Slope:** 126-121.
Comments: "Great old track . . . Positive experience in all respects . . . Great character. . . Very tough, subtle greens . . . Old Donald Ross subtleties . . . Current owner doing great job in rehab of course . . . New watering system . . . New holes a plus . . . Sadly remodeled course to get more money from real estate . . . Destroyed Mr. Ross . . . Used to be the best until three Donald Ross holes were replaced."

★★★½ HEATHERWOODE GOLF CLUB
Springboro—PU—513-748-3222 (15 mi. from Dayton).
Season: March-Dec. **High:** May-Sept. **Caddies:** No.
Green fee: $20-$49. **Credit cards:** V, AMEX, MC.
Lodging on site: No. **Reduced fees:** No.
Unrestricted walking: No. **Range:** Yes (grass).
Holes: 18. **Par:** 71. **Yards:** 6,730-5,069. **Slope:** 122-112.
Comments: "New, interesting. . . Top-shelf layout. . . Outstanding from championship tees . . . Well groomed. . . Good facilities. . . Wonderful attitude. . . Some funky holes."

★★★½ HUESTON WOODS STATE PARK GOLF COURSE
Oxford—R—513-624-0518 (30 mi. from Cincinnati).
Season: April-Oct. **High:** Summer. **Caddies:** No.
Green fee: $20-$49. **Credit cards:** V, MC.
Lodging on site: Yes. **Reduced fees:** Twilight Play.
Unrestricted walking: No. **Range:** Yes (grass).
Holes: 18. **Par:** 72. **Yards:** 7,030-5,186. **Slope:** 132.
Comments: "Enjoyable. . . Beautiful. . . Lots of woods. . . Very long for seniors . . . Don't play unless you can carry it 185 yards . . . Condition could be better . . . Tweak it a little and it'd be great. . . For the price, it's great . . . Great weekday values . . . Poor service. . . Allows cut-ins at 10th tee . . . State highways are in better shape."

★★★★ INDIAN SPRINGS GOLF CLUB
Mechanicsburg—PU—513-834-2111 (30 mi. from Columbus).
Season: March-Oct. **High:** Summer. **Caddies:** No.
Green fee: $20-$49. **Credit cards:** V, MC.

Lodging on site: No. **Reduced fees:** Weekdays, Twilight Play.
Unrestricted walking: Yes. **Range:** Yes (grass).
Holes: 18. **Par:** 72. **Yards:** 7,138-5,780. **Slope:** 125-121.
Comments: "Country club caliber course . . . Stern test . . . Whole bag of shotmaking . . . True greens. . . Not well known, but good . . . Good test for all levels . . . Well done, well maintained. . . Hope they can keep it up."

JACK NICKLAUS SPORTS CENTER
Mason—PU—513-398-7700 (25 mi. from Cincinnati).
Season: March-Dec. **High:** May-Sept. **Caddies:** No.
Credit cards: V, AMEX, DISC, MC.
Lodging on site: No. **Reduced fees:** Weekdays.
Unrestricted walking: Yes. **Range:** Yes (grass).
THE BRUIN COURSE*
Green fee: Under $20. **Holes:** 18. **Par:** 61. **Yards:** 3,428-3,428.
★★★ THE GRIZZLY COURSE
Green fee: $20-$49. **Holes:** 18. **Par:** 71. **Yards:** 6,731-5,256.
Slope: 131-115.
Comments: "Good resort course . . . Best of the best. . . Challenging, but playable for all handicaps . . . Sporty. . . Well maintained. . . Easy from the regular tees, a monster from the backs . . . Good pro shop. . . Considerate staff . . . Not terribly challenging . . . Overpriced, hard to get on . . . Poor management, big egos . . . Congested . . . Tourist trap . . . Easy walking."

★★ LICKING SPRINGS TROUT & GOLF CLUB
Newark—PU—614-366-2770 (35 mi. from Columbus).
Season: April-Oct. **High:** Summer. **Caddies:** No.
Green fee: Under $20. **Credit cards:** V, MC.
Lodging on site: No. **Reduced fees:** Weekdays.
Unrestricted walking: Yes. **Range:** No.
Holes: 18. **Par:** 72. **Yards:** 6,317-5,035. **Slope:** 117-117.

★★★ MAUMEE BAY STATE PARK GOLF COURSE
Oregon—R—419-836-9009 (10 mi. from Toledo).
Season: April-Oct. **High:** May-Sept. **Caddies:** No.
Green fee: $20-$49. **Credit cards:** All Major.
Lodging on site: Yes. **Reduced fees:** Weekdays, Low Season,
Twilight Play.
Unrestricted walking: No. **Range:** Yes (grass).
Holes: 18. **Par:** 72. **Yards:** 6,941-5,221. **Slope:** 129-118.
Comments: "Good new links-style course . . . Rough is maturing. Give it two years . . . Courteous staff . . . Price too high for state park course."

★★½ OXBOW GOLF & COUNTRY CLUB
Belpre—PU—614-423-6771, 800-423-0443 (120 mi. from Columbus).
Season: Year-round. **High:** April-Oct. **Caddies:** No.
Green fee: Under $20. **Credit cards:** V, MC.
Lodging on site: No. **Reduced fees:** Weekdays.
Unrestricted walking: Yes. **Range:** Yes (grass).
Holes: 18. **Par:** 71. **Yards:** 6,558-4,858. **Slope:** 117-109.

★★★ PIPESTONE GOLF CLUB
Miamisburg—PU—513-866-4653 (8 mi. from Dayton).
Season: March-Nov. **High:** Summer. **Caddies:** No.
Green fee: $20-$49. **Credit cards:** V, MC.
Lodging on site: No. **Reduced fees:** Low Season.
Unrestricted walking: Yes. **Range:** Yes (grass).
Holes: 18. **Par:** 72. **Yards:** 6,939-5,207. **Slope:** 137-121.
Comments: "New, needs maturing . . . Will get better, rates too high . . . Too many parallel fairways . . . A few holes too severe for elderly and high handicappers . . . Personnel indifferent, course too new to be this complacent."

★★★½ QUAIL HOLLOW RESORT
Concord—R—216-352-6201, 800-792-0258 (45 mi. from Cleveland).
Season: April-Nov. **High:** May-Sept. **Caddies:** No.
Green fee: $50-$99. **Credit cards:** All Major.
Lodging on site: Yes. **Reduced fees:** Weekdays, Low Season.
Unrestricted walking: No. **Range:** Yes (grass).
Holes: 18. **Par:** 72. **Yards:** 6,712-4,389. **Slope:** 130-109.
Comments: "One of the best public courses in northeast Ohio . . . A fall spectacle . . . Great condition but costly . . . Prices too high because of Nike Tour."

★★★ROYAL AMERICAN LINKS GOLF CLUB
Galena—PU—614-965-1215 (10 mi. from Columbus).
Season: March-Dec. **High:** Summer. **Caddies:** No.
Green fee: $20-$49. **Credit cards:** V, MC.
Reduced fees: Weekdays, Low Season, Twilight Play.
Unrestricted walking: Yes. **Range:** Yes (grass).
Holes: 18. **Par:** 72. **Yards:** 6,809-5,171. **Slope:** 126-111.
Comments: "Challenging links course . . . Fast greens . . . Water everywhere . . . A lake that has a golf course on it . . . If not windy, an easy course . . . Inconsistent . . . Still developing character."

★★★SAWMILL CREEK GOLF & RACQUET CLUB
Huron—PU—419-433-3789 (60 mi. from Cleveland).
Season: April-Oct. **High:** Summer. **Caddies:** No.
Green fee: $20-$49. **Credit cards:** V, AMEX, MC.
Lodging on site: Yes. **Reduced fees:** Resort Guests.
Unrestricted walking: Yes. **Range:** No.
Holes: 18. **Par:** 71. **Yards:** 6,813-5,416. **Slope:** 128-120.
Comments: "Tom Fazio course on Lake Erie. . . Outstanding . . . Flat but demanding . . . Long when wet. . . Good par 3s. . . Could be better maintained . . . Terrible front 9. . . Some weird holes. . . Back isn't bad."

★★★SLEEPY HOLLOW GOLF COURSE
Brecksville—PU—216-526-4285 (15 mi. from Cleveland).
Season: March-Dec. **High:** May-Sept. **Caddies:** No.
Green fee: Under $20. **Credit cards:** V, MC.
Lodging on site: No. **Reduced fees:** No.
Unrestricted walking: Yes. **Range:** Yes (mats).
Holes: 18. **Par:** 71. **Yards:** 6,500-5,815. **Slope:** 124-122.
Comments: "Hilly. . . Tough . . . Not what it used to be . . . Greens should be more consistent . . . Prefer faster greens."

TAM O'SHANTER GOLF COURSE
Canton—PU—216-477-5111, 800-462-9964 (20 mi. from Akron).
Season: March-Dec. **High:** May-Sept. **Caddies:** No.
Green fee: Under $20. **Credit cards:** V, MC.
Lodging on site: No. **Reduced fees:** No.
Unrestricted walking: Yes. **Range:** Yes (mats).
★★½ DALES COURSE
Holes: 18. **Par:** 70. **Yards:** 6,569-5,384. **Slope:** 110-109.
Comments: "Fine public course . . . Good for average and below-average golfers . . . Needs more definition, some bunkering."
★★½ HILLS COURSE
Holes: 18. **Par:** 70. **Yards:** 6,385-5,076. **Slope:** 104-102.
Comments: "Always in great condition. . . Superb drainage. . . Water disappears from greens within minutes of a downpour."

TURKEYFOOT LAKE GOLF LINKS*
FIRST/SECOND/THIRD 9s
Akron—PU—216-644-5971.
Season: Year-round. **High:** April-Oct. **Caddies:** No.
Green fee: Under $20. **Credit cards:** No.

ERRY GOLF COURSE
—PU—614-645-2582 (10 mi. from Columbus).
Season: Year-round. **High:** May-Aug. **Caddies:** No.
Green fee: $20-$49. **Credit cards:** V, MC.
Reduced fees: Weekdays, Low Season, Twilight Play.
Unrestricted walking: No. **Range:** Yes (grass).
Holes: 18. **Par:** 72. **Yards:** 6,636-5,440. **Slope:** 114.
Comments: "Ordinary, a few memorable holes . . . Holes run very close together . . . Greens and fairways not maintained as well as would be expected . . . Could stand to let rough grow higher . . . Links courses don't work in central Ohio. There's not enough wind."

★★★½ THE VINEYARD GOLF COURSE
Cincinnati—PU—513-474-3007.
Season: March-Nov. **High:** May-Sept. **Caddies:** No.
Green fee: $20-$49. **Credit cards:** No.
Lodging on site: No. **Reduced fees:** Weekdays, Twilight Play.
Unrestricted walking: Yes. **Range:** No.
Holes: 18. **Par:** 71. **Yards:** 6,789-4,747. **Slope:** 129-113.
Selected as runner-up for Best New Public Course of 1987 by GOLF DIGEST.
Comments: "Exceptional public course. . . A favorite . . . Very pretty . . . Classy. . . Always challenging and different . . . Tough second shots . . . A couple of holes in so-so shape, generally real nice. . . Every aspect of club is outstanding, especially the service . . . Pleasant experience . . . Like a private club . . . Absolutely tops in greeting golfers . . . For the price you can't beat it . . . Best bargain in Cincy . . . 10-minute intervals for tee times . . . A couple of nice holes, otherwise overrated . . . Greens on two par 3s are poorly designed. . . Higher cost than others."

WEATHERWAX GOLF COURSE
Middletown—PU—513-425-7886 (20 mi. from Dayton).
Season: Year-round. **High:** May-Oct. **Caddies:** No.
Green fee: Under $20. **Credit cards:** No.
Lodging on site: No. **Reduced fees:** No.
Unrestricted walking: Yes. **Range:** Yes (grass).
★★★ VALLEYVIEW/HIGHLANDS COURSE
Holes: 18. **Par:** 72. **Yards:** 6,756-5,253. **Slope:** 120-117.
Comments: "Pretty good, not great . . . Water everywhere . . . Great price . . . Maintenance could be better."
★★★ WOODSIDE/MEADOWS COURSE
Holes: 18. **Par:** 72. **Yards:** 7,174-5,669. **Slope:** 116-112.
Comments: "Nice course, nice value . . . Fun course with good variety . . . Well run . . . Excellent in all ways . . . Too long for seniors."

WHETSTONE COUNTRY CLUB*
Caledonia—PU—614-389-4343 (45 mi. from Columbus).
Season: April-Oct. **High:** May-Sept. **Caddies:** No.
Green fee: Under $20. **Credit cards:** V, MC.
Lodging on site: No. **Reduced fees:** Weekdays.
Unrestricted walking: Yes. **Range:** Yes (grass).
Holes: 18. **Par:** 72. **Yards:** 6,674-5,023. **Slope:** 120-111.

OKLAHOMA

ADAMS MUNICIPAL GOLF COURSE*
Bartlesville—PU—918-337-5313 (50 mi. from Tulsa).
Season: Year-round. **High:** April-Sept. **Caddies:** No.
Green fee: Under $20. **Credit cards:** V, MC.
Lodging on site: No. **Reduced fees:** Weekdays, Twilight Play.
Unrestricted walking: Yes. **Range:** Yes (grass).
Holes: 18. **Par:** 72. **Yards:** 6,819–5,655. **Slope:** 119-112.

★★★★FOREST RIDGE GOLF CLUB
Broken Arrow—PU—918-357-2282 (10 mi. from Tulsa).
Season: Year-round. **High:** April-Oct. **Caddies:** No.
Green fee: $50-$99. **Credit cards:** V, AMEX, DISC, MC.
Reduced fees: Weekdays, Low Season, Twilight Play.
Unrestricted walking: No. **Range:** Yes (grass).
Holes: 18. **Par:** 72. **Yards:** 7,069-5,341. **Slope:** 134-112.
Comments: "Perfect . . . Impeccable . . . The best daily fee in Oklahoma
. . . Tough, need accuracy . . . Nice but hot . . . Challenging course . . .
Every hole seems to play uphill . . . Well laid out . . . Holes don't intrude
upon one another . . . Too difficult for the average golfer . . . Needs better
distance markers . . . Rye fairways are great except when they yellow in
August . . . Expensive for the area . . . Courteous treatment . . . You feel
like you're on an exclusive club . . . Need drinking fountains on course."

FOUNTAINHEAD STATE PARK GOLF COURSE*
Checotah—R—918-689-3209 (60 mi. from Tulsa).
Season: Year-round. **High:** March-Oct. **Caddies:** No.
Green fee: Under $20. **Credit cards:** V, DISC, MC.
Lodging on site: Yes. **Reduced fees:** Weekdays, Twilight Play.
Unrestricted walking: Yes. **Range:** Yes (grass).
Holes: 18. **Par:** 72. **Yards:** 6,919-5,470. **Slope:** 112-110.

★★★KICKINGBIRD GOLF COURSE
Edmond—PU—405-341-5350 (15 mi. from Oklahoma City).
Season: Year-round. **High:** May-Sept. **Caddies:** No.
Green fee: Under $20. **Credit cards:** No.
Lodging on site: No. **Reduced fees:** Twilight Play.
Unrestricted walking: Yes. **Range:** Yes (grass).
Holes: 18. **Par:** 71. **Yards:** 6,785-4,649. **Slope:** 127-117.
Comments: "Tough public course . . . Treelined with rolling hills . . . Lots
of trees . . . Blind shots in heavy oaks . . . Utilize forecaddies on some holes
. . . Recently redid both 9s, good job . . . Excellent conditions . . . Great
bent-grass greens . . . Excellent facilities and staff . . . Original home of the
5-hour round . . . No drinking water to be found anywhere."

LINCOLN PARK GOLF COURSE
Oklahoma City—PU—405-424-1421.
Season: Year-round. **High:** April-Aug. **Caddies:** Yes.
Green fee: Under $20. **Credit cards:** No.
Lodging on site: No. **Reduced fees:** Twilight Play.
Unrestricted walking: Yes. **Range:** Yes (grass).
★½ EAST COURSE
Holes: 18. **Par:** 70. **Yards:** 6,508-5,855. **Slope:** 120-112.
Comments: "Old, very good layout . . . Just upgraded, looks great . . .
Short par 70, playable . . . Easier than the West . . . Unexciting . . . Full of
city hacks."
★★½ WEST COURSE
Holes: 18. **Par:** 70. **Yards:** 6,508-5,673. **Slope:** 121-115.
Comments: "Good routing . . . Hilly and rolling . . . Good greens . . .
More difficult than the East . . . Superior service . . . New staff are upgrad-
ing already excellent facility . . . Best for the money in the city . . . Family
attractions nearby . . . Inexpensive and slow."

PAGE BELCHER GOLF COURSE
Tulsa—PU—918-446-1529.
Season: Year-round. **High:** Spring/Fall. **Caddies:** No.
Green fee: Under $20. **Credit cards:** No.
Lodging on site: No. **Reduced fees:** Twilight Play.
Unrestricted walking: Yes. **Range:** Yes (grass).

★★½ **OLDE PAGE COURSE**
Holes: 18. **Par:** 71. **Yards:** 6,826-5,532. **Slope:** 121-118.
Comments: "One of the best public facilities around . . . Old style . . . Not too tight . . . Big wide greens . . . More spacious than Stone Creek . . . Good for average golfers . . . Needs some TLC."

★★★½ **STONE CREEK COURSE**
Holes: 18. **Par:** 71. **Yards:** 6,539-5,144. **Slope:** 126-127.
Runner-up for Best New Public Course of 1988 by GOLF DIGEST.
Comments: "Outstanding . . . Stylish . . . Many mounds, much water . . . Excellent mixture . . . Great zoysia-grass fairways . . . 'Trick or treat' greens . . . Requires thinking and shotmaking skills . . . Can walk and enjoy . . . Too long to walk."

SHANGRI-LA GOLF RESORT
Afton—R—918-257-4204, 800-331-4060 (75 mi. from Tulsa).
Season: Year-round. **High:** April-Oct. **Caddies:** No.
Green fee: $50-$99. **Credit cards:** V, AMEX, MC.
Lodging on site: Yes. **Reduced fees:** Weekdays, Low Season, Resort Guests, Twilight Play.
Unrestricted walking: No. **Range:** Yes (grass).

★★★½ **BLUE COURSE**
Holes: 18. **Par:** 72. **Yards:** 7,012-5,975. **Slope:** 132-126.
Comments: "Best-kept secret in the U.S. . . . Beautiful lakeside setting . . . Memorable holes . . . Challenging and fun . . . Long, tight . . . Bring a big stick . . . Tough putting . . . Will eat a hacker's lunch . . . Pro shop outstanding . . . Great place for a vacation . . . A little pricey but first class."

★★★ **GOLD COURSE**
Holes: 18. **Par:** 70. **Yards:** 5,932-4,571. **Slope:** 123-112.
Comments: "Short, but very difficult greens . . . Six par 3s, six par 4s and six par 5s . . . Great set of par 3s . . . Two great water holes . . . Toughest 5,900 yards you'll ever play."

★★★ SILVERHORN GOLF CLUB
Oklahoma City—PU—405-752-1181.
Season: Year-round. **High:** April-Oct. **Caddies:** No.
Green fee: $20-$49. **Credit cards:** V, AMEX, MC.
Reduced fees: Weekdays, Low Season, Twilight Play.
Unrestricted walking: Yes. **Range:** Yes (grass).
Holes: 18. **Par:** 71. **Yards:** 6,768-4,943. **Slope:** 128-113.
Comments: "Miniature version of Forest Ridge . . . Narrow driving areas . . . Subtle greens . . . Classy . . . Country club atmosphere . . . Courteous staff . . . People know how to treat you . . . Worth the extra money . . . Bad fairways, no drainage . . . Roughs unplayable . . . Too many lay-up holes . . . Needs some trees and traps . . . Extremely slow play."

★★½ SOUTH LAKES GOLF COURSE
Jenks—PU—918-299-0176 (3 mi. from Tulsa).
Season: Year-round. **High:** April-Sept. **Caddies:** No.
Green fee: Under $20. **Credit cards:** No.
Lodging on site: No. **Reduced fees:** Twilight Play.
Unrestricted walking: Yes. **Range:** Yes (grass).
Holes: 18. **Par:** 71. **Yards:** 6,340-5,242. **Slope:** 113-99.
Comments: "Short holes, big greens . . . But has character . . . Allows run ups . . . Fairways in poor condition . . . Great for walking . . . Great for high handicappers . . . Short to a fault."

SUNSET HILLS GOLF COURSE*
Guymon—PU—405-338-7404 (120 mi. from Amarillo, Tex.).
Season: Year-round. **High:** Summer. **Caddies:** No.
Green fee: Under $20. **Credit cards:** No.
Lodging on site: No. **Reduced fees:** Weekdays, Twilight Play.
Unrestricted walking: Yes. **Range:** Yes (mats).
Holes: 18. **Par:** 71. **Yards:** 6,700-5,204. **Slope:** 108-105.

TEXOMA STATE PARK GOLF COURSE*
Kingston—R—405-564-3333 (40 mi. from Ardmore).
Season: Year-round. **High:** Summer. **Caddies:** No.
Green fee: Under $20. **Credit cards:** V, DISC, MC.
Lodging on site: Yes. **Reduced fees:** Weekdays, Resort Guests,
Twilight Play.
Unrestricted walking: Yes. **Range:** Yes (grass).
Holes: 18. **Par:** 71. **Yards:** 6,128-5,145. **Slope:** 112-108.

TROSPER PARK GOLF COURSE*
Oklahoma City—PU—405-677-8874.
Season: Year-round. **High:** March-Sept. **Caddies:** No.
Green fee: Under $20. **Credit cards:** No.
Lodging on site: No. **Reduced fees:** Twilight Play.
Unrestricted walking: Yes. **Range:** Yes (grass).
Holes: 18. **Par:** 72. **Yards:** 6,928-6,450. **Slope:** 118-116.

★★UNIVERSITY OF OKLAHOMA GOLF COURSE
Norman—PU—405-325-6716 (20 mi. from Oklahoma City).
Season: Year-round. **High:** April-Oct. **Caddies:** No.
Green fee: Under $20. **Credit cards:** No.
Lodging on site: No. **Reduced fees:** Twilight Play.
Unrestricted walking: Yes. **Range:** Yes (grass).
Holes: 18. **Par:** 72. **Yards:** 6,905-5,341. **Slope:** 123-116.
Comments: "Great Perry Maxwell layout, bad fairways . . . Difficult small
greens . . . Dried up goat patch . . . Needs irrigation system . . . Needs a
face-lift . . . Avoid during Dog Days."

WESTWOOD PARK GOLF COURSE*
Norman—PU—405-321-0433 (15 mi. from Oklahoma City).
Season: Year-round. **High:** April-Aug. **Caddies:** No.
Green fee: Under $20. **Credit cards:** V, DISC, MC.
Lodging on site: No. **Reduced fees:** Weekdays.
Unrestricted walking: Yes. **Range:** Yes (grass).
Holes: 18. **Par:** 70. **Yards:** 6,015-5,525. **Slope:** 108-120.

OREGON

★BATTLE CREEK GOLF COURSE
Salem—PU—503-585-1402.
Season: Year-round. **High:** April-Sept. **Caddies:** No.
Green fee: $20-$49. **Credit cards:** V, MC.
Lodging on site: No. **Reduced fees:** Weekdays.
Unrestricted walking: Yes. **Range:** No.
Holes: 18. **Par:** 72. **Yards:** 6,025-4,935. **Slope:** 109-109.
Comments: "Parallel fairways . . . Dangerously tight . . . Beware stray shots."

BLACK BUTTE RANCH GOLF CLUB
Black Butte Ranch—R—503-595-6689, 800-399-2322.
Season: March-Nov. **High:** Summer. **Caddies:** No.
Green fee: $20-$49. **Credit cards:** V, MC, AMEX, DISC.
Lodging on site: Yes. **Reduced fees:** Low Season.
Unrestricted walking: Yes. **Range:** Yes (grass).
★★★½ BIG MEADOW COURSE
Holes: 18. **Par:** 72. **Yards:** 6,870-5,716. **Slope:** 126-115.
Comments: "Most scenic in Oregon . . . Great setting against the Cascades . . . Beautiful woodlands . . . Beautiful mountain views . . . Short and tricky . . . OK, but not great . . . Too many tricks . . . Too long to travel just for golf . . . Great lodge but expensive."
★★★½ GLAZE MEADOW COURSE
Holes: 18. **Par:** 72. **Yards:** 6,560-5,616. **Slope:** 128-120.
Comments: "Equally picturesque . . . More variety than Big Meadow . . . More difficult than its sister . . . Best in the area . . . Lots to offer . . . Great views . . . Definitely not for walkers . . . Super quality for the price . . . Time in summer to play both courses in one day."

★★BROADMOOR GOLF COURSE
Portland—PU—503-281-1337.
Season: Year-round. **High:** April-Oct. **Caddies:** No.
Green fee: Under $20. **Credit cards:** V.
Reduced fees: Weekdays, Low Season, Twilight Play.
Unrestricted walking: Yes. **Range:** Yes (grass).
Holes: 18. **Par:** 72. **Yards:** 6,498-5,384. **Slope:** 122-110.
Comments: "Good public course . . . Not too long . . . Water and trees . . . Willow-lined fairways . . . Lousy drainage . . . Turns to mud in rain."

EAGLE CREST RESORT
Redmond—R—503-923-4653.
Season: Year-round. **High:** May-Oct. **Caddies:** No.
Green fee: $20-$49. **Credit cards:** V, MC.
Lodging on site: Yes. **Reduced fees:** No.
Unrestricted walking: No. **Range:** Yes (grass).
★★★EAGLE CREST COURSE
Holes: 18. **Par:** 72. **Yards:** 6,673-5,395. **Slope:** 123-109.
Comments: "Good use of natural terrain . . . Setting makes it interesting . . . Most beautiful in Oregon . . . Underrated . . . Need long irons to score."
EAGLE RIDGE COURSE*
Holes: 18. **Par:** 72. **Yards:** 6,477-4,773. **Slope:** 123.
New course opened fall of 1993.

★★★½ EASTMORELAND GOLF COURSE
Portland—PU—503-775-2900.
Season: Year-round. **High:** May-Sept. **Caddies:** No.
Green fee: Under $20. **Credit cards:** No.
Lodging on site: No. **Reduced fees:** Weekdays.
Unrestricted walking: Yes. **Range:** Yes (mats).
Holes: 18. **Par:** 72. **Yards:** 6,629-5,646. **Slope:** 123-116.
Ranked in First 25 of America's 75 Best Public Courses by GOLF DIGEST.

Comments: "Lovely old course . . . Heavily treed . . . Lots of water on back 9 . . . Terrific back 9 . . . Demanding . . . Wide variety of shots . . . Best, fastest greens in town . . . One of the best munies in the country . . . Great condition for amount of play . . . Too crowded but outstanding . . . Very soggy in spring."

★★★EMERALD VALLEY GOLF COURSE
Creswell—PU—503-895-2174 (10 mi. from Eugene).
Season: Year-round. **High:** July-Aug. **Caddies:** No.
Green fee: $20-$49. **Credit cards:** V, AMEX, MC.
Reduced fees: Weekdays, Low Season, Twilight Play.
Unrestricted walking: Yes. **Range:** Yes (mats).
Holes: 18. **Par:** 72. **Yards:** 6,873-5,803. **Slope:** 129-129.
Comments: "Nice . . . Not too tough . . . Easy to find . . . Very good price . . . Very good food . . . Worth the drive."

★★★FOREST HILLS GOLF COURSE
Cornelius—PU—503-357-3347 (25 mi. from Portland).
Season: Year-round. **High:** May-Sept. **Caddies:** No.
Green fee: $20-$49. **Credit cards:** V, MC.
Lodging on site: No. **Reduced fees:** No.
Unrestricted walking: Yes. **Range:** Yes (mats).
Holes: 18. **Par:** 72. **Yards:** 6,173-5,673. **Slope:** 122-114.
Comments: "Tremendous layout . . . Nicely wooded traditional design . . . Lots of fun . . . Lots of variety and character . . . Small greens . . . Very hilly back side . . . Some demanding blind shots . . . Underrated . . . In the city but off the beaten path . . . A favorite . . . Overplayed."

★★GEARHART GOLF LINKS
Gearhart—PU—503-738-3538 (85 mi. from Portland).
Season: Year-round. **High:** May-Oct. **Caddies:** No.
Green fee: $20-$49. **Credit cards:** V, MC.
Lodging on site: Yes. **Reduced fees:** No.
Unrestricted walking: Yes. **Range:** No.
Holes: 18. **Par:** 72. **Yards:** 6,089-5,882. **Slope:** 112-123.
Comments: "Old-fashioned links . . . On sand dunes near the ocean . . . Rolling moundy fairways . . . Always ocean breezes . . . Used to be the best greens on Oregon coast . . . Has let course go . . . Greens are terrible."

GLENDOVEER GOLF COURSE
Portland—PU—503-253-7507.
Season: Year-round. **High:** March-Oct. **Caddies:** No.
Green fee: Under $20. **Credit cards:** V, MC.
Lodging on site: No. **Reduced fees:** Weekdays.
Unrestricted walking: Yes. **Range:** Yes (mats).
★★½ EAST COURSE
Holes: 18. **Par:** 72. **Yards:** 6,319-5,142. **Slope:** 119-115.
Comments: "Challenging hills . . . Lots of trees . . . Tall trees . . . Trees make it tough . . . Too heavily played to be maintained decently."
★½ WEST COURSE
Holes: 18. **Par:** 73. **Yards:** 5,803-5,117. **Slope:** 111-106.
Comments: "Easy course, good for novice golfers . . . Flat, back-and-forth design . . . Hilly on some holes . . . Heavy, heavy play."

HERON LAKES GOLF COURSE
Portland—PU—503-289-1818.
Season: Year-round. **High:** June-Sept. **Caddies:** No.
Green fee: Under $20. **Credit cards:** No.
Lodging on site: No. **Reduced fees:** Weekdays.
Unrestricted walking: Yes. **Range:** Yes (grass).

★★★GREENBACK COURSE
Holes: 18. **Par:** 72. **Yards:** 6,565-5,938. **Slope:** 124-115.
Ranked in Third 25 of America's 75 Best Public Courses by GOLF DIGEST.

Comments: "Water, water everywhere . . . Huge greens . . . Every shot offers options and challenges . . . Holds up despite tons of play . . . Fine views of Mt. Hood . . . Best buy in Oregon . . . Great course, but less challenging than Great Blue."

★★★½ GREAT BLUE COURSE
Holes: 18. **Par:** 72. **Yards:** 6,916-6,056. **Slope:** 132-122.
Comments: "Great test for all . . . A linksy, target-style course . . . Lots of water . . . Lots of options . . . Take a deep breath, take your best shot . . . Tougher than it looks from the outside . . . Poor clubhouse."

★½ JUNIPER GOLF CLUB
Redmond—PU—503-548-3121 (130 mi. from Portland).
Season: Year-round. **High:** March-Oct. **Caddies:** No.
Green fee: $20-$49. **Credit cards:** V, MC.
Lodging on site: No. **Reduced fees:** Weekdays, Low Season.
Unrestricted walking: Yes. **Range:** Yes (grass).
Holes: 18. **Par:** 72. **Yards:** 6,525-5,598. **Slope:** 124-115.

★★ KAH-NEE-TAH RESORT GOLF CLUB
Warm Springs—R—503-553-1112, 800-831-0100.
Season: Year-round. **High:** March-Sept. **Caddies:** No.
Green fee: $20-$49. **Credit cards:** All Major.
Lodging on site: Yes. **Reduced fees:** Low Season.
Unrestricted walking: Yes. **Range:** Yes (grass).
Holes: 18. **Par:** 72. **Yards:** 6,352-5,195. **Slope:** 123-116.
Comments: "Very remote . . . High, hot, dry, windy . . . Sagebrush rough . . . Maintenance is not constant . . . Only other thing to do here is swim . . . Not worth the drive."

★½ MERIWETHER NATIONAL GOLF CLUB
Hillsboro—PU—503-648-4143.
Season: Year-round. **High:** March-Oct. **Caddies:** No.
Green fee: Under $20. **Credit cards:** No.
Lodging on site: No. **Reduced fees:** No.
Unrestricted walking: No. **Range:** Yes (grass).
Holes: 18. **Par:** 72. **Yards:** 6,716-5,846. **Slope:** 116-115.
Comments: "Awful condition . . . Under water during winter months . . . Gets dry and hard by end of summer."

★ MOUNTAIN HIGH GOLF COURSE
Bend—PU—503-382-1111.
Season: April-Nov. **High:** June-Oct. **Caddies:** No.
Green fee: $20-$49. **Credit cards:** V, MC.
Lodging on site: No. **Reduced fees:** Low Season, Twilight Play.
Unrestricted walking: Yes. **Range:** Yes (mats).
Holes: 18. **Par:** 72. **Yards:** 6,649-5,556. **Slope:** 126-126.
Comments: "Most unfair island green ever."

★½ PROGRESS DOWNS GOLF COURSE
Beaverton—PU—503-646-5166.
Season: Year-round. **High:** April-Oct. **Caddies:** No.
Green fee: Under $20. **Credit cards:** All Major.
Lodging on site: No. **Reduced fees:** Weekdays.
Unrestricted walking: Yes. **Range:** Yes (mats).
Holes: 18. **Par:** 71. **Yards:** 6,426-5,626. **Slope:** 112-115.
Comments: "Average public course . . . Maintenance could be better . . . Busiest course in Portland . . . Chronic slow play."

PUMPKIN RIDGE GOLF CLUB
Cornelius—PU—503-647-9977 (20 mi. from Portland).
Season: Year-round. **High:** May-Sept. **Caddies:** No.
Green fee: $50-$99. **Credit cards:** V, DISC, MC.
Lodging on site: No. **Reduced fees:** Weekdays.

GREAT VALUE

Unrestricted walking: Yes. Range: Yes (grass).

★★★★½ GHOST CREEK COURSE

Holes: 18. Par: 71. Yards: 6,839-5,326. Slope: 140-121.

Selected Best New Public Course of 1992 by GOLF DIGEST. Club also has 18-hole Witch Hollow Course open only to members.

Comments: "Best in Oregon . . . Best in the west . . . The sky's the limit . . . A beauty . . . Wonderful design . . . Fantastic . . . Great track . . . Like a top level private club . . . Several ways to play each hole . . . Tough, fair, varied . . . Beautifully conditioned . . . Expensive for the area . . . Definitely not overpriced."

★★½ THE RESORT AT THE MOUNTAIN
THISTLE/FOXGLOVE/PINECONE 9s

Welches—R—503-622-3151, 800-669-4653 (45 mi. from Portland).

Season: Year-round. High: March-Nov. Caddies: No.

Green fee: $20-$49. Credit cards: All Major.

Lodging on site: Yes. Reduced fees: Weekdays, Low Season, Resort Guests, Twilight Play.

Unrestricted walking: Yes. Range: No.

Holes: 27. Par: 36/36/34. Yards: 3,351/3,092/2,681.

Comments: "Three good 9s . . . Not a pushover . . . Newest 9 is best . . . Scenery can't be beat . . . Great vacation spot."

★★★RIVER'S EDGE GOLF COURSE

Bend—R—503-389-2828, 800-547-3928.

Season: Year-round. High: Summer. Caddies: No.

Green fee: $20-$49. Credit cards: All Major.

Lodging on site: Yes. Reduced fees: Low Season, Resort Guests, Twilight Play.

Unrestricted walking: Yes. Range: Yes (grass).

Holes: 18. Par: 72. Yards: 6,647-5,380. Slope: 136-135.

Comments: "Much improved with new back 9."

★★½ ROSE CITY MUNICIPAL GOLF CLUB

Portland—PU—503-253-4744.

Season: Year-round. High: Summer. Caddies: No.

Green fee: Under $20. Credit cards: No.

Lodging on site: No. Reduced fees: Weekdays.

Unrestricted walking: Yes. Range: No.

Holes: 18. Par: 72. Yards: 6,455-5,619. Slope: 118-117.

★★★SALEM GOLF CLUB

Salem—PU—503-363-6652.

Season: Year-round. High: April-Sept. Caddies: No.

Green fee: $20-$49. Credit cards: V, MC.

Lodging on site: No. Reduced fees: No.

Unrestricted walking: Yes. Range: No.

Holes: 18. Par: 72. Yards: 6,203-5,408. Slope: 118-110.

Comments: "Good old course . . . Outstanding variety . . . Narrow, tree-lined . . . Steeped in tradition . . . Truly fun course . . . A bit crowded . . . Play is slow because of so much use . . . Can get spongy . . . Okefenokee in the springtime!"

★★★SALISHAN GOLF LINKS

Gleneden Beach—R—503-764-3632, 800-452-2300 (59 mi. from Salem).

Season: Year-round. High: June-Oct. Caddies: No.

Green fee: $20-$49. Credit cards: All Major.

Lodging on site: Yes. Reduced fees: Low Season.

Unrestricted walking: Yes. Range: Yes (mats).

Holes: 18. Par: 72. Yards: 6,439-5,693. Slope: 128-127.

Ranked 73rd in America's 75 Best Resort Courses by GOLF DIGEST.

Comments: "Front and back very distinct . . . Two different 9s . . . Ocean links and forest holes . . . Mountain and sea . . . Tough course in wind and rain . . . Panoramic ocean views . . . Rustic luxury . . . Best dining on the coast . . . Silly par 3s on back 9."

★★★★½ SANDPINES

Florence—R—503-997-1940 (67 mi. from Eugene).
Season: Year-round. **High:** June-Oct. **Caddies:** Yes.
Green fee: $20-$49. **Credit cards:** V, MC.
Lodging on site: No. **Reduced fees:** Twilight Play.
Unrestricted walking: Yes. **Range:** Yes (grass).
Holes: 18. **Par:** 72. **Yards:** 6,954-5,346. **Slope:** 129-111.
Selected Best New Public Course of 1993 by GOLF DIGEST.
Comments: "Wow! A winner . . . Gotta be Best New . . . Hard to beat . . . Great, right on the dunes . . . This is a beauty . . . Dunes make it unique . . . Exceptional . . . Great, true putting greens . . . They got this one right . . . A real bargain."

★★SANTIAM GOLF CLUB

Stayton—PU—503-769-3485 (12 mi. from Salem).
Season: Year-round. **High:** May-Sept. **Caddies:** No.
Green fee: $20-$49. **Credit cards:** No.
Lodging on site: No. **Reduced fees:** Weekdays.
Unrestricted walking: Yes. **Range:** Yes (mats).
Holes: 18. **Par:** 72. **Yards:** 6,385-5,553. **Slope:** 115-122.
Comments: "Plain Jane course . . . Flat, walkable, interesting . . . Outstanding when you consider it was built by volunteers."

SUNRIVER LODGE

Sunriver—R—503-593-1221, 800-962-1770 (150 mi. from Portland).
Season: April-Oct. **High:** Summer. **Caddies:** No.
Green fee: $50-$99. **Credit cards:** V, AMEX, DISC, MC.
Lodging on site: Yes. **Reduced fees:** Low Season, Resort Guests, Twilight Play.
Unrestricted walking: Yes. **Range:** Yes (grass).

★★★★NORTH COURSE

Holes: 18. **Par:** 72. **Yards:** 6,880-5,446. **Slope:** 131-118.
Ranked 20th in America's 75 Best Resort Courses by GOLF DIGEST.
Comments: "Wonderful . . . Beautiful . . . Interesting . . . Extremely playable . . . Good test of golfing skills . . . Lacks nothing . . . One of Oregon's best . . . Great, hard to find . . . Comfortable setting . . . Nice view of Mt. Bachelor . . . Relaxing if you tee off early . . . Pay once, play all day . . . Nothing special . . . Overcrowded . . . Hard to walk . . . Must dodge goose droppings . . . Tourists everywhere . . . Priced higher than rest of the area."

★★★SOUTH COURSE

Holes: 18. **Par:** 72. **Yards:** 6,960-5,847. **Slope:** 130-116.
Comments: "Outstanding . . . Wonderful golf . . . Just a touch under the North . . . Best resort in Oregon . . . Way overpriced . . . Always crowded in summer."

★★★★TOKATEE GOLF CLUB

Blue River—PU—503-822-3220 (47 mi. from Eugene).
Season: Feb.-Nov. **High:** May-Sept. **Caddies:** No.
Green fee: $20-$49. **Credit cards:** V.
Lodging on site: No. **Reduced fees:** No.
Unrestricted walking: Yes. **Range:** Yes (grass).
Holes: 18. **Par:** 72. **Yards:** 6,817-5,651. **Slope:** 126-115.
Ranked in First 25 of America's 75 Best Public Courses by GOLF DIGEST.
Comments: "Majestic . . . A true jewel . . . Wilderness beauty . . . Another picture perfect . . . Oregon beauty . . . Some terrific holes . . . Tougher

than it looks . . . Very playable . . . Can walk . . . Beautiful setting with
mountain views . . . View is terrific . . . Hard to explain what makes this so
unique and satisfying, but it is sheer pleasure . . . Pure magic."

★★★½ TRYSTING TREE GOLF CLUB

Corvalis—PU—503-752-3332 (90 mi. from Portland).
Season: Year-round. **High:** Summer. **Caddies:** No.
Green fee: $20-$49. **Credit cards:** No.
Lodging on site: No. **Reduced fees:** Twilight Play.
Unrestricted walking: Yes. **Range:** Yes (grass).
Holes: 18. **Par:** 72. **Yards:** 7,014-5,516. **Slope:** 129-118.
Course owned by Oregon State University.
Comments: "Great links experience . . . Rolling terrain along the river . . .
Looks easy—Not! . . . Underrated, undiscovered . . . Try this one . . .
Unknown except to OSU students . . . Greenkeeper does a great job . . .
Inexpensive . . . Young, may be good someday with tree growth and other
hazards added, but pretty blah now."

★★½ BUCK HILL GOLF CLUB
WHITE/RED/BLUE 9s
Buck Hill Falls—PU—717-595-7730 (100 mi. from Philadelphia).
Season: April-Nov. **High:** Summer. **Caddies:** No.
Green fee: $50-$99. **Credit cards:** V, AMEX, MC.
Lodging on site: No. **Reduced fees:** Low Season, Twilight Play.
Unrestricted walking: No. **Range:** Yes (grass).
Holes: 27. **Par:** 36/34/36. **Yards:** 3,282/2,842/3,114.
Comments: "Great forgotten 27 holes . . . It's Donald Ross . . . Restoration would do wonders . . . Needs watering system . . . Nothing put back into it to improve the place."

CEDARBROOK GOLF COURSE
Belle Vernon—PU—412-929-8300 (30 mi. from Pittsburgh).
Season: Year-round. **High:** April-Oct. **Caddies:** No.
Green fee: $20-$49. **Credit cards:** V, MC.
Lodging on site: No. **Reduced fees:** Low Season, Twilight Play.
Unrestricted walking: No. **Range:** Yes (grass).
GOLD COURSE*
Holes: 18. **Par:** 72. **Yards:** 6,700-5,211. **Slope:** 135-123.
RED COURSE*
Holes: 18. **Par:** 71. **Yards:** 6,100-4,556. **Slope:** 118-107.

★★★½ CENTER VALLEY CLUB
Center Valley—PU—215-791-5580 (12 mi. from Allentown).
Season: Year-round. **High:** May-Aug. **Caddies:** No.
Green fee: $20-$49. **Credit cards:** V, MC.
Lodging on site: No. **Reduced fees:** Weekdays, Twilight Play.
Unrestricted walking: No. **Range:** Yes (grass).
Holes: 18. **Par:** 72. **Yards:** 6,904-4,932. **Slope:** 135-107.
Comments: "Great layout . . . Outstanding eye appeal . . . High standards of maintenance . . . A lot of fun . . . Courteous staff . . . Front 9 sand and mounds, back 9 water and more water . . . Could use a map . . . Several poorly designed holes . . . Unmarked hidden hazards . . . Unfair."

★★★½ CHAMPION LAKES GOLF COURSE
Bolivar—PU—412-238-5440 (50 mi. from Pittsburgh).
Season: March-Nov. **High:** Summer. **Caddies:** No.
Green fee: $20-$49. **Credit cards:** No.
Lodging on site: No. **Reduced fees:** Weekdays.
Unrestricted walking: Yes. **Range:** No.
Holes: 18. **Par:** 71. **Yards:** 6,608-5,556. **Slope:** Unrated.
Comments: "Outstanding . . . Difficult but fun . . . Prettiest in western Pennsylvania . . . Use your head on front 9 . . . Added new tees to back 9. OK! . . . Attentive employees . . . A couple of poor holes."

★★★★COUNTRY CLUB AT WOODLOCH SPRINGS
Hawley—R—717-685-2100 (40 mi. from Scranton).
Season: April-Oct. **High:** Summer.
Green fee: $20-$49. **Credit cards:** V, AMEX, MC.
Lodging on site: Yes. **Reduced fees:** Weekdays, Twilight Play.
Unrestricted walking: No. **Range:** Yes (grass).
Holes: 18. **Par:** 72. **Yards:** 6,579-4,973. **Slope:** 143-130.
Comments: "Beautiful scenery, super maintenance . . . Many hazards . . . Many tricky holes . . . Many forced carries . . . Worst example of target golf ever . . . Unfair especially to short hitters."

GREAT VALUE

CROSS CREEK RESORT
Titusville—R—814-827-9611 (25 mi. from Erie).
Season: April-Oct. **High:** Summer. **Caddies:** No.
Green fee: Under $20. **Credit cards:** V, DISC, MC.
Lodging on site: Yes. **Reduced fees:** Weekdays, Low Season.
Unrestricted walking: No. **Range:** Yes (mats).

★★½ NORTH COURSE
Holes: 18. **Par:** 70. **Yards:** 6,495-5,285. **Slope:** 112-108.
Comments: "Greens extremely difficult . . . Fast and contoured . . . Hard to hold . . . Putting is a real adventure . . . Course eased somewhat for heavy play . . . Well maintained . . . A complete resort . . . Lodging and food very reasonable . . . Gourmet food and clean rooms."
SOUTH COURSE*
Holes: 9. **Par:** 36. **Yards:** 3,238-2,449.

★½ DOWNINGTON COUNTRY CLUB
Downington—PU—215-269-2000 (25 mi. from Philadelphia).
Season: Year-round. **High:** May-Sept. **Caddies:** No.
Green fee: $20-$49. **Credit cards:** V, AMEX, MC.
Reduced fees: Weekdays, Low Season, Twilight Play.
Unrestricted walking: No. **Range:** Yes (mats).
Holes: 18. **Par:** 72. **Yards:** 6,585-5,665. **Slope:** 120-115.
Comments: "Wonderful course . . . Excellent design . . . Fun to play, especially the par 3s . . . Poorly kept."

★★★ EDGEWOOD IN THE PINES GOLF COURSE
Drums—PU—717-788-1101 (22 mi. from Wilkes-Barre).
Season: March-Dec. **High:** May-Sept. **Caddies:** No.
Green fee: $20-$49. **Credit cards:** No.
Lodging on site: No. **Reduced fees:** Weekdays, Low Season.
Unrestricted walking: No. **Range:** No.
Holes: 18. **Par:** 72. **Yards:** 6,721-5,184. **Slope:** Unrated.
Comments: "Thinker's course . . . Very long and narrow . . . Lots of trees . . . Like Florida, without the water . . . Well maintained . . . Beautiful in fall . . . Long waits, long rounds. Always . . . Parallel fairways can be dangerous."

★½ FERNWOOD RESORT & COUNTRY CLUB
Bushkill—R—717-588-9500, 800-233-8103 (80 mi. from New York City).
Season: April-Nov. **High:** Summer. **Caddies:** No.
Green fee: $20-$49. **Credit cards:** All Major.
Lodging on site: Yes. **Reduced fees:** Weekdays, Resort Guests, Twilight Play.
Unrestricted walking: No. **Range:** Yes (grass).
Holes: 18. **Par:** 72. **Yards:** 6,208-5,086. **Slope:** 125-115.
Additional 9-hole par-3 course.
Comments: "Keeps your game straight . . . Greens are murder . . . Too sloped . . . Gimmicked up . . . Waste of time and money."

★★ FIVE PONDS GOLF CLUB
Warminster—PU—215-956-9727 (10 mi. from Philadelphia).
Season: Jan.-Dec. **High:** April-Oct. **Caddies:** No.
Green fee: $20-$49. **Credit cards:** V, MC.
Reduced fees: Weekdays, Low Season, Twilight Play.
Unrestricted walking: No. **Range:** Yes (grass).
Holes: 18. **Par:** 71. **Yards:** 6,760-5,430. **Slope:** 121-117.
Comments: "OK course, needs more trees and variety . . . Great driving range and putting green . . . Doesn't adhere to tee times . . . Interested only in selling tickets."

★★★ FOXCHASE GOLF CLUB
Stevens—PU—717-366-3673 (15 mi. from Lancaster).
Season: Year-round. **High:** April-Oct. **Caddies:** No.
Green fee: $20-$49. **Credit cards:** V, MC.
Lodging on site: No. **Reduced fees:** Weekdays.
Unrestricted walking: Yes. **Range:** Yes (grass).
Holes: 18. **Par:** 72. **Yards:** 6,620-4,690. **Slope:** 113-102.
Comments: "Very nice . . . Lush . . . First class . . . Plush fairways, tall-grass hazards . . . Can only get better . . . Not long enough from whites—

driver-sand wedge almost every hole . . . Too crowded . . . Gets boring . . .
Must prepay for tee times."

★½ GLEN BROOK COUNTRY CLUB

Stroudsburg—R—717-421-3680.
Season: March-Nov. **High:** Summer. **Caddies:** No.
Green fee: $20-$49. **Credit cards:** V, MC.
Lodging on site: Yes. **Reduced fees:** Weekdays, Resort Guests,
Twilight Play.
Unrestricted walking: No. **Range:** Yes (grass).
Holes: 18. **Par:** 72. **Yards:** 6,536-5,234. **Slope:** 123-117.
Comments: "Good course . . . Best in the Poconos . . . Typical mountain
course —lost ball is lost . . . Well kept . . . New super is doing a great job
. . . Too wet in spring."

★★★½ GOLF CLUB AT HIDDEN VALLEY

Hidden Valley—R—814-443-6454, 800-458-0175 (60 mi. from Pittsburgh).
Season: April-Nov. **High:** Summer. **Caddies:** No.
Green fee: $50-$99. **Credit cards:** V, AMEX, DISC, MC.
Lodging on site: Yes. **Reduced fees:** Weekdays, Low Season, Resort
Guests, Twilight Play.
Unrestricted walking: No. **Range:** Yes (mats).
Holes: 18. **Par:** 72. **Yards:** 6,579-5,097. **Slope:** 142-129.
Comments: "Beautiful mountain setting . . . Breathtaking views . . . Play
in the fall . . . Extremely hilly . . . Difficult . . . Fair test . . . Slow greens
. . . Poor 'get-on, get-off' attitude."

★★★ GREENCASTLE GREENS GOLF CLUB

Greencastle—PU—717-597-1188 (75 mi. from Baltimore).
Season: Jan.-Dec. **High:** May-Sept. **Caddies:** No.
Green fee: $20-$49. **Credit cards:** V, MC.
Reduced fees: Weekdays, Low Season, Twilight Play.
Unrestricted walking: No. **Range:** Yes (mats).
Holes: 18. **Par:** 72. **Yards:** 6,332-5,350. **Slope:** 122-124.
Comments: "Excellent layout . . . Every hole different and beautiful . . .
Could someday be a top course . . . Hilly . . . Use all your clubs . . . Hard
greens . . . Island green on par-4 10th . . . Not in the best shape . . . Too
many right-to-left holes . . . Save your bucks, poor value."

★★★ HAWK VALLEY GOLF CLUB

Denver—PU—215-445-5445, 800-522-4295 (20 mi. from Lancaster).
Season: Year-round. **High:** April-Oct. **Caddies:** No.
Green fee: $20-$49. **Credit cards:** V, AMEX, MC.
Lodging on site: No. **Reduced fees:** No.
Unrestricted walking: No. **Range:** No.
Holes: 18. **Par:** 72. **Yards:** 6,628-5,414. **Slope:** 132-119.
Comments: "Average public course . . . Good conditions . . . Good out-
ward half . . . Firm greens . . . Playable terrain . . . No long carries . . . Any
golfer should lower his average score on this course . . . Needs a range . . .
Very hospitable . . . Hard to find but worth the search."

HERSHEY COUNTRY CLUB

Hershey—R—717-533-2464 (15 mi. from Harrisburg).
Season: March-Nov. **High:** April-Sept. **Caddies:** Yes.
Green fee: $50-$99. **Credit cards:** All Major.
Lodging on site: Yes. **Reduced fees:** No.
Unrestricted walking: No. **Range:** Yes (grass).
★★★ EAST COURSE
Holes: 18. **Par:** 71. **Yards:** 7,061-5,645. **Slope:** 128-127.
Comments: "Very good . . . Great, just great . . . Challengingly long . . .
Longest course from the whites, ever . . . Liked this more than famous West
. . . One of the finest maintained in the area . . . Disappointed in course
condition . . . Not as refined as the West . . . Not very interesting . . . Too
many holes alike."

★★★½ WEST COURSE
Holes: 18. **Par:** 73. **Yards:** 6,860-5,908. **Slope:** 131-127.
Comments: "Grand old course . . . One of the gems of Pennsylvania . . . Great in every respect . . . Almost as good as chocolate . . . Very mature . . . Treelined . . . A lot of good holes . . . Not a lot of water . . . A real joy . . . Love to play on Hershey's front yard."

★★★HERSHEY PARKVIEW GOLF COURSE
Hershey—PU—717-534-3450.
Season: April-Nov. **High:** April-Sept. **Caddies:** No.
Green fee: $20-$49. **Credit cards:** V, AMEX, DISC, MC.
Reduced fees: Weekdays, Low Season, Twilight Play.
Unrestricted walking: No. **Range:** Yes (grass).
Holes: 18. **Par:** 70. **Yards:** 6,103-4,871. **Slope:** 121-107.
Comments: "One of the best public courses in Pennsylvania . . . Tough, old-style course . . . Short . . . Narrow . . . Much water . . . Tight and sporty . . . New immaculate greens . . . Best course of its length . . . Recent changes have downgraded the course . . . No longer cheap."

★★½ LINDEN HALL GOLF COURSE
Dawson—PU—412-529-7543 (37 mi. from Pittsburgh).
Season: Year-round. **High:** March-Nov. **Caddies:** No.
Green fee: $20-$49. **Credit cards:** All Major.
Lodging on site: Yes. **Reduced fees:** Weekdays, Low Season.
Unrestricted walking: Yes. **Range:** No.
Holes: 18. **Par:** 72. **Yards:** 6,675-5,900. **Slope:** Unrated.
Comments: "Like playing on a carpet . . . Course is fine, but play is extremely slow due to overbooking . . . Hills too much for some . . . Needs more maintenance . . . Needs a driving range . . . Bugs around water hazards are annoying."

★★½ MILL RACE GOLF & CAMPING RESORT
Benton—PU—717-925-2040 (125 mi. from Philadelphia).
Season: Year-round. **High:** May-Sept. **Caddies:** No.
Green fee: $20-$49. **Credit cards:** V, MC.
Reduced fees: Weekdays, Low Season, Resort Guests, Twilight Play.
Unrestricted walking: No. **Range:** Yes (grass).
Holes: 18. **Par:** 70. **Yards:** 6,096-4,791. **Slope:** 126-122.
Comments: "Intriguing . . . Pleasant experience . . . Superior to others in immediate area . . . Nice, has plenty of water . . . Short and level but fun . . . Position counts . . . Tends to stay wet . . . Layout is easy, price is high."

★★★MOUNT AIRY LODGE GOLF COURSE
Mount Pocono—R—717-839-8811 (30 mi. from Scranton).
Season: April-Nov. **High:** May-Aug. **Caddies:** No.
Green fee: $50-$99. **Credit cards:** V, AMEX, DISC, MC.
Lodging on site: Yes. **Reduced fees:** Resort Guests, Twilight Play.
Unrestricted walking: No. **Range:** Yes (mats).
Holes: 18. **Par:** 72. **Yards:** 7,123-5,711. **Slope:** Unrated.
Course consists of holes patterned after Sports Illustrated's selections of "The Best 18 Holes in America."
Comments: "An ultimate challenge . . . Some of the best holes you can play . . . Many great holes . . . Beautiful . . . Difficult but great . . . Well maintained . . . Good value with golf package . . . Pro shop is lost in the 1950s . . . What a crazy course . . . Doesn't live up to its billing as 'The Best 18' . . . First hole is awful . . . Unfair, blind shots everywhere . . . Too many unreachable par 4s . . . Greens and tees poor . . . They've let this go to the dogs . . . Slow greens . . . Six hours to play in carts."

★★★THE MOUNTAIN LAUREL RESORT
White Haven—R—717-443-8411, 800-458-5921 (70 mi. from Philadelphia).
Season: April-Nov. **High:** June-Oct. **Caddies:** No.
Green fee: $20-$49. **Credit cards:** All Major.

Lodging on site: Yes. **Reduced fees:** Weekdays, Low Season, Resort Guests, Twilight Play.
Unrestricted walking: No. **Range:** Yes (grass).
Holes: 18. **Par:** 72. **Yards:** 6,800-5,900. **Slope:** Unrated.
Comments: "Very scenic . . . Nice water holes . . . Tough in the wind . . . , Fair layout, great superintendent . . . Trying to bring it to the top . . . OK, but not if you're traveling from any distance."

MOUNTAIN MANOR INN & GOLF CLUB
Marshall's Creek—R—717-223-1290 (80 mi. from Philadelphia).
Season: April-Nov. **High:** May-Oct. **Caddies:** No.
Green fee: $20-$49. **Credit cards:** No.
Lodging on site: Yes. **Reduced fees:** Weekdays, Resort Guests, Twilight Play.
Unrestricted walking: Yes. **Range:** Yes (mats).
★★★BLUE/YELLOW COURSE
Holes: 18. **Par:** 71. **Yards:** 6,233-5,080. **Slope:** 115-115.
Comments: "Flat . . . In good shape . . . Great course for seniors . . . Enjoyable for any type of golfer . . . Operators very polite and accommodating."
★★★ORANGE/SILVER COURSE
Holes: 18. **Par:** 73. **Yards:** 6,426-5,146. **Slope:** 132.
Comments: "Nice mix of holes on all four 9s . . . Orange and Silver very challenging . . . Orange outstanding . . . Silver even harder . . . A legitimate par 6 . . . A never-ending par 6 . . . Mountain courses . . . Impossible to walk."

★★½ OVERLOOK GOLF COURSE
Lancaster—PU—717-569-9551.
Season: Year-round. **High:** May-Sept. **Caddies:** No.
Green fee: $20-$49. **Credit cards:** V, MC.
Lodging on site: No. **Reduced fees:** Low Season, Twilight Play.
Unrestricted walking: Yes. **Range:** No.
Holes: 18. **Par:** 70. **Yards:** 6,100-4,902. **Slope:** 116-108.
Comments: "Mature public course . . . Very well kept . . . Open . . . Easy . . . No rough . . . Recently improved conditions . . . Very busy."

★★★½ PENN NATIONAL GOLF COURSE
Fayetteville—PU—717-352-2193, 800-221-7336.
Season: Year-round. **High:** April-Oct. **Caddies:** No.
Green fee: $20-$49. **Credit cards:** V, MC.
Lodging on site: Yes. **Reduced fees:** Weekdays, Low Season, Resort Guests, Twilight Play.
Unrestricted walking: No. **Range:** Yes (grass).
Holes: 18. **Par:** 72. **Yards:** 6,919-5,331. **Slope:** 131-116.
Comments: "Little known . . . Well kept . . . Very enjoyable . . . Very interesting . . . All skill levels will enjoy . . . Beautiful rural setting . . . Excellent greens . . . People are the greatest."

PENN STATE UNIVERSITY GOLF COURSE
University Park—PU—814-865-4653 (90 mi. from Harrisburg).
Season: April-Oct. **High:** May-Sept. **Caddies:** No.
Green fee: $20-$49. **Credit cards:** V, DISC, MC.
Lodging on site: No. **Reduced fees:** Resort Guests, Twilight Play.
Unrestricted walking: Yes. **Range:** Yes (mats).
BLUE COURSE*
Holes: 18. **Par:** 72. **Yards:** 6,825-5,450. **Slope:** Unrated.
WHITE COURSE*
Holes: 18. **Par:** 70. **Yards:** 6,250-5,850. **Slope:** Unrated.

POCONO MANOR INN & GOLF CLUB
Pocono Manor—R—717-839-7111, 800-233-8150 (20 mi. from Scranton).
Season: April-Nov. **High:** May-Oct. **Caddies:** No.
Green fee: $20-$49. **Credit cards:** V, AMEX, MC.

Lodging on site: Yes. **Reduced fees:** Weekdays, Resort Guests, Twilight Play.
Unrestricted walking: No. **Range:** Yes (grass).

★★EAST COURSE
Holes: 18. **Par:** 72. **Yards:** 6,480-6,113. **Slope:** Unrated.
Comments: "Mountainous . . . A few blind shots . . . Gimmicky holes . . . Overpriced, overplayed, undermaintained . . . Has gone downhill in recent years . . . Stuffy employees not helpful . . . That 77-yard par 3 is pretty tricky. Honest!"

★½ WEST COURSE
Holes: 18. **Par:** 72. **Yards:** 6,857-5,706. **Slope:** Unrated.
Comments: "Interesting . . . Very fair . . . Good for all levels and ages . . . Needs work conditionwise . . . Almost a cow pasture . . . A watering system would be nice . . . Took 5½ hours to play."

★★★½ QUICKSILVER GOLF CLUB
Midway—PU—412-796-1811 (18 mi. from Pittsburgh).
Season: March-Dec. **High:** Summer. **Caddies:** No.
Green fee: $50-$99. **Credit cards:** V, AMEX, MC.
Lodging on site: No. **Reduced fees:** No.
Unrestricted walking: No. **Range:** Yes (grass).
Holes: 18. **Par:** 72. **Yards:** 7,120-5,067. **Slope:** 145-115.
Comments: "Quiet . . . Hilly . . . Very long . . . Length alone does not make a good golf course . . . Not scenic . . . Expensive . . . Overrated . . . It's no $50 course."

★★★½ RIVERSIDE GOLF COURSE
Cambridge Springs—PU—814-398-4537 (18 mi. from Erie).
Season: March-Oct. **High:** Summer. **Caddies:** No.
Green fee: Under $20. **Credit cards:** V, MC.
Reduced fees: Weekdays, Low Season, Twilight Play.
Unrestricted walking: No. **Range:** Yes (grass).
Holes: 18. **Par:** 70. **Yards:** 6,113-5,232. **Slope:** 116-117.
Comments: "Good variety of holes . . . Nicely manicured . . . Long and lush . . . Don't get in the rough."

★★★½ ROYAL OAKS GOLF COURSE
Lebanon—PU—717-274-2212 (15 mi. from Hershey).
Season: Year-round. **High:** April-Nov. **Caddies:** No.
Green fee: $20-$49. **Credit cards:** V, DISC, MC.
Lodging on site: No. **Reduced fees:** Twilight Play.
Unrestricted walking: No. **Range:** Yes (grass).
Holes: 18. **Par:** 71. **Yards:** 6,542-4,687. **Slope:** 118-115.
Comments: "Fantastic layout . . . Great design . . . Good balance of difficulty . . . Best new course in central Pennsylvania . . . Needs time to mature . . . Quickly maturing."

★★★SEVEN SPRINGS MOUNTAIN RESORT GOLF COURSE
Champion—R—814-352-7777 (50 mi. from Pittsburgh).
Season: April-Oct. **High:** May-Sept. **Caddies:** No.
Green fee: $50-$99. **Credit cards:** V, DISC, MC.
Lodging on site: Yes. **Reduced fees:** Weekdays, Low Season, Resort Guests, Twilight Play.
Unrestricted walking: No. **Range:** Yes (grass).
Holes: 18. **Par:** 71. **Yards:** 6,360-4,934. **Slope:** 116-111.
Comments: "Good mountain golf . . . Nice scenery . . . Nice atmosphere . . . Priced too high . . . Thick with sneaker crowd in tank tops . . . I've seen better operations at municipals for a fraction of the fee."

★★★SHAWNEE INN
BLUE/RED/WHITE 9s
Shawnee-on-Delaware—R—717-421-1500, 800-742-9633 (75 mi. from New York City). **Season:** April-Nov. **High:** Summer. **Caddies:** No.
Green fee: $50-$99. **Credit cards:** All Major.

Lodging on site: Yes. **Reduced fees:** Weekdays, Low Season, Resort Guests, Twilight Play.
Unrestricted walking: No. **Range:** Yes (mats).
Holes: 27. **Par:** 36/36/36. **Yards:** 3,468/3,362/3,227.
Most of the holes are located on an island in the middle of the Delaware River.
Comments: "Historic layout . . . Three 9s, great variety, challenging greens . . . 24 of 27 holes on an island in the Delaware River . . . Wonderful for all golfers . . . Good shape . . . Fantastic mountain scenery . . . Some great holes . . . Good resort . . . Nice package plans . . . Needs better maintenance . . . Some traps would help."

★★½ SKYTOP LODGE GOLF CLUB
Skytop—R—717-595-7401, 800-345-7759 (50 mi. from Scranton).
Season: April-Oct. **High:** Summer. **Caddies:** No.
Green fee: $20-$49. **Credit cards:** All Major.
Lodging on site: Yes. **Reduced fees:** No.
Unrestricted walking: No. **Range:** No.
Holes: 18. **Par:** 71. **Yards:** 6,256-5,683. **Slope:** 121-122.
Comments: "Small fast greens . . . Poorly maintained fairways . . . Too high a price . . . No real public access."

★★★½ STONE HEDGE COUNTRY CLUB
Tunkhannock—PU—717-836-5108 (22 mi. from Scranton).
Season: April-Dec. **High:** May-Aug. **Caddies:** No.
Green fee: $20-$49. **Credit cards:** No.
Reduced fees: Weekdays, Low Season, Twilight Play.
Unrestricted walking: No. **Range:** Yes (grass).
Holes: 18. **Par:** 71. **Yards:** 6,506-4,992. **Slope:** 124-122.
Comments: "Top layout . . . Front extremely long . . . Back is narrow and windy . . . Fast greens . . . A challenge for all . . . Young course . . . Great potential . . . Still developing, could be first class."

SUGARLOAF GOLF CLUB*
Sugarloaf—PU—717-384-4097.
Season: March-Nov. **High:** July-Aug. **Caddies:** No.
Green fee: Under $20. **Credit cards:** V, MC.
Lodging on site: No. **Reduced fees:** No.
Unrestricted walking: No. **Range:** Yes (grass).
Holes: 18. **Par:** 72. **Yards:** 6,795-5,565. **Slope:** 122-120.

★★★ TAMIMENT RESORT & COUNTRY CLUB
Tamiment—R—717-588-6652 (90 mi. from New York City).
Season: April-Nov. **High:** May-Sept. **Caddies:** No.
Green fee: $20-$49. **Credit cards:** All Major.
Lodging on site: Yes. **Reduced fees:** Weekdays, Resort Guests, Twilight Play.
Unrestricted walking: No. **Range:** No.
Holes: 18. **Par:** 72. **Yards:** 6,858-5,598. **Slope:** 130-124.
Comments: "Good layout . . . Long, tough . . . A killer from the back tees . . . Very heavy rough . . . Very difficult greens . . . Hilly . . . Carts a must . . . No maintenance, dirt tees . . . Too much clover . . . Very slow play . . . First fairway is a ski slope in winter."

★★★★ TOFTREES RESORT
State College—R—814-238-7600 (200 mi. from Pittsburgh).
Season: March-Dec. **High:** Summer. **Caddies:** No.
Green fee: $50-$99. **Credit cards:** All Major.
Lodging on site: Yes. **Reduced fees:** Weekdays, Low Season, Twilight Play.
Unrestricted walking: No. **Range:** Yes (grass).
Holes: 18. **Par:** 72. **Yards:** 7,018-5,567. **Slope:** 134-126.
Comments: "Magnificent . . . Scenic challenge . . . Fast greens, professional quality . . . Watch the slopes of the fairways . . . Excellent maintenance . . . High fees, but worth it . . . Excellent resort . . . Friendly staff."

VALLEY GREEN PUBLIC GOLF COURSE*
Etters—PU—717-938-4200 (15 mi. from Harrisburg).
Season: Year-round. **High:** April-Oct. **Caddies:** No.
Green fee: $20-$49. **Credit cards:** V, MC.
Reduced fees: Weekdays, Low Season, Twilight Play.
Unrestricted walking: Yes. **Range:** No.
Holes: 18. **Par:** 71. **Yards:** 6,000-5,079. **Slope:** 112-110.

★★WATER GAP COUNTRY CLUB
Delaware Water Gap—PU—717-476-0200 (70 mi. from New York City).
Season: March-Nov. **High:** July-Sept. **Caddies:** No.
Green fee: $20-$49. **Credit cards:** All Major.
Lodging on site: Yes. **Reduced fees:** Weekdays.
Unrestricted walking: No. **Range:** No.
Holes: 18. **Par:** 72. **Yards:** 6,186-5,175. **Slope:** 125-114.
Comments: "A real antique. Walter Hagen still holds course record . . .
Poor design . . . Dries up in summer . . . Tees and traps neglected . . . No
grass . . . Don't go when it's been dry . . . Layout does not warrant snooti-
ness of membership . . . Less than polite at times . . . Expensive for a
mediocre course."

WHITE DEER PARK & GOLF COURSE
Montgomery—PU—717-547-2186 (90 mi. from Harrisburg).
Season: Year-round. **High:** May-Sept. **Caddies:** No.
Green fee: Under $20. **Credit cards:** V, MC.
Lodging on site: No. **Reduced fees:** Twilight Play.
Unrestricted walking: Yes. **Range:** Yes (grass).
★★★CHALLENGE COURSE
Holes: 18. **Par:** 72. **Yards:** 6,608-4,727. **Slope:** 133-115.
Comments: "New . . . Fairways still filling in . . . Distances from greens to
tees are terrible . . . Needs cart paths."
★★VINTAGE COURSE
Holes: 18. **Par:** 72 . **Yards:** 6,397-4,847. **Slope:** 122-120.
Additional 9-hole executive course also available.
Comments: "A favorite has been ruined with new construction."

★★★WILKES-BARRE GOLF CLUB
Willkes-Barre—PU—717-472-3590.
Season: April-Nov. **High:** Summer. **Caddies:** No.
Green fee: $20-$49. **Credit cards:** V, AMEX, MC.
Reduced fees: Weekdays, Low Season, Twilight Play.
Unrestricted walking: No. **Range:** Yes (grass).
Holes: 18. **Par:** 72. **Yards:** 6,912-5,690. **Slope:** 125-117.
Comments: "Very nice public course, will get better once irrigation starts
working . . . New superintendent improving course a bunch . . . Best in the
area . . . Increasingly difficult to get tee times . . . Long, not very exciting."

★★★★WYNCOTE GOLF CLUB
Oxford—PU—215-932-8900 (50 mi. from Philadelphia).
Season: March-Nov. **High:** May-Oct. **Caddies:** No.
Green fee: $20-$49. **Credit cards:** V, DISC, MC.
Lodging on site: No. **Reduced fees:** Weekdays.
Unrestricted walking: No. **Range:** Yes (mats).
Holes: 18. **Par:** 72. **Yards:** 7,012-5,454. **Slope:** 128-126.
Comments: "Wonderful . . . A hidden gem . . . Great design features . . .
Tough . . . You'll need great approach shots . . . Very playable . . . Virtual-
ly no play on it right now . . . Still a little young . . . Best public course in
Oxford/Delaware County area . . . Green fee slightly high but worth it."

SUPER VALUE

CRANSTON COUNTRY CLUB*
Cranston—PU—401-826-1683 (10 mi. from Providence).
Season: March-Dec. **High:** April-Oct. **Caddies:** No.
Green fee: $20-$49. **Credit cards:** No.
Lodging on site: No. **Reduced fees:** Weekdays, Twilight Play.
Unrestricted walking: Yes. **Range:** No.
Holes: 18. **Par:** 71. **Yards:** 6,750-5,499. **Slope:** 124-120.

★★★½ EXETER COUNTRY CLUB
Exeter—PU—401-295-1178 (15 mi. from Warwick).
Season: March-Nov. **High:** Summer. **Caddies:** No.
Green fee: $20-$49. **Credit cards:** V, MC.
Lodging on site: Yes. **Reduced fees:** Low Season, Twilight Play.
Unrestricted walking: Yes. **Range:** Yes (grass).
Holes: 18. **Par:** 72. **Yards:** 6,919-5,733. **Slope:** 123-115.
Comments: "Pleasant . . . Nice Sunday afternoon course . . . Enjoyable, not too tough . . . One of the best in the state . . . Best public course in the state . . . Closest thing to a private course . . . Some interesting holes . . . Pretty, with covered bridges . . . One pretty hole by the ocean . . . Out-9 is just long, in-9 required thoughtful play . . . Lots of water on back 9 . . . Demanding drives over water hazards . . . Beautiful greens . . . Best public greens in Rhode Island . . . Inconsistent greens . . . Occasional slow play . . . Usually hit and wait . . . Hard walking."

★★FOSTER COUNTRY CLUB
Foster—PU—401-397-7750 (24 mi. from Providence).
Season: April-Dec. **High:** Summer. **Caddies:** No.
Green fee: Under $20. **Credit cards:** V, MC.
Lodging on site: No. **Reduced fees:** Weekdays.
Unrestricted walking: Yes. **Range:** No.
Holes: 18. **Par:** 72. **Yards:** 6,187-5,499. **Slope:** 114-112.
Comments: "Eleven easy, wide open holes, seven tight and tricky holes . . . Loads of fun . . . Great shape . . . Few traps . . . Uneven greens . . . Too tricky . . . Needs a sprinkler system . . . Difficult for first-timer to locate the correct greens . . . Don't like the last two holes, both par 3s."

★★½ GREEN VALLEY COUNTRY CLUB
Portsmouth—PU—401-847-9543.
Season: Year-round. **High:** May-Oct. **Caddies:** No.
Green fee: $20-$49. **Credit cards:** V, MC.
Lodging on site: No. **Reduced fees:** Weekdays, Twilight Play.
Unrestricted walking: Yes. **Range:** Yes (grass).
Holes: 18. **Par:** 71. **Yards:** 6,850-5,515. **Slope:** 120-Unrated.
Comments: "Good test . . . Long . . . Wide open . . . Firm greens . . . Usually very windy . . . Fairways and greens need work . . . All the grass is too long . . . Holes lack distinctive features . . . Fair amenities."

★★★LAUREL LANE GOLF COURSE
West Kingston—PU—401-783-3844 (30 mi. from Providence).
Season: March-Dec. **High:** Summer. **Caddies:** No.
Green fee: Under $20. **Credit cards:** No.
Reduced fees: Weekdays, Low Season, Twilight Play.
Unrestricted walking: Yes. **Range:** No.
Holes: 18. **Par:** 71. **Yards:** 5,801-5,416. **Slope:** 113-115.
Comments: "Short but challenging . . . Easy open front, narrow hard back . . . Truly challenging back 9 . . . Many bogs . . . Best shape in years . . . Great people run the course . . . Great 'after hours' bargain green fee . . . Dull course . . . Not well designed . . . Just average . . . Not usually in good condition . . . Will not challenge better players."

★★½ **TRIGGS MEMORIAL GOLF COURSE**
Providence—PU—401-272-4653.
Season: Year-round. **High:** Summer. **Caddies:** No.
Green fee: $20-$49. **Credit cards:** V, MC.
Lodging on site: No. **Reduced fees:** No.
Unrestricted walking: Yes. **Range:** No.
Holes: 18. **Par:** 72. **Yards:** 6,796-5,386. **Slope:** 126.
Comments: "Donald Ross, enough said . . . Great Donald Ross, but miserably maintained . . . What a shame . . . Very rough around the edges . . . At one time was very good, but now little or no upkeep . . . Bad fairways . . . Needs water badly . . . Poor greens . . . Sand traps should be called rock quarries . . . Not user friendly."

★★½ **WINNAPAUG COUNTRY CLUB**
Westerly—PU—401-596-1237 (40 mi. from Providence).
Season: Year-round. **High:** Summer. **Caddies:** No.
Green fee: $20-$49. **Credit cards:** All Major.
Lodging on site: Yes. **Reduced fees:** Twilight Play.
Unrestricted walking: No. **Range:** Yes (mats).
Holes: 18. **Par:** 72. **Yards:** 6,248-5,158. **Slope:** 113-110.
Comments: "Classic Donald Ross . . . Most improved course in Rhode Island . . . Most unusual but fun . . . Varied terrain and conditions . . . A little of everything . . . Very playable . . . Great Ross greens . . . Unforgiving greens . . . Narrow fairways . . . Sidehill lies . . . Nice long-distance ocean views . . . Fun to play . . . But too much play."

★★★ARCADIAN SHORES GOLF CLUB
Myrtle Beach—R—803-449-5217, 800-248-9228.
Season: Year-round. **High:** Spring/Fall. **Caddies:** No.
Green fee: $50-$99. **Credit cards:** V, AMEX, MC.
Lodging on site: Yes. **Reduced fees:** Low Season, Resort Guests.
Unrestricted walking: No. **Range:** Yes (grass).
Holes: 18. **Par:** 72. **Yards:** 6,938-5,294. **Slope:** 136-116.
Comments: "Outstanding . . . Great natural beauty . . . Very pretty and challenging . . . Full test of skill. Even alligators seem to agree . . . Trouble everywhere . . . No hidden surprises . . . Exceptional staff . . . Despite amount of traffic, very well maintained . . . Hyper-rangers."

★★AZALEA SANDS GOLF CLUB
North Myrtle Beach—PU—803-272-6191, 800-253-2312.
Season: Year-round. **High:** March-May. **Caddies:** No.
Green fee: $20-$49. **Credit cards:** V, MC.
Lodging on site: No. **Reduced fees:** Resort Guests.
Unrestricted walking: No. **Range:** No.
Holes: 18. **Par:** 72. **Yards:** 6,902-5,172. **Slope:** 121-116.
Comments: "Beautiful . . . Relaxing . . . Very forgiving . . . Well organized . . . Very pleasant experience . . . Long for short hitters . . . Greens were in bad shape."

BAY TREE GOLF PLANTATION
North Myrtle Beach—R—803-249-1487, 800-845-6191.
Season: Year-round. **High:** March-April. **Caddies:** No.
Green fee: $20-$49. **Credit cards:** V, MC.
Lodging on site: Yes. **Reduced fees:** Low Season, Resort Guests, Twilight Play.
Unrestricted walking: No. **Range:** Yes (grass).

★★½ GOLD COURSE
Holes: 18. **Par:** 72. **Yards:** 6,942-5,264. **Slope:** 135-117.
Comments: "Best of the three Bay Trees . . . Friendly in spite of volume of play . . . Average in all areas . . . Terrible condition."

★★½ GREEN COURSE
Holes: 18. **Par:** 72. **Yards:** 7,044-5,362. **Slope:** 135-116.
Comments: "Good layout . . . Fun to play . . . Seemed to play longer than yardages indicated . . .Course condition varies drastically . . . Staff very professional."

★★½ SILVER COURSE
Holes: 18. **Par:** 72. **Yards:** 6,871-5,417. **Slope:** 131-116.
Comments: "Enjoyable . . . Needs work, a little scruffy . . . Expensive . . . Assembly-line attitude . . . Bay Tree's a mediocre threesome."

★★★BEACHWOOD GOLF CLUB
North Myrtle Beach—PU—803-272-6168, 800-526-4889.
Season: Year-round. **High:** Spring/Fall. **Caddies:** No.
Green fee: $20-$49. **Credit cards:** V, AMEX, MC.
Lodging on site: No. **Reduced fees:** Low Season.
Unrestricted walking: No. **Range:** Yes (grass).
Holes: 18. **Par:** 72. **Yards:** 6,825-6,344. **Slope:** 121-117.
Comments: "Good course anybody can play . . . Nice, gives everyone a chance . . . Good for one's ego . . . Enjoyable day . . . Worth playing . . . Well maintained . . . Allows walking in afternoons . . . People were great . . . Not enough yardage markers."

★★★½ BLACKMOOR GOLF CLUB
Murrells Inlet—PU—803-650-5555 (15 mi. from Myrtle Beach).
Season: Year-round. **High:** Spring/Fall. **Caddies:** No.
Green fee: $50-$99. **Credit cards:** V, MC.
Lodging on site: No. **Reduced fees:** Low Season, Resort Guests.
Unrestricted walking: No. **Range:** Yes (grass).

Holes: 18. **Par:** 72. **Yards:** 6,714-4,807. **Slope:** 126-115.
Comments: "One very pretty course . . . Playable, inviting . . . Has good flow, all the shots . . . A finesse course . . . Well designed and well maintained . . . Good tee placements for ladies . . . One of the top 5 at the Beach . . . Enjoyable for the 90s shooter . . . Back 9 very unusual . . . Many blind dogleg par 4s . . . Too many tricky holes."

★★½ BUCK CREEK GOLF PLANTATION
MEADOW/CYPRESS/TUPELO 9s
North Myrtle Beach—PU—803-399-2660, 800-344-0982.
Season: Year-round. **High:** Spring/Fall. **Caddies:** No.
Green fee: $20-$49. **Credit cards:** V, MC.
Reduced fees: Low Season, Resort Guests, Twilight Play.
Unrestricted walking: No. **Range:** Yes (grass).
Holes: 27. **Par:** 36/36/36. **Yards:** 3,306/3,445/3,420.
Comments: "Three 9s, all different, all good . . . Nice place to play . . . Lots of water . . . Tight, trouble . . . Enjoyable . . . Cypress 9 especially interesting . . . Watch for bugs . . . Not user-friendly . . . Fairways are rounded, balls bounce toward water . . . Swamp golf is out."

BURNING RIDGE GOLF CLUB
Conway—PU—803-247-0538, 800-833-0337 (8 mi. from Myrtle Beach).
Season: Year-round. **High:** Feb.-April/Oct.-Nov. **Caddies:** No.
Green fee: $20-$49. **Credit cards:** V, MC.
Reduced fees: Low Season, Resort Guests, Twilight Play.
Unrestricted walking: No. **Range:** Yes (grass).
★★★EAST COURSE
Holes: 18. **Par:** 72. **Yards:** 6,780-4,524. **Slope:** 128-111.
Comments: "Good challenge . . . Too much trouble . . . Overcrowded."
★★★WEST COURSE
Holes: 18. **Par:** 72. **Yards:** 6,714-4,831. **Slope:** 122-114.

CAROLINA SPRINGS GOLF CLUB*
WILLOWS/PINES/CEDARS 9s
Fountain Inn—PU—803-862-3551 (10 mi. from Greenville).
Season: Year-round. **High:** April-Oct. **Caddies:** No.
Green fee: $20-$49. **Credit cards:** V, MC.
Reduced fees: Weekdays, Low Season, Twilight Play.
Unrestricted walking: Yes. **Range:** Yes (grass).
Holes: 27. **Par:** 36/36/36. **Yards:** 3,391/3,424/3,252.

★★★½ CEDAR CREEK GOLF CLUB
Aiken—PU—803-648-4206 (20 mi. from Augusta, Ga.).
Season: Year-round. **High:** March-June. **Caddies:** No.
Green fee: $20-$49. **Credit cards:** V, AMEX, MC.
Lodging on site: No. **Reduced fees:** Weekdays, Low Season.
Unrestricted walking: No. **Range:** Yes (grass).
Holes: 18. **Par:** 72. **Yards:** 7,206-5,231. **Slope:** 125-115.
Comments: "Fantastic . . . Good challenge . . . Very well manicured . . . Nice course to play the weekend before Masters . . . Severe terrain . . . Holes nestled among home sites."

★½ CHARLESTON MUNICIPAL GOLF COURSE
Charleston—PU—803-795-5856.
Season: Year-round. **High:** March-May. **Caddies:** No.
Green fee: Under $20. **Credit cards:** V, AMEX, MC.
Reduced fees: Weekdays, Low Season, Twilight Play.
Unrestricted walking: Yes. **Range:** Yes (grass).
Holes: 18. **Par:** 72. **Yards:** 6,411/5,202. **Slope:** 112-114.
Comments: "Straight, flat, little water . . . Very inexpensive . . . Boring . . . Would make a good rice plantation."

SOUTH CAROLINA

★★★CHARLESTON NATIONAL COUNTRY CLUB
Mount Pleasant—PU—803-884-7799 (9 mi. from Charleston).
Season: Year-round. **High:** Spring/Fall. **Caddies:** No.
Green fee: $20-$49. **Credit cards:** V, MC.
Reduced fees: Weekdays, Low Season, Twilight Play.
Unrestricted walking: No. **Range:** Yes (grass).
Holes: 18. **Par:** 72. **Yards:** 6,928-5,103. **Slope:** 132-115.
Comments: "Amazing . . . Challenging, interesting ocean course . . .
Many, long forced carries over marsh . . . Plays solid even from members'
tees . . . Too bad Hurricane Hugo wiped out so many trees . . . Coming
back after Hugo . . . Hugo's wrath was a gift to the public-access world . . .
No facilities . . . Too many blind hazards."

THE CLUB AT SEABROOK ISLAND
Johns Island—R—803-768-2529, 800-845-2457 (18 mi. from Charleston).
Season: Year-round. **High:** April-July/Oct.-Nov. **Caddies:** No.
Green fee: $50-$99. **Credit cards:** V, AMEX, DISC, MC.
Lodging on site: Yes. **Reduced fees:** Low Season.
Unrestricted walking: No. **Range:** Yes (grass).
★★★CROOKED OAKS COURSE
Holes: 18. **Par:** 72. **Yards:** 6,970-5,250. **Slope:** 126-119.
Comments: "Undiscovered east coast treasure . . . Oaks and moss . . .
Very friendly . . . Southern charm."
★★★OCEAN WINDS COURSE
Holes: 18. **Par:** 72. **Yards:** 6,805-5,524. **Slope:** 130-127.
Comments: "One of the nicest resorts on the East Coast . . . Love this
course! . . . Very difficult on windy day."

★★COLONIAL CHARTERS GOLF CLUB
Longs—PU—803-249-8809 (3 mi. from North Myrtle Beach).
Season: Year-round. **High:** Spring/Fall. **Caddies:** No.
Green fee: $20-$49. **Credit cards:** All Major.
Lodging on site: Yes. **Reduced fees:** Low Season, Twilight Play.
Unrestricted walking: No. **Range:** Yes (grass).
Holes: 18. **Par:** 72. **Yards:** 6,901-6,372. **Slope:** 127-120.
Comments: "It's playable . . . A dog track. Lay-up shots everywhere . . .
Looks like too many architects spoiled the broth."

★★★COUNTRY CLUB AT EDISTO
Edisto Island—R—803-869-2561, 800-845-8500 (40 mi. from Charleston).
Season: Year-round. **High:** March-Nov. **Caddies:** No.
Green fee: $20-$49. **Credit cards:** All Major.
Lodging on site: Yes. **Reduced fees:** Low Season, Twilight Play.
Unrestricted walking: No. **Range:** No.
Holes: 18. **Par:** 71. **Yards:** 6,212-5,254. **Slope:** 118-114.
Comments: "Tropical layout . . . Very tight, lots of water . . . Accuracy a
must . . . Fun vacation course . . . Poor greens."

★★★COUNTRY CLUB OF BEAUFORT
Beaufort—PU—803-522-1605, 800-869-1617 (45 mi. from Savannah, Ga.).
Season: Year-round. **High:** Spring/Fall. **Caddies:** No.
Green fee: $20-$49. **Credit cards:** V, AMEX, MC.
Lodging on site: No. **Reduced fees:** Twilight Play.
Unrestricted walking: Yes. **Range:** Yes (grass).
Holes: 18. **Par:** 72. **Yards:** 6,506-4,880. **Slope:** 118-115.
Comments: "An abundance of wildlife."

★★★★COUNTRY CLUB OF CALLAWASSIE
DOGWOOD/MAGNOLIA/PALMETTO 9s
Ridgeland—PU—803-785-7888, 800-221-8431.
Season: Year-round. **High:** Spring/Fall. **Caddies:** No.
Green fee: $50-$99. **Credit cards:** V, AMEX, MC.
Lodging on site: No. **Reduced fees:** Low Season.

Unrestricted walking: No. **Range:** Yes (grass).
Holes: 27. **Par:** 36/36/36. **Yards:** 3,519/3,545/3,411.
Comments: "Original 18 is Magnificent . . . New 9 is a further improvement . . . First class all the way . . . Beautiful vistas, great challenge."

★★★COUNTRY CLUB OF HILTON HEAD
Hilton Head Island—PU—803-681-4653.
Season: Year-round. **High:** Spring/Fall. **Caddies:** No.
Green fee: $50-$99. **Credit cards:** All Major.
Lodging on site: No. **Reduced fees:** Low Season, Resort Guests.
Unrestricted walking: No. **Range:** Yes (grass).
Holes: 18. **Par:** 72. **Yards:** 6,919-5,373. **Slope:** 132-123.
Comments: "Very enjoyable, playable . . . Prettiest I've seen . . . Several outstanding holes . . . Best course on Hilton Head for late afternoon tee times . . . Not unusual to be alone on the course . . . Designed for carts . . . Sometimes bad greens."

★★★½ CROWFIELD GOLF & COUNTRY CLUB
Goose Creek—PU—803-764-4618.
Season: Year-round. **High:** Spring/Fall. **Caddies:** No.
Green fee: $20-$49. **Credit cards:** V, MC.
Reduced fees: Weekdays, Low Season, Twilight Play.
Unrestricted walking: No. **Range:** Yes (grass).
Holes: 18. **Par:** 72. **Yards:** 7,003-5,682. **Slope:** 134-115.
Comments: "A sleeper . . . Excellent track . . . Tough, but fair . . . Good value for money . . . If driving up I-95, don't pass it by . . . Nice course, but there are better, cheaper courses around . . . Narrow. Hooks or slices equal lost balls . . . Too much space between greens and tees . . . Too many gimmicky mounds."

★★CYPRESS BAY GOLF CLUB
Little River—PU—803-249-1025, 800-833-6337 (8 mi. from Myrtle Beach).
Season: Year-round. **High:** Spring/Fall. **Caddies:** No.
Green fee: $20-$49. **Credit cards:** V, MC.
Reduced fees: Weekdays, Low Season, Resort Guests, Twilight Play.
Unrestricted walking: No. **Range:** No.
Holes: 18. **Par:** 72. **Yards:** 6,502-5,004. **Slope:** 115-110.
Comments: "Typical Myrtle Beach golf . . . Not in the best of shape."

DEER TRACK GOLF RESORT
Surfside Beach—R—803-650-2146, 800-548-9186
(5 mi. from Myrtle Beach).
Season: Year-round. **High:** Spring/Fall. **Caddies:** No.
Green fee: $20-$49. **Credit cards:** V, MC.
Lodging on site: Yes. **Reduced fees:** Low Season, Resort Guests, Twilight Play.
Unrestricted walking: No. **Range:** Yes (grass).
★★½ NORTH COURSE
Holes: 18. **Par:** 72. **Yards:** 7,203-6,511. **Slope:** 126-121.
Comments: "Good service . . . Gets too much play."
★★SOUTH COURSE
Holes: 18. **Par:** 71. **Yards:** 6,916-6,143. **Slope:** 126-119.
Comments: "Unmarked water hazards . . . 'Hairy' greens . . . Wouldn't go out of my way to play it again . . . Should have left it a swamp."

★★★½ DUNES WEST GOLF CLUB
Mt. Pleasant—PU—803-856-9000 (11 mi. from Charleston).
Season: Year-round. **High:** Spring/Fall. **Caddies:** No.
Green fee: $20-$49. **Credit cards:** V, AMEX, MC.
Lodging on site: No. **Reduced fees:** Weekdays, Low Season.
Unrestricted walking: No. **Range:** No.
Holes: 18. **Par:** 72. **Yards:** 6,850-6,500. **Slope:** 131-128.
Comments: "Beautiful new course. . . Fair . . . Excellent though short. . . Local knowledge helps . . . Stay tuned. This will be heard from."

★★EAGLE NEST GOLF CLUB
North Myrtle Beach—PU—803-249-1449, 800-543-3113.
Season: Year-round. **High:** March-April. **Caddies:** No.
Green fee: $20-$49. **Credit cards:** V, MC.
Reduced fees: Low Season, Resort Guests, Twilight Play.
Unrestricted walking: No. **Range:** Yes (grass).
Holes: 18. **Par:** 72. **Yards:** 6,901-5,105. **Slope:** 120-116.
Comments: "Haven't seen or had an eagle yet . . . Great use of natural elements . . . Nice place to play . . . Excellent finishing holes . . . Just finish the last 3 with pars! . . . Middle-of-the-road course recently . . . Nice staff, but forgettable course."

★½ FALCON'S LAIR GOLF COURSE
Walhalla—PU—803-638-0000 (40 mi. from Greenville).
Season: Year-round. **High:** May-Sept. **Caddies:** No.
Green fee: $20-$49. **Credit cards:** V.
Lodging on site: No. **Reduced fees:** Weekdays.
Unrestricted walking: Yes. **Range:** Yes (grass).
Holes: 18. **Par:** 72. **Yards:** 6,980-5,238. **Slope:** 124-113.
Comments: "Narrow, mountainous . . . Immaculate greens, but poor fairways . . . Too many creeks."

★★½ GATOR HOLE GOLF COURSE
North Myrtle Beach—PU—803-249-3543.
Season: Year-round. **High:** Spring/Fall. **Caddies:** No.
Green fee: $50-$99. **Credit cards:** V, MC.
Lodging on site: No. **Reduced fees:** Low Season.
Unrestricted walking: No. **Range:** Yes (grass).
Holes: 18. **Par:** 70. **Yards:** 6,000-5,000. **Slope:** 116-122.
Comments: "Tough little track, could be outstanding with just a little more care . . . Surprisingly good . . . Fair course for anybody . . . Challenging par-3 18th over water . . . Good, cheap, overplayed . . . Not much on amenities . . . Not customer-oriented."

THE GOLF PROFESSIONALS CLUB
Beaufort—R—803-524-3635 (40 mi. from Hilton Head).
Season: Year-round. **High:** March-May. **Caddies:** No.
Green fee: $20-$49. **Credit cards:** All Major.
Lodging on site: Yes. **Reduced fees:** Low Season, Resort Guests, Twilight Play.
Unrestricted walking: No. **Range:** Yes (grass).
½ CHAMPIONS COURSE
Holes: 18. **Par:** 72. **Yards:** 6,811-5,241. **Slope:** 124-119.
½ PLAYERS COURSE
Holes: 18. **Par:** 72. **Yards:** 5,929-5,192. **Slope:** 104-107.
Comments: "Absolutely terrible!"

★★★★HARBOUR TOWN GOLF LINKS
Hilton Head Island—R—803-842-1892, 800-955-8337.
Season: Year-round. **High:** March-Nov. **Caddies:** No.
Green fee: $100 and up. **Credit cards:** V, AMEX, DISC, MC.
Lodging on site: Yes. **Reduced fees:** Low Season, Resort Guests, Twilight Play.
Unrestricted walking: No. **Range:** Yes (grass).
Holes: 18. **Par:** 71. **Yards:** 6,912-5,019. **Slope:** 136-117.
Site of PGA Tour's annual Heritage Classic. Ranked 70th in America's 100 Greatest Courses and 9th in America's 75 Best Resort Courses by GOLF DIGEST.
Comments: "Outstanding . . . What a golf course should be . . . Must be able to play a lot of different shots . . . Small greens, but I can't hit large ones either . . . Maybe someday there'll be a par-3 course with par 3s like these . . . Great finishing hole . . . The pros earn their money here . . . Expensive, but worth it . . . Pleasant staff . . . Good course, but resort prices . . . Top notch, too expensive . . . Overrated and overpriced . . . Never in shape . . .

Disappointing . . . Poor condition for its reputation . . . Horrible greens except during the Heritage . . . Played just to say I played it . . . Too expensive for what you get . . . Cost is insulting . . . Too costly for terribly slow play . . . Five hours plus, in carts!"

★★★★ HEATHER GLEN GOLF LINKS
NO. 1/NO. 2/NO. 3 NINES

North Myrtle Beach—PU—803-249-9000, 800-868-4536.
Season: Year-round. **High:** Feb.-March. **Caddies:** No.
Green fee: $50-$99. **Credit cards:** All Major.
Lodging on site: No. **Reduced fees:** No.
Unrestricted walking: No. **Range:** Yes (grass).
Holes: 27. **Par:** 36/36/36. **Yards:** 3,400/3,408/3,383.
Original 18 named Best New Public Course of 1987 and ranked in Second 25 of America's 75 Best Public Courses by GOLF DIGEST.
Comments: "All 27 are delightful . . . Interesting . . . Exceptional . . . Well designed for all handicaps . . . Different, unique holes . . . Strategy is the key . . . Super challenge . . . Super finishing hole . . . Toughest bunkers on the Strand . . . Well groomed . . . Smooth operations . . . So picturesque you forget to play golf . . . The way golf should be experienced . . . Should be on everyone's Myrtle Beach list . . . Some trick holes . . . Loved it, but green fee is ridiculous."

★★★½ HERITAGE CLUB

Pawleys Island—PU—803-626-5121, 800-552-2660.
Season: Year-round. **High:** Spring/Fall. **Caddies:** No.
Green fee: $50-$99. **Credit cards:** V, AMEX, MC.
Lodging on site: No. **Reduced fees:** Low Season.
Unrestricted walking: No. **Range:** Yes (grass).
Holes: 18. **Par:** 71. **Yards:** 7,100-5,325. **Slope:** 137-115.
Ranked in Second 25 of America's 75 Best Public Courses by GOLF DIGEST.
Comments: "A jewel . . . One of the best in Myrtle Beach . . . Blends in perfectly with surroundings . . . Feel like you're the only group on the front 9 . . . Beautiful course in good shape . . . A course for risk-takers . . . Has a special aura . . . Driving into course reminds you of 'Magnolia Lane' . . . Great course for all players, but getting pricey . . . Too many forced carries if wind is blowing . . . Several unfair landing areas . . . Treats players like cattle . . . Gives impression of barely tolerating guests . . . So impolite! They don't seem to realize there are 80 other courses to play here."

★★ HERON POINT GOLF CLUB
Myrtle Beach—PU—803-448-6664.
Season: Year-round. **High:** Spring/Fall. **Caddies:** No.
Green fee: $20-$49. **Credit cards:** V, MC.
Reduced fees: Low Season, Resort Guests, Twilight Play.
Unrestricted walking: No. **Range:** Yes (grass).
Holes: 18. **Par:** 72. **Yards:** 6,599-6,151. **Slope:** 121-116.

★★★½ HICKORY KNOB STATE PARK RESORT
McCormick—PU—803-391-2450 (50 mi. from Augusta, Ga.).
Season: Year-round. **High:** April-Sept. **Caddies:** No.
Green fee: Under $20. **Credit cards:** V, MC.
Lodging on site: Yes. **Reduced fees:** Weekdays, Twilight Play.
Unrestricted walking: Yes. **Range:** Yes (grass).
Holes: 18. **Par:** 72. **Yards:** 6,560-4,905. **Slope:** 119-120.
Comments: "Tight, fair, challenging . . . Scenic venue . . . Uncrowded . . . Well maintained for a state park . . . Good value . . . Best around."

★★★½ HILTON HEAD NATIONAL GOLF CLUB
Hilton Head Island—PU—803-842-5900 (30 mi. from Savannah, Ga.).
Season: Year-round. **High:** March-April/Oct.-Nov. **Caddies:** No.
Green fee: $50-$99. **Credit cards:** V, AMEX, MC.
Reduced fees: Weekdays, Low Season, Resort Guests, Twilight Play.
Unrestricted walking: No. **Range:** Yes (grass).

Holes: 18. **Par:** 72. **Yards:** 6,779–5,589. **Slope:** 124–115.
Comments: "Attractive . . . Good condition . . . Fun course, very fair . . .
Nice greens . . . Multiple tee placements allow for a creative round . . . One
of Gary Player's best . . . Friendly staff . . . Too short from white tees . . .
Too wet for links course . . . Too much money."

★★½ INDIAN WELLS GOLF CLUB
Garden City—PU—803-651-1505 (12 mi. from Myrtle Beach).
Season: Year-round. **High:** March-April. **Caddies:** No.
Green fee: $20–$49. **Credit cards:** V, MC.
Reduced fees: Low Season, Resort Guests, Twilight Play.
Unrestricted walking: No. **Range:** Yes (grass).
Holes: 18. **Par:** 72. **Yards:** 6,624–4,872. **Slope:** 125–118.
Comments: "Lots of water . . . Poor greens . . . Excellent value, never
crowded."

★★★ INDIGO CREEK GOLF CLUB
Garden City—PU—803-650-0381, 800-833-6337.
Season: Year-round. **High:** Spring/Fall. **Caddies:** No.
Green fee: $20–$49. **Credit cards:** V, MC.
Reduced fees: Low Season, Resort Guests, Twilight Play.
Unrestricted walking: No. **Range:** Yes (grass).
Holes: 18. **Par:** 72. **Yards:** 6,744–4,921. **Slope:** 128–120.
Comments: "Playable by both average and good players . . . High handi-
cappers won't enjoy it . . . Too much water . . . Too many waste bunkers
and carries."

★★★★ INDIGO RUN GOLF CLUB
Hilton Head—PU—803-689-2200.
Season: Year-round. **High:** March-May/Oct. **Caddies:** No.
Green fee: $20–$49. **Credit cards:** All Major.
Lodging on site: No. **Reduced fees:** Low Season, Twilight Play.
Unrestricted walking: No. **Range:** Yes (grass).
Holes: 18. **Par:** 72. **Yards:** 7,014–4,974. **Slope:** 132–119.
Comments: "Very good for a new layout . . . Fun . . . Staff terrific."

(GREAT VALUE)

★★★ ISLAND WEST GOLF CLUB
Hilton Head Island—PU—803-757-6660.
Season: Year-round. **High:** April-Oct. **Caddies:** No.
Green fee: $50–$99. **Credit cards:** V, MC.
Reduced fees: Low Season, Resort Guests, Twilight Play.
Unrestricted walking: No. **Range:** Yes (grass).
Holes: 18. **Par:** 72. **Yards:** 6,803–4,938. **Slope:** 129–124.
Comments: "Wonderful layout . . . Seemed very long, but isn't . . . Excel-
lent shape . . . Rough needs maturing . . . Attentive staff . . . Best value in
the off season . . . Blah! No character."

KIAWAH ISLAND RESORT
Kiawah Island—R—803-768-2121, 800-654-2924 (21 mi. from Charleston).
Season: Year-round. **High:** Spring/Fall. **Caddies:** No.
Green fee: $50–$99. **Credit cards:** All Major.
Lodging on site: Yes. **Reduced fees:** Low Season, Resort Guests.
Unrestricted walking: No. **Range:** Yes (grass).
★★★ MARSH POINT COURSE
Holes: 18. **Par:** 71. **Yards:** 6,334–6,007. **Slope:** 126–120.
Comments: "Leisurely course . . . Short, but fun . . . Easy, but interesting
. . . Lots of water . . . 13 water holes . . . Demanding small greens . . .
Alligators on the cart paths! . . . Delightful for average golfer . . . Excellent
golf packages . . . Good bargain winter rates."
★★★★ THE OCEAN COURSE
Green fee: $100 and up. **Reduced fees:** Resort Guests.
Holes: 18. **Par:** 72. **Yards:** 7,371–6,244. **Slope:** 145–126.
Selected Best New Resort Course of 1991 and ranked 3rd in America's 75

Best Resort Courses by GOLF DIGEST. Site of 1991 Ryder Cup.

Comments: "Extraordinary . . . Outstanding . . . What a natural design . . . Best ocean course in the East . . . The Pebble Beach of the East Coast . . . Pete Dye's best . . . A real golf experience . . . They don't get much better . . . The new standard of difficulty in golf design. PGA West not even close . . . Toughest course in the world . . . Too difficult for all but the very best golfers . . . Best course ever played . . . Good once . . . Exposed, lots of wind . . . Too hard for amateurs when windy and cold . . . Bring your shag balls . . . Great breakfast in clubhouse . . . Poor selection of clothes in pro shop . . . Far too difficult to be enjoyable . . . Far too expensive to be enjoyable . . . Worth it . . . Same as Wild Dunes, but more costly . . . Brutal . . . Can't figure out what they had in mind, a test of golf, or of willpower?"

★★★½ OSPREY POINT COURSE

Green fee: $50–$99. **Reduced fees:** Resort Guests.

Holes: 18. **Par:** 72. **Yards:** 6,678–6,244. **Slope:** 124–118.

Ranked 54th in America's 75 Best Resort Courses by GOLF DIGEST.

Comments: "Excellent Fazio design . . . Playable to all levels . . . Easiest of the Kiawah courses . . . Beautiful . . . One of the best . . . As nice as any in the Low Country . . . Very immaculate . . . Staff extremely sharp . . . Long distances between holes . . . A long way out for just an average round."

★★★½ TURTLE POINT COURSE

Green fee: $50–$99. **Reduced fees:** Low Season, Resort Guests.

Holes: 18. **Par:** 72. **Yards:** 6,914–6,489. **Slope:** 132–127.

Ranked 44th in America's 75 Best Resort Courses by GOLF DIGEST.

Comments: "A true challenge . . . Very pretty . . . Underrated . . . Would you believe it? A playable Nicklaus course . . . Best Nicklaus ever . . . Better than The Ocean Course . . . Well run . . . If you don't have a long iron game, stay home . . . Slightly tight at places . . . Three ocean holes are fantastic . . . A good test, a 'should play' . . . Pro shop prices high."

★½ KINGS GRANT COUNTRY CLUB

Summerville—PU—803-873-7110 (25 mi. from Charleston).

Season: Year-round. **High:** Year-round. **Caddies:** No.

Green fee: Under $20. **Credit cards:** V, MC.

Lodging on site: No. **Reduced fees:** Weekdays.

Unrestricted walking: Yes. **Range:** Yes (grass).

Holes: 18. **Par:** 72. **Yards:** 6,712–5,025. **Slope:** 115–115.

Comments: "Very interesting design . . . Poor upkeep, does not take advantage of its potential."

★★★LAKE MARION GOLF CLUB

Santee—PU—803-854-2554, 800-344-6543 (50 mi. from Charleston).

Season: Year-round. **High:** March-May. **Caddies:** No.

Green fee: $20–$49. **Credit cards:** V, MC.

Lodging on site: No. **Reduced fees:** No.

Unrestricted walking: No. **Range:** Yes (grass).

Holes: 18. **Par:** 72. **Yards:** 6,615–5,254. **Slope:** 117–112.

Comments: "Heavy traffic . . . Well maintained for the number of players . . . Nice staff . . . Very friendly, down to earth."

THE LEGENDS

Myrtle Beach—PU—803-236-9318, 800-552-2660.

Season: Year-round. **High:** Sept.-Nov./Feb.-May. **Caddies:** No.

Green fee: $50–$99. **Credit cards:** V, AMEX, MC.

Lodging on site: No. **Reduced fees:** Low Season.

Unrestricted walking: No. **Range:** Yes (grass).

★★★★HEATHLAND COURSE

Holes: 18. **Par:** 71. **Yards:** 6,785–5,115. **Slope:** 127–121.

Ranked 14th in South Carolina by GOLF DIGEST.

Comments: "Excellent links course . . . Wonderful layout . . . A different look . . . Forgiving . . . Pull out the driver without fear . . . Great fun . . . Worth playing . . . A cheap trip to Scotland. . . Fun when windy . . . Always windy . . . Best of the Legends complex . . . Best in Myrtle Beach

... Busy, but organized staff ... Smooth operation ... Starter area too crowded ... Imitation Scottish links is too cute ... Now I'm really convinced I don't want to play golf in Scotland."

★★★ MOORLAND COURSE

Holes: 18. **Par:** 72. **Yards:** 6,799-4,905. **Slope:** 140-127.

Comments: "Tough if not in fairways ... All gimmicks, no golf. .. Too tricked up ... P.B. Dye went too far ... Artificial mounds and bunkers everywhere ... Not at all natural ... Not playable by average golfer ... Loved clubhouse, not course ... Very friendly, helpful people ... Hurried atmosphere."

★★★½ PARKLAND COURSE

Holes: 18. **Par:** 72. **Yards:** 7,170-5,570. **Slope:** 138-127.

Comments: "Nice new layout ... Decisions abound ... Good daily double with Heathland ... Wish I was a member there ... A disorganized disaster at the starter's shack ... Long distances between holes ... Not all it's cracked up to be ... Mowing crew needs manners ... Legends is best 54-hole complex anywhere."

★★★ THE LINKS AT STONO FERRY

Hollywood—PU—803-763-1817 (15 mi. from Charleston).
Season: Year-round. **High:** Spring/Fall. **Caddies:** No.
Green fee: $20-$49. **Credit cards:** V, MC.
Reduced fees: Weekdays, Low Season, Twilight Play.
Unrestricted walking: No. **Range:** Yes (grass).
Holes: 18. **Par:** 72. **Yards:** 6,606-4,928. **Slope:** 115-119.
Comments: "Not a back breaker ... Nice layout, slow greens ... Reasonable, fine shape, worth the trip ... Busy, but cheap ... Best for the money in Charleston ... $12 includes cart in summer ... Poor hitting areas, lousy greens ... Bring bug spray."

★★★ LITCHFIELD COUNTRY CLUB

Pawleys Island—R—803-237-3411 (60 mi. from Charleston).
Season: Year-round. **High:** March-April/Oct. **Caddies:** No.
Green fee: $20-$49. **Credit cards:** V, AMEX, DISC, MC.
Lodging on site: Yes. **Reduced fees:** Low Season, Resort Guests.
Unrestricted walking: No. **Range:** Yes (grass).
Holes: 18. **Par:** 72. **Yards:** 6,752-5,264. **Slope:** 120-119.
Comments: "Fair, but challenging ... Some long carries, long distances between holes ... Too long for average players ... Outstanding accommodations."

★★★½ LONG BAY CLUB

Longs—PU—803-399-2222, 800-422-7274.
Season: Year-round. **High:** March-April/Oct. **Caddies:** No.
Green fee: $50-$99. **Credit cards:** V, DISC, MC.
Lodging on site: No. **Reduced fees:** Low Season, Resort Guests.
Unrestricted walking: No. **Range:** Yes (grass).
Holes: 18. **Par:** 72. **Yards:** 7,021-5,598. **Slope:** 137-120.
Ranked 15th in South Carolina by GOLF DIGEST.
Comments: "Great course, needs clubhouse. .. Designed by and suitable for Nicklaus. .. Nicklaus makes you play every shot... I used all my clubs. .. Nicklausmania! Gimmicks and greens widths that run opposite to approach shots. .. Lunarscape. .. Elevated target greens that won't accept shots. .. Too long for a 14-handicapper. .. Hard greens, always in poor shape. .. Poor drainage. .. Needs better maintenance. .. Love those waste areas. .. Jack's waste bunkers are killers. .. Waste bunkers serve as cart paths. .. Too hard for weekenders. .. Ugliest course I ever played. .. Even Jack makes a mistake."

MYRTLE BEACH NATIONAL GOLF CLUB

Myrtle Beach—PU—803-448-2308, 800-344-5590.
Season: Year-round. **High:** March-April/Oct. **Caddies:** No.
Green fee: $20-$49. **Credit cards:** V, AMEX, MC.

Lodging on site: No. **Reduced fees:** Low Season, Resort Guests.
Unrestricted walking: No. **Range:** Yes (grass).

★★★½ NORTH COURSE
Holes: 18. **Par:** 72. **Yards:** 6,759-4,982. **Slope:** 125-113.
Comments: "Good, lots of water . . . Super nice . . . Outstanding facility
. . . Staff is excellent . . . A real factory . . . Meat-market treatment."

★★★½ SOUTHCREEK COURSE
Holes: 18. **Par:** 72. **Yards:** 6,416-4,723. **Slope:** 123-109.
Comments: "Short treelined course . . . Open and deceiving, with water in
all the right spots . . . Friendly, fun layout . . . Fairly short course where
distance wins."

★★★ WEST COURSE
Holes: 18. **Par:** 72. **Yards:** 6,866-5,307. **Slope:** 119-109.
Comments: "A real delight . . . Not too difficult, but fun . . . Always in
good condition, always busy . . . Very straight and boring."

★★★ MYRTLE WEST GOLF CLUB
North Myrtle Beach—PU—803-249-1478, 800-842-8390.
Season: Year-round. **High:** Spring/Fall. **Caddies:** No.
Green fee: $20-$49. **Credit cards:** V, MC.
Lodging on site: No. **Reduced fees:** Low Season, Twilight Play.
Unrestricted walking: No. **Range:** Yes (grass).
Holes: 18. **Par:** 72. **Yards:** 6,787-6,191. **Slope:** 132-118.
Comments: "Great course . . . Great greens . . . Super clubhouse."

MYRTLEWOOD GOLF CLUB
Myrtle Beach—PU—803-449-5134, 800-283-3633.
Season: Year-round. **High:** Spring/Fall. **Caddies:** No.
Green fee: $50-$99. **Credit cards:** V, AMEX, DISC, MC.
Lodging on site: No. **Reduced fees:** Low Season, Resort Guests.
Unrestricted walking: No. **Range:** Yes (grass).

★★★ PALMETTO COURSE
Holes: 18. **Par:** 72. **Yards:** 6,957-5,305. **Slope:** 121-117.
Comments: "Best course in Myrtle Beach . . . Great finishing hole . . .
Two great finishing holes . . . Great staff."

★★★½ PINEHILLS COURSE
Holes: 18. **Par:** 72. **Yards:** 6,640-4,906. **Slope:** 125-115.
"Newly remodeled . . . Much improved . . . A nice place to start after a cold
winter . . . Staff is excellent."

★★★½ NORTHWOODS GOLF CLUB
Columbia—PU—803-786-9242 (60 mi. from Charlotte, N.C.).
Season: Year-round. **High:** May-June/Sept.-Nov. **Caddies:** No.
Green fee: $20-$49. **Credit cards:** V, AMEX, MC.
Lodging on site: No. **Reduced fees:** Weekdays, Low Season.
Unrestricted walking: No. **Range:** Yes (grass).
Holes: 18. **Par:** 72. **Yards:** 6,800-4,954. **Slope:** 122-118.
Comments: "A good P.B. Dye layout . . . Excellent greens . . . Always in
great shape . . . Walkable, fun . . . No weak points . . . Staff insists you be
treated as a valued guest."

★★½ OAK HILLS GOLF CLUB
Columbia—PU—803-735-9830.
Season: Year-round. **High:** April-Aug. **Caddies:** No.
Green fee: $20-$49. **Credit cards:** V, MC.
Lodging on site: No. **Reduced fees:** No.
Unrestricted walking: No. **Range:** Yes (grass).
Holes: 18. **Par:** 72. **Yards:** 6,894-4,574. **Slope:** 122-110.
Comments: "Fair layout, fair greens . . . Course never in good shape . . .
Rocks in fairways and rough . . . Staff only cares about bottom-line profits
. . . Ch-ching! . . . From the price, they think a lot of their course."

★★½ OAK POINT GOLF COURSE
Johns Island—PU—803-768-7431 (20 mi. from Charleston).
Season: Year-round. **High:** March-Nov. **Caddies:** No.
Green fee: $20-$49. **Credit cards:** V, MC.
Lodging on site: No. **Reduced fees:** Low Season.
Unrestricted walking: No. **Range:** Yes (grass).
Holes: 18. **Par:** 72. **Yards:** 6,759-4,671. **Slope:** 132-121.
Formerly called Hope Plantation Golf Club.
Comments: "Newer course, needs work . . . Perfect greens . . . New owners have really made this nice . . . Near Kiawah, but much less money . . . Too many poorly designed holes . . . Some holes unfair . . . Blind hazards . . . Poor shape . . . Expensive at any price."

★★½ OLD SOUTH GOLF LINKS
Hilton Head Island—PU—803-785-5353.
Season: Year-round. **High:** March-April/Oct. **Caddies:** No.
Green fee: $50-$99. **Credit cards:** V, AMEX, MC.
Lodging on site: No. **Reduced fees:** Low season, Twilight Play.
Unrestricted walking: No. **Range:** Yes (grass).
Holes: 18. **Par:** 72. **Yards:** 6,772-4,776. **Slope:** 129-123.
Comments: "Very pretty . . . Very playable . . . Spectacular holes . . . The opposite of blah . . . A real sleeper . . . Few long carries . . . Not a 'power game' course . . . Mid-handicappers can play from championship tees . . . Always in excellent shape . . . Very crowded."

★★★½ OYSTER REEF GOLF CLUB
Hilton Head Island—PU—803-681-7717.
Season: Year-round. **High:** Spring/Fall. **Caddies:** No.
Green fee: $50-$99. **Credit cards:** V, AMEX, DISC, MC.
Lodging on site: No. **Reduced fees:** Low Season.
Unrestricted walking: No. **Range:** Yes (grass).
Holes: 18. **Par:** 72. **Yards:** 7,027-5,288. **Slope:** 131-118.
Comments: "Terrific . . . Beautiful, fair . . . Tough, honest . . . One of the best on the island . . . Has become very expensive."

PALMETTO DUNES RESORT
Hilton Head—R—803-785-1138, 800-827-3006.
Season: Year-round. **High:** March-April/Oct. **Caddies:** No.
Green fee: $50-$99. **Credit cards:** AMEX, MC.
Lodging on site: Yes. **Reduced fees:** Low Season, Resort Guests.
Unrestricted walking: No. **Range:** Yes (grass).
★★★½ ARTHUR HILLS COURSE
Holes: 18. **Par:** 72. **Yards:** 6,651-4,999. **Slope:** 127-113.
Comments: "A gem . . . Classic Arthur Hills . . . A shotmaker's course . . . Best on Hilton Head . . . Very hard for average golfers . . . Target golf with bad targets . . . Spotty condition."
★★★GEORGE FAZIO COURSE
Holes: 18. **Par:** 70. **Yards:** 6,873-5,273. **Slope:** 132-127.
Comments: "Excellent layout . . . Nice track . . . Best of the lot . . . Long par 4s . . . Too tough for resort play . . . Good, but too many players . . . Treated us like they did not want us there . . . Greens in horrid shape."
★★½ ROBERT TRENT JONES COURSE
Holes: 18. **Par:** 72. **Yards:** 6,710-5,425. **Slope:** 123-123.
Comments: "Tenth hole plays toward the ocean . . . Only a glimpse of the sea . . . Not too interesting . . . Dull, boring and ugly . . . Far too expensive . . . Has become a golf factory."

PALMETTO HALL PLANTATION
Hilton Head Island—R—803-689-4100, 800-827-3006.
Season: Year-round. **High:** April-Oct. **Caddies:** No.
Green fee: $50-$99. **Credit cards:** V, AMEX, MC.
Lodging on site: No. **Reduced fees:** Low Season, Resort Guests.
Unrestricted walking: No. **Range:** Yes (grass).

SOUTH CAROLINA

★★★★ARTHUR HILLS COURSE
Holes: 18. **Par:** 72. **Yards:** 6,918-4,956. **Slope:** 132-117.
Comments: "The hidden gem of Hilton Head . . . Perfect condition . . . The best back 9 in golf . . . Great finishing hole . . . Nos. 9 and 18 too tough for public play."

★★ROBERT CUPP COURSE
Holes: 18. **Par:** 72. **Yards:** 7,079-5,220. **Slope:** 141-120.
Comments: "Tortured layout . . . Geometric design is awful . . . One big computer glitch . . . Too bizarre . . . Second hole is absurd . . . Who ever heard of pyramids in a South Carolina marsh? . . . Too cute . . . Several unfair greens . . . Not for the traditionalist."

★★PATRIOTS POINT LINKS
Mt. Pleasant—PU—803-881-0042 (2 mi. from Charleston).
Season: Year-round. **High:** Spring/Fall. **Caddies:** No.
Green fee: Under $20. **Credit cards:** V, AMEX, MC.
Reduced fees: Weekdays, Low Season, Twilight Play.
Unrestricted walking: No. **Range:** Yes (grass).
Holes: 18. **Par:** 72. **Yards:** 6,838-5,562. **Slope:** 118-113.
Comments: "Beautiful oceanside course at a good price . . . Wonderful walking course . . . Very busy . . . Well kept . . . Plain, mostly parallel fairways . . . Too easy."

★★★½ PINE LAKES INTERNATIONAL COUNTRY CLUB
Myrtle Beach—R—803-449-6459, 800-446-6817.
Season: Year-round. **High:** March-May/Oct.-Nov. **Caddies:** No.
Green fee: $50-$99. **Credit cards:** V, AMEX, MC.
Lodging on site: No. **Reduced fees:** No.
Unrestricted walking: No. **Range:** Yes (grass).
Holes: 18. **Par:** 71. **Yards:** 6,709-5,376. **Slope:** 125-122.
Comments: "Oldie, but goodie, a pleasure to play . . . Oldest course in Myrtle Beach, a gentlemen's course . . . Nice place . . . Excellent . . . Classy . . . Unique, traditional course . . . A one-time unforgettable experience . . . The best in golf hospitality . . . Super treatment . . . The ultimate in golfing enjoyment . . . Outstanding service . . . Excellent clam chowder . . . They simply treat you great . . . Inconsistently maintained . . . Pretentious . . . All glitz . . . Lots of frills, bang for buck questionable . . . Six-hour rounds."

★½ PINELAND PLANTATION GOLF CLUB
Mayesville—PU—803-659-4359 (15 mi. from Sumter).
Season: Year-round. **High:** March-May. **Caddies:** No.
Green fee: $20-$49. **Credit cards:** V, MC.
Reduced fees: Weekdays, Low Season, Twilight Play.
Unrestricted walking: Yes. **Range:** Yes (grass).
Holes: 18. **Par:** 72. **Yards:** 7,084-5,307. **Slope:** 122-119.
Comments: "Poorly kept . . . Needs much work."

PORT ROYAL GOLF CLUB
Hilton Head—R—800-925-3508.
Season: Year-round. **High:** March-May/Oct. **Caddies:** No.
Green fee: $50-$99. **Credit cards:** V, AMEX, MC.
Lodging on site: Yes. **Reduced fees:** Low Season, Resort Guests, Twilight Play.
Unrestricted walking: No. **Range:** Yes (grass).

★★½ BARONY COURSE
Holes: 18. **Par:** 72. **Yards:** 6,530-5,253. **Slope:** 124-115.
Comments: "Yawn."

★★★PLANTER'S ROW COURSE
Holes: 18. **Par:** 72. **Yards:** 6,520-5,126. **Slope:** 128-116.
Comments: "A favorite . . . Finishing holes are terrific . . . Is overshadowed by the island's biggies . . . Expensive."

SOUTH CAROLINA

★★★ROBBER'S ROW COURSE
Holes: 18. **Par:** 72. **Yards:** 6,711-5,299. **Slope:** 126-114.
Being redesigned in 1994.
Comments: "Nice resort layout . . . Reduced prices and walking after 2 p.m. . . . Tight fairways make it hard."

★★½ POSSUM TROT GOLF CLUB
North Myrtle Beach—PU—803-272-5341, 800-626-8768.
Season: Year-round. **High:** March-April/Oct. **Caddies:** No.
Green fee: $20-$49. **Credit cards:** V, AMEX, MC.
Lodging on site: No. **Reduced fees:** Low Season, Twilight Play.
Unrestricted walking: No. **Range:** Yes (grass).
Holes: 18. **Par:** 72. **Yards:** 6,966-5,160. **Slope:** 118-111.
Comments: "Fun course . . . Heavy play . . . Good warm-up for rest of Myrtle Beach . . . Good prices, pretty good shape . . . Great hospitality . . . Cheap for the Beach."

★RACCOON RUN GOLF CLUB
Myrtle Beach—PU—803-650-2644.
Season: Year-round. **High:** Feb.-April/Oct.-Nov. **Caddies:** No.
Green fee: $20-$49. **Credit cards:** No.
Lodging on site: No. **Reduced fees:** Low Season.
Unrestricted walking: No. **Range:** No.
Holes: 18. **Par:** 73. **Yards:** 7,349-6,804. **Slope:** 120-116.
Comments: "Poorly maintained . . . Play only if looking for cheap golf."

★★★½ RIVER CLUB
Pawleys Island—R—803-237-8755 (60 mi. from Charleston).
Season: Year-round. **High:** March-April/Oct. **Caddies:** No.
Green fee: $20-$49. **Credit cards:** V, AMEX, DISC, MC.
Lodging on site: Yes. **Reduced fees:** Low Season, Resort Guests.
Unrestricted walking: No. **Range:** No.
Holes: 18. **Par:** 72. **Yards:** 6,677-5,084. **Slope:** 125-120.
Comments: "Top marks for design . . . Challenging, but fair . . . Scenic."

★★★RIVER FALLS PLANTATION
Duncan—PU—803-949-3750 (10 mi. from Greenville).
Season: Year-round. **High:** April-Aug. **Caddies:** No.
Green fee: $20-$49. **Credit cards:** V, MC.
Lodging on site: No. **Reduced fees:** Low Season.
Unrestricted walking: No. **Range:** Yes (grass).
Holes: 18. **Par:** 72. **Yards:** 6,734-5,702. **Slope:** 127-116.
Comments: "Very, very pretty . . . Hard . . . Get rid of the love grass."

★★★RIVER HILLS GOLF & COUNTRY CLUB
Little River—PU—803-399-2100, 800-264-3810.
Season: Year-round. **High:** April-Oct. **Caddies:** No.
Green fee: $20-$49. **Credit cards:** V, MC.
Lodging on site: No. **Reduced fees:** Low Season.
Unrestricted walking: No. **Range:** Yes (grass).
Holes: 18. **Par:** 72. **Yards:** 6,829-4,861. **Slope:** 133-120.
Comments: "Never tire of this one . . . Nice elevation changes . . . 11 through 14 and 17th are among best Myrtle has to offer . . . Nice layout, friendly staff . . . Overbooked . . . Greens are shaky at best, sparse."

★★★RIVER OAKS GOLF PLANTATION
OTTER/BEAR/FOX 9s
Myrtle Beach—PU—803-236-2222, 800-762-8813.
Season: Year-round. **High:** Spring/Fall. **Caddies:** No.
Green fee: $20-$49. **Credit cards:** V, MC.
Reduced fees: Weekdays, Low Season, Resort Guests, Twilight Play.
Unrestricted walking: No. **Range:** Yes (grass).
Holes: 27. **Par:** 36/36/36. **Yards:** 3,445/3,432/3,346.

Comments: "Neat, challenging, fun . . . Wide range in types of holes . . . They keep it mowed . . . Very good value . . . One to play more than once when visiting the Grand Strand."

★★ROLLING HILLS GOLF CLUB
Aynor—PU—803-358-4653, 800-633-2380 (35 mi. from Myrtle Beach).
Season: Year-round. **High:** Spring/Fall. **Caddies:** No.
Green fee: $20-$49. **Credit cards:** V, MC.
Lodging on site: No. **Reduced fees:** Low Season, Resort Guests.
Unrestricted walking: No. **Range:** Yes (grass).
Holes: 18. **Par:** 72. **Yards:** 6,749-5,178. **Slope:** 120-109.
Comments: "Don't bother . . . Give it back to the cows."

★★★SANTEE NATIONAL GOLF CLUB
Santee—R—803-854-3531, 800-448-0152 (45 mi. from Charleston).
Season: Year-round. **High:** March-April/Oct. **Caddies:** No.
Green fee: $20-$49. **Credit cards:** V, DISC, MC.
Lodging on site: Yes. **Reduced fees:** Low Season.
Unrestricted walking: No. **Range:** Yes (grass).
Holes: 18. **Par:** 72. **Yards:** 6,800-6,150. **Slope:** 121-114.
Comments: "Terrific bent-grass greens . . . Good design for shorter hitters . . . Age will make it great . . . Another good value . . . Find it. An excellent experience . . . They cater to golfers . . . Very heavy traffic."

★★SEA GULL GOLF CLUB
Pawleys Island—PU—803-448-5931, 800-833-6337.
Season: Year-round. **High:** Feb.-May/Sept.-Nov. **Caddies:** No.
Green fee: $20-$49. **Credit cards:** V, MC.
Lodging on site: Yes. **Reduced fees:** Low Season.
Unrestricted walking: No. **Range:** No.
Holes: 18. **Par:** 72. **Yards:** 6,910-5,250. **Slope:** 128-115.
Comments: "Playable by all . . . Uncrowded . . . Course in poor shape."

SEA PINES PLANTATION
Hilton Head—R—803-842-1894, 800-845-6131.
Season: Year-round. **High:** Spring/Fall. **Caddies:** No.
Green fee: $50-$99. **Credit cards:** V, AMEX, DISC, MC.
Lodging on site: Yes. **Reduced fees:** Resort Guests, Twilight Play.
Unrestricted walking: No. **Range:** Yes (grass).
★★½ OCEAN COURSE
Holes: 18. **Par:** 72. **Yards:** 6,614-5,284. **Slope:** 125-111.
Comments: "Nice layout, some fine holes . . . Great teaching staff . . . Run-of-the-mill resort course . . . Getting too expensive."
★★½ SEA MARSH COURSE
Holes: 18. **Par:** 72. **Yards:** 6,515-5,054. **Slope:** 120-123.
Comments: "Generally a good experience . . . Showing a little wear and tear . . . New greens, cartpaths and irrigation . . . Lots of water, some alligators."

★★★SHADOWMOSS PLANTATION GOLF CLUB
Charleston—PU—803-556-8251, 800-338-4971.
Season: Year-round. **High:** March-May. **Caddies:** No.
Green fee: Under $20. **Credit cards:** V, AMEX, MC.
Reduced fees: Weekdays, Low Season, Resort Guests.
Unrestricted walking: No. **Range:** Yes (grass).
Holes: 18. **Par:** 72. **Yards:** 6,701-5,169. **Slope:** 123-120.
Comments: "Nice course . . . Fair . . . Good value . . . Too much water . . . Too much development . . . Hugo was there."

★★★SHIPYARD GOLF CLUB
GALLEON/BRIGANTINE/CLIPPER 9s
Hilton Head Island—R—803-686-8802, 800-925-3508.
Season: Year-round. **High:** Spring/Fall. **Caddies:** No.

Green fee: $50-$99. **Credit cards:** V, MC.
Lodging on site: Yes. **Reduced fees:** Low Season, Resort Guests.
Unrestricted walking: No. **Range:** Yes (grass).
Holes: 27. **Par:** 36/36/36. **Yards:** 3,364/3,352/3,466.
Comments: "Interesting mix of holes . . . Some great ones . . . Much water, tight fairways . . . Bring your scuba gear . . . Scenic . . . Plantation has everything . . . More fun, less stuffy than Sea Pines."

★★★½ SURF GOLF AND BEACH CLUB
North Myrtle Beach—PU—803-249-1524, 800-765-7873.
Season: Year-round. **High:** Spring/Fall. **Caddies:** No.
Green fee: $50-$99. **Credit cards:** V, MC.
Lodging on site: No. **Reduced fees:** Low Season.
Unrestricted walking: No. **Range:** Yes (grass).
Holes: 18. **Par:** 72. **Yards:** 6,842-5,178. **Slope:** 126-111.
Comments: "Fine old course . . . Absolutely beautiful . . . Interesting lay-out . . . Excellent greens . . . You never tire of it . . . One of the best on the Strand . . . Great care, Southern hospitality . . . Made me feel as though it was my home course . . . Overpriced for tourists . . . Slicer's nightmare. Most doglegs to the left ever seen."

★★★★½ TIDEWATER GOLF CLUB
North Myrtle Beach—PU—803-249-3829, 800-446-5363.
Season: Year-round. **High:** Spring/Fall. **Caddies:** No.
Green fee: $50-$99. **Credit cards:** V, AMEX, MC.
Lodging on site: Yes. **Reduced fees:** Low Season.
Unrestricted walking: No. **Range:** Yes (grass).
Holes: 18. **Par:** 72. **Yards:** 7,020-4,765. **Slope:** 134-127.
Selected Best New Public Course of 1990 and ranked 8th in South Carolina by GOLF DIGEST.
Comments: "Excellent . . . Tough, but enjoyable . . . Leaning toward too tough . . . Probably the best course ever played . . . Without doubt the best in Myrtle Beach . . . No gimmicks . . . Play it every time I'm in South Carolina . . . One of the best, but expensive . . . Solid course, too pricey for area . . . Excellent and they know it. And they charge for it . . . Must play once . . . Who cares about the cost? . . . Range is as plush as the course . . . Staff very friendly . . . Most overpriced course ever played . . . Hilton Head prices in Myrtle Beach . . . Staff said excessive green fee was to keep play down! . . . Good course, but doesn't deserve No. 1 in Myrtle Beach rankings . . . Slow play a problem . . . Too much back-and-forth driving to reach holes."

★★WATERWAY HILLS GOLF CLUB
OAKS/LAKES/RAVINE 9s
Myrtle Beach—PU—803-449-6488.
Season: Year-round. **High:** March-April/Oct. **Caddies:** No.
Green fee: $20-$49. **Credit cards:** V, AMEX, MC.
Lodging on site: No. **Reduced fees:** Low Season, Resort Guests.
Unrestricted walking: No. **Range:** Yes (grass).
Holes: 27. **Par:** 36/36/36 **Yards:** 3,271/3,190/3,149.
Comments: "Unique entrance on ski lift over waterway . . . Nice people, superior staff . . . Very unspectacular . . . First holes on waterway unfair . . . One of the worst . . . Bad condition, the ride across water isn't worth it."

★★½ WEDGEFIELD PLANTATION COUNTRY CLUB
Georgetown—PU—803-546-8587 (35 mi. from Myrtle Beach).
Season: Year-round. **Caddies:** No.
Green fee: $20-$49. **Credit cards:** V, MC.
Lodging on site: No. **Reduced fees:** No.
Unrestricted walking: No. **Range:** Yes (grass).
Holes: 18. **Par:** 72. **Yards:** 6,705-5,249. **Slope:** 123-119.
Comments: "Pedestrian, needs grooming . . . Was getting facelift last time I played."

SOUTH CAROLINA

★★★THE WELLMAN CLUB
Johnsonville—PU—803-386-2521 (35 mi. from Florence).
Season: Year-round. **High:** March-April. **Caddies:** No.
Green fee: $20-$49. **Credit cards:** V, MC.
Lodging on site: Yes. **Reduced fees:** Weekdays, Low Season.
Unrestricted walking: No. **Range:** Yes (grass).
Holes: 18. **Par:** 72. **Yards:** 7,032-6,428. **Slope:** 123-120.
Comments: "A hidden gem . . . Worth the trouble to find . . . Need to fix
some drainage problems."

WILD DUNES RESORT
Isle of Palms—R—803-886-2164, 800-845-8880 (12 mi. from Charleston).
Season: Year-round. **High:** Spring/Fall. **Caddies:** No.
Green fee: $50-$99. **Credit cards:** V, AMEX, DISC, MC.
Lodging on site: Yes. **Reduced fees:** Low Season, Resort Guests.
Unrestricted walking: No. **Range:** Yes (grass).
★★★HARBOR COURSE
Holes: 18. **Par:** 70. **Yards:** 6,446-5,900. **Slope:** 124-117.
Comments: "Well-conditioned shotmaker's course . . . Just as nice as the
Links . . .Different, but fun . . . Improved by Hurricane Hugo . . . Too
expensive for the experience."
★★★★LINKS COURSE
Holes: 18. **Par:** 72. **Yards:** 6,722-6,131. **Slope:** 131-121.
Ranked 100th in America's 100 Greatest Courses and 13th in America's 75
Best Resort Courses by GOLF DIGEST.
Comments: "A great course . . . Outstanding . . . Gorgeous . . . Beautiful
all the way around . . . Good test of golf, unique . . . Ocean views . . .
Always windy, very hard to score . . . I would like to walk it . . . Not the
same course as before Hurricane Hugo . . . Somewhat overrated, saved by
oceanside holes . . . Nice clubhouse/restaurant . . . Too expensive."

WILD WING PLANTATION
Myrtle Beach—PU—803-347-9464, 800-736-9464.
Season: Year-round. **High:** Spring/Fall. **Caddies:** No.
Green fee: $50-$99. **Credit cards:** V, AMEX, DISC, MC.
Reduced fees: Low Season, Resort Guests, Twilight Play.
Unrestricted walking: No. **Range:** Yes (grass).
AVOCET COURSE*
Holes: 18. **Par:** 72. **Yards:** 7,127-5,298. **Slope:** 128.
Comments: "Newest at Wild Wing . . . Incredible bent-grass
greens . . . Many two-tiered greens, one 100-yard-long green
serves two holes . . . Fairways still rough, bent-grass greens OK."
★★★★HUMMINGBIRD COURSE
Holes: 18. **Par:** 72. **Yards:** 6,853-5,168. **Slope:** 131-123.
Comments: "Beautiful, challenging course . . . A little expensive . . . Fan-
tastic clubhouse . . . Look for a PGA tournament held there in the
future . . . No coolers allowed . . . Discourteous grounds people."
★★★★WOOD STORK COURSE
Holes: 18. **Par:** 72. **Yards:** 7,044-5,409. **Slope:** 126-121.
Comments: "Heavily wooded, beautiful . . . Great greens
. . . Firm . . . Immaculate conditions . . . First-class operation . . . Real treat
to play . . . A keeper . . . Largest practice putting green on the Strand . . .
Friendly, most accommodating . . . Outstanding facility . . . Wild Wing
courses are 'must plays' when in Myrtle Beach."

★★★WILLBROOK PLANTATION GOLF CLUB
Pawleys Island—R—803-237-4900 (60 mi. from Charleston).
Season: Year-round. **High:** March-April/Oct. **Caddies:** No.
Green fee: $50-$99. **Credit cards:** V, AMEX, DISC, MC.
Lodging on site: Yes. **Reduced fees:** Low Season, Resort Guests.
Unrestricted walking: No. **Range:** Yes (grass).
Holes: 18. **Par:** 72. **Yards:** 6,674-4,694. **Slope:** 127-118.

Comments: "Great course. . . Little known in Myrtle Beach. . . Pleasant atmosphere, fine course. . . Conditions improving with recent drainage additions. . . A course for all skills."

★★★½ THE WITCH

Conway—PU—803-448-1300 (5 mi. from Myrtle Beach).
Season: Year-round. **High:** Spring/Fall. **Caddies:** No.
Green fee: $50-$99. **Credit cards:** V, MC.
Lodging on site: No. **Reduced fees:** Low Season.
Unrestricted walking: No. **Range:** Yes (grass).
Holes: 18. **Par:** 71. **Yards:** 6,702-4,812. **Slope:** 133-121.
Comments: "Terrific isolation in wild, swampy outback . . . A 'witch' to the player and the billfold . . . Great use of natural wetlands terrain . . . Super layout . . . Excellent . . . Lots of character building . . . A delight to play for all levels, but demands local knowledge . . . Fun course, loads of trouble . . . Tough, but interesting . . . Terrific. Don't miss it . . . Needs to mature just a little . . . Front 9 is superior, back 9 is too contrived . . . Too far from greens to tees . . . Great people, too."

★★½ ELMWOOD GOLF COURSE
Sioux Falls—PU—605-339-7092.
Season: April-Oct. **High:** May-Sept. **Caddies:** No.
Green fee: Under $20. **Credit cards:** V, MC.
Lodging on site: No. **Reduced fees:** Weekdays.
Unrestricted walking: Yes. **Range:** Yes (grass).
Holes: 18. **Par:** 72. **Yards:** 6,850-5,737. **Slope:** 129-123.
Ranked 5th in South Dakota by GOLF DIGEST.
Also has 9-hole East Course.
Comments: "Lots of timber . . . Ego deflater . . . Perfect walking course
. . . Drains poorly . . . Airport proximity is bothersome . . . Overplayed
. . . OK if you need to kill time."

FOX RUN GOLF COURSE*
Yankton—PU—605-665-8456 (70 mi. from Sioux Falls).
Season: March-Nov. **High:** June-Aug. **Caddies:** No.
Green fee: Under $20. **Credit cards:** V, MC.
Lodging on site: No. **Reduced fees:** Weekdays.
Unrestricted walking: Yes. **Range:** Yes (grass).
Holes: 18. **Par:** 72. **Yards:** 6,696-5,209. **Slope:** 122-108.
Comments: "New course . . . Playable . . . When it matures, watch out!"

★★★½ HILLCREST GOLF & COUNTRY CLUB
Yankton—PU—605-665-4621 (70 mi. from Sioux Falls).
Season: April-Oct. **High:** May-Aug. **Caddies:** No.
Green fee: $20-$49. **Credit cards:** No.
Lodging on site: No. **Reduced fees:** Weekdays.
Unrestricted walking: Yes. **Range:** Yes (grass).
Holes: 18. **Par:** 72. **Yards:** 6,874-5,725. **Slope:** 130-126.
Comments: "Challenging . . . Well maintained . . . Great staff."

★★★LAKEVIEW GOLF COURSE
Mitchell—PU—605-996-1424.
Season: April-Oct. **High:** June-Aug. **Caddies:** No.
Green fee: Under $20. **Credit cards:** V, MC.
Lodging on site: No. **Reduced fees:** No.
Unrestricted walking: Yes. **Range:** Yes (grass).
Holes: 18. **Par:** 72. **Yards:** 6,670-5,808. **Slope:** 123-115.
Comments: "Was only 9, now a great 18 . . . Old part is treelined, new
part is open . . . Very nice, well-groomed, reasonably priced, enjoyable."

★★★★MEADOWBROOK GOLF COURSE
Rapid City—PU—605-394-4191.
Season: Year-round. **High:** May-Sept. **Caddies:** No.
Green fee: Under $20. **Credit cards:** No.
Lodging on site: No. **Reduced fees:** Weekdays.
Unrestricted walking: Yes. **Range:** Yes (grass).
Holes: 18. **Par:** 72. **Yards:** 7,054-5,603. **Slope:** 138-130.

Ranked 2nd in South Dakota by GOLF DIGEST.
Comments: "Beautiful, tough, must think at all times . . . Fair, interesting
. . . Difficult, with a variety of challenges . . . Great staff, will accommodate
your tourist schedule and get you on . . . Avoid weekend crowds."

★★★½ WILLOW RUN GOLF COURSE
Sioux Falls—PU—605-335-5900 (1 mi. from Sioux Falls).
Season: April-Oct. **High:** June-Aug. **Caddies:** No.
Green fee: Under $20. **Credit cards:** V, MC.
Lodging on site: No. **Reduced fees:** Twilight Play.
Unrestricted walking: Yes. **Range:** Yes (grass).
Holes: 18. **Par:** 71. **Yards:** 6,500-4,915. **Slope:** 127-119.
Comments: "Excellent use of hazards . . . Memorable holes . . . A bit up
and down . . . In great shape, greens very fast . . Friendly atmosphere . . .
Good test, great shop . . . One of the best east of the Missouri River."

★½ BANEBERRY GOLF CLUB
White Pine—R—615-674-2500, 800-951-4663 (30 mi. from Knoxville).
Season: Year-round. **High:** March-Oct. **Caddies:** No.
Green fee: Under $20. **Credit cards:** V, AMEX, MC.
Lodging on site: Yes. **Reduced fees:** Weekdays.
Unrestricted walking: Yes. **Range:** Yes (grass).
Holes: 18. **Par:** 71. **Yards:** 6,720-4,748. **Slope:** 124-114.
Comments: "Good play for the dollar . . . Not much . . . Boring . . . Wide fairways . . . Houses and condos too close! . . . Maintenance very poor . . . Good packages."

★★BENT CREEK GOLF RESORT
Gatlinburg—R—615-436-3947, 800-251-9336 (45 mi. from Knoxville).
Season: Year-round. **High:** April-Oct. **Caddies:** No.
Green fee: $20-$49. **Credit cards:** All Major.
Lodging on site: Yes. **Reduced fees:** Low Season, Resort Guests, Twilight Play.
Unrestricted walking: No. **Range:** Yes (grass).
Holes: 18. **Par:** 72. **Yards:** 6,202-5,111. **Slope:** 127-117.
Comments: "Longer, flowing front 9 . . . Is beautiful, nice . . . Funky back 9 . . . A disappointment . . . Terrible . . . Full of trick shots . . . It's 'Mickey Mouse' . . . Back should be redesigned . . . A nightmare . . . Insect repellent a must . . . Food and accommodations barely adequate."

★★★BIG CREEK GOLF CLUB
Millington—PU—901-353-1654 (5 mi. from Memphis).
Season: Year-round. **High:** May-Sept. **Caddies:** No.
Green fee: Under $20. **Credit cards:** V, MC.
Lodging on site: No. **Reduced fees:** Twilight Play.
Unrestricted walking: Yes. **Range:** Yes (grass).
Holes: 18. **Par:** 72. **Yards:** 7,056-5,086. **Slope:** 121-111.
Comments: "Well-kept Memphis secret . . . Very fair, good greens . . . New owners have done a great job . . . Friendly staff, good facilities."

★★BRAINERD GOLF COURSE
Chattanooga—PU—615-855-2692 (90 mi. from Atlanta).
Season: Year-round. **High:** April-Oct. **Caddies:** No.
Green fee: $20-$49. **Credit cards:** V, MC.
Lodging on site: No. **Reduced fees:** Weekdays.
Unrestricted walking: No. **Range:** No.
Holes: 18. **Par:** 72. **Yards:** 6,468-4,983. **Slope:** 119-118.
Comments: "Glorified pitch and putt . . . Was run-down, is getting better."

★★★★BRIARWOOD GOLF COURSE
Crab Orchard—R—615-484-5285 (60 mi. from Knoxville).
Season: Year-round. **High:** April-Oct. **Caddies:** No.
Green fee: $20-$49. **Credit cards:** V, AMEX, DISC, MC.
Lodging on site: Yes. **Reduced fees:** Weekdays, Low Season.
Unrestricted walking: No. **Range:** Yes (grass).
Holes: 18. **Par:** 72. **Yards:** 6,689-5,021. **Slope:** 132-123.
Highest golf course in Tennessee at elevation of 2,700 feet.
Comments: "Fantastic views . . . Spectacular in fall . . . Most exciting . . . Great fun . . . Lovely to play . . . Breathtaking . . . Impossible to walk . . . No longer an undiscovered beauty . . . Difficult for novices."

★½ BUFFALO VALLEY GOLF COURSE
Unicoi—PU—615-928-1022, 800-882-1096 (3 mi. from Johnson City).
Season: Year-round. **High:** June-Aug. **Caddies:** No.
Green fee: Under $20. **Credit cards:** V, MC.
Lodging on site: Yes. **Reduced fees:** No.
Unrestricted walking: Yes. **Range:** Yes (grass).

Holes: 18. **Par:** 72. **Yards:** 6,802-5,106. **Slope:** 119-111.
Comments: "Very, very rough . . . Many bad holes."

★COUNTRY HILLS GOLF COURSE
Hendersonville—PU—615-824-1100 (12 mi. N. of Nashville).
Season: Year-round. **High:** March-Oct. **Caddies:** No.
Green fee: Under $20. **Credit cards:** V, AMEX, MC.
Reduced fees: Weekdays, Low Season, Twilight Play.
Unrestricted walking: No. **Range:** Yes (grass).
Holes: 18. **Par:** 70. **Yards:** 6,150-5,017. **Slope:** 119-114.
Comments: "Very hilly . . . Too many blind shots . . . The dogleg redefined . . . Par-5 6th poorly designed."

DEAD HORSE LAKE GOLF COURSE*
Knoxville—PU—615-693-5270.
Season: Year-round. **High:** April-Oct. **Caddies:** No.
Green fee: $20-$49. **Credit cards:** V, DISC, MC.
Lodging on site: No. **Reduced fees:** Weekdays.
Unrestricted walking: No. **Range:** No.
Holes: 18. **Par:** 71. **Yards:** 6,180-5,655. **Slope:** 116-110.

★★★EGWANI FARMS GOLF COURSE
Rockford—PU—615-970-7132 (8 mi. from Knoxville).
Season: March-Dec. **High:** May-Oct. **Caddies:** No.
Green fee: $20-$49. **Credit cards:** V, MC.
Lodging on site: No. **Reduced fees:** Weekdays.
Unrestricted walking: No. **Range:** Yes (grass).
Holes: 18. **Par:** 72. **Yards:** 6,708-4,680. **Slope:** 126-113.
Comments: "Good course, links-type feel . . . Best-conditioned course in east Tennessee . . . Quality but expensive . . . Overpriced for such a bland layout . . . Price holds down crowds nicely."

FAIRFIELD GLADE RESORT
Fairfield Glade—R—615-484-7521 (60 mi. from Knoxville).
Season: Year-round. **High:** April-Oct. **Caddies:** No.
Lodging on site: Yes. **Reduced fees:** Low Season, Twilight Play.
Unrestricted walking: No. **Range:** Yes (grass).
★★★½ HEATHERHURST GOLF CLUB PINE/CREEK/MOUNTAIN 9s
615-484-3799.
Green fee: $20-$49. **Credit cards:** All Major.
Holes: 27. **Par:** 36/36/36. **Yards:** 3,074/3,298/3,297.
Comments: "Very playable . . . Wide fairways, short par 5s . . . Don't go if it's wet . . . How can water stand on a mountaintop?"
★★★★STONEHENGE GOLF CLUB
615-484-3731.
Green fee: $50-$99. **Credit cards:** All Major.
Holes: 18. **Par:** 72. **Yards:** 6,549-5,000. **Slope:** 131-124.
Selected Best New Resort Course of 1985 by GOLF DIGEST.
Ranked 14th in America's 75 Best Resort Courses by GOLF DIGEST.
Comments: "Great place . . . Fine operation . . . One of best in Southeast . . . Beautiful . . . Incredible . . . Great bent-grass fairways . . . Always soft, wet . . . Plays long . . . Fast bent greens . . . Almost perfect . . . Back 9 gorgeous . . . Front can't match back . . . Carts not allowed on fairways, like walking 36 holes . . . Count on slow play."

★★★½ FALL CREEK FALLS GOLF COURSE
Pikeville—PU—615-881-5706 (70 mi. from Chattanooga).
Season: Year-round. **High:** May-Oct. **Caddies:** No.
Green fee: Under $20. **Credit cards:** V, AMEX, MC.
Lodging on site: Yes. **Reduced fees:** Low Season.
Unrestricted walking: Yes. **Range:** Yes (grass).

Holes: 18. **Par:** 72. **Yards:** 6,669-6,051. **Slope:** 127-126.
Ranked in Third 25 of America's 75 Best Public Courses by GOLF DIGEST.
Comments: "One of the best . . . Peaceful mountain setting . . . Miles from anywhere . . . Very pretty . . . Most holes isolated in forest . . . Lots of wildlife . . . No water, lots of sand . . . Great place for families . . . State park rates are a good value."

FORREST CROSSING GOLF COURSE*
Franklin—PU—615-794-9400 (20 mi. from Nashville).
Season: Year-round. **High:** April-Oct. **Caddies:** No.
Green fee: $20-$49. **Credit cards:** V, MC.
Lodging on site: No. **Reduced fees:** Weekdays, Twilight Play.
Unrestricted walking: No. **Range:** Yes (grass).
Holes: 18. **Par:** 72. **Yards:** 6,968-5,011. **Slope:** 125-114.

★★½ GATLINBURG GOLF COURSE
Pigeon Forge—PU—615-453-3912 (35 mi. from Knoxville).
Season: Year-round. **High:** April-Oct. **Caddies:** No.
Green fee: $20-$49. **Credit cards:** No.
Lodging on site: No. **Reduced fees:** No.
Unrestricted walking: No. **Range:** No.
Holes: 18. **Par:** 72. **Yards:** 6,281-4,718. **Slope:** 123-114.
Comments: "Nice . . . Scenic and dramatic . . . Contrasting 9s . . . First 9 dull, second 9 mountainous with great views . . . Par-3 12th has 250-foot drop from tee to green . . . Made for sales brochures, not for play."

THE GOLF CLUB AT SHILOH FALLS*
Pickwick Dam—PU—901-689-5050 (100 mi. from Memphis).
Season: Year-round. **High:** April-Oct. **Caddies:** No.
Green fee: $20-$49. **Credit cards:** V, AMEX, MC.
Lodging on site: Yes. **Reduced fees:** Resort Guests, Twilight Play.
Unrestricted walking: No. **Range:** Yes (grass).
Holes: 18. **Par:** 72. **Yards:** 6,810-5,300. **Slope:** Unrated.

★★★½ GRAYSBURG HILLS GOLF COURSE
Chuckey—PU—615-234-8061 (12 mi. from Greenville).
Season: Year-round. **High:** April-Oct. **Caddies:** No.
Green fee: Under $20. **Credit cards:** V, MC.
Lodging on site: No. **Reduced fees:** Weekdays.
Unrestricted walking: Yes. **Range:** Yes (grass).
Holes: 18. **Par:** 72. **Yards:** 6,834-5,562. **Slope:** 126-117.
Comments: "Tops! . . . A family-run jewel . . . Really special . . . Out of the way, a must to play . . . Some great holes . . . True running greens . . . Needs more trees . . . Winds start blowing at 11 a.m. You can set your watch by it."

★★HARPETH HILLS GOLF COURSE
Nashville—PU—615-862-8493 (9 mi. from Nashville).
Season: Year-round. **High:** April-Sept. **Caddies:** No.
Green fee: Under $20. **Credit cards:** No.
Lodging on site: No. **Reduced fees:** No.
Unrestricted walking: Yes. **Range:** Yes (grass).
Holes: 18. **Par:** 72. **Yards:** 6,850-5,223. **Slope:** 126-124.
Comments: "Best public course in Nashville . . . Wide fairways, big greens . . . Cheap price, cheap course . . . Too crowded . . . Abused . . . Just rebuilt, is maturing into an outstanding course."

★★★½ HERMITAGE GOLF CLUB
Old Hickory—PU—615-847-4001 (5 mi. from Nashville).
Season: Year-round. **High:** March-Oct. **Caddies:** No.
Green fee: $20-$49. **Credit cards:** V, AMEX, DISC, MC.
Lodging on site: No. **Reduced fees:** Twilight Play.
Unrestricted walking: No. **Range:** Yes (grass).

Holes: 18. **Par:** 72. **Yards:** 6,775-5,475. **Slope:** 122-120.
Site of LPGA's Sara Lee Classic.
Comments: "Excellent . . . Wonderful . . . Absolutely beautiful . . . Impeccably maintained . . . Great place to play . . . I got a rain check for 9 holes! . . . Good mix of holes . . . Nice view of Cumberland River from several holes . . . Play it just before the Sara Lee Classic . . . All you want from the back tees . . . Best value in Nashville."

★½ IRONWOOD GOLF COURSE
Cookeville—PU—615-528-2331 (85 mi. from Nashville).
Season: Year-round. **High:** April-Oct. **Caddies:** No.
Green fee: Under $20. **Credit cards:** V, DISC, MC.
Lodging on site: No. **Reduced fees:** No.
Unrestricted walking: Yes. **Range:** Yes (grass).
Holes: 18. **Par:** 72. **Yards:** 6,311-5,972. **Slope:** 123-119.
Comments: "Hard, mounded greens . . . Short par 5s . . . Don't go out of your way."

LEGENDS CLUB OF TENNESSEE
Franklin—PU—615-790-1300 (10 mi. from Nashville).
Season: Year-round. **High:** March-Oct. **Caddies:** No.
Green fee: $50-$99. **Credit cards:** All Major.
Reduced fees: Weekdays, Low Season, Resort Guests.
Unrestricted walking: No. **Range:** Yes (grass).
Home of the Tennessee PGA, Tennessee Golf Association and Tennessee Golf Hall of Fame Museum.
★★★★ NORTH COURSE
Holes: 18. **Par:** 72. **Yards:** 7,190-5,333. **Slope:** 132-119.
Comments: "Expensive but awesome . . . Lots of sand, tough but fair . . . Best greens you'll ever putt . . . Longer than South Course but less imaginative . . . Gimmicky mounded fairways . . . Treats public players like private club members."
★★★★ SOUTH COURSE
Holes: 18. **Par:** 71. **Yards:** 7,113-5,292. **Slope:** 129-121.
Comments: "Great test, beautiful clubhouse . . . Lots of sand, tough but fair . . . Good mix of obstacles . . . Best yardage markers in Tennessee . . . Could have highest prices in Nashville . . . Too many holes look alike . . . When all those trees grow in, both will be stunning."

★★★ MONTGOMERY BELL STATE PARK GOLF COURSE
Burns—PU—615-797-2578 (30 mi. from Nashville).
Season: Year-round. **High:** May-July. **Caddies:** No.
Green fee: Under $20. **Credit cards:** V, AMEX, MC.
Lodging on site: Yes. **Reduced fees:** No.
Unrestricted walking: Yes. **Range:** Yes (grass).
Holes: 18. **Par:** 71. **Yards:** 6,056-4,994. **Slope:** 121-116.
Comments: "Another good state park course . . . Hilly, tight, modest length . . . Much improved recently . . . Laid out for long left-to-right tee shots . . . Don't play if you hit a draw."

★★½ NASHBORO VILLAGE GOLF COURSE
Nashville—PU—615-367-2311.
Season: Year-round. **High:** March-Oct. **Caddies:** No.
Green fee: $20-$49. **Credit cards:** V, AMEX, MC.
Lodging on site: Yes. **Reduced fees:** Weekdays, Low Season, Resort Guests.
Unrestricted walking: No. **Range:** Yes (grass).
Holes: 18. **Par:** 72. **Yards:** 6,887-5,485. **Slope:** 134-129.
Comments: "Good old standby . . . No memorable holes . . . Slow play."

★★★ ORGILL PARK GOLF COURSE
Millington—PU—901-872-3610 (10 mi. from Memphis).
Season: Year-round. **High:** April-Oct. **Caddies:** No.

Green fee: Under $20. **Credit cards:** V, MC.
Lodging on site: No. **Reduced fees:** Weekdays.
Unrestricted walking: Yes. **Range:** Yes (grass).
Holes: 18. **Par:** 70. **Yards:** 6,284-4,574. **Slope:** 113-108.
Comments: "Best value in west Tennessee . . . Excellent conditions for a government course . . . Fairways better than local country clubs . . . You need to see . . . A bit short . . . Zero sand traps."

PARIS LANDING GOLF CLUB*
Buchanan—PU—901-644-1332 (45 mi. from Clarksville).
Season: Year-round. **High:** Spring/Fall. **Caddies:** No.
Green fee: $20-$49. **Credit cards:** V, AMEX, MC.
Lodging on site: Yes. **Reduced fees:** No.
Unrestricted walking: Yes. **Range:** Yes (grass).
Holes: 18. **Par:** 72. **Yards:** 6,612-5,410. **Slope:** 126-Unrated.

★★★★RIVER ISLANDS GOLF CLUB
Kodak—PU—615-933-0100, 800-347-4837 (24 mi. from Gatlinburg).
Season: Year-round. **High:** April-Oct. **Caddies:** No.
Green fee: $20-$49. **Credit cards:** V, MC.
Reduced fees: Weekdays, Low Season, Twilight Play.
Unrestricted walking: No. **Range:** Yes (grass).
Holes: 18. **Par:** 72. **Yards:** 7,002-4,873. **Slope:** 133-118.
Comments: "Difficult Arthur Hills design . . . Tough, lots of trees and water . . . Outstanding use of river site . . . Lots of river crossings . . . Three holes on an island . . . Unique, challenging, playable . . . Great par 3s . . . Keep this one a secret."

★★★½ ROAN VALLEY GOLF ESTATES
Mountain City—PU—615-727-7931 (85 mi. from Knoxville).
Season: April-Nov. **High:** May-Sept. **Caddies:** No.
Green fee: $20-$49. **Credit cards:** V, MC.
Lodging on site: Yes. **Reduced fees:** Low Season.
Unrestricted walking: No. **Range:** No.
Holes: 18. **Par:** 72. **Yards:** 6,736-4,370. **Slope:** 122-107.
Comments: "Beautiful . . . Miles from nowhere . . . Very mountainous, you need the cart . . . A fun 5½ hours."

★★★½ SPRINGHOUSE GOLF CLUB
Nashville—R—615-871-7759.
Season: Year-round. **High:** April-Oct. **Caddies:** No.
Green fee: $50-$99. **Credit cards:** All Major.
Lodging on site: Yes. **Reduced fees:** No.
Unrestricted walking: No. **Range:** Yes (grass).
Holes: 18. **Par:** 72. **Yards:** 7,007-5,126. **Slope:** 133-118.
Part of the Opryland amusement park complex.
Comments: "Outstanding hotel course . . . Amazing what money can do to a flood plain . . . Lots of water to contend with . . . Different, links play . . . Pro staff second to none . . . Contrived 'Hershey Kiss' mounds everywhere . . . Forced carries everywhere . . . Pure target golf, not enjoyable . . . Great clubhouse, mediocre course."

★★★STONEBRIDGE GOLF COURSE
Memphis—PU—901-382-1886.
Season: Year-round. **High:** Spring/Fall. **Caddies:** No.
Green fee: $20-$49. **Credit cards:** V, AMEX, MC.
Lodging on site: No. **Reduced fees:** Weekdays.
Unrestricted walking: No. **Range:** Yes (grass).
Holes: 18. **Par:** 71. **Yards:** 6,788-5,012. **Slope:** 133-Unrated.
Comments: "Excellent subdivision course . . . Well-kept, nice bent-grass greens . . . Interesting, several challenges . . . Unattractive par 3s . . . Out-of-bounds right and left on every hole."

★★THREE RIDGES GOLF COURSE
Knoxville—PU—615-687-4797.
Season: Year-round. **High:** April-Sept. **Caddies:** No.
Green fee: Under $20. **Credit cards:** V, AMEX, DISC, MC.
Lodging on site: No. **Reduced fees:** Weekdays, Twilight Play.
Unrestricted walking: Yes. **Range:** Yes (grass).
Holes: 18. **Par:** 72. **Yards:** 6,825-5,200. **Slope:** 128-121.
Comments: "Challenging, fairways still thin . . . Good practice facilities
. . . Good bunkers . . . Too many bunkers for a muny . . . Difficult to walk
. . . Nos. 10 and 11 should be redone . . . Spotty conditions."

TWO RIVERS GOLF COURSE*
Nashville—PU—615-889-2675.
Season: Year-round. **High:** April-Sept. **Caddies:** No.
Green fee: Under $20. **Credit cards:** No.
Lodging on site: No. **Reduced fees:** No.
Unrestricted walking: Yes. **Range:** No.
Holes: 18. **Par:** 72. **Yards:** 6,595-5,336. **Slope:** 120-116.

WARRIOR'S PATH STATE PARK*
Kingsport—PU—615-323-4990 (100 mi. from Knoxville).
Season: Year-round. **High:** Summer. **Caddies:** No.
Green fee: Under $20. **Credit cards:** V, AMEX, MC.
Lodging on site: No. **Reduced fees:** Weekdays.
Unrestricted walking: Yes. **Range:** Yes (grass).
Holes: 18. **Par:** 72. **Yards:** 6,581-5,428. **Slope:** 115-117.

WHITTLE SPRINGS GOLF COURSE*
Knoxville—PU—615-525-1022.
Season: Year-round. **High:** Jan.-Sept. **Caddies:** No.
Green fee: Under $20. **Credit cards:** No.
Lodging on site: No. **Reduced fees:** No.
Unrestricted walking: Yes. **Range:** Yes (grass).
Holes: 18. **Par:** 70. **Yards:** 6,000-4,884. **Slope:** 110-106.
Oldest course in the city of Knoxville.

★★★½ WILLOW CREEK GOLF CLUB
Knoxville—PU—615-675-0100.
Season: Year-round. **High:** April-Oct. **Caddies:** No.
Green fee: $20-$49. **Credit cards:** V, AMEX, MC.
Lodging on site: No. **Reduced fees:** Weekdays, Low Season.
Unrestricted walking: No. **Range:** Yes (grass).
Holes: 18. **Par:** 72. **Yards:** 6,936-5,557. **Slope:** 124-119.
Host to the Nike Tour's Knoxville Open.
Comments: "A total golf challenge . . . A 'must play' . . . Best back 9 in
east Tennessee . . . Perfectly maintained year-round . . . Some great holes,
some dull ones . . . Five hours of 'cart golf.' "

★★★WINDTREE GOLF COURSE
Mt. Juliet—PU—615-754-4653 (15 mi. from Nashville).
Season: Year-round. **High:** April-Sept. **Caddies:** No.
Green fee: $20-$49. **Credit cards:** V, AMEX, MC.
Reduced fees: Weekdays, Low Season, Twilight Play.
Unrestricted walking: No. **Range:** Yes (grass).
Holes: 18. **Par:** 72. **Yards:** 6,669-5,245. **Slope:** 126-117.
Comments: "An up-and-comer . . . Not far from great . . . Nice changes
in elevation . . . Back 9 especially hilly . . . Great par 3s . . . . . . An 'Atta-
boy' for their efforts to speed play . . . Most interestingly designed greens
I've played . . . Greens have awful 'novelty gag' depressions in them . . .
Greens just need some windmills."

BARTON CREEK RESORT & COUNTRY CLUB

Austin—R—512-329-4000, 800-336-6158.

Season: Year-round. **High:** March-Nov. **Caddies:** No.
Green fee: $50-$99. **Credit cards:** All Major.
Lodging on site: Yes. **Reduced fees:** Weekdays, Low Season.
Unrestricted walking: Yes. **Range:** Yes (grass).

★★CRENSHAW-COORE COURSE

Holes: 18. **Par:** 71. **Yards:** 6,678-4,843. **Slope:** 116-110.
Comments: "Quirky . . . Fun and fair . . . My kind of minimal architecture . . . Scottish style in Hill country . . . Not as difficult as the Fazio . . . Greens almost too big . . . Too many blind shots, unfair greens . . . Dig it up and start over."

★★★★½ FAZIO COURSE

Green fee: $100 and up.
Holes: 18. **Par:** 72. **Yards:** 6,956-5,098. **Slope:** 130-118.
Ranked 60th in America's 100 Greatest Golf Courses and ranked 21st in America's 75 Best Resort Courses by GOLF DIGEST 1992.
Comments: "An original . . . Most esthetic course in Texas . . . Best in Texas, bar none . . . Great example of Tom Fazio's spirit . . . Super in every way . . . Not ridiculously hard . . . Nos. 9 and 18 are great holes . . . Caves! Waterfalls! Magnificent . . . A-1 accommodations . . . Top notch in every aspect . . . Out of reach in cost for most of us."

★★★½ PALMER-LAKESIDE COURSE

Lake Travis—R—210-693-4589, 800-888-2257 (7 mi. from Austin).

Season: Year-round. **High:** March-Nov. **Caddies:** No.
Green fee: $50-$99. **Credit cards:** All Major.
Lodging on site: No. **Reduced fees:** Weekdays, Low Season.
Unrestricted walking: Yes. **Range:** Yes (grass).
Holes: 18. **Par:** 71. **Yards:** 6,622-5,063. **Slope:** 123-110.
Comments: "Well-kept secret . . . Excellent . . . Well balanced . . . Like Augusta National, no rough . . . Always in fantastic shape . . . View from the clubhouse is incredible . . . Miles from lodging . . . Worth the drive from Austin . . . Unnecessary out-of-bounds stakes."

★★★BAY FOREST GOLF COURSE

LaPorte—PU—713-471-4653 (10 mi. from Houston).

Season: Year-round. **High:** Sept.-Oct. **Caddies:** No.
Green fee: Under $20. **Credit cards:** V, MC.
Lodging on site: No. **Reduced fees:** Twilight Play.
Unrestricted walking: Yes. **Range:** Yes (grass).
Holes: 18. **Par:** 72. **Yards:** 6,872-6,235. **Slope:** 126-122.
Comments: "Nicely-maintained muny . . . Extremely reasonable fees . . . Three par 3s on front, three par 5s on back . . . Lots of water . . . Almost impossible to get tee times."

BEAR CREEK GOLF WORLD

Houston—PU—713-859-8188.

Season: Year-round. **High:** Summer/Fall. **Caddies:** No.
Green fee: $20-$49. **Credit cards:** V, MC, AMEX.
Lodging on site: No. **Reduced fees:** Twilight Play.
Unrestricted walking: No. **Range:** Yes (grass).

★★★MASTERS COURSE

Holes: 18. **Par:** 72. **Yards:** 7,131-6,188. **Slope:** 133-123.
Ranked in Second 25 of America's 75 Best Public Courses by GOLF DIGEST.
Comments: "Great traditional-style course, long and tough . . . Interesting, well-kept, fair test . . . Mucho trees and water, straight shots only . . . Nine and 18 hard finishers . . . Best in Houston area . . . Most overrated course in Houston . . . Mandatory carts a serious drawback . . . Much better maintained in past years . . . Greens need work . . . They don't move the pins often enough."

★★PRESIDENTS COURSE

Unrestricted walking: Yes.
Holes: 18. **Par:** 72. **Yards:** 6,562-6,115. **Slope:** 110-107.

Comments: "Beginner's course . . . Confidence builder . . . Wide and forgiving . . . Too flat . . . Too dry . . . Too easy . . . Floods easily . . . One big driving range . . . Lots of wear and tear, high fee for the area."
CHALLENGER COURSE*
Unrestricted walking: Yes.
Holes: 18. **Par:** 66. **Yards:** 5,295-4,097. **Slope:** 103-99.

★★½ BLACKHAWK GOLF CLUB
Pflugerville—PU—512-251-9000 (10 mi. from Austin).
Season: Year-round. **High:** March-July. **Caddies:** No.
Green fee: $20-$49. **Credit cards:** V, AMEX, MC.
Lodging on site: No. **Reduced fees:** Twilight Play.
Unrestricted walking: No. **Range:** Yes (grass).
Holes: 18. **Par:** 72. **Yards:** 7,103-5,538. **Slope:** 123-121.
Comments: "Affordable . . . Not that interesting . . . Flat, few trees . . . Greens were patchy . . . Bent greens are a bust."

★★★★ BUFFALO CREEK GOLF CLUB
Rockwall—PU—214-771-4003 (20 mi. from Dallas).
Season: Year-round. **High:** April-Oct. **Caddies:** No.
Green fee: $20-$49. **Credit cards:** V, AMEX, MC.
Reduced fees: Weekdays, Low Season, Twilight Play.
Unrestricted walking: No. **Range:** Yes (grass).
Holes: 18. **Par:** 71. **Yards:** 7,018-5,209. **Slope:** 133-113.
Comments: "Great new course . . . Outstanding . . . Can't be beat . . . Nice terrain . . . Has character . . . Tough but interesting . . . Excellent playability . . . Perfect greens . . . Best in Dallas area, maybe the state . . . Fine Morrish/Weiskopf design, but too expensive for a small town."

★★★½ CEDAR CREEK GOLF COURSE
San Antonio—PU—210-695-5050.
Season: Year-round. **High:** Year-round. **Caddies:** No.
Green fee: $20-$49. **Credit cards:** No.
Lodging on site: No. **Reduced fees:** No.
Unrestricted walking: Yes. **Range:** Yes (mats).
Holes: 18. **Par:** 72. **Yards:** 7,150-6,629. **Slope:** 132-118.
Comments: "No one would believe this is a muny . . . Best new muny in San Antonio . . . In the U.S. . . . Great layout . . . Few level lies . . . Rocky rough . . . Greens need work . . . Some blind shots . . . They let fivesomes out. Not good . . . Six hours, even on a weekday."

CHASE OAKS GOLF CLUB
★★★½ BLACKJACK COURSE
Plano—PU—214-517-7777.
Season: Year-round. **High:** March-Nov. **Caddies:** No.
Green fee: $20-$49. **Credit cards:** V, AMEX, DISC, MC.
Lodging on site: No. **Reduced fees:** Low Season, Twilight Play.
Unrestricted walking: No. **Range:** Yes (grass).
Holes: 18. **Par:** 72. **Yards:** 6,811-6,292. **Slope:** 139-134.
Also has 9-hole Sawtooth Course featuring separate sets of tees for front and back.
Comments: "Outstanding course with cost in reach of everyone . . . A real treat . . . Country club atmosphere . . . Shotmaker's course. . . . Pretty but unfair . . . Some trick holes but solid over all . . . Get rid of half the moguls . . . Need to play it twice to understand hitting areas . . . Great practice facility . . . Does not allow carts off paths . . . Miles from greens to next tees."

★★★½ CIRCLE C GOLF CLUB
Austin—PU—512-288-4297.
Season: Year-round. **High:** Spring/Fall. **Caddies:** No.
Green fee: $20-$49. **Credit cards:** V, AMEX, MC.
Lodging on site: No. **Reduced fees:** Weekdays, Twilight Play.
Unrestricted walking: No. **Range:** Yes (grass).

Holes: 18. **Par:** 72. **Yards:** 6,859-5,236. **Slope:** 122-120.
Comments: "Excellent . . . True Hill Country course . . . Very courteous pro shop . . . Four putts possible on several holes."

★★½ CLUB DEL LAGO

Montgomery—R—409-582-6100, 800-833-3078 (50 mi. from Houston).
Season: Year-round. **High:** May-Oct. **Caddies:** No.
Green fee: $20-$49. **Credit cards:** All Major.
Lodging on site: Yes. **Reduced fees:** Weekdays, Resort Guests, Twilight Play.
Unrestricted walking: Yes. **Range:** Yes (grass).
Holes: 18. **Par:** 71. **Yards:** 6,907-6,467. **Slope:** 122-113.
Comments: "Open, easy, interesting . . . Relaxing track . . . Fun for anyone . . . No. 9 is very tough . . . Needs work on fairways . . . Boring."

★★★COLUMBIA LAKES

West Columbia—R—409-345-5455 (50 mi. from Houston).
Season: Year-round. **High:** Spring/Fall. **Caddies:** No.
Green fee: $50-$99. **Credit cards:** All Major.
Lodging on site: Yes. **Reduced fees:** Weekdays, Low Season, Resort Guests.
Unrestricted walking: Yes. **Range:** Yes (grass).
Holes: 18. **Par:** 72. **Yards:** 6,997-6,300. **Slope:** 131-125.
Comments: "Good layout, fun course, use every club in the bag . . . Great undulating greens . . . Not much imagination . . . Weak holes on back 9."

★★COUNTRY VIEW GOLF CLUB

Lancaster—PU—214-227-0995 (15 mi. from Dallas).
Season: Year-round. **High:** May-Aug. **Caddies:** No.
Green fee: Under $20. **Credit cards:** V, MC.
Lodging on site: No. **Reduced fees:** Weekdays, Twilight Play.
Unrestricted walking: Yes. **Range:** Yes (mats).
Holes: 18. **Par:** 71. **Yards:** 6,610-5,048. **Slope:** 116-116.
Comments: "Not very impressive . . . Too many elevated greens . . . Great people . . . Very helpful . . . Maintenance on the rebound."

★½ CRYSTAL FALLS GOLF COURSE

Leander—PU—512-259-5855 (14 mi. from Austin).
Season: Year-round. **High:** April-Oct. **Caddies:** No.
Green fee: Under $20. **Credit cards:** V, MC.
Reduced fees: Weekdays, Low Season, Twilight Play.
Unrestricted walking: Yes. **Range:** Yes (grass).
Holes: 18. **Par:** 72. **Yards:** 6,654-6,164. **Slope:** 126-122.
Comments: "Meanest, most unfair course I've ever played . . . Built on the side of a mountain, literally . . . Nothing but sloping fairways and blind shots . . . No rough, just fairway and brush . . . It's even got blind par 3s! . . . Terrible shape."

CYPRESSWOOD GOLF CLUB

Spring—PU—713-821-6300 (15 mi. from Houston).
Season: Year-round. **High:** Spring/Fall. **Caddies:** No.
Green fee: $20-$49. **Credit cards:** V, AMEX, MC.
Lodging on site: No. **Reduced fees:** Weekdays, Twilight Play.
Unrestricted walking: Yes. **Range:** Yes (grass).
★★★CREEK COURSE
Holes: 18. **Par:** 72. **Yards:** 6,930-5,549. **Slope:** 124-113.
Comments: "Wide open, challenging yet very enjoyable . . . Always in good shape . . . Good use of terrain . . . Creek is the better of the two."
★★★CYPRESS COURSE
Holes: 18. **Par:** 72. **Yards:** 6,906-5,602. **Slope:** 123-111.
Comments: "Both courses are great . . . Rolling terrain with heavily wooded pine trees . . . Both 18s are a good value . . . Cypress is one of the best public courses in Texas."

★★½ DELAWARE SPRINGS GOLF CLUB
Burnet—PU—512-756-8471 (50 mi. from Austin).
Season: Year-round. **High:** Year-round. **Caddies:** No.
Green fee: Under $20. **Credit cards:** V, AMEX, DISC, MC.
Lodging on site: No. **Reduced fees:** Twilight Play.
Unrestricted walking: No. **Range:** Yes (grass).
Holes: 18. **Par:** 72. **Yards:** 6,850-5,000. **Slope:** 121-108.

FIREWHEEL GOLF PARK
Garland—PU—214-205-2795 (25 mi. from Dallas).
Season: Year-round. **High:** May-Sept. **Caddies:** No.
Green fee: $20-$49. **Credit cards:** V, AMEX, MC.
Reduced fees: Weekdays, Low Season, Twilight Play.
Unrestricted walking: Yes. **Range:** Yes (grass).
★★★LAKES COURSE
Holes: 18. **Par:** 71. **Yards:** 6,625-5,215. **Slope:** 126-110.
Comments: "Short, scenic, well bunkered, interesting . . . Makes you play a lot of shots . . . Tough on first timers . . . Lots of sand and water . . . Many blind shots . . . Nicer than the Old . . . Not as good as the Old . . . Greens have improved . . . Maintenance no longer a problem . . . Now first class with new greenkeeper."
★★★OLD COURSE
Holes: 18. **Par:** 72. **Yards:** 7,054-5,692. **Slope:** 129-117.
Comments: "A classic . . . Appealing setting . . . Private-club atmosphere . . . Could hold a national publinx . . . Great test when wind blows . . . Hospitable staff."

★★★FOREST CREEK GOLF CLUB
Round Rock—PU—512-388-2874 (18 mi. from Austin).
Season: Year-round. **High:** April-July. **Caddies:** No.
Green fee: $20-$49. **Credit cards:** V, AMEX, MC.
Lodging on site: No. **Reduced fees:** Low Season, Twilight Play.
Unrestricted walking: Yes. **Range:** Yes (grass).
Holes: 18. **Par:** 72. **Yards:** 7,084-5,600. **Slope:** 132-121.
Comments: "Pleasant surprise . . . Challenging and fun . . . No forced tee shots . . . Best public course in Austin area."

FOUR SEASONS RESORT & CLUB
Irving—R—214-717-2530 (5 mi. from Dallas).
Season: Year-round. **High:** Spring/Fall. **Caddies:** No.
Green fee: $100 and up. **Credit cards:** All Major.
Lodging on site: Yes. **Reduced fees:** No.
Unrestricted walking: No. **Range:** Yes (grass).
Club also has private Cottonwood Valley 18.
★★½ TOURNAMENT PLAYERS COURSE
Holes: 18. **Par:** 70. **Yards:** 6,899-5,340. **Slope:** 135-116.
Site of PGA Tour's Byron Nelson Classic.
Comments: "Manicured to the hilt. What else would you expect where the pros play? . . . Best at tournament time . . . Disappointing . . . Long boring typical TPC . . . Front 9 has no character . . . Course needs two more par 5s . . . If only we could walk . . . You'll need a loan for green fee . . . Phenomenal hotel."

★½ FOX CREEK GOLF COURSE
Hempstead—PU—409-826-2131 (40 mi. from Houston).
Season: Year-round. **High:** March-Sept. **Caddies:** No.
Green fee: Under $20. **Credit cards:** V, MC.
Lodging on site: No. **Reduced fees:** Weekdays, Twilight Play.
Unrestricted walking: Yes. **Range:** Yes (grass).
Holes: 18. **Par:** 70. **Yards:** 5,750-4,680. **Slope:** Unrated.
Comments: "Very short . . . Dull . . . A real pasture . . . Water on almost every hole . . . How bad is it? First hole is a par 3."

★★½ GALVESTON ISLAND MUNICIPAL GOLF COURSE
Galveston—PU—409-744-2366 (45 mi. from Houston).
Season: Year-round. **High:** June-Aug. **Caddies:** No.
Green fee: Under $20. **Credit cards:** V, AMEX, MC.
Lodging on site: No. **Reduced fees:** Weekdays, Twilight Play.
Unrestricted walking: No. **Range:** Yes (grass).
Holes: 18. **Par:** 72. **Yards:** 6,969-5,407. **Slope:** 115-121.
Comments: "Not laid out well . . . Too much water . . . Water on all 18 holes . . . Narrow fairways not needed for such windy conditions . . . Too far between holes to carry a bag . . . Poor pro shop."

GARDEN VALLEY GOLF RESORT
Lindale—R—903-882-6107, 800-443-8577 (80 mi. from Dallas).
Season: Year-round. **High:** March-Oct. **Caddies:** No.
Green fee: $50-$99. **Credit cards:** V, AMEX, MC.
Lodging on site: Yes. **Reduced fees:** Low Season.
Unrestricted walking: No. **Range:** Yes (grass).
★★★★DOGWOOD COURSE
Holes: 18. **Par:** 72. **Yards:** 6,754-6,269. **Slope:** 132-126.
Comments: "The Augusta National of Texas . . . A great find in the middle of nowhere . . . Beautiful . . . Outstanding pines . . . Expertly maintained . . . Too bad you can't walk it . . . Condos are great."
★★½ HUMMINGBIRD COURSE
Green fee: Under $20. **Reduced fees:** Seniors, Guests, Twilight Play.
Unrestricted walking: Yes.
Holes: 18. **Par:** 71. **Yards:** 6,446-5,955. **Slope:** Unrated.
Comments: "Have let it go some since completing Dogwood . . . Has potential with some work."

★★GRAPEVINE GOLF COURSE
Grapevine—PU—817-481-0421 (10 mi. from Dallas).
Season: Year-round. **High:** April-Sept. **Caddies:** No.
Green fee: Under $20. **Credit cards:** V, MC.
Lodging on site: No. **Reduced fees:** No.
Unrestricted walking: Yes. **Range:** Yes (grass).
Holes: 18. **Par:** 72. **Yards:** 6,953-6,503. **Slope:** 113-113.
Comments: "Great course on upswing after years of slight neglect . . . Toughest tee time in the Metroplex . . . Not challenging, bad shape . . . Only a few good holes . . . A poor man's course: poor layout, poor maintenance . . . Bad floods periodically hurt course . . . Greens in terrible shape, less than cordial atmosphere . . . Costs higher than most other munys . . . Great potential, poorly run."

★★★½ HILL COUNTRY GOLF CLUB
San Antonio—R—210-520-4040.
Season: Year-round. **High:** Year-round. **Caddies:** No.
Green fee: $50-$99. **Credit cards:** All Major.
Lodging on site: Yes. **Reduced fees:** Weekdays, Resort Guests.
Unrestricted walking: No. **Range:** Yes (grass).
Holes: 18. **Par:** 72. **Yards:** 6,913-4,781. **Slope:** 136-Unrated.
Comments: "Best new course in San Antonio . . . In the United States . . . Too pricey for average golfer."

HORSESHOE BAY RESORT & CONFERENCE CENTER
Horseshoe Bay—R—800-531-5105 (47 mi. from Austin).
Season: Year-round. **High:** March-Nov. **Caddies:** No.
Green fee: $50-$99. **Credit cards:** V, MC, DISC.
Lodging on site: Yes. **Reduced fees:** Weekdays, Low Season, Resort Guests.
Unrestricted walking: No. **Range:** Yes (grass).
★★★★APPLEROCK COURSE
Holes: 18. **Par:** 72. **Yards:** 6,999-5,480. **Slope:** 134-117.
Selected Best New Resort Course of 1986 by GOLF DIGEST. Plays along shoreline of Lake LBJ.

257

Comments: "Superb . . . Most fun ever . . . Terrain a plus . . . Less punishing than Ram Rock . . . Suited for the average golfer . . . Deer late in the day . . . Some weak par 4s on back . . . Poor food service."

★★★★RAM ROCK COURSE

Holes: 18. **Par:** 71. **Yards:** 6,946-5,306. **Slope:** 137-121.

Ranked 40th in America's 75 Best Resort Courses by GOLF DIGEST.

Comments: "A very fine test . . . Extremely well bunkered . . . Perfect greens . . . Difficult . . . Hardest ever . . . So hard! Why is it so fun? . . . Bring your knee pads . . . Best Hill Country views in Texas . . . Incredible attention to landscaping details . . . Rock work alone is worth the trip . . . Plush facilities . . . Restaurants are only negative."

★★★½ SLICK ROCK COURSE

Holes: 18. **Par:** 72. **Yards:** 6,834-5,832. **Slope:** 125-115.

Comments: "Very playable, well maintained . . . Three great finishing holes . . . Easiest of the three . . . Best greens . . . Incredible, tremendous waterfall on No. 14 . . . Simply great."

HYATT BEAR CREEK GOLF & RACQUET CLUB

DFW Airport—R—214-615-6800 (20 mi. from Dallas).

Season: Year-round. **High:** April-Nov. **Caddies:** No.

Green fee: $20-$49. **Credit cards:** All Major.

Lodging on site: Yes. **Reduced fees:** Low Season, Twilight Play.

Unrestricted walking: Yes. **Range:** Yes (grass).

★★★½ EAST COURSE

Holes: 18. **Par:** 72. **Yards:** 6,670-6,282. **Slope:** 127-114.

Comments: "Deceptive, well bunkered . . . Hilly, tight . . . Enjoyed it immensely . . . But staying on cart paths slows play . . . Planes a pain! . . . Noisy . . . Pro shop has good selection of merchandise."

★★★½ WEST COURSE

Holes: 18. **Par:** 72. **Yards:** 6,670-5,630. **Slope:** 130-121.

Comments: "A player's layout . . . Slightly better than the East . . . Jets drive you crazy."

INDIAN CREEK GOLF CLUB

Carrollton—PU—214-492-3620 (15 mi. from Dallas).

Season: Year-round. **High:** Year-round. **Caddies:** No.

Green fee: $20-$49. **Credit cards:** V, MC.

Lodging on site: No. **Reduced fees:** Weekdays, Twilight Play.

Unrestricted walking: Yes. **Range:** Yes (grass).

★★★CREEK COURSE

Holes: 18. **Par:** 72. **Yards:** 7,218-4,967. **Slope:** Unrated.

Comments: "Good course, well maintained . . . Difficult and fair . . . Last three holes are tough . . . Target golf. Lots of long carries . . . Better than Lakes but no bent greens . . . Dollar for dollar the best around . . . Very slow play . . . Course has too much trouble for average players."

★★★LAKES COURSE

Holes: 18. **Par:** 72. **Yards:** 7,060-5,367. **Slope:** 122-114.

Comments: "Wonderful . . . Good test, some gorgeous holes . . . Tons of lakes . . . If hydrophobic, stay away . . . Look out for No. 9 . . . Can play tough when wind blows . . . Best bent-grass greens of any public course . . . Best value in DFW . . . Floods too much . . . Every hole looks the same . . . Unreasonable carts-on-paths rule."

★★★IRON HORSE GOLF COURSE

N. Richland Hills—PU—817-485-6666 (2 mi. from Fort Worth).

Season: Year-round. **High:** Year-round. **Caddies:** No.

Green fee: $20-$49. **Credit cards:** V, AMEX, MC.

Lodging on site: No. **Reduced fees:** Weekdays, Twilight Play.

Unrestricted walking: Yes. **Range:** Yes (grass).

Holes: 18. **Par:** 70. **Yards:** 6,580-5,684. **Slope:** 130-114.

Comments: "Very nice . . . Super layout . . . Excellent variety of par 4s . . . Sharp doglegs . . . Great bargain . . . Don't tell anyone about this jewel . . . On too small a parcel . . . Golf ball eater . . . Golfers seen as dollar signs."

★★½ JIMMY CLAY GOLF COURSE
Austin—PU—512-444-0999.
Season: Year-round. **High:** March-Aug. **Caddies:** No.
Green fee: Under $20. **Credit cards:** V, AMEX, MC, DISC.
Lodging on site: No. **Reduced fees:** Weekdays, Twilight Play.
Unrestricted walking: Yes. **Range:** Yes (grass).
Holes: 18. **Par:** 72. **Yards:** 6,857-6,368. **Slope:** Unrated.
Comments: "Old Austin standby . . . Well maintained for muny, reasonably challenging . . . Usually breezy, easy to walk . . . Wide open for hackers . . . Great place to start the game."

LAKEWAY RESORT
Austin—R—512-261-7573, 800-525-3929.
Season: Year-round. **High:** Spring/Fall. **Caddies:** No.
Green fee: $20-$49. **Credit cards:** V, AMEX, MC.
Lodging on site: Yes. **Reduced fees:** Weekdays.
Unrestricted walking: Yes. **Range:** Yes (grass).
★★½ LIVE OAK COURSE
Holes: 18. **Par:** 72. **Yards:** 6,643-5,472. **Slope:** 121-122.
Comments: "Flat, tree lined . . . Not bad, not great . . . Pretty predictable . . . Forgettable . . . Very poor greens . . . No sand . . . Run down."
★★½ YAUPON COURSE
Holes: 18. **Par:** 72. **Yards:** 6,565-5,032. **Slope:** 123-119.
Comments: "Nice and relaxing . . . Deer along many fairways . . . Severely up and down . . . Numerous blind shots . . . Bring a bulldozer."

★★½ LIONS MUNICIPAL GOLF COURSE
Austin—PU—512-477-6963.
Season: Year-round. **High:** June-Aug. **Caddies:** No.
Green Fee: Under $20. **Credit cards:** No.
Lodging on site: No. **Reduced fees:** Twilight Play.
Unrestricted walking: Yes. **Range:** Yes (mats).
Holes: 18. **Par:** 71. **Yards:** 6,001-4,931. **Slope:** 118-Unrated.
Comments: "The best little muny in Texas . . . An Austin favorite . . . Short n' sweet . . . Older and better . . . Huge oaks . . . Easy to walk . . . No one can stay away from this gem . . . 16th is called Hogan's hole . . . Only its conditioning is questionable."

★★★½ MARRIOTT'S GOLF CLUB AT FOSSIL CREEK
Fort Worth—PU—817-847-1900.
Season: Year-round. **High:** March-Oct. **Caddies:** No.
Green fee: $50-$99. **Credit cards:** V, AMEX, MC.
Reduced fees: Weekdays, Low Season, Twilight Play.
Unrestricted walking: No. **Range:** Yes (grass).
Holes: 18. **Par:** 72. **Yards:** 6,865-5,066. **Slope:** 131-111.
Comments: "Incredible . . . One of the best . . . Best in Fort Worth . . . A little of everything . . . A real pleasure . . . Attracts golfers who take care of the course . . . Nice job, Arnie . . . Great hot dogs . . . The grill closes at 2 p.m. . . . Slowest course on earth . . . The prices! Ouch!"

★★ MEMORIAL PARK GOLF COURSE
Houston—PU—713-862-4033.
Season: Year-round. **High:** April-Aug. **Caddies:** No.
Green fee: Under $20. **Credit cards:** No.
Lodging on site: No. **Reduced fees:** Weekdays, Twilight Play.
Unrestricted walking: Yes. **Range:** Yes (grass).
Holes: 18. **Par:** 72. **Yards:** 7,380-6,140. **Slope:** Unrated.
Comments: "Great muny . . . Flat, easy walk, lots of trees . . . Historic . . . Long and beat up . . . You can grip-it-and-rip-it here . . . Can't beat the price . . . Could be the best in Houston with any care at all . . . Needs a lot of attention . . . Too old to care . . . Raise the fee! This needs maintenance money . . . Course revenues just go into city fund. Not good."

TEXAS

★★MORRIS WILLIAMS GOLF CLUB
Austin—PU—512-926-1298.
Season: Year-round. **High:** Jan-Oct. **Caddies:** No.
Green fee: Under $20. **Credit cards:** V, MC, DISC.
Lodging on site: No. **Reduced fees:** Weekdays, Twilight Play.
Unrestricted walking: Yes. **Range:** Yes (grass).
Holes: 18. **Par:** 72. **Yards:** 6,636-5,273. **Slope:** 121-117.
Comments: "Windy old Austin muny, hilly with medium trees . . . Tight in spots, open in others . . . On airport glidepath . . . Planes over putts . . . A major distraction . . . Turf too thin in areas . . . Fairways need work."

★★★OLD ORCHARD GOLF CLUB
BARN/RANGE/STABLES 9s
Richmond—PU—713-277-3300 (10 mi. from Houston).
Season: Year-round. **High:** March-Oct. **Caddies:** No.
Green fee: $50-$99. **Credit cards:** V, AMEX, MC.
Lodging on site: No. **Reduced fees:** Twilight Play.
Unrestricted walking: No. **Range:** Yes (grass).
Holes: 27. **Par:** 36/36/36. **Yards:** 3,564/3,363/3,324.
Comments: "Interesting, old-style layout . . . Cut from pecan orchard . . . Very nice . . . First class . . . Well groomed . . . Finest daily-fee course in Houston area . . . Barn and Stables the best 9s . . . Range 9 too open . . . Real ranch house is now restaurant . . . Too much traffic . . . Overpriced . . . Not worth what they charge."

★★★★PAINTED DUNES DESERT GOLF COURSE
El Paso—PU—915-821-2122.
Season: Year-round. **High:** Spring/Fall. **Caddies:** No.
Green fee: Under $20. **Credit cards:** V, AMEX, MC.
Lodging on site: No. **Reduced fees:** Weekdays, Twilight Play.
Unrestricted walking: Yes. **Range:** Yes (grass).
Holes: 18. **Par:** 72. **Yards:** 6,925-6,162. **Slope:** 135-122.
Comments: "Wonderful 'desert-style' layout . . . With no hills! . . . Beautiful . . . Outstanding condition . . . What a surprise . . . In a word, Awesome! . . . Fast bent-grass greens . . . Pro shop great . . . Best value in golf . . . All public courses should be like this . . . Still lacks some amenities . . . Too hot in summer to play without shade trees."

★★★PECAN VALLEY GOLF CLUB
San Antonio—PU—210-333-9018, 800-336-3418.
Season: Year-round. **High:** Spring/Fall. **Caddies:** No.
Green fee: $20-$49. **Credit cards:** V, AMEX, MC.
Reduced fees: Weekdays, Low Season, Resort Guests, Twilight Play.
Unrestricted walking: No. **Range:** Yes (grass).
Holes: 18. **Par:** 71. **Yards:** 7,074-5,621. **Slope:** 136-118.
Ranked in Second 25 of America's 75 Best Public Courses by GOLF DIGEST. Site of 1968 PGA Championship.
Comments: "Majestic . . . Excellent layout . . . A quality course . . . A classic beauty . . . Lots of tradition . . . Tight . . . A zillion pecan trees . . . In better shape every year . . . Very friendly . . . Country club atmosphere without the price . . . Tremendous experience when in shape . . . Still nice but sad . . . Needs updating . . . Greens need work, bigtime."

★★PLANTATION RESORT GOLF CLUB
Frisco—PU—214-335-4653 (20 mi. from Dallas).
Season: Year-round. **High:** Year-round. **Caddies:** No.
Green fee: $20-$49. **Credit cards:** V, AMEX, MC.
Lodging on site: No. **Reduced fees:** Weekdays, Twilight Play.
Unrestricted walking: No. **Range:** Yes (grass).
Holes: 18. **Par:** 72. **Yards:** 6,382-5,945. **Slope:** 122-117.
Comments: "Flat and easy, shoot lights out . . . Boring target golf . . . Too short. Driver-wedge, driver-wedge . . . Good practice course."

★★★½ THE RANCH COUNTRY CLUB
AT STONEBRIDGE RANCH
McKinney—PU—214-540-2200 (25 mi. from Dallas).
Season: Year-round. **High:** March-Oct. **Caddies:** No.
Green fee: $50-$99. **Credit cards:** V, MC.
Lodging on site: Yes. **Reduced fees:** Weekdays, Low Season,
Twilight Play.
Unrestricted walking: No. **Range:** Yes (grass).
Holes: 18. **Par:** 72. **Yards:** 7,087-5,053. **Slope:** 130-117.
Comments: "Classy . . . Outstanding . . . Exceptional . . . Lush . . .
Tough from the tips . . . Tough in the wind . . . Tough but fair . . . Big fast
greens . . . Worth every cent . . . Not the prettiest."

RANCHO VIEJO RESORT & COUNTRY CLUB
Rancho Viejo—R—210-350-4359 (7 mi. from Brownsville).
Season: Year-round. **High:** Oct.-May. **Caddies:** No.
Green fee: $20-$49. **Credit cards:** All Major.
Lodging on site: Yes. **Reduced fees:** Resort Guests.
Unrestricted walking: No. **Range:** Yes (grass).
★★EL ANGEL COURSE
Holes: 18. **Par:** 70. **Yards:** 6,647-5,331. **Slope:** 119-115.
Comments: "Good greens and fairways, could be more difficult . . . Tough
in the wind . . . Below-average design . . . Minimal maintenance."
★★½ EL DIABLO COURSE
Holes: 18. **Par:** 70. **Yards:** 6,899-5,700. **Slope:** 121-123.
Comments: "Very flat, sand traps make it a devil . . . Good fairways and
greens . . . Fair course conditions . . . Good course for the Valley but over-
priced . . . Fine resort but prices escalating."

★★★½ RATLIFF RANCH GOLF LINKS
Odessa—PU—915-368-4653.
Season: Year-round. **High:** April-Sept. **Caddies:** No.
Green fee: Under $20. **Credit cards:** V, AMEX, MC.
Lodging on site: No. **Reduced fees:** Weekdays, Twilight Play.
Unrestricted walking: Yes. **Range:** Yes (grass).
Holes: 18. **Par:** 72. **Yards:** 6,800-6,243. **Slope:** 122-117.
Comments: "Excellent design . . . Best layout around Odessa . . . Funky
greens."

★★★½ RAYBURN COUNTRY CLUB & RESORT
BLUE/GOLD/GREEN 9s
Sam Rayburn—R—800-882-1442 (50 mi. from Lufkin).
Season: Year-round. **High:** March-Nov. **Caddies:** No.
Green fee: $20-$49. **Credit cards:** V, AMEX, MC, DISC.
Lodging on site: Yes. **Reduced fees:** Weekdays, Low Season.
Unrestricted walking: No. **Range:** Yes (grass).
Holes: 27. **Par:** 36/36/36. **Yards:** 3,361/3,370/3,358.
Comments: "Three 9s, three famous designers . . . An east Texas favorite
. . . Beautiful piney woods . . . Better since members became owners . . .
Lodging and restaurant outstanding . . . Best bargain going."

★★RIVERCHASE GOLF CLUB
Coppell—PU—214-462-8281 (5 mi. from Dallas).
Season: Year-round. **High:** April-Oct. **Caddies:** No.
Green fee: $20-$49. **Credit cards:** V, AMEX, MC.
Reduced fees: Weekdays, Low Season, Twilight Play.
Unrestricted walking: No. **Range:** Yes (mats).
Holes: 18. **Par:** 71. **Yards:** 6,592-6,041. **Slope:** 124-114.
Comments: "Design problems . . . No trees, wide open . . . Winds control
everything . . . Dull . . . No atmosphere . . . Huge electrical towers go
through course . . . Definitely not a $45 course."

★★½ RIVERSIDE GOLF COURSE
Austin—PU—512-389-1070.
Season: Year-round. **High:** May-June. **Caddies:** No.
Green fee: Under $20. **Credit cards:** All Major.
Reduced fees: Weekdays, Low Season, Twilight Play.
Unrestricted walking: Yes. **Range:** No.
Holes: 18. **Par:** 71. **Yards:** 6,500-5,700. **Slope:** 122-118.
Comments: "Harvey Penick's old course . . . Where Crenshaw learned to putt . . . Retains only some old Austin Country Club holes . . . Some great holes, some strange ones . . . Fun but floods easily . . . Only enough maintenance to get by . . . Diligently working to return it to glory days."

★★½ RUNAWAY BAY GOLF CLUB
Runaway Bay—R—817-575-2228 (45 mi. from Fort Worth).
Season: Year-round. **High:** April-Oct. **Caddies:** No.
Green fee: Under $20. **Credit cards:** V, AMEX, MC.
Lodging on site: Yes. **Reduced fees:** Weekdays, Resort Guests, Twilight Play.
Unrestricted walking: Yes. **Range:** Yes (grass).
Holes: 18. **Par:** 71. **Yards:** 6,690-6,290. **Slope:** 116-114.
Comments: "Must attack the greens, no bump-and-runs due to heavy fringes . . . Never crowded . . . New owners much better."

★★★★ SOUTHWYCK GOLF CLUB
Pearland—PU—713-436-9999 (10 mi. from Houston).
Season: Year-round. **High:** Spring/Fall. **Caddies:** No.
Green fee: $20-$49. **Credit cards:** V, AMEX, MC.
Lodging on site: No. **Reduced fees:** Weekdays, Twilight Play.
Unrestricted walking: No. **Range:** Yes (grass).
Holes: 18. **Par:** 72. **Yards:** 7,015-6,010. **Slope:** 123-116.
Comments: "Nice surprise . . . Superior links-type design . . . Scotland south of Houston . . . Different play from different tees . . . Brutal with wind, easy without . . . Real challenge with that high rough . . . Great practice area . . . No shade, not walkable . . . Too contrived and unnatural."

★★★½ SQUAW VALLEY GOLF COURSE
Glen Rose—PU—817-897-7956, 800-831-8259 (60 mi. from Fort Worth).
Season: Year-round. **High:** March-Oct. **Caddies:** No.
Green fee: $20-$49. **Credit cards:** All Major.
Lodging on site: No. **Reduced fees:** Weekdays, Twilight Play.
Unrestricted walking: Yes. **Range:** Yes (grass).
Holes: 18. **Par:** 72. **Yards:** 7,062-6,288. **Slope:** 130-119.
Comments: "Front resembles links, back more traditional . . . Weak front, too many mounds, wide open . . . Back 9 much better . . . In trees . . . Crosses Squaw Creek six times . . . A little out of the way but worth the drive . . . Well maintained."

SUGARTREE GOLF CLUB*
Dennis—PU—817-441-8643 (30 mi. from Fort Worth).
Season: Year-round. **High:** April-Oct. **Caddies:** No.
Green fee: $20-$49. **Credit cards:** V, AMEX, MC.
Lodging on site: No. **Reduced fees:** Weekdays, Twilight Play.
Unrestricted walking: Yes. **Range:** Yes (grass).
Holes: 18. **Par:** 71. **Yards:** 6,750-6,230. **Slope:** 138-126.
Comments: "One heck of a challenge . . . Hardest unknown course around . . . Beautiful course with ecology in mind . . . A real treasure, lovingly maintained, in the middle of nowhere . . . Everything you could want . . . Serious Fort Worth golfers think nothing of driving an hour to play here."

★★★ TANGLEWOOD RESORT & COUNTRY CLUB
Pottsboro—R—903-786-4140, 800-833-6569 (70 mi. from Dallas).
Season: Year-round. **High:** April-Oct. **Caddies:** No.
Green fee: $20-$49. **Credit cards:** V, AMEX, MC, DISC.
Lodging on site: Yes. **Reduced fees:** Weekdays.

Unrestricted walking: No. **Range:** Yes (grass).
Holes: 18. **Par:** 72. **Yards:** 6,946–4,953. **Slope:** 119-104.
Comments: "Great resort course for average golfer."

★★★ TAPATIO SPRINGS RESORT & COUNTRY CLUB
Boerne—R—210-537-4197, 800-999-3299 (20 mi. from San Antonio).
Season: Year-round. **High:** March/Oct. **Caddies:** No.
Green fee: $50-$99. **Credit cards:** No.
Lodging on site: Yes. **Reduced fees:** Resort Guests.
Unrestricted walking: No. **Range:** Yes (mats).
Holes: 18. **Par:** 72. **Yards:** 6,500–6,150. **Slope:** 122-116.
Also has a 9-hole executive course.
Comments: "Fine resort course . . . Nice Hill Country setting . . . Majestic views . . . Deer roam the course . . . Remote, nice getaway . . . Very nice for the whole family . . . Pleasant surprise . . . Most hospitable . . . Hasn't recovered from hard times . . . Not worth the time or money."

TENISON PARK GOLF COURSE
Dallas—PU—214-670-1402.
Season: Year-round. **High:** May-Sept. **Caddies:** No.
Green fee: Under $20. **Credit cards:** No.
Lodging on site: No. **Reduced fees:** Weekdays, Twilight Play.
Unrestricted walking: Yes. **Range:** No.
★★½ EAST COURSE
Holes: 18. **Par:** 72. **Yards:** 6,802-5,444. **Slope:** 123-Unrated.
Comments: "Good course, very reasonable fee . . . A lot of water, no sand . . . Par 5s are birdie holes . . . Nice layout, poor upkeep . . . Good staff for a muny . . . Security can be a problem, don't play alone."
★★½ WEST COURSE
Holes: 18. **Par:** 72. **Yards:** 6,902-5,747. **Slope:** 121-Unrated.
Comments: "Fun to imagine Trevino hustling here . . . Difficult, no frills . . . Better of the two . . . Beware hilly back 9 . . . Has potential but poorly maintained . . . Some very inexpensive touchups would improve both courses a great deal."

★★★½ TOUR 18
Humble—PU—713-540-1818 (20 mi. from Houston).
Season: Year-round. **High:** Spring/Fall. **Caddies:** Yes.
Green fee: $50-$99. **Credit Cards:** V, AMEX, MC, DISC.
Lodging on Site: No. **Reduced fees:** Twilight Play.
Unrestricted walking: No. **Range:** No.
Holes: 18. **Par:** 72. **Yards:** 6,807-5,583. **Slope:** 126-113.
Course consists of attempted duplicates of 18 famous golf holes.
Comments: "What fun! . . . A great idea . . . Unique concept . . . A novelty . . . Every hole wonderfully different . . . The next best thing to the real thing . . . Traditionalists will hate it, but it's the only chance I'll ever get to play Amen Corner . . . We'll see lots more of these soon . . . Opened too soon . . . Layout exceeds condition . . Greens are bumpy . . . Fun golf but no soul . . . Overhyped . . . Totally manufactured . . . Priced as a tourist attraction . . . Trying to make all their money back at once . . . Green fee too high for a return bout."

★½ TWIN WELLS GOLF COURSE
Irving—PU—214-438-4340 (5 mi. from Dallas).
Season: Year-round. **High:** March-Dec. **Caddies:** No.
Green fee: Under $20. **Credit cards:** V, MC.
Reduced fees: Weekdays, Low Season, Twilight Play.
Unrestricted walking: Yes. **Range:** Yes (mats).
Holes: 18. **Par:** 72. **Yards:** 6,636-6,239. **Slope:** 117-113.
Comments: "Blah . . . No character . . . Floodplain . . . Always underwater . . . Could be much better . . . Will be OK when trees grow in . . . Easy to get lost, need markers to next tees . . . Below average snack bar."

★★★½ WATERWOOD NATIONAL RESORT & COUNTRY CLUB

Huntsville—R—409-891-5050, 800-441-5211 (90 mi. from Houston).
Season: Year-round. **High:** April-Nov. **Caddies:** No.
Green fee: $20-$49. **Credit cards:** All Major.
Lodging on site: Yes. **Reduced fees:** Weekdays, Low Season, Resort Guests, Twilight Play.
Unrestricted walking: No. **Range:** Yes (grass).
Holes: 18. **Par:** 71. **Yards:** 6,872-6,258. **Slope:** 142-132.
Ranked 6th in Texas by GOLF DIGEST.
Comments: "Great price for a tough Pete Dye course . . . Finest layout in Texas . . . Too much from back tees . . . Impossible . . . Toughest I've seen . . . Will destroy your confidence . . . Only a couple of bad greens keep it from stardom . . . No. 14 a great par 3 . . . Conditioning has slipped."

★★½ WEDGEWOOD GOLF COURSE

Conroe—PU—409-539-4653 (60 mi. from Houston).
Season: Year-round. **High:** Spring/Fall. **Caddies:** No.
Green fee: $20-$49. **Credit cards:** V, AMEX, MC.
Lodging on site: No. **Reduced fees:** Twilight Play.
Unrestricted walking: Yes. **Range:** Yes (grass).
Holes: 18. **Par:** 72. **Yards:** 6,817-5,825. **Slope:** 134-122.
Comments: "Hilly course in average shape . . . Undulating fairways and 90-degree doglegs . . . Good bent-grass greens . . . World's tightest fairways, blind tee shots, fast greens, sand, water. What's not to love? . . . Too tight, too many blind shots . . . Target golf to the max . . . Not tough, just tricked up . . . Always shooting over hills and around corners . . . Almost unfair . . . Designed to eat balls . . . No room for errors . . . Blind shots every hole . . . Very hard walking."

★★½ WOODLAND HILLS GOLF COURSE

Nacogdoches—PU—409-564-2762 (120 mi. from Houston).
Season: Year-round. **High:** April-Aug. **Caddies:** No.
Green fee: Under $20. **Credit cards:** V, MC.
Lodging on site: No. **Reduced fees:** Weekdays, Twilight Play.
Unrestricted walking: Yes. **Range:** Yes (grass).
Holes: 18. **Par:** 72. **Yards:** 6,672-6,218. **Slope:** 123-114.
Comments: "Much improved recently."

THE WOODLANDS RESORT & COUNTRY CLUB

The Woodlands—R—713-367-1100 (22 mi. from Houston).
Season: Year-round. **High:** Spring/Fall. **Caddies:** No.
Green fee: $20-$49. **Credit cards:** All Major.
Lodging on site: Yes. **Reduced fees:** Weekdays, Low Season, Twilight Play.
Unrestricted walking: No. **Range:** Yes (grass).
★★★NORTH COURSE
Holes: 18. **Par:** 72. **Yards:** 6,881-6,339. **Slope:** 126-122.
Comments: "Best golf resort in Texas . . . Much better than Tour 18 for the same price . . . Traditional design . . . Excellent condition always . . . Too many players, not enough personnel . . . Never seen so much sand."
★★★★TPC AT THE WOODLANDS
713-367-7285.
Green fee: $50-$99.
Holes: 18. **Par:** 72. **Yards:** 7,045-6,387. **Slope:** 135-127.
Site of PGA Tour's annual Houston Open.
Comments: "Super fun . . .Good test of skill from any tee, but a little overpriced compared to other good courses close by . . . Great course, high rates . . . In terrific shape . . . No bad lies . . . Fun even in the wind and rain . . . Great 17th and 18th . . . Worth the cost a couple of times a year . . . Too tough . . . Emphasis is on how far you can hit the ball . . . Disappointing, touted too much . . . Typical punishing TPC-style course, water everywhere . . . Overpriced for what you get."

★★★½ BOUNTIFUL CITY GOLF COURSE
Bountiful—PU—801-298-6040 (9 mi. from Salt Lake City).
Season: March-Nov. **High:** April-Aug. **Caddies:** No.
Green fee: Under $20. **Credit cards:** V.
Lodging on site: No. **Reduced fees:** Weekdays.
Unrestricted walking: Yes. **Range:** No.
Holes: 18. **Par:** 71. **Yards:** 6,485-5,224. **Slope:** 117-115.
Comments: "True mountain course . . . Beautiful views of the Great Salt Lake . . . Fun to play."

★★½ DAVIS PARK GOLF COURSE
Fruit Heights—PU—801-546-4154 (20 mi. from Salt Lake City).
Season: Feb.-Dec. **High:** March-Sept. **Caddies:** No.
Green fee: Under $20. **Credit cards:** V, MC.
Lodging on site: No. **Reduced fees:** No.
Unrestricted walking: Yes. **Range:** Yes (grass).
Holes: 18. **Par:** 71. **Yards:** 6,500-5,295. **Slope:** 117-114.
Comments: "Beautiful mature layout . . . Like putting on a glass tabletop . . . Great pro shop."

★★½ EAST BAY MUNICIPAL GOLF COURSE
Provo—PU—801-379-6612 (45 mi. from Salt Lake City).
Season: March-Nov. **High:** June-Aug. **Caddies:** No.
Green fee: Under $20. **Credit cards:** No.
Lodging on site: No. **Reduced fees:** No.
Unrestricted walking: Yes. **Range:** Yes (mats).
Holes: 18. **Par:** 71. **Yards:** 6,800-4,900. **Slope:** 119-106.

★★½ GLENDALE GOLF COURSE
Salt Lake City—PU—801-974-2403.
Season: March-Oct. **High:** April-July. **Caddies:** No.
Green fee: Under $20. **Credit cards:** V, MC.
Lodging on site: No. **Reduced fees:** Weekdays.
Unrestricted walking: Yes. **Range:** Yes (grass).
Holes: 18. **Par:** 72. **Yards:** 6,939-5,930. **Slope:** 117.

★★★½ GREEN SPRING GOLF COURSE
Washington—PU—801-673-7888 (2 mi. from St. George).
Season: Year-round. **High:** Feb.-May. **Caddies:** No.
Green fee: $20-$49. **Credit cards:** V, MC.
Lodging on site: No. **Reduced fees:** Low Season, Twilight Play.
Unrestricted walking: Yes. **Range:** Yes (grass).
Holes: 18. **Par:** 71. **Yards:** 6,717-5,042. **Slope:** 131-118.
Comments: "What scenery! . . . Surrounded by hills whose hues change with the angle of the sun . . . Just beautiful . . . Summer rates I can afford . . . Exceptionally fast greens . . . Hefty climbs on the back . . . A mix of very good, very poor holes . . . Too much trouble . . . Target, target, target."

★★★ HOMESTEAD GOLF CLUB
Midway—R—801-654-1485, 800-327-7220 (50 mi. from Salt Lake City).
Season: April-Nov. **High:** June-Sept. **Caddies:** No.
Green fee: $20-$49. **Credit cards:** All Major.
Lodging on site: Yes. **Reduced fees:** Weekdays, Low Season, Resort Guests, Twilight Play.
Unrestricted walking: Yes. **Range:** Yes (grass).
Holes: 18. **Par:** 72. **Yards:** 6,971-5,131. **Slope:** 135-118.
Comments: "Scenic . . . Excellent setting . . . Very challenging . . . But don't try to buy a drink afterward."

★★★ MOUNT OGDEN GOLF COURSE
Ogden—PU—801-629-8700 (30 mi. from Salt Lake City).
Season: March-Nov. **High:** April-Oct. **Caddies:** No.

Green fee: Under $20. **Credit cards:** No.
Lodging on site: No. **Reduced fees:** No.
Unrestricted walking: Yes. **Range:** Yes (grass).
Holes: 18. **Par:** 71. **Yards:** 6,390-5,051. **Slope:** 119.
Comments: "Many altitude changes . . . Very hard to walk . . . Narrow doglegs . . . Lots of trees . . . Tough little course."

★★★ PARK CITY MUNICIPAL GOLF COURSE
Park City—PU—801-649-8701 (30 mi. from Salt Lake City).
Season: April-Oct. **High:** May-Sept. **Caddies:** No.
Green fee: $20-$49. **Credit cards:** V, MC, DISC.
Lodging on site: No. **Reduced fees:** Low Season.
Unrestricted walking: Yes. **Range:** Yes (grass).
Holes: 18. **Par:** 72. **Yards:** 6,754-5,600. **Slope:** 127-123.

★★★½ PARK MEADOWS GOLF CLUB
Park City—R—801-649-2460 (30 mi. from Salt Lake City).
Season: May-Oct. **High:** June-Sept. **Caddies:** No.
Green fee: $50-$99. **Credit cards:** V, AMEX, MC.
Lodging on site: No. **Reduced fees:** Low Season, Twilight Play.
Unrestricted walking: No. **Range:** Yes (grass).
Holes: 18. **Par:** 72. **Yards:** 7,413-5,816. **Slope:** 132-118.
Comments: "No course in Utah like this one . . . Fun Nicklaus . . . Built for pros . . . Virtually treeless . . . Very long, plays much shorter due to altitude . . . Flat, but loaded with bunkers."

★★ ST. GEORGE GOLF CLUB
St. George—PU—801-634-5854 (110 mi. from Las Vegas).
Season: Year-round. **High:** Jan.-April. **Caddies:** No.
Green fee: $20-$49. **Credit cards:** No.
Lodging on site: No. **Reduced fees:** No.
Unrestricted walking: Yes. **Range:** No.
Holes: 18. **Par:** 73. **Yards:** 7,211-5,216. **Slope:** 126-114.

★★½ SOUTHGATE GOLF CLUB
St. George—PU—801-628-0000 (130 mi. from Las Vegas).
Season: Year-round. **High:** Jan.-April. **Caddies:** No.
Green fee: Under $20. **Credit cards:** V, MC.
Lodging on site: No. **Reduced fees:** Low Season.
Unrestricted walking: Yes. **Range:** Yes (mats).
Holes: 18. **Par:** 70. **Yards:** 6,100-4,463. **Slope:** 119-106.
Comments: "Front 9 a bore . . . Challenging new back 9 . . . Back is a brute . . . Best driving range in the state . . . Exceptional staff and facilities."

★★★★ SUNBROOK GOLF CLUB
St. George—PU—801-634-5866 (120 mi. from Las Vegas).
Season: Year-round. **High:** Jan-May. **Caddies:** No.
Green fee: $20-$49. **Credit cards:** V, MC.
Lodging on site: No. **Reduced fees:** Low Season.
Unrestricted walking: Yes. **Range:** Yes (grass).
Holes: 18. **Par:** 72. **Yards:** 6,800-5,286. **Slope:** 129-121.
Comments: "A little gem . . . Beautiful vistas . . . Plenty of variety . . . Five or six signature holes . . . Cliff holes . . . Great island green par 3 . . . Try No. 13 from the back tees . . . Well groomed . . . Walking allowed, but only the fittest should consider it."

★★★ TRI-CITY GOLF COURSE
American Fork—PU—801-756-3594 (20 mi. from Salt Lake City).
Season: March-Nov. **High:** May-Aug. **Caddies:** No.
Green fee: Under $20. **Credit cards:** No.
Lodging on site: No. **Reduced fees:** No.
Unrestricted walking: Yes. **Range:** Yes (grass).
Holes: 18. **Par:** 72. **Yards:** 7,077-6,304. **Slope:** 125.
Comments: "A tough test . . . Demanding tee shots . . . Narrow but fair."

★★★★ VALLEY VIEW GOLF COURSE

Layton—PU—801-546-1630 (15 mi. from Salt Lake City).
Season: March-Oct. **High:** May-Sept. **Caddies:** No.
Green fee: Under $20. **Credit cards:** V, MC.
Lodging on site: No. **Reduced fees:** No.
Unrestricted walking: Yes. **Range:** Yes (grass).
Holes: 18. **Par:** 72. **Yards:** 7,084-5,755. **Slope:** 123.
Comments: "Best course in the valley . . . Best muny in Utah . . . Pure muny . . . Beautiful . . . Immaculate . . . Lots of variety . . . Could be a hard walk for some people."

(SUPER VALUE)

★★★½ WASATCH STATE PARK GOLF CLUB
CANYON/LAKE/MOUNTAIN 9s

Midway—PU—801-654-0532. (50 mi. from Salt Lake City)
Season: April-Nov. **High:** July-Aug. **Caddies:** No.
Green fee: Under $20. **Credit cards:** V, MC.
Lodging on site: No. **Reduced fees:** No.
Unrestricted walking: Yes. **Range:** Yes (grass).
Holes: 27. **Par:** 36/36/36. **Yards:** 3,519/3,423/3,289.
Comments: "Three very different 9s . . . Stick to the Lake and Canyon . . . Can see wildlife during evening rounds."

★★½ WEST RIDGE GOLF COURSE

West Valley City—PU—801-966-4653.
Season: March-Nov. **High:** June-Aug. **Caddies:** No.
Green fee: Under $20. **Credit cards:** All Major.
Lodging on site: No. **Reduced fees:** Weekdays.
Unrestricted walking: Yes. **Range:** Yes (grass).
Holes: 18. **Par:** 71. **Yards:** 6,734-5,027. **Slope:** 125-118.

★★★½ WINGPOINTE GOLF COURSE

Salt Lake City—PU—801-575-2345.
Season: March-Dec. **High:** June-Aug. **Caddies:** No.
Green fee: $20-$49. **Credit cards:** V, MC.
Lodging on site: No. **Reduced fees:** Weekdays.
Unrestricted walking: Yes. **Range:** Yes (grass).
Holes: 18. **Par:** 72. **Yards:** 7,189-6,420. **Slope:** 130-121.
Comments: "Spiffy new links design . . . Best new course ever . . . Hard . . . Definitely a comer . . . Could host a U.S. Open from the back tees."

★★★½ WOLF CREEK RESORT GOLF COURSE

Eden—R—801-745-3365 (14 mi. from Ogden).
Season: March-Nov. **High:** May-Sept. **Caddies:** No.
Green fee: Under $20. **Credit cards:** V, AMEX, MC.
Lodging on site: Yes. **Reduced fees:** Weekdays, Low Season, Resort Guests, Twilight Play.
Unrestricted walking: Yes. **Range:** No.
Holes: 18. **Par:** 72. **Yards:** 6,845-5,332. **Slope:** 134-127.
Comments: "Spectacular views . . . Starkly different 9s . . . Greens slickest anywhere in state . . . Can eat up the high handicapper."

★★★BASIN HARBOR GOLF CLUB
Vergennes—R—802-475-2309 (30 mi. from Burlington).
Season: May-Oct. **High:** July-Aug. **Caddies:** Yes.
Green fee: $20-$49. **Credit cards:** V, MC.
Lodging on site: Yes. **Reduced fees:** Low Season, Resort Guests, Twilight Play.
Unrestricted walking: No. **Range:** Yes (grass).
Holes: 18. **Par:** 72. **Yards:** 6,513-5,745. **Slope:** 122-116.
Comments: "Wonderful . . . Scenic . . . Enjoyable . . . Very fair layout, always an option . . . Well kept, new holes are a challenge . . . Great lake views . . . Great condition now that carts are kept off fairways . . . Easy to walk . . . You can fly in . . . Food out of sight."

★★★COUNTRY CLUB OF BARRE
Barre—PU—802-476-7658.
Season: April-Nov. **High:** June-Aug. **Caddies:** No.
Green fee: $20-$49. **Credit cards:** V, MC.
Lodging on site: No. **Reduced fees:** No.
Unrestricted walking: Yes. **Range:** Yes (grass).
Holes: 18. **Par:** 71. **Yards:** 6,149-5,900. **Slope:** 123-116.
Comments: "Scenic . . . Tight, small greens . . . Treelined . . . Deceptive . . . Hilly back . . . Many blind greens."

★★½ CROWN POINT COUNTRY CLUB
Springfield—PU—802-885-1010.
Season: April-Oct. **High:** June-Sept. **Caddies:** No.
Green fee: $20-$49. **Credit cards:** V, MC.
Lodging on site: No. **Reduced fees:** Weekdays, Twilight Play.
Unrestricted walking: Yes. **Range:** Yes (grass).
Holes: 18. **Par:** 72. **Yards:** 6,572-6,120. **Slope:** 123-119.
Comments: "Nice New England setting . . . Had to wait for deer crossing . . . Vermont manicure . . . No fairway watering . . . Bunkers need sand."

★★★½ GLENEAGLES GOLF COURSE
Manchester Village—R—802-362-3223 (60 mi. from Albany, NY).
Season: May-Oct. **High:** July-Aug. **Caddies:** No.
Green Fee: $50-$99. **Credit cards:** All Major.
Lodging on site: Yes. **Reduced Fees:** Weekdays, Resort Guests, Twilight Play.
Unrestricted Walking: No. **Range:** No.
Holes: 18. **Par:** 71. **Yards:** 6,423-5,082. **Slope:** 129-117.
Course on the grounds of the Equinox Resort Hotel.
Comments: "Wonderful setting . . . Marvelously scenic . . . Since remodeling, course is beautiful . . . Renovation a big improvement . . . Will be great when it grows in . . . Recently remodeled to its detriment, made easier to please tourists . . . Pricey but worth splurging . . . Good but overpriced."

★★½ HAYSTACK GOLF CLUB
Wilmington—PU—802-464-8301.
Season: May-Nov. **High:** July-Oct. **Caddies:** No.
Green fee: $50-$99. **Credit cards:** V, AMEX, MC.
Lodging on site: No. **Reduced fees:** Weekdays.
Unrestricted walking: No. **Range:** Yes (grass).
Holes: 18. **Par:** 72. **Yards:** 6,500-6,000. **Slope:** 125-120.
Comments: "Good layout . . . Good condition . . . Food is tops . . . Why bother? For the same fee, go elsewhere."

★★½ KILLINGTON GOLF COURSE
Killington—R—802-422-4100 (100 mi. from Burlington).
Season: May-Oct. **High:** July-Aug. **Caddies:** No.
Green fee: $20-$49. **Credit cards:** V, MC.
Lodging on site: Yes. **Reduced fees:** Twilight Play.
Unrestricted walking: Yes. **Range:** No.

Holes: 18. **Par:** 72. **Yards:** 6,326-5,170. **Slope:** 126-123.
Comments: "Unique golf experience . . . Pure Vermont . . . Cut right out of a mountain side . . . Deceiving distances . . . Some unfair landing areas . . . Often wet, sloppy . . . Add 10 strokes to your usual score . . . Don't walk . . . Course built to accommodate mountain goats . . . Steep trails should not mean steep green fee."

★★★MOUNT SNOW GOLF CLUB
West Dover—R—802-464-5642, 800-451-4211 (30 mi. from Brattleboro).
Season: May-Oct. **High:** July-Sept. **Caddies:** No.
Green fee: $20-$49. **Credit cards:** V, AMEX, MC.
Lodging on site: Yes. **Reduced fees:** Weekdays, Low Season, Resort Guests, Twilight Play.
Unrestricted walking: Yes. **Range:** Yes (grass).
Holes: 18. **Par:** 72. **Yards:** 6,894-6,443. **Slope:** 130-127.
Ranked 5th in Top 5 Courses in Vermont by GOLF DIGEST.
Comments: "Pretty, lush conditions . . . Hilly—tough to walk . . . Best value for the money . . . Gets a lot of play, needs more maintenance . . . Poor drainage . . . Too slow! Golf school slows it down."

NEWPORT COUNTRY CLUB*
Newport—PU—802-334-2391 (80 mi. from Burlington).
Season: April-Oct. **High:** July-Aug. **Caddies:** No.
Green fee: $20-$49. **Credit cards:** V, MC.
Lodging on site: No. **Reduced fees:** Twilight Play.
Unrestricted walking: Yes. **Range:** Yes (grass).
Holes: 18. **Par:** 72. **Yards:** 6,117-5,312. **Slope:** 120-111.

★★★½ RUTLAND COUNTRY CLUB
Rutland—PU—802-773-3254.
Season: May-Oct. **High:** June-Aug. **Caddies:** No.
Green fee: $20-$49. **Credit cards:** V, MC.
Lodging on site: No. **Reduced fees:** No.
Unrestricted walking: No. **Range:** No.
Holes: 18. **Par:** 70. **Yards:** 6,062-5,761. **Slope:** 125-122.
Comments: "Tough short course . . . Great greens . . . Great shape . . . Rolling terrain, but walkable . . . Beautiful vistas . . . Great staff."

★★½ STOWE COUNTRY CLUB
Stowe—R—802-253-4893 (30 mi. from Burlington).
Season: May-Oct. **High:** July-Sept. **Caddies:** Yes.
Green fee: $20-$49. **Credit cards:** All Major.
Lodging on site: Yes. **Reduced fees:** Twilight Play.
Unrestricted walking: Yes. **Range:** Yes (grass).
Holes: 18. **Par:** 72. **Yards:** 6,200-5,346. **Slope:** 122-115.
Comments: "Nice vacation course . . . Good fairways, good greens, good clubhouse . . . Lovely spot, hilly terrain . . . Views beautiful, especially in autumn . . . Excellent choice for mini-vacation . . . A disappointment."

★★★STRATTON MOUNTAIN COUNTRY CLUB
LAKE/MOUNTAIN/FOREST 9s
Stratton Mountain—R—802-297-4114 (45 mi. from Rutland).
Season: May-Oct. **High:** July-Sept. **Caddies:** Yes.
Green fee: $50-$99. **Credit cards:** V, MC.
Lodging on site: Yes. **Reduced fees:** Low Season, Resort Guests.
Unrestricted walking: No. **Range:** Yes (mats).
Holes: 27. **Par:** 36/36/36. **Yards:** 3,325/3,277/3,201.
Site of the LPGA's McCall's Classic.
Comments: "Great golf, great skiing . . . Super atmosphere, good shape . . . Lovely views . . . Forest and Mountain more interesting than Lake . . . Mountain 9 tough to walk . . . Watch for buried rocks . . . Best resort in Vermont . . . Best golf school . . . Improved since LPGA started playing here . . . Stratton Inn was truly falling apart."

VERMONT

★★★SUGARBUSH GOLF COURSE
Warren—PU—802-583-2722 (45 mi. from Burlington).
Season: May-Oct. **High:** June-Oct. **Caddies:** No.
Green fee: $20-$49. **Credit cards:** V, AMEX, MC.
Lodging on site: Yes. **Reduced fees:** Weekdays, Low Season, Resort Guests, Twilight Play.
Unrestricted walking: No. **Range:** Yes (mats).
Holes: 18. **Par:** 72. **Yards:** 6,524-5,187. **Slope:** 128-119.
Comments: "Classic Robert Trent Jones mountain layout . . . Great views, dramatic holes, severe penalties for poor shots . . . Tough but fair . . . Whole area is wonderful . . . Long hikes from green to tee . . . Take a cart."

★½WEST BOLTON GOLF CLUB
Jericho—PU—802-434-4321 (25 mi. from Burlington).
Season: April-May/Oct. **High:** June-Aug. **Caddies:** No.
Green fee: Under $20. **Credit cards:** V, MC.
Lodging on site: No. **Reduced fees:** Weekdays, Twilight Play.
Unrestricted walking: Yes. **Range:** No.
Holes: 18. **Par:** 70. **Yards:** 5,432-5,009. **Slope:** 109-103.
Comments: "Very short . . . Tiny greens . . . Only a few good holes, not that well maintained . . . Has potential."

★★½WILLISTON GOLF CLUB
Williston—PU—802-878-3747 (7 mi. from Burlington).
Season: May-Nov. **High:** July-Aug. **Caddies:** No.
Green fee: Under $20. **Credit cards:** V, MC.
Lodging on site: No. **Reduced fees:** Twilight Play.
Unrestricted walking: Yes. **Range:** No.
Holes: 18. **Par:** 69. **Yards:** 5,620-4,753. **Slope:** 118-106.
Comments: "Short but tricky . . . Very scenic . . . Family owned, nicely managed . . . Has everything, white sand, water, woods . . . Flowers around trees . . . Tends to play slow . . . Too many par 3s on the back."

★★★½WOODSTOCK COUNTRY CLUB
Woodstock—R—802-457-2114 (140 mi. from Boston).
Season: May-Nov. **High:** July-Sept. **Caddies:** No.
Green fee: $50-$99. **Credit cards:** V, AMEX, MC.
Lodging on site: Yes. **Reduced fees:** Weekdays, Resort Guests, Twilight Play.
Unrestricted walking: Yes. **Range:** Yes (grass).
Holes: 18. **Par:** 69. **Yards:** 6,001-5,202. **Slope:** 121-117.
Comments: "Tight old course . . . Picturesque . . . Trout stream weaves through it, will whisk ball away quickly . . . Outstanding clubhouse and personnel . . . Bring money."

★★½ BELMONT GOLF COURSE
Richmond—PU—804-266-4929 (12 mi. from Richmond).
Season: Year-round. **High:** April-Oct. **Caddies:** No.
Green fee: Under $20. **Credit cards:** No.
Lodging on site: No. **Reduced fees:** Twilight Play.
Unrestricted walking: Yes. **Range:** No.
Holes: 18. **Par:** 71. **Yards:** 6,400-5,990. **Slope:** 126-122.
Formerly Hermitage Country Club, site of the 1949 PGA Championship.
Comments: "Cheap, cheap, cheap . . . Great staff . . . Good value, but poorly maintained . . . Not kept up . . . No driving range."

★★ BIRKDALE GOLF CLUB
Chesterfield—PU—804-734-8800 (15 mi. from Richmond).
Season: Year-round. **High:** April-Sept. **Caddies:** No.
Green fee: $20-$49. **Credit cards:** V, MC.
Reduced fees: Weekdays, Low Season, Resort Guests.
Unrestricted walking: No. **Range:** Yes (grass).
Holes: 18. **Par:** 71. **Yards:** 6,550-4,459. **Slope:** 122.
Comments: "Good new course . . . It's coming around . . . Decent greens . . . Lots of clay, not much grass."

★½ BOW CREEK GOLF COURSE
Virginia Beach—PU—804-431-3763 (5 mi. from Norfolk).
Season: Year-round. **High:** April-Sept. **Caddies:** No.
Green fee: Under $20. **Credit cards:** V, MC.
Lodging on site: No. **Reduced fees:** No.
Unrestricted walking: Yes. **Range:** Yes (grass).
Holes: 18. **Par:** 70. **Yards:** 5,917-5,181. **Slope:** 114-104.
Comments: "Short, tight . . . Plays well, nothing special . . . Challenges short game."

★★½ BRYCE RESORT GOLF COURSE
Basye—R—703-856-2124 (90 mi. from Washington, D.C.).
Season: March-Nov. **High:** April-Sept. **Caddies:** No.
Green fee: $20-$49. **Credit cards:** V, MC.
Lodging on site: Yes. **Reduced fees:** Weekdays, Twilight Play.
Unrestricted walking: No. **Range:** Yes (grass).
Holes: 18. **Par:** 71. **Yards:** 6,290-5,240. **Slope:** 122-120.
Comments: "Enjoyable."

★★★ CAVERNS COUNTRY CLUB
Luray—PU—703-743-7111 (80 mi. from Washington, D.C.).
Season: Year-round. **High:** April-Oct. **Caddies:** No.
Green fee: $20-$49. **Credit cards:** V, MC.
Lodging on site: No. **Reduced fees:** No.
Unrestricted walking: Yes. **Range:** Yes (grass).
Holes: 18. **Par:** 72. **Yards:** 6,400-5,499. **Slope:** 117-120.
Comments: "Fine course . . . Very nice . . . Hilly . . . Challenging . . . Attractive Blue Ridge scenery . . . Tough first hole . . . Single walk-ons accepted . . . 'Mountain goat' course."

★★★ THE CROSSINGS GOLF CLUB
Glen Allen—PU—804-261-0000 (8 mi. from Richmond).
Season: Year-round. **High:** March-Nov. **Caddies:** No.
Green fee: $20-$49. **Credit cards:** V, MC.
Reduced fees: Weekdays, Low Season, Twilight Play.
Unrestricted walking: No. **Range:** Yes (grass).
Holes: 18. **Par:** 72. **Yards:** 6,619-5,626. **Slope:** 126-128.
Comments: "Very nice undiscovered track . . . Short, playable for all . . . Challenging for all levels, but fair . . . Picturesque . . . Very well maintained . . . Above average fee, but worth it . . . Low course, often wet . . . Nondescript . . . Very hard on seniors because of cart rule . . . Carts not allowed on fairways."

FORD'S COLONY
Williamsburg—R—804-258-4130 (50 mi. from Richmond).
Season: Year-round. **High:** Spring/Fall. **Caddies:** No.
Green fee: $50-$99. **Credit cards:** V, AMEX, MC.
Reduced fees: Weekdays, Low Season, Resort Guests, Twilight Play.
Unrestricted walking: No. **Range:** Yes (mats).
★★★½ **BLUE/GOLD COURSE**
Holes: 18. **Par:** 71. **Yards:** 6,769-4,815. **Slope:** 124-109.
Comments: "Love at first sight . . . Beautiful . . . Very well maintained
. . . Great design . . . One of the best . . . Fun to play . . . Stay out of the
Bermuda rough . . . Too expensive . . . Mediocre condition . . . Too
crowded . . . A factory."
RED/WHITE COURSE*
Holes: 18. **Par:** 72. **Yards:** 6,755-5,614. **Slope:** 126-119.
Comments: "Incredible experience . . . Excellent condition . . . Wonderful
staff . . . A perfect place to retire . . . Incredibly expensive."

GOLDEN HORSESHOE GOLF CLUB
Williamsburg—R—804-220-7696, 800-447-8679 (50 mi. from Richmond).
Season: Year-round. **High:** Spring/Fall. **Caddies:** No.
Green fee: $50-$99. **Credit cards:** V, AMEX, DISC; MC.
Lodging on site: Yes. **Reduced fees:** Resort Guests.
Unrestricted walking: No. **Range:** Yes (grass).
★★★★½ **GOLD COURSE**
Holes: 18. **Par:** 71. **Yards:** 6,700-5,159. **Slope:** 137-120.
Ranked 30th in America's 75 Best Resort Courses by GOLF DIGEST.
Comments: "Marvelous design . . . A classic . . . Not to be missed . . .
Most beautiful course ever . . . Lovely Trent Jones . . . Tough traditional
golf course . . . Best course in Virginia . . . Greatest set of par 3s on one
course you'll ever see . . . Difficult finishing holes . . . Exceptionally main-
tained . . . Ride slowly so you don't miss the scenery . . . Difficult to play
because entire course is roped off, tee to green . . . Too hard for short
knockers . . . Expensive . . . It's Williamsburg prices."
★★★½ **GREEN COURSE**
Holes: 18. **Par:** 72. **Yards:** 7,120-5,350. **Slope:** 134-109.
Ranked 5th in Virginia by GOLF DIGEST.
Comments: "Tough and beautiful . . . Tight with difficult forced carries
. . . Straightforward, no gimmicks . . . Shows its youth, but great potential
. . . Rugged, but enjoyable . . . A delight to play . . . Steep prices . . .
Expensive, but prestigious."

★★★ HANGING ROCK GOLF CLUB
Salem—PU—703-398-7275 (2 mi. from Roanoke).
Season: Year-round. **High:** April-Oct. **Caddies:** No.
Green fee: $20-$49. **Credit cards:** V, MC.
Reduced fees: Low Season, Resort Guests, Twilight Play.
Unrestricted walking: No. **Range:** Yes (grass).
Holes: 18. **Par:** 73. **Yards:** 6,828-4,463. **Slope:** 125-106.
Comments: "Young course . . . Nothing memorable . . . Needs seasoning
. . . Great potential . . . Gimmicky . . . Some yardages suspect."

★★★½ HELL'S POINT GOLF COURSE
Virginia Beach—PU—804-721-3400.
Season: Year-round. **High:** April-Sept. **Caddies:** No.
Green fee: $20-$49. **Credit cards:** V, MC.
Reduced fees: Weekdays, Low Season, Twilight Play.
Unrestricted walking: No. **Range:** Yes (grass).
Holes: 18. **Par:** 72. **Yards:** 6,766-5,003. **Slope:** 130-116.
Comments: "For golf lovers . . . Interesting . . . Hard . . . Tight . . . Best
public course in Virginia Beach . . . Fun, challenging, long between some
holes . . . Very good value with afternoon specials."

THE HOLLOWS GOLF CLUB*
Montpelier—PU—804-798-2949 (10 mi. from Richmond).
Season: Year-round. **High:** April-Oct. **Caddies:** No.
Green fee: Under $20. **Credit cards:** No.
Reduced fees: Weekdays, Low Season, Twilight Play.
Unrestricted walking: Yes. **Range:** Yes (grass).
Holes: 18. **Par:** 72. **Yards:** 6,557-5,088. **Slope:** 118-108.

THE HOMESTEAD
Hot Springs—R—800-336-5771 (80 mi. from Roanoke).
Season: April-Oct. **High:** April-Oct. **Caddies:** No.
Green fee: $50-$99. **Credit cards:** V, MC, AMEX.
Lodging on site: Yes. **Reduced fees:** Low Season.
Unrestricted walking: No. **Range:** Yes (grass).

(SUPER VALUE)

★★★★½ CASCADES COURSE
Holes: 18. **Par:** 70. **Yards:** 6,566-5,448. **Slope:** 136.
Ranked 95th in America's 100 Greatest Golf Courses and 12th in America's
75 Best Resort Courses by GOLF DIGEST.
Comments: "Super course . . . Fabulous . . . Unforgetable . . . Worth
playing 100 times . . . A shotmaker's delight . . . Each hole truly outstanding . . . Great tradition . . . Best course in Virginia . . . Finest mountain
course in the East . . . My favorite in the U.S. . . . Among the world's very
best . . . Take a deep breath when you start, another when you're done."

★★★HOMESTEAD COURSE
Holes: 18. **Par:** 71. **Yards:** 5,957-5,150. **Slope:** 115.
Comments: "Very short . . . OK, but not great . . . First-rate
accommodations."

★★★½ LOWER CASCADES COURSE
Holes: 18. **Par:** 72. **Yards:** 6,619-4,726. **Slope:** 127.
Comments: "Fun . . . Fair . . . Beautiful . . . Diverse . . . Excellent golf
. . . Open course with mountain views . . . Great companion to the Cas-
cades . . . Two or three weak holes, otherwise superb."

★★½ HONEY BEE GOLF CLUB
Virginia Beach—PU—804-471-2768 (10 mi. from Norfolk).
Season: Year-round. **High:** April-Oct. **Caddies:** No.
Green fee: $20-$49. **Credit cards:** V, MC.
Lodging on site: No. **Reduced fees:** Weekdays, Low Season.
Unrestricted walking: No. **Range:** Yes (grass).
Holes: 18. **Par:** 70. **Yards:** 6,075-5,667. **Slope:** 123-119.
Comments: "Short, but challenging . . . Many interesting little holes . . .
Excellent greens . . . Lots of straight holes . . . Ball placement is critical . . .
Good for the money."

★★KEMPSVILLE GREENS GOLF COURSE
Virginia Beach—PU—804-474-8441 (6 mi. from Norfolk).
Season: Year-round. **High:** May-Sept. **Caddies:** No.
Green fee: Under $20. **Credit cards:** No.
Lodging on site: No. **Reduced fees:** Low Season.
Unrestricted walking: Yes. **Range:** Yes (mats).
Holes: 18. **Par:** 70. **Yards:** 5,478-4,538. **Slope:** 114-94.
Comments: "Great greens, narrow fairways . . . Houses on both sides of
fairways . . . Terrible back 9 . . . 1980s renovations destroyed a nice course."

KINGSMILL GOLF CLUB
Williamsburg—R—804-253-3906.
Season: Year-round. **High:** Spring/Fall. **Caddies:** No.
Green fee: $50-$99. **Credit cards:** V, AMEX, DISC, MC.
Lodging on site: Yes. **Reduced fees:** Low Season, Resort Guests,
Twilight Play.
Unrestricted walking: No. **Range:** Yes (grass).
★★★PLANTATION COURSE
Holes: 18. **Par:** 72. **Yards:** 6,605-4,880. **Slope:** 126-108.

Also a 9-hole par-3 course.

Comments: "Very good course . . . In great shape . . . Not for the weak of heart . . . 18th green is wild . . . Great golf resort . . . Weak counterpart to River Course."

★★★½ RIVER COURSE

Holes: 18. **Par:** 71. **Yards:** 6,797-4,606. **Slope:** 137-109.

Comments: "Great track . . . Championship caliber . . . Beautiful layout . . . Very scenic . . . Enjoyed back 9 especially . . . Interesting historical markers . . . Very tough for the bogey golfer, but worth it for the beauty . . . Generally overrated . . . Most holes have a muny feel . . . Very hard for short hitter . . . Tremendously overpriced."

★½ LAKE WRIGHT GOLF COURSE

Norfolk—PU—804-461-2246.

Season: Year-round. **High:** Sept-May. **Caddies:** No.
Green fee: Under $20. **Credit cards:** All Major.
Lodging on site: Yes. **Reduced fees:** Resort Guests.
Unrestricted walking: No. **Range:** Yes (mats).
Holes: 18. **Par:** 70. **Yards:** 6,174-5,874. **Slope:** 116-107.

Comments: "Decent short course . . . Wide open . . . Terrible atmosphere in clubhouse . . . Cow pasture next to the interstate."

★★★½ LANSDOWNE GOLF CLUB

Lansdowne—R—703-729-4071, 800-541-4801
(40 mi. from Washington, D.C.).

Season: Year-round. **High:** April-Oct. **Caddies:** No.
Green fee: $50-$99. **Credit cards:** V, AMEX, DISC, MC.
Lodging on site: Yes. **Reduced fees:** Weekdays, Low Season.
Unrestricted walking: No. **Range:** Yes (grass).
Holes: 18. **Par:** 72. **Yards:** 7,040-5,213. **Slope:** 126-134.

Comments: "Front 9 OK, back 9 magnificent . . . Front 9 ordinary, back 9 spectacular and tough . . . Immaculate playing conditions . . . Pricey, but worth it . . . Far too expensive."

★★★★ OLDE MILL GOLF COURSE

Laurel Fork—R—703-398-2211 (90 mi. from Roanoke).

Season: March-Nov. **High:** May-Oct. **Caddies:** No.
Green fee: $20-$49. **Credit cards:** V, MC.
Lodging on site: Yes. **Reduced fees:** Weekdays, Low Season, Resort Guests, Twilight Play.
Unrestricted walking: No. **Range:** Yes (grass).
Holes: 18. **Par:** 72. **Yards:** 6,833-4,876. **Slope:** 121-134.

Comments: "A beautiful hidden jewel in the Appalachian Range . . . Spectacular scenery . . . Hilly . . . Much water . . . Each hole has its own personality . . . Hard to find, worth the effort . . . So undiscovered you can easily play 36 a day . . . Enjoyable . . . Keeps you smiling."

★½ OLE MONTEREY GOLF CLUB

Roanoke—PU—703-563-0400.

Season: Year-round. **High:** April-Oct. **Caddies:** No.
Green fee: $20-$49. **Credit cards:** No.
Lodging on site: No. **Reduced fees:** Weekdays.
Unrestricted walking: No. **Range:** No.
Holes: 18. **Par:** 71. **Yards:** 6,712-6,287. **Slope:** 116-112.

Comments: "Not in great shape . . . Poor condition . . . Clover covered . . . Bad clubhouse."

★★ RED WING LAKE GOLF COURSE

Virginia Beach—PU—804-437-4845 (16 mi. from Norfolk).

Season: Year-round. **High:** April-Sept. **Caddies:** No.
Green fee: Under $20. **Credit cards:** No.
Lodging on site: No. **Reduced fees:** No.
Unrestricted walking: Yes. **Range:** Yes (grass).
Holes: 18. **Par:** 72. **Yards:** 7,080-5,285. **Slope:** 125-102.

Comments: "Good layout . . . Fairly long . . . Great finishing par 5s on both 9s . . . Poorly maintained . . . Poor conditions regularly . . . Greens are too thick . . . Overplayed . . . Marshals need to take care of slow play."

★★½ RIVER'S BEND COUNTRY CLUB
Chester—SP—804-530-1000 (15 mi. from Richmond).
Season: Year-round. **High:** April-Sept. **Caddies:** No.
Green fee: $20-$49. **Credit cards:** V, MC.
Lodging on site: No. **Reduced fees:** Weekdays, Low Season.
Unrestricted walking: No. **Range:** Yes (grass).
Holes: 18. **Par:** 71. **Yards:** 6,671-4,932. **Slope:** 132-117.
Comments: "Great course . . . Beautiful course . . . Strange layout . . . Front 9 tight, back 9 a pasture."

★★½ SHANNON GREEN GOLF COURSE
Fredericksburg—R—703-786-8385, 800-682-1049
(50 mi. from Washington, D.C.).
Season: Year-round. **High:** April-Aug. **Caddies:** No.
Green fee: $20-$49. **Credit cards:** V, AMEX, MC.
Lodging on site: Yes. **Reduced fees:** Weekdays, Low Season, Resort Guests, Twilight Play.
Unrestricted walking: No. **Range:** Yes (grass).
Holes: 18. **Par:** 72. **Yards:** 6,970-5,512. **Slope:** 135-124.
Comments: "Great layout . . . Sneaky long . . . Not always well maintained . . . Course conditions very inconsistent . . . In terrible shape . . . Wretched maintenance . . . Course undergoing modifications."

★★THE SHENVALEE
OLDE/CREEK/MILLER 9s
New Market—R—703-740-9930 (115 mi. from Washington, D.C.).
Season: Year-round. **High:** April-Oct. **Caddies:** No.
Green fee: Under $20. **Credit cards:** V, AMEX, MC.
Lodging on site: Yes. **Reduced fees:** Weekdays, Low Season, Resort Guests, Twilight Play.
Unrestricted walking: No. **Range:** Yes (grass).
Holes: 27. **Par:** 36/35/36. **Yards:** 3,030/3,328/3,267.
Comments: "Fun course . . . Interesting layout . . . Fairly short . . . Great new 9 . . . Staff makes you feel welcome."

★★★SLEEPY HOLE GOLF COURSE
Suffolk—PU—804-538-4100 (5 mi. from Portsmouth).
Season: Year-round. **High:** May-Oct. **Caddies:** No.
Green fee: Under $20. **Credit cards:** V, MC.
Lodging on site: No. **Reduced fees:** Weekdays.
Unrestricted walking: Yes. **Range:** Yes (grass).
Holes: 18. **Par:** 72. **Yards:** 6,700-5,121. **Slope:** 123-108.
Comments: "Very challenging public course . . . Excellent golf . . . A must for any player . . . Best closing hole in the Tidewater area . . . Fun course, dogs serve as forecaddies, find lost balls . . . Unbelievably low prices . . . Not in good shape . . . Was let go after LPGA stopped playing there."

★★★SYCAMORE CREEK GOLF COURSE
Manakin-Sabot—PU—804-784-3544 (10 mi. from Richmond).
Season: Year-round. **High:** April-Oct. **Caddies:** No.
Green fee: $20-$49. **Credit cards:** V, MC.
Reduced fees: Weekdays, Low Season, Twilight Play.
Unrestricted walking: No. **Range:** Yes (grass).
Holes: 18. **Par:** 70. **Yards:** 6,256-4,431. **Slope:** 124-111.

THE TIDES INN
Irvington—R—804-438-5501 (65 mi. from Richmond).
Season: March-Jan. **High:** Spring/Fall. **Caddies:** Yes.
Green fee: $20-$49. **Credit cards:** V, MC.
Lodging on site: Yes. **Reduced fees:** Weekdays, Low Season, Resort

Guests, Twilight Play.
Unrestricted walking: Yes. **Range:** Yes (grass).
★★★½ **GOLDEN EAGLE GOLF CLUB**
Holes: 18. **Par:** 72. **Yards:** 6,963-5,384. **Slope:** 130.
Comments: "One of Virginia's best-kept secrets . . . Extremely long . . . Narrow . . . Long carries on second shots . . . Very difficult for average golfers . . . Awesome shape . . . Fun course, can walk . . . Great couples getaway . . . Deserves a high ranking."

THE TIDES LODGE
Irvington—R—804-438-6000, 800-248-4337 (65 mi. from Richmond).
Season: March-Jan. **High:** Spring/Fall. **Caddies:** Yes.
Green fee: $20-$49. **Credit cards:** V, MC.
Lodging on site: Yes. **Reduced fees:** Weekdays, Low Season, Resort Guests, Twilight Play.
Unrestricted walking: Yes. **Range:** Yes (grass).
★★★ **TARTAN COURSE**
Holes: 18. **Par:** 72. **Yards:** 6,323-5,310. **Slope:** 124-116.
Course has a unique practice par-3 hole before the 1st.
Comments: "Classic . . . Nice sporty course . . . Reasonable . . . Quirky . . . 18th hole was shortened . . . Outstanding amenities."

WINTERGREEN RESORT
Wintergreen—R—804-325-2200, 800-325-2200 (43 mi. from Charlottesville). **Season:** April-Oct. **High:** May-Oct. **Caddies:** No.
Green fee: $50-$99. **Credit cards:** V, AMEX, MC.
Lodging on site: Yes. **Reduced fees:** Weekdays, Low Season, Resort Guests.
Unrestricted walking: No. **Range:** Yes (grass).
★★★½ **DEVILS KNOB GOLF CLUB**
Holes: 18. **Par:** 70. **Yards:** 6,576-5,101. **Slope:** 126-118.
Comments: "Mountain golf at its best . . . Spectacular . . . Beautiful views . . . Very tight, requires accuracy . . . Leave the driver home . . . Tough greens . . . Greens configurations unfair . . . Too short . . . Too narrow . . . No 'feel' to the course."
★★★★ **STONEY CREEK GOLF COURSE**
Holes: 18. **Par:** 72. **Yards:** 7,005-5,500. **Slope:** 132-125.
Selected as runner-up for Best New Resort Course of 1989 and ranked 34th in America's 75 Best Resort Courses by GOLF DIGEST.
Comments: "Lovely design . . . Beautiful setting . . . Unmatched in fall . . . Super test . . . One of the finest . . . Long, open, big greens that roll good . . . Very good, but hard . . . Better than Devil's Knob . . . Top-notch golf resort . . . Stay on the mountain when temperature is above 80."

★★½ ALDERBROOK GOLF & YACHT CLUB
Union—R—206-898-2560 (30 mi. from Olympia).
Season: Year-round. **High:** June-Sept. **Caddies:** No.
Green fee: $20-$49. **Credit cards:** V, MC.
Lodging on site: Yes. **Reduced fees:** Weekdays, Low Season, Resort Guests, Twilight Play.
Unrestricted walking: Yes. **Range:** Yes (mats).
Holes: 18. **Par:** 72. **Yards:** 6,326-5,500. **Slope:** 122-125.
Comments: "Inconsistent . . . It's got serious problems."

★★★½ APPLE TREE GOLF COURSE
Yakima—PU—509-966-5877 (140 mi. from Seattle).
Season: March-Nov. **High:** June-Sept.. **Caddies:** No.
Green fee: $20-$49. **Credit cards:** V, MC.
Lodging on site: No. **Reduced fees:** Low Season, Twilight Play.
Unrestricted walking: Yes. **Range:** Yes (grass).
Holes: 18. **Par:** 72. **Yards:** 6,892-5,428. **Slope:** 130-128.
Comments: "Fun course . . . Only a challenge when rough is up . . . Some interesting holes . . . Apple island green 17th fun to play."

★★★ AVALON GOLF CLUB
NORTH/WEST/SOUTH 9s
Burlington—PU—206-757-1900, 800-624-0202 (55 mi. from Seattle).
Season: Year-round. **High:** May-Oct. **Caddies:** Yes.
Green fee: $20-$49. **Credit cards:** V, MC.
Reduced fees: Weekdays, Low Season, Resort Guests, Twilight Play.
Unrestricted walking: Yes. **Range:** Yes (grass).
Holes: 27. **Par:** 36/36/36. **Yards:** 3,396/3,201/3,375.
Comments: "What variety . . . North and West are the best . . . Very good design for good players."

★½ BATTLE CREEK GOLF COURSE
Marysville—PU—206-659-7931 (30 mi. from Seattle).
Season: Year-round. **High:** April-Sept. **Caddies:** No.
Green fee: $20-$49. **Credit cards:** No.
Lodging on site: No. **Reduced fees:** Weekdays.
Unrestricted walking: Yes. **Range:** Yes (grass).
Holes: 18. **Par:** 73. **Yards:** 6,575-5,286. **Slope:** 133-132.
Also has 9-hole par-3 course.
Comments: "Terrible . . . Terrible tees . . . Terrible greens . . . Greens hopelessly bad . . . Rocky roughs . . . One par 3 stuck behind a boulder . . . A favorite of guys in swim trunks and tank tops."

★½ CEDARCREST MUNICIPAL GOLF COURSE
Marysville—PU—206-659-3566.
Season: Year-round. **High:** May-Sept. **Caddies:** No.
Green fee: Under $20. **Credit cards:** No.
Lodging on site: No. **Reduced fees:** No.
Unrestricted walking: Yes. **Range:** No.
Holes: 18. **Par:** 70. **Yards:** 5,474-4,905. **Slope:** 115-118.
Comments: "End-of-the-month golf course. Play it only when you haven't got enough cash to play elsewhere."

★★★½ CLASSIC GOLF & COUNTRY CLUB
Spanaway—PU—206-847-4440, 800-924-9557 (5 mi. from Tacoma).
Season: Year-round. **High:** May-Sept. **Caddies:** No.
Green fee: $20-$49. **Credit cards:** V, AMEX, MC.
Lodging on site: No. **Reduced fees:** Weekdays, Twilight Play.
Unrestricted walking: Yes. **Range:** Yes (grass).
Holes: 18. **Par:** 72. **Yards:** 6,793-5,580. **Slope:** 133-121.
Comments: "Good course with lots of variation and challenges . . . Easy for intelligent golfers . . . Too crowded . . . Too high priced for its immature conditions."

★★½ THE CREEK AT QUALCHAN GOLF COURSE
Spokane—PU—509-448-9317.
Season: April-Nov. **High:** June-Aug. **Caddies:** No.
Green fee: Under $20. **Credit cards:** V, MC.
Lodging on site: No. **Reduced fees:** No.
Unrestricted walking: Yes. **Range:** Yes (grass).
Holes: 18. **Par:** 72. **Yards:** 6,577-5,533. **Slope:** 124-120.
Comments: "Each drive makes each hole moderate or severe . . . Still new, still poor grass."

★★★★DESERT CANYON GOLF RESORT
Orondo—R—509-784-1111, 800-258-4173 (15 mi. from Wenatchee).
Season: March-Nov. **High:** May-Sept. **Caddies:** No.
Green fee: $20-$49. **Credit cards:** V, MC.
Lodging on site: Yes. **Reduced fees:** Low Season.
Unrestricted walking: No. **Range:** Yes (grass).
Holes: 18. **Par:** 72. **Yards:** 7,500-4,800. **Slope:** 127-104.

Comments: "Great target golf . . . Best in Washington already . . . Reminds me of Troon North . . . Very long. Has a downhill 670-yard par 5 . . . Fun but slow."

★★★DUNGENESS GOLF & COUNTRY CLUB
Sequim—PU—206-683-6344, 800-447-6826 (60 mi. from Seattle).
Season: Year-round. **High:** April-Sept. **Caddies:** No.
Green fee: $20-$49. **Credit cards:** V, MC.
Reduced fees: Weekdays, Low Season, Twilight Play.
Unrestricted walking: Yes. **Range:** Yes (grass).
Holes: 18. **Par:** 72. **Yards:** 6,378-5,400. **Slope:** 121-117.
Comments: "Surprisingly fun . . . Good retiree golf . . . It doesn't rain much in the banana belt . . . Can be difficult if windy . . . Watch out for sea crabs . . . They have a 'sea crab' bunker."

★★★½ HARBOUR POINTE GOLF CLUB
Mukilteo—PU—206-355-6060 (25 mi. from Seattle).
Season: Year-round. **High:** June-Sept. **Caddies:** No.
Green fee: $20-$49. **Credit cards:** V, MC.
Reduced fees: Weekdays, Low Season, Twilight Play.
Unrestricted walking: Yes. **Range:** Yes (grass).
Holes: 18. **Par:** 72. **Yards:** 6,862-6,024. **Slope:** 137-124.
Selected Best New Public Course of 1991 by GOLF DIGEST.
Comments: "Exciting . . . Excellent mix of water and woods . . . Two different 9s . . . Flat watery front, hilly back . . . Terrible greens . . . Hybrid grass never worked . . . Never grew in . . . A drag . . . Good design but should be better maintained, especially for the price . . . Too spendy . . . Caters to the best-dressed."

★★★★INDIAN CANYON GOLF COURSE
Spokane—PU—509-747-5353.
Season: March-Nov. **High:** June-Sept. **Caddies:** No.
Green fee: Under $20. **Credit cards:** No.
Lodging on site: No. **Reduced fees:** Twilight Play.
Unrestricted walking: Yes. **Range:** Yes (grass).
Holes: 18. **Par:** 72. **Yards:** 6,296-5,318. **Slope:** 127-123.
Ranked in First 25 of America's 75 Best Public Courses by GOLF DIGEST.
Comments: "Old highly-ranked legend is aging beautifully . . . Great public course at very reasonable price . . . Best public links around . . . No. 1 public in the Pacific Northwest . . . Hilly . . . Lush . . . Very tight . . . Bring your straight stick . . . A real test of stamina."

★½ JEFFERSON PARK GOLF COURSE
Seattle—PU—206-762-4513.
Season: Year-round. **High:** March-Oct. **Caddies:** No.
Green fee: Under $20. **Credit cards:** V, MC.

WASHINGTON

Lodging on site: No. **Reduced fees:** Twilight Play.
Unrestricted walking: Yes. **Range:** Yes (mats).
Holes: 18. **Par:** 70. **Yards:** 6,019-5,449. **Slope:** 115-112.
Also 9-hole executive course on site.
Comments: "Nice view of Seattle . . . Only way to get a tee time is to work there . . . Only I-5 gets more traffic."

★★★★½ KAYAK POINT GOLF COURSE
Stanwood—PU—206-652-9676, 800-562-3094 (45 mi. from Seattle).
Season: Year-round. **High:** May-Sept. **Caddies:** No.
Green fee: $20-$49. **Credit cards:** V, MC.
Lodging on site: No. **Reduced fees:** Weekdays.
Unrestricted walking: Yes. **Range:** Yes (grass).
Holes: 18. **Par:** 72. **Yards:** 6,719-5,332. **Slope:** 133-128.
Ranked in Second 25 of America's 75 Best Public Courses by GOLF DIGEST.
Comments: "Wonderful up-in-the-woods layout . . . Unbelievable . . . Beauty and grace . . . Cut through the forest . . . Real tight . . . Bring your entire golf game . . . As tough as a day is long . . . Can score with irons off tees . . . Long tee to green . . . Long walks from greens to tees . . . Best place to play in Puget Sound area . . . Best in Snohomish County . . . Probably the best county-owned course in the U.S. . . . Just not well known yet . . . Tough on short hitters . . . Pro shop/counter staff couldn't be friendlier."

★★★ LAKE PADDEN GOLF CLUB
Bellingham—PU—206-738-7400 (65 mi. from Seattle).
Season: Year-round. **High:** Apr-Sept. **Caddies:** No.
Green fee: Under $20. **Credit cards:** V, MC.
Lodging on site: No. **Reduced fees:** No.
Unrestricted walking: Yes. **Range:** Yes (grass).
Holes: 18. **Par:** 72. **Yards:** 6,580-6,300. **Slope:** 122-118.
Comments: "Good looking . . . Not long, kind of wet . . . Lots of players."

★★★ LAKE SPANAWAY GOLF COURSE
Tacoma—PU—206-531-3660.
Season: Year-round. **High:** May-Sept. **Caddies:** No.
Green fee: Under $20. **Credit cards:** No.
Lodging on site: No. **Reduced fees:** Weekdays.
Unrestricted walking: Yes. **Range:** Yes (mats).
Holes: 18. **Par:** 72. **Yards:** 6,787-5,935. **Slope:** 129-126.
Comments: "Very good medium-priced course . . . Best public course in Puget Sound . . . Plain, stuffy and unkempt."

★½ LAKE WILDERNESS GOLF COURSE
Maple Valley—PU—206-432-9405 (13 mi. from Renton).
Season: Year-round. **High:** June-Sept. **Caddies:** No.
Green fee: Under $20. **Credit cards:** V, MC.
Reduced fees: Weekdays, Low Season, Twilight Play.
Unrestricted walking: Yes. **Range:** No.
Holes: 18. **Par:** 70. **Yards:** 5,495-4,767. **Slope:** 122-120.
Comments: "The worst in Washington . . . Glorified pitch and putt."

★½ LIPOMA FIRS GOLF COURSE
Puyallup—PU—206-841-4396, 800-649-4396 (10 mi. from Tacoma).
Season: Year-round. **High:** June-Sept. **Caddies:** No.
Green fee: Under $20. **Credit cards:** No.
Reduced fees: Weekdays, Low Season, Twilight Play.
Unrestricted walking: Yes. **Range:** Yes (mats).
Holes: 18. **Par:** 72. **Yards:** 6,847-6,200. **Slope:** 124-119.
Comments: "No topsoil . . . Don't take divots . . . Too many rocks . . . A club damager . . . Needs to grow up."

★★★★McCORMICK WOODS GOLF COURSE

Port Orchard—PU—206-895-0130, 800-323-0130 (20 mi. from Tacoma).
Season: Year-round. **High:** April-Oct. **Caddies:** No.
Green fee: $20-$49. **Credit cards:** V, MC.
Reduced fees: Weekdays, Low Season, Twilight Play.
Unrestricted walking: Yes. **Range:** Yes (grass).
Holes: 18. **Par:** 72. **Yards:** 7,012-5,299. **Slope:** 139-120.
Ranked in Second 25 of America's 75 Best Public Courses, GOLF DIGEST.
Comments: "Serene . . . Spectacular . . . What golf is all about . . . As
good as any in Puget Sound . . . Best test in the state . . . My favorite . . .
Real fun . . . Just a treat to play . . . A large scale course . . . Front 9 may be
the best 9 in Washington . . . So many doglegs, premium is on accuracy . . .
Tough pin placements . . . Roughs are native, bring a lot of balls . . . Mt.
Rainier backdrop makes one par 3 almost spiritual . . . Worth the cost."

★★MEADOW PARK GOLF COURSE

Tacoma—PU—206-473-3033.
Season: Year-round. **High:** May-Sept. **Caddies:** No.
Green fee: Under $20. **Credit cards:** V, MC.
Lodging on site: No. **Reduced fees:** Weekdays.
Unrestricted walking: Yes. **Range:** Yes (mats).
Holes: 18. **Par:** 71. **Yards:** 6,093-5,763. **Slope:** 114-111.

★★½ NORTH SHORE GOLF COURSE

Tacoma—PU—206-838-3660, 800-447-1375.
Season: Year-round. **High:** May-Sept. **Caddies:** No.
Green fee: $20-$49. **Credit cards:** V, AMEX, MC.
Reduced fees: Weekdays, Low Season, Twilight Play.
Unrestricted walking: Yes. **Range:** Yes (mats).
Holes: 18. **Par:** 71. **Yards:** 6,305-5,442. **Slope:** 127-126.
Comments: "Old course . . . Plain clubhouse . . . Good marshals . . . A bit
pricey."

★★★½ PORT LUDLOW GOLF COURSE
TIDE/TIMBER/TRAIL 9s

Port Ludlow—R—206-437-0272, 800-732-1239 (40 mi. from Seattle).
Season: Year-round. **High:** May-Sept. **Caddies:** No.
Green fee: $50-$99. **Credit cards:** V, AMEX, MC.
Reduced fees: Low Season, Resort Guests, Twilight Play.
Unrestricted walking: Yes. **Range:** Yes (grass).
Holes: 27. **Par:** 36/36/36. **Yards:** 3,357/3,430/3,418.
Tide/Timber Course ranked 46th in America's 75 Best Resort Courses by
GOLF DIGEST.
Comments: "Classic Washington course in tall firs . . . Well designed,
beautiful to play . . . A good test. A great vacation . . . Beautifully main-
tained . . . But maintenance crew is understaffed . . . New Trail 9 is a great
addition . . . Is very, very tough . . . New 9 is ridiculous . . . Too many
blind drives . . . Always seems to be soggy."

★★RIVERBEND GOLF COMPLEX

Kent—PU—206-854-3673 (20 mi. from Seattle).
Season: Year-round. **High:** March-Oct. **Caddies:** No.
Green fee: Under $20. **Credit cards:** V, MC.
Lodging on site: Yes. **Reduced fees:** Weekdays, Low Season,
Twilight Play.
Unrestricted walking: Yes. **Range:** Yes (mats).
Holes: 18. **Par:** 72. **Yards:** 6,603-5,485. **Slope:** 120-124.
Comments: "Flat but long . . . Plays tough but fair . . . Lots of water . . .
Greens need work . . . Too many hackers, no trees to hide behind."

★★★★SEMIAHMOO GOLF & COUNTRY CLUB

Blaine—R—206-371-7005 (33 mi. from Vancouver B.C.).
Season: Year-round. **High:** May-Oct. **Caddies:** No.
Green fee: $50-$99. **Credit cards:** V, AMEX, MC.

Lodging on site: Yes. **Reduced fees:** Weekdays, Low Season, Resort Guests, Twilight Play.
Unrestricted walking: Yes. **Range:** Yes (mats).
Holes: 18. **Par:** 72. **Yards:** 7,005-5,288. **Slope:** 130-123.
Selected Best New Resort Course of 1987 and ranked 18th in America's Best Resort Courses by Golf Digest.
Comments: "Oceanic beauty . . . Wooded setting . . . Well laid out, good separation between fairways, nice traps . . . A wonderful golf experience . . . Just excellent . . . Incredible. But you pay . . . Worth the high cost . . . Terrific design for all players . . . Looks ferocious, plays gently . . . Don't play, just take pictures."

★★★SNOHOMISH GOLF CLUB
Snohomish—PU—206-568-2676 (20 mi. from Seattle).
Season: Year-round. **High:** May-Sept. **Caddies:** No.
Green fee: Under $20. **Credit cards:** V, MC.
Lodging on site: No. **Reduced fees:** Weekdays.
Unrestricted walking: Yes. **Range:** Yes (grass).
Holes: 18. **Par:** 72. **Yards:** 6,858-6,315. **Slope:** 126-121.
Comments: "Older course . . . Trees and more trees . . . A driver's course . . . You'll not find a longer course for the money . . . Good variety of holes . . . Forget about a weekend spot on the starter's sheet."

★★½ SUDDEN VALLEY GOLF & COUNTRY CLUB
Bellingham—R—206-734-6435 (50 mi. from Vancouver, BC).
Season: Year-round. **High:** May-Oct. **Caddies:** No.
Green fee: $20-$49. **Credit cards:** V, MC.
Lodging on site: Yes. **Reduced fees:** Weekdays, Low Season, Resort Guests, Twilight Play.
Unrestricted walking: Yes. **Range:** Yes (grass).
Holes: 18. **Par:** 72. **Yards:** 6,550-5,627. **Slope:** 129-126.
Comments: "Nice variation between 9s . . . Flat front, hilly back . . . Nice but pricey . . . Poor maintenance for the price."

★★½ TUMWATER VALLEY GOLF CLUB
Tumwater—PU—206-943-9500 (1 mi. from Olympia).
Season: Year-round. **High:** April-Sept. **Caddies:** No.
Green fee: $20-$49. **Credit cards:** V, MC.
Lodging on site: No. **Reduced fees:** Low Season, Twilight Play.
Unrestricted walking: Yes. **Range:** Yes (mats).
Holes: 18. **Par:** 72. **Yards:** 7,162-5,854. **Slope:** 122-123.
Comments: "Excellent, plus it's next door to the Olympia Brewery! . . . A little too wet . . . Plays long . . . Always muddy . . . Believe it or not, this course needs water . . . Hard greens . . . Great driving range."

★★½ VETERANS MEMORIAL GOLF COURSE
Walla Walla—PU—509-527-4507 (280 mi. from Seattle).
Season: Year-round. **High:** April-Sept. **Caddies:** No.
Green fee: Under $20. **Credit cards:** No.
Lodging on site: No. **Reduced fees:** No.
Unrestricted walking: Yes. **Range:** Yes (grass).
Holes: 18. **Par:** 72. **Yards:** 6,311-5,732. **Slope:** 114-121.

WEST VIRGINIA

★★★½ CACAPON RESORT STATE PARK GOLF COURSE
Berkeley Springs—R—304-258-1022 (25 mi. from Winchester).
Season: Year-round. **High:** April-Oct. **Caddies:** No.
Green fee: Under $20. **Credit cards:** V, AMEX, MC.
Lodging on site: Yes. **Reduced fees:** Low Season.
Unrestricted walking: Yes. **Range:** Yes (grass).
Holes: 18. **Par:** 72. **Yards:** 6,940-5,510. **Slope:** 121-116.
Comments: "Relaxing setting . . . Beautiful scenery . . .Long hitters like it
. . . Better than Virginia's Lansdowne at less than half the price . . . Best deal
in the area . . . A bargain, but run by bureaucrats . . . Needs to be better
maintained, otherwise excellent . . . Two or three holes have bad greens . . .
Bugs a nuisance in early morning."

★★★CANAAN VALLEY RESORT GOLF COURSE
Davis—R—304-866-4121, 800-622-4121 (31 mi. from Elkins).
Season: April-Nov. **High:** Summer. **Caddies:** No.
Green fee: $20-$49. **Credit cards:** V, AMEX, DISC, MC.
Lodging on site: Yes. **Reduced fees:** No.
Unrestricted walking: Yes. **Range:** Yes (grass).
Holes: 18. **Par:** 72. **Yards:** 6,982-6,436. **Slope:** 125-119.
Comments: "Wide open, inexpensive . . . Outstanding greens . . . Out-
standing conditions . . . You will enjoy this . . . Lots of wildlife."

★★★½ GLADE SPRINGS RESORT
Daniels—R—304-763-2000, 800-634-5233 (13 mi. from Beckley).
Season: Year-round. **High:** April-Oct. **Caddies:** No.
Green fee: $20-$49. **Credit cards:** V, AMEX, MC.
Lodging on site: Yes. **Reduced fees:** Weekdays, Low Season, Resort
Guests, Twilight Play.
Unrestricted walking: No. **Range:** Yes (grass).
Holes: 18. **Par:** 72. **Yards:** 6,941-6,176. **Slope:** 135-129.
Ranked 5th in West Virginia by GOLF DIGEST.
Comments: "A diamond in coal country . . . Nicely maintained . . . Very
nice clubhouse, food and drink."

THE GREENBRIER
White Sulphur Springs—R—304-536-7851, 800-624-6070
(75 mi. from Roanoke, Va.).

Season: Year-round. **High:** April-Oct. **Caddies:** Yes.
Green fee: $50-$99. **Credit cards:** V, AMEX, MC.
Lodging on site: Yes. **Reduced fees:** Low Season.
Unrestricted walking: No. **Range:** Yes (grass).
★★★★½ GREENBRIER COURSE
Holes: 18. **Par:** 72. **Yards:** 6,681-5,280. **Slope:** 136-123.
Ranked 33rd in America's 75 Best Resort Courses by GOLF DIGEST.
Comments: "Hello, Mr. Nicklaus! . . . What a thrill . . . Spectacular . . .
Very strong . . . Not 1 weak hole . . . No breathers . . . Difficult but
beautiful . . . Too difficult . . . Not for beginners . . . A Nicklaus resort
course disaster . . . Impeccable service . . . Wonderful caddies . . . Wonder-
ful staff . . . Expensive but worth it."
★★½ LAKESIDE COURSE
Holes: 18. **Par:** 70. **Yards:** 6,336-5,175. **Slope:** 121-115.
Comments: "Fairways are fabulous . . . Par 3s most challenging . . . Cad-
dies available . . . Great for 25-handicappers."
★★★★OLD WHITE COURSE
Holes: 18. **Par:** 70. **Yards:** 6,640-5,658. **Slope:** 128-126.
Ranked 2nd in West Virginia by GOLF DIGEST.
Comments: "Great course . . . Everybody's favorite . . . Wide fairways,
very tough greens . . . Overpriced . . . Makes for expensive scenery."

LAKEVIEW RESORT & CONFERENCE CENTER
Morgantown—R—304-594-2011, 800-624-8300 (90 mi. from Pittsburgh).
Season: Year-round. **High:** April-Oct. **Caddies:** No.

Green fee: $20-$49. **Credit cards:** All Major.
Lodging on site: Yes. **Reduced fees:** Weekdays, Low Season, Resort Guests. **Unrestricted walking:** No. **Range:** Yes (mats).

★★★½ LAKEVIEW COURSE

Holes: 18. **Par:** 72. **Yards:** 6,760-5,432. **Slope:** 130-118.
Ranked 4th in West Virginia by GOLF DIGEST.
Comments: "Very scenic . . . Enjoyable course . . . Challenging from No. 1 to 18 . . . As nice as you can get . . . Pure golfing pleasure . . . Guests are treated like owners . . . Beautiful vistas . . . Don't forget to look around . . . Excellent food and lodging . . . Reasonably priced."

★★MOUNTAINVIEW COURSE

Holes: 18. **Par:** 72. **Yards:** 6,447-5,242. **Slope:** 119-122.
Comments: "Very hilly . . . Tight . . . Too many sidehill problems."

OGLEBAY PARK

Wheeling—PU—304-243-4051, 800-752-9436 (70 mi. from Pittsburgh).
Season: Year-round. **High:** April-Sept. **Caddies:** Yes.
Green fee: Under $20. **Credit cards:** V, AMEX, DISC, MC.
Lodging on site: Yes. **Reduced fees:** No.
Unrestricted walking: Yes. **Range:** Yes (grass).

★½ CRISPIN GOLF COURSE

Holes: 18. **Par:** 71. **Yards:** 5,700-5,670. **Slope:** 103-108.
Comments: "Well-deserved ego boost after Speidel course . . . Conditions very poor."

★★★½ SPEIDEL GOLF COURSE

304-243-4050.
Season: March-Dec. **High:** May-Sept.
Green fee: $20-$49. **Reduced fees:** Resort Guests.
Holes: 18. **Par:** 71. **Yards:** 7,000-5,515. **Slope:** 126-120.
Ranked 3rd in West Virginia by GOLF DIGEST.
Comments: "Great course . . . Always green, thick and tough . . . Tough but fair . . . Hard-to-read greens . . . Mountainous terrain . . . Very difficult . . . Bring a mountain goat . . . Use a cart . . . You'll take a lickin' . . . Play is very slow, rangers needed . . . Not good for below-average golfers."

★★½ PIPESTEM STATE PARK RESORT GOLF COURSE

Pipestem—R—304-466-1800, 800-225-5982 (189 mi. from Charlotte, N.C.). **Season:** Year-round. **High:** May-Sept. **Caddies:** No.
Green fee: Under $20. **Credit cards:** V, AMEX, MC.
Lodging on site: Yes. **Reduced fees:** Low Season.
Unrestricted walking: Yes. **Range:** Yes (grass).
Holes: 18. **Par:** 72. **Yards:** 6,884-6,131. **Slope:** 129-123.
Has 9-hole par-3 course.
Comments: "Excellent resort course . . . Play it again and again . . . Always in great shape . . . People as friendly as the course . . . Great value . . . Only fair conditioning . . . Poor greens."

★★½ TWIN FALLS RESORT STATE PARK GOLF COURSE

Mullens—PU—304-294-4000, 800-225-5982 (25 mi. from Beckley).
Season: Year-round. **High:** May-Aug. **Caddies:** No.
Green fee: Under $20. **Credit cards:** V, AMEX, MC.
Lodging on site: Yes. **Reduced fees:** Low Season.
Unrestricted walking: Yes. **Range:** No.
Holes: 18. **Par:** 71. **Yards:** 6,382-5,202. **Slope:** 122-112.
Comments: "In the middle of nowhere, but a very good challenge."

★★½ THE WOODS RESORT

Hedgesville—R—304-754-7222 (90 mi. from Washington D.C.).
Season: Year-round. **High:** Summer. **Caddies:** No.
Green fee: $20-$49. **Credit cards:** V, AMEX, MC.
Lodging on site: Yes. **Reduced fees:** No.
Unrestricted walking: No. **Range:** Yes (mats).
Holes: 18. **Par:** 72. **Yards:** 6,534-5,273. **Slope:** 121-109.
Third 9 under construction.

★★½ ABBEY SPRINGS GOLF COURSE

Fontana on Geneva Lake—R—414-275-6111 (60 mi. from Milwaukee).
Season: April-Nov. **High:** June-Sept. **Caddies:** No.
Green fee: $50-$99. **Credit cards:** V, AMEX, MC.
Lodging on site: No. **Reduced fees:** No.
Unrestricted walking: No. **Range:** Yes (grass).
Holes: 18. **Par:** 72. **Yards:** 6,466-5,439. **Slope:** 133-129.
Comments: "Pretty but short . . . Narrow fairways, steep hillside greens
. . . So-so front, challenging back . . . Difficult to walk . . . Has three
drivable par 4s . . . Too tight, slow play."

★★ ALPINE RESORT GOLF COURSE
RED/WHITE/BLUE 9s

Egg Harbor—R—414-868-3232 (60 mi. from Green Bay).
Season: May-Oct. **High:** July-Aug. **Caddies:** No.
Green fee: Under $20. **Credit cards:** V, MC.
Lodging on site: Yes. **Reduced fees:** Resort Guests, Twilight Play.
Unrestricted walking: Yes. **Range:** No.
Holes: 27. **Par:** 35/35/36. **Yards:** 2,849/3,198/3,009.
Comments: "Quaint . . . Very scenic . . . Good resort course, fast play . . .
No rough, no water . . . Recent improvements are noteworthy . . . Nothing
special . . . Keep alert for balls from adjacent holes . . . Hard fairways, poor
traps . . . A hackers' convention . . . One gimmick cliff hole . . . Make sure
the tram is working, it's a heart attack to the top."

BLACKWOLF RUN

Kohler—R—414-457-4446 (55 mi. from Milwaukee).
Season: April-Oct. **High:** Summer. **Caddies:** No.
Green fee: $50-$99. **Credit cards:** V, AMEX, MC, DISC.
Lodging on site: Yes. **Reduced fees:** Low Season, Twilight Play.
Unrestricted walking: Yes. **Range:** Yes (grass).

★★★★ MEADOW VALLEYS COURSE

GREAT VALUE

Holes: 18. **Par:** 72. **Yards:** 7,142-5,065. **Slope:** 143-125.
Pete Dye design. Ranked 4th in Wisconsin by GOLF DIGEST.
Comments: "Surprising, interesting contrast to River Course . . . Almost
as terrific as River . . . Back 9 is the finest I've played . . . From arrival to
departure, a truly great experience . . . Tough, beautiful, immaculate . . .
Terrific, a bit overpriced . . . No place better . . . Good value but high priced
. . . Staff was outstanding . . . Very polite, helpful . . . Worth a 6-hour drive
. . . Expensive but they treat you well . . . Very penal . . . Rough unfair for
average golfer . . . Requires thought and execution . . . Execute Pete Dye!"

★★★★★ RIVER COURSE

SUPER VALUE

Holes: 18. **Par:** 72. **Yards:** 6,991-5,090. **Slope:** 151-128.
Also a Pete Dye design. Ranked 31st in America's
100 Greatest Courses by GOLF DIGEST.
Comments: "The Best . . . Brutal, beautiful, toughest course ever . . .
Great challenge, great scenery . . . Would pay to just walk it . . . Greatest
test of game management, bar none . . . As good as it gets . . . Bring your
camera . . . Wonderful, scenic, tough . . . Heaven! . . . Outstanding . . .
Nos. 5 through 13 are the best run of 9 holes ever seen . . . A 'Must Play' . . .
Class operation from the range to the pro shop . . . Not a weak hole . . .
One of Pete Dye's best, he didn't ruin the land . . . Mother Nature's best . . .
Simply the best public course in America . . . A major someday? . . . Pure
target golf, no forgiveness."

★★★½ BROWN COUNTY GOLF COURSE

Oneida—PU—414-497-1731 (4 mi. from Green Bay).
Season: April-Oct. **High:** Summer. **Caddies:** No.
Green fee: Under $20. **Credit cards:** V.
Lodging on site: No. **Reduced fees:** No.
Unrestricted walking: Yes. **Range:** Yes (grass).
Holes: 18. **Par:** 72. **Yards:** 6,729-5,814. **Slope:** 133-127.
Ranked in Second 25 of America's 75 Best Public Courses by GOLF DIGEST.

Comments: "Exceptional for a county course . . . Textbook public operation . . . Great value . . . A challenging gem . . . Too bad you can only play it five months a year . . . Fairways and greens need work . . . Needs yardage markers . . . Best secret in Wisconsin. Shhhh."

★★★ BROWN DEER GOLF COURSE
Milwaukee—PU—414-352-8080.
Season: April-Dec. **High:** Summer. **Caddies:** No.
Green fee: $20-$49. **Credit cards:** V, MC.
Lodging on site: No. **Reduced fees:** No.
Unrestricted walking: Yes. **Range:** Yes (mats).
Holes: 18. **Par:** 71. **Yards:** 6,763-5,965. **Slope:** 130-131.
Comments: "Great county course . . . Good value . . . Tough par 4s . . . Not many traps, cheap green fee . . . Not the course it once was, but still fun . . . Greater Milwaukee Open here? No way! . . . A mistake . . . Should never be allowed to host GMO in 1994 . . . Once a county course, always a county course . . . GMO should improve the course . . . Will be even better once GMO is there . . . Being restored beyond former glory."

★★★½ CEDAR CREEK COUNTRY CLUB
Onalaska—PU—608-783-8100 (150 mi. from Minneapolis).
Season: April-Nov. **High:** May-Aug. **Caddies:** No.
Green fee: $20-$49. **Credit cards:** V, MC.
Lodging on site: No. **Reduced fees:** Weekdays.
Unrestricted walking: Yes. **Range:** Yes (grass).
Holes: 18. **Par:** 71. **Yards:** 6,751-5,240. **Slope:** 132-123.
Comments: "Newer course . . . Beautiful bent grass all around . . . Consistently well maintained. A lot of fun . . . The 'hill holes' are great . . . Don't walk them . . . Will be a true test in 10 years . . . Outstanding service."

CHASKA GOLF COURSE*
Appleton—PU—414-757-5757 (90 mi. from Milwaukee).
Season: April-Oct. **High:** Summer. **Caddies:** No.
Green fee: Under $20. **Credit cards:** V, MC.
Lodging on site: No. **Reduced fees:** Twilight Play.
Unrestricted walking: Yes. **Range:** Yes (grass).
Holes: 18. **Par:** 72. **Yards:** 6,854-5,847. **Slope:** 128-118.

★½ CHERRY HILLS GOLF COURSE
Sturgeon Bay—R—414-743-3240 (45 mi. from Green Bay).
Season: Year-round. **High:** Summer. **Caddies:** No.
Green fee: $20-$49. **Credit cards:** V, MC.
Lodging on site: Yes. **Reduced fees:** Weekdays, Low Season, Resort Guests, Twilight Play.
Unrestricted walking: Yes. **Range:** Yes (grass).
Holes: 18. **Par:** 72. **Yards:** 6,200-5,400. **Slope:** 119-123.
Comments: "Hilliest course ever . . . So-so. Big price, bad shape . . . Stones in the fairways . . . Poorly designed greens . . . Some bad holes."

FOX HILLS RESORT GOLF COURSES
Mishicot—R—414-755-2831, 800-955-7615 (25 mi. from Green Bay).
Season: April-Nov. **High:** Summer. **Caddies:** No.
Green fee: $20-$49. **Credit cards:** V, AMEX, MC, DISC.
Lodging on site: Yes. **Reduced fees:** Weekdays, Low Season, Twilight Play.
Unrestricted walking: Yes. **Range:** Yes (grass).
CLASSIC COURSE*
FRONT/BACK/BLUE 9s
Holes: 27. **Par:** 36/36/35. **Yards:** 3,094/3,280/3,130.
★★½ FOX HILLS NATIONAL GOLF CLUB
Holes: 18. **Par:** 72. **Yards:** 7,017-5,366. **Slope:** 136-124.
Comments: "Imitation links . . . Secret not known by many . . . Has a British feel . . . No trees, wear sunscreen . . . Waste bunkers hold water . . .

Maintenance a problem . . . Very boring, too many forced carries . . . Touted as a links-style course. Not even close! . . . Lousy clay pasture, artificially hard."

GENEVA NATIONAL GOLF CLUB
Lake Geneva—R—414-245-7010 (45 mi. from Milwaukee).
Season: April-Oct. **High:** May-Sept. **Caddies:** No.
Green fee: $50-$99. **Credit cards:** V, AMEX, MC.
Lodging on site: Yes. **Reduced fees:** Weekdays, Low Season, Resort Guests.
Unrestricted walking: No. **Range:** Yes (grass).
★★★½ **PALMER COURSE**
Holes: 18. **Par:** 72. **Yards:** 7,171-4,904. **Slope:** 140-122.
Ranked 6th in Wisconsin by GOLF DIGEST.
Comments: "Excellent new course, cut out of woods . . . A player's course, no tricks . . . Will be a great one . . . Very beautiful but didn't make good use of ample land . . . Pretty, but 11 blind tee shots? Come on! . . . First-class service . . . Great facilities."
★★★½ **TREVINO COURSE**
Holes: 18. **Par:** 72. **Yards:** 7,120-5,193. **Slope:** 137-124.
Ranked 9th in Wisconsin by GOLF DIGEST.
Comments: "Incredible course, great design . . . Great elevation changes, demands concentration . . . Fader's dream . . . Great natural terrain, starters are outstanding . . . Greens like concrete . . . Better than Palmer Course . . . It's a coin toss as to which course I preferred."

THE GOLF COURSES OF LAWSONIA
Green Lake—PU—414-294-3320, 800-558-8898 (40 mi. from Oshkosh).
Season: April-Oct. **High:** Summer. **Caddies:** No.
Green fee: $50-$99. **Credit cards:** All Major.
Lodging on site: Yes. **Reduced fees:** Twilight Play.
Unrestricted walking: No. **Range:** Yes (grass).
★★★★ **LINKS COURSE**
Holes: 18. **Par:** 72. **Yards:** 6,764-5,778. **Slope:** 130-114.
Ranked in Third 25 of America's 75 Best Public Courses by GOLF DIGEST.
Comments: "One of the most wondrous courses in America . . . 1920s course with huge elevated greens . . . Memorable . . . Outstanding . . . A classic . . . Takes you back to yesteryear . . . The way it used to be . . . No other course like it . . . Super elevated greens . . . Par 3s are unique . . . A treat, and cheap! . . . Quality personnel and service . . . Pro shop merchandise and restaurant overpriced."
★★★★ **THE WOODLANDS COURSE**
Holes: 18. **Par:** 72. **Yards:** 6,618-5,106. **Slope:** 129-120.
Comments: "Good modern course . . . Toughest 18 you'll ever play . . . Terrific ambiance, with deer prancing through fairways. But some greens aren't up to speed . . . Lovely scenery . . . If you're not straight, bring plenty of ammo . . . First-class facilities at a sensible price . . . For overall enjoyment, one of the top 5 ever . . . Only Blackwolf is better."

GRAND GENEVA RESORT
Lake Geneva—R—414-248-8811 (45 mi. from Milwaukee).
Season: April-Oct. **High:** May-Sept. **Caddies:** No.
Green fee: $50-$99. **Credit cards:** V, AMEX, MC.
Lodging on site: Yes. **Reduced fees:** Weekdays, Twilight Play.
Unrestricted walking: No. **Range:** Yes (grass).
Previously known as Americana Lake Geneva Resort.
★★★ **THE BRIAR PATCH COURSE**
Holes: 18. **Par:** 71. **Yards:** 6,900-4,950. **Slope:** 130-117.
Comments: "Dye/Nicklaus course that's fun from any set of tees . . . Great links style . . . Like playing a British Open course . . . Not the quality it once was . . . Less interesting since some of the wilderness has been removed."
★★★½ **THE BRUTE COURSE**
Holes: 18. **Par:** 72. **Yards:** 7,200-5,400. **Slope:** 135-122.
Comments: "More challenging than Briar Patch . . . Long course, fast

greens . . . Huge greens . . . Well named . . . Boring, driver, 3-wood all day . . . Run-down resort . . . Property recently sold. Needs money but layout is superb . . . Old facilities, need maintenance."

★★★★ LAKE ARROWHEAD GOLF COURSE

Nekoosa—PU—715-325-2929 (15 mi. from Wisconsin Rapids).
Season: April-Oct. **High:** May-Sept. **Caddies:** No.
Green fee: $20-$49. **Credit cards:** V, MC.
Lodging on site: Yes. **Reduced fees:** Weekdays, Low Season, Twilight Play.
Unrestricted walking: Yes. **Range:** Yes (grass).
Holes: 18. **Par:** 72. **Yards:** 6,624-5,213. **Slope:** 135-125.
Comments: "One of the best in the area . . . Wonderfully laid out and maintained. A gem . . . Excellent course, not bad on the wallet . . . Course and staff are A-plus . . . SentryWorld without the flowers . . . Better than SentryWorld, by far . . . Worth the drive . . . Wear your Desert Storm khakis, lots of sand!"

★½ LAKE LAWN LODGE GOLF COURSE

Delavan—R—414-728-7950, 800-338-5253 (45 mi. from Milwaukee).
Season: April-Oct. **High:** May-Sept. **Caddies:** No.
Green fee: $50-$99. **Credit cards:** All Major.
Lodging on site: Yes. **Reduced fees:** Resort Guests, Twilight Play.
Unrestricted walking: No. **Range:** Yes (grass).
Holes: 18. **Par:** 70. **Yardage:** 6,418-5,215. **Slope:** 120-107.
Comments: "Layout lacks interest . . . Greens and tees too close together . . . Improved considerably in past several years . . . Redesign has made it quite acceptable."

★★★ MASCOUTIN GOLF CLUB

Berlin—PU—414-361-2360 (20 mi. from Oshkosh).
Season: April-Oct. **High:** July-Sept. **Caddies:** No.
Green fee: $20-$49. **Credit cards:** V, MC.
Lodging on site: No. **Reduced fees:** Low Season, Twilight Play.
Unrestricted walking: No. **Range:** Yes (grass).
Holes: 18. **Par:** 72. **Yards:** 6,821-5,339. **Slope:** 123-116.
Comments: "Nice mature public course . . . All-around high quality . . . Beautiful hilltop views . . . Best greens in the state . . . People are nice, fairways below average . . . Needs a better pro shop."

★★★½ NORTHWOOD GOLF CLUB

Rhinelander—PU—715-282-6565 (55 mi. from Wausau).
Season: April-Oct. **High:** Summer. **Caddies:** No.
Green fee: $20-$49. **Credit cards:** V, MC.
Lodging on site: No. **Reduced fees:** No.
Unrestricted walking: Yes. **Range:** Yes (grass).
Holes: 18. **Par:** 72. **Yards:** 6,719-5,338. **Slope:** 135-127.
Comments: "A surprise . . . Unbelievable . . . A true test, two island greens, slick greens . . . Extremely tight . . . Not much room for error . . . Don't miss the fairways . . . Not for the everyday golfer . . . Most fairways slope toward treelined rough . . . Bring a compass."

★½ OLYMPIA RESORT & SPORTS CENTER

Oconomowoc—R—414-567-2577, 800-558-9573 (40 mi. from Milwaukee).
Season: April-Nov. **High:** Summer. **Caddies:** No.
Green fee: $20-$49. **Credit cards:** V, AMEX, MC.
Lodging on site: Yes. **Reduced fees:** Weekdays, Twilight Play.
Unrestricted walking: Yes. **Range:** Yes (grass).
Holes: 18. **Par:** 71. **Yards:** 6,482-6,215. **Slope:** 116-114.
Comments: "Rather plain and open . . . Poorly maintained . . . Has slipped downhill . . . Facilities were dirty . . . Outstanding recovery under new owners . . . Now OK."

★★THE RIDGES GOLF CLUB
Wisconsin Rapids—PU—715-424-1111 (100 mi. from Madison).
Season: April-Oct. **High:** Summer. **Caddies:** No.
Green fee: Under $20. **Credit cards:** V, MC.
Lodging on site: Yes. **Reduced fees:** Weekdays, Twilight Play.
Unrestricted walking: Yes. **Range:** Yes (grass).
Holes: 18. **Par:** 72. **Yards:** 6,400-5,300. **Slope:** 130-126.
Comments: "Front 9 average . . . A pasture . . . Back 9 a tight challenge
. . . Fantastic . . . Out of the Twilight Zone . . . Fun golf."

★★★★SENTRYWORLD
Stevens Point—PU—715-345-1600 (100 mi. from Milwaukee).
Season: April-Nov. **High:** Summer. **Caddies:** No.
Green fee: $50-$99. **Credit cards:** V, AMEX, MC.
Lodging on site: No. **Reduced fees:** Low Season.
Unrestricted walking: Yes. **Range:** Yes (grass).
Holes: 18. **Par:** 72. **Yards:** 7,055-5,197. **Slope:** 144-130.
Ranked in First 25 of America's 75 Best Public Courses by GOLF DIGEST.
Comments: "A perfect experience . . . Golf among the flower beds . . . Ex-
cellent flower gardens . . . The colors are great . . . Course was designed by
Better Homes and Gardens . . . Has gone downhill in past couple of years
but still excellent . . . Not up to its former status . . . Coming back to life.
Now in great shape . . . Haagen-Dazs malts at the turn!"

★★★THE SPRINGS GOLF CLUB RESORT
Spring Green—R—608-588-7707, 800-822-7774 (35 mi. from Madison).
Season: Year-round. **High:** Summer. **Caddies:** No.
Green fee: $20-$49. **Credit cards:** V, DISC, MC.
Lodging on site: Yes. **Reduced fees:** No.
Unrestricted walking: No. **Range:** Yes (grass).
Holes: 18. **Par:** 72. **Yards:** 6,700-6,100. **Slope:** 132-124.
New 9 by Roger Packard and Andy North will open in spring of '94.
Comments: "Many improvements made . . . Used to be outstanding, was
redesigned to accommodate condos . . . Rates have doubled in two years
. . . Beautiful spot spoiled by condos and commercialism . . . Not in good
shape at all . . . Lots of bugs."

★★★½ TRAPPERS TURN GOLF CLUB
Wisconsin Dells—R—608-253-7000, 800-221-8876 (50 mi. from Madison).
Season: April-Oct. **High:** Summer. **Caddies:** No.
Green fee: $20-$49. **Credit cards:** V, MC.
Lodging on site: Yes. **Reduced fees:** Weekdays, Low Season, Resort
Guests, Twilight Play.
Unrestricted walking: No. **Range:** No.
Holes: 18. **Par:** 72. **Yards:** 6,363-5,043. **Slope:** 126-120.
Comments: "Super layout . . . Good combo of links and woods . . . Hilly,
scenic . . . Three great finishing holes . . . Great little course and value . . .
Never a dull moment . . . Nice people . . . Very friendly."

★★★★½ UNIVERSITY RIDGE GOLF COURSE
Verona—PU—608-845-8704, 800-897-4343 (8 mi. from Madison).
Season: April-Oct. **High:** Summer. **Caddies:** No.
Green fee: $20-$49. **Credit cards:** V, AMEX, MC.
Lodging on site: No. **Reduced fees:** Low Season, Twilight Play.
Unrestricted walking: Yes. **Range:** Yes (grass).
Holes: 18. **Par:** 72. **Yards:** 6,857-5,005. **Slope:** 142-121.
Ranked 3rd in state by GOLF DIGEST. Owned by Univ. of Wisconsin.
Comments: "Contrasting 9s . . . Combines links and traditional holes into
one . . . Beyond words . . . Has it all . . . Great wooded holes . . . Gor-
geous, almost too tough in places . . . Frequently two routes to a green . . .
What a beauty! What a value! . . . Closest thing to Blackwolf I've seen . . .
Will be up there with the best . . . Outstanding service and personnel . . .
Too pricey for being supported by a university."

GREAT VALUE

★½ AIRPORT GOLF COURSE
Cheyenne—PU—307-637-6418.
Season: Year-round. **High:** May-Oct. **Caddies:** No.
Green fee: Under $20. **Credit cards:** V, MC.
Lodging on site: No. **Reduced fees:** Twilight Play.
Unrestricted walking: Yes. **Range:** Yes (grass).
Holes: 18. **Par:** 70. **Yards:** 6,121-5,661. **Slope:** 99-113.
Comments: "Front is short, narrow . . . Back is long, wide open . . . Takes 5 hours to play, every time."

★★★ BUFFALO GOLF CLUB
Buffalo—PU—307-684-5266.
Season: March-Nov. **High:** May-Aug. **Caddies:** No.
Green fee: Under $20. **Credit cards:** V, MC.
Lodging on site: No. **Reduced fees:** No.
Unrestricted walking: Yes. **Range:** Yes (grass).
Holes: 18. **Par:** 71. **Yards:** 6,556-5,512. **Slope:** 114-116.
Comments: "Always an excellent time . . . Hard course to walk."

★★½ CASPER GOLF CLUB
Casper—PU—307-234-2405.
Season: March-Nov. **High:** May-Aug. **Caddies:** No.
Green fee: Under $20. **Credit cards:** No.
Lodging on site: No. **Reduced fees:** Weekdays.
Unrestricted walking: Yes. **Range:** Yes (grass).
Holes: 18. **Par:** 70. **Yards:** 6,234-5,472. **Slope:** 112-112.

★★½ DOUGLAS CONVERSE GOLF CLUB
Douglas—PU—307-358-5099 (48 mi. from Casper).
Season: Year-round. **High:** May-Sept. **Caddies:** No.
Green fee: Under $20. **Credit cards:** No.
Lodging on site: No. **Reduced fees:** No.
Unrestricted walking: Yes. **Range:** Yes (grass).
Holes: 18. **Par:** 71. **Yards:** 6,400-6,100. **Slope:** 107-103.
Comments: "Never crowded."

★★ FRANCIS E. WARREN AFB GOLF COURSE
Francis E. Warren AFB—PU—307-775-3556 (1 mi. from Cheyenne).
Season: Year-round. **High:** April-Oct. **Caddies:** No.
Green fee: Under $20. **Credit cards:** V, MC.
Lodging on site: Yes. **Reduced fees:** Weekdays, Twilight Play.
Unrestricted walking: Yes. **Range:** Yes (grass).
Holes: 18. **Par:** 72. **Yards:** 6,665-5,199. **Slope:** 105-103.
Comments: "Good military course open to the public . . . Needs more maintenance."

GLENN (RED) JACOBY GOLF COURSE*
Laramie—PU—307-745-3111.
Season: April-Oct. **High:** May-Aug. **Caddies:** No.
Green fee: Under $20. **Credit cards:** No.
Lodging on site: No. **Reduced fees:** No.
Unrestricted walking: Yes. **Range:** Yes (grass).
Holes: 18. **Par:** 70. **Yards:** 6,533-5,338. **Slope:** 109-108.
Course owned by University of Wyoming.

GREEN HILLS MUNICIPAL GOLF COURSE*
Worland—PU—307-347-8972 (160 mi. from Billings, Mont.).
Season: April-Oct. **High:** April-July. **Caddies:** No.
Green fee: Under $20. **Credit cards:** No.
Lodging on site: No. **Reduced fees:** Weekdays.
Unrestricted walking: Yes. **Range:** Yes (grass).
Holes: 18. **Par:** 72. **Yards:** 6,444-5,104. **Slope:** 113-95.

WYOMING

★★★★**JACKSON HOLE GOLF & TENNIS CLUB**
Jackson—PU—307-733-3111.
Season: May-Oct. **High:** Summer. **Caddies:** No.
Green fee: $20-$49. **Credit cards:** V, AMEX, MC.
Lodging on site: No. **Reduced fees:** Low Season, Twilight Play.
Unrestricted walking: No. **Range:** Yes (grass).
Holes: 18. **Par:** 72. **Yards:** 7,168-6,783. **Slope:** 133-124.
Ranked 10th in America's 75 Best Resort Courses by GOLF DIGEST.
Comments: "Very close to Heaven . . . How can you go wrong with the
Grand Tetons as a background? . . . Great mountains, good course . . . Flat,
in a river floodplain . . . Overhyped."

(GREAT VALUE)

KENDRICK MUNICIPAL GOLF COURSE*
Sheridan—PU—307-674-8148 (140 mi. from Billings, Mont.).
Season: April-Oct. **High:** May-July. **Caddies:** No.
Green fee: Under $20. **Credit cards:** No.
Lodging on site: No. **Reduced fees:** No.
Unrestricted walking: Yes. **Range:** Yes (grass).
Holes: 18. **Par:** 72. **Yards:** 6,800. **Slope:** 116-113.

★★★**OLIVE GLENN GOLF & COUNTRY CLUB**
Cody—PU—307-587-5551 (125 mi. from Billings, Mont.).
Season: April-Oct. **High:** Summer. **Caddies:** No.
Green fee: $20-$49. **Credit cards:** MC.
Lodging on site: No. **Reduced fees:** Low Season.
Unrestricted walking: Yes. **Range:** Yes (grass).
Holes: 18. **Par:** 72. **Yards:** 6,880-5,654. **Slope:** 124-120.
Ranked 4th in Wyoming by GOLF DIGEST.
Comments: "Scenic . . . Set in Buffalo Bill country."

★★★★**TETON PINES COUNTRY CLUB & RESORT**
Jackson—R—307-733-1733, 800-238-2223.
Season: May-Oct. **High:** Summer. **Caddies:** Yes.
Green fee: $50-$99. **Credit cards:** All Major.
Lodging on site: Yes. **Reduced fees:** Low Season, Resort Guests,
Twilight Play.
Unrestricted walking: No. **Range:** Yes (grass).
Holes: 18. **Par:** 72. **Yards:** 7,403-5,480. **Slope:** 137-117.
Ranked 49th in America's 75 Best Resort Courses by GOLF DIGEST.
Comments: "What marvelous scenery . . . One of the best resorts I've ever
stayed . . . One of the best courses I've ever played . . . Excellent in all
respects . . . Don't care what you guys say. It's better than Jackson Hole . . .
More interesting water holes . . . Better greens."

Note: The 800 toll-free numbers listed might not connect to locations outside Canada.

NEWFOUNDLAND

TWIN RIVERS GOLF COURSE*
Port Blanford—R—709-543-2626, 800-461-0808 (150 mi. from St. John's).
Season: May-Nov. **High:** July-Aug. **Caddies:** No.
Green fee: $20-$49. **Credit cards:** All Major.
Lodging on site: Yes. **Reduced fees:** No.
Unrestricted walking: Yes. **Range:** Yes (grass).
Holes: 18. **Par:** 71. **Yards:** 6,546-5,433. **Slope:** Unrated.
Comments: "Super . . . Long, but scenic . . . Hard to get to . . . Very short season . . . Walkers can enjoy."

PRINCE EDWARD ISLAND

★★★★BRUDENELL RIVER PROVINCIAL GOLF COURSE
Montague—R—902-652-2342 (35 mi. from Charlottetown).
Season: May-Oct. **High:** Summer. **Caddies:** No.
Green fee: $20-$49. **Credit cards:** V, MC.
Lodging on site: Yes. **Reduced fees:** Low Season.
Unrestricted walking: Yes. **Range:** Yes (grass).
Holes: 18. **Par:** 72. **Yards:** 6,517-5,082. **Slope:** Unrated.
Comments: "One of the best in eastern Canada . . . Extremely well groomed . . . Tricky greens . . . One course I've seen with six par 5s, six par 4s and six par 3s . . . Out of the way . . . Priced right . . . Great facilities . . . Worth the drive . . . A must."

★★★GREEN GABLES GOLF COURSE
Cavendish—PU—902-963-2488 (28 mi. from Charlottetown).
Season: May-Oct. **High:** July-Aug. **Caddies:** No.
Green fee: $20-$49. **Credit cards:** V, MC.
Reduced fees: Weekdays, Low Season, Twilight Play.
Unrestricted walking: Yes. **Range:** Yes (grass).
Holes: 18. **Par:** 72. **Yards:** 6,331-5,296. **Slope:** Unrated.
Comments: "Interesting . . . Enjoyable . . . Nice mature layout . . . Small greens, difficult to hold . . . Wide, fun, playable by a wide spectrum of abilities . . . Watch those water hazards. Red clay banks very slippery."

★★½ MILL RIVER PROVINCIAL GOLF COURSE
O'Leary—R—902-859-2238 (75 mi. from Charlottetown).
Season: May-Oct. **High:** June-Sept. **Caddies:** No.
Green fee: $20-$49. **Credit cards:** V, MC.
Lodging on site: Yes. **Reduced fees:** Low Season.
Unrestricted walking: Yes. **Range:** Yes (grass).
Holes: 18. **Par:** 72. **Yards:** 7,001-6,503. **Slope:** Unrated.
Comments: "Superb short course . . . Demanding . . . Accuracy required . . . Varying terrain . . . Long walks green to tee. Take a cart . . . Good family place . . . Uncrowded. Unhurried."

STANHOPE GOLF & COUNTRY CLUB*
Stanhope—PU—902-672-2842 (12 mi. from Charlottetown).
Season: May-Oct. **High:** July-Aug. **Caddies:** No.
Green fee: $20-$49. **Credit cards:** V.
Lodging on site: No. **Reduced fees:** Weekdays, Low Season.
Unrestricted walking: Yes. **Range:** Yes (grass).
Holes: 18. **Par:** 72. **Yards:** 6,439-5,785. **Slope:** Unrated.
Comments: "A great test . . . Wind always a factor . . . Slow play, undistinguished design."

NEW BRUNSWICK

★★★THE ALGONQUIN GOLF COURSE
St. Andrews—R—506-529-3062 (60 mi. from Saint John).
Season: May-Oct. **High:** July-Aug. **Caddies:** No.
Green fee: $20-$49. **Credit cards:** All Major.
Lodging on site: Yes. **Reduced fees:** Low Season, Resort Guests,
Twilight Play.
Unrestricted walking: Yes. **Range:** Yes (grass).
Holes: 18. **Par:** 72. **Yards:** 6,474-5,949. **Slope:** Unrated.
Comments: "Olden-time course . . . Donald Ross, remodeled . . . Worthwhile . . . Scotland on the east coast of Canada . . . Can see the ocean from most holes . . . Good variety . . . Both short and long irons a must . . . Small tough greens . . . In one of the most beautiful towns in North America . . . Needs better maintenance."

NOVA SCOTIA

★★★★CAPE BRETON HIGHLANDS GOLF LINKS
Ingonish Beach—PU—902-285-2600 (70 mi. from Sydney).
Season: May-Oct. **High:** July-Aug. **Caddies:** Yes.
Green fee: $20-$49. **Credit cards:** V, MC.
Lodging on site: Yes. **Reduced fees:** Twilight Play.
Unrestricted walking: Yes. **Range:** No.
Holes: 18. **Par:** 72. **Yards:** 6,596-5,664. **Slope:** 139.
Comments: "Golf Heaven on earth . . . Outstanding . . . Incredible . . . Very challenging . . . Just wonderful . . . Only one adjective fits—sublime . . . One of the world's best . . . What golf should be—fabulous views, great layout, not overconditioned and golfers walk . . . A walk in the woods . . . Too long a walk between holes . . . Bring your hiking boots . . . Easternmost course in North America . . . Long drive for a fun layout . . . Stay at the Keltic Lodge . . . Pro shop doesn't measure up to course."

DUNDEE RESORT GOLF COURSE*
West Bay—R—902-345-2649, 800-565-5660 (200 mi. from Halifax).
Season: May-Nov. **High:** July-Sept. **Caddies:** No.
Green fee: $20-$49. **Credit cards:** All Major.
Lodging on site: Yes. **Reduced fees:** Weekdays, Resort Guests,
Twilight Play.
Unrestricted walking: Yes. **Range:** No.
Holes: 18. **Par:** 72. **Yards:** 6,475-5,236. **Slope:** 135.

★★★½ THE PINES RESORT HOTEL GOLF CLUB
Digby—R—902-245-4104 (150 mi. from Halifax).
Season: May-Oct. **High:** July-Aug. **Caddies:** No.
Green fee: $20-$49. **Credit cards:** V.
Lodging on site: Yes. **Reduced fees:** Weekdays.
Unrestricted walking: Yes. **Range:** No.
Holes: 18. **Par:** 71. **Yards:** 6,308-5,856. **Slope:** 121.
Comments: "Great backgrounds . . . Average length . . . Narrow fairways . . . Demanding holes . . . Most enjoyable . . . Old-style hospitality . . . Never too busy . . . Best reception from a pro shop ever."

QUEBEC

★★★½ LE CHATEAU MONTEBELLO
Montebello—R—819-423-4653 (50 mi. from Ottawa).
Season: May-Oct. **High:** Summer. **Caddies:** No.
Green fee: $20-$49. **Credit cards:** V, AMEX, MC.
Lodging on site: Yes. **Reduced fees:** Weekdays, Low Season.
Unrestricted walking: No. **Range:** Yes (grass).
Holes: 18. **Par:** 70. **Yards:** 6,240-5,620. **Slope:** Unrated.
Comments: "Outstanding recently renovated old Stanley Thompson de-

sign . . . Super old layout . . . Difficult . . . Not too long . . . Very tight fairways . . . Beautifully treed . . . Very scenic . . . Considerable elevation changes . . . Wonderful colors in fall . . . Great old log cabin hotel . . . No. 9 is a wild par 4 . . . 9 is a farce . . . Course redesign poorly done."

★★★½ LE CLUB DE GOLF CARLING LAKE
Brownsburg—R—514-476-1212 (100 mi. from Montreal).
Season: May-Oct. **High:** Summer. **Caddies:** No.
Green fee: $20-$49. **Credit cards:** V, AMEX, MC.
Lodging on site: Yes. **Reduced fees:** Weekdays, Low Season, Twilight Play.
Unrestricted walking: No. **Range:** No.
Holes: 18. **Par:** 72. **Yards:** 6,691-5,352. **Slope:** Unrated.
Comments: "A genuine secret . . . Great scenery, great holes . . . Short front, long back . . . Built on a mountainside, spectacular in fall . . . A few very tough holes . . . New lodging a plus."

★★LE GOLF CHANTECLER
Ste. Adele—PU—514-229-3742, 800-363-2587 (30 mi. from Montreal).
Season: May-Oct. **High:** Summer. **Caddies:** No.
Green fee: $20-$49. **Credit cards:** AMEX, MC.
Lodging on site: Yes. **Reduced fees:** Weekdays, Low Season.
Unrestricted walking: No. **Range:** No.
Holes: 18. **Par:** 70. **Yards:** 6,280-6,110. **Slope:** Unrated.
Comments: "Fine little short course . . . Poorly maintained."

★★★GRAY ROCKS GOLF COURSE
St. Jovite—R—819-425-2771, 800-567-6744 (90 mi. from Montreal).
Season: May-Oct. **High:** July-Aug. **Caddies:** No.
Green fee: $20-$49. **Credit cards:** V, AMEX, MC.
Lodging on site: Yes. **Reduced fees:** Weekdays, Low Season, Resort Guests, Twilight Play.
Unrestricted walking: Yes. **Range:** Yes (grass).
Holes: 18. **Par:** 72. **Yards:** 6,320-5,785. **Slope:** 127-120.
Comments: "Old, beautifully maintained vacation spot . . . Hilly setting . . . OK course, a long way from Montreal . . . A great week of golf."

★★★MANOIR RICHELIEU
Pointe-au-Pic—R—418-665-3703, 800-463-2613 (90 mi. from Quebec).
Season: May-Oct. **High:** July-Aug. **Caddies:** No.
Green fee: $20-$49. **Credit cards:** All Major.
Lodging on site: Yes. **Reduced fees:** No.
Unrestricted walking: Yes. **Range:** No.
Holes: 18. **Par:** 70. **Yards:** 6,255-5,980. **Slope:** Unrated.
Comments: "Great Canadian hospitality . . . Scenery a distraction . . . Lots of hills . . . Some holes too easy."

OWL'S HEAD GOLF COURSE*
Mansonville—R—514-292-3666 (80 mi. from Montreal).
Season: May-Oct. **High:** June-Aug. **Caddies:** No.
Green fee: $20-$49. **Credit cards:** V, MC.
Lodging on site: Yes. **Reduced fees:** Weekdays, Low Season, Twilight Play.
Unrestricted walking: Yes. **Range:** Yes (mats).
Holes: 18. **Par:** 72. **Yards:** 6,705-5,295. **Slope:** Unrated.

ONTARIO

DEERHURST RESORT
Huntsville—R—705-789-2381 (130 mi. from Toronto).
Season: May-Nov. **High:** July-Aug. **Caddies:** No.
Green fee: $50-$99. **Credit cards:** All Major.
Lodging on site: Yes. **Reduced fees:** Resort Guests, Twilight Play.
Unrestricted walking: No. **Range:** Yes (grass).

DEERHURST HIGHLANDS GOLF CLUB*
Holes: 18. **Par:** 72. **Yards:** 7,011-5,393. **Slope:** 140.
Comments: "World class . . . Almost perfect . . . One of the very best in Canada . . . Great variety of holes . . . Great mixture . . . Each hole is unique . . . Challenging for all levels . . . Fees double those of nearby courses."

★★★DEERHURST LAKESIDE GOLF CLUB
705-789-7878, 800-461-4393.
Green fee: $20-$49. **Unrestricted walking:** Yes.
Holes: 18. **Par:** 65. **Yards:** 4,667-3,737. **Slope:** Unrated.
Comments: "Short, undulating track . . . Great improvement over the last 5 years . . . Clearly inferior to Deerhurst Highlands."

★★DON VALLEY GOLF COURSE
Toronto—PU—416-392-2465.
Season: April-Nov. **High:** July-Aug. **Caddies:** Yes.
Green fee: $20-$49. **Credit cards:** V, AMEX, MC.
Lodging on site: No. **Reduced fees:** Twilight Play.
Unrestricted walking: Yes. **Range:** Yes (grass).
Holes: 18. **Par:** 71. **Yards:** 6,300-6,150. **Slope:** Unrated.
Comments: "Decent layout . . . In scenic river valley . . . Small fast greens . . . Many water and bunker hazards . . . Inexpensive but busy . . . Very busy . . . No tee times . . . Long waits, slow play."

★★★★GLEN ABBEY GOLF CLUB
Oakville—PU—416-844-1800 (25 mi. from Toronto).
Season: April-Oct. **High:** Summer. **Caddies:** No.
Green fee: $50-$99. **Credit cards:** V, AMEX, MC.
Lodging on site: No. **Reduced fees:** Low Season.
Unrestricted walking: No. **Range:** Yes (grass).
Holes: 18. **Par:** 73. **Yards:** 7,102-5,577. **Slope:** Unrated.
Home of the Canadian Open.
Comments: "Fantastic . . . Best in Canada . . . Nicklaus' 1st design, still one of his 10 best . . . Superb fairways . . . Superb condition . . . Great back 9 . . . Six tough valley holes . . . Keeps play moving at excellent speed . . . Fact it's home to Canadian Open is its biggest draw . . . Fun playing where the pros play . . . Front 9 very ordinary . . . No hole the pros play should be as easy as No. 5 . . . Good shape prior to Canadian Open, so-so after . . . Delusions of grandeur . . . Minimum 6-hour rounds . . . A struggle for the average player . . . Overrated, overpriced . . . Questionable service . . . Only interested in your money . . . You're paying for the name."

★★½ HOCKLEY VALLEY RESORT
Orangeville—R—519-942-0754 (40 mi. from Toronto).
Season: April-Nov. **High:** June-Aug. **Caddies:** No.
Green fee: $50-$99. **Credit cards:** All Major.
Lodging on site: Yes. **Reduced fees:** Weekdays, Low Season, Resort Guests, Twilight Play.
Unrestricted walking: No. **Range:** Yes (mats).
Holes: 18. **Par:** 70. **Yards:** 6,391-4,646. **Slope:** Unrated.
Comments: "Nice valley course . . . Some premium on target golf . . . Treelined, a real challenge . . . Fabulous scenery . . . Best in the fall . . . Front is hard, back is easy . . . Very hilly . . . Cart is an essential . . . Just not there yet . . . Very disappointing . . . A ski resort turned golf club."

★★½ KANATA LAKES GOLF & COUNTRY CLUB
Kanata—PU—613-592-1631 (10 mi. from Ottawa).
Season: May-Oct. **High:** June-Aug. **Caddies:** No.
Green fee: $20-$49. **Credit cards:** V, MC.
Lodging on site: No. **Reduced fees:** No.
Unrestricted walking: Yes. **Range:** Yes (mats).
Holes: 18. **Par:** 70. **Yards:** 6,730-5,388. **Slope:** Unrated.
Comments: "Built around housing . . . Long walks greens to tees . . . Monster par-5 finishing hole."

LIONHEAD GOLF & COUNTRY CLUB
Brampton—PU—416-455-4900 (6 mi. from Toronto).
Season: April-Nov. **High:** May-Oct. **Caddies:** No.
Green fee: $100 and up. **Credit cards:** V, AMEX, MC.
Lodging on site: No. **Reduced fees:** Low Season.
Unrestricted walking: No. **Range:** Yes (grass).
★★**THE LEGENDS**
Holes: 18. **Par:** 72. **Yards:** 7,198-5,730. **Slope:** Unrated.
★★**THE MASTERS**
Holes: 18. **Par:** 72. **Yards:** 7,035-5,553. **Slope:** Unrated.

★★**MAPLES OF BALLANTRAE LODGE & GOLF CLUB**
Stouffville—R—416-640-6077 (35 mi. from Toronto).
Season: April-Dec. **High:** June-Sept. **Caddies:** No.
Green fee: $20-$49. **Credit cards:** V, MC.
Lodging on site: Yes. **Reduced fees:** Weekdays, Low Season, Resort Guests, Twilight Play.
Unrestricted walking: Yes. **Range:** Yes (grass).
Holes: 18. **Par:** 72. **Yards:** 6,499-5,195. **Slope:** Unrated.
Comments: "Great early season warm-up . . . Heavily wooded course that permits bump and run . . . Severely sloped fairways, uneven lies . . . Tough dogleg par 4s . . . Very pleasant . . . Last three holes are great . . . Nice finishing holes, but mostly boring."

★★★½ **MONTERRA GOLF CLUB**
Collingwood—R—705-445-0231 (106 mi. from Toronto).
Season: May-Oct. **High:** May-Oct. **Caddies:** No.
Green fee: $20-$49. **Credit cards:** V, AMEX, MC.
Lodging on site: Yes. **Reduced fees:** Resort Guests, Twilight Play.
Unrestricted walking: Yes. **Range:** Yes (mats).
Holes: 18. **Par:** 72. **Yards:** 6,581-5,139. **Slope:** Unrated.
Comments: "Tremendous . . . Scenic northern location . . . A Thomas McBroom delight . . . Real tough, a real experience . . . Very memorable . . . Requires all the shots. Must think . . . Lakes and ravines really add to the design . . . Last season's twilight rate was the bargain of the century . . . Too much Dye-like mounding and hazards."

★★★**OSPREY VALLEY HEATHLANDS GOLF COURSE**
Alton—PU—416-454-4653 (20 mi. from Toronto).
Season: April-Dec. **High:** May-Sept. **Caddies:** Yes.
Green fee: $20-$49. **Credit cards:** V, AMEX, MC.
Reduced fees: Weekdays, Resort Guests, Twilight Play.
Unrestricted walking: Yes. **Range:** No.
Holes: 18. **Par:** 71. **Yards:** 6,810-5,248. **Slope:** Unrated.
Comments: "Young links-type course . . . Very attractive . . . Solid newcomer . . . Only requires some maturity."

★★½ **PHEASANT RUN GOLF CLUB**
SOUTHERN UPLAND/MIDLANDS/HIGHLANDS 9s
Sharon—PU—416-898-3917 (40 mi. from Toronto).
Season: April-Nov. **High:** April-Nov. **Caddies:** No.
Green fee: $20-$49. **Credit cards:** V, MC.
Lodging on site: No. **Reduced fees:** Weekdays, Twilight Play.
Unrestricted walking: Yes. **Range:** Yes (grass).
Holes: 27. **Par:** 35,36,37. **Yards:** 2,926/3,132/3,328.
Comments: "Tight, treelined fairways . . . Sidehill lies . . . Large, slow greens . . . New holes feature fierce doglegs . . . Watch for pheasants."

★★½ **PINESTONE GOLF COURSE**
Haliburton—R—705-457-3444, 800-461-0357 (130 mi. from Toronto).
Season: May-Oct. **High:** Summer. **Caddies:** No.
Green fee: $20-$49. **Credit cards:** All Major.
Lodging on site: Yes. **Reduced fees:** Low Season, Resort Guests, Twilight Play.

Unrestricted walking: Yes. **Range:** No.
Holes: 18. **Par:** 71. **Yards:** 6,023-5,533. **Slope:** Unrated.
Comments: "Located in beautiful cottage country . . . Good layout . . . A little short . . . Tight, tight fairways . . . Questionable condition . . . Getting better each year . . . Needs practice range and decent putting green."

★★½ UPPER CANADA GOLF COURSE
Morrisburg—R—613-543-2003 (50 mi. from Montreal).
Season: April-Nov. **High:** Summer. **Caddies:** No.
Green fee: $20-$49. **Credit cards:** All Major.
Reduced fees: Weekdays, Low Season, Twilight Play.
Holes: 18. **Par:** 72. **Yards:** 6,922-6,008. **Slope:** Unrated.
Comments: "Very pretty . . . Some fascinating holes along river on back 9 . . . Well marshaled . . . Not considered a great course in Ottawa . . . Not costly . . . Watch out for geese."

★★★★WHIRLPOOL GOLF COURSE
Niagara Falls—PU—416-356-1140.
Season: March-Nov. **High:** Summer. **Caddies:** No.
Green fee: $20-$49. **Credit cards:** V, AMEX, DISC, MC.
Lodging on site: No. **Reduced fees:** Low Season, Twilight Play.
Unrestricted walking: Yes. **Range:** No.
Holes: 18. **Par:** 72. **Yards:** 6,994-6,495. **Slope:** 130-124.
Comments: "Just great . . . Strong layout . . . Tough track . . . Best in Ontario . . . Super long par 3s, short par 5s . . . Big greens . . . Room for errors . . . Terrific maintenance . . . Best-conditioned public course within 50 miles of Buffalo . . . Most private clubs are not as well kept . . . Maintained by college horticulture students . . . Nice enough, no big deal . . . Slow play left bad taste in my mouth."

MANITOBA

★★★½ CLEAR LAKE GOLF COURSE
Onanole—PU—204-848-4653 (60 mi. from Brandon).
Season: May-Oct. **High:** July-Aug. **Caddies:** No.
Green fee: $20-$49. **Credit cards:** V, MC.
Lodging on site: No. **Reduced fees:** Low Season, Twilight Play.
Unrestricted walking: Yes. **Range:** No.
Holes: 18. **Par:** 72. **Yards:** 6,070. **Slope:** Unrated.
Formerly Wasagaming Golf Course.
Comments: "Another Manitoba gem . . . Nice and scenic, but too many blind shots . . . So many hills and valleys there are no level lies."

★★★FALCON BEACH GOLF COURSE
Whiteshell Park—PU—204-349-2554 (80 mi. from Winnipeg).
Season: April-Oct. **High:** July-Aug. **Caddies:** No.
Green fee: $20-$49. **Credit cards:** V.
Lodging on site: No. **Reduced fees:** Weekdays, Twilight Play.
Unrestricted walking: Yes. **Range:** Yes (grass).
Holes: 18. **Par:** 72. **Yards:** 6,964-5,917. **Slope:** Unrated.
Comments: "Is in beautiful shape and challenging for the price."

★★★½ HECLA GOLF COURSE
Riverton—R—204-475-2354 (110 mi. from Winnipeg).
Season: May-Oct. **High:** Summer. **Caddies:** No.
Green fee: $20-$49. **Credit cards:** All Major.
Lodging on site: Yes. **Reduced fees:** Twilight Play.
Unrestricted walking: Yes. **Range:** Yes (grass).
Holes: 18. **Par:** 72. **Yards:** 6,678-5,535. **Slope:** Unrated.
Comments: "Wonderful rustic experience . . . Carved out of the wilderness . . . Has severely raised prices during past three years."

CANADA

★½ JOHN BLUMBERG GOLF COURSE
Winnipeg—PU—204-888-8860.
Season: April-Nov. **High:** June-Sept. **Caddies:** No.
Green fee: Under $20. **Credit cards:** V, AMEX, MC.
Lodging on site: No. **Reduced fees:** Twilight Play.
Unrestricted walking: Yes. **Range:** Yes (mats).
Holes: 18. **Par:** 71. **Yards:** 6,343-5,844. **Slope:** 118-115.
Additional 9-hole, par-34, 2,739-yard course.

★★★½ LINKS AT QUARRY OAKS
Steinbach—PU—204-326-4653 (35 mi. from Winnipeg).
Season: April-Oct. **High:** July-Aug. **Caddies:** No.
Green fee: $20-$49. **Credit cards:** V, AMEX, MC.
Lodging on site: No. **Reduced fees:** Weekdays, Twilight Play.
Unrestricted walking: Yes. **Range:** Yes (grass).
Holes: 18. **Par:** 72. **Yards:** 6,524-5,422. **Slope:** Unrated.
Comments: "Potential to be a top Canadian layout . . . Course is nice, but walks between holes too long . . . Exceptional service."

SASKATCHEWAN

★★★½ WASKESIU GOLF COURSE
Prince Albert National Park—PU—306-663-5300
(50 mi. from Prince Albert).
Season: May-Sept. **High:** June-Aug. **Caddies:** No.
Green fee: $20-$49. **Credit cards:** V, AMEX, MC.
Reduced fees: Weekdays, Low Season, Twilight Play.
Unrestricted walking: Yes. **Range:** Yes (mats).
Holes: 18. **Par:** 70. **Yards:** 6,051-5,710. **Slope:** Unrated.
Comments: "$20 for Stanley Thompson! . . . Short, but hilly, so it plays long . . . Not one level lie . . . No water, but heavy forest and bears."

ALBERTA

★★★½ BANFF SPRINGS HOTEL GOLF COURSE
RUNDLE/TUNNEL/SULPHUR 9s
Banff—R—403-762-6801 (75 mi. from Calgary).
Season: May-Oct. **High:** June-Aug. **Caddies:** No.
Green fee: $50-$99. **Credit cards:** All Major.
Lodging on site: Yes. **Reduced fees:** Low Season, Twilight Play.
Unrestricted walking: No. **Range:** Yes (mats).
Holes: 27. **Par:** 36/35/36. **Yards:** 3,174/3,452/3,269.
Comments: "Astonishing location . . . Scenic, challenging . . . Moose and elk . . . Can't get better than this . . . Everyone needs to play here once . . . Great course, outstanding setting . . . Original was fabulous . . . Sulphur and Rundle 9s are great. Tunnel isn't . . . Rearrangement of holes was a mistake . . . Don't care for the changes."

★★★½ D'ARCY RANCH GOLF CLUB
Okotoks—PU—403-938-4455 (15 mi. from Calgary).
Season: April-Oct. **High:** May-Sept. **Caddies:** No.
Green fee: $20-$49. **Credit cards:** V, AMEX, MC.
Lodging on site: No. **Reduced fees:** Twilight Play.
Unrestricted walking: Yes. **Range:** Yes (mats).
Holes: 18. **Par:** 72. **Yards:** 6,919-5,529. **Slope:** 126-113.
Comments: "Great use of a natural site . . . Very fair . . . Target golf, deep rough . . . Always windy . . . Well maintained . . . Excellent facilities."

★★★½ HERITAGE POINTE GOLF & COUNTRY CLUB
THE POINTE/THE DESERT/THE HERITAGE 9s
De Winton—PU—403-256-2002 (10 mi. from Calgary).
Season: April-Nov. **High:** Summer. **Caddies:** No.

Green fee: $20-$49. **Credit cards:** V, AMEX, MC.
Lodging on site: No. **Reduced fees:** Twilight Play.
Unrestricted walking: Yes. **Range:** Yes (mats).
Holes: 27. **Par:** 36/36/36. **Yards:** 3,335/3,520/3,506.
Comments: "Best in Alberta . . . Three choice 9s . . . Like playing Scotland . . . Difficult forced carries . . . Penal rough . . . Some blind shots, many lost balls . . . 5-irons off some tees . . . Interesting, but not fun . . . Needs some design tune-up . . . Not yet playable."

★★★½ JASPER PARK LODGE GOLF CLUB

Jasper—R—403-852-3400 (210 mi. from Edmonton).
Season: April-Oct. **High:** Summer. **Caddies:** No.
Green fee: $20-$49. **Credit cards:** All Major.
Lodging on site: Yes. **Reduced fees:** Low Season, Twilight Play.
Unrestricted walking: Yes. **Range:** Yes (grass).
Holes: 18. **Par:** 71. **Yards:** 6,598-6,037. **Slope:** Unrated.
Comments: "Still a classic . . . The grand mountain course of Canada . . . Very hilly . . . No rough . . . Fairly easy . . . Poor maintenance . . . Sand traps require attention . . . Pretentious price . . . They're going to redo it."

KANANASKIS COUNTRY GOLF COURSE

Kananaskis Village—PU—403-591-7272 (55 mi. from Calgary).
Season: May-Oct. **High:** Summer. **Caddies:** No.
Green fee: $20-$49. **Credit cards:** V, AMEX, MC.
Lodging on site: Yes. **Reduced fees:** Weekdays.
Unrestricted walking: Yes. **Range:** Yes (grass).

★★★★ MT. KIDD COURSE

Holes: 18. **Par:** 72. **Yards:** 7,049-5,539. **Slope:** Unrated.
Comments: "Splendid all around . . . Exceptional location . . . Unexcelled scenery . . . Memorable holes . . . Great shape . . . Great test of skill . . . Most reasonable green fee in Canada . . . Can't beat it . . . Too flat to be called a mountain course . . . Should not be missed."

★★★★ MT. LORETTE COURSE

Holes: 18. **Par:** 72. **Yards:** 7,102-5,429. **Slope:** Unrated.
Comments: "Other half of Canada's greatest golf value . . . Absolutely beautiful . . . Mountain backdrop the most beautiful sight in golf . . . Golfer's paradise . . . Longer and tougher than Kidd brother . . . Every variety of hole . . . Great par 3s . . . Precision is the word here . . . Lots of water . . . Exceptional walking course."

★★½ REDWOOD MEADOWS GOLF & COUNTRY CLUB

Calgary—PU—403-949-3663.
Season: May-Oct. **High:** June-Sept. **Caddies:** No.
Green fee: $20-$49. **Credit cards:** V, MC.
Lodging on site: No. **Reduced fees:** No.
Unrestricted walking: Yes. **Range:** Yes (grass).
Holes: 18. **Par:** 72. **Yards:** 6,965-6,108. **Slope:** Unrated.
Comments: "Rustic, but well groomed . . . Front a bit dull . . . Could have used more water . . . Back in foothills OK . . . Inconsistent conditioning."

★★★½ WOLF CREEK GOLF RESORT
WEST/EAST/SOUTH 9s

Ponoka—R—403-783-6050.
Season: April-Oct. **High:** Summer. **Caddies:** Yes.
Green fee: $20-$49. **Credit cards:** V, AMEX, MC.
Lodging on site: No. **Reduced fees:** No.
Unrestricted walking: Yes. **Range:** Yes (grass).
Holes: 27. **Par:** 35/35/35. **Yards:** 3,302/3,516/3,214.
Comments: "British links in western Canada . . . In middle of nowhere . . . Punishing . . . Lots of long carries over rough . . . Extremely hard . . . Gimmicky . . . Play silver tees and keep it straight."

CANADA

BRITISH COLUMBIA

★★★½ **CASTLEGAR GOLF CLUB**
Castlegar—PU—604-365-5006 (350 mi. from Vancouver).
Season: April-Oct. **High:** June-Sept. **Caddies:** No.
Green fee: $26 (cart extra $23). **Credit cards:** V, MC.
Lodging on site: No. **Reduced fees:** No.
Unrestricted walking: Yes. **Range:** Yes (mats).
Holes: 18. **Par:** 72. **Yards:** 6,677-6,265.
Comments: "Very hilly course . . . Many doglegs . . . Tall pines dot many of the fairways."

★★★½ **CHATEAU WHISTLER GOLF CLUB**
Whistler—R—604-938-2095 (65 mi. from Vancouver).
Season: May-Oct. **High:** Summer. **Caddies:** No.
Green fee: $50-$99. **Credit cards:** All Major.
Lodging on site: Yes. **Reduced fees:** Low Season, Resort Guests, Twilight Play.
Unrestricted walking: No. **Range:** No.
Holes: 18. **Par:** 72. **Yards:** 6,635-5,157. **Slope:** Unrated.
Selected Best New Canadian Course of 1993 by GOLF DIGEST.
Comments: "Outstanding . . . Most beautiful course in Canada . . . Don't pass this one by."

★★★ **CORDOVA BAY GOLF COURSE**
Victoria—PU—604-658-4444.
Season: Year-round. **High:** May-Sept. **Caddies:** No.
Green fee: $20-$49. **Credit cards:** V, AMEX, MC.
Reduced fees: Weekdays, Low Season, Twilight Play.
Unrestricted walking: Yes. **Range:** Yes (mats).
Holes: 18. **Par:** 72. **Yards:** 6,628-5,211. **Slope:** Unrated.
Comments: "You'll use every club . . . Nice for walking."

★★★ **EAGLE POINT GOLF & COUNTRY CLUB**
Kamloops—PU—604-573-2453 (180 mi. from Vancouver).
Season: March-Oct. **High:** May-Sept. **Caddies:** No.
Green fee: $20-$49. **Credit cards:** V, MC.
Lodging on site: Yes. **Reduced fees:** Weekdays, Low Season, Resort Guests.
Unrestricted walking: Yes. **Range:** Yes (mats).
Holes: 18. **Par:** 72. **Yards:** 6,762-6,006. **Slope:** Unrated.

★★ **FAIRMONT HOT SPRINGS RESORT**
Fairmont—R—604-345-6514, 800-663-4979 (180 mi. from Calgary).
Season: March-Nov. **High:** Summer. **Caddies:** No.
Green fee: $20-$49. **Credit cards:** All Major.
Lodging on site: Yes. **Reduced fees:** Resort Guests, Twilight Play.
Unrestricted walking: Yes. **Range:** No.
Holes: 18. **Par:** 72. **Yards:** 6,505-5,554. **Slope:** Unrated.
Comments: "Too many condos . . . Too many sloping lies . . . Too many repeat holes."

★★★½ **GALLAGHERS CANYON GOLF RESORT**
Kelowna—PU—604-861-4240 (200 mi. from Vancouver).
Season: April-Oct. **High:** May-Sept. **Caddies:** No.
Green fee: $20-$49. **Credit cards:** V, MC.
Lodging on site: No. **Reduced fees:** Twilight Play.
Unrestricted walking: Yes. **Range:** Yes (grass).
Holes: 18. **Par:** 72. **Yards:** 6,950-5,700. **Slope:** Unrated.
Additional 9-hole, par-32 course.
Comments: "Good mountain setting . . . Hilly . . . Brilliant, especially for shotmaking."

★★★½ KOKANEE SPRINGS GOLF RESORT
Crawford Bay—R—604-227-9362 (160 mi. from Spokane).
Season: April-Oct. **High:** Summer. **Caddies:** No.
Green fee: $20-$49. **Credit cards:** V, AMEX, DISC, MC.
Lodging on site: Yes. **Reduced fees:** Resort Guests, Twilight Play.
Unrestricted walking: Yes. **Range:** Yes (grass).
Holes: 18. **Par:** 71. **Yards:** 6,537-5,747. **Slope:** Unrated.
Comments: "Undiscovered jewel . . . Championship design . . . Good fun
. . . Isolated . . . Spectacular scenery . . . Short par 4s . . . Tough greens."

★★½ OLYMPIC VIEW GOLF COURSE
Victoria—PU—604-474-3671.
Season: Year-round. **High:** May-Oct. **Caddies:** No.
Green fee: $20-$49. **Credit cards:** All Major.
Reduced fees: Weekdays, Low Season, Twilight Play.
Unrestricted walking: Yes. **Range:** Yes (mats).
Holes: 18. **Par:** 72. **Yards:** 6,475-5,182. **Slope:** 137.
Comments: "Beautiful . . . Ocean views are great . . . Outstanding bent-
grass greens . . . Tight scenic target golf . . . We walked off after 9."

★★★½ PREDATOR RIDGE GOLF RESORT
Vernon—PU—604-542-3436.
Season: March-Nov. **High:** Summer. **Caddies:** No.
Green fee: $20-$49. **Credit cards:** V, AMEX, MC.
Lodging on site: No. **Reduced fees:** Low Season, Twilight Play.
Unrestricted walking: Yes. **Range:** Yes (grass).
Holes: 18. **Par:** 73. **Yards:** 7,156-5,475. **Slope:** Unrated.
Comments: "Championship target golf . . . Among the top 5 in British
Columbia . . . Great value . . . Good for long shotmaking."

★★★RIVERSHORE GOLF COURSE
Kamloops—PU—604-573-4622.
Season: March-Nov. **High:** April-Sept. **Caddies:** No.
Green fee: $20-$49. **Credit cards:** V, MC.
Lodging on site: Yes. **Reduced fees:** Low Season, Resort Guests,
Twilight Play.
Unrestricted walking: Yes. **Range:** Yes (mats).
Holes: 18. **Par:** 72. **Yards:** 7,007-5,445. **Slope:** Unrated.
Comments: "A Trent Jones classic . . . Beautiful backdrops . . . One of the
best . . . Fairways of silk, greens of felt . . . Fairly flat, links style . . . Don't
walk, river is a real river . . . Uninspiring."

★★★½ THE SPRINGS AT RADIUM GOLF COURSE
Radium Hot Springs—PU—604-347-6444, 800-667-6444
(90 mi. from Banff).
Season: April-Oct. **High:** July-Aug. **Caddies:** No.
Green fee: $20-$49. **Credit cards:** V, MC.
Lodging on site: No. **Reduced fees:** Weekdays.
Unrestricted walking: Yes. **Range:** Yes (grass).
Holes: 18. **Par:** 72. **Yards:** 6,717-5,163. **Slope:** Unrated.
Comments: "Probably the best all-round course in Canada . . . Wonderful
scenery . . . Extremely hospitable . . . Too pricey"

★★★WHISTLER GOLF CLUB
Whistler—R—604-932-3280 (75 mi. from Vancouver).
Season: May-Oct. **High:** Summer. **Caddies:** No.
Green fee: $50-$99. **Credit cards:** V, AMEX, MC.
Lodging on site: Yes. **Reduced fees:** Weekdays, Low Season, Resort
Guests, Twilight Play.
Unrestricted walking: Yes. **Range:** Yes (mats).
Holes: 18. **Par:** 72. **Yards:** 6,397-5,343. **Slope:** Unrated.
Comments: "Arnold Palmer did a good job . . . Scenic Glacier mountain
. . . Unusually scruffy for big time golf."